The Grass Roots

The Grass Roots

Readings in State and Local Government

Erwin C. Buell *North Texas State University*

William E. Brigman *Florida State University*

Scott, Foresman and Company

Library of Congress Catalog Card No. 68-27031
Copyright © 1968 by Scott, Foresman and Company, Glenview, Illinois 60025
All Rights Reserved. Printed in the United States of America.
Regional offices of Scott, Foresman and Company are located in
Atlanta, Dallas, Glenview, Palo Alto, and Oakland, N.J.

Preface

The more than 100,000 state and local governments in the United States collectively spend more than twice as much as the national government, and the rate of growth in their expenditures in recent years has been more than twice that of the national government. Traditionally, it has been the local governments that have supplied the basic services of health, education, and welfare to American citizens, and despite the shadow cast across these governments by the well-publicized activities of the national government, they are still a vital element in American life.

The Grass Roots: Readings in State and Local Government is based on a recognition of this vitality and a dissatisfaction with the traditional structural approach to state and local government found in most texts and collected reading materials. Our selection is based on the assumption that it is impossible to understand government without an appreciation of the political context in which the governmental structure operates. The focal point of this collection of materials is thus the interrelationship of government and politics. While maintaining an emphasis on structural considerations, we have made an attempt through case studies and other relevant materials to emphasize the functional and political aspects of state and local government.

Erwin C. Buell
William E. Brigman

Contents

CHAPTER IV   THE LEGISLATURE   189

CHAPTER V   THE OFFICE OF GOVERNOR   260

CHAPTER VI   THE ADMINISTRATION   313

Introduction

Two decades ago it was fashionable to discuss the obsolescence of federalism as a form of government and the eventual demotion of the states to the status of administrative units of the central government. To many observers the trend was clear and logical. They viewed the states as unnecessary, as performing a duplicating and overlapping role. The United States had begun as a federal union in 1789 with a constitution containing division of power and authority. The powers of the central government were stated in Article I, Section 8 of the Constitution, and all powers not granted to the central government or denied to the states were retained by the states (Tenth Amendment). Almost immediately after the creation of the new central government, the struggle for power between the newly formed government and the older states had begun. Much of the controversy centered around the interpretation of the powers of the new government, especially the implied powers clause of the Constitution. As will be explained in Chapter II, this broad interpretation opened an avenue for the expansion of the new central government's activities. By 1930 it appeared to many observers that the central government was on the verge of completely overshadowing the state and local governments by continued encroachment into areas previously assumed to be the exclusive domain of the state governments. The expansion of the regulatory function of the central government had a real impact on state activity; however, the expansion of the grants-in-aid programs of the 1930's and post-World War II had an even greater impact. It was through the grants-in-aid programs that the central government projected itself most directly into areas of state concern.

The much anticipated decline of the state and local governments as independent political and governing units has not occurred, however. In fact, the importance of local government has increased rather than decreased. It is true that all levels of government (national, state, and local) have increased functions and expenditure in recent years, but at the present time the state and local expenditures are increasing more rapidly than the expenditures of the national government. It is anticipated that by the 1970's state and local expenditures may outstrip national expenditures (see Chapter II).

While few, if any, areas of state and local activity are completely immune to intervention by the federal government, the states do exercise primary control over many aspects of the daily lives of their inhabitants. The states and their subdivisions spend much more for education, highways, health, public welfare, and police and fire protection than does the national government.

While state and local governments have not declined in importance, there *has* been a significant alteration in the structure of the government of the United States through the development of *cooperative federalism*. The concept of *dual federalism* — i.e., a belief that both the national and state governments are sovereign in certain areas and that the other governments must not encroach in the reserved area — has fallen into disuse today. Instead, the different levels of government cooperate in many fields to perform services for their citizens. For instance, transportation, urban renewal, old-age assistance, airport construction, education, employment opportunities, and retraining programs are dealt with by both federal and local governments. The extent of intergovernmental involvement is increasing; at the present time approximately 12 per cent of the monies expended by the state and local governments are given through federal grants-in-aid and other federal allocations.[1] In addition, the national government directly finances many projects (such as hospitals for veterans) that relieve some of the burden of the states.

This overlapping of functions by various levels of government has altered the neat, formal division of power between the central government and the states which the advocates of dual federalism consider to be the essence of federalism. For such advocates, any sharing of power among the national and state governments is a decline in state power. Thus, from this point of view, federalism and the states are being destroyed and no amount of growth in state and local services can obscure the fact. However, even these critics of cooperative federalism cannot deny that the state and local governments today are performing many more functions than in the past.

With cooperative federalism the states still have a vital function because they can operate with more flexibility and respond to a wider variety of needs than can a more centralized government. The states serve as laboratories for the solution of problems and produce significant contributions in many areas. For instance, agencies such as the

---

[1]James A. Maxwell, *Financing State and Local Government* (Washington: The Brookings Institute, 1965), appendix, Table A-1.1.

Federal Deposit Insurance Corporation resulted from state experimentation, and the federal unemployment and disability compensation programs had beginnings in state programs. In addition, state and local governments have served as important training grounds for leaders in other levels of government. From the time of Thomas Jefferson to the present, many have argued that local government is the strongest bulwark of democracy.

Despite the many forceful arguments for state and local governments and despite the rapid growth of these governments since 1930, they have many problems. The Commission on Intergovernmental Relations, which was established under President Eisenhower, and was sympathetic to the states, found many pressing needs. Most basic, according to the Commission, was the need for structural modifications to allow efficient operation of the state and local governments. Many state constitutions are outmoded and place too many detailed limitations on the scope of legislative powers. In addition, many legislative sessions are too short. Significant steps have been taken in newer state constitutions to remedy these weaknesses, and movements are under way in several states for major revisions of existing constitutions. Governor John Connally of Texas has recently called for a complete revision of the Texas constitution and a commission has been appointed to begin the work. Legislative changes resulting from the reapportionment of state legislatures give promise of vast improvements in this aspect of state government.

The Commission also concluded that few states had an adequate executive branch. As a result of the weak executive, the Commission saw "a tendency for groups of professional administrators in a single, specialized field working at national, state and local levels to become a more or less independent government of their own."[2] As will be noted in Chapter IV, significant advancement has been made by some states to strengthen the executive, either formally or informally.

The Commission also found structural problems at the local level— too many local governments, but not enough local government. Greater home rule would alleviate some of the problems, but home rule is not the solution to the growing problems of metropolitan areas. Because metropolitan areas sprawl far beyond the boundaries of the cities which serve as their core, no adequate governmental organization exists to perform the necessary services for the entire area. In many cases metropolitan areas extend into more than one state, further complicating the jurisdictional problems. The national government has made money available to interstate metropolitan areas to encourage these areas to seek cooperative solutions to their common problems. Some states are

---

[2]The Commission on Intergovernmental Relations, *A Report to the President for Transmittal to Congress* (Washington: U.S. Government Printing Office, 1955), p. 44.

also aware of the problems of metropolitan areas and larger cities, and they are seeking solutions. In Texas, for example, money has been made available to the larger cities, some counties, and the metropolitan areas for research into urban and metropolitan problems.

In summary, the state and local governments have shown a remarkable capacity for growth since the end of World War II, and at present they face major problems because of this rapid growth. If these governments fail to solve their problems and meet the new demands placed upon them by their residents, power will shift to the national government.

The readings selected for this anthology are designed to illustrate and evaluate the present structure and operations of the state and local governmental and political systems, to pose some alternatives, and to highlight some of the problems that must be faced and overcome.

Chapter I

The State
Political
System

Each state political system is a fundamental unit of the political and governmental system of the United States and each occupies the same constitutional relationship to the central government and to each other. In addition, each of the states has basically the same formal structure of government. All have a division of governmental powers between the executive, the legislature, and the courts. With the exception of Nebraska, all have a bicameral legislature.

Despite these important similarities in formal governmental structure, Harvey Mansfield demonstrates that "The States are Different" in such factors as size, climate, ethnic and religious composition, population density, and extent and type of industrialization. Equally important, each state political system is a product of its inheritance. This inheritance has created not only interstate differences, but intrastate differences as well. For example, many southern and border states such as North Carolina, Kentucky, and Missouri have regional differences extending back to the issue of slavery and the Civil War. Such internal differences are the essence of state politics and make each state political system unique.

Charles Press and Charles R. Adrian in "Why Our State Governments Are Sick" suggest that the states are the prisoners of their heritage. They argue that "the ideology to which decision makers are beholden is not appropriate as a yardstick against which to judge proposed public policies for today because it is appropriate for a rural, small-town, pre-industrial society rather than for our contemporary urban society." The result, they assert, is ineffective, "sick" state governments, which can be remedied only by major structural changes.

Norton Long's "Aristotle and the Study of Local Government" implicitly conflicts with Adrian and Press' pleas for structural alterations. Noting that "[t]he inappropriateness, for the solution of major current problems, of our existing structure of state and local governments is a common lament of citizen, scholar, and public official," Long suggests that "much of the action of the formal government is mere ratification of decisions made by . . . holders of social power."

According to Long, the real meaning of politics lies in "[t]he interrelations between the geographically separated ruling classes, the differences in their composition, the formal legal constitutions through and alongside which they operate, the varying ethics that legitimatize their power, and the revolutionary movements for altering their composition, winning recognition for new elements, or overthrowing them. . . ."

THE STATES ARE DIFFERENT

HARVEY C. MANSFIELD

Harvey Mansfield is professor of government, Columbia University. He is a contributor to *The Fifty States and Their Local Governments* (1967) and has served as a consultant to the Commission on Intergovernmental Relations and various other agencies.

No two states are the same, not even the Dakotas. Texas has over 100 times the area, and New York nearly 50 times the population of Delaware, but Delaware stands at the head of the list in individual income per capita. The population of the nation has doubled in the past half century, but some states have virtually stood still while others—Florida, Arizona, California—have multiplied several times over. The composition of some individual state populations has changed as much as their numbers in the same period. This is not any longer the result of immigration—though half a million Puerto Ricans have moved into New York since World War II—but rather of interstate migration. The great migrations of the nineteenth and early twentieth centuries from Europe have been dwarfed by the effects of automobiles and hard-surfaced roads. As many people have moved into California since the 1940 census as now live in Indiana. Movements within states, from the farms to the cities and from one city to another, though harder to measure, have probably been taking place on even a greater scale. Under the stimulus

From *The Forty-eight States* by Harvey C. Mansfield (New York: Columbia University Press, 1956), pp. 15-19. Reprinted by permission of the publisher.

of industrialization and urbanization, and the development of new resources and new technologies, sections and regions have been transformed by processes that ignore state lines. No major power in history, working under the conditions of a free society, has infused a common loyalty into so vast and varied a citizenry; but little of that loyalty attaches to the states of the citizens' temporary domicile.

State boundaries are apparently immutable, and logically indefensible. Rivers that unite have been chosen to divide economically integrated areas. Since the issue of free soil and slave became moot, the justification for most state lines has been purely historical, the accidental result of surveyors' lines on maps of land not yet surveyed. An industrial and urban society finds state lines chiefly a bother.

Within living memory it was practical politics to think of many states and sections in terms of common commodity interests — the cotton states, the silver states, the wheat states. While more than traces of these identifications persist, the list of states with any single prevailing interest of that sort is steadily dwindling. The southwest has supplanted the southeast in cotton production. The resort industries have changed the complexions of Florida, Arizona, and Nevada, and are making headway in New Hampshire. Vermont and Wisconsin remain faithful to the oleomargarine tax, but in Ohio and elsewhere the introduction of soybeans has fatally divided the dairymen's rank. Oil has made Texas something more than one big cattle ranch, and is just now dissolving the homogeneous wheat economy of North Dakota. But probably the greatest of these regional transformations has taken place in the South, in the wake of the developing chemical, textile, paper pulp, and other industries, the TVA, army camps, and so on. One discernible and significant consequence of this general trend toward economic diversification in the post-depression years has been a marked amelioration in the previously sharp differences in per capita income as between states. Substantial differences remain, . . . but the range from Delaware to Mississippi is now less than three to one. Far greater disparities than this can be found among the counties in most states.

Within living memory also, it was practical politics to count the governments of a considerable number of states as subsidiary instruments of one or another of the great industrial and transportation corporations that dominated the business world at the turn of the century. A classical example was California, where for many years what was good for the Southern Pacific was good enough for the state. Here again, diversification has been one among several influences tending to emancipate state governments from monopolistic control. DuPont is still in Delaware and Anaconda in Montana; but Delaware has a personal income tax and Montana a corporation net income tax. The Pennsylvania Railroad has been successful in the past three biennial legislative sessions in preventing the passage of an Ohio enabling act, sought by the steel, coal, and rubber industries, for a conveyor belt to run from the Ohio River to Lake Erie; but the Railroad is no match for the trucking lobbies there or in its home state. State governments have more freedom of action and decision in a pluralist society.

State politics, and therefore governments, are profoundly affected by the balance of urban and rural interests within their borders. Three or four characteristic patterns occur frequently enough to be classified. In over a dozen states, one metropolitan city—a Providence, a Baltimore, a New Orleans—stands politically arrayed against the rest of the state. Such a city often decides the governorship and other statewide election races. It is always underrepresented in the legislature. Outside the South it usually has a party majority opposite to that of the rest of the state, though its business leaders are frequently allied on economic issues with the rural legislative leaders. Rarely is the big city the state capital—witness Chicago and New York City. In another half dozen or more states a bipolar rivalry between two major cities, dividing both parties, is the key to the state's politics. In Pennsylvania, Missouri, and California, for example, the two U.S. Senate seats are regularly allotted to the two leading cities, the governor must beware of too close identification with either, and the rural legislators play off both against each other in a state capital which is a small neutral city. Again, in states as different as Connecticut and Texas, a number of cities, each with its local machine but no one or two of them predominant, find common interests in some general issues of urbanism, yet fail to form any durable alliance against the rural areas. Finally, there are the states—Connecticut, New Jersey, Maryland, Virginia, Wisconsin—adjoining a huge metropolis in another state. In each of these an important section of the state consists of well-to-do "dormitory" suburbs whose commuter inhabitants are absorbed in the life of the big city of the neighboring state. They are interested in the politics of their "home" states chiefly for their bearing on the outcome of presidential elections.

WHY OUR STATE GOVERNMENTS ARE SICK

CHARLES PRESS AND CHARLES R. ADRIAN

Charles Press is professor of political science, Michigan State University. He is author of *Main Street Politics* (1962) and co-author of *State Manuals, Blue Books, and Election Results* (1962). Charles R. Adrian is professor of political science, University of California, Riverside. His publications include *Governing Our Fifty States and Their Communities* (1963), *Governing Urban America; Structure, Politics and Administration* (1955), and, with Oliver P. Williams, *Four Cities; A Study in Comparative Policy Making* (1963).

State governments are sick. In recent years there have been exposés of prison riots, snake-pit mental facilities, "death trap" and "speed trap" highway traffic regulations, state mining regulations, court and police procedures, and out-dated divorce laws. Almost every year someone attracts attention by writing a book critical of one of the activities for which state government has responsibility. These who defend state governments must apologize for such practices as those of legislators in New Hampshire who hire out as ushers at race tracks; or for the wholesale turnover of state personnel that occurs after an election in border states such as Kentucky and West Virginia; or for the generally weak performance of Southern governors (as compared with many Southern mayors) in response to the school integration order of the Supreme Court. These examples are not representative of universal state practices, but they are common enough to place state government a poor second when specialists make a comparison of quality between it and Federal or most municipal government operations. A decade ago President Eisenhower said he wished to return a number of governmental functions to the states. Not only professional Democrats greeted his proposal as a "give-away" of the nation's resources; many others assumed that substituting state for Federal supervision would mean a shift from regulation in the interest of consumers to that of producers.

Certainly the weaknesses plaguing state governments can not all be traced to one source. Some result from the operation of a federal system. Competition among states tends to drive standards to the level of the lowest common denominator and encourages cut-rate practices such as Nevada's gambling and divorce industries. A good many of the worst weaknesses of state government, however, are unnecessary. These recognized shortcomings, we believe, are traceable to the failure of state governments to reflect the modern viewpoints held by a large majority

From "Why Our State Governments Are Sick" by Charles Press and Charles R. Adrian. Reprinted from *The Antioch Review*, XXIV: 2, 194-165, copyright 1964, the Antioch Press.

of their citizens. We charge that ideas dominant among the decision makers for state governments lack *timeliness*. By this we mean that the ideology to which decision makers are beholden is not appropriate as a yardstick against which to judge proposed public policies for today because it is appropriate for a rural, small-town, pre-industrial society rather than for our contemporary urban society. Furthermore, it is outmoded because many of its assumptions are based on folk beliefs rather than on the scientific study of psychology, psychiatry, economics, engineering, and other fields that have advanced rapidly in recent decades. (Advocates of the archaic small-town ideology, we should add, are not necessarily themselves small-town dwellers. They may live in large cities or in suburbs. Despite their urban life experiences, some persons, because of career success which they attribute to the older ideology, to childhood teachings, to early life in a small town, to a deliberate revolt against urbanism, or to lack of education, subscribe to the belief system of the small town.) The concepts of reality that dominate policy making in most states are out-of-date by at least half a century.

Crisis Amid Plenty

Daily headlines announce that a number of states are in financial difficulties. Indiana and Ohio recently cut back services severely to live within their income, while in New Jersey until a short time ago both parties had planks in their platforms opposing any new taxes. The posture of state legislatures in respect to taxes illustrates well the quality of their guiding ideologies. Meat-axe economizing is occurring at a time when, as John Kenneth Galbraith has illustrated, the private economy is full of frills. But to hear some state politicians tell it, one would imagine their state park, library, and water pollution budgets must be cut to the bone to head off widespread starvation, to keep tax-impoverished citizens out of soup lines, to prevent the ride over the hill to the poorhouse. To argue this way is patent foolishness in an economy where motor boat sales are skyrocketing, people feel deprived unless they own a movie camera, and student cars on high school and university parking lots are shinier and newer than those owned by many of their teachers. The last time such nonsense was taken seriously was in the 1920's.

Michigan has received a good deal of publicity for its financial sickness, and it provides a case study for the diagnosis of the disease. The state entered the post-war period with a tidy treasury surplus. In 1946 a constitutional amendment took two and one-half cents of the three-cent state sales tax and handed it over to the cities, villages, townships, and school districts, which were then in serious financial trouble. Within a few years, however, the state encountered financial difficulties. Several times attempts were made to increase state revenues, but almost always the governor and the state Senate could not agree on a tax program. In

1959, when crisis could no longer be side-stepped, they fought each other in a year-long, nationally publicized battle. State bills went unpaid, and some state employees had a paycheck delayed. After a year of struggle, one cent was added to the state sales tax. It is clear that this was not enough, for the state immediately began to suffer from an austerity budget under which universities turned away qualified students, the mental health program (especially rehabilitation of patients) was seriously set back, and a reduction in personnel was made necessary in many agencies, including the state police.

Common explanations for these developments include the argument that there was "too much" party competition, or that the state was a "welfare paradise," or that Michigan had a worker-oriented government which lacked "good business sense." At the heart of the deadlock, however, was an ideological clash. A spokesman for one side was Governor G. Mennen Williams, who was first elected in 1948 and who served an unprecedented six terms in office. He and his Democratic cohorts ran on a platform calling for personal and corporate income taxes. Steadily through the 1950's the Democrats gained strength in state government. After the election in 1958 the score on state offices filled by election was as follows: the Democrats had captured every executive office, held a top-heavy majority on the four statewide boards dealing with education, a majority on the Supreme Court, and an even split in the House, which was apportioned so as to give smaller districts roughly an eight-seat bonus. Few party organizations can claim a popular mandate of this extent, and perhaps for this reason Williams and his Democratic following felt justified in fighting for their program. Nevertheless, the state Senate had a twenty-two to twelve Republican majority. Democrats pointed out that their twelve members represented more citizens than the twenty-two Republicans and that the twelve Democrats had received more total votes than the twenty-two Republicans, but this line of argument did not make the latter more willing to compromise.

The Senate battled mightily with the Governor in the manner of the House of Lords fighting the wrong-headed popular majority—and easily won the war. A legislative sales-tax plan was finally adopted because the state desperately needed more funds.

Representation of Political Traditions

The composition of most state legislatures is defended because it is representative of both area and population. (The idea is, incidentally, one borrowed from the Federal government where it seems to work well.) Yet, almost every state can provide startling examples of "rotten boroughs" based on area representation. In Vermont, a town with less than a hundred residents has the same representation as the state's largest city, a difference in representation of about 600 to one. New Jersey provides a classic case, for the price of its post-war constitution of 1947 was leaving the state Senate undisturbed. In this body each county has one representative: Cape May, with a population of less than 40,000, has the same number of legislators as Essex County, with a population approaching one million.

Why is the national government not faced with the same problem concerning timeliness? Each state has two senators. The 1960 ratio at its extreme between New York and Nevada was 122 to one. As League of Women Voters spokeswomen are fond of saying, when 122 voters in New York equal one in Nevada, the situation is "obviously unfair and undemocratic." Yet the system works reasonably well in terms of the timeliness of legislation, and few seriously suggest changing it. The usual justification for the Senate's representative ratio takes the form of legal mumbo-jumbo; states, the argument goes, are semi-sovereign, while counties or other sub-units of a state are not. But this seems to us to sidestep the crucial point.

The United States Senate, despite its lack of mathematical equality in representation, comes fairly close to representing the mood of the nation – closer, many would argue, than the House of Representatives, which was intended to represent population. The United States Senate is, in fact, *timely*. Only a minority of its members could be described as of the group that had to be "dragged, kicking and screaming, into the twentieth century," as Adlai Stevenson once put it.

Turning to the states, one finds a different picture. There the unapportioned house commonly is dominated by "the old guard," which is likely to boast that its members are "watch-dogs of the treasury." In an inspired phrase, the journalist and lobbyist Olga Moore once described a legislator from among this group in her home state of Wyoming as having a "look of consecrated negativism." Most of these long-time stalwarts probably have little to worry about in elections. Leon Epstein, in a study of Wisconsin, found that the safe districts (which he defined as consistently favoring one party by over sixty per cent of the vote) were also those districts that had few primary fights. These are generally the kinds of districts the legislative old guard represents.

Because of a lack of apportionment, a small minority in the state becomes a top-heavy majority in its legislature. What kind of minority is over-represented? Clearly it is that of the small-town and agricultural minority devoted to a belief system that was popularly dominant prior to the Great Depression, but that has since become an atypical ideology. Duane Lockard, writing of Rhode Island, noted that its state Senate was the last bastion of conservative Republican strength, but argued that this situation produced an advantage gained only by putting a millstone around the neck of the party. In Northern states this dominant legislative bloc is generally Republican while in Southern and Border states it is Democratic. In neither case, however, does it co-operate well with the state-wide leaders of its own party. In Florida, former Governor Leroy Collins faced the same kind of problem as did Governor Nelson Rockefeller in New York, though each was—on paper—being supported by a legislative majority from his own party.

Sometimes legislative leaders devoted to the small-town ideology test their personal strength in state-wide races. The results are revealing. In Michigan, for example, the state senator who quite appropriately claimed to have masterminded in 1959 the legislative torpedoing of an income tax sought to run for governor in 1960. He put a large mock torpedo on the top of his car and toured the state seeking votes in the Republican primary. The first election-year opinion poll published by the Detroit *News* reported he was the favorite of less than ten per cent of the Republican voters. Shortly afterwards he decided to drop out of the gubernatorial primary and leave the "modern" Republican unchallenged. Meanwhile the majority floor leader of the Senate announced that he was a member of the John Birch Society, a revelation that was not greeted with great enthusiasm by Republicans who were interested in seeking state-wide office.

The type of archaic ideology legislative leaders express is often carelessly defined and ascribed to farmers who are sometimes said to constitute a "hayseed brigade." The image is misleading. Most legislative leaders were born in and reside in small towns. They are lawyers, real estate dealers, insurance men, and merchants. Even where districts are primarily agricultural, the dirt farmer, who is himself unable to run for an office that would take him away from the land for increasingly long periods each year, often votes for a candidate from a nearby trading center. Most such legislators seem to have gotten their start in small-town government and at some time have held a county office. The county-seat connection may explain why so many of them are from one of the smaller rather than the middle-sized towns in the district. The distinction made here between farmer and small-town dweller is, we believe, of importance. The legislative oligarchy is recruited in most states from small-town fish who reflect a large image while cruising around in little ponds. The political traditions of the small-town environment have had a notable effect on state government, and they have consistently supported archaic beliefs. The farmer, unlike the village merchant, has for more than a century seen government as an institution that can aid the citizen with his problems. And while he is often suspicious of the big-city businessman and factory worker, he is also far more of an experimental empiricist than is the small-town dweller.

In the 1930's, a fight over the Supreme Court raged at the national level. The justices were attacked as "nine old men," though in fact some of the most conservative were not among the oldest. But after 1937, the Supreme Court became *timely* without changing its structure. It did so as a reaction to the Roosevelt "packing" plan and the blandishments of the Chief Justice, Charles Evans Hughes. It became much too timely, in fact, for the tastes of some observers. The legislatures need a similar kind of change toward timeliness if states are to take their place with national and municipal governments as units reflecting contemporary popular concerns. The problem is not necessarily one of apportioning on the basis of strict population. We can settle for some consideration of area in apportionment if only the viewpoints represented are evolved in response to twentieth-century conditions and problems. As matters now stand, most contemporary state legislatures have inherited the discarded mantle and way of thinking of the pre-1937 Supreme Court.

The Choice of Political Traditions

The problem we have been discussing is one of viewpoint or political tradition. A political tradition is not easily changed; the ideas that are part of it have been formed as a result of life's experiences. When a political generation has undergone a period of trial under a novel set of conditions, the mood that results is worked into political programs, and if that political generation becomes a national majority, it is espoused by one of the major parties. This program is their definition of social justice and at the time of its birth purports to liberate the common man. Each of the important political eras of our history can be interpreted as the breakthrough of a new political generation, of its view of desirable public policies and of social justice.

An early political perspective that still has some relevance for state government was that formed on the frontier in the period of Andrew Jackson. Jackson, in 1824, received the most popular votes for the presidency but was denied the office by what he and his followers regarded as another manipulation of an Eastern Seaboard aristocracy. In 1828, he marshalled the newly enfranchised electorate of the common man to swamp the candidate of the East, John Quincy Adams. Jackson and his followers fashioned a political viewpoint that was meant to smash all political oligarchies before they had a chance to develop by applying the principle of rotation in office. State governments still bear the marks of this view: in the requirements for a great number of elected officials; frequent elections; short terms of office; laws against succession in office; and the spoils system of patronage, the moral justification of which is that no bureaucrat should ever feel he owns his office and that any citizen of ordinary intelligence is capable of handling any government job. Most people still respond somewhat favorably to the old Jacksonian rallying cries. They have lost most of their attractiveness, however, under the impact of changing conditions. Today we pay lip service to, but do not uncritically accept, these old theories, and this skepticism is but one step away from complete unbelief. We have reorganized most of our municipal governments, and the "little Hoover commissions" of the

1950's supported the rejection of Jacksonianism on the state level. The last remnants of the frontier view are to be found in the complex, much criticized governments of villages, townships, and counties.

The development of each new political ideology seems to follow the movement of the population frontier. Each set of ideas reflects the views of those who at the moment of its creation were the dynamic part of American society. By the end of the Civil War, a great part of the population had shifted from the wilderness to the small towns. As the potentialities of industrial society were revealed, their possibilities were seized upon by the new American majority, those living in the smaller cities and villages. The young men from these places built a new and mighty society for America and in the process formed a new political ideology.

The key to the small-town tradition is the Horatio Alger myth. Many a small-town boy has re-enacted it in detail: Thomas Edison, Will Rogers, Henry Ford, Harvey Firestone, together with an impressive number of presidents, governors, generals, and writers. The promise of this new ideology was that a young man could make good on nothing more than personal ability, pluck, thrift, hard work, and moral worth, with perhaps a little — but only a little — luck thrown in. The objective was not to find a safe and secure spot in some large organization but to be one's own boss and to succeed on one's own merits.

The attitude toward government that followed from this belief system was, of course, that government should not spoil the process by interfering with it or by making wasteful expenditures that would deplete the capital of the entrepreneur. If government did little more than its traditional functions of keeping order and enforcing civil contracts, leaving other decisions in private hands, the land would flow with milk, honey, and useful industrial artifacts such as automobiles, zippers, and packaged breakfast foods.

This political perspective blended with the older frontier view of distrust of the expert or professional. It placed heavy reliance on conventional wisdom or "common sense." Especially in government, the virtuous amateur, or jack-of-all-trades, was trusted over the specialist with professional concepts or standards.

The small town is no longer dominant, however. The descendants of its entrepreneurs are now living in the metropolis or its suburbs. The cream of small-town creativity has soured as small-town vitality has diminished. The importance of this fact is so great for our subject that it will shortly be dealt with in more detail.

After the Horatio Alger ideology, the next political breakthrough came as Americans moved to the large city during and after World War I. The political budding of this majority was brought about by such men as Al Smith; it flowered in the New Deal. Samuel Lubell, in the *Future of American Politics*, has described how the elements of the Roosevelt coalition merged once they had been given impetus by the Great Depression. The experiences of those who lived in the cities led them to reject the small-town view as irrelevant and impractical. Urbanites embraced a social-service state ideology. The sons and daughters of urbanite immigrants believed that failure was not simply the consequence of personal inability or immorality. They felt that sweatshops, dumbbell tenements, Jim Crow regulations, city streets serving as children's playgrounds, or monopolies could be changed only by government. The traditional social controls of the small town—neighborhood gossip and personal morality—no longer were sufficient in the city. The urbanite wanted workmen's compensation, wages-and-hours legislation, abolition of child labor, inspection of milk and food, adequate control of the conditions of work for women, fire and safety regulations in factories, and a host of other public policies that could only be accomplished through state action.

This welfare or social-service viewpoint has not yet spent itself. The Kennedy campaign of 1960 echoed the slogans of the New and Fair Deals. The unsolved problem of medical care remains, as do the unfinished battle over civil rights, and the expanding problems of the technologically unemployed (President Johnson's war on poverty). However, American life styles have changed again since the end of World War II. America has discovered the suburbs. The emerging majority now consists of white-collar organization men from nation-wide corporations rather than blue-collar workers and small-business entrepreneurs. The new majority has yet to make its dramatic breakthrough into the national political scene, but the outlines of its political slant are already familiar on the local level. It is evidenced in a desire to avoid conflict and partisanship, a preference for political independence, and a willingness to split party tickets, a taste for blandness, a championing of the technical efficiency of civil service, a deference to the opinions of the "expert," and an emphasis on selected welfare functions such as education and mental health. Probably the greatest impact of the new political viewpoint on the state level will be in the encouragement it gives to professionalism in government.

The Fruits of the Small-Town Political Tradition

To return to the major point of analysis, our argument is that state government is suffering from an overdose of the small-town political ideology, a viewpoint that no longer is appropriate for contemporary society and business. Legislators who hold this viewpoint are occasionally used by large industry to avoid government regulation and to secure preferred labor laws. The legislative laissez-faire viewpoint is not, however, one that is purchased; anyone so cynical as to think so seriously misjudges the situation. The small-town contingent sincerely believes in its traditions. To the beleagured small-town legislators in an un-friendly modern world of cities, it often seems as if they are themselves the last stronghold of sanity and morality. These men grew up in the last days of glory for the small-town viewpoint and they accepted it wholeheartedly. Herbert Hoover once said that the years before World War I were the best time to be alive in America or to be alive, in fact, in any nation at any point in history—which is, everything considered, quite a broad statement. But the world Hoover idolized could not sur-vive in the face of the even greater demand for the material goods the American Way seemed to offer to citizens. In 1916, as Henry Ford applied the assembly-line approach to mass production in Detroit's suburban Highland Park, the present generation of small-town legis-lators was passing through adolescence. To these men, small-town values were very real. As is the case with all of us, the ideas adopted at this period of one's life are among the hardest to change. They still color the small-town concept of reality.

During World War I and in the 1920's, population shifts tipped the scales in favor of the industrial cities. The presidency fell to the Demo-crats in 1932, and the New Deal followed. Big Steel, General Motors, and the Supreme Court surrendered in 1937, and within five years even Ford was unionized. The axis of the world, as Oliver Wendell Holmes once said, continued to be driven through every small town in America. But by the end of World War II, these places consisted mainly of those who did not want to try to advance under the new rules. (We hasten to concede that there continued to be many individual exceptions.) The small-town viewpoint, now on the defensive, sometimes achieves a shrill note with irrational overtones. Low taxes and simplicity in state govern-ment are the goal for a group of legislators who see most modern-day conditions as a mammoth conspiracy against their views of truth and beauty. Big-city schemers seem to surround them. Legislators of the small town paint pictures—in a day of widespread prosperity and the most conspicuous forms of consumption—of the beleaguered and al-most bankrupt taxpayer who cannot afford to have rivers unpolluted, or mental institutions with rehabilitation facilities for their patients, or highway systems designed to minimize the danger of head-on crashes.

One political analyst, describing the small-town legislative bloc in his own state said, "They have 'tantrums' for a platform." And this nicely sums up the decline of what once was the most dynamic political viewpoint in America. A querulousness about governmental "frills" is almost all that remains of the once proud doctrine of small-town in-dividualism. State legislatures, as currently established, are made to order for a group with this ideology. To gain their ends, they do not need to formulate alternative programs; they need only the power to block action and hence to stagnate government.

Because legislation and, in more than two-thirds of the states, constitutional amendments as well can be proposed only with its approval, the small-town bloc will often levy a special price when it agrees to act. This is the most obvious result of its control. A study in Connecticut, for example, described a state-aid formula constructed so that towns with less than 500 population received $27.19 per student while cities of over 100,000 received $4.95 per student. In Colorado, Denver schools with an enrollment of 90,000 received $2,300,000 under the state-aid formula while the schools of nearby Jefferson County with 72,000 fewer children enrolled received $100,000 more in state aid. The same pattern is frequently repeated in state aid for local roads, welfare grants, police protection, library facilities, and almost every other purpose. Richard Neuberger, when he was a state senator in Oregon, noticed that a bill to exempt rural mail carriers (usually residents of small towns) from state gasoline taxes passed overwhelmingly. When he proposed that some help be given urban mailmen who were more underpaid and had to walk, he was greeted with guffaws. This pattern of special gimmicks for the over-represented is repeated in the drawing of representative district lines for the United States Congress. Urban areas are seriously shortchanged in a way that has its effect on the national scene as well. A 1964 decision of the United States Supreme Court calling for equal population in House districts may change this pattern. It is now too early to know.

This self-interest aspect of small-town dominance is often irritating, but this is the least important of the effects. Urban areas are rich enough to carry small-town residents on their backs, and to some extent such a pattern is justified. Just as New York taxes are spent in Mississippi and North Dakota, so taxes from urban areas should probably be spent to bring facilities in smaller communities up to modern standards. But there is another more serious set of issues that represents a mixture of small-town morality and small-town selfishness. The opposition to the child-labor amendment sprang from such mixed motives. Children were a source of labor in small towns and on farms. Federal control was considered wrong, and besides, work for children was thought to be "character building." Probably the most obvious issue is the reluctant recognition of the need for government regulation. The price of small-town leaders' support for new legislation is often a rider that exempts towns of less than some figure acceptable to them. One study of Alabama by Murray Havens found small-town legislators exempting from regulation those barbers who worked only on Saturdays, presumably those working in the county seat when the farmers came in. In matters affecting the small-town businessmen, the mixed motives of the small-town attitude are frequently manifested. Legislators have valiantly tried to handicap chain-stores, both in order to help the small-town merchant and because they regard chains a threat to small businessmen generally. The Utah legislature in the 1940's passed anti-chain legislation. When put to a state-wide vote on a referendum, the bill was defeated by a four to one margin. The small-town crusade against trading stamps and the refusal of legislatures in states like New York to accept Federal funds at the price of eliminating billboards on freeways are examples. In the latter case, the fear was openly expressed that without billboards motorists would pass the small town by.

However, probably the most debilitating effect of the small-town ideology on state government today is the attempt to apply to all citizens the morality of small-town life of a half-century ago. At base, this morality holds that those who succeed will do so without help because they deserve to succeed. Those who do not, then, deserve to fail. In Minnesota, for example, a small-town representative once announced that he opposed a civil rights bill, explaining that when he was young he had been orphaned and he felt all citizens should make their own way by themselves, as he had done, for this would "build character." In the South, as an Alabama study of legislative voting has illustrated, it is the small-town legislator who favors last stands on segregation. His urban colleagues, for the most part, have reluctantly concluded that the South must, as best it can, move into the twentieth-century world. The news stories of small-town violence over civil rights confirm this finding. The same attitudes are frequently reflected on prohibition and Sunday "blue" laws. Repeal is the only amendment to the United States Constitution that has been submitted to specially elected state conventions. This procedure was followed primarily because the Roosevelt administration felt state legislatures might not agree to repeal, despite the fact that repeal was able to secure two-thirds majorities in each house of Congress and was quickly adopted by the state conventions.

Small-town morality is particularly harsh on matters involving labor, welfare, and crime, where the fear is one of coddling the undeserving. During the Great Depression, the principal small-town spokesman in the Minnesota Senate announced that "there is no need for a wide-open relief allowance in this state." He argued for state loans rather than grants to counties, even though thousands of families were on the edge of starvation and the counties were virtually bankrupt. He favored a bill granting *one-tenth* of the amount requested by the urban, liberal governor, Floyd B. Olson. It need scarcely be added that while governors do tend to inflate their budget requests, none comes close to padding 1000 per cent. In Franklin Roosevelt's term as Governor of New York, professional criminologists at the Governor's suggestion proposed revision of the criminal code. Leading the fight against the revision was a state Senator who favored a tough approach because, he said, there was "too much sentiment for the convict class." The outrage expressed in the California Senate when Governor Edmund (Pat) Brown stayed the execution of Caryl Chessman is another illustration of this attitude. One of the legislators with a small-town background argued that Brown's action provided grounds for impeaching the Governor. His stance offered no direct economic payoff for him—he acted from deep belief and tradition. The same attitude is reflected in the treatment of mental health patients. The small-town legislators generally favor custody over treatment—that is, locking up mental patients and criminals rather than spending funds on expensive psychiatric rehabilitation. The condition of our mental hospitals and prisons often reflects this judgment. Small-town morality finds no place for suspected academic or intellectual dreamers. In Maine, legislators refused a grant for legislative assistants who would be of help to themselves because the college instructor supervising the program has "extreme ideas." The suspect was, in fact, a Republican and his "extreme ideas" appear to have existed only in a proposal he had made for reorganizing Maine's archaic county governments.

Alcoholism in the small-town view should not be viewed as an illness. Rather, alcoholics are "drunks" and every small town has at least one specimen; he is regarded as morally weak. The small town's ideological bias also favors right-to-work laws, fights public housing, and works to ferret out "parlor pinks" from the universities. In welfare matters, non-urban legislators produce such legislation as Nebraska's homestead lien law, which confiscates all or part of the value of the home of the old-age assistance recipient at his death, or the means test to demonstrate need before aid is given, or the requirement of publication of lists of recipients as was once devised by the Indiana legislature. In Louisiana, the legislature—over the protest of professionals—sought to deny aid for dependents of unwed mothers who had any additional children out of marriage. All of these laws are aimed at what is considered to be the moral "slacker."

A distrust of the professional is also basic to the concepts of small-town moralism. The trained specialist is regarded as a "fuzzy-minded" idealist, an over-educated fool, rather than a practical worker. State legislatures are notorious for gutting civil service systems. More is involved than the simple desire to provide jobs for the county courthouse gangs; there is a deepfelt ideological distrust of government employees who attempt, through specialized skills, to handle the complex problems facing urban America. This attitude is potentially among the most destructive to effective state government, for it involves a notion that urban problems are imagined rather than real, that they can be best handled if government does nothing and if those who do not live moral, upright lives are allowed to suffer until they change their ways.

No industrial corporation could flourish if a group on its board of directors with this attitude towards professionalism held a veto, and no state government that uses the simple and archaic morality of the small town as a point of departure can cope effectively with modern problems.

Action Related to the Problem

The commonplace reform proposal is one for reapportioning state legislatures strictly by population. In 1958, a United States District Court directed the Minnesota legislature to reapportion according to the state constitution. (Like many state legislatures, it had not honored constitutional provisions and had not reapportioned itself for forty-five years.) In the 1961 tradition-shattering Tennessee decision (Baker *v.* Carr), the United States Supreme Court decided that the Federal courts did have jurisdiction over apportionment questions and might consider injury to urbanites resulting from archaic apportioning systems. Legally, the case affected only those states that had not apportioned according to their constitutional provisions, but it was only the first of many decisions related to representation formulas.

Another method for achieving representation by population is the use of the initiative. Thirteen states have this method available for changing their constitutions. (In the past, however, California and Michigan have used the initiative to freeze inequality into their constitutions rather than eliminate it.)

We believe there is a solution to state archaism short of the mammoth efforts required to achieve apportionment strictly according to population. The problem is one of representing political views formed in response to twentieth-century urban conditions and problems. To do this not every district need necessarily be mathematically equal in size. If other viewpoints receive representation enough to offset the antedeluvian small-town ideology, the necessary result would be achieved. Adding to the representation of cities or suburbs would achieve this. Another method of diluting the small-town viewpoint in the legislature would be to increase the size of legislative districts so that each legislator would have some urban constituents. This is what had kept the United States Senate timely, even though that body is not selected on the basis of representation by population. House districts, on the other hand, have been planned by state legislative leaders to over-represent small towns. A third method for helping offset the small-town viewpoint in state legislatures might be to leave present districts as they are but to elect in addition a half dozen or more legislators on a state-wide, at-large basis. This would have the advantage of preserving the old district lines and sense of community while breaking down the disproportionate small-town hold. Another method — most drastic — would simply be to abolish the unapportioned house of the legislature and base the other on population.

The most important of all strategies, we believe, is to focus public attention on the real problem. Once the stakes are clear to the urban majority, a change will occur, for the tools are at hand. It is quite possible that along the way the urban areas may lose individual battles but in the end win the war, just as Franklin Roosevelt did in his 1937 fight with the Supreme Court. Gordon Baker has pointed out that suburbanites are even more drastically under-represented than are voters in the core cities of metropolitan area. The 1960 census showing population losses in many large cities has emphasized this fact. The emerging majority fights some of the battles of the last great majority as well as its own.

We think timeliness is the major problem facing state government. Today our legislatures over-represent a political tradition devised for small-town living in the last century. This viewpoint does not fit the wants of most members of today's society. Old-fashioned political cures for modern problems work about as well as do the medical home remedies of the 1890's. The followers of the small-town political tradition must be given the status of a legitimate minority rather than being enthroned as the dominant policy makers. Until such a change in the political balance of power is made, our state governments will remain sick, sick, sick.

ARISTOTLE AND THE STUDY OF LOCAL GOVERNMENT

NORTON E. LONG

Norton E. Long is a professor at Brandeis University. He is a member of the Joint Center of Urban Studies, Massachusetts Institute of Technology and Harvard University. Several of his writings have been collected in *The Policy* (1962).

Professor Louis Hartz has argued that American political life has been characterized by a massive acceptance of a Lockean ethic. Implicit in this ethic is a justification for a given "ordering of offices": a certain type of ruling class and its recruitment and a set of supporting economic and social institutions. The bearers of this ethic are driven to seek its institutionalization through society. The United States is certainly no tight little city-state, but a continent with wide variation in social and economic conditions. Local heresies from the central conception of the good life are inevitable. And yet, looking at the formal "ordering of the offices," the legal structure of the subpolities of the American polity, there is an apparent monotonous uniformity that makes most texts in state and local government arid in the extreme. Does this mean that the overriding ethic of the national polity has indeed informed the political subdivisions, as in Aristotelian theory it ideally should? Or does it mean that political scientists, despite Aristotle's example to the contrary, have con-

From "Aristotle and the Study of Local Government," Norton E. Long, *Social Research*, XXIV (Autumn 1957), 295-310. Reprinted by permission of the author and *Social Research*.

fined themselves merely to the legal constitution, and have neglected the social-economic and the ethical?

In view of the continental sweep of American politics, we can expect state and local governments to show a wide deviation from the national norm, to have individual constitutions in the Aristotelian sense, with significant differences that cannot be adequately described in the strong- mayor, weak-mayor, city-manager, and commission legal typology that divides our municipal Gaul into four unequal parts. V. O. Key has urged, and in his *Southern Politics* has begun to make respectable, a recognition of the deviant that has hitherto been the province of the muckraker and the journalist rather than of the orthodox political scientist. A comparative approach would open a rich mine of local "constitutions," varying from the narrowest oligarchy to the freest democracy, and from the most brutal tyranny to a near philosopher-king. A recent *Saturday Evening Post* headlined a story, "Tyrant in Texas," the story of George Parr, so-called Duke of Duval County. This regime lasted for years, under the forms of law. Bell County, Kentucky, killed its opponents with impunity and dominated the courts, and its tyranny was finally overthrown only from without. The Imperial Valley in California exhibits a brutal oligarchy that tolerates no nonsense from its helots. The investigations of the La Follette Civil Liberties Committee documented the deviant local constitutions. The company towns of the nineteenth century not only illustrate the concentration of economic and political power in a ruling oligarchy or tyranny, but provide a classic example of the transition of oligarchy to a broader based polity.

Thus, under the deceptive uniformity of an apparently similar legal structure, a wide range of actual variance appears in the "constitutions" of our local governments. And it is under these "constitutions" that many, if not most, people have to live the most significant parts of their lives. We have no adequate information as to these "actual constitutions," the degree of their prevalence in their different forms, and the extent to which they cover, for practical purposes, the political life of those subject to them. We are even in the dark as to any cumulative trends.

It may be disquieting to realize that, in respects important for significant groups of the population, the American government that counts is oligarchical or tyrannical rather than democratic. The implications for the superior levels of government of variant constitutions below are serious. As Madison pointed out, an advantage that the expanse of the country gives to federalism is the possibility of restricting political contagion to the infected governmental cell, walling it off, and, after rallying the healthy corpuscles, restoring the normative order. Another advantage lies in the capacity to tolerate, under the cloak of lip service to the respectable national norm, wide deviations in practice dictated by differing social and economic situations.

Yet local government on the firing line must be a major determinant of the realities at the national level. Caciquism, the rule of local chieftains, made a mockery of parliamentary democracy in eastern Europe, parts of Italy, Spain, and South America. Perhaps the *tutelle administrative* of France may indicate the real possibility of centralized national democracy unsupported by extensive local foundations. Or one may see in France's apathetic masses a result that Burke foresaw in a metaphysical constitution that denies the necessity of mediating institutions between individual and nation. Surely the trends of our local constitutions, as they develop toward a more extensive prevalence of oligarchy, democracy, or ochlocracy, and their variants, are highly significant for the future of state and national government.

Each local jurisdiction, with important powers of police, justice, and taxation, can resemble a feudatory, with high, middle, and low justice; can constitute a little world for some, if not all, of its inhabitants; and can as truly represent a way of life as ancient Athens. The Aristotelian view sees the relationship between levels of government as most importantly a hierarchy of increasingly more self-sufficient ethical associations, until in the state self-sufficiency is attained. A part of the reason for the more primitive associations entering into the higher is military and economic, but by themselves these motives would not constitute a sufficient bond to produce a new political unity. Thus a NATO, or even an EDC, does not constitute a state, nor will a private or public international coal-and-steel cartel produce one. A community or friendship for business may produce a cartel or an International Rotary, a similar association for defense may produce a military alliance, but by themselves these purposes are insufficient to structure a political union. For this, according to Aristotle, a commonly shared and participated-in conception of a good life is essential.

The significance of this for local government, and its relation to the higher levels of government, lies in the widely felt differences regarding the importance of the various communities' purposes. The sense of the significance of the community's ethical value varies as between communities, and as between inhabitants of the same community. Thus a citizen of Quebec may find his provincial loyalty far more meaningful than his Canadian citizenship. Robert E. Lee, wending his way sadly back to his native Virginia, illustrates a type of conflict that reaches beyond the formal context of legal federalism. The scale of areal and governmental loyalties has a wide range of possibilities. While secession may not be a realistic possibility for Yorkville Nazis, a species of spiritual and even politically effective secession can occur. Nullification is not just a Southern states-rights phenomenon, and the non-enforcement of federal and state law is a significant aspect of political geography.

Not only may citizens of local governments limit or even cut their allegiance to state and national governments, by apathy and neglect, if not outright revolt; also at the local level they may exhibit little or no allegiance. Many an ardent young progressive is condemned to live in the Republican desert of an otherwise charming suburb. The split between the local citizens and the purely national citizens is a common problem of party politics. Thus the question of who are and who are not citizens is more than a mere legalism, although legal right is not without relevance. A most significant question of citizenship is that asking who participates in the ethical conception of the good life, embodied in the constitution of the community, and how the community's institutions, both formal and informal, are designed to effectuate participation.

If Aristotle, Plato, the Catholic church, the American Legion, the totalitarian states, and many others are right in the critical political importance they assign to education, then the educational systems, both formal and informal, that characterize our communities are of central significance. These institutions not only indoctrinate youth in the spirit of the polity; they also serve in part to separate the men of gold from the men of silver and the men of brass. The free and easy Periclean high school of the older small community mixed all social classes, nationalities, races, and religions in a school whose creed was likely to be Locke and Jefferson with a dash of the Napoleonic gospel that every private carries a marshal's baton in his knapsack.

A principal political effect of the motor car and the bedroom suburb has been the one-class school. For certain racial and national minorities, segregation and the peculiar operations of the real-estate trade had already, to some extent, produced this independently in the larger cities. The extent to which a countertrend at institutions of higher learning may overcome the influence of early education is problematic. In so far as churches, boy scouts, other youth organizations are an important factor in the role training and indoctrination of youth, they well warrant study. Each community has a system of educational institutions to indoctrinate youth in the spirit of the polity and confirm them in the principle of distributive justice by which role allocation is justified.

The political effect of parochialization of the schools is widely recognized. Yet study of the school system as a "brute fact" of American politics, and as much so as the party system, is avoided — and at the cost of losing that refreshing and serene realism that characterizes Greek political thought. We may, and in fact as disciples of Locke we must, reject the Aristotelian identification of politics with pedagogy. The ideal of the state as a glorified Rugby is incompatible with a political philosophy that refuses to see the individual and society as reaching their fulfillment in the state. But while rejecting the metaphysical idea of the ethical ultimacy of the state, and its corollary that the state should be an all-inclusive educational institution, we must acknowledge the important political functions of education.

The struggle for the minds of men is a pervasive and never ending battle. Recently the newspapers of an Ohio city rebuked the local leaders of the AFL for seeking to organize the schoolteachers with the avowed intent of getting across to the students a point of view sympathetic to labor. The union leaders replied to the outraged rebuke that this was the only way they had to break the monopoly of their opponents on the formal educational system. The process of education is central to the indoctrination of the young and the recruitment of the governing class. It complements and sometimes competes with the family, the church, and other social organizations that perform similar functions.

For Aristotle the key to the constitution is the governing class. Here is the human embodiment of the constitution. It spells out in clearly legible "big letters" what may be obscure or hidden in the legal constitution. The governing class represents or appears to represent the qualities that exemplify the conception of the good life that informs the constitution. Its members are looked up to and admired, since they most fully reflect the ideal. Their position is felt to be just, to be legitimate, because in terms of the particular constitution it is just that the richest, the most noble, the most learned, should rule.

The institutions of the society, if it is to be stable, must buttress and reinforce the principle of legitimacy. So viewed, ideally, all institutions are shaped to give effect to an ethical norm; viewed in another respect, all institutions are shaped to support the claims of a particular governing class. Thus the Federalist parson and pedagogue justified the government of the wise and the good, who turned out to be the rich and the well born. Art, literature, religion, and manners, and the social structures through which they operate, are pregnant with political consequences. They serve to support or undermine a given political order. As Irving Babbitt once remarked, all great revolutions are preceded by a revolution in the dictionary. The key value terms of a society undergo a change, sapping the symbols of legitimacy of a given order.

Governments, local and state, may range from a tight oligarchy of wealth to a demagogic mass dictatorship. For the most part, pure forms are rare. As Aristotle pointed out, there are many claims to political power: wealth, free birth, numbers, noble birth, military prowess, and the like. All of these have a real but limited justice. A stable constitution requires that no single claim prevail, and that at least wealth be tempered by numbers. In fact, this mixed government or polity is best achieved through the predominance of the middle class. Where the rich confront the poor with little or no middle class between them, the city is divided into irreconcilable armed camps. A sociological and economic substructure is necessary to support a given constitution, and that constitution will be radically altered by economic change, as from a peasant democracy to an urban proletariat. Thus Aristotle recognizes that ruling class, legal constitution, ethical order, and economy are interdependent.

Changes in one aspect have significant consequences for all others in the dynamic equilibrium of the constitution.

When we apply Aristotle's conception of constitution to state and local governments, each unit of government may be conceived of as possessed of a ruling class. From the composition and character of this ruling class emerges the real nature of the local government's constitution, as opposed to the formal legal order. The holders of political office represent a small fraction of the ruling class; the offices of the formal political order may be among the less important in the community. The separation of church and state, of politics and economics, veils some of the jagged peaks of the pyramid of power. The princes of the church, the presidents of the banks, the editors of the newspapers, the manufacturers, the labor-union leaders, the leaders of society, of fraternal organizations, of nationality and racial groups are not, as such, officers of the formal government. But if government be regarded as a decision-making process, much of the action of the formal government is mere ratification of decisions made by these holders of social power. For this reason Marx and his followers have maintained that bourgeois democracy is a fraud, in which the pseudo-equality of the ballot box hides the realities of the unequal distribution of power. As John Adams wrote to Jefferson, there are nobles in Boston as well as in Madrid.

Conservatives in the early American state constitutional conventions protested again and again that abolition of the property qualification for office or suffrage would prove pernicious or nugatory. Property was an indestructible part of political power, and failure to recognize it in the constitution would lead either to a demagogic assault on wealth or to the devising of informal means whereby wealth would achieve its inevitable influence in the power structure of the community. To the realists of the eighteenth and early nineteenth centuries the struggle between the rich and the poor, the few and the many, seemed as invariant a problem of politics as it did to Plato and Aristotle. The opponents of the Daniel Shays, while doubtless seeking to provide in the constitution an instrumentality for the solution of common social problems, frequently argued in terms reminiscent of the pages of Thucydides. Their advocacy was couched in the language of frightened oligarchs seeking to band themselves together in a league to furnish mutual aid and comfort against one another's threatening democracies.

The wisdom of the fathers is full of reference to the bloody social politics of the republics of antiquity. In no respect does their political science seem more faulty than in its gloomy prophecies that political democracy means social democracy, and social democracy means class war. On the other hand, the twin inventions of representation and federalism — in which the authors of the *Federalist* set considerable stock as so extending the feasible territorial limits of free government as to diffuse and dilute interests, and so break the force of faction — have appeared to succeed beyond their fondest hopes. Given their dour view of the nature of man, the Federalists could scarcely have dreamed that our cities and local governments would be so free of the mischief of faction as would appear from contemporary textbooks. One would never gather from a text on local government that the prime fact of politics is the struggle of classes, or that the central question of government is the ruling class.

The gulf between Aristotle and the eighteenth-century realists, on the one hand, and contemporary political science on the other is vividly apparent in the preoccupation of the former with stasis and the problems of class rule, and our present attitude of avoidance or indifference toward these issues. In part, this difference of approach results from a belief that the phenomena of class struggle, which are fundamental in Aristotelian analysis, are simply not exemplified in the American scene. In part, it is due to a belief in a fundamental social-harmony theory, similar to that of classical economics. This view results in a conception of a system of political laissez faire in which, as in economic laissez faire, no one rules. Free political competition exists in much the same way as free economic competition.

A more realistic view would see our political organization as a system that, while differing in part, is nonetheless comparable to a system of Greek city-states or to the feudal lordships and free cities of the Middle Ages, clusters of power and local government under varying degrees of external control. In Aristotle's sense, each local government may, and often will, have a ruling class of its own, once independent and now subject to or participant in a ruling class of the new more comprehensive political unit. Looked at historically and analytically, there is a continuum between the independent small governments of one period and the local governments embraced in the empires and nation-states of succeeding epochs. The cycle of building larger aggregates may halt and reverse itself, bringing about the renewed independence of lesser communities; or both the process of aggregation and that of disintegration may go forward at the same time, interacting together. Thus the study of state formation and international relations joins hands with the study of local government.

Secession, separatism, colonial nationalism, revolution, and imperialism are pervasive categories of political analysis. The ethical self-sufficiency of the community and the supremacy and independence of its ruling class are two aspects of statehood that local governments approach as limits. If they are attained, local governments become independent states; if lost, they become incorporated in larger units.

Ethical self-sufficiency means in practice that a political community possesses ideal goals whose significance for the politically decisive part of the community transcends the goals of any more or less inclusive community. The supremacy of the ruling class is derived from its commonly accepted relation to those goals from which it derives its legitimatized power. In practice, the community may possess both ethical self-sufficiency and a ruling class of its own and still fail of political independence. The captivity of the Jews under Babylon and Rome is a case in point. Ireland and Poland in recent history were incorporated as foreign bodies into alien sovereignties. But in Hobbes' terms they indeed formed "worms in the body politic." In any event, the material conditions of independent statehood depend in part on the surrounding facts of other powers.

The ethical self-sufficiency or the ideal goals of communities can be regarded as technologies for permitting large-scale cooperation, both by giving a decisive number of inhabitants participating roles and by structuring and legitimatizing a ruling class and its roles — creating an area and a personnel with shared legitimate power. The possibility of creating such goals with an appropriate ruling group is decisive not only for the creation of larger state structures in the international sphere, but equally for the solution of metropolitan problems internally. Of course, in either the international or the domestic sphere, problems may be "solved" by the force of conquest or fiat. Even here, however, the transformation of might into an accepted and acceptable right remains.

The inappropriateness, for the solution of major current problems, of our existing structure of state and local governments is a common lament of citizen, scholar, and public official. The satellite suburb entrenched in its baneful legal autonomy, the rotten-borough state, the under-represented urban population, all exemplify the conflict between the dynamics of change and the statics of a vested interest in the institutional status quo, with its passing ideals and its challenged power structure. Just as internal local government structures are menaced by the sweep of change, so the international state structure itself, in its embodiment of a bygone distribution of power and purposes, is challenged by new and legally unrecognized facts and forces.

The process of adjustment of institutional structure to the emerging new facts of life may proceed more peacefully within states, where there exists a more or less accepted mechanism for the transfer of power, than between states, where commonly accepted instrumentalities for adjustment and the saving of face are lacking. In the extreme case, and always as a real alternative, there remains the possibility of revolution in the one case and war in the other. A major achievement of political institutions is to make possible the non-violent adaptation of the status quo to the necessities of change.

Edward Hallett Carr, in his *Twenty Years Crisis*, has well expressed the problem of politics as the institutionalization of peaceful change. In this sense war and revolution are extreme means necessitated by the failure of institutions to adapt to major new facts of power. One does not have to share in Carr's apparent worship of the "bitch goddess success" to appreciate the force of this position. From it, as from that of Marx and Aristotle, the assumption of the normality of "social harmony," that underlies much economic and political analysis, seems naive, hypocritical, or pollyanna. Thus a study of American politics that focuses on parties and elections is, while important, radically insufficient, open to the same criticism that Marx leveled at the economists. It assumes the permanence of the system and therefore neglects the dynamics of its structure. It neglects the dynamics of political structure. The evisceration of politics by abstracting from its vital Aristotelian elements, now isolated in sociology and economics, accounts in part for the emptiness and insufficiency of analysis.

For Aristotle the ruling class and revolution were two of the main concepts of political analysis. Investigation guided by these concepts inevitably leads to concern for the realities of social power, its acquisition, distribution, limits, transfer, and loss. Power capabilities, a term we glibly bandy about in the analysis of international relations, has equal meaning in terms of local, state, and national government. The process of political change can be fruitfully viewed from the standpoint of changes in the composition and techniques of the ruling class, its relation to the value symbols of the society, and the dynamics of economic and cultural change.

There is certainly room for the important study of the politics and technology of cooperation. In the larger sense, however, this is a subcategory of the greater process of the dynamics of group adjustment. And even in the study of supposedly instrumental politics — as for example the fringe problem of metropolitan cities — the structure of a local ruling class and the possibility of galvanizing it into effective action is a decisive element for success. The differing fortunes of urban redevelopment in Pittsburgh — where the Mellon family and its leading scion, Richard Mellon, exert an effective hegemony — and in those communities with a jealous group of contending notables bear witness to the very everyday and very practical consequences of the structure of the local ruling class.

The emergence of labor leaders as powerholders without social status constitutes a source of instability for local constitutions and local ruling classes. Whether they will be crushed or ignored, or admitted to the country clubs and the honor-laden posts of our society, is on the agenda of history. The nationality leaders, from the Boston Irish to the Slavonians, have fought a long-drawn battle for inclusion into the upper ranks of the status system. When Harvard College conferred an honorary degree on Cardinal O'Connell of Boston the reconciliation of State Street with Lake Street was finally ratified.

The basic adjustment of the ruling class to new facts of power, compelling the admission of new elements and signalizing the decline of old, is not always easy, and sometimes is violent. The La Follette Civil Liberties Committee records the violent objection to the emergence of union power.

Sometimes the problems of intergroup adjustment approximate those with which we are painfully familiar in international life. The Negro population strains at the dikes of segregation with all the pent-up energy of a nation seeking its place in the sun. Quite literally it seeks to conquer living space, space that cannot be purchased. Violence is a technique that lies ready at hand. Despite feelings of guilt, in terms of both the plutocratic principle of justice — they have the money — and the democratic principle — they are fellow citizens — those next to the problem, feeling menaced, deny Negroes membership in a community controlled by these principles. The prevention of warfare depends on the institutionalized technique of mobilizing the neutrals.

But the solution will require granting the same accolade to the Negro leaders that has been accorded other nationality groups by the ruling class. Failing that, the Negroes would remain a community within a community, struggling for a recognition that can finally be accorded only by the ruling class. In an important sense the Negroes as a group are excluded from becoming fully participating citizens, and thus are fair game for the revolutionary appeal of communists and alien agents. Symbolic participation in community acceptance, through the leaders' attainment of social-status positions, is a major attribute of citizenship in a mass state. Thus the ruling class becomes a medium for the representation of groups and the resolution of their conflicts. It may be a far more significant center of representation than city council or legislature.

The composition, interrelation, and changes of local ruling classes give significance to the local election returns. The president of the Central Labor Union Council and the archbishop do not change with the elections. What difference, then, do the elections make? How does the apparent change in formal political power relate to and affect the real distribution of social power? The political institutions are not only a device for doing the day-by-day work of meeting commonly accepted needs; they are also a mechanism for facilitating the peaceful readjustment of the balance of social power. The legal structure may obstruct or facilitate this. It may be more accessible to some groups, some levels of government, some agencies of government than to others, in their struggle for recognition and change. And the contest will be carried on in private organizations whose decisions may frequently outweigh the public in importance.

The concept of the ruling class provides a corrective for the superficialities of the formal legal order as a true description of the actualities of political power; and the Aristotelian analysis of revolutions provides a more searching analysis of political process than our preoccupation with formal elections. The seeming inapplicability of city-state experience to the macroscopic phenomena of the nation-state has served to limit Aristotelian analysis to the office of a profound but tenuous philosophic inspiration.

That this should have occurred despite the deep appreciation of early American theorists for the classic categories of analysis is in all probability due to the great appeal of both the facts and the myth of classless society. As Professor Hartz has pointed out, American experience has been peculiar in having a democratic revolution without the necessity of overthrowing a feudal order. The absence of class consciousness may well bé due, as Professor Hartz contends, not only to the bounty of nature but even more to the fact that the middle class, never made class-conscious by struggle with a nobility, has failed to tutor the workers in their "historic" role.

Surely a part of the reason for the failure of political science to make use of the concept of the ruling class is the disrepute of Marxism and its works, and the crudity of much of vulgar Marxism. The Italian realists, such as Mosca, have remained curiosities from which to quote an occasional line with approval, but despite even the enormous vogue of Pareto they have failed to stimulate systematic study and reorientation. Elite studies there have been, but these have had the appearance of being esoteric when they have not been damned as antidemocratic.

The Aristotelian conceptions of citizen, constitution, and ruling class can be transferred from the city-state to an examination of the phenomena of government at local, state, and national levels, and even of politics, including the international. To raise the question of who are citizens, and in what sense, at each level of government, is to pin-point crucial political issues that legal categories neglect and obscure. A functional conception of citizenship is as fruitful as a functional conception of party membership.

That a city like New York may best be regarded as made up largely of resident alien merchants and mechanics, gathered for trade and pleasure, and therefore lacking in civic motivation may explain some of the necessities of its government. That the ruling class of town X are branch-plant managers taking their orders from Pittsburgh and hoping to be promoted elsewhere is a more vital political fact than the town's possession of a city-manager form of government, though the two may be related. The suburban residence of large elements of a metropolitan ruling class, and its ethos of irresponsibility, may be a more potent cause of central city disintegration than would be revealed by any analysis of the multiplicity of legal jurisdictions. Rural domination of state legislatures and the orientation of urban masses toward Washington and the presidency are deeply related to the current institutional technique for bolstering oligarchic power.

The interrelations between the geographically separated ruling classes, the differences in their composition, the formal legal constitutions through and alongside which they operate, the varying ethics that legitimatize their power, and the revolutionary movements for altering their composition, winning recognition for new elements, or overthrowing them — these are the vital stuff of politics. Their investigation can give real meaning to the shadowy phenomena of legal structures and elections, pointing to the large and cumulative phenomena and escaping the mere flux of the headlines.

Chapter II

Federal-
State
Relations

The American federal system of government, as conceived by the founding fathers, was designed to provide for the operation of two levels of government exercising power over the nation's affairs. The genius of the American system is that it has provided a distribution of powers between two levels of government without institutionalizing the distribution into self-limiting and exclusive compartments. The Constitution does not spell out the specific role of each level of government; it provides certain guide lines but no clear definitions. Herein lies the source of much of the controversy over the years as to the nature of the American federal system and the proper roles of the two levels of government. In addition, this lack of strict boundaries contributes to the adaptability of the system to new circumstances and needs.

American federalism has developed along no clear line, and the quest for definitive answers as well as generalizations has continued from the beginning to the present. Article I, section 8 of the Constitution enumerates certain powers of the federal government and implies the existence of other powers. The Supreme Court, in *McCulloch* v. *Maryland,* gave an expansive interpretation of the elastic clause, which can be used to justify those other powers. In addition, the enumerated or implied powers to tax, to charter corporations, and to institute certain regulatory laws are exercised by the federal government as concurrent powers with the states. The Constitution places certain limitations on the states as well as on the national government, but it does not clearly define all of the areas of national operation. Whatever the intent of the founding fathers as stated in the Constitution concerning the roles of the two levels of government, federalism has become a dynamic process, providing a means for change and not a static concept that fixes national and state responsibility in particular areas of operation.

The Tenth Amendment, which provides that "the powers not delegated to the United States by the Constitution, nor prohibited by it to the States, are reserved to the States respectively, or to the people," has been a mainstay of those advocating a strict separation of roles. The Amendment, however, has not been interpreted by the Supreme Court as restricting the role of the federal government if the action of the federal government is justified under its delegated or implied powers.

Changes in the actual roles of both levels of government have followed the demands of the people (with some delays imposed by the courts). These demands, in turn, have usually been the outgrowth of changes in the patterns of life brought about by such developments as industrialization, urbanization, and metropolitanization. Changes in the American scene have caused stresses in the political system, but they have not prevented the quest for solutions. For example, in an attempt to solve problems associated with change, federal activities have grown from incidental aid programs prior to World War I to massive grants-in-aid programs in the depression years and post-World War II period. The enlargement of the federal sphere has most frequently resulted from the inability or unwillingness of the states to act. However, the growth of federal powers has not precluded the development of strong state governments, and the states continue to spend an ever-increasing percentage of the total national product—in part, because of federal grants-in-aid.

The nature of American federalism has changed tremendously in the twentieth century, with much greater emphasis being placed in recent years on cooperation. Presidents, governors, and legislators have been aware of the need for change. Action taken by the national government through the Second Hoover Commission, the Committee on Intergovernmental Relations, the Joint Federal-State Action Committee, the Committee on Governmental Operation of the House of Representatives, and the President's Commission on National Goals illustrate the federal government's awareness of the need for a change in the nature of federal-state relations.

The articles in this chapter have been selected to illustrate the development, nature, and problems of American federalism. In the article "The Federal System," Morton Grodzins defines federalism as "a device for dividing decisions and functions of government," and emphasizes the cooperative nature of American federalism in the twentieth century. He insists that its entire history has been one of sharing power rather than of strict division of power between the central government and the states; the division of power is more akin to a marble cake than to a layer cake. Grodzins illustrates the trend away from the study of federalism in strictly legalistic terms—a trend which substitutes a concept of cooperative federalism for that of a sharp division of powers—and he points out that attempts to unwind the federal system and define specific areas of power have largely failed. Examples from the federal assumption of state Revolutionary War debts to the present grants-in-aid system reveal the cooperative nature of American federalism. Action by the Executive, Congress, and the Courts has improved the effectiveness of the cooperative nature of federalism, and there has been little historical evidence that the three branches of government have seriously considered federalism as a strict separation of roles. Grodzins states that it would be "a misjudgment of our history and our present situation to believe that a neat separation of governmental functions could take place without drastic alterations in our society and system of government." He is concerned not only with the development of cooperative federalism from a historical perspective but also with the political nature of the present system of sharing. Suggested goals for the system of sharing are evaluated, and the strengths and weaknesses of American federalism are examined.

A serious problem of the federal system, stemming from federal-state fiscal relations, is explored in the second article, by former Governor John Anderson of Kansas. This article highlights one of the most serious problems faced by state administrations—that of finding revenue for ever expanding programs. Governor Anderson points out that whereas federal expenditures are actually leveling off, state and local expenditures continue to rise. It is possible that by the 1970's, state and local expenditures will surpass federal expenditures. If this occurs, a serious adjustment in income resources between the states' governments and the federal government must take place. Anderson explores a number of alternatives and discusses the flaws in each before concluding that a system of tax rebates by the federal government to the states would be the most favorable solution.

A number of proposals for tax rebates have been supported in Congress and have generally had the support of governors. However, many mayors of larger cities have raised serious objections to unrestricted federal grants to states. Under the present program much of the money is channeled directly into major cities. Mayors often feel that under an unrestricted tax rebate system to the state government, the cities would not fare as well as they do under the present grants-in-aid programs. This poses a problem of state-local relations which will be considered in a later chapter.

The federal government has depended upon the system of grants-in-aid to assist the states in meeting their present obligations for increased services as well as to spur the states to undertake new programs which are considered essential to the national interest. The aid technique enables the federal government to enter into a partnership with the states without encroaching upon the reserved powers of the states. In this manner the federal government is able to maintain national standards, to balance or distribute the financial burden of government, and to bring the centralized taxing, borrowing, and monetary powers of the United States to bear on national problems. This can be done through the decentralized spending agencies of the states.

During the past thirty years there has been a recognizable trend to increase the amount spent through grants-in-aid as well as a proliferation of programs. The bulk of the increased spending has gone to the traditional areas such as agriculture, education, highways, public welfare, and housing, but an increasing amount has been allocated to post-World War II programs, including airport construction, hospital construction, urban redevelopment, watershed protection and flood prevention, and urban planning, as well as many programs to promote improved health care.

Grants-in-aid have accomplished much good, but the programs have also raised serious problems in federal-state relationships. The federal policy makers feel that guidelines are necessary if the objectives of the programs are to be achieved. The states, however, have rightly felt that these guidelines have often been an unnecessary intrusion into their affairs. In some instances they have caused serious problems in decision making at the state and local level, and have resulted in priorities being given to federally supported programs while support of other local programs which should have high priorities is lessened.

Former Governor Alfred E. Driscoll of New Jersey discusses some of the problems of grants-in-aid in his article "The Biggest Con Game in Politics," placing emphasis on a few of the most important grants. He makes a strong case against the entire program by emphasizing the often unrealistic nature of federal regulations concerning the use of grants-in-aid. More specifically, he points out that regulation and the requirements for federal approval of local plans often do not take into consideration local conditions and needs. He suggests that the programs are wasteful and that this waste may be due to the high cost of federal administration, overpayment to states due to state duplicity, or federal specifications for programs.

Finally, the former Governor questions the effect of federal grants-in-aid upon the initiative of state and local governments to face their problems and seek realistic solutions at the local level. With cases to support his arguments, Governor Driscoll amply illustrates the serious problems raised by the grants-in-aid approach—federal-state fiscal relation (that is, waste), intrusion into local affairs, erosion of local initiative, and dislocation of local fiscal management.

While Driscoll argues that the trend has gone too far and that the state should be given more power and autonomy, there are others who are more extreme in their views and who have more fundamental objections to the expanding role of the federal government. These advocates insist upon a limited central government, and they oppose most of the giant federal-state programs as exceeding the constitutional grant of powers to the central government. As strict constructionists, they see a real danger in big government at any level. One of the most lucid presentations of this position is contained in the article "The Case for 'States' Rights' " by James Jackson Kilpatrick.

Mr. Kilpatrick envisions the federal system in a fundamentally different fashion than do a majority of today's policy makers. His article is not merely an appeal to return to the Jeffersonian concept of "that government is best which governs least," but also for a strict construction of the Constitution. It is Kilpatrick's argument that centralization is a threat to individual liberty, and a restraint to the role of the states in experimentation and diversity in the solution of problems. Subscribing to the compact theory that the union was formed by the states and the states are the sources of political power, he cites the Tenth Amendment to strengthen his case. In addition, he makes a strong appeal for limited government at all levels of government.

There *are* arguments to justify the establishment of guidelines. The major objectives of establishing national standards, distributing the financial burden of government, and equalizing services in certain critical areas necessitate the establishment of guidelines and a degree of federal control.

Interstate relations comprise another important aspect of the American federal system. The Constitution lays the basis for interstate cooperation, and as the nation develops and becomes more complex, a multitude of problem areas develop which defy solution on an individual state basis. Although interstate cooperation may take many forms and may be applied to many interstate problems, this chapter uses two of the best-known forms—the interstate compact and the uniform commercial code—to serve as examples of successful methods of coming to grips with interstate problems and to illustrate the possibilities of interstate cooperation in the solution of common problems.

Bernard D. Kolasa's article on the New York Port Authority describes one of the most successful interstate compacts. The Constitution permits states to enter into compacts on common problems with the consent of Congress. These compacts make possible the solution of regional interstate problems at a lower level. Kolasa's article points up the new significance of the interstate compact in view of the national trend of interstate urbanization and metropolitanization. The author discusses a growing concern over the use of the compact and its future significance for interstate-federal relations.

The final article, "The Uniform Commercial Code: What Is Accomplished —What Remains" by William A. Schnader, is concerned with the development of uniform commercial codes by states. We need only to allude to the rapid development of interstate business enterprises to pinpoint the need for such codes. The article describes what has been accomplished in this area thus far, but more importantly it points out what has yet to be done. Mr. Schnader poses a very serious question: "Are they [states] going to delay in making the Uniform Commercial Code the law of every state until Congress is forced by the pressure from business and financial interests all over the country to regulate such transactions as sales, the negotiation of commercial paper, the issuance of letters of credit, and most of the other facets of commercial law with which the code deals?" It is generally recognized that such defaults by states have led to the expansion of federal activity in other spheres. To logically argue the issue of states rights the states must take action to satisfy the legitimate demands of their people.

THE FEDERAL SYSTEM

MORTON GRODZINS

The late Morton Grodzins was professor of political science and director of the Federalism Workshop, University of Chicago. His books include *Government and Housing in Metropolitan Areas* (1958).

Federalism is a device for dividing decisions and functions of government. As the constitutional fathers well understood, the federal structure is a means, not an end. The pages that follow are therefore not concerned with an exposition of American federalism as a formal, legal set of relationships. The focus, rather, is on the purpose of federalism, that is to say, on the distribution of power between central and peripheral units of government.

The Sharing of Functions

The American form of government is often, but erroneously, symbolized by a three-layer cake. A far more accurate image is the rainbow or marble cake, characterized by an inseparable mingling of differently colored ingredients, the colors appearing in vertical and diagonal strands and unexpected whirls. As colors are mixed in the marble cake, so functions are mixed in the American federal system. Consider the health officer, styled "sanitarian," of a rural county in a border state. He embodies the whole idea of the marble cake of government.

The sanitarian is appointed by the state under merit standards established by the federal government. His base salary comes jointly from state and federal funds, the county provides him with an office and office amenities and pays a portion of his expenses, and the largest city in the county also contributes to his salary and office by virtue of his appointment as a city plumbing inspector. It is impossible from moment to moment to tell under which governmental hat the sanitarian operates. His work of inspecting the purity of food is carried out under federal standards; but he is enforcing state laws when inspecting commodities that have not been in interstate commerce; and somewhat perversely he also acts under state authority when inspecting milk coming into the county from producing areas across the state border. He is a federal officer when impounding impure drugs shipped from a neighboring state; a federal-state officer when distributing typhoid immunization serum; a state officer when enforcing standards of industrial hygiene; a state-local officer when inspecting the city's water supply; and (to complete the

Morton Grodzins, "The Federal System" from *Goals for Americans*, pp. 265-282, © 1960 by The American Assembly, Columbia University, New York, New York. Reprinted by permission of Prentice-Hall, Inc., Englewood Cliffs, New Jersey. [Footnotes omitted.]

circle) a local officer when insisting that the city butchers adopt more hygienic methods of handling their garbage. But he cannot and does not think of himself as acting in these separate capacities. All business in the county that concerns public health and sanitation he considers his business. Paid largely from federal funds, he does not find it strange to attend meetings of the city council to give expert advice on matters ranging from rotten apples to rabies control. He is even deputized as a member of both the city and county police forces.

The sanitarian is an extreme case, but he accurately represents an important aspect of the whole range of governmental activities in the United States. Functions are not neatly parceled out among the many governments. They are shared functions. It is difficult to find any governmental activity which does not involve all three of the so-called "levels" of the federal system. In the most local of local functions — law enforcement or education, for example — the federal and state governments play important roles. In what, *a priori*, may be considered the purest central government activities — the conduct of foreign affairs, for example — the state and local governments have considerable responsibilities, directly and indirectly.

The federal grant programs are only the most obvious example of shared functions. They also most clearly exhibit how sharing serves to disperse governmental powers. The grants utilize the greater wealth-gathering abilities of the central government and establish nation-wide standards, yet they are "in aid" of functions carried out under state law, with considerable state and local discretion. The national supervision of such programs is largely a process of mutual accommodation. Leading state and local officials, acting through their professional organizations, are in considerable part responsible for the very standards that national officers try to persuade all state and local officers to accept.

Even in the absence of joint financing, federal-state-local collaboration is the characteristic mode of action. Federal expertise is available to aid in the building of a local jail (which may later be used to house federal prisoners), to improve a local water purification system, to step up building inspections, to provide standards for state and local personnel in protecting housewives against dishonest butchers' scales, to prevent gas explosions, or to produce a land use plan. States and localities, on the other hand, take important formal responsibilities in the development of national programs for atomic energy, civil defense, the regulation of commerce, and the protection of purity in foods and drugs; local political weight is always a factor in the operation of even a post office or a military establishment. From abattoirs and accounting through zoning and zoo administration, any governmental activity is almost certain to involve the influence, if not the formal administration, of all three planes of the federal system.

Attempts to Unwind the Federal System

Within the past dozen years there have been four major attempts to reform or reorganize the federal system: the first (1947-49) and second (1953-55) Hoover Commissions on Executive Organization; the Kestnbaum Commission on Intergovernmental Relations (1953-55); and the Joint Federal-State Action Committee (1957-59). All four of these groups have aimed to minimize federal activities. None of them has recognized the sharing of functions as the characteristic way American governments do things. Even when making recommendations for joint action, these official commissions take the view (as expressed in the Kestnbaum report) that "the main tradition of American federalism [is] the tradition of separateness." All four have, in varying degrees, worked to separate functions and tax sources.

The history of the Joint Federal-State Action Committee is especially instructive. The committee was established at the suggestion of President Eisenhower, who charged it, first of all, "to designate functions which the States are ready and willing to assume and finance that are now performed or financed wholly or in part by the Federal Government." He also gave the committee the task of recommending "Federal and State revenue adjustments required to enable the States to assume such functions."

The committee subsequently established seemed most favorably situated to accomplish the task of functional separation. It was composed of distinguished and able men, including among its personnel three leading members of the President's cabinet, the director of the Bureau of the Budget, and ten state governors. It had the full support of the President at every point, and it worked hard and conscientiously. Excellent staff studies were supplied by the Bureau of the Budget, the White House, the Treasury Department, and, from the state side, the Council of State Governments. It had available to it a large mass of research data, including the sixteen recently completed volumes of the Kestnbaum Commission. There existed no disagreements on party lines within the committee and, of course, no constitutional impediments to its mission. The President, his cabinet members, and all the governors (with one possible exception) on the committee completely agreed on the desirability of decentralization-via-separation-of-functions-and-taxes. They were unanimous in wanting to justify the committee's name and to produce action, not just another report.

The committee worked for more than two years. It found exactly two programs to recommend for transfer from federal to state hands. One was the federal grant program for vocational education (including practical-nurse training and aid to fishery trades); the other was federal grants for municipal waste treatment plants. The programs together cost the federal government less than $80 million in 1957, slightly more than two per cent of the total federal grants for that year. To allow the states to pay for these programs, the committee recommended that they be allowed a credit against the federal tax on local telephone calls. Calculations showed that this offset device, plus an equalizing factor, would give every state at least 40 per cent more from the tax than it received from the federal government in vocational education and sewage disposal grants. Some states were "equalized" to receive twice as much.

The recommendations were modest enough, and the generous financing feature seemed calculated to gain state support. The President recommended to Congress that all points of the program be legislated. None of them was, none has been since, and none is likely to be.

A Point of History

The American federal system has never been a system of separated governmental activities. There has never been a time when it was possible to put neat labels on discrete "federal," "state," and "local" functions. Even before the Constitution, a statute of 1785, reinforced by the Northwest Ordinance of 1787, gave grants-in-land to the states for public schools. Thus the national government was a prime force in making possible what is now taken to be the most local function of all, primary and secondary education. More important, the nation, before it was fully organized, established by this action a first principle of American federalism: the national government would use its superior resources to initiate and support national programs, principally administered by the states and localities.

The essential unity of state and federal financial systems was again recognized in the earliest constitutional days with the assumption by the federal government of the Revolutionary War debts of the states. Other points of federal-state collaboration during the Federalist period concerned the militia, law enforcement, court practices, the administration of elections, public health measures, pilot laws, and many other matters.

The nineteenth century is widely believed to have been the preeminent period of duality in the American system. Lord Bryce at the end of the century described (in *The American Commonwealth*) the federal and state governments as "distinct and separate in their action." The system, he said, was "like a great factory wherein two sets of machinery are at work, their revolving wheels apparently intermixed, their bands crossing one another, yet each set doing its own work without touching or hampering the other." Great works may contain gross errors. Bryce was wrong. The nineteenth century, like the early days of the republic, was a period principally characterized by intergovernmental collaboration.

Decisions of the Supreme Court are often cited as evidence of nineteenth century duality. In the early part of the century the Court, heavily weighted with Federalists, was intent upon enlarging the sphere of national authority; in the later years (and to the 1930's) its actions were in the direction of paring down national powers and indeed all governmental authority. Decisions referred to "areas of exclusive competence" exercised by the federal government and the states; to their powers being "separate and distinct;" and to neither being able "to intrude within the jurisdiction of the other."

Judicial rhetoric is not always consistent with judicial action, and the Court did not always adhere to separatist doctrine. Indeed, its rhetoric sometimes indicated a positive view of cooperation. In any case, the Court was rarely, if ever, directly confronted with the issue of cooperation *vs.* separation as such. Rather it was concerned with defining permissible areas of action for the central government and the states; or with saying with respect to a point at issue whether any government could take action. The Marshall Court contributed to intergovernmental cooperation by the very act of permitting federal operations where they had not existed before. Furthermore, even Marshall was willing to allow interstate commerce to be affected by the states in their use of the police power. Later courts also upheld state laws that had an impact on interstate commerce, just as they approved the expansion of the national commerce power, as in statutes providing for the control of telegraphic communication or prohibiting the interstate transportation of lotteries, impure foods and drugs, and prostitutes. Similar room for cooperation was found outside the commerce field, notably in the Court's refusal to interfere with federal grants in land or cash to the states. Although research to clinch the point has not been completed, it is probably true that the Supreme Court from 1800 to 1936 allowed far more federal-state collaboration than it blocked.

Political behavior and administrative action of the nineteenth century provide positive evidence that, throughout the entire era of so-called dual federalism, the many governments in the American federal system continued the close administrative and fiscal collaboration of the earlier period. Governmental activities were not extensive. But relative to what governments did, intergovernmental cooperation during the last century was comparable with that existing today.

Occasional presidential vetoes (from Madison to Buchanan) of cash and land grants are evidence of constitutional and ideological apprehensions about the extensive expansion of federal activities which produced widespread intergovernmental collaboration. In perspective, however, the vetoes are a more important evidence of the continuous search, not least by state officials, for ways and means to involve the central government in a wide variety of joint programs. The search was successful.

Grants-in-land and grants-in-services from the national government were of first importance in virtually all the principal functions undertaken by the states and their local subsidiaries. Land grants were made to the states for, among other purposes, elementary schools, colleges, and special educational institutions; roads, canals, rivers, harbors, and railroads; reclamation of desert and swamp lands; and veterans' welfare. In fact whatever was at the focus of state attention became the recipient of national grants. (Then, as today, national grants established state emphasis as well as followed it.) If Connecticut wished to establish a program for the care and education of the deaf and dumb, federal money in the form of a land grant was found to aid that program. If higher education relating to agriculture became a pressing need, Congress could dip into the public domain and make appropriate grants to states. If the need for swamp drainage and flood control appeared, the federal government could supply both grants-in-land and, from the Army's Corps of Engineers, the services of the only trained engineers then available.

Aid also went in the other direction. The federal government, theoretically in exclusive control of the Indian population, relied continuously (and not always wisely) on the experience and resources of state and local governments. State militias were an all-important ingredient in the nation's armed forces. State governments became unofficial but real partners in federal programs for homesteading, reclamation, tree culture, law enforcement, inland waterways, the nation's internal communications system (including highway and railroad routes), and veterans' aid of various sorts. Administrative contacts were voluminous, and the whole process of interaction was lubricated, then as today, by constituent-conscious members of Congress.

The essential continuity of the collaborative system is best demonstrated by the history of the grants. The land grant tended to become a cash grant based on the calculated disposable value of the land, and the cash grant tended to become an annual grant based upon the national government's superior tax powers. In 1887, only three years before the frontier was officially closed, thus signalizing the end of the disposable public domain, Congress enacted the first continuing cash grants.

A long, extensive, and continuous experience is therefore the foundation of the present system of shared functions characteristic of the American federal system, what we have called the marble cake of government. It is a misjudgment of our history and our present situation to believe that a neat separation of governmental functions could take place without drastic alterations in our society and system of government.

Dynamics of Sharing: The Politics of the Federal System

Many causes contribute to dispersed power in the federal system. One is the simple historical fact that the states existed before the nation. A second is in the form of creed, the traditional opinion of Americans that expresses distrust of centralized power and places great value in the strength and vitality of local units of government. Another is pride in locality and state, nurtured by the nation's size and by variations of regional and state history. Still a fourth cause of decentralization is the sheer wealth of the nation. It allows all groups, including state and local governments, to partake of the central government's largesse, supplies room for experimentation and even waste, and makes unnecessary the tight organization of political power that must follow when the support of one program necessarily means the deprivation of another.

In one important respect, the Constitution no longer operates to impede centralized government. The Supreme Court since 1937 has given Congress a relatively free hand. The federal government can build substantive programs in many areas on the taxation and commerce powers. Limitations of such central programs based on the argument, "it's unconstitutional," are no longer possible as long as Congress (in the Court's view) acts reasonably in the interest of the whole nation. The Court is unlikely to reverse this permissive view in the foreseeable future.

Nevertheless, some constitutional restraints on centralization continue to operate. The strong constitutional position of the states—for example, the assignment of two senators to each state, the role given the states in administering even national elections, and the relatively few limitations on their law-making powers—establish the geographical units as natural centers of administrative and political strength. Many clauses of the Constitution are not subject to the same latitude of interpretation as the commerce and tax clauses. The simple, clearly stated, unambiguous phrases—for example, the President "shall hold his office during the term of four years"—are subject to change only through the formal amendment process. Similar provisions exist with respect to the terms of senators and congressmen and the amendment process. All of them have the effect of retarding or restraining centralizing action of the federal government. The fixed terms of the President and members of Congress, for example, greatly impede the development of nation-wide, disciplined political parties that almost certainly would have to precede continuous large-scale expansion of federal functions.

The constitutional restraints on the expansion of national authority are less important and less direct today than they were in 1879 or in 1936. But to say that they are less important is not to say that they are unimportant.

The nation's politics reflect these decentralizing causes and add some of their own. The political parties of the United States are unique. They seldom perform the function that parties traditionally perform in other countries, the function of gathering together diverse strands of power and welding them into one. Except during the period of nominating and electing a president and for the essential but non-substantive business of organizing the houses of Congress, the American parties rarely coalesce power at all. Characteristically they do the reverse, serving as a canopy under which special and local interests are represented with little regard for anything that can be called a party program. National leaders are elected on a party ticket, but in Congress they must seek cross-party support if their leadership is to be effective. It is a rare president during rare periods who can produce legislation without facing the defection of substantial numbers of his own party. (Wilson could do this in the first session of the sixty-third Congress; but Franklin D. Roosevelt could not, even during the famous hundred days of 1933.) Presidents whose parties form the majority of the congressional houses must still count heavily on support from the other party.

The parties provide the pivot on which the entire governmental system swings. Party operations, first of all, produce in legislation the basic division of functions between the federal government, on the one hand, and state and local governments, on the other. The Supreme Court's permissiveness with respect to the expansion of national powers has not in fact produced any considerable extension of exclusive federal functions. The body of federal law in all fields has remained, in the words of Henry M. Hart, Jr. and Herbert Wechsler, "interstitial in its nature," limited in objective and resting upon the principal body of legal relationships defined by state law. It is difficult to find any area of federal legislation that is not significantly affected by state law.

In areas of new or enlarged federal activity, legislation characteristically provides important roles for state and local governments. This is as true of Democratic as of Republican administrations and true even of functions for which arguments of efficiency would produce exclusive federal responsibility. Thus the unemployment compensation program of the New Deal and the airport program of President Truman's administration both provided important responsibilities for state governments. In both cases attempts to eliminate state participation were defeated by a cross-party coalition of pro-state votes and influence. A large fraction of the Senate is usually made up of ex-governors, and the membership of both houses is composed of men who know that their re-election depends less upon national leaders or national party organization than upon support from their home constituencies. State and local officials are key members of these constituencies, often central figures in selecting candidates and in turning out the vote. Under such circumstances, national legislation taking state and local views heavily into account is inevitable.

Second, the undisciplined parties affect the character of the federal system as a result of senatorial and congressional interference in federal administrative programs on behalf of local interests. Many aspects of the legislative involvement in administrative affairs are formalized. The Legislative Reorganization Act of 1946, to take only one example, provided that each of the standing committees "shall exercise continuous watchfulness" over administration of laws within its jurisdiction. But the formal system of controls, extensive as it is, does not compare in importance with the informal and extralegal network of relationships in producing continuous legislative involvement in administrative affairs.

Senators and congressmen spend a major fraction of their time representing problems of their constituents before administrative agencies. An even larger fraction of congressional staff time is devoted to the same task. The total magnitude of such "case work" operations is great. In one five-month period of 1943 the Office of Price Administration received a weekly average of 842 letters from members of Congress. If phone calls and personal contacts are added, each member of Congress on the average presented the OPA with a problem involving one of his constituents twice a day in each five-day work week. Data for less vulnerable agencies during less intensive periods are also impressive. In 1958, to take only one example, the Department of Agriculture estimated (and underestimated) that it received an average of 159 congressional letters per working day. Special congressional liaison staffs have been created to service this mass of business, though all higher officials meet it in one form or another. The Air Force in 1958 had, under the command of a major general, 137 people (55 officers and 82 civilians) working in its liaison office.

The widespread, consistent, and in many ways unpredictable character of legislative interference in administrative affairs has many consequences for the tone and character of American administrative behavior. From the perspective of this paper, the important consequence is the comprehensive, day-to-day, even hour-by-hour, impact of local views on national programs. No point of substance or procedure is immune from congressional scrutiny. A substantial portion of the entire weight of this impact is on behalf of the state and local governments. It is a weight that can alter procedures for screening immigration applications, divert the course of a national highway, change the tone of an international negotiation, and amend a social security law to accommodate local practices or fulfill local desires.

The party system compels administrators to take a political role. This is a third way in which the parties function to decentralize the American system. The administrator must play politics for the same reason that the politician is able to play in administration: the parties are without program and without discipline.

In response to the unprotected position in which the party situation places him, the administrator is forced to seek support where he can find it. One ever-present task is to nurse the Congress of the United States, that crucial constituency which ultimately controls his agency's budget and program. From the administrator's view, a sympathetic consideration of congressional requests (if not downright submission to them) is the surest way to build the political support without which the administrative job could not continue. Even the completely task-oriented administrator must be sensitive to the need for congressional support and to the relationship between case work requests, on one side, and budgetary and legislative support, on the other. "You do a good job handling the personal problems and requests of a Congressman," a White House officer said, "and you have an easier time convincing him to back your program." Thus there is an important link between the nursing of congressional requests, requests that largely concern local matters, and the most comprehensive national programs. The administrator must accommodate to the former as a price of gaining support for the latter.

One result of administrative politics is that the administrative agency may become the captive of the nation-wide interest group it serves or presumably regulates. In such cases no government may come out with effective authority: the winners are the interest groups themselves. But in a very large number of cases, states and localities also win influence. The politics of administration is a process of making peace with legislators who for the most part consider themselves the guardians of local interests. The political role of administrators therefore contributes to the power of states and localities in national programs.

Finally, the way the party system operates gives American politics their over-all distinctive tone. The lack of party discipline produces an openness in the system that allows individuals, groups, and institutions (including state and local governments) to attempt to influence national policy at every step of the legislative-administrative process. This is the "multiple-crack" attribute of the American government. "Crack" has two meanings. It means not only many fissures or access points; it also means, less statically, opportunities for wallops or smacks at government.

If the parties were more disciplined, the result would not be a cessation of the process by which individuals and groups impinge themselves upon the central government. But the present state of the parties clearly allows for a far greater operation of the multiple crack than would be possible under the conditions of centralized party control. American interest groups exploit literally uncountable access points in the legislative-administrative process. If legislative lobbying, from committee stages to the conference committee, does not produce results, a cabinet secretary is called. His immediate associates are petitioned. Bureau chiefs and their aides are hit. Field officers are put under pressure. Campaigns are instituted by which friends of the agency apply a secondary influence on behalf of the interested party. A conference with the President may be urged.

To these multiple points for bringing influence must be added the multiple voices of the influencers. Consider, for example, those in a small town who wish to have a federal action taken. The easy merging of public and private interest at the local level means that the influence attempt is made in the name of the whole community, thus removing it from political partisanship. The Rotary Club as well as the City Council, the Chamber of Commerce and the mayor, eminent citizens and political bosses — all are readily enlisted. If a conference in a senator's office will expedite matters, someone on the local scene can be found to make such a conference possible and effective. If technical information is needed, technicians will supply it. State or national professional organizations of local officials, individual congressmen and senators, and not infrequently whole state delegations will make the local cause their own. Federal field officers, who service localities, often assume local views. So may elected and appointed state officers. Friendships are exploited, and political mortgages called due. Under these circumstances, national policies are molded by local action.

In summary, then, the party system functions to devolve power. The American parties, unlike any other, are highly responsive when directives move from the bottom to the top, highly unresponsive from top to bottom. Congressmen and senators can rarely ignore concerted demands from their home constituencies; but no party leader can expect the same kind of response from those below, whether he be a President asking for congressional support or a congressman seeking aid from local or state leaders.

Any tightening of the party apparatus would have the effect of strengthening the central government. The four characteristics of the system, discussed above, would become less important. If control from the top were strictly applied, these hallmarks of American decentralization might entirely disappear. To be specific, if disciplined and program-oriented parties were achieved: (1) It would make far less likely legislation that takes heavily into account the desires and prejudices of the highly decentralized power groups and institutions of the country, including the state and local governments. (2) It would to a large extent prevent legislators, individually and collectively, from intruding themselves on behalf of non-national interests in national administrative programs. (3) It would put an end to the administrator's search for his own political support, a search that often results in fostering state, local, and other non-national powers. (4) It would dampen the process by which individuals and groups, including state and local political leaders, take advantage of multiple cracks to steer national legislation and administration in ways congenial to them and the institutions they represent.

Alterations of this sort could only accompany basic changes in the organization and style of politics which, in turn, presuppose fundamental changes at the parties' social base. The sharing of functions is, in fact, the sharing of power. To end this sharing process would mean the destruction of whatever measure of decentralization exists in the United States today.

Goals for the System of Sharing

The Goal of Understanding

Our structure of government is complex, and the politics operating that structure are mildly chaotic. Circumstances are ever-changing. Old institutions mask intricate procedures. The nation's history can be read with alternative glosses, and what is nearest at hand may be furthest from comprehension. Simply to understand the federal system is therefore a difficult task. Yet without understanding there is little possibility of producing desired changes in the system. Social structures and processes are relatively impervious to purposeful change. They also exhibit intricate interrelationships so that change induced at point "A" often produces unanticipated results at point "Z." Changes introduced into an imperfectly understood system are as likely to produce reverse consequences as the desired ones.

This is counsel of neither futility nor conservatism for those who seek to make our government a better servant of the people. It is only to say that the first goal for those setting goals with respect to the federal system is that of understanding it.

Two Kinds of Decentralization

The recent major efforts to reform the federal system have in large part been aimed at separating functions and tax sources, at dividing them between the federal government and the states. All of these attempts have failed. We can now add that their success would be undesirable.

It is easy to specify the conditions under which an ordered separation of functions could take place. What is principally needed is a majority political party, under firm leadership, in control of both Presidency and Congress, and, ideally but not necessarily, also in control of a number of states. The political discontinuities, or the absence of party links, (1) between the governors and their state legislatures, (2) between the President and the governors, and (3) between the President and Congress clearly account for both the picayune recommendations of the Federal-State Action Committee and for the failure of even those recommendations in Congress. If the President had been in control of Congress (that is, consistently able to direct a majority of House and Senate votes), this alone would have made possible some genuine separation and devolution of functions. The failure to decentralize by order is a measure of the decentralization of power in the political parties.

Stated positively, party centralization must precede governmental decentralization by order. But this is a slender reed on which to hang decentralization. It implies the power to centralize. A majority party powerful enough to bring about ordered decentralization is far more likely to choose in favor of ordered centralization. And a society that produced centralized national parties would, by that very fact, be a society prepared to accept centralized government.

Decentralization by order must be contrasted with the different kind of decentralization that exists today in the United States. It may be called the decentralization of mild chaos. It exists because of the existence of dispersed power centers. This form of decentralization is less visible and less neat. It rests on no discretion of central authorities. It produces at times specific acts that many citizens may consider undesirable or evil. But power sometimes wielded even for evil ends may be desirable power. To those who find value in the dispersion of power, decentralization by mild chaos is infinitely more desirable than decentralization by order. The preservation of mild chaos is an important goal for the American federal system.

Oiling the Squeak Points

In a governmental system of genuinely shared responsibilities, disagreements inevitably occur. Opinions clash over proximate ends, particular ways of doing things become the subject of public debate, innovations are contested. These are not basic defects in the system. Rather, they are the system's energy-reflecting life blood. There can be no permanent "solutions" short of changing the system itself by elevating one partner to absolute supremacy. What can be done is to attempt to produce conditions in which conflict will not fester but be turned to constructive solutions of particular problems.

A long list of specific points of difficulty in the federal system can be easily identified. No adequate congressional or administrative mechanism exists to review the patchwork of grants in terms of national needs. There is no procedure by which to judge, for example, whether the national government is justified in spending so much more for highways than for education. The working force in some states is inadequate for the effective performance of some nation-wide programs, while honest and not-so-honest graft frustrates efficiency in others. Some federal aid programs distort state budgets, and some are so closely supervised as to impede state action in meeting local needs. Grants are given for programs too narrowly defined, and over-all programs at the state level consequently suffer. Administrative, accounting and auditing difficulties are the consequence of the multiplicity of grant programs. City officials complain that the states are intrusive fifth wheels in housing, urban redevelopment, and airport building programs.

Some differences are so basic that only a demonstration of strength on one side or another can solve them. School desegregation illustrates such an issue. It also illustrates the correct solution (although not the most desirable method of reaching it): in policy conflicts of fundamental importance, touching the nature of democracy itself, the view of the whole nation must prevail. Such basic ends, however, are rarely at issue, and sides are rarely taken with such passion that loggerheads are reached. Modes of settlement can usually be found to lubricate the squeak points of the system.

A pressing and permanent state problem, general in its impact, is the difficulty of raising sufficient revenue without putting local industries at a competitive disadvantage or without an expansion of sales taxes that press hardest on the least wealthy. A possible way of meeting this problem is to establish a state-levied income tax that could be used as an offset for federal taxes. The maximum level of the tax which could be offset would be fixed by federal law. When levied by a state, the state collection would be deducted from federal taxes. But if a state did not levy the tax, the federal government would. An additional fraction of the total tax imposed by the states would be collected directly by the federal government and used as an equalization fund, that is, distributed among the less wealthy states. Such a tax would almost certainly be imposed by all states since not to levy it would give neither political advantage to its public leaders nor financial advantage to its citizens. The net effect would be an increase in the total personal and corporate income tax.

The offset has great promise for strengthening state governments. It would help produce a more economic distribution of industry. It would have obvious financial advantages for the vast majority of states. Since a large fraction of all state income is used to aid political subdivisions, the local governments would also profit, though not equally as long as cities are under-represented in state legislatures. On the other hand, such a scheme will appear disadvantageous to some low-tax states which profit from the in-migration of industry (though it would by no means end all state-by-state tax differentials). It will probably excite the opposition of those concerned over governmental centralization, and they will not be assuaged by methods that suggest themselves for making both state and central governments bear the psychological impact of the tax. Although the offset would probably produce an across-the-board tax increase, wealthier persons, who are affected more by an income tax than by other levies, can be expected to join forces with those whose fear is centralization. (This is a common alliance and, in the nature of things, the philosophical issue rather than financial advantage is kept foremost.)

Those opposing such a tax would gain additional ammunition from the certain knowledge that federal participation in the scheme would lead to some federal standards governing the use of the funds. Yet the political strength of the states would keep these from becoming onerous. Indeed, inauguration of the tax offset as a means of providing funds to the states might be an occasion for dropping some of the specifications for existing federal grants. One federal standard, however, might be possible because of the greater representation of urban areas in the constituency of Congress and the President than in the constituency of state legislatures: Congress might make a state's participation in the offset scheme dependent upon a periodic reapportionment of state legislatures.

The income tax offset is only one of many ideas that can be generated to meet serious problems of closely meshed governments. The fate of all such schemes ultimately rests, as it should, with the politics of a free people. But much can be done if the primary technical effort of those concerned with improving the federal system were directed not at separating its interrelated parts but at making them work together more effectively. Temporary commissions are relatively inefficient in this effort, though they may be useful for making general assessments and for generating new ideas. The professional organizations of government workers do part of the job of continuously scrutinizing programs and ways and means of improving them. A permanent staff, established in the President's office and working closely with state and local officials, could also perform a useful and perhaps important role.

The Strength of the Parts

Whatever governmental "strength" or "vitality" may be, it does not consist of independent decision-making in legislation and administration. Federal-state interpenetration here is extensive. Indeed, a judgment of the relative domestic strength of the two planes must take heavily into account the influence of one on the other's decisions. In such an analysis the strength of the states (and localities) does not weigh lightly. The nature of the nation's politics makes federal functions more vulnerable to state influence than state offices are to federal influence. Many states, as the Kestnbaum Commission noted, live with "self-imposed constitutional limitations" that make it difficult for them to "perform all of the services that their citizens require." If this has the result of adding to federal responsibilities, the states' importance in shaping and administering federal programs eliminates much of the sting.

The geography of state boundaries, as well as many aspects of state internal organization, are the products of history and cannot be justified on any grounds of rational efficiency. Who, today, would create major governmental subdivisions the size of Maryland, Delaware, New Jersey, or Rhode Island? Who would write into Oklahoma's fundamental law an absolute state debt limit of $500,000? Who would design (to cite only the most extreme cases) Georgia's and Florida's gross under-representation of urban areas in both houses of the legislature?

A complete catalogue of state political and administrative horrors would fill a sizeable volume. Yet exhortations to erase them have roughly the same effect as similar exhortations to erase sin. Some of the worst inanities — for example, the boundaries of the states, themselves — are fixed in the national constitution and defy alteration for all foreseeable time. Others, such as urban under-representation in state legislatures, serve the over-represented groups, including some urban ones, and the effective political organization of the deprived groups must precede reform.

Despite deficiencies of politics and organizations that are unchangeable or slowly changing, it is an error to look at the states as static anachronisms. Some of them—New York, Minnesota, and California, to take three examples spanning the country—have administrative organizations that compare favorably in many ways with the national establishment. Many more in recent years have moved rapidly towards integrated administrative departments, state-wide budgeting, and central leadership. The others have models-in-existence to follow, and active professional organizations (led by the Council of State Governments) promoting their development. Slow as this change may be, the states move in the direction of greater internal effectiveness.

The pace toward more effective performance at the state level is likely to increase. Urban leaders, who generally feel themselves disadvantaged in state affairs, and suburban and rural spokesmen, who are most concerned about national centralization, have a common interest in this task. The urban dwellers want greater equality in state affairs, including a more equitable share of state financial aid; non-urban dwellers are concerned that city dissatisfactions should not be met by exclusive federal, or federal-local, programs. Antagonistic, rather than amiable, cooperation may be the consequence. But it is a cooperation that can be turned to politically effective measures for a desirable upgrading of state institutions.

If one looks closely, there is scant evidence for the fear of the federal octopus, the fear that expansion of central programs and influence threatens to reduce the states and localities to compliant administrative arms of the central government. In fact, state and local governments are touching a larger proportion of the people in more ways than ever before; and they are spending a higher fraction of the total national product than ever before. Federal programs have increased, rather than diminished, the importance of the governors; stimulated professionalism in state agencies; increased citizen interest and participation in government; and, generally, enlarged and made more effective the scope of state action. It may no longer be true in any significant sense that the states and localities are "closer" than the federal government to the people. It is true that the smaller governments remain active and powerful members of the federal system.

Central Leadership: The Need for Balance

The chaos of party processes makes difficult the task of presidential leadership. It deprives the President of ready-made congressional majorities. It may produce, as in the chairmen of legislative committees, power-holders relatively hidden from public scrutiny and relatively protected from presidential direction. It allows the growth of administrative agencies which sometimes escape control by central officials. These are prices paid for a wide dispersion of political power. The cost is tolerable because the total results of dispersed power are themselves desirable and because, where clear national supremacy is essential, in foreign policy and military affairs, it is easiest to secure.

Moreover, in the balance of strength between the central and peripheral governments, the central government has on its side the whole secular drift towards the concentration of power. It has on its side technical developments that make central decisions easy and sometimes mandatory. It has on its side potent purse powers, the result of superior tax-gathering resources. It has potentially on its side the national leadership capacities of the presidential office. The last factor is the controlling one, and national strength in the federal system has shifted with the leadership desires and capacities of the chief executive. As these have varied, so there has been an almost rhythmic pattern: periods of central strength put to use alternating with periods of central strength dormant.

Following a high point of federal influence during the early and middle years of the New Deal, the post-war years have been, in the weighing of central-peripheral strength, a period of light federal activity. Excepting the Supreme Court's action in favor of school desegregation, national influence by design or default has not been strong in domestic affairs. The danger now is that the central government is doing too little rather than too much. National deficiencies in education and health require the renewed attention of the national government. Steepening population and urbanization trend lines have produced metropolitan area problems that can be effectively attacked only with the aid of federal resources. New definitions of old programs in housing and urban redevelopment, and new programs to deal with air pollution, water supply, and mass transportation are necessary. The federal government's essential role in the federal system is that of organizing, and helping to finance, such nation-wide programs.

The American federal system exhibits many evidences of the dispersion of power not only because of formal federalism but more importantly because our politics reflect and reinforce the nation's diversities-within-unity. Those who value the virtues of decentralization, which writ large are virtues of freedom, need not scruple at recognizing the defects of those virtues. The defects are principally the danger that parochial and private interests may not coincide with, or give way to, the nation's interest. The necessary cure for these defects is effective national leadership.

The centrifugal force of domestic politics needs to be balanced by the centripetal force of strong presidential leadership. Simultaneous strength at center and periphery exhibits the American system at its best, if also at its noisiest. The interests of both find effective spokesmen. States and localities (and private interest groups) do not lose their influence opportunities, but national policy becomes more than the simple consequence of successful, momentary concentrations of non-national pressures: it is guided by national leaders.

CAN THE STATE LIVE ON CRUMBS?

Extension of Remarks of Hon. Karl E. Mundt of South Dakota in the Senate of the United States

Mr. MUNDT. Mr. President, as a member of the Senate Subcommittee on Intergovernmental Relations, and a charter member of the President's Advisory Commission on Intergovernmental Relations, my attention has been sharply focused on the compelling seriousness of the need of study and attention to the area of intergovernmental relations and our Federal system today.

Appearing in the Saturday Review for January 9, 1965, is an excellent statement of Federal-State fiscal relations by former Gov. John Anderson, of Kansas, who until recently was a member of the Advisory Commission on Intergovernmental Relations. Many of the conclusions Governor Anderson has reached are the same as those reached by our subcommittee. Because of the pressing need for more effort in developing greater fiscal capacity and tax effort at all levels of government in our Federal system, I ask unanimous consent that Governor Anderson's article be printed in the Appendix of the *Congressional Record.*

There being no objection, the article was ordered to be printed in the *Record,* as follows:

The Challenge of Prosperity: Can the State Live on Crumbs? — What Happens When Washington Cuts Into the Pie of Local Revenue

JOHN ANDERSON

The choices which Americans must make over the next 2 or 3 years concerning the critical question of Federal-State fiscal relations will greatly affect the future nature of the Federal system. The best way to begin a

Reprinted from *The Congressional Record,* February 19, 1965, A. pp. 728-730. Mr. Anderson's remarks originally appeared as "The Challenge of Prosperity: Can the State Live on Crumbs?—What Happens When Washington Cuts into the Pie of Local Revenue," in the *Saturday Review,* January 9, 1965. Reprinted by permission of the author, *Saturday Review,* and the Center for Democratic Institutions.

consideration of Federal and State fiscal relations is to sort out the salient facts about Federal, State, and local governmental revenues and expenditures. Some of these facts are startling and all of them have serious implications for the future. (By "serious" I do not necessarily mean "discouraging.") But first, some facts and figures:

1. Amazing as it may sound to some, Federal expenditure needs are leveling off while at the same time State and local expenditures are continuing to skyrocket.

2. By 1970 or thereabouts, barring drastic changes in the international situation, annual State and local expenditures will have passed total Federal expenditures, including those for defense and foreign aid. In the fiscal year 1963 Federal expenditures for civilian government totaled about $30 billion, in comparison to State and local outlays of $64 billion. I would guess that by 1971 State and local expenditures will have reached $120 billion, compared with a Federal budget of $110 to $115 billion by that time.

3. State and local government employment is rising steeply. These governments now have about 7,500,000 employees, compared with 2,500,000 Federal employees.

4. During the past decade State and local outlays grew more than 8 percent annually, or double the growth rate of the national income.

5. During the past decade State and local governments have had to increase tax rates repeatedly. At the Federal level there have been two large tax cuts, in 1954 and 1964, with talk of more good things to come.

6. State and local debt increased by 170 percent from 1952 to 1962, with over $80 billion outstanding at the end of the period.

7. The most costly functions at the State and local level have been and will continue to be those of education, roads, health and welfare.

8. Taxes by all governments took about 25 percent of the gross national product in 1952, and the same proportion a decade later. However, the share taken by the State and local government continues to rise and the Federal share continues to decline.

9. In round figures, the State-local tax take is made up of 45 percent property taxes; 12 percent income taxes (most of which are only mildly graduated, if at all); 15 percent general sales taxes; 13 percent gasoline and motor vehicle taxes; and 15 percent miscellaneous, such as cigarette, liquor, and inheritance taxes.

10. Federal grants-in-aid continue to grow apace in both magnitude and variety. This aid tripled between the years 1952 and 1962. It now stands at $11 billion. The last Congress alone added between 10 and 30 new grant programs, depending on what one calls a separate program category.

11. The rate of tax mortality among State and local political leaders is very high. A Governor or mayor must raise taxes in order to meet his increasing responsibilities—but he is often voted out of office for doing

so. Were he to choose to cut services rather than to raise taxes he would also be likely to get kicked out—so he usually tries to raise taxes at the beginning rather than the middle of his term. Also, we are told continually that any further increases in State and local taxes will drive industry out of the State or discourage new industry from coming in. In other words, political and economic pressures at the State and local levels are against tax increases.

12. We are told that Federal revenues are likely to outstrip expenditure needs over the next few years, with a budgetary surplus the likely result unless new domestic spending programs are undertaken by the Federal Government or unless the Federal debt is reduced.

These 12 basic facts generally tell where we have been, where we are now, and where we are tending in Federal-State fiscal relations. The essence of what they tell us is this:

The responsibilities for nonmilitary public services in government over the next few years are going to fall largely on State and local levels of governments. However, State and local revenue systems are much less responsive to economic growth than is the Federal revenue system. Consequently, State and local expenditure needs are going to outstrip revenues at current rates, while it appears that at the Federal level revenue at current rates is going to outstrip expenditure needs. The big question before us is: "Which of several alternate courses should be taken?"

An obvious possibility is to utilize judiciously any Federal budgetary surpluses for reductions in the debt or reductions in tax rates, according to the economic outlook at the time. It may be the result of an outdated Puritan ethic even to consider the reduction of debt. But I think we would all agree that, in years of full employment and firm or rising prices, an application of Federal surpluses to debt retirement would not be unduly deflationary.

On the other hand, to confine the use of Federal surpluses solely to Federal tax reductions or to debt retirement is objected to on two grounds. First, it does nothing in a direct sense to ease the pinch on State and local governments. Second, if Federal tax rates are steadily reduced, and State and local taxes continue to increase, the result will be increased burdens upon property and consumption taxes, and lessened burdens on income taxes.

A second possibility is to utilize Federal surpluses for the initiation of some new and large Federal grant-in-aid programs in areas having a strong element of national interest. Some of the obvious fields would be education, highways, and mental health. It is not difficult to dredge up several other fields of State and local activity in which Federal financial assistance would be welcome.

However, this approach meets with some strong objections. In the first place, Federal aid in these new fields would inevitably be accompanied by Federal controls. Our existing Federal aid programs are accompanied by controls. New ones would be, too. In the second place, at Federal, State, and local levels we are approaching the limits of manageability in the variety and complexity of Federal grant programs. We can add new ones, but getting rid of old ones is practically impossible.

As the Advisory Commission on Intergovernmental Relations has observed, "there is nothing so permanent as a temporary grant-in-aid." Many thoughtful people are coming to the conclusion that there must be simpler and better ways of making future Federal funds available to the States.

A third possibility is to initiate the concept of an unconditional Federal grant to the States — often referred to as a "block grant." The difficulty with this approach in the past has been that its advocates have coupled it with simultaneous elimination of present Federal grants. In addition to other arguments against such an approach, it is not feasible from a political standpoint. It would be hard enough to get Congress to agree with the concept of an unconditional grant; it would be impossible to get it to carry on a corollary fight with all of the interest groups that are involved in the existing program grants.

In our new situation of projected Federal surpluses, however, the possibility is advanced of initiating a block grant to the States to be used for virtually any purpose except highways and with no matching or other strings attached, leaving undisturbed the existing pattern of Federal grants in the various program areas. This approach has the advantage of administrative simplicity and a transfer of Federal funds to the States without accompanying controls. Furthermore, to the extent desired, the distribution of such a grant could be keyed to the fiscal capacity of the various States so that any desired degree of equalization between low- and high-income States could be accomplished. This general approach seems to be the one most favored by the administration.

The principal argument against this approach is the alleged lack of political feasibility. Specifically, how could one persuade Congress to turn loose billions of dollars of Federal funds each year, without any specifications as to their use by the recipient States?

Another argument is advanced against this type of approach; namely, that local governments, as well as State governments, should receive unconditional Federal grants and that the sharing of these funds between State and local governments should not be left to the discretion of the individual State. However, as a Governor, I cannot subscribe to this argument.

In the first place, the local governments are subdivisions of the State and operate under the provisions of State constitutions and statutes. Secondly, the division of responsibilities and, consequently, fiscal burdens between State and local governments, varies from State to State. Thirdly, no yardstick exists by which Federal funds could be distributed directly to localities on anything other than a per capita basis, because we have no measures by which to compare fiscal capacities of local government on a nationwide basis. Finally, the reapportionment of State legislatures on the basis of one man, one vote, may relieve some of the fears that the Federal funds would be disproportionately divided.

A fourth possibility would be to ease the State-local tax bind by means of a credit against the Federal personal income tax for State and local taxes paid. Such a credit would necessarily be less than 100 percent but would cover all State and local taxes. This would leave it up to each State and local government to determine the most equitable taxation method to be employed in meeting the massive increases in State and local expenditures, but at the same time would make it possible for a designated portion of such tax increases to be borne indirectly by the Federal Government. This would make tax raising more politically feasible at the State and local levels. It would also meet the argument of local governments that they should not have to depend on the State for a distribution of Federal aid. It is also one of the most politically feasible of all the approaches from the standpoint of the Congressman or Senator because it combines a Federal tax reduction with automatic help to State and local governments.

This approach, however, is open to the objection that it would be regressive in nature and would not benefit the people who pay State and local taxes — particularly sales taxes — but whose incomes are not sufficiently high to place them in a Federal tax bracket. This argument could be partially met by having the credit apply in a decreasing scale as one moves up in the tax brackets.

A fifth alternative would be to rebate a percentage of Federal income taxes to the State of collection. This has been proposed at various times in Congress. It would be a tax sharing rather than a tax credit arrangement. It would be simple to administer and would leave State and local governments free to chart their future policies on taxes and expenditures. However, it is objected to on the ground that existing fiscal disparities among the States could not be recognized in the rebate arrangement. New York and California, for example, being relatively high-income States with many citizens paying taxes in the higher Federal brackets, would get back a much larger per capita share than would low-income States.

I have attempted to describe briefly the present Federal-State fiscal situation, the major trends, and some alternate proposals for improving the balance in the fiscal relationships between our various levels of government. Up to this point, I have tried to be completely objective in stating the problem and in presenting the arguments for and against the various solutions that have been suggested.

At this point I would like to give you my own views on the most desirable path to be pursued.

Unlike some, I do not view the Federal tax system as ideal, either from the standpoint of equity or from the standpoint of maximum encouragement to economic growth. The corporate income tax rate is still at a high level. I am confident that further reductions in the corporate income tax would, for the most part, find their way into new investment in plant and equipment. Investment in new plant by private enterprise is an ideal stimulant to growth.

Next, I should explain the absence from the list of the five foregoing alternatives of a proposal that has been viewed fondly by many Governors over the years — that of exchanging some Federal tax sources for some existing Federal grants-in-aid. While I would like to see something of this sort accomplished, I and all of my fellow Governors know that it is neither equitable nor feasible. It was tried a few years ago during the Eisenhower administration when it was proposed that the Federal telephone tax be repealed and this tax source turned over to the States, while at the same time a group of grants-in-aid equal to the amount of Federal telephone tax be discontinued — leaving it to the States to pick up the responsibility for the functions formerly aided.

This plan collapsed when it became apparent that the transfer of the tax source would aid the wealthy States most and the poor States least, while the cessation of the grants would hurt the wealthy States least and the poor States most. Governors and Congressmen alike lost little time in turning their backs on that one.

I think that, whatever steps are taken to provide increased Federal aid to the States, the implication should not be left that the States and local governments can relax and stop trying to improve their respective revenue systems. The States are not trying to duck their responsibility; they recognize that much remains to be accomplished in strengthening the structure of State government and improving their tax systems, particularly with regard to the local property tax.

Now, let's get to the heart of the matter. Which of the five possibilities would be best for the States and best for the Nation, and what are the political feasibilities?

It is always an easy answer to say that the best government is that which is closest to the people. It is also easy to say, and it always sounds good, that Federal bureaucracy will be our downfall and that our strength lies in a strong free enterprise system.

These statements may be true, but what virtue they have lies in their generality.

It seems to me we must rely on a combination of programs in the fiscal fields — active in strengthening the State and local governments, yet utilizing, when needed, the combined strength of financial resources of the entire Nation.

If we reach the point of Federal tax surplus, we should not only consider tax reductions, but also apply some of the surplus to debt reduction.

I favor a rebate or tax-sharing program, the objections notwithstanding. It seems to me that such a tax-sharing program could be effective in strengthening the State governments and thwarting the ever-increasing trend toward centralized control. Such tax sharing should not preclude continued use of grant-in-aid programs. While I favor tax sharing over grant-in-aid programs, because of the extensive controls attached to some of the latter, I think it extremely likely that the Federal Government will favor a block grant plan so as to give States with lower gross State products relatively larger amounts of money, probably in combination with tax cuts and added grant programs.

There should be few strings attached except the requirement for a well-developed State spending plan. Performance should be measured, perhaps annually.

Every State will have to put more energy, talent, and money into planning, because the Federal money will likely go to education, environment control, perhaps urban and rural renewal. These will be fields of endeavor for both State and local governments. They will therefore require exceptional planning activities.

A Federal tax return program might be a major catalyst. Long overdue, it is needed to initiate regional thinking and action on public problems. Despite the practical difficulties in arranging useful cooperation among present groups across political boundaries, regional solutions are clearly mandatory, with the likelihood that political obstacles will be readily overcome when sizable rebate funds are the incentive.

The Midwestern Governors' Association is currently working toward effective regional cooperation in the fields of equalization in Federal defense spending, in research and development, and in the interstate cooperation for utilization of graduate and professional school facilities in the colleges and universities by means of reciprocal contracts. Mental health programs and penal programs are also being explored for regional cooperative effects.

These trends point in one direction—the need for more management-trained and professional staff people in State and local government. Finding these people, integrating them into State governments, and paying for their services will be a major problem, and State governments must then compete with private industry, universities, Federal Government, and other institutions for the same people. The market will remain tight for another 7 to 10 years, because of the population-age distribution. States may want to consider contracting out some of their problems to skilled groups throughout the country.

Perhaps the Federal Government can be prevailed upon to distribute back to the States some of the talented people it now employs, along with money. This might have a considerable beneficial effect on the "brain drain" that is now such a major issue among many States. It could also mean that States like Kansas might celebrate the return of ex-patriates who have left Kansas to work in the Federal establishment because of the lack of challenging, adequately reimbursed, opportunities at home.

All these points are supported by the increasing regard and responsibility with which the voting public views government solutions to public problems. More professionals in State government should further enhance in the public mind the stature and status of government employment.

There is, of course, no easy solution, no pat formula. I hope my remarks may be interpreted as being related to a great opportunity to realize the federalist idea of solving the local problems at the local level, and utilizing the combined resources of all the people in solving the interstate problems for the common good.

THE BIGGEST CON GAME IN POLITICS

ALFRED E. DRISCOLL WITH CHARLES STEVENSON

Alfred E. Driscoll is a former governor of New Jersey. He is now a corporation executive.

The people of Kansas City thought they were getting free money when the federal government gave them a grant-in-aid to help pay for improving their airport. But, as usual in such cases, the Government also insisted on taking over as boss—so the cost turned out to be higher than if Kansas City had spent municipal funds alone.

Why? For one thing, Washington said that a sand base was needed on which to pour concrete. Masterminding from a thousand miles away, the federal government refused to believe that the airport, dredged out of the Missouri River, was itself a sand base upon which city engineers had satisfactorily laid concrete for years. An official job had to be done the official way: *four inches of river sand had to be scraped off the airport, hauled away, and replaced with four inches of similar sand that was purchased and hauled in.*

This is typical of the grants-in-aid confidence game—a con game which is growing every year. This fiscal year it is adding upward of five billion dollars to our federal tax bill!

It is high time we as a nation woke up to what is happening. Here

Reprinted from Alfred E. Driscoll, with Charles Stevenson, "The Biggest Con Game in Politics," *The Reader's Digest*, December 1956, pp. 33-38, and January 1957, pp. 63-67. Copyright 1956 by The Reader's Digest Assn., Inc.

are the documented, though little-known, facts. They are facts out of my own experience as Governor of New Jersey; facts reported by other governors at meetings of the National Governors' Conference; facts from the testimony of experts before Congressional investigating committees; facts from the findings of a Presidential commission, of which I had the honor to be vice-chairman.

Grants-in-aid are nothing more than our own taxes which federal bureaus distribute to states and localities for specified services, usually with the requirement that the recipients put up some matching cash. The original purpose was to encourage states to undertake nationally important programs which they would later operate by themselves. However, since the '20's, when such aid totaled only about 100 million dollars a year and went chiefly into roads, grants have developed into the fastest-growing gimmick in politics. Today they embrace some 50 different programs: for airports, education, relief, sewage plants, even traveling libraries. They cut across every function of local and state government, both worthy and superfluous, piling up duplicated services and needless expenses which we would never tolerate if we paid for them directly.

Grants are popular simply because, ever since the New Deal, politicians have kidded us into believing they are gifts that somebody else pays for. Yet every time we reach out for one of these prize packages we end up paying more for what we get than if we spent local money alone.

The Governors' Conferences have repeatedly demanded that Congress curtail grants and proportionately reduce federal taxes so the states could pay their own way at great savings. One of President Eisenhower's first acts in the White House was to ask Congress to create the investigating commission on which I served. This Commission on Intergovernmental Relations piled up irrefutable evidence of waste and extravagance. Yet, in spite of all this, pressure groups and politicians, lacking the ability or courage to sell their projects to their own hometown or home-state constituents for financing at home, prevail upon Congress to hand out more and more federal tax money.

"Don't quote me as criticizing that airport case," a Kansas City official said recently. "We've got to get along with Washington. And if we don't grab this free money somebody else will."

Free money? To qualify for a federal grant of up to half the cost of airport work, a locality must subject itself to dictation which runs up heavy extra costs. The Department of Labor decrees the wages which must be paid—wages which, according to evidence uncovered by the President's commission, are often unexplainably and unrealistically high compared with those paid for other work. Contractors have to wait so long for their Government payments—an average of six months for the whole United States, up to a year and a half in some areas—that they "deliberately increase their bids" to compensate.

Clayton, N.M., last year succeeded finally in collecting cash due it under a 1949 airport agreement. It collected only because Congress passed special legislation directing that the payment be made. The Government had refused to settle up because, after construction was completed, it decided to disapprove plans and specifications which it had earlier approved.

"In most cases a community could build an adequate facility for less than its half-share of the federal-aid project," says Missouri's state aviation chief. But Toledo, Ohio, is the only city which has had the initiative to finance its own airport since federal subsidies became available a decade ago. Toledo, with four million dollars of its own, constructed an airport which it estimates would have cost up to *three* times as much with federal aid. President Eisenhower was so pleased that he sent his personal congratulations.

The woes that afflict airport construction are common to most grant programs. Many of these programs were justified at the start in order to meet a temporary condition or to unite the states in working for a common goal. Nevertheless, because of the cherished illusion that cash from the federal treasury is free, these grants are almost always added to, never cut back.

Federal aid to vocational education, for example, was begun in 1917 because there weren't enough mechanics to man World War I industry. Since then, unions and manufacturers have undertaken training programs of their own, and state and local governments are generally doing the job that needs to be done. Yet this federal grant is still handed out every year.

Only one fourth of the pupils aided by these funds receive instruction in trades and industries, however. Almost half the enrollment is now in *home economics*. And the administration of the federal program has become so elaborate that states are required to keep track of 13 different sub-funds, each of which must be separately spent and accounted for!

Years ago Congress wanted the states to do more about public health, so it began appropriating grants for this purpose. Today, though the states are spending ten times as much as they receive from the federal government, the grants continue. Moreover, they are pigeon-holed into five inflexible categories, each for a different disease. The result is that state governors must spend the money for these particular diseases, even though the need may be greater for some other. The President's commission found that such inflexibility actually has tended to restrict, rather than assist, progress in public health.

On top of this inefficiency is the expense: nine regional U.S. Public Health Service offices, each boasting its own medical director, medical programs consultant, sanitary engineer, dental consultant, nursing consultant, public health representative, hospital program director.

Investigators for our commission reported that almost everywhere the recipients of federal grants feel that this cash "need not be spent very carefully because it didn't cost anything." The fact is that the grabbing for this easy-come cash pushed the annual *visible* bill for grants from 126 million dollars in 1934 to nearly four billion dollars for the fiscal year beginning last July 1. On top of this the last Congress passed new and liberalized programs which will add another billion and a half dollars to grants spending for the year. *We all pay this sum in our federal taxes.*

Moreover, everybody must pay additional federal taxes to cover *concealed* costs in grants. As Representative Charles A. Halleck puts it, "Out in Indiana we find that, by the time our money goes to Washington and is sent back, the dollars shrink."

One reason for this shrinkage is the seldom-mentioned federal administrative cost. It takes a lot of money just to process the grants. Our commission found that every time a dollar is granted to a city for slum clearance, some 22½ cents is consumed as the federal overhead expense of making the dollar available. For low-cost housing the brokerage fee is estimated at 39.9 cents. Nobody knows for sure what the *total* administrative cost is. Not one cent of it appears in over-all Treasury reports on grants-in-aid as a charge against the giveaway programs.

Another concealed fraud lies in taxes collected in the name of a certain program but not entirely spent for the advertised purpose. The highway aid which Congress "gives" to the states comes from a gas tax passed in 1932 as an "emergency" measure. Three billion dollars of these taxes have never gone back to build roads.

At their annual conferences the state governors have unanimously demanded that Congress repeal this gas tax. They have insisted that with this source of revenue they could build the nation's roads without *any* U.S. aid.

There is no doubt that the states could build more cheaply. Washington State just couldn't afford to construct a vehicular tunnel the way the U.S. Bureau of Public Roads said it must be done if its grants were used to meet part of the cost. So the state saved money by using its own funds and the specifications of its own engineers.

And then the waste.

One of the functions of the U.S. Office of Education has been to help build schools in areas temporarily overpopulated because of federal defense work. However, House Appropriations Committee investigators discovered that instead of merely enabling states to meet their construction costs the agency, "contrary to law," grossly overpaid state after state.

California told the Office of Education that it needed $852 per pupil to build elementary schools. It was handed $1420 per pupil. Mississippi said its normal construction cost $682 per pupil. The Government offered it $830 per pupil, two weeks later jumped this to $1040, then hiked the ante again. Pascagoula, Miss., wound up with an "emergency minimum facility" of 12 elementary classrooms costing $379,000. The building contained cut-stone decorations, flagstoned entrances, terrazzo floors, glazed-brick walls, black-marbel windowsills.

John E. Burton, vice-president of Cornell University, told a Congressional committee that when he was budget director for New York State he felt compelled to approve spending grants that his state didn't need, simply because "officials in Washington are displeased if there's any money left over."

A common misconception is that grant money is doled out basically to help poorer areas provide essential services they can't otherwise afford. This isn't so. Since qualifying for a grant usually means putting up matching funds, the biggest returns go to those states which repudiate economy and, at the sacrifice of real requirements, put the bulk of their cash into Washington-blessed programs designed to produce handouts at the expense of somebody else.

Our federally aided relief program is an example. At the outset, grants for relief helped to bring about long-overdue better care for needy folk, especially the elderly. The original purpose was to help these persons *temporarily,* until they could qualify for old-age insurance. Since then, however, the federal government has increased its share of the cost from less than 25 percent to well over 50 percent. Moreover, Congress and the Social Security Administration have permitted individual states to raid these funds to provide payments based not so much on need as on the philosophy that it is good politics to pension people even if they're not in real need. So the more people to whom cash is to be distributed, the more giveaway funds the Government provides. Result: despite the greatest employment and prosperity in history and the stepped-up protection of old-age insurance, old-age relief rolls today are more than twice as big as at the depth of the Depression.

The actions of certain states are largely to blame for this. For instance, through the years the federal government has made a relief payment to Louisiana in behalf of all persons 65 years old whom the state wanted to qualify as needy. Some of these "needy" persons have owned businesses, enjoyed $5000-a-year incomes and had comfortably fixed adult children who could assist them. Thus the state has been able to kite its grants to *52 million dollars a year more than it contributes to the kitty.* U.S. grants for relief average $248.27 for every person 65 years old in the entire state. The state distributes this cash from your taxes and mine to nearly six out of every ten older persons who live within its borders.

By the same method Oklahoma adds $2.52 of federal money to every dollar it pays out for grants—$182 for every older person in its population. California, one of the wealthiest states, collects at the rate of $109 per older person. In contrast, New Jersey, which pays the sixth-highest benefits in the nation, gets only $17 per elderly person from the federal government—because it limits this relief to people who really need it.

A task force of the President's commission found that if we distributed our federal relief grants so as to equalize the burden between rich and poor states, instead of as giveaway gravy, we could save $661,717,000 a year on this item alone. It would cut our national relief bill in half.

Even the states which enjoy distributing other people's cash must themselves lose in the long run, for the federal encouragement to loose spending requires ever-increasing local matching funds. In 1948 the voters of Washington State were lured into an easy-come pension for persons not actually in need. They were led to believe that Uncle Sam would pick up the tab. But in spite of immense grants, the program not only ate up 32 million dollars then in the state's general funds but put the state 44 million dollars in the red. The law was repealed only after the authorities were left without funds to care properly for persons most requiring aid.

Nevertheless, in the face of all this, Congress and its pressure groups continue to offer fake gifts. At the last session, Congress authorized 500 million dollars' worth of grants for cities which want sewage-treatment plants but have looked to Washington to pay the bill. Local government has so lost the initiative to help itself that President Eisenhower had to issue a warning: "I urge that no community with sufficient resources to construct a needed sewage-treatment project without federal aid postpone that construction simply because of the prospect of a possible federal grant. It should be clearly understood that federal aid will not be available to all communities."

By the record there is no profit in blindly depending upon grants to finance shared extravagances in the false belief that we're spending somebody else's cash. Says James F. Byrnes, speaking from a lifetime as legislator, federal official and most recently as Governor of South Carolina: "Whenever a state or county receives a grant which officials can spend without the responsibility of collecting the money by taxes, you are certain to have extravagance."

Let us destroy this free-money myth before it destroys us.

Eight years ago the U.S. Bureau of Employment Security threatened to cut off millions of dollars in grants-in-aid to the states of Washington and California. The grants had been paid for wholly out of taxes on local payrolls; passed back to the states, they were supposed to finance unemployment insurance programs under the states' own laws. In accordance with these laws, both states had refused to pay compensation to maritime workers whose union was on strike. The Bureau declared this a violation of federal standards.

With its whole insurance program jeopardized, Washington State paid up. California fought all the way to its supreme court, which upheld the state. Still the Bureau persevered. On its complaint U.S. Labor Department hearings were held in judgment of the court's decision. California was not let off the bureaucratic hook until last April when the Secretary of Labor decided that the state had been right all along.

Such interference with our right to manage our home-town, home-county, home-state affairs haunts more than 50 different state and local programs financed with federal grants-in-aid.* President Eisenhower's Commission on Intergovernmental Relations has found that since the idea of going to Uncle Sam for "free money" became popular back in New Deal days, grants have increased until with matching funds they accounted in a single year for an average 25 percent of all state budgets — 46 percent in the case of Missouri.

These grants were originally intended by Congress to interest the states in starting nationally important programs, and to strengthen state administrations until they could stand alone. But under the excuse that federal supervision is required to safeguard public funds, the federal bureaus dispensing the funds have used the power of the dollar to establish themselves in permanent control over segments of state and local government.

The U.S. Bureau of Public Assistance in the Social Security Administration is an example. Troops of auditors, inspectors and overseers fan out from this Bureau into ten regional offices scattered across the United States, thence into 3000 state and local offices to tell 65,000 nonfederal relief workers how to run their business. State and local officials must conform to an ever-changing loose-leaf manual containing nearly 1000 pages of rules and regulations. These extend to instructing state officials to make no investigation of a relief applicant without his approval. Officials are told to rely on the applicant's own information instead of making "unproductive visits to the home, relatives or references."

"The present machinery has become intolerable," says Philip Vogt, welfare administrator at Omaha, Neb. He points to no less than 60 different forms which must be filled out and to 341 replies which may be required of a single applicant for aid. Nebraska, he says, had to abandon its own law and financing of medical care for the destitute because of the expense and complicated procedures demanded under federal supervision.

Each of six separate divisions of this one branch of the Social Security Administration has assigned itself overlapping, even competing authority over the states. Their organization chart shows one division's job is to "prepare instructions to state agencies." Another "formulates policies for development of state staffs." A third "reviews state plan

---

*See "The Biggest Con Game in Politics," *The Reader's Digest*, December, 1956 [pp. 63-68].

material" and "conducts the continuing review of state and local administration." And so on through a fourth, fifth and sixth division.
Researchers from Temple University reported to President Eisenhower that "the bulk of these activities is not required by any statutory
responsibility vested in the federal agency." The agency's clear duty has
been to make federal cash available to the states as long as they adhere to
certain broad federal principles, and to give technical aid on request.
Instead, staffs of social workers have pyramided themselves to establish
their own welfare world.

Despite President Eisenhower's efforts to control the situation, long-
established policies of bureaucratic interference still shape the administration of relief in every town.

In Washington State the Bureau of Public Assistance was able to
obstruct for months the hiring of investigators to track down fathers who
faked desertion so that their wives could collect aid in the name of their
dependent children. Even when Congress, in answer to nation-wide
protests, enacted a law requiring state authorities to pass along the
names of such "deserters" for prosecution, the Bureau cautioned employes against busying themselves with "police functions."

The Bureau says it is wrong—New York once tried it—for a state to
make a relief recipient sign a statement certifying his eligibility every
time he collects a relief check because this "may cause a reluctance to
accept assistance." The Bureau once cut off Indiana's 21-million-dollar-
a-year grant because the state authorized public inspection of its rolls to
get rid of chiselers. When Congress passed a special act to repay Indiana
and encourage other states to follow Indiana's lead, since it had resulted
in big savings, the Bureau continued to protest. Its own printed regulations still call on the states to pass such airtight secrecy laws as to prevent
"any" information about a relief client from being made available even
to a court despite a subpoena or court order.

A study committee of the President's commission declares that the
system under which the relief grants are handled has "weakened, rather
than strengthened, state and local government, which are the very heart
of democracy."

It is much the same story in other federal agencies that dispense
grants. All emphasize the same multitudinous procedures, the same
costly inflexibility and inevitable bureaucratic domination.

The Children's Bureau requires state officials to study 58 pages of
instructions and forms just to learn how to request grants for assistance
to crippled children. For years it has denied funds to Arizona, contending the state is guilty of racial discrimination because it doesn't
provide hospital care for Indian children on reservations, although these
government wards are already cared for under a similar program conducted by the Indian Bureau and the Public Health Service.

Los Angeles voters became so angry at freewheeling activity in their town by the U.S. Public Housing Administration that they demanded a halt in a city-wide referendum. But they couldn't get rid of this agency until Congress stepped in and twice specifically outlawed any spending by it in defiance of a community's wishes.

Grants for public works can bring as much woe as those for social welfare. The U.S. Bureau of Public Roads has more than 1700 employes just to ride herd on federally aided construction performed by capable state engineers. And it plans to employ 900 more. While I was Governor of New Jersey, the state was spending 61 million dollars of its own funds in a year for roads. Nevertheless, the Bureau sought to withhold grants because the state wasn't spending as large a percentage of its gas taxes on highways as it had done in 1934, when actual expenditures were less than 25 million dollars.

Our New Jersey Turnpike never could have been built if we had not defied this Bureau all the way to Congress. We had started to build a free cross-state highway, using state taxes and federal grants, but after sinking ten million dollars into rights-of-way and grading for a one-mile stretch, it became plain that the route could be completed only as a specially financed toll road. But the Bureau of Public Roads, which will not participate in toll roads, refused to permit the state to transfer the U.S. funds already used to other free highways then being constructed. It also refused to let the state reimburse it in cash. Then the Bureau ruled that because of the federal cash in the original one-mile section it would be illegal to charge tolls on the pike. We had to obtain special legislation from Congress nullifying the Bureau's stand before the state could put the highway into use.

Federal bureaus often exert an inexcusable influence on state employes. When I was Governor, federal employes would phone our workers, urging them to high-pressure Congress for bigger appropriations. Then our employes would call the federal people and ask them to pressure us to increase matching funds.

In state after state evidence of similar abuses has been uncovered by the President's commission. The most widespread complaint was that federal employes handling grants use their dollar authority to transfer the allegiance of state staffs from their own elected officials to the federal organization.

The commission found that in Washington State, for example, "as more sizable sums have been given by the federal government, actual control of activities within the state has shifted to program professionals. A contract in regard to the school lunch program is not one the state makes; it is made directly between the state educational agency and the U.S. Department of Agriculture. Heavy emphasis is placed on 'What will the federals approve?' rather than 'What is in the best interests of the state?' Many of [the governor's] key department heads answer more directly to federal administrators than to him."

When Massachusetts moved recently to put groundskeepers, janitors and other custodial employes of its state university under civil service, the U.S. Government informed the governor that this was political interference with academic freedom and that the state thereby jeopardized its right to receive further land-grant funds for education.

Amid such instances, one would think that Congressional attention would be given to curtailing grants.

THE CASE FOR "STATES' RIGHTS"

JAMES JACKSON KILPATRICK

James Jackson Kilpatrick is editor of the *Richmond* (Virginia) *News Leader* and author of *The Sovereign States: Notes of a Citizen of Virginia* (1957).

> What has destroyed the liberty and the rights of man in every government which has ever existed under the sun? The generalizing and concentrating all cares and powers into one body, no matter whether of the autocrats of Russia or France, or of the aristocrats of a Venetian Senate.
> THOMAS JEFFERSON to Joseph C. Cabell (1816)

It offers a small footnote to the semantic confusion of our times that an essayist, assigned to prepare "the case for States' rights," must begin by saying that he does not propose to talk about States' rights. The States have very few rights. They have a right to equal representation in the United States Senate, and they have a right to be protected against invasion; but by and large, as the Ninth and Tenth Amendments make clear in their perfect choice of nouns, people have rights; States have powers. We may go a step further, and remark that today the people have fewer rights and the States have smaller powers than they possessed at one time, and we shall not be far from the mark in surmising that the cause of the former is an effect of the latter.

I would express certain convictions at the outset. Government, it seems to me, ought always to be seen clearly for what it is: A necessary evil. And the more it is thought to be necessary, the more it is bound to become evil. I do not use "evil" here to mean debauched or corrupt, though I believe such a charge could be maintained. I mean rather that government feeds upon the storehouse of man's freedom, and the more this precious granary is drawn down and nibbled away, the less remains to sustain us. I hold that all governments are oppressive; they are distinguished only by this, that some are more oppressive than others.

Reprinted from *A Nation of States*, ed. Robert A. Goldwin (Chicago: Rand McNally & Co., 1963), pp. 88-105. Copyright © 1961, 1963 by the Public Affairs Conference Center, Kenyon College. [Footnotes omitted.]

When I am told that our government, among all the powers of the earth, is the most free, I am minded to say that it is merely the least despotic. From what little I can read of history, and what I can perceive of our own day, I conclude that man always has existed in a condition of conflict with the state. It is inherent in the nature of man, whose first impulse is to act; it is inherent in the nature of the state, whose first duty is to restrain. A long time ago, when he was writing more poetically than politically, Jefferson put it down that governments exist to secure those unalienable rights that do indeed comprise man's inheritance here on earth—the rights to life, liberty, and the pursuit of happiness. But it has not worked out that way. In practice, governments frequently have secured our rights by judiciously taking them away, and acts of injustice to the individual have won easy sanction in the name of the common good. Let any friend of liberty read the Supreme Court's recent decisions in the Baltimore and Dayton sanitation cases, and ask himself if the citizen's right to be free from unreasonable searches and seizures has here been secured.

The chief problem of government in a free society is to keep this conflict between man and the state, the one pulling, the other hauling, under some sort of effective control, so that society moves forward and men find slight disposition to chafe under the restraints put upon them. All governments must preserve law and order; national governments must provide for the common defense. Beyond those essentials, we advance with less sureness. A large function of government is to promote the general welfare; and it is here that those of us who are styled as inexactly "conservatives" as we are mistakenly termed "States' righters" would plead for caution. "I am not a friend to very energetic government," Jefferson once remarked to Madison. "It is always oppressive."

The great men who long ago preceded us in this inquiry comprehended this conflict, this tension, with perfect clarity. They did not view the central government, as it is the custom to view it in the United States today, as a firm but loving paterfamilias, or in a less elegant image, as a comfortable sow with a hundred million teats. "Free government is founded in jealousy and not in confidence," cried the Kentucky Resolution. The authors of that Resolution had gazed upon the face of tyranny and knew it well; in forming their own free Republic, they brought to the creative act the accumulated wisdom of the great men who had preceded them. They *knew*, in a deep way that contemporary political philosophers do not seem to know, the conditions that historically have contributed to greatness in nations and to happiness in man. The examples of Babylonia and Greece and Rome were fresh and commanding precepts for the delegates who met that summer in Philadelphia. It is impossible to pursue their deliberations, or to read the debates of the ratifying conventions that followed thereafter in the States, without developing a profound respect for the wisdom, the intelligence, and the sure sense of history that imbued the men who conceived our form of union. It was a small assembly that wrote the Constitution, Tocqueville observed, but it contained "the finest minds and the noblest characters that had ever appeared in the New World."

In that just appraisal lies the first argument I would make in behalf of "the case for States' rights." Truly there were giants in our earth in those days. We ought to honor them. By what presumption—by what giddy conceit—do today's political scientists, uneducated editors, witless politicians, and other ignorami assert a superior wisdom? I travel to Washington with some frequency, and I gaze from the House galleries at the awesome scene below. A few good men excepted, it offers only a milling gaggle of chiropractors, foot doctors, country clowns, elevated plumbers, and second-rate lawyers—and these, God save the mark, are the statesmen who would discard the charter of our liberties! When a mood of flagellation comes over me, and the *Congressional Record* is not at hand, I read some of the learned quarterlies and other leaf-rakings from the academic grove. These are not as funny as the *Record,* but they are more pompous and arrogant; and I recall Burke's biting comment upon the literary men, politicians, and gauzy divines who encouraged the French Revolution:

> *They have no respect for the wisdom of others; but they pay it off by a very full measure of confidence in their own. With them it is a sufficient motive to destroy an old scheme of things, because it is an old one. As to the new, they are in no sort of fear with regard to the duration of a building run up in haste; because duration is no object to those who think little or nothing has been done before their time, and who place all their hopes in discovery. They conceive, very systematically, that all things which give perpetuity are mischievous, and therefore they are at inexpiable war with all establishments.*

For my own part, I should like to remain decently obedient to Aristotle's counsel, in *Politics* (Book II), not to disregard the experience of ages. Jefferson, Mason, and Henry, to name but three of Virginia's forebears, dealt in eternal verities; to the surpassing truth of their repeated warnings against excessive centralism, our own busy philosophers have responded with no more than a few evasive falsehoods. It is said that times have changed, and the world has become smaller, and time has been telescoped into some remarkable units known as "short hours" or "short years." It is said that the dangers to the survival of civilization have become much greater. And on the broad subject of expanding government, we are told disarmingly, and in a sort of folksy grammar, that we have nothing to fear from big government for government, after all, is nobody but us.

To these familiar rationalizations, I say, nonsense! *Plus ça change, plus c'est la même chose.* Now we fly to London in five or six of those short hours; we converse by satellites that circle the globe; tomorrow the inanities of television will be bounced from the moon. But let us not be deceived into supposing that the traveler's journey is different, or that the human heart speaks in a new way, or that the old immutable laws of political behavior can be summarily amended or repealed. There is a sea change that comes over men raised from private life to public office, and if this is most clearly observed in Federal judges, it is manifest in other magistrates also. They become a part of that vast, shapeless, formless, ectoplasmic mass known as *government,* and they find themselves — even the good men — aligned in an antithetical relationship: the governed, and the governors. If this relationship normally is pleasant and benevolent, if government accomplishes much that is, provisionally, good, the abuses of power remain a constant threat. Governments exist, Calhoun observed, to restrain men; and therefore we have constitutions, to restrain governments.

Our fathers comprehended these elementary truths; they mastered their lessons in a contemplative period when public leaders had priceless assets we deny our public men today: time to think, time to read, time to watch the seasons from a mountaintop in Albemarle. The last book I happened to put aside, of a recent afternoon, was a volume of Jefferson's letters; the first book I happened to pick up after dinner was Harry Truman's autobiography; and I was impressed, as any man must be, by the thought of how far we have advanced from Monticello — advanced, that is to say, as Southerners speak of their army in the last days of the Confederacy, to the rear.

Plainly, it is not enough merely to honor the founding fathers for their amazing genius, or to observe with Burke that men who lose respect for their ancestors are likely to command none from their posterity. Coming closer to the point, and this is my second contention, I submit that we should respect their political handiwork also. The Constitution is not without fault; some of its provisions are archaic, and some of its language is ambiguous, and needs have developed — as Washington and Jefferson foresaw — for some desirable amendments. But it is still the supreme law of the land. We ought to obey it implicitly. And both in its basic provisions, and in the underlying political philosophy these provisions reflect, the Constitution remains to this day what Tocqueville termed it, "the most perfect federal constitution that ever existed."

Even the briefest examination into these basic provisions, in terms of the case for States' rights, will disclose certain political truths the high priests of centralization cannot exorcise by the sweet smoke of pedantry. Our Union was formed by the States, acting as States; all political powers exercised by the central government come by delegation from the States; the States alone have inherent powers, while the central government has none—save those it has assumed by usurpation. If the structure of our government ever is to be altered in any essential respect, the States will have to do it. This ultimate sovereign power—"the will to enact, the power to execute," as John Taylor of Carolina termed it—resides finally with the States. If the Union ever were to be dissolved, it would be as a consequence of State action; and the States would survive.

The objective student of the Constitution who undertakes to read our charter in terms of the State and central government relationship may be astonished at what he finds. Before he is well launched into Article I, he is brought up short by the fact that members of the House of Representatives are chosen not "by the people," but by "the people of the several States." The lower chamber was intended to represent people by the numbers, but the notable fact is that no congressional district stretches across a State line. These districts are fixed by State authority.

Who are these "people of the several States" who are to elect the Representatives? What authority fixes their qualifications to vote? Why, plainly, "the electors in each State shall have the qualifications requisite for electors of the most numerous branch of the State legislature." What of a candidate for the House? He must be at least twenty-five years old; he must have been at least seven years a citizen—but to these fairly universal standards, one more is added: He must be an inhabitant of that State "in which" he shall be chosen.

I put "in which" in quotation marks in order to emphasize a subtle but significant distinction that appears in the following section as to Senators. A Senator must be at least thirty; he must have been nine years a citizen; and he must be an inhabitant of that State "for which" he shall be chosen. The deliberate choice of prepositions points up both the equality of States and the role of Senators. Until the unfortunate adoption of the Seventeenth Amendment in 1913, Senators were chosen by State legislatures and served in effect as State ambassadors. And thinking rapidly over half a century of Senate history, I am inclined to believe the great Senators since 1913 most likely would have been named by their State legislatures if the Seventeenth Amendment never had been adopted; the senatorial mediocrities, for the most part, have been second-raters who owed their election to a gift for gab and never would have made it without the process of popular election.

Pursuing the constitutional provisions as to States, one finds the entire Constitution strung upon a thread of State responsibilities and restraints. The very words "State" or "States" appear more than ninety times; the word "nation," in reference to the United States of America, never appears at all. Our Republic three times is referred to as "this Union" and once as "the land," but every other reference is simply to "the United States"—and the proper noun is always treated as a plural noun.

The longer one reflects upon the Constitution, and upon the writings of the founding fathers, the more apparent two political truths become. The first deals with the source of political power; the second deals with the restraints upon power. The advocate of "States' rights" would like to be heard on both of them.

It is astonishing how many persons in public life never have grasped — or even thought about — the origin and abiding location of political power in the United States. This power now flows from fifty identical springs, filling fifty separate but identical reservoirs. And whatever powers may be vested, now or hereafter, in the central government, these powers must flow upward from the State reservoirs. The flow never goes the other way. If beginning students of the Constitution were asked to understand one truth only of their government, they could not do better than to begin with this: *The Constitution acts upon the States in a prohibitory fashion only.*

This is not true of the Constitution's action upon the central government. The Constitution both authorizes the central government to do certain things, and prohibits the central government from doing certain things, but at no point does the Constitution authorize or permit the States to do anything. As a consequence, members of the Congress embarking upon some legislative scheme must ask themselves two questions: (1) Are we permitted to do this under the Constitution? and (2) Are we prohibited from doing this under the Constitution? The States have no such problems. They have all powers to begin with. Their search is for a prohibition only, and if they find nothing *in the Constitution* prohibiting them from a particular course of action, they are free to proceed.

The Tenth Amendment makes this clear beyond peradventure. It is the key that unlocks every mystery of our form of government; it is the very polar star of our fundamental charter. "The powers [let us note the noun] not delegated [let us note the verb] to the United States by the Constitution [let us pause especially upon that prepositional phrase], nor prohibited by it [the antecedent of "it" is "Constitution"] to the States, are reserved to the States respectively [there is profound meaning in that adverb] or to the people."

Why was this amendment demanded, in New Hampshire no less than in Virginia, in Rhode Island no less than in South Carolina? The object was to give expression to the underlying philosophy of the people on whom this Constitution was to act directly. *They meant to restrain.* They knew, as Jefferson remarked, that "the natural progress of things is for liberty to yield and government to gain ground," and they hoped to create a government that would gain as little such ground as possible. Thus, it will be observed that the Constitution is in many ways a very negative document. Wherever there is a giving, there is almost always a snatching back; the whole instrument abounds in "noes," "nots," "neithers," and "nors." The list of prohibitions flatly imposed upon the central government is long, but when the framers had finished their work, the States found the list not yet long enough, so they added ten broad amendments more. The prohibitions imposed by the States upon their own exercise of power, especially in the tenth section of Article I, are scarcely less impressive.

This self-evident desire to restrain *all* government pervades the entire document. Ours was to be a *limited* government. That was the whole reason the framers enumerated the powers vested in the Congress, with such tedious care that the power to punish counterfeiting is separated from the power to coin money, and the power to support an army is not joined by even a conjunction to the power to maintain a navy. Here every separate sentence is numbered; every particular power is spelled out. And what a mockery it is of their prudent labors to see men contend for the absurd notion that the power to lay taxes "to provide for the general welfare" vests the Congress with the power to do whatever Congress pleases! Such a construction reduces the Constitution to blank paper; it arrogates to judges and to congressmen the bumptious authority claimed by Humpty-Dumpty, to whom words meant what he chose them to mean, and neither more nor less. If all powers were delegated to the central government, then none remained exclusively with the States; the bulk of the Constitution is mere surplusage, and the Tenth Amendment is a fraud; the authors of *The Federalist* were masters of deceit, and the written English language is become the babble of idiots. Yet these are the ends the advocates of centralization would put upon us: the reversal of the flow of power, the upending of our structure, so that the foundation is on top and the gables down below; they would have us abandon the restraints and limitations that long ago were laid upon the States by the States themselves, and imposed on their central government by their own joint action.

Now, all of this is not to suggest that the United States do not comprise a "nation." Of course they do. Neither is it to suggest that some sharp line always has separated the powers delegated from the powers reserved. From the beginning, there has been a blurring and a mixing; the popular image of two governmental spheres, each rotating perfectly in its own separate orbit, touching but never overlapping, has nothing in history to commend it. Nevertheless, the dual structure remains, and a full understanding of this concept is imperative to any understanding of how our Republic functions.

"The people of the United States constitute one nation, under one government, and this government, *within the scope of the powers with which it is invested,* is supreme," wrote Chief Justice Chase in 1868. "On the other hand, the people of each State comprise a State, having its own government, and endowed with all the functions essential to separate and independent existence. *The States disunited might continue to exist.*

Without the States in union, there could be no such political body as the United States."

Notice Chase's careful qualification: The central government is supreme "within the scope of the powers with which it is invested." And whence came this investiture? Not from the people in one great body. The powers of the central government, as Madison pointed out in the Virginia Convention of 1787, came from "the people as composing thirteen sovereignties." That is to say, the powers came from the States.

Yet a statement of this truth implies no hostility to a strong national government. The Federal government is our government; we owe obedience and allegiance to it. The plan of our fathers, and it was a good plan, was simply to assure the people the best of both worlds—a central government strong enough to act boldly and powerfully in the preservation of national security and in the promotion of truly national interests, yet not so strong that it would swallow up the administration of those local and domestic responsibilities which the people wanted kept close at hand.

Tocqueville put it simply. The federal system was created, he observed, "with the intention of combining the different advantages which result from the magnitude and the littleness of nations," and he went on to describe these advantages as he perceived them in America:

> *In great centralized nations the legislator is obliged to give a character of uniformity to the laws, which does not always suit the diversity of customs and of districts; as he takes no cognizance of special cases, he can only proceed upon general principles; and the population are obliged to conform to the requirements of the laws, since legislation cannot adapt itself to the exigencies and the customs of the population, which is a great cause of trouble and misery. This disadvantage does not exist in confederations; Congress regulates the principal measures of the national government, and all the details of the administration are reserved to the provincial legislatures. One can hardly imagine how much this division of sovereignty contributes to the well-being of each of the States that compose the Union.*

At a later point, I want to touch upon the troubles that arise when the central government ceases to heed "the diversity of customs and of districts." Here I would dwell a little longer upon the political insight, as I conceive it, that went into the structure of our government. The founding fathers wanted not only to restrain all governments. *They wanted also to preserve that sense of close community which is the starting point of political well-being.* Burke, in his *Reflections on the Revolution in France,* put it this way: "To be attached to the subdivision, to love the little platoon we belong to in society, is the first principle (the germ as it were) of public affections. It is the first link in the series by which we proceed towards a love to our country, and to mankind."

Let that sense of community be dulled or lost, and something precious is abandoned. Let local powers atrophy, and State prerogatives decline, and the wellspring of patriotism inevitably must run thin. For this sense of community, unless it is nurtured at home, cannot flourish and retain its simple vitality in a "community" that stretches from Maine to Hawaii and from the Florida keys to the Alaskan tundra.

Yet it is not necessary to rely upon metaphysical reasons for urging a return to the balance of powers conceived by the founding fathers and written into a supreme law that must be obeyed until the States themselves amend it. There are sound political reasons also. And the foremost of these is that the separate States ought to remain free—as free as possible—to engage in experiment and innovation. I appreciate the argument that this freedom of political action may not promote the most efficient government; it may not be the best for Getting Things Done. But it permits us to avoid the blighting curse of uniformity and regimentation which must always be the foe of creative political thought.

I know of no one who has summed up this position more admirably that Mr. Justice Harlan, in the notable dissenting opinion he wrote in the Roth-Alberts case in 1957. Two men had been convicted for trafficking in obscene materials, Roth under the Federal postal laws, Alberts under the State law of California. A majority of the court voted to uphold both sentences. Harlan objected. He was ready to concur in Alberts' conviction, for this was under State law; and the court's function, in judging the constitutionality of such a statute, was not to decide whether California's policy were wise, or whether the assumptions underlying the State's obscenity law were sound. "Nothing in the Constitution requires California to accept as truth the most advanced and sophisticated psychiatric opinion." The first question was whether the Constitution prohibited California from enacting the law; if not, the Court's only remaining duty was to decide whether Alberts had been denied due process at his trial.

Satisfied that California had the power to enact, and that no reversible error had occurred in the trial itself, Harlan willingly affirmed this judgment. But the companion Roth case was something else. I should like to quote at some length from this dissent, for Harlan's comments, while they necessarily dealt with the narrow and unsavory case before the court, also embraced some of the broad principles that go into the case for States' rights. He said:

> *We are faced here with the question whether the Federal obscenity statute, as construed and applied in this case, violates the First Amendment to the Constitution. To me, this question is of quite a different*

*order than one where we are dealing with State legislation under the
Fourteenth Amendment. I do not think it follows that State and Federal powers in this area are the same.* . . .

The Constitution differentiates between those areas of human conduct subject to the regulation of the States and those subject to the powers of the Federal government. The substantive powers of the two governments, in many instances, are distinct. . . .

The Federal government has, for example, power to restrict seditious speech directed against it, because that Government certainly has the substantive authority to protect itself against revolution. But in dealing with obscenity we are faced with the converse situation, for the interests which obscenity statutes purportedly protect are primarily entrusted to the care, not of the Federal government, but of the States. Congress has no substantive power over sexual morality. Such powers as the Federal government has in this field are but incidental to its other powers, here the postal power, and are not of the same nature as those possessed by the States, which bear direct responsibility for the protection of the local moral fabric. . . .

Not only is the federal interest in protecting the nation against pornography attenuated, but the dangers of federal censorship in this field are far greater than anything the States may do. It has often been said that we have, in the forty-eight States, forty-eight experimental social laboratories. . . . *Different States will have different attitudes toward the same work of literature. The same book which is freely read in one State might be classed as obscene in another. And it seems to me that no overwhelming danger to our freedom to experiment and to gratify our tastes in literature is likely to result from the suppression of a borderline book in one of the States, so long as there is no nationwide suppression of the book, and so long as other States are free to experiment with the same or bolder books.*

Quite a different situation is presented, however, where the Federal government imposes the ban. The danger is perhaps not great if the people of one State, through their legislature, decide that "Lady Chatterley's Lover" goes so far beyond the acceptable standards of candor that it will be deemed offensive and non-sellable, for the State next door is still free to make its own choice. But the dangers to free thought and expression are truly great if the Federal government imposes a blanket ban over the nation on such a book. The prerogative of the States to differ on their ideas of morality will be destroyed, the ability of the States to experiment will be stunted. The fact that the people of one State cannot read some of the works of D. H. Lawrence seems to me, if not wise or desirable, at least acceptable. But that no person in the United States should be allowed to do so seems to me to be intolerable, and violative of both the letter and the spirit of the First Amendment.

It is precisely this intolerable end that lies down the path of centralization in the United States. I have strong reservations about extension of the franchise in Georgia and Kentucky to young men and women of eighteen, for I incline to the view that the franchise should not be broadened, but restricted. Yet I am delighted to see them undertake the experiment. If my prejudice be in error, it may be abandoned in the light of their successful experience; but there would be no way of learning this on a small scale if the Congress, by some distortion of its power to alter State regulations prescribing the manner of holding elections, were to extend the franchise overnight to all eighteen-year-olds everywhere. By the same token, I have been interested to see Nevada experiment with divorce laws that are liberal, and South Carolina adhere to divorce laws that are strict. Much has been learned through the varying approaches of the separate States to problems of forestry, stream pollution, conditions of labor, and public education. In a thousand areas of human conduct, the States and their constituent localities constantly are experimenting, and this political ferment—this bubbling vitality—seems to me absolutely essential to the continued strength of the Republic as a whole.

One of the reasons for the success of this system is that the States and the localities must always be closer to the people than the central government. In stating this view, I respectfully differ from one of my brother essayists, who paints a pretty picture of the intimacy that exists, especially in the case of the farmer, between the Federal government and the individual citizen. It is a pretty picture, but a false one. On my own observations (apart from the common observation of mankind), I would find him clearly wrong. Several years ago, in a manifestation of that particular lunacy to which newspapermen historically are prone, I undertook to run a chicken farm. The county agent was indeed a source of comfort, and the home-demonstration worker could be summoned to educate my wife in the mysteries of a churn. But only in a very narrow and technical sense were these neighborly plenipotentiaries ministers of the Federal government. In their appointment and in their daily activities, they were "county people," different in every way from the regional inspectors of the Commodity Credit Corporation sent out to measure one's acres of wheat. Nor were the ministrations of even the county agents and soil conservation committeemen (locally elected) the be-all and end-all of farm life. Of far greater importance were the local schools, and the local tax rate, and the widening of the road that led to the country store. The government that counted most, because we felt the greatest sense of community with it, was the government at the courthouse, and the government at the State Capitol.

A part of this feeling rests in the belief that local government can be controlled in a way that the central government cannot be controlled. Restraints can be applied close at hand, through the devices of referendum and recall, that cannot be applied far away. The county commissioner dwells low on Olympus, and the local alderman is accessible in ways that United States Senators and Cabinet Secretaries are not accessible. When a citizen of Virginia travels to the Capitol at Richmond, he travels with a sure sense of participation and of community; he speaks to the committees of the General Assembly, supporting or opposing particular legislation, as a fellow-citizen in the community of four million that is Virginia. When he travels to the Capitol at Washington, by contrast, he feels insecurity gnawing at his vitals. He finds the palace ringed by the glassy castles of potent baronies—the Machinists, the Mineworkers, the Educationists—and the marbled catacombs of the Senate Office Building are filled with total strangers. In this distant opulence, he stands subdued.

It is out of this sense of helplessness that the citizen draws his prudent fear of "Federal control." He sees Federal control as as inescapable corollary of "Federal aid." He knows that it cannot possibly be otherwise. Nor is he the least impressed by the remonstrances of political doctors who assure him that the history of numerous grant-in-aid programs fails to support his apprehension.

I am told that Federal controls never have been oppressive, and that Federal outlays almost invariably are administered by State and local functionaries in whom our trust may be freely reposed. I am told that I am conjuring mere spectres and seeing things in the dark. John Marshall long ago (in McCulloch *v.* Maryland, 1819) struck through these specious assurances with a famous line. The tax levied by Maryland upon the Bank of the United States was not large; Mr. McCulloch could have paid it and the Bank would not have gone under. But it was not the particular tax that mattered. It was the power to tax, for "the power to tax involves the power to destroy." And Marshall, agreeing for once with Jefferson, scoffed at the idea of having *confidence* in the States to exercise this power wisely:

> If the States may tax one instrument employed by the government in the execution of its powers, they may tax any and every other instrument. They may tax the mail; they may tax the mint; they may tax patent rights; they may tax the papers of the custom-house; they may tax judicial process; they may tax all the means employed by the government, to an excess which would defeat all the ends of government. This was not intended by the American people. They did not design to make their government dependent upon the States.

The same line of reasoning exactly persuades me to sound a warning against the growing absorption of responsibilities by the central government. It never was intended for the people to be dependent upon Washington, either. If the central government can aid our disabled, and pension our old people, and succour our illegitimate children; if it can fill our fish ponds and level our slums; if it can build our highways and lay our sewers and vaccinate our children and finance our college students, it can dominate our lives in such a way that freedom is lost altogether. It is *the power to control* that is to be feared; and this power to control follows the Federal dollar as surely as that famous lamb accompanied little Mary. And it will follow us to school one day if the principle of general aid to public education, and especially to teacher salaries, ever is approved by the Congress.

Coming events cast long shadows. I see the penumbra approaching and I feel the damp wind cold on my neck. Let the man who imagines there are "no controls" study the disbursement of hospital construction grants under the Hill-Burton Act. Let him gaze upon the thick manual of federally approved regulations by which the interstate highways must be constructed uniformly. Let him ponder the effect of the wage controls decreed under the Davis-Bacon Act — 40,000 local determinations a year, and every one of them controlling what shall be paid carpenters, pipefitters, and common laborers. We have lately had the example of what is known euphemistically as the National Defense Education Act, and I find in it incipiently the very philosophy that seems to me so dangerous; for these grants are intended chiefly for students agreeable to studying what the government wants them to study — science, and mathematics, and foreign languages. We have opened our classroom door, like the flap of the nomad's tent, to a very large camel. I see in the history of legislation under the commerce clause what lies ahead in education; for the regulation of commerce that began with the steamboats of Gibbons and Ogden has expanded until even the window washers on a local office building are the objects of Federal control. The scholarship program that begins with a subtle hint of what should be learned will yet end in effective control of what shall be taught, and to whom, and by whom, and in what sort of buildings.

It was to this sort of *immoderate* greatness that Gibbon attributed the decline of Rome. It is to this sort of faceless nationalizing, to these idiot yells for *equality*, that our own Republic may yet succumb. Long ago a petty despot, troubled by insurrection in his realm, sent an envoy to Periander for advice. The Ambracian tyrant did not reply directly. He took the envoy into a cornfield, and with a sharp blade lopped off the tallest ears until all stalks were standing level. The despot's solution, he meant to say, lay in chopping down the strong to equality with the weak, for when all men are equal none can excel.

The hard counsel of Periander is lost upon some of the more naïve envoys of today's zealous centralizers, but we may be sure it is not wasted on their masters. Their god is the brutal bulldozer, squat as a pagan idol, whose function is to bring down the mountains and to fill up the valleys. They fear excellence as they abhor ineptitude. The diversity of the States offends their pretty sense of order, and from the comfortable living rooms of Scarsdale they weep tears for Mississippi.

The worst fate that could befall this Republic would be for the centralists to impose upon this broad land a Procrustean uniformity that would impoverish the Hudson Valley to enrich the catfish Yazoo. If our strength be in union, it lies first in apartness. This concept is the spark that kindled the American flame; it is the very soul of our Republic, and we ought never to trade it off to the centralist Mephistopheles who promises a beautiful Utopia but would deliver a dreary Hell.

In thus contending for a tightly limited central government, no thoughtful States' righter would want to be misunderstood. If he urges the importance of the Tenth Amendment, he urges with equal vigor the propriety of Article I, Section 8. In matters of foreign policy, in the waging of war, in the coinage of money, in the full and efficient operation of all those delegated powers that are in fact national in their scope—in all of these, the advocate of strict construction yields to the central authority gladly. He is not asking that Delaware be admitted to NATO, or that a first reliance in some war with Russia be placed on the Georgia militia.

He is urging simply that we cherish a reasoned veneration for established institutions, and that we preserve a decent obedience to the form and spirit and meaning of the Constitution. He knows that fallible man will err, and he conceives it better to risk wrongs imposed upon one State than to hazard misjudgments that fall upon fifty. He is no foe of "national greatness." He is merely convinced that national greatness may best be achieved by building upon the solid foundation of personal liberty, individual attainment, and local responsibility erected by the wisest men the Republic will ever know.

INTERSTATE COMPACTS AND CONGRESS: THE PORT OF NEW YORK AUTHORITY CASE

BERNARD D. KOLASA

Bernard D. Kolasa did the research on which this article is based while working for a Ph.D. at the University of Nebraska.

Congress has given its consent more or less automatically to interstate compacts over the years, but some have received extremely close examination, as in the case of the Interstate Oil Compact and the Atlantic States Marine Fisheries Compact. Congress also has established conditions under which it has given consent to others. Until recently, however, Congress has paid relatively little attention to interstate compacts; its

From "Interstate Compacts and Congress: The Port of New York Authority," Bernard D. Kolasa, *State Government*, Autumn 1964, pp. 251-263. Reprinted by permission of the author and The Council of State Governments. [Footnotes omitted.]

almost automatic approval, along with its lack of interest in events subsequent to approval, has helped to encourage use of compacts to solve problems that were regional rather than statewide in scope.

The Port of New York Authority

Creation of the Port of New York Authority in 1921 was a significant step in the use of the authority device as a tool of state and local government to cope with problems of an expanding urban and industrial society. "The most important single event in the rise of an interstate compact agency was probably the establishment and success of the Port of New York Authority, based on the Compact of 1921." The Port Authority furnished the framework upon which subsequent authorities were patterned.

The situation in the New York port was congested and chaotic; the piers and wharves were on the New York side, the railroads on the New Jersey side, both separated by water, necessitating literage and carfloat service. During World War I the gravity of this situation was emphasized, and public spirited groups and citizens took steps to attempt to correct it. The legislatures of the two states approved a joint New York-New Jersey Commission to study the problem. In 1918 it presented a report calling for a permanent bi-state administrative agency with powers to undertake the necessary steps to bring some semblance of order into the port area. The agency was finally approved by both states in the compact of 1921, but was delegated fewer powers than the commission had recommended.

The Port Authority was given no taxing or assessing power and was forbidden to pledge the credit of either state without its consent; the Authority was permitted to borrow money through the use of bonds. It received no powers to enforce its plans, but had wide powers of persuasion, recommendation and petition. It was empowered to construct, lease or operate any terminal or transportation facility, and to this end to own, lease or operate any property in the port-district, needing, however, the consent of a governmental body for any property owned by that body. The Commissioners comprising the Authority were to function as a board, with free rein to draw up by-laws, and to hire employees, as well as determine their qualifications and duties. The states were to determine the method of selection and removal of the Commissioners. The Authority could make rules and regulations governing port improvement, subject to the concurrence of both state legislatures. Finally, any additional powers could be granted to the Port Authority upon the concurrence of both state legislatures.

A Comprehensive Plan adopted in 1922 did nothing more than set forth in detail some of the specific improvements that were to be carried out, along with the general principles governing port development. No powers were granted in addition to those given by the compact of the previous year.

The Port Authority's early efforts were disappointing, since it was unable to get the railroads to cooperate with its plans for port development. Turning to bridges and tunnels, bus, truck, air and marine terminals, it met with more success. The legislatures granted additional powers which enabled the authority to enter into these varied fields. The new authorizations included condemnation powers, establishment of a reserve fund which allowed the pooling of funds so that all facilities became part of one unit, perpetual toll collecting rights, rule-making powers with reference to Authority facilities, giving Port Authority bonds the same status as other municipal bonds and securities, maintenance power over facilities, resale power, immunity from taxation, and in-lieu-of-tax payments.

In this way, the Authority has been able to grow and prosper, always able to find a ready market for its bonds at very favorable interest rates. It has become a billion dollar enterprise, despite its lack of taxing or assessing power and the prohibition against pledging the credit of either state without the state's consent.

The Port Authority follows the board structure in its operation. Its six Commissioners (three from each state, appointed by their respective Governors for six-year terms) are responsible for setting general policy. Administration is under the direction of an Executive Director. Most of the work is done within committees, but issues are fully discussed at the board meetings before formal actions are taken on committee actions.

All minutes are forwarded to the Governors of the two states. Actions of the board take effect unless vetoed by the Governors within ten days. If a Governor does not return the minutes within the prescribed time, the action takes effect.

The two legislatures, of course, have full control over the actions of the Port Authority through their power to amend or alter the compact by concurrent legislation.

The Port Authority and Congress

The Port Authority was created under a compact between New York and New Jersey, falling under the compact clause of the United States Constitution which requires congressional consent for such agreements. Congress gave its assent, but beyond this left the Port Authority on its own, a procedure which Congress had generally followed in respect to all compacts receiving its approval.

Events within the past few years have changed the situation rather drastically, as Congress is becoming more interested in compacts, both before and after approval; the Port Authority has the dubious distinction of generating the most recent controversy touching upon the relationship between Congress and bi-state agencies created under the compact clause.

Congressional Authorization for Creation of the Authority

In the resolution consenting to the compact of 1921, Congress added the following provision:

> *Resolved by the Senate and House of Representatives of the United States of America in Congress assembled, that the consent of Congress is hereby given to the said agreement, and to each and every part thereof: Provided, That nothing therein contained shall be construed as impairing or in any manner affecting any right or jurisdiction of the United States in and over the region which forms the subject of said agreement.*
>
> *Sec. 2 That the right to alter, amend, or repeal this resolution is hereby expressly reserved.*

Congress consented to the Comprehensive Plan, but provided in the preamble of the resolution that consent is "subject always to the approval of the officers and agents of the United States as required by Acts of Congress touching the jurisdiction and control of the United States over matters, or any part thereof, covered by this resolution. . . ." At the end of the resolution the same provision was added as to the consent to the compact reserving jurisdiction and the right to amend or alter the consent, and in addition:

> *Provided further, That no bridges, tunnels, or other structures shall be built across, under, or in any of the waters of the United States, and no change shall be made in the navigable capacity or condition of any such waters, until the plans therefore have been approved by the Chief of Engineers and the Secretary of War.*

The Port Authority abided by the last provision, and all of its bridge and tunnel projects were approved by Congress or the appropriate executive officials. Beyond this the Port Authority exercised a free hand, and Congress turned its attention to other matters as the Authority grew and prospered.

Friction Between the Authority and Congress

An attempt for congressional action. In 1952 the Port Authority announced that it had decided to lease space, to industry and retail outlets, of unused portions of air terminals under its jurisdiction. Jersey City and Hudson County, already irked because they had not been represented on the Port Authority's board, and feeling that the Authority was exceeding its powers, attempted to bring congressional pressure upon it. Accordingly, Representative Sieminski (D., N.J.) introduced House Joint Resolution No. 375, the purpose of which was to "rescind consent of Congress to the compact or agreement between the State of New York and the State of New Jersey creating the Port of New York Authority. . . ."

Hearings were held in May 1952 before a subcommittee of the Committee of the Judiciary, chaired by Representative Emanuel Celler (D., N.Y.). Proponents of the resolution furnished the committee with no new disclosures, but merely presented old arguments that toll collections were excessive, that an independent audit was needed, and that the Authority's reserves were excessive. The committee felt that the states were the proper ones to take action in this circumstance and that to rescind Congress' consent to the compact would only bring chaos and disorder into the port district, and solve none of the problems. A long list of eminent witnesses, including former Governors and Senators of both states, convincingly defended the Port Authority's position.

Needless to say, the resolution was not reported out of committee. The resolution had not called for an investigation of the question of the Authority's exceeding its powers, or for an inquiry of the Authority itself, but called for the outright withdrawal of congressional consent. This move to repeal consent was putting the "cart before the horse," and the committee was completely averse to abolishing the Authority without any alternate agency having been designated to continue the operation of its facilities. The drastic objective of the proponents of the resolution was one of the most important contributory causes for the resolution's defeat. If it had merely called for a thorough investigation of the Authority it might have had a chance of passage.

Congress investigates the Authority. In December 1959, the Port Authority announced that it was studying the possibility of using the Great Swamp in Morris County, New Jersey, for a proposed jet airport. The site, about twenty-five miles from New York City, is a combination of swampland and small residential towns. The announcement set off a wave of protest from residents in the area, and the Port Authority found itself in another controversy. Representative Celler, at the request of some of the New Jersey delegation, introduced House Joint Resolution No. 615, which would have amended the Port Authority compact resolution to: (1) require advance congressional consent to any state action which amended or supplemented the compact; (2) require submission to Congress of all reports to the state legislatures; (3) permit congressional committees to demand relevant information, inspect books and records, and view any Authority facility.

The Judiciary Committee, under Representative Celler's chairmanship, proceeded to investigate the Port Authority, but was unable to obtain the information it desired. Mr. Celler then introduced Resolution No. 350, authorizing the committee to use its subpoena power in connection with matters "involving the activities and operations of interstate compacts." The resolution was passed. Officials of the Port Authority were subpoenaed, along with certain documents which consisted of inter-office memos, internal financial reports, and other internal administrative documents. The officials appeared before a subcommittee of the Judiciary Committee, but refused to produce certain documents pertaining to the internal administration of the Port Authority because they had been ordered not to do so by the Governors of both states who felt the subcommittee was exceeding its jurisdiction. The subcommittee then voted to cite the three for contempt of Congress.

On August 23, 1960 the House adopted the resolution citing the three for contempt, and the Justice Department filed an "information" against the Authority's Executive Director, Austin J. Tobin. Tobin alone was charged, because it was conceded that he would turn over the requested documents if the judge ruled against him. In December Representative Celler brought his subcommittee to New York and held week-long hearings into the activities of the Port Authority. The investigation shed no new light on the subject, but rather turned into a personality clash between Celler and the Authority, each advancing charges and countercharges. Nothing of substance resulted from the hearing.

Contempt of Congress proceedings in court. The contempt case came before Judge Luther W. Youngdahl in January 1961 in the United States District Court for the District of Columbia. The wheels were now set in motion for the greatest battle the Port Authority had fought at any time during its forty-year existence. The case would test the contentions of Congress and the Port Authority as to the extent to which Congress may inquire into the operations of an interstate agency created under an interstate compact.

Proponents of the Authority argued that it was a bi-state agency created by a compact between New York and New Jersey. Consent of Congress did not create the Authority, for it was created by the states party to the compact; they endowed it with its powers and jurisdiction. "If the ruling in *Virginia* v. *Tennessee* still has meaning, Congress' consent merely attested to its conviction that the compact does not infringe on federal powers and jurisdictions." If the congressional power to investigate were upheld, a dangerous precedent would be set which proponents contended would extend congressional authority to all compact agencies and state agencies as well. The Port Authority had cooperated with the federal government in the past; it had sought approval of those federal officials necessary for undertaking new projects. The Federal Aviation Agency audited and had investigative powers over airports which the Authority controlled, and thus there was adequate protection of federal interests. If any corrections were to be made, they should have been made by the states rather than the federal government, as the Authority was a state agency, not a federal one.

It is a well-known judicial doctrine that Congress has power to investigate only in those areas where it can legislate. Recently, in *Barenblatt* v. *United States*, the Supreme Court said:

> *Broad as it is, the power is not however, without limitation. Since Congress may only investigate into those areas in which it may potentially legislate or appropriate, it cannot inquire into matters which are within the exclusive province of one of the other branches of government.*

Therefore even the clause in the consent legislation by which Congress retained the right to "alter, amend, or repeal" the terms of its consent is meaningless if these powers of alteration or amendment are not based on express or implied powers of Congress. In other words, Congress cannot confer upon itself the legislative power merely by its own action.

There is, under the *dictum* of *Virginia* v. *Tennessee*, a "gray-zone" in which agreements or compacts may be made by states without congressional consent if they do not tend "to the increase of political power in the states, which may encroach upon or interfere with the just supremacy of the United States."

Thus the congressional investigation could only be upheld if the investigation was in an area in which Congress had the express or implied power to legislate, or if the compact, as such, tended to increase state power and thus encroach on federal power. Opponents argued that Congress was justified in its investigation because of the vast federal interest involved in the area of interstate commerce. But the entire matter involved many other aspects which called for caution:

> *Investigation may be required, therefore, both to evaluate the need for supplementary legislation and to impose more subtle controls on agency officials. But a countervailing argument suggests that Congress should use its investigating powers sparingly. Interstate agreements often deal with multistate problems which might otherwise be considered the responsibility of the federal government. State officials who negotiate interstate agreements are frequently aware of this fact, and may be induced in part, by a desire to preserve traditional state authority over the problem area. The prospect of increased federal interference could have a strong inhibitory effect on interstate cooperation. If it does the national interest may be harmed on balance, for any reduction in state action will ultimately lead to demands for increases in federal activity and expenditures.*

District Court Decision

On June 15, 1961 Judge Youngdahl handed down his decision, one which was not a cause for rejoicing for the Port Authority. Mr. Tobin was found guilty of contempt and was sentenced to thirty days and fined $100.

Mr. Tobin based his defense on five grounds: (1) the subcommittee had not been authorized to conduct an investigation in which it could call for the disputed documents; (2) the subject matter or pertinency of the documents had not been made sufficiently clear to him; (3) there had not been a proper legislative purpose in conducting the inquiry; (4) the documents were privileged and immune from congressional demand; (5) he was merely obeying superior orders from the two Governors.

The Court refuted all five contentions in finding Mr. Tobin guilty of contempt. Looking to the debates and the resolution which gave the Judiciary Committee power over interstate compacts, the Court could not find that any limits had been prescribed.

> There is no doubt that the diverse and extensive operations of the Port Authority cut across a great many areas of Federal concern. Precisely because this is so, it is not unreasonable to assume that both for the purposes of internal efficiency and to prevent undue burdens on the Authority, Congress might focus its visitorial powers with respect to the Authority in a single committee.

The subject matter of the investigation was twofold as presented by the Chairman in his opening statement: to determine whether the Authority was functioning as envisioned by Congress when it consented to the compact and Comprehensive Plan; and, whether it was exercising the tasks assigned it in a manner that showed sufficient concern for federal interests. The ultimate purpose was to determine whether Congress should alter, amend, or repeal its consent. The Court was satisfied that it was proven that the documents requested were pertinent to the subject-matter under investigation, and that this pertinency was made clear to Mr. Tobin so that he could decide if there had been a proper connection between the request and the subject matter. Since there had not been any congressional investigation of the relationship of the Authority to Congress for more than forty years, it was not possible for the committee to explain the subject matter in full detail.

> To say that it was required to delineate with ultimate precision elements of Federal interests which the inquiry might reveal to be adversely affected would be to require the committee, in effect, to have stated its subject in the narrow terms of the conclusions it might later reach. This was obviously impossible.

Looking to the reservation clause—the power to "alter, amend, or repeal"—the Court found that the legislative pronouncement and debates at the time of enactment showed the clause was not an automatic, purposeless gesture, since it was felt that the port affected the entire nation.

> *In view of the frank recognition that the Port of New York is a 'national asset' and that Congress has responsibility under the Compact clause to "exercise national supervision" over compacts, it is clear to the Court that the power of Congress to legislate pursuant to the reservations must be co-extensive any with threat to national interests caused by activities of the Authority.*

The Court refused to look for motives behind the investigation; for to impugn the motives of the committee would be to do so for the entire House, because it had passed the contempt resolution. It was granted by the Court that certain of the documents requested may have had immunity, but here the Court had to weigh the balance between Congress' needs for them and the injuries to the compact and to the federal system which might result from disclosure. The Court could not say that in no circumstance could this immunity be given to documents of a compact agency; in this case, however, it held that the balance was in favor of disclosure of the documents.

> *It cannot be emphasized too strongly that the conclusion reached here is the result of a balancing of the unique facts of the case. In a future situation involving this agency or another, the factors will have to be weighed afresh, and clearly relevant will be the way in which the powers here recognized are exercised.*

Mr. Tobin, it was said, could only claim a valid defense that he was obeying superior orders if he had been deprived of the physical ability to produce the documents, if the letters constituted a legal justification for his refusal to produce the documents, or if the letters caused his default to lack the proper willfulness. The records had not been removed by the Governors from Mr. Tobin's power either before or after the letters. Secondly, "the letters' objective was either to compel the committee to confer with the Governors before the inquiry proceeded, or to insure default on the subpoena to precipitate a court test of the committee's power to demand the subpoenaed material," and therefore did not constitute a legally sufficient justification for refusal to disclose the documents. Finally, the letters were efforts to justify Mr. Tobin's position, and were thus more a matter of ratification of this position than a command to assume it.

In conclusion the Court cautioned:

The fact that the Court decides that Congress has the power *to request the documents here subpoenaed and to investigate this compact agency is neither carte blanche to excessive use of that power nor an excuse for failure by the committee to re-examine the relative necessity and desirability of some of its requests and the manner in which it conducts its hearings. As the Court has previously indicated, one of the controlling factors in this case is that this is the first full probe into the Port Authority ever conducted by Congress.*

The New York Times commented editorially after the decision:

Representative Celler would compel it [the Authority] to get Congressional approval of every new bus terminal it wanted to build, every pier to be constructed, every airport, every bridge. Thus Congressmen as far away as Hawaii and Alaska would be usurping the State's power of decision over local improvements, only because the agency for their construction happened to be a bi-state rather than a single-state authority.

The Port Authority, with its fine record of accomplishment, is not above criticism or investigation. . . . But there is an important principle of jurisdiction here involved. . . . The appeal that is being taken concerns large constitutional questions that must be answered.

Commenting on the decision, a legal periodical was satisfied with Judge Youngdahl's reasoning, seeing his balancing of federal and state interests as a proper solution to the issue.

Congress may investigate interstate compacts as a preliminary step to enacting legislation, but such information will not be available if state interests outweigh the federal need for disclosure. Further, properly administered compact agencies would not seem to be restricted unduly in investigations initiated to secure information relating to valid federal interests if the investigations are not conducted for solely political ends and if the investigating committees do not attempt to use the documents to give unwarranted publicity to agency activities.

Appeal Proceedings and Decision

The Port Authority promptly appealed Judge Youngdahl's ruling to the United States Court of Appeals for the District of Columbia. Thomas E. Dewey, counsel for the Authority, argued that the agency was a state entity and that congressional consent given in 1921 was irrevocable. The government contended that the Port Authority was partly federal and partly state, and thus Congress had power to investigate it. "The question whether the New York-New Jersey agency is a Federal or state agency and what investigatory powers Congress has regarding it are prime issues in the Tobin case."

On June 8, 1962 the three-judge Court of Appeals unanimously overruled the District Court's conviction of Mr. Tobin for contempt of Congress. The opinion was less than what both sides had hoped for, in that the Court avoided the broad constitutional questions involved in the case, interpreting the House resolution narrowly and concluding that it did not authorize an investigation as extensive as the subcommittee attempted to undertake.

> *And so, in view of the fact that we consider it our duty to avoid, if possible, constitutional adjudication, we read these authorizing resolutions to mean that the Judiciary Committee was empowered to conduct an investigation calling for documents relating to actual 'activities and operations' of the Authority rather than for all the administrative communications, internal memoranda, and other intra-Authority documents demanded by the subpoena in question.*

The Court was not unaware of the seriousness and possible ramifications of the questions presented by the dispute. To illustrate what constitutional issues would have had to be decided to affirm the conviction it discussed at length appellant's argument that Congress does not have the power to "alter, amend or repeal" its consent to an interstate compact.

The Court granted that Congress could attach conditions to its consent to the formation of an interstate compact; however, any condition must in itself be constitutional. In other words, Congress cannot confer such power upon itself by legislative fiat.

> *In the present case, therefore, Congress' express reservation of the right 'to alter, amend or repeal' its initial consent to the creation of the Authority is meaningless unless Congress has the power under the Constitution 'to alter, amend or repeal' its consent to an interstate compact. The compact clause of the Constitution does not specifically confer such power on Congress. . . . Since no such power appears expressly in the compact clause, any holding that it exists and that Congress possesses it must be predicated on the conclusion that it exists as an implied power.*

The fact that Congress possessed plenary powers specified in the Constitution which would be sufficient to protect federal interests caused the Court to be "even less inclined to reach the constitutional issues involved here." Further, the Court recognized the serious ramifications of a holding that Congress did have the implied power "to alter, amend or repeal" consent to a compact. "No doubt the suspicion of even potential impermanency would be damaging to the very concept of interstate compacts."

Speaking to appellant's argument that congressional consent once given becomes irrevocable, the Court held that this did not mean that the states are free of the Constitution. An operational compact (as the one creating the Port Authority) as opposed to a static one (e.g., boundary line settlement) does not leave Congress without power to control its conduct. Congress possesses plenary powers—in the fields of interstate commerce and national defense—which enable it to supervise and regulate the activities of compacts to preserve federal interests. The Court found appellant's argument that Congress can adequately protect federal interests without going to the extreme of rescinding its consent "not unpersuasive." It conceded that the power "to alter, amend or repeal" is not of universal applicability; e.g., Congress could not at some future date withdraw its consent to a boundary line settlement.

Thus the Court pointed out in detail just one of the many constitutional questions raised by the dispute and the gravity and seriousness which their resolution involved. But it did not answer these questions. Inasmuch as the proceeding at bar was a criminal one, the Court felt constrained to grant the defendant every legal right, and for this reason was reluctant to pass upon broad questions of civil law within the framework of reviewing a criminal conviction. "Undoubtedly the questions presented to us properly demand resolution, but we should not and cannot permit this appeal for answers blind us to our duty of administering criminal justice according to traditional concepts."

> *A contempt of Congress prosecution is not the most practical method of inducing courts to answer broad questions broadly. Especially is this so when the answers sought necessarily demand far-reaching constitutional adjudications. To avoid such constitutional holdings is our duty, particularly in the area of the right of Congress to inform itself. Consequently, when Congress authorizes a committee to conduct an investigation, the courts have adopted the policy of construing such resolutions of authority narrowly, in order to obviate the necessity of passing on serious constitutional questions.*

Therefore, the first question to be answered was whether Congress gave the committee the authority to conduct the sweeping investigation undertaken. Examining the resolutions, the Court held that the House did not intend the authorization to include the internal operations of the Port Authority. The fact that Congress had never before attempted an investigation of such scope, an investigation which was certain to provoke the serious and difficult constitutional questions involved, led the Court to conclude that if it had intended to do so "it would have spelled out this intention in words more explicit than the general terms found in the authorizing resolutions under consideration."

In conclusion, the Court reiterated Judge Youngdahl's plea that Congress in the future find some other means to settle broad constitutional questions, advancing the suggestion that it allow these questions to be settled by declaratory judgement. Both Courts had found it unfortunate that it was necessary to treat a person as a criminal, who obviously was not, in order to raise constitutional questions for adjudication.

The Supreme Court refused to review the case upon the request of the Government, the Court of Appeals decision thus standing.

Conclusion

It may indeed be frustrating to a good many to find that after all of the subcommittee's action and the legal processes in the courts, some broad constitutional questions concerning the relationship between Congress and an interstate agency created under an interstate compact are still unanswered. Nevertheless, certain fairly definite conclusions can be drawn from the proceedings of the past few years.

First of all, it can be said that Congress, at least now if not before, may be acutely aware of the potentialities of the compact device. What at one time may be given scant attention is more likely to be analyzed before Congressional approval and watched afterward with a view of protecting federal interests from encroachment.

Secondly, a case can be made for congressional power to investigate an interstate authority like the Port of New York Authority down to the most intimate detail (as evidenced by the District Court's ruling). The Port Authority's intimate connection with interstate commerce, coupled with the Supreme Court's interpretation of the commerce clause in favor of federal authority, lends credence to the belief that, with the issues properly presented, the Court might favor the federal power over that of the state and/or the Port Authority. This belief, however, is weakened by the *dictum* in the Appeals Court decision asserting that congressional power over interstate compacts is not plenary. The Court spent some time examining the constitutional questions involved and the gravity of their effects, and although it avoided any expression as to their outcome, it recognized the issues' intimate connection with the federal system. With such large issues at stake — along with the Court's recognition that means, other than an investigation of internal operation, exist to protect federal interests — the commerce power does not loom so strongly in reference to the Port of New York Authority.

Thirdly, although it is too early to determine definitely, one can speculate on the effects of the Port Authority experience. The compact device has been a useful tool in attacking problems on a higher than intrastate level but a lower than national level. This sort of "regionalism" is a development of American federalism much more in evidence than in the past, and can have great impact upon its future. For instance, one area where interstate compacts could have a greater usefulness than up to now is in interstate metropolitan areas. An interstate compact providing for a metropolitan government for the Chicago-Gary area, or the St. Louis area, would be a step in solving the growing problems of expanding metropolitan areas. The difficulties involved, legal, political, and psychological are great enough to restrain one from seeing such an arrangement in the near future. Nevertheless, this is only one example of the potential use of the compact device. Meantime, compacts now are serving for action on a number of metropolitan area problems.

The great resistance in many quarters to a growing federal government can provide some cause for positive counteraction through the compact device. Accepting the concept of cooperative federalism, and using the compact device with the state and the federal government acting as partners, one can see the development of regional arrangements which combine resources of both the states and the federal government while keeping government "close to home." As has been mentioned, the responsibilities which many of these interstate compacts have assumed would, in their absence, fall upon the federal government. Thus the advantages of the device to both the states and the federal government seem evident. It is not unreasonable to feel that Congress possibly realizes this, inasmuch as it has not taken any steps to date to raise the constitutional questions within the terms of the Appeals Court decision in the Port of New York Authority case, i.e., steps authorizing, with a clear intent, the committee to secure the internal records of the Authority.

Let no one think that the compact device will solve all problems. But the compact device has provided indications of what can be done, and it deserves to be tried on a broader scale. If the states truly are "governmental laboratories" now is the time to put the possibilities of the compact approach under the microscope. If the states are losing their power at the expense of a centralizing national government, as many contend, they have increased incentive to exercise initiative and bold leadership in order to carry out the demands of twentieth century America. As many state leaders have emphasized, decrying "centralization by the national government at the expense of the states," while resting only on traditional procedures of the states, will not meet the challenge of the age.

THE UNIFORM COMMERCIAL CODE:
WHAT IS ACCOMPLISHED – WHAT REMAINS

WILLIAM A. SCHNADER

William A. Schnader is a former attorney general of Pennsylvania. He was president of the National Conference of Commissioners on Uniform State Laws and a member of the original editorial board for the Uniform Commercial Code.

Are the states going to surrender to Congress one more field in which they have hitherto had a free hand? Are they going to delay in making the Uniform Commercial Code the law of every state until Congress is forced by pressure from business and financial interests all over the country to regulate such transactions as sales, the negotiation of commercial paper, the issuance of letters of credit, and most of the other facets of commercial law with which the code deals? And, even if the fifty states enact the Commercial Code, will individual state action, as in the making of scores of nonuniform amendments, indicate to those calling for adequate solutions that the states cannot satisfactorily continue to function in what has thus far been an important area of states' rights?

That these questions are not mere figments of the imagination was rather definitely demonstrated by the fact that in the 1930's a federal sales act was introduced in Congress because the Uniform Sales Act (a) had not been universally enacted by the states and (b) was not fluid enough to take account of new practices in trade and commerce which had developed since the act was drafted many years before, and which were continuing to develop at a more rapid pace than ever. It was only because the late Karl N. Llewellyn, then Chairman of the Commercial Arts Section of the National Conference of Commissioners on Uniform State Laws, assured the proponents of the federal sales act that the Uniform Sales Act would be modernized, that they agreed to withdraw the federal act and give the conference another opportunity to show what it could accomplish.

What the Code Is

Here let us stop for a moment to review what the Uniform Commercial Code is.

It is a code regulating a great variety of commercial transactions, all of them of first importance. The code takes the place of all or parts

From "The Uniform Commercial Code: What is Accomplished—What Remains," William A. Schnader, *State Government,* Winter 1963, pp. 49-53. Reprinted by permission of the author and The Council of State Governments. [Footnotes omitted.]

of nine uniform acts which had been promulgated by the National Conference of Commissioners on Uniform State Laws before the task of preparing the code was undertaken, in 1942. These acts were the Uniform Sales Act, the Negotiable Instruments Law, the Uniform Bills of Lading Act, the Uniform Warehouse Receipts Act, the Uniform Stock Transfer Act, the Uniform Conditional Sales Act, the Uniform Trust Receipts Act, the Uniform Written Obligations Act, and the Uniform Fiduciaries Act.

The Commercial Code deals with sales; commercial paper; bank deposits and collections; letters of credit; bulk sales; documents of title, including warehouse receipts and bills of lading; investment securities; and secured transactions, including sales of accounts, contract rights and chattel paper.

Although the code is long, it is not nearly as long as the combined length of all of the acts it supersedes. The code, moreover, deals with several subjects which were never covered by uniform legislation. These additional subjects are bank deposits and collections, letters of credit and bulk sales. There are 400 sections in the code, but the nine uniform acts previously listed, which are superseded in whole or in part by it, contained 492 sections. When these facts are kept in mind, the code's size is not at all stupendous.

Why a Single Code?

The question naturally arises, why was it necessary to abandon the nine uniform acts, some of which were enacted by every state in the Union?

There are several answers. First, the most important uniform commercial acts which are being superseded were drafted in the early part of this century and modeled after English legislation, which had been drafted still earlier. They were not adapted to the business practices which followed in the wake of the tremendous development of methods of communication and transportation that has characterized the past forty years. In addition, some of the acts were drafted rather hurriedly. By the year 1940, eighty of the 198 sections of the Negotiable Instruments Law had different meanings in different states because the highest courts of different states had construed them differently. Finally, experience had taught the Commissioners on Uniform State Laws that, while they might propose sets of amendments to these several uniform acts, legislatures were slow to pass the amendments and bring the acts up to date.

Therefore it was felt that it would be much more feasible, if the states were to remain in control of this field of legislation — the regulation of commercial transactions — to embody in one great Commercial Code all of the important facets of commercial law. It was thought that it would be much easier to have the code amended from time to time than it would be to have six or eight separate uniform acts, each dealing with one phase of commercial law, kept up to date by the process of amendment.

Whether this will prove to be true only the future will tell.

Development of the Code; First Enactments

The Uniform Commercial Code was proposed in 1940. Shortly afterward, the American Law Institute and the National Conference of Commissioners on Uniform State Laws undertook the task as a joint project. An Editorial Board consisting of representatives of both bodies was created, and the code was drafted under its supervision. There were draftsmen for each of the articles of the code, and there were committees of advisers to assist the draftsmen as the work progressed. The code was almost the sole subject on the agenda at meetings of the Institute and the Conference for at least five years, and during most of those years there were two joint meetings each year. At last, in the fall of 1952, at a joint meeting of the Commissioners and the Institute, the code was finally adopted by them. Promptly thereafter it was endorsed by the American Bar Association.

When the Pennsylvania legislature met in 1953, the code was one of the first bills introduced, and it was the first bill to be enacted and signed by the Governor — Act No. 1 of the 1953 session, which appears on page 3 of the 1953 laws.

It was hoped that New York also would enact the code in 1953. However, the New York legislature referred it for study to its expert statutory drafting agency, the New York Law Revision Commission.

That action by the New York legislature effectively stopped the progress of the code for the time being. Everyone outside of Pennsylvania awaited the verdict of the New York commission. That verdict was announced in February, 1956. The commission's conclusion was that a code of commercial law was entirely feasible, but that in its then form the Uniform Commercial Code was not ready for passage by the New York legislature.

The staffs of the code's Editorial Board and the New York commission were in constant communication while the New York study was proceeding, so that the board was not surprised by the New York pronouncement. It immediately resumed work, reviewed the recommendations made by the New York commission, and in the fall of 1956 promulgated a revised Uniform Commercial Code. The revised code was introduced into the Massachusetts legislature early in 1957, and was enacted in September, 1957, to become effective on October 1, 1958.

Recent Enactments; State Amendments

Enactments of the code did not really gain momentum until 1961. Kentucky enacted it in 1958, Connecticut and New Hampshire in 1959 and Rhode Island in 1960. Then, in 1961, Wyoming, Arkansas, New Mexico, Ohio, Oregon, Oklahoma, Illinois and New Jersey became code states, and they were followed in 1962 by Georgia, Alaska, New York and Michigan. Meantime, in 1959, the Pennsylvania Legislature completely reenacted the code, substituting the revised for the original version.

While it is true that the eighteen states which have enacted the code will have, generally speaking, the same law regulating commercial transactions when their codes all become effective, it is also true that in some of the states a number of nonuniform amendments have, to some extent, impaired the chief value of the code, which is UNIFORMITY in state law regulating commercial transactions.

That the nonuniform amendments are by and large of a freakish nature is evident from the fact that only one section of the code has been amended in as many as ten states. This is Section 9–401, which relates to the place of filing financing statements. Unfortunately, the section was promulgated with a number of alternatives, and the alternatives were published in the Official Text in a manner which was highly confusing. That is being corrected in a new edition of the Official Text which is about to be published.

One section of the code was amended in seven states and another in six. Three sections were amended in five states, four sections in four states and five sections in three states. The remaining amendments modified the same sections of the code in not more than two states. In most cases there is little similarity between the language or substance of amendments made by two or more states to the same section of the code. Also, there is a great disparity in the total number of nonuniform amendments made by each of the eighteen enacting states.

Pennsylvania, with more than eight years' experience under the code, has in its present code only one variation from the 1958 Official Text. The banking, business and financial interests and the credit associations in Pennsylvania were completely satisfied with the original code. There is no demand anywhere in Pennsylvania for the code's revision. The revised version was substituted for the original in 1959 solely in the interest of uniformity.

Turning now to the other states, we find that Alaska and Michigan each have but one variation from the Official Text. Illinois has only three, Kentucky and New Mexico have four each, and the other states have larger numbers.

Work of the Editorial Board

In an effort to stop the making of miscellaneous unauthorized amendments to satisfy the draftsmen's vagaries in a single state, the suggestion was made in 1961 that a "Permanent Editorial Board for the Uniform Commercial Code" be established. An application was made by the American Law Institute to the Maurice and Laura Falk Foundation of Pittsburgh for a fund, the income of which would endow the work of such a board. The fund was granted and the board was created early in 1962. It will review the code not less often than once in five years and, with the approval of the Executive Committees of the National Conference of Commissioners on Uniform State Laws and of the American Law Institute, will make recommendations for amendments to the code to keep it up to date. This board will also examine and report on any unauthorized amendments which are made by the states which either have enacted the code or will enact it in the future.

The Permanent Editorial Board and three subcommittees have studied all amendments to the code made in the eighteen enacting states.

As of October 31, 1962, the board made its Report No. 1. It recommended twenty-three amendments to the code, offered three new optional provisions, and rearranged the alternative provisions in Section 9 – 401 in such a way as to render them more understandable. It also rejected 180 amendments made by the eighteen states and gave its reasons for rejecting them.

It should be made clear that the fact that the Permanent Editorial Board is recommending several dozen amendments at this time does not mean that it is going to recommend amendments with great frequency or in large numbers henceforth.

The code as a whole was reviewed by the original Editorial Board in 1956 after the report of the New York Law Revision Commission became available. Until 1962 there had been no further official review of the entire code. The agreement between the conference and the institute enjoins the Permanent Editorial Board to promulgate a minimum number of amendments and places strict limits on the board's jurisdiction. There is no danger whatever that the board will undertake to write a new code.

Looking to the Future

Of the thirty-two states which have not enacted the code, only five seem to have done nothing whatever looking toward its enactment. The code will be introduced into the legislatures of many of the remaining twenty-seven states in 1963, and it is safe to predict that when the 1963 sessions have come to an end there will be no less than thirty code states—and those of us who have been assiduously urging the universal adoption of the code by the states certainly hope that the number will be greater.

Need for Uniformity Emphasized

We cannot urge too strongly that the texts of the codes introduced into and enacted by 1963 legislatures be the 1962 Official Text with no variations. This will be the 1958 Official Text with the amendments recently promulgated by the Permanent Editorial Board.

In the eighteen states which have enacted the code there is substantial work to be done to make the codes conform to the 1962 Official Text. We do not understand the fear which has been expressed in some quarters that legislatures will resent having the most recently promulgated amendments introduced in 1963 and being asked to repeal all nonuniform amendments—or to state it differently to "clean up" their codes.

The Commercial Code project would never have been undertaken except in an effort to bring about UNIFORMITY in state law regulating commercial transactions. Unless the importance of this is emphasized all around, then, of course, a legislature may be annoyed by the introduction of a bill to bring the code of its particular state up to date, especially if it is only a year or so ago that the code was enacted. On the other hand, it would seem that the banking, business and financial interests of every state would want to see their legislature take whatever steps may be necessary to press forward toward the goal of UNIFORMITY.

As a result of the passage by eighteen states of the Uniform Commercial Code and its non-passage by thirty-two, the law regulating commercial transactions is less uniform today than it has been for many, many years. It is, of course, true that a majority of the states which are included among the ten states that lead in volume in practically all categories of manufacturing, business and finance have enacted the code. However, this is not enough. If the objective is to be met, *all* of the states must enact the code and *all* of them must enact it as promulgated and without any nonuniform variations from the Official Text.

We use the word "must" because, with the increasing tempo of business and finance, it is unthinkable that American businessmen and financiers will tolerate much longer a system under which the law relating to exactly the same transaction differs from state to state. So many businesses are today conducted in more than one state that, unless the states show by prompt and uniform adoption of the Commercial Code that they can and will handle this important field of legislation to meet modern conditions, Congress, we are convinced, will step in and add the regulation of commercial transactions to the many fields formerly occupied by state and local governments but now pre-empted by federal legislation. Federal legislation would, of course, be confined to transactions "in or affecting interstate commerce"; but we know from previous experience that this would be a most flexible limitation.

Only timely and uniform action by the states will save to them the regulation of commercial transactions.

Chapter III

Political Parties
and
Pressure Groups

The American party system is characterized by decentralization of power. In reality there is no national political party, but rather an alliance of state or local political parties. The state and local parties are inevitably affected by the course of national politics, but the effect is not uniform.

Only in the highly competitive two-party states such as California, Pennsylvania, and Delaware is there a clear parallel between national politics and state politics. In states with a weak two-party system such as Michigan, Ohio, Massachusetts, and Connecticut, the effect of national politics is limited to particular issues or personalities. There is even less effect in the one-party states of the South and in Vermont and New Hampshire.

The level of interparty competition is a major factor in the operation of state government and politics. A highly competitive system tends to reduce friction between the executive and legislative branches if both branches are controlled by the same party. Even when different parties control the executive and legislative branches, internal dissension within the parties is limited. Generally, the lower the leven of competition between the parties the greater the tendency of the parties to fragment or develop factions.

The level of interparty competition and corresponding political party power structure reflect the political history of the state. California, for example, developed a strong anti-party sentiment earlier in the century and as a result the structure of the Democratic party of California is quite weak. In "California Politics: The Search for Power" James Q. Wilson describes the resultant shift of political power to officeholders and various

Democratic "clubs" to fill the vacuum created by the absence of a hierarchical party structure.

The atrophy of party organizations in Massachusetts is based on ethnic, religious, and geographic rivalry. In "The Atrophy of Party Organization in Massachusetts," Murray B. Levin outlines some of the results of fragmented political power and argues that "[d]isciplined, responsible government is possible only if public officials have the political power necessary to execute their duties." The fragmentation of parties in Massachusetts "tends to make legislators easy prey for powerful groups in search of political favors."

Thus the nature of the political party system and the structure of the governmental system are major factors in the operation of pressure groups. In "St. Louis Politics: Relationships Among Interests, Parties and Governmental Structure," Robert H. Salisbury examines the configurations of power, interests, and governmental structures in St. Louis. He suggests that the two major interest groups have managed to stay within one political party by concentrating on different levels of government. Thus the formal structure of government significantly affects the form and intensity of conflict among interests.

The range of interests found in St. Louis is paralleled on the state level in most states. The specific "Issues and Pressure Groups in the State of Washington" are described by Daniel M. Ogden, Jr., and Hugh A. Bone. They state that there are three principal types of pressure groups in most states — service groups which advance the social, economic, or religious interests of their members, political action groups organized primarily for political purposes, and goal-directed groups which are usually temporary coalitions seeking a fairly specific goal.

The tactics of these three types of pressure groups differ, depending upon their objectives and the type of political system in which they operate. In a highly competitive two-party system power tends to move to the governor and the party leaders, and pressure groups must work at this level to be effective. "The 'Engineering of Consent' — A Case Study" by Robert Bendiner is an account of a battle between two major pressure groups — the railroads and the truckers — in the competitive political system of Pennsylvania. The techniques of creating an illusion of "public opinion" by creating, supporting, and infiltrating interested, but apparently unbiased, organizations are graphically described.

In a system with less competition the tactics of the pressure groups would be different. In a one-party system committee chairmen and leaders of the different factions within the party would be more powerful and they would be the targets of pressure-group persuasion. Although interest-group tactics must be compatible with the structure of the political system, some tactics are effective in a variety of political situations. Edward F. Cooke illustrates such a tactic in his article "Research: An Instrument of Political Power," which describes the activities of the Pennsylvania Economy League, a highly successful lobby working under the guise of a nonpartisan research organization studying the requirements of "good" government.

CALIFORNIA POLITICS: THE SEARCH FOR POWER

JAMES Q. WILSON

James Q. Wilson is associate professor of government, Harvard University. His works include *Negro Politics: The Search for Leadership* (1960) and *Urban Renewal: The Record and the Controversy* (1966).

California politics has been less a struggle and more a search for power. The reforms instituted by an earlier group of amateurs and progressives in part stimulated and in part frustrated the present generation of volunteers. By effectively destroying local party organization, these "reforms" provided the opportunity for the present club movement; by removing elective officials from dependence on the party, they prevented club movement from winning a complete victory.

Partisan activity continues to be deeply molded by the anti-party legacy of Hiram Johnson and the statutory restrictions on political parties enacted over forty years ago. Johnson and his followers in the progressive wing of the dominant Republican party sought to break the hold of the Southern Pacific Railroad over the government of the state by curbing, through legislation, the party machinery which translated economic into political power. In the desire to eliminate a bad party, party itself was all but destroyed. A direct primary law had, in 1909, already supplanted the party convention as a means of selecting nominees. After Johnson's Lincoln-Roosevelt League captured control of the Republican party by taking advantage of the direct primary system, it moved in the legislature to insure that never again would a political party be strong in the state. Between 1911 and 1913, a presidential primary election and the direct election of United States senators were authorized, straight-ticket party voting was made laborious by eliminating the party circle from the ballot, the legal party organization was fragmented and reduced to impotence, all city and county elected posts were made non-partisan, and cross-filing was introduced. The result was the creation of a political vacuum which has never been filled.

There is no integrated party structure in the state. Two party organs are recognized by law, but they bear only the slightest relationship to each other. The state central committee of each party is composed, for the most part, of the party's nominees for public office and

Reprinted from *The Amateur Democrat* by James Q. Wilson (pp. 96-109) by permission of The University of Chicago Press. Copyright © 1962 by The University of Chicago Press. [Footnotes omitted.]

their appointees; the county central committees, on the other hand, are composed of members elected by the voters from small (either assembly or county supervisor) districts. Neither body is organically related to the other, and the law has little to say about what relationships ought to exist except to require that the county central committees "shall have charge of the party campaign under the direction of the state central committee." Of crucial importance is the fact that not only are the two bodies not part of a single party hierarchy (as they would be, for example, if the state committee were composed of delegates from the county committee), but they consist of groups which have an inevitable conflict of interest.

The state central committee is dominated by the incumbent elective officials in the party. It consists of 706 members, all but 58 of whom are either party nominees (one for each of the 162 partisan offices in the state) or their appointees (three for each nominee, or a total of 648). The remaining 58 members, a tiny minority, are the chairmen of the county central committees of California's 58 counties. Not only is representation on the state committee heavily weighted in favor of elective officials and nominees, but it is dominated by nominees for legislative, rather than executive, offices. There are only six statewide executive officers, but there are eighty assemblymen and forty state senators. Nominees for the state legislature thus control 480 seats on the committee, while nominees for executive posts control only 24. Further, nominees who win office and who stand for re-election year after year are able to retain seats for themselves and their appointees on the committee for long periods of time, whereas unsuccessful nominees serve only two years and then are replaced by a new set of nominees (except for those few times when defeated candidates stand again for election). This means that incumbent officeholders tend to acquire seniority and a fund of experience in and knowledge about committee affairs that usually enables them to exercise leadership in this group. In 1961, a law was passed which strengthened even further the power of the incumbents by increasing the number of committee members each could name from three to five.

The county central committees, on the other hand, are dominated by elected members. The Los Angeles County Democratic Central Committee, the largest in the state, consists of 249 members, 217 of whom are elected in primaries for two-year terms, seven from each assembly district. The remaining 32 are the party's nominees for assemblymen and state senator from the county. These nominees, who usually control the state central committee, are a small minority on the county committee. Whereas the chairman of the state committee is almost always either an officeholder or the appointee of one, the chairmen of the county committees rarely are. The elected county committeemen are the only party officials chosen directly by the voters. This election is, of course, hardly a deliberative process of any consequence. Owing to the lengthy and complicated California ballot and the absence of party control over the electorate in primaries, the choice of county committeemen is, in the words of many party leaders, a "hopeless lottery" in which the sound of one's name and the nature of one's occupation, together with one's position on the ballot in the list of candidates for that post, are the most important factors in determining election to the committee. Nevertheless, despite the fact that the average county committeeman is almost entirely unknown to the voters and owes his post as much to chance as to ability, he is placed—by virtue of his election—in a position which inescapably gives him a point of view different from that of the state legislators and congressmen who control the state committee.

Not only are the two official party organs predestined to conflict, but in addition the legal party lacks any base in city or county politics. Affairs at the local level are by and large non-partisan. Legally, the city does not exist for the party organization, and there is little patronage in city government with which to strengthen party organization even if the parties could successfully intervene in local affairs.

Most important, however, the official party organs have relatively little power. To decentralization and internal conflict is added impotence. The state committee by law cannot take part in primary contests, and only recently have the county committees, by a lower court test, won a cloudy right to make pre-primary endorsements. But even local endorsements by a county committee are often unimportant, for there is no official party organization in the precincts that could make effective the decisions of the leadership. The Elections Code prescribes in careful detail what the state central committee may do. It meets every two years, principally to elect officers. Although contests for these offices are often heated, in a committee with so many members and in a state with so few means for assembling political power, it becomes extremely difficult to control the election process. Further, the law requires that the chairmanship of the committee be alternated between the northern and southern parts of the state. This means not only that no state committee chairman can succeed himself, but also that for this and other reasons, the party organization is split in half. North and south function virtually as separate political entities. The state committee has two vice-chairmen, one from each region. In effect, when the chairman is from the north, party affairs in the south are conducted, not by the chairman, but the vice-chairman for Southern California, and vice versa. There can never be a single statewide party chairman with influence commensurate with his title, nor can there be, except under the most fortuitous circumstances based on informal personal understandings, any real continuity of party leadership.

The Los Angeles County Committee is probably the most active in the California Democratic party. In comparison to many other county committees, some of which scarcely ever meet and a few of which lack a full complement of members, it is exceptionally effective. In comparison with a county party organization in a large eastern city, however, it is feeble and inconsequential. An active member of it, addressing a meeting of its executive committee, urged it to be more active in certain party affairs. "Twelve to fifteen years ago," he observed, "the County Committee was a laughing stock. We have grown in stature some, and we want to grow even more. Not many years ago, hardly any politician would even talk to us. Now, many will. We have to up-grade ourselves."

In cities where parties are strong, that strength results from the existence of an effective precinct organization, the ability to determine who shall be the party's nominees, and control of the patronage resources of the government. In California, all three of these sources of strength are lacking. There is no precinct organization within the regular party, no way to deliver nominations to endorsed candidates at the local level, no way even to make endorsements at the state level, and parties are excluded from city and county affairs. Only from the state and national governments may the parties receive patronage. In California, the merit system is effective at the state as well as the local level, and only a few desirable jobs, most of them judicial appointments, are available to state officers. Edmund G. "Pat" Brown, a Democrat who later became governor, told an interviewer that there were no more than six hundred political appointments available to the top state official. Most of the discretionary appointments are to honorific posts which carry no pay. Judgeships and department heads, under the control of the governor, and inheritance tax appraiserships, under the purview of the controller, are almost the only important state patronage.

But even these meager resources are not used to build party strength. Because of the factional character of Democratic politics, patronage must be distributed to competing leaders and rival groups. There is enough patronage to make these forces struggle for it, but not enough to compel them to follow a single leader. Further, the elective officials who control these jobs are concerned with re-election. Knowing that the prospects for building a strong organization are almost nil under present laws, jobs are awarded in order to reward personal supporters and overcome objections to re-election rather than to consolidate political strength in a single organization. Indeed, elective officers, both Democratic and Republican, are keenly aware that a strong party would weaken their own authority and place burdensome constraints upon them. This gives them additional reasons for spending patronage in a way one powerful California party leader termed "unwise." The state controller told an interviewer that criticisms of his practice in awarding inheritance tax appraiserships, many of which are very lucrative, were known to him. But he defended giving such jobs to persons who in some cases were weak Democrats or even known Republicans. "To make appointments only to strong party workers in the Democratic organization would make it appear as if I were attempting too consciously to build a political machine. We don't want it to look machine-like, so I am spreading the appointments around so that as a result, some Republicans and weak Democrats get them."

After the Democrats won five of the six statewide offices in 1958, no central patronage-dispensing office was created, much to the disgust of party functionaries. A powerful member of the State Central Committee observed glumly:

> *What he [the Governor] needs to do is to pick a State Chairman and back him — decide who is going to get the patronage and centralize the control of it in somebody . . . with continuity. . . . For a while there we were trying to run all this through one man, but [the Governor] keeps pulling the rug out from under him. For a while I was handling all the patronage, and then the Governor would make a couple of appointments himself to people he had to satisfy, and there I'd be, standing on a bare floor with no clothes on. . . . He won't designate one person to handle this.*

These debilitating factors have been aggravated by others. Until 1954, it was possible for one candidate to file for nomination in the primaries of both parties without indicating his party affiliation on the ballot. Cross-filing, in the view of every writer on the subject, undoubtedly reduced party organization to very nearly an empty charade. Effective in 1954, the law was changed to require that party membership be shown on the ballot after the name of each candidate. The results were dramatic. In 1952, 72 per cent of all elective offices had been won in the primary by cross-filed candidates who captured the nomination of both parties. In 1954, after the introduction of the party label, only 26 per cent were decided in the primary. Having won the nomination, many Democrats were then able to go on to the general election and, drawing on the Democrats' four-to-three lead in registration, turn Republicans out. (In 1954, the number of Democrats in the state senate increased from eleven to sixteen, and in the state assembly from twenty-six to thirty-two.) In 1959, the legislature abolished cross-filing altogether.

Consequences of Party Weakness

Given the rapid growth and high mobility of California's population, it is questionable whether an effective precinct organization could have been constructed even if the formal party machinery had been legally strong and patronage plentiful. It has been estimated that about one-fourth of the persons in the state did not live at their present address one year ago. Organizing the grass roots when the population turnover is so high would be exceptionally difficult under the best of circumstances.

The principal consequence of this political vacuum in California is that any number of persons, groups, and community organizations seek to fill the void and that in the effort to establish themselves, these forces endeavor not so much to wrest power from those who hold it as to create power where none has existed before. The search for power in this fluid situation, in which the formal party apparatus is both incomplete and fragmented, is an extraordinarily difficult and taxing enterprise. But it offers great rewards to skilful men who have the ability to manipulate large groups of people and the energy to struggle for intangible ends in a highly uncertain situation. The absence of a hierarchical party, with authority clearly distributed in some regularized pattern, means that men with ability but little seniority can rise rapidly. Paul Ziffren, the former Democratic national committeeman from California, rose to that office almost out of nowhere, his talents more than compensating for his lack of preliminary work in the lower ranks of the party and his recent arrival in the state from Illinois. Joseph L. Wyatt, Jr., became the second president of the California Democratic Council after having lived in the state only eight years. Jesse M. Unruh, one of the two or three most powerful politicians in the state, Speaker of the Assembly and head of the Kennedy presidential campaign in Southern California in 1960, was just thirty-eight years old and a member of the assembly only since 1954.

This is true throughout the party. An able young leader who had risen quickly observed:

> *Power accrues to him who works hard and becomes known as a leader. If you're willing to be vigorous and active, if you're willing to do the work, sooner or later you're going to become known as a leader. It's inevitable. Leadership tends to go to the person most active, and thus power goes by default to the person most interested in obtaining it.*

There is no table of organization to fill, and hence no energy-sapping career ladder which requires new arrivals to wait at the lower levels until party leaders die or resign. "The party is young and in flux," said a rising young leader. But this same flux which has as its advantage the creation of opportunities has as its price the creation of uncertainty. Those most anxious to attain power are least confident that they have it or know where it can be found. No matter how high they rise, claims are always made on their authority by others and decisions must always be shared with many. Since decision-making is highly decentralized and based in great measure on persuasion and consensus, those most influential in making decisions are those most adept at persuading and creating the correct mood or set of expectations. A majority of the 249 members of the Los Angeles County Committee must be persuaded (threats are almost useless) in order to endorse a primary candidate for the least important offices. To choose a state chairman, the votes or proxies of a majority of 706 state central committeemen must be obtained.

The absence of a clear party organization, with easily visible and generally recognized leadership, means that roles are vague and tend to overlap. Conflict is intensified simply by the multiplication of the number of people who can advance some claim to having their views considered. Deprived of formal responsibilities, leaders of county committees often fall to wondering just what they are supposed to do. Said one in Los Angeles:

> *What are we supposed to do? What is power? We are supposed to have it, but we don't seem to. The Election Code gives us the right to conduct the affairs of the party in Los Angeles County under the general direction of the State Committee. But the State Committee tends to be meaningless as a source of direction. We really don't know what we are supposed to do down here.*

"Capturing control" of the county committee is almost an empty phrase. There is not enough at stake in control of that committee, or indeed in the control of any party organ, to justify the effort or to make the results significant. A young, ambitious leader may well be able, after a heated fight, to become chairman of the Los Angeles County Committee. But he would not find that he could then speak as the "leader" of the Democratic party in Los Angeles County, and should he attempt to do so, others would laugh at him. A California political scientist recently commented:

> *The [county] committee commands little respect, manifests a high degree of disagreement, and, because of a rigid California code, is generally hamstrung in its operations. As a result, county central committeemen, frustrated by their inability to act, are reduced to the status of party caretaker, content to discuss issues, mold empty plans, and contemplate the disadvantages of ineffective organization.*

Committee members are fully aware of their weak position. As a result, there is a high absentee rate at meetings even though the law stipulates that anyone who is absent more than three times without an excuse forfeits his seat. At every meeting of the committee, new members are selected to fill such vacancies. Over 38 per cent of the members of the 1960 Los Angeles County Committee had not been members of the previous committee. Nearly two out of every five members had either resigned, not sought re-election, or been defeated. In 1950, one student discovered that there was no contest for county committee seats in about 36 of California's 58 counties. In another study made in 1956, over one-third of a random sample of all county committeemen (of both parties) had held their seat for one year or less. The same can be said for the state committee. Only 32.3 per cent of the members of the 1954 Democratic State Central Committee had served on the 1952 committee. Few county committeemen receive the kind of reward which could be expected by their counterparts in many eastern states. In 1956, only 2.2 per cent of a sample of county committeemen (of both parties) gave their occupation as government employee or officeholder. An active member of the Los Angeles County Committee, chairman of one of its subcommittees, noted that some influential members opposed the county chairman, but little had been done.

> *The turnover is so high and the lack of interest is so great that nobody thinks it's worth much to organize an effective campaign against him. There has never been any well-programmed opposition to the present leadership of the County Committee. The reasons for that are, first of all, the Committee is so big and the county is so large that it's almost impossible to organize it to do anything. And secondly, it's simply not worth the effort it would take to control it. If you control the committee, what do you have? Just a large, unwieldy body in which most people don't even take any interest at all.*

The incomplete and disjointed nature of the party organization makes the crucial question of party finance a perplexing one. With no clear center of political gravity and no recognized leadership, many party agencies and individuals raise money in independent and often conflicting ways. With the lack of a patronage-sustained precinct organization, abundant campaign funds are vital. Yet precisely because the legal party apparatus is ineffective, donors are often reluctant to give any sizable contribution to a committee which carries little weight. Unions, businesses, and individuals with interests they are anxious to advance are far more likely to give money directly to candidates, particularly incumbent candidates. A person who both spent funds on behalf of a local special-interest group and served on the county committee told an interviewer that it would be absurd to consider giving much to the party organs. "You might as well throw your money away. . . . If you have any money to give, you give it to the individual candidate directly." Lacking adequate funds, the party committees find it even harder to control party nominations. Each prospective nominee first decides whether he can find a personal finance chairman who can raise the money he needs; if he can, he need rarely worry about having the approval of the county committee, for a failure to win its support would not be very costly in terms of withheld funds.

The decentralization of party finance has in the past, at least, given inordinate influence to certain generously endowed interests which found that money could provide more influence than party control. In recent years this has changed somewhat, with the public exposure of some of the more notorious donors, a tendency toward greater organization and routinization of party finance, and the growth of the extra-legal party groups which have been sources of volunteer labor that reduced somewhat the need for large sums in campaigns.

All of these factors — the high turnover of county and state committee members, the diffuseness of political power, the weakness of the legal party machinery, and the tendency of political funds to go directly to incumbent candidates — have served to enhance the position of the elective officials. In the past, these men have often been the only visible sign of party life at all, and even today, despite the partisan revitalization, they have as large or larger a claim to influence within the party as anyone. Such influence has often been used to keep the party weak and divided, for this condition removes one restraint on their freedom of action and permits the broad appeal to voters which has been so successful in the past. One of the themes of this study will be the fundamental conflict between elective officials and the amateur politicians who make up the California Democratic Council, but it should be remembered that this tension between incumbent and party workers existed long before the creation of the CDC. Earl Warren found that the Republican state organization was of little help to his candidacy and its intervention reduced the effectiveness of his bipartisan appeal. He rejected its pre-primary support and refused to become identified with it in the election campaign. Democrats have been somewhat more partisan, in an effort to capitalize on the Democratic lead in registration, but even they have looked upon the party as a group which should work hard and remain silent. In 1951, and again in 1961, the legislature passed a bill which, if the Governor had signed it, would have allowed each nominee for state office to appoint some members to his county central committee. In effect, this would have converted the county committees into smaller replicas of the state central committee.

THE ATROPHY OF PARTY ORGANIZATION
IN MASSACHUSETTS

Murray B. Levin

Murray B. Levin is professor of government, Boston University. His works include *The Alienated Voter: Politics in Boston* (1960).

As we have mentioned, the ethnic, religious, and geographical factors in Massachusetts politics account, in part, for the feudalization of the Democratic party and the moderate liberalism (and at times conservatism) of its supporters. The ecological basis of Massachusetts politics also accounts, in part, for the relatively greater stability and centralization of the minority Republican party. The feudalization of the Democratic party is also a result of the ideological divergence of the several blocs that compose the party. Setting aside President Kennedy and the peculiar blend of Harvard, New Deal, and "lace-curtain Irish" heritage he represents, the Democratic party of Massachusetts is split into five major groups, whose political ideologies vary widely. They are:

1. A small group of ardent New Dealers who wish to expand state services in the fields of education, mental health, and public welfare, and who recognize that these programs require increased taxation. The New Dealers' leadership is drawn from a small but articulate community of intellectuals, professional men, and a very few labor leaders. Their strength is limited by the fact that many who share their views (people associated with universities, a fair number of the skilled engineers and technical personnel in such industries as electronics, and a group of small businessmen) vote Republican on the state level and Democratic on the national level.

2. A small group of moderate liberals who favor expansion of state services and vigorously defend civil rights. They hesitate, however, to endorse significant tax increases, preferring moderate gains in public services commensurate with the expansion of the economy.

3. A larger group of "job-conscious" Democrats. Although vaguely committed to the goals laid down in the party platform, this group is interested in government chiefly as a source of income or prestige for themselves or their friends. Its members tend to think in terms of jobs, low-number license plates, and other favors of various kinds. Their activities are not necessarily corrupt (patronage and corruption may be distinct). The bulk of these job-conscious Democrats are lawyers or insurance men who use political influence to make business contacts and

From *The Compleat Politician* by Murray B. Levin (Indianapolis: The Bobbs-Merrill Co., Inc., 1962), condensed and adapted from pp. 38-54, 58-63, 68-70. Reprinted by permission of the publisher. [Footnotes omitted. Originally titled "Democrats and Republicans: The Atrophy of Party Organization."]

secure positions on the state payroll. A few regard politics as an opportunity to work with and for people they like, regardless of political issues.

4. A very large group of "Al Smith Democrats," who form the broad base of the party. These Democrats are essentially what James MacGregor Burns calls "bread-and-butter liberals"; that is, they are concerned with immediate economic gains for the working class. John Fitzgerald Kennedy was one for much of his congressional career. The Al Smith Democrats often believe that the national party is too "leftish." Many of them deserted Adlai Stevenson in 1952 and 1956 and were not unfavorably disposed to Senator Joseph McCarthy. They also look with disfavor on the "internationalism" of the party and its "friendly" relations with Great Britain. They usually oppose increased taxation on the state level, unless party leaders can demonstrate some urgent need.

5. A small group of strongly conservative Democrats who identify with the party simply by the historical accident of birth, rather than by ideological conviction. Their views on governmental matters are dramatically similar to those of the conservative segments of the Republican state party.

In contrast to the Democratic party, conflicts among the Republicans tend to center on problems of political strategy rather than political philosophy. The Bay State Republicans are a microcosm of the national party. That is, they fall into three categories, exemplified by such national figures as Nelson Rockefeller, Richard Nixon, and Barry Goldwater, as follows:

1. A small group of liberals who look to Rockefeller as their national leader. They are represented by a few outspoken and articulate leaders in the state legislature who argue that if the party is to regain its strength it should be friendly to labor, advocate the expansion of some important state services, and stoutly champion civil liberties. This group is strongly opposed by the "Old Guard."

2. A very large group, the party core, that accepts the moderate conservatism typified by President Eisenhower but whose state heroes are such "blue bloods" as Saltonstall, Lodge, and Herter. This group accepts Nixon, respects Rockefeller, and is somewhat dubious about Goldwater. Although its members venerate prestigious Brahmins, the leading Republicans in the state legislature and most of the "working politicians" in the party are what are called "swamp Yankees"—that is, white Anglo-Saxon Protestants who have money or professional prestige but not "blue blood." The party core consists largely of middle-class Protestant suburbanites who are cautious about spending but who nevertheless believe that some of the programs suggested by liberal Republicans warrant investigation and possibly endorsement (if they do not result in heavier taxes).

3. A small group of ultra-conservatives who find Goldwater's views congenial and who stress the need for a very distinctive stand in opposi-

tion to the Democrats, especially on economy in government. They favor minimal governmental "interference" and a "return" to the "virtues" of *laissez faire*, thrift, and individual initiative.

There are, in addition to these ideologically distinctive groups, a number of ethnic-oriented revisionists within the GOP (equivalent to the "job-conscious" and "Al Smith Democrats") who are more concerned with the "image" of the party than with its policy. The ethnic-oriented Republicans argue that the party must broaden its ethnic and religious base by endorsing some candidates who are not Protestant and Anglo-Saxon. This group supported George Fingold and promoted the candidacy of John Volpe for the governorship in 1960. Ethnic-oriented Republicans can be found in all the major groups within the party. Unlike the Democrats, who resolve their group differences, often noisily, in public during primary campaigns, the Republicans manage to "harmonize" their differences within the party caucus and are thus able to present a "united" front to the voters.

Before analyzing the manner in which the parties operate in the state legislature, it is necessary to examine in greater detail the feudalization of the Democratic organization and the relative unity of the Republican organization.

In his distinguished work *American State Politics,* V. O. Key, Jr., notes, "Over a period of a half century party organizations have seriously deteriorated. Their decay has been associated with the rise of the direct primary system of nomination." The fact that the Democratic party organization in Massachusetts has disintegrated more than its Republican counterpart although both must operate with the same pre-primary convention system suggests that factors other than the direct primary contribute to the atrophy of party organization. We can appraise the viability of a party organization on the basis of three criteria: (1) its ability to prevent primary fights, (2) its ability to control finances and patronage, and (3) its ability to develop a working base at the grass-roots level.

A party organization that is highly centralized and disciplined should be able to prevent, or at least minimize, challenges to convention endorsees during the primaries. The Republicans have been far more successful than the Democrats in protecting their endorsees from such challenges. Table 1 shows the number of candidates in the Republican and Democratic primaries who competed for state-wide offices from 1950 to 1960.

Since 1950, 100 Democrats have competed for their party's nominations while only 64 Republicans have competed for Republican nominations. The Democratic organization often has been unable to force the various party leaders to accept the decision of the convention. Since 1952, when the Republican party resorted to the pre-primary conven-

TABLE 1. NUMBER OF CANDIDATES IN PRIMARY CONTESTS FOR STATEWIDE OFFICES, BY PARTIES (1950-60)*

Office	Democrats 1950	1952	1954	1956	1958	1960	Republicans 1950	1952	1954	1956	1958	1960
Governor	1†	1†	2	2	1†	7	6	1	1†	1	3	1
Lt. Governor	5†	6†	1	3	1†	2	5	1	1†	1	1	1
Sec. of State	8†	1†	1†	2†	1†	3	7	1	1	1	1	1
Treasurer	1†	7†	3	5†	2†	6	2	2	1	1	1	2
Auditor	1†	1†	1†	1†	1†	2†	2	1	1	1	1	1
Attorney General	4†	4†	1	2	2	1†	5	1	1†	1†	1	1
U.S. Senator	—	1	3	—	—	3	—	1†	1†	—	—	1†

* Duane Lockard compiled this table for the years 1950-56. The authors "completed" the table for the period 1958-60. We wish to thank Mr. Lockard and his publishers, the Princeton University Press, for their kind permission to reproduce this table from Lockard, *New England Politics* (Princeton, N.J.: Princeton University Press, 1959), p. 133.
† Indicates races in which incumbents were involved.

tion, only two Republicans have opposed the endorsee. Since 1954, when the Democratic party endorsed candidates in pre-primary conventions, 33 individuals have opposed endorsees.

One of the reasons that the Democratic party has had so much difficulty in preventing challenges to the convention endorsee is that many endorsed candidates have very common Irish names. In several instances, individuals who happened to have the same last name (and sometimes the same first name and middle initial) as an endorsee have been tempted to run, and have in fact run, on the theory that massive confusion of the voters might result in their election. The classic case of what is commonly known in Massachusetts as "the name's the same" is that of one John Francis Kennedy, who ran against the Democratic party endorsee for state treasurer in 1952, 1956, and 1958, winning each time. In the 1960 gubernatorial contest, Kennedy ran against the convention endorsee, Joseph Ward, who remarked, when estimating Kennedy's chances, "He has a magic name, and believe me, a name in politics is like Ivory Soap in business, or like Coca Cola. Once the American people have accepted it, it is pretty difficult to have them accept something else." One of Ward's advisers who was worried by Kennedy's "appeal" stated to the authors:

> *It's tough enough for them [the voters] to find out who the candidates for governor and president and senator may be, and so at that level the name becomes terribly important, just the familiarity of the name, the reaction to the name. It doesn't even have to be "Kennedy."*

V. O. Key, Jr., has compiled "the saga of the Hurleys in Massachusetts," which illustrates the tribulations of the Democratic party leaders and "the name's the same":

In 1930 Francis X. Hurley won the Democratic nomination for auditor and Charles F. Hurley won the Democratic nomination for treasurer. Both went on to victory and in 1932 were renominated and re-elected. Four years of publicity for the Hurley name gave it a political potency. In 1934, as Charles F. Hurley, unsuccessful in his bid for convention endorsement for governor, had to be content with a renomination for treasurer, one Joseph L. Hurley turned up on the scene and won the nomination for lieutenant-governor. Elected as lieutenant-governor, he shared the stage with Treasurer Hurley for a couple of years and the name of Hurley became more and more of a household word. The two Hurleys, Charles F. and Joseph L., vied in 1936 for the convention endorsement for governor. Charles F. won the nod and Joseph L. disappeared from the limelight. The magic of the name Hurley seeped over into the Republican ranks and, also in 1936, the Republicans endorsed and nominated a William E. Hurley for treasurer, the post held by the Democrat, Charles F. Hurley, now running for governor. Simultaneously, the Democratic convention proposed J. C. Scanlon for the treasury post, but one James M. Hurley won the primary nomination for the place that had been so adequately filled by Charles F. Hurley. Mr. Charles F. Hurley went on to win the governorship but his colleague Mr. James M. Hurley, of Marlborough, fell before the campaign of Mr. William E. Hurley, the Boston Republican.

The fact that so many candidates challenge the Democratic convention endorsee leads to bitter primary fights characterized by mutual character assassination, and the bitterness of the primary fight causes some followers of losing Democratic candidates to abstain from voting or support a Republican in the general election. The ethnic diversity of the Democratic constituency and the "in-fellow" feeling of the ethnic-group members undoubtedly heighten the bitterness of Democratic primaries, particularly when Italo-American oppose Irish-American candidates. The primary election that we shall analyze is a classic example of this type, in which the convention endorsee, Joseph Ward, an "outstate" American of Irish descent, was opposed by three other Irish Americans, two Italo-Americans, and one Yankee Protestant. The successful Republican candidate in the general election, John Volpe, an Italo-American, won partly because of the support of many non-Irish Democrats who objected to the "all green" ticket endorsed by their party. In contrast to the Democrats with their hotly contested primaries, the Republicans, whose convention endorsee is customarily unopposed, enter the general election "unsmeared," at least by each other.

It is also possible to evaluate the strength of a party organization on the basis of its ability to control its funds. Strong party organizations are able to centralize fund-raising efforts and control the disbursements for expenses. Here too, the Republican organization is far more successful than its opposition. Lockard points out that in the bitter campaign of 1954 "most of the Republican money was spent by the state committee and little by the organizations directly associated with the leading candidates. The reverse was true with the Democrats. . . . Roughly the same situation prevailed in 1952." This was also true in the 1960 elections. The Republican party customarily collects money through the central organization, which then proceeds to distribute it to local organizations as it sees fit. This control of the purse is, of course, an awesome device for enforcing party discipline in the hands of the state committee. Most of the money spent by Democratic organizations in local communities is collected in the local communities by the local organizations. Each Democratic candidate raises his own funds in whatever way he can and with little or no direction or control from the state committee. Quite often the Democratic candidate who survives a bitter primary fight has exhausted his resources. Republicans, who are uncontested in the primary, are able to preserve their financial strength for the general election.

The ultimate test of a vigorous and centralized party organization is its ability to sustain working organizations at the ward and precinct level and "force" them to support the convention endorsee. In this respect too, the Republicans are far more successful than the Democrats. We have already pointed out that the Democratic organization has not been very successful in preventing challenges in the primary and that it is divided regionally and ethnically. Lockard writes:

> *The Democratic organization in fact seems at times to be nothing at all. . . . Personal organizations are numerous and various strong men often go their own way without regard for other candidates in a campaign. In a good many areas, particularly in the small Republican towns, there is no Democratic organization of any kind. In some smaller urban centers where there are Democratic majorities, the party organization may practically give way to labor groups who do most of the work of campaigning. The lack of constant contact between the central party and the local units has tended to result in the atrophy of some local units, and if the central organization has not atrophied it has certainly suffered badly from weakness born of internal division.*

On the local level, the Republicans are frequently better organized than the Democrats. This does not mean that Republican organization in the smaller cities and towns is adequate; it means simply that what leadership there is tends to think in terms of its relationship to the state organization more than do the Democrats, who, with locally loyal followings, think in terms of "every man for himself." In most of the larger cities, Republican organizations are weak or nonexistent. In

Boston, for example, the GOP as an organization is impotent in all but two or three of the city's 22 wards. Until recent years, prestigious party leaders were able to determine the Republican ticket with little opposition.

The feudalization of the Democratic party organization and the relative unity of the Republicans also result from the belief held by many Republicans that they have little chance of winning statewide contests. The Republicans can maintain some semblance of unity because their minority status discourages challengers to the convention endorsee and forces the party to unite. The Democrats, on the other hand, believe that they are likely to win most of the contests for statewide office. This whets the appetite of potential candidates, who are willing to defy the convention and develop organizations of their own. The degree of internal cleavage within a state party organization is related to the party's strength in the electorate.

During the period 1916-30, Democrats in Massachusetts believed (and correctly so) that they had little chance of winning many statewide contests. For this reason, relatively few notables within the party attempted to establish rival organizations. If we measure party unity during these years using the same criteria we used above, the Democratic party is unified, the Republican party is feudalized.

Despite the relatively superior Republican organization, there is little doubt that a majority (perhaps 55%) of the voters in Massachusetts identify in some way with the Democratic party. The overwhelming victories of the Democratic party in recent years in the state legislature indicate this. If the Democrats could overcome the mutual hostility of ethnic groups and so unite them, the Republicans would be able to maintain their current position only in their safest districts. The natural advantages of the Democratic party, however, are dissipated by continuous primary warfare, a plethora of candidates with the "right" name, the Boston-*vs.*-outstate antagonism, and the taint of corruption—all serious problems which can be dealt with only after some awakening of interest in responsible party organization.

Because it is not the nominal "majority" party, the Republican party is forced to pursue a strategy of divide-and-conquer; the party stands to do best if it nominates ethnically balanced slates, continues to force investigations of corrupt practices by the incumbent Democrats, and maintains its superior organization. The gubernatorial elections of 1960, with which we are concerned, illustrate the interplay of these forces so far as election strategy is concerned. Before turning to the 1960 elections, however, it is necessary to examine briefly the operation of parties in the state legislature and the incidence of corruption in Massachusetts public life, because the legislative record of the incumbents and corruption in public life were the prime issues of the 1960 elections.

Party Influence in the General Court

We have been using the concept "political party" in two senses. At times we have used it to refer to that group of voters who consider themselves party members. The vast majority of voters who make up the Democratic and the Republican "parties" in Massachusetts (and other states) are politically active only on election day, although many view political issues during the intervals between elections in a predictably partisan fashion. This group can be called the "party-in-the-electorate." As we have said, the Democratic "party-in-the-electorate" is a loose coalition of ethnic groups which are, at best, moderately liberal; the Republican "party-in-the-electorate," is predominantly Anglo-Saxon, Protestant, and moderately conservative. We have also used the term "political party" to refer to the relatively small group of active, professional political workers who maintain the party organization (i.e., the members of the state central committee, the members of the ward and town committees, and the active workers at the grass roots). The Democratic "party-organization" is feudalized and relatively ineffectual. The Republican "party-organization," in comparison, is relatively centralized and disciplined. The "party-in-the-electorate" includes the apathetic and the active.

The term "political party," however, may also refer to groups within the government (Democratic and Republican state legislators, governors, senators, and congressmen). The "party-in-the-government" may be quite distinct from the "party-organization" and may espouse an ideology that is somewhat different from that held by the amorphous blocs that make up the "party-in-the-electorate." Such, as we shall see, is the case in Massachusetts.

Despite the feudal character of the Democratic "party-organization" and the ethnic diversity of the Democratic "party-in-the-electorate," the Democratic "party-in-the-government" is relatively solid, unified, and disciplined with respect to such issues as labor-management relations; health, welfare, and education; taxation; governmental operations; and the regulation of the economy. Democratic legislators tend to unite in support of the so-called liberal position; Republican legislators tend to unite in favor of the "conservative" position. The national party "philosophy" and the expressed wishes of national party leaders tend to be reference points for large numbers of state legislators. Massachusetts, in fact, ranks near the top of the American states with respect to the level of party cohesion in the state legislature. It is not unusual, for example, for the majorities of the two parties to take opposite sides on approximately 80 to 85 per cent of all roll-call votes in a given legislative session.

One state legislator summarized the conflict between the "parties-in-the-government" by remarking that "an issue supported by labor is a Democratic party issue, and an issue supported by management is a Republican party issue." A close relationship exists between the Massachusetts AFL-CIO and the Massachusetts Democratic party. In some districts, the local labor unions are the major source of funds for Democratic legislators and for aspirants seeking to unseat Republicans "unfriendly to labor." Only two or three Republicans are regarded as "friendly" by the AFL-CIO, which publishes an "Official Labor Record of the Massachusetts Legislature" for each session. Republicans consistently score "wrong" on labor-management bills from the viewpoint of labor. The major bills on which interparty divisions have occurred in recent years are those concerning increases in workmen's compensation, maximum unemployment-insurance benefits, provisions of the minimum-wage law, and state action in labor disputes; all these bills were supported by Democrats and opposed by Republicans. Business organizations, such as the Associated Industries of Massachusetts and the Greater Boston Chamber of Commerce, usually oppose increases in workers' compensation and unemployment insurance, and most Republican legislators agree with them.

As Democratic strength in the legislature has grown, however, labor has had more trouble with its ally. The unions have never lobbied successfully for a "cash sickness" bill (i.e., one that would provide a state insurance fund to cover unemployment due to illness). The insurance companies (perhaps the most powerful lobby in Massachusetts) have consistently opposed the bill. The united Republicans, combined with a significant number of Democratic "defectors," have managed to block the bill. The political alignments of the labor-industry battle remain, therefore, less than certain. In the 1960 session, for example, a bill requiring registration of imported strikebreakers was passed with strong Democratic support (a distinct victory for labor). Another AFL-CIO-sponsored bill (to provide unemployment compensation to strikers after six weeks) was defeated when half the Democratic legislators responded to industry's argument that employers would be financing strikes against themselves. Seventy-six Republicans voted against the bill and only three for it; 66 Democrats were against the proposal while 62 favored it.

In addition to supporting most pro-labor bills, the Democrats tend to unite in favor of welfare legislation, particularly increased old-age assistance, aid for retarded children, and the expansion of state facilities for the mentally disturbed. The Republicans split occasionally in their response to these measures, but their position over the years has been basically "conservative." The division between the two parties on problems of taxation is much less sharp than on labor-management or welfare problems. The GOP has consistently opposed tax increases, particularly taxes on income. The Republicans feel that the revenue from increased taxes on income or a sales tax (if passed) ought to be used to relieve property taxes rather than to expand "state bureaucracy." They also oppose the graduation of the income tax, while the Democrats and organized labor favor it. The position of the Democrats on other aspects of the tax problem is less unified. Traditionally, the party has opposed a sales tax; in 1957-60, it split down the middle on Governor Furcolo's proposed limited sales tax. On the key vote in 1957, a small majority of Democrats voted with the Governor; the margin of defeat was provided by the Republicans. This occurred despite the fact that most Republican businessmen and newspapers were strongly in favor of the bill.

Since the 1940's, the Democrats have strongly advocated extensions of civil rights, including fair-employment laws and laws forbidding discrimination in college admissions and in housing. A sizable minority of Republicans has usually voted with the Democrats. The Republicans, however, are more favorably disposed toward the extension and protection of civil liberties. With some help from a small band of vocal Democrats, the Republicans generally lead the fight for the enactment of most bills advocated by the Civil Liberties Union of Massachusetts, such as those providing for curbing of police wire-tapping and the protection of the individual from sweeping investigations by committees seeking out Communists. In recent years, some of the Democratic leaders have shown a growing concern for civil liberties.

Local issues, which often cut across party lines, cause more defections within the parties than any other area of legislation. For example, outstate Republicans vote as a body to retain curbs on Boston's city government, while the few Republicans from Boston vote for greater "home rule." The same alignment characterizes the Democratic vote on this issue. The high degree of "independent" voting on local issues reflects the fact that his constituency is often a more significant reference point for a state representative than is his party.

The cohesion of the parties in the state legislature is remarkable given the amorphous character of the Democratic "party-in-the-electorate," the atrophy of the Democratic organization, and the absence of a unified political philosophy among Democratic ethnic groups, on the one hand, and the Rockefeller-Nixon-Goldwater division that exists among Republican voters, on the other. Several factors, which are themselves interrelated, must be considered in attempting to account for the cohesiveness of the parties in the legislature. These include the closeness of party competition, the differences between typical Republican and Democratic constituencies, differences in the occupational backgrounds of Republican and Democratic legislators, and differences among the types of lobby allied with each party. In addition to these factors, the enormous power and prestige of the speaker of the Massachusetts House of Representatives and the president of the Massachusetts Senate must be taken into account.

For the 15 years preceding the 1958 state elections, the party division in the legislature was often highly competitive, as is shown in Tables 2 and 3.

TABLE 2. THE PARTY DIVISION OF THE MASSACHUSETTS HOUSE OF REPRESENTATIVES, 1943-62 (TOTAL SEATS: 240)

	Republicans	Democrats
1943-44	143	97
1945-46	138	102
1947-48	144	96
1949-50	118	122
1951-52	116	124
1953-54	124	116
1955-56	112	128
1957-58	108	132
1959-60	95	145
1961-62	85	155

TABLE 3. THE PARTY DIVISION OF THE MASSACHUSETTS SENATE, 1943-62 (TOTAL SEATS: 40)

	Republicans	Democrats
1943-44	26	14
1945-46	23	17
1947-48	24	16
1949-50	20	20
1951-52	22	18
1953-54	25	15
1955-56	21	19
1957-58	21	19
1959-60	16	24
1961-62	14	26

Close competition of parties induces legislators to stay with their party, for a relatively small number of "defections" in such a situation may seriously affect the strength of the party and hence an individual legislator's prospects for patronage and personal promotion. To desert one's party when the party balance is extremely close is to risk castigation as unreliable and denunciation as a traitor. Lockard has pointed out that the re-election of an individual legislator in a close district " . . . may be tied in closely with the chances of the gubernatorial candidate, who must in part run on his party's legislative record. To the extent that the record of the party is an issue in campaigns, the party must concentrate on making at least a reasonable record of legislative action." This fact often compels the legislator to support his party. But the impact of close party competition on party regularity is also shown by the fact that since 1958, when the Democrats took a commanding lead in the House of Representatives, the number of Democratic "defectors" has greatly increased.

The closeness of party competition, however, does not fully explain the case; the party division in the United States Congress is often close, but there is less cohesion among party members in Congress than in the Massachusetts state legislature. Perhaps the most important factor leading to party cohesion is the similarity among the several constituencies from which each party draws most of its support. "Like-minded legislators," Lockard suggests, "will come from similar districts and if the party's legislators are drawn from widely differing constituencies the degree of cohesion will accordingly be less." State legislators, like United States congressmen, must cater to local constituencies, regardless of the party position on an issue. If, then, most of the Democrats in the state legislature represent relatively similar constituencies, one would expect a high degree of cohesion in the Democratic party. And such is, in fact, the case—for both parties in Massachusetts. As we have said, the majority of the Democrats represent constituencies which are urban, Catholic, and lower-middle to middle class. The majority of the Republicans represent districts which are suburban or rural, Protestant, and middle to upper-middle class. A "typical" Republican constituency has a much greater proportion of owner-occupied dwelling units than does a "typical" Democratic constituency. MacRae has pointed out that "those representatives who come from districts that are most typical of their parties tend to show the highest 'party loyalty' on roll calls." He has also shown that

> The extent of party deviation in each party is greatest in districts that are atypical of one's own party, and are most like those of the opposing party. The Democrats from high owner-occupancy districts tend on the average to vote more like Republicans, and the Republicans from low owner-occupancy districts tend to vote more like Democrats.

Party cohesion may also result from the fact that Republican and Democratic representatives tend to be drawn from quite different occupations. V. O. Key, Jr., has shown, for example, that the "typical Republican" background is "business-managerial" whereas the "typical Democratic" background is "sales-clerical." The greater concern of the Republicans with ideological aims (conservatism) is explained by Lockard, who suggests that "a greater number of Republicans who go to the legislature have a very definite 'stake' in the community, which makes their conservatism a natural position." It is this "stake" in business and property of Republican legislators and many of their constituents that makes the Republican party the party of conservatism. The labor orientation of Democratic representatives and their constituents obviously adds motive power to the "liberalism" of the party. Except when the local needs of constituencies divide intraparty interests on specific issues, this general differentiation of the parties makes for cohesion within each party.

The separatism and cohesion of the parties in the state legislature may also be explained as both cause and consequence of the types of lobby that finance and pressure the parties. According to Lockard, the most significant groups supporting the Democratic party are labor and such reform organizations as Americans for Democratic Action (ADA). The most significant lobbies supporting the Republican party are "the public utility interests, the real estate lobby, the Associated Industries of Massachusetts (the local version of the NAM), the Chamber of Commerce, the insurance companies, and the Massachusetts Federation of Taxpayers' Associations. All these groups have easy access to the leaders of the Republican party." The lobbyists for these groups, however, work closely with the more conservative Democrats when it is advantageous for them to do so. This formidable alignment not only indicates that a conservative-liberal split does exist in the General Court but accounts, in part, for its continued existence.

The high degree of party discipline in the state legislature is also a consequence of the power and prestige of the speaker of the House and the president of the Senate. The speaker and the president have the power to designate the chairmen of all committees and to appoint all members, thus determining the party composition of every committee. They also have the power to depose any chairman or remove any committee member at any time without showing cause. All investigations undertaken by either body must be approved by its Committee on Rules. The speaker of the House and the president of the Senate serve as chairmen of their respective Committees on Rules. They also have the power to "seat" any member at any time with cause. It is obvious that their power is considerable. The speaker of the House and the president of the Senate can and do use their power to enforce party discipline and maintain control over the legislature.

Despite the existence of fairly distinctive orientations for the "parties-in-the-government," the major issue in recent elections so far as the voters are concerned has been the apparently massive and pervasive corruption in public life at all levels of Massachusetts government. For political commentators in this country and abroad, Boston and Massachusetts politics have become prime examples of the kinds of corruption and conflict of interest that too frequently degrade American local and state government. Any analysis of politics in the Bay State is naive, incomplete, and highly inaccurate if it does not include an examination of forms and causes of corruption in Massachusetts public life. . . .

Some idea of the nature and extent of corruption and conflicts of interest in Massachusetts public life was provided by William H. Wells, a reporter for the *Boston Globe,* in a series of 12 articles analyzing the problem in Massachusetts. In his final article, Wells summarized his findings:

> *The corrupt and questionable activities that permeate the common-wealth's political life are, like the iceberg, largely submerged and difficult to disclose.*
>
> *While the guilty escape punishment, the honest majority of legis-lators and government employees are tarnished by suspicion and rumor.*
>
> *Only fact-finders armed with the power of subpoena can hope to break the pattern that stretches from towns and cities through the executive departments into the Legislature and into the courts. Conflict-of-interest legislation that would provide such power to an enforcement team is now in the General Court under study.*
>
> *Meanwhile these things have happened:*

■ *Engineers and consultants have paid off legislators and highway officials to obtain contracts.*

■ *Governor's councilors have done business with the state and traded votes for promises of future jobs.*

■ *Government employees quit state service to work for firms with whom they did business on behalf of the state.*

■ *Probate judges awarded trustee positions to relatives and friends.*

■ *Lawyer-legislators voted on bills to raise the pay of judges before whom they practice.*

■ *Officials with regulatory powers received cash benefits from testi-monial dinners attended by those whose affairs they regulate.*

■ *Legislators and state employees received commissions for selling performance bonds on state contracts.*

■ *Lawyer-legislators practiced before state agencies.*

■ *Legislators who are insurance brokers sold insurance to the state.*

■ *Government employees and legislators profited through land-takings for state highways.*

■ *Town employees dominated representative town meetings and voted their own pay raises.*

■ *Community road superintendents rented equipment to the commu-nities they served.*

■ *Friends and relatives of politicians and the politicians themselves were on the payrolls of state agencies and public authorities.*

■ *They were also on the payrolls of firms doing business with these agencies and authorities.*

■ *An attorney general and assistant attorneys general represented clients in cases against the state.*

■ *City councilmen intervened to secure performance bonds and insurance from contractors dealing with their cities.*

■ *Assessors fixed valuations on properties of firms in which they had an interest or for which they worked — or as realtors owned property which they assessed.*

■ *Labor officials sat on boards negotiating with the unions for which they worked or which they represented.*

■ *Legislators fought for legislation benefiting their own businesses.*

■ *Attempts to uncover such activities encounter a maze of interlocking conflict situations.*

■ *A legislator does business with a state agency but the agency head is a party to the wrong-doing and conceals any record of the transaction.*

■ *A governor's councilor does business with an agency head who owes his appointment to the councilor's vote.*

■ *Private business officials, lawyers, judges, legislators, executive department heads will all be parties to the same act of wrong-doing and owe their income to each other's goodwill.*

According to Wells, conflicts of interest are common in local as well as state government.

Town and city governments are as infested with unethical activities as the state government — in some cases more so.

Real estate men double as assessors; contractors who are highway superintendents do public business with their own firms; town counsel represent private clients against their communities; city councilmen have interests in firms doing business with the city; individuals and families dominate communities by holding most of the public jobs. . . .

One way in which local police chiefs and captains help their "friends" is through the ticket fix — making certain these friends are not brought to court for minor law infractions.

The protection given illegal activities by some police officers has been demonstrated in revelations of establishments selling liquor after hours within sight of patrolmen — of state and Federal police forced to conduct vice raids that should have been conducted by local police.

Even school systems are not immune. The placing of contracts for school equipment, for school construction and for school bus service has been carried out in some communities with private profit motivating school officials and committeemen.

Policemen and firemen maintaining a construction business on the side and using their contacts made at work to obtain company contracts.

Town officials selling insurance to the community.

City councilmen and highway superintendents leasing trucks and other equipment to the community.

The varieties of civic corruption are known to every resident of a suburban or rural town or city. The hard-fisted rule of the urban boss has given way to the more sophisticated maneuvering of city employees who know the angles.

These examples of conflict of interest are relatively trivial compared to the wrong-doing in the Metropolitan District Commission, which is in charge of parks and parkways, water, and sewage-disposal in and around Boston. An inquiry by the State Senate has resulted in the conviction, on criminal charges, of the MDC Chairman, an associate MDC Commissioner, and a state representative. Anthony Lewis, of the *New York Times*, gave the following examples of the inquiry's findings:

> [*The MDC*] *paid a swimming coach $5,000 for a report on the "desirable characteristics of a pool" it was going to build. The Senate inquiry said the need for such advice was "obscure, because MDS has already built several pools."*
>
> *Another consultant on a different swimming pool was paid $17,000. All he did, according to the investigators, was to use specifications that had been given to him free by a pool manufacturer and, in suggesting a bathhouse design, to copy the plan of another commission bathhouse.*
>
> *The investigating committee found that the commission had ordered items from contractors that it did not need, apparently to make contracts more profitable. One contract required the contractor to supply a $1,000 calculating machine "for which there was no use at the site," according to the committee.*
>
> *A constant practice of the district commission was to break its projects into contracts of less than $1,000 each. The Senate committee suggested that the reason was that state law requires competitive bidding on all contracts of more than $1,000.*
>
> *Contractors, the investigating committee said, "billed the MDC without regard to the fair value of the work done or a fair profit to themselves. Each took as a yardstick the starting point of $1,000 [and] picked some figure as close to $1,000 as their courage permitted."*
>
> *The committee found that on some jobs the contractors had done no work, and on most jobs only part of the contracted project. In "an overwhelming majority" of instances, the committee said, the work done "was sloppy, shoddy, unworkmanlike and an outright public disgrace."*
>
> *The head of the agency, Commissioner John E. Maloney, was also the 40 per cent owner of an insurance agency that received many commissions on the agency's performance bonds.*
>
> *Charles J. McCarty, an associate commissioner, was the local distributor for one kind of highway guard rail. The MDC bought large quantities of this kind of rail, producing net profits of about 60 per cent for the distributing company on each sale.*

Activities of the Massachusetts Department of Public Works have also been investigated (1960) by a committee of the State Senate. A report of the investigating committee ("which was widely denounced as a whitewash") indicated that it was a common practice for the Department to split up contracts in pieces of less than $1,000 so that it could award them without competitive bidding. The report also noted that surveyors had received payment for working on the day of a blizzard. It criticized J. L. Hayden, a consulting engineer, because he was unable to show how he had arrived at the figure of $84,000, which he had charged the state for one job. Firms in which Hayden had an interest reached nearly $2,500,000 from the state in consulting fees over a three-year period. Prior to this investigation, the federal government had begun to investigate prices paid by the Department of Public Works for "rights of way" on highways that are partially financed by federal funds. In 1960, the Federal Bureau of Public Roads froze all federal monies assigned to Massachusetts for landtakings. A subcommittee of the United States House of Representatives has investigated landtakings in Massachusetts, and three individuals (including a prominent Democratic politician) have been convicted on charges of conspiring to defraud the federal government of more than $30,000.

Perhaps the shabbiest aspect of Massachusetts public life has to do with public servants who have served or are now serving time in federal or state penal institutions or who have been convicted of various crimes. During the early stages of his career, James M. Curley successfully campaigned from jail for re-election as a Boston alderman. In 1945 Curley ran for mayor of Boston while under indictment for mail fraud and won the largest plurality any candidate had received for that office. Curley was ultimately convicted and served time in a federal penitentiary. In 1956 Massachusetts had the unique distinction of becoming the first state in the union to elect to Congress an individual who had served a term in a federal penitentiary while in office. Thomas J. Lane, a Democrat from Lawrence, Massachusetts, was found guilty in 1956 of willfully evading payment of $38,543 in federal income taxes over a three-year period. He served four months in the Federal Correctional Institution in Danbury, Connecticut. Fifteen days after his release from prison Lane was returned to his old seat in the House of Representatives by a margin of 87,332 to 48,154 votes. He was re-elected in 1958 and 1960. Currently serving in the Massachusetts House of Representatives is Charles Iannello, a Democrat of Boston, who has been tried, convicted, and sentenced to one year in the house of correction on charges of larceny from the state in connection with work performed for the Metropolitan District Commission by a firm owned by Iannello and members of his family. Representative Iannello's case is now on appeal. He was re-elected in November 1960 (while under indictment) by a margin of more than two to one. Former United States Attorney Elliot

Richardson reports that "Boston radio and television station WBZ . . .
made random phone calls to residents of . . . Iannello's district in
Boston's South End after he had been sentenced to a year of jail. . . .
Of twenty voters called, eighteen said they would vote for Iannello
again." . . .

Personal Politics and the Structure of Massachusetts Government

We have suggested that politicians in Massachusetts play the political
game as it was played in the nineteenth century because the structure of
government in the Commonwealth has in many respects remained unchanged since that time. The abuses of the present have evolved from
and continue to deal with peculiarities of the past. Current party programs, party principles, and party discipline are matters of secondary
importance. Issues in the state legislature are very often resolved, not
in terms of party positions or on the merits of cases, but rather in terms
of a complex network of friendships, opportunities, enmities, courtesies,
slights, etc. One state representative, who has served four terms in the
Great and General Court, described the operation of the House of Representatives to the authors as follows:

> . . . *The legislature is a different world, and it is a club. It's an area,
> and the longer you're there the more you get used to being there and
> you become alienated in a sense from the outside world. You begin to
> talk a language of your own. You begin to discuss constituents in a
> more or less impersonal manner. The talk is in a large measure about
> "how many summer jobs did you get?" You're there a long time and you
> begin to observe the personalities of the other people that are there and
> it's almost like being in the army. You live with your buddies here and
> this becomes your world and there's a certain feeling and obligation
> that we're all there to help each other and protect each other. I suppose
> much like the medical societies exist to take care of their own first, and
> there's this feeling which we have among ourselves, that we work very
> hard, and that we're entitled to some satisfaction for what we do
> and . . . we don't feel any qualms about a legislator being given a
> job and that sort of thing. But the world outside is not something that
> we're really alerted to. . . . Very often I think we're way behind the
> feelings of our constituents—you know the old saying that politicians
> are fifty years behind their times—I think there's something to that be-
> cause we feel we got in by a certain method and we've taken our course
> and we might as well stick on that course and why look for change and
> why fight for change. . . .
> I think there are a certain amount of pressures [upon legislators].
> Well, of course, if there are no skeletons in the closet I don't suppose
> there can be much in the way of pressure, but there's some other infor-*

mal pressures. Many times somebody will say, "Well, why get involved in that — why look into that — you know you're not going to make yourself very popular around here by doing it," and very often people succumb to that kind of talk. You want to be a good fellow and you want the others to say hello and joke and sit . . . next to you and have a feeling of comradeship — . . . you want to be part of the gang, you want to participate and contribute to the esprit de corps. *You can't do that if you're going to strike out on your own and yell for things which . . . in the minds of many legislators — not only legislators but politicians, in the minds of political people who have influence over legislators — may be a very unpopular thing to do. So the pressure is really one of being accused of being a nonconformist within the legislature. I suppose the legislator is in many instances a greater example of conformity than in any other body. You talk about the conformity on the outside but you have it in the legislature.*

He went on to describe the policy of *quid pro quo* that characterizes the relationships of legislators:

. . . The fact . . . that the whole legislature is run on a personal basis leaves a lot of room for back-scratching and for "put this man on and I'll see that this man gets in that department," or "I know so-and-so up in this department that's looking for a job and maybe we can work him into another job but at the same time, if I do that for you or for your cousin up there, why don't you do something for my friend down here?" I think there's a good deal of that. I think really this is one of the problems that the legislature faces and which prevents the legislature from doing the best possible job it could do in the way of legislation. If we had a strong party government outside the legislature, this wouldn't have to happen. . . .

The system of personal exchanges of favors results in weakening of the parties, which in turn makes it difficult for the voter to fix responsibility for party action or to perceive the real reason a particular representative voted with or against his party. Fragmentation of the parties tends to make legislators easy prey for powerful groups in search of political favors. The result in many instances is a government of men, not of laws. But the exchange of personal favors does not necessarily result in corruption and conflict of interest. Bartering of favors on a personal basis characterizes the actions of many representatives in many state legislatures in this country; indeed, it appears to be part of the democratic process. In Massachusetts, however, the evidence indicates that the exchange of personal favors between influential individuals has all but replaced government by parties. Consequently, party responsibility has decreased and corruption increased.

Disciplined, responsible government is possible only if public officials have the political power necessary to execute their duties. Political power in Massachusetts, however, is fragmented — indeed, it is atomized. The governor is hamstrung by a plethora of archaic checks and balances which often prevent him from controlling key officials in his own branch of government. Indeed, he must often work with department heads who, appointed by a previous governor, may be members of the opposition party. The governor's council, established in the eighteenth century to check and advise the governor, is a vestigial organ which performs no useful service to the community. The bureaucracy, an anarchic collection of 177 separate units, is a model of administrative chaos. Many boards, commissions, and public authorities, which are beyond the effective control of the governor or the legislature, operate as independent (and thus irresponsible) centers of power. This fragmentation of political power makes for irresponsible parties and personal politics — an atmosphere conducive to *quid pro quo* and corruption.

ST. LOUIS POLITICS: RELATIONSHIPS AMONG INTERESTS, PARTIES, AND GOVERNMENTAL STRUCTURE*

ROBERT H. SALISBURY

Robert H. Salisbury is associate professor of political science, Washington University. He is a contributor to *Functions and Policies of American Government* (1967).

Political scientists have been troubled in recent years by just what it is they mean when they talk about a political party. Whether the discussion concentrates on the American scene or includes comparative data from other countries, the ambiguity of party as an analytical tool remains. Particularly difficult and very largely untouched by specific empirical analysis are the relationships which connect core party organizations, the social and economic interest group configuration, and the formal governmental structure of a community. Whereas some political scientists have assumed the crucial importance of the formal structure in shaping the political life of the community, others have tended to regard structure as largely irrelevant and to argue instead that the only

From "St. Louis Politics: Relationships Among Interests, Parties, and Governmental Structure" by Robert Salisbury, *Western Political Quarterly*, XIII:2 (June 1960), 498-507. Reprinted by permission of the University of Utah, copyright owners.
*Material for this paper has been drawn from a larger study of St. Louis politics in which the writer is engaged in association with G. Robert Blackburn.

significant variables were embraced in interest group activity. This paper will offer a synopsis of the situation in one city, St. Louis, Missouri, in an effort to suggest the ways in which the three factors mentioned are interrelated.

The burden of the argument here is that a somewhat peculiar bifurcated structure of local government plays a crucial role in shaping the nature and scope of political conflict in the city. Two broad interest groupings in St. Louis, each composed of rather loosely allied groups and each pursuing different sets of goals in the political arena, are enabled to live under the same party label by the fact that each grouping can control one segment of the governmental structure and from that control secure the portion of its goals most vital to it. Neither group gains complete satisfaction thereby, but the consequence is that the two groups are not forced into the full range of sharp competition that a more centralized and monolithic structure might require.

The Interests

The constellation of social and economic interests which make up the body politic of St. Louis is like in some ways and in some ways unlike that of other major American cities. In common with other metropolitan centers, the St. Louis area has experienced rapid growth in the post-World War II period, but unlike most other cities, this growth has taken place almost entirely outside the city limits, which were fixed by constitutional provision in 1876. The growth of the St. Louis area, further, has not kept pace with many other parts of the country, particularly because the hinterland of the city has not grown much. Consequently, St. Louis business leaders have been concerned to bring new industry to the city, and this effort has spurred the desire, shared by other metropolises, to solve traffic and transit problems, to renovate and rehabilitate slum areas, and to revive the downtown business district.

In common with many cities, St. Louis has experienced a great influx of Negroes and "mountain whites" in recent years with a resulting increased demand for various types of municipal services. As elsewhere, these "new immigrants" play the same role in relation to ward organizations of the party that nationality groups did in past decades. The tight and inflexible boundaries of the city have, at the same time, meant that St. Louis has lost upper income population to the suburbs. The combination of an increasingly lower income population and the desire to attract new industry and therefore to keep tax rates at reasonable levels has left the city in almost perpetual financial embarrassment in the postwar period, an embarrassment alleviated only by the imposition of an earnings tax of 1 per cent on all income.

If one looks at the major economic interests in the city, one can begin with familiar categories, labor and business, and discover some degree of conflict between these two groups. Yet no analysis can explain St. Louis politics satisfactorily by relying solely upon labor-management conflict. Labor, for example, is not monolithic. The largest unions are the Teamsters, the Building Trades, the Machinists, and the Auto Workers, while a number of smaller unions also play some role. These unions differ considerably in their local political significance. The Teamsters are the most active locally and the most controversial. They have a fairly fully articulated set of goals for St. Louis which includes general expansion of services for low income groups and which emphasizes heavily the betterment of race relations and equality for Negroes. The militance of the Teamsters, with its ideological flavor, is in contrast to the unphilosophical bread-and-butter concerns of the Building Trades which seek jobs and contracts and find that extensive political alliances are of great assistance in securing these goals. They are not really interested in most of the program of the Teamsters, and the Teamster leaders sometimes express contempt for the unconcern with policy exhibited by the "pork chop" unions. Nevertheless, each group finds that under present conditions their channels of action often bring them into working agreements with each other on political questions. The UAW and the Steelworkers differ from each of the two types of labor groups mentioned above, since they are largely unconcerned with local politics. Their union interests are not much affected by decisions in the local arena, and though their leaders sometimes go through political motions, neither these unions nor the management of the plants where they work are normally active on the St. Louis political scene.

The business community is likewise divided along a number of lines. Dominating the public view are the industrial, banking, and commercial leaders of locally controlled large businesses, the "downtown" business community. These are the men who need more industrial development in the city, these are the men who have significant stakes in the rehabilitation of the slums and the consequent revival of the core city, and these are the men who also form the social elite of the city. The interests of this configuration are articulated by the metropolitan daily press, and they are identified with "Progress" and "Good Government," while they are against the "Politicians." The bulk of the middle and upper-middle income residents of the city and the professional, religious, and educational leadership tend strongly to identify their interests with those of this business elite.

The small business community, on the other hand, does not. Composed of small downtown enterprises like parking lot operators and of neighborhood commercial establishments, this group is concerned with specific, individual treatment at the hands of governmental authority. Specific tax measures, provision of stop signs, regulation of on- and off-street parking, zoning, and the like are their primary goals, and they very often line up with organized labor groups in political alliance against the "downtown" interests.

The social composition of the city is noteworthy in two main respects, the impact of the Negro influx and the ethnic make-up of the city. More than one-fourth of the city's population today is Negro, and Negroes are achieving increasing political power. Six wards of the city's twenty-eight are represented by Negroes, and significant influence is exerted in at least three others. Desegregation of swimming pools, schools, and, to some extent, of places of public accommodation has followed the rise of Negroes to influence. Until the New Deal and again during most of the 1940's the Negro community was predominantly Republican, but since 1949 Negro wards have produced overwhelming margins for any candidate bearing the Democratic label.

Nationality groups have not played as important a role in St. Louis politics as in many cities. St. Louis experienced a large German immigration and a significant Irish immigration during the mid-nineteenth century. For decades these two groups formed the backbone of the Republican and Democratic parties respectively. But the "late immigrants" from Eastern and Southern Europe largely by-passed St. Louis in favor of the heavy industrial centers. Thus the European "ethnics" in the city have had nearly a century to become assimilated, and today, except for one Italian ward, it is difficult to find many traces of genuine nationality identification. The heavily Catholic religious heritage of St. Louis remains, but national origin seems to have little meaning in St. Louis politics.

St. Louis thus displays two broad configurations of interests. On one side are the locally oriented labor unions, Negroes, neighborhood businessmen, and lower income people generally. This grouping focuses its attention primarily on the specific bread-and-butter issues of jobs, stop signs, spot zoning, and the like, and exhibits a sharp antipathy toward any suggestion of increased tax rates. Downtown business interests and the middle and upper-middle income residents, on the other hand, are primarily interested in broader policy questions — economic growth, urban renewal — and their approach to problems of fiscal solvency is more sympathetic to the needs for more tax revenue.

The Structure of Government

The structure of St. Louis government is *sui generis* in many respects. The city is governed under a charter adopted by the voters in 1914. Some important aspects of the city's business, however, are not under home rule control. The police department, for example, is controlled by a Board of Police Commissioners appointed by the governor, and a

Board of Election Commissioners is similarly appointed. Originally, the device was adopted to enable a pro-Southern state administration to have police control in a Unionist city. Later it allowed a Democratic state administration to have patronage to dispense in a normally Republican city. The contemporary significance of this arrangement is quite different as will be noted later. In the city a moderately strong mayor administers nearly ten thousand employees of whom he can appoint some seventeen without regard to civil service requirements. An elected comptroller acts jointly with the mayor and the president of the Board of Aldermen, elected at large, to form the Board of Estimate and Apportionment which prepares the city budget, a budget which the Board of Aldermen may cut but not increase. The budget includes in its provisions many of the most vital policy decisions affecting the city, and the mayor is certainly the key figure in its preparation. The Board of Aldermen is composed of the president and twenty-eight representatives elected one each from the twenty-eight wards. The mayor and the members of the Board of Aldermen each serve four-year terms. The aldermen, of course, must pass all ordinances for the city, but even though a majority of the Board often opposes the mayor on policy issues, the latter clearly dominates the policy-making process.

Almost entirely separate from this portion of the city government are the so-called "county offices." St. Louis, like Baltimore, is not a part of any county. Nevertheless, under state law, the functions ordinarily performed by county officials must be performed in St. Louis by officials like sheriff, collector of revenue, license collector, recorder of deeds, magistrates, and others who are elected by the voters and are completely outside the control of the city administration or the city charter. These officials make few policy decisions of any importance, but taken together they provide nearly one thousand non-civil service jobs, and, as one of the few remaining sources of patronage in the city, they are prizes of great importance to those who are interested in patronage.

The Board of Education should also be mentioned here. It, too, is outside the budgetary control of the city. The Board is elected separately and its tax rate is determined through separate referendum elections. It, too, controls a substantial pool of patronage jobs in its building and maintenance departments, and patronage rather than educational policy is the major issue in Board of Education elections.

Thus the structure of St. Louis government contains two largely separate sets of offices. One is centered in the mayor's office and is the natural focus of attention for those interested in broad problems of municipal policy. The other is based upon the county offices, Board of Education, and Board of Aldermen and consists essentially of a patronage pool and a means for securing individual favor with very little responsibility for policy.

The Party Situation

St. Louis has undergone two rather remarkable political metamorphoses during the past three decades. The first it shared with many other metropolitan centers, the change from consistent Republicanism to overwhelming Democracy as the New Deal coalition produced sizable pluralities on the local level. The shift to the Democrats embraced practically all elements of the community, but perhaps the most notable changes took place among the Negroes, and among many of the German areas of the city. Silk stocking and delivery wards alike went Democratic during the thirties. But although the state and national Democratic tickets continued to carry the city comfortably, during the next decade, from 1941 to 1949, the Republicans returned to power on the local scene. We need not examine the reasons for this switch except to note that it took in much of the city, especially the Negroes, and it was backed by much of downtown business and the metropolitan press. This Republican swing carried the party into the mayor's office (by a two-to-one majority in 1945), swept the Board of Aldermen nearly clean of Democrats, and helped elect Republicans to Congress, although the Democrats hung on to some local offices and Roosevelt won handily.

The period of Republican control ended in 1949, however, and since that time the Democratic sweep of all offices at all levels, save only a maximum of four aldermanic seats, has been complete. This time the Negro wards shifted overwhelmingly to the Democrats and have shown no sign of defecting despite that tendency in some other cities. The upper income areas — smaller now than formerly — have shown remarkable Democratic strength, largely undisturbed by the Eisenhower era. The lower income sections of the city, which include the Negro areas, are staunchly Democratic, to the extent that the Republicans are badly demoralized and have difficulty in finding either candidates or money to make a serious race for any political office in the community.

Yet this cyclical variation in the fortunes of the two parties does not conform to the configuration of interests in the community. As outlined above, the city is broadly divided along some sort of quasi-class basis into two groupings; labor, low income, small, neighborhood business, and at least recently Negroes, against large downtown business, the forces of "Progress," with the daily papers as spokesmen and the so-called "newspaper wards" as sources of voting strength. This general division of the community interests has not changed greatly during the past decade except perhaps as the proportion of Negroes has increased while the old German Republicans have lost their ethnic identity. But these changes surely do not account for (a) the massive shifts in the strength of each party over a relatively short period of time, or (b) the absence of fairly sharp and relatively even competition between the two parties for local office. For this latter fact is perhaps most prominent; namely, that when one party has been dominant, the other party is moribund. This is especially true of the Republicans since 1949. With a constellation of interests that normally might be expected to support Republican candidates, the latter lose by margins exceeding three-to-one.

Interest, Party, and Structure in St. Louis

We cannot here go into all the reasons for the variation in party fortunes and the recent lack of Republican success. But we do want to examine the forms of institutionalization of this division of interests in the community. If it has not taken the form of inter-party conflict, how has it been expressed? The answer is that two fairly distinct groupings have appeared *within* whichever party was dominant in a particular period, one representing the larger business groups, the newspaper ward areas, and the forces of "Progress" generally, while the other is characterized by the "Politicians" who are spokesmen for a medley of lower income, labor, small business, and minority groups. Such a division was notable within the Republican ranks during the late 1940's. Such a division is quite obvious within the Democratic ranks today. *This division is not only one of conflict over economic and social interests in the community, it is also manifested in the formal structure of government.*

In both the Republican and the Democratic parties the intra-party division has followed essentially the same lines. On the one side, the downtown business groups and the other interests associated with them have found their representation in the office of mayor primarily, usually with co-operation from the comptroller and the president of the Board of Aldermen. All these officials are elected on a city-wide basis with substantial newspaper attention to their campaigns which tend to cost considerable sums of money for publicity. These three, forming the Board of Estimate and Apportionment, make the key fiscal decisions of the city, and, however hard they try, the Board of Aldermen can alter these decisions only at the margins. Moreover, the mayor, as mentioned before, is by all odds the most significant policy-making official in the city. It is policy, of course, with which the large business constellation is concerned—broad civic policy affecting the location of industry, general tax rates, availability of full city services, the social climate of the community necessary to attract technical personnel for their businesses, and the social climate of the community necessary to preserve the status of an old-line, social elite whose autonomy of local operation is being eroded by the nationalization of business and labor alike. It is this group which wants civic reform and civil service, which sponsors the many Citizens Committees to study local problems, and so on. The group is not reactionary or even particularly conservative in the usual meanings of those terms. Some of its leaders are liberal Democrats on the national scene, and many are outspoken defenders of equality for Negroes on all levels. Its co-operation with organized labor is never more than luke-warm, but again, on the national scene, the Teamsters and the Building Trades, the dominant labor groups locally, are not noted for their liberalism.

The other side is likewise focused on a set of public officials, the holders of the "county offices," supplemented by the dominant group on the Board of Aldermen. The county offices are filled in city-wide elections too, thus giving them the same formal constituency as the mayor and his associates. But these elections are not attended by wide publicity, they are held in conjunction with November general elections instead of the municipal elections in the spring, and the chief requisite of victory is a dependable vote delivered by an effective ward organization. The newspapers take little part in these elections and correspondingly have little influence on them. Instead they are dominated by the so-called "delivery wards" of the city, generally, the lower income and Negro wards. Again this was true when the Republicans controlled these offices as well as now when the Democrats are supreme.

The complex of interests which supports these political leaders also finds it important to have influence with the aldermen. In the wards inhabited by lower income residents aldermen are selected in the same way as the county office-holders; nomination dependent largely upon the support of the ward committeemen and election dependent upon an effective ward organization. Many county office-holders are also ward committeemen and the alliance between these elements of the core party organization is firm. By and large, this element of the party is not particularly concerned with broad social or economic policy as such. It is concerned rather with the immediate needs of effective ward organization, and these needs are not notably different today than they traditionally have been. Patronage remains the lifeblood of the organization and, of course, the county offices are sources of significant patronage in the city. Consequently, control of these offices is vital to the organization. For the same reason, control of the Board of Education is important. More than that, however, the county office element of the party is concerned with the needs of its electoral supporters as the latter interpret these needs. This means broadly *individual favor*. Jobs are crucial, but so also are specific contracts for building contractors, stop signs and parking regulations, assistance in getting into a public housing project, route location for a throughway, and so on. Assistance for individuals in need, the classic basis of urban political organization, remains the basis for this wing of the party, and such assistance is necessarily funneled through the particular set of offices which this wing seeks to control; jobs through the county offices and Board of Education, and individual attention from the Board of Aldermen achieved through a log-rolling system known locally as aldermanic courtesy. These are the concerns of

Negroes, low income groups, the politically active elements of the local labor movement, and of many kinds of small businesses. Thus there is not much question of which element in the party these groups will support in a situation of conflict between the two party groups.

One interesting thing about this division, both of interests in the city and of offices, is that conflict between the two groupings is minimized. The group focused on the mayor is not interested in patronage, although from time to time its conception of good government requires that it advocate the further extension of civil service. By the same token, the county office group and many of its electoral supporters are profoundly indifferent to most matters of public policy. Aldermanic courtesy does create conflict, since the granting of individual favors—e.g., a stop sign in front of a confectionery—often runs counter to broader policy concerns—e.g., a master traffic plan. Nevertheless, there are many areas of policy and of patronage where each element of the party is content to let the other element control. Each group needs the other. The county office people need the financial support for their precinct workers which the mayor-led group contributes to the party. The mayoral group needs the support of the delivery wards to get many of its policy goals put into effect. This mutual need is sufficient at least to permit the two groups to share the same party label, and perhaps to require it.

But there is always latent and sometimes manifest conflict between the two groups. Issues like the distribution of the tax load, recognition of labor organizations among municipal employees, and particularly charter reform, which might threaten the existence of the patronage offices, all activate not only the office-holders within the party but, more importantly, bring into operation most of the interest groups in the community which ally with one or the other faction. On such questions the mayoral group is sharply opposed by the majority of the aldermen as well as by the dominant elements in the city committee of the party, the ward committeemen-county office forces. The tendency toward conflict is reinforced by the fact that each group tends to view the other as an unholy conspiracy aimed at destroying its opponents. As it happens in St. Louis this conflict often takes the geographical form of what is nearly a north-south split with the south side and west end supporting the mayoral faction while the north side is the heart of the county office group strength.

A word should be said about the rather special effect that the structure of the police department, headed by a Board appointed by the governor, has on the political scene. Two consequences are apparent. In the first place, influence with the police department follows from influence with the governor, and consequently, successful gubernatorial candidates are much sought after figures in St. Louis politics. Secondly, although the police department is run on the merit system, there is a substantial amount of patronage available in the form of assignments and promotions. This patronage is, of course, of more interest to the county office group than to the mayoral group and the former seeks it more assiduously. In this quest the county office group joins forces with the representatives from St. Louis to the state legislature in an alliance that is facilitated by the dependence of the state legislators upon ward committeeman endorsement in order to win office. The close liaison between the state delegation and the county office forces means that the county offices themselves, established by state statute, are safe, and that the desires of the city administration for new state legislation will often get a cool reception from a state delegation allied with the opposing faction of the party. When the St. Louis delegation to the legislature is not united in behalf of the city's demands, they have little chance of passage, and policy requests from the St. Louis administration are blocked most often not by rural opposition, as so often is alleged, but by the county office faction of the St. Louis party.

Perhaps there is no way to prove categorically that the formal structure of government is the crucial variable in determining the particular form which the interest conflict in St. Louis politics has taken. Certainly the total political process in the city is complex. Yet it can scarcely be doubted that if the county offices did not exist and their meager functions were performed by regular administrative agencies of the city, the contending interest groupings in the city would have to find other channels for the satisfaction of their needs. Without the county offices there would be no patronage and hence ward organizations would be weakened. In that event, those interest groups, notably labor, which now work through the ward organizations, would be forced to play an even more direct role in the political process than they do now. Without the county offices there would be only one really important office through which to exert political power, for whatever purposes, and that would be the office of mayor. The aldermen, without effective ward organizations, would need to turn more directly to the interest groups of their wards, and again the conflict between the two broad interest configurations of the city would become more open. If the office of mayor became the chief and virtually the only prize for the contending groups, then it would seem that at least two consequences would follow, given the interest group line-up as it now exists in St. Louis. First, the two groupings which now form factions within the party would divide into two separate parties. This process might be slow. It might be effected through the use of "Blue Ribbon" slates running against "politician" slates, or it might in time result in the revival of the Republican party. In any case, the conflict would be more open than it is now. Secondly, it would be more continuous and involve a broader range of issues. Whereas now there is a substantial area of autonomous operation left to each faction, if the mayor's office were the only prize, then victory and the battle to achieve victory would cover all the issues in which the two sets of interests are even potentially in conflict. Either one side would win or it would lose, and there would be none of the present partial victories for both sides, which, however frustrating they are sometimes, at least give some satisfactions and some basis for compromise and mediation to each group.

If the present alignment of interests were altered in any significant way, a development which the militant and volatile character of the Teamsters and the increasing numbers and self-consciousness of Negroes make possible, the significance either of the present structure or of any alternative arrangements would be altered too. Under the present conditions, however, this analysis seems to be valid and, indeed, is confirmed by each major political event in the city. Any discussion of the effects of a really different structure, of course, must be speculative, since the proposal to change the structure so as to abolish the county offices will be met with sharp resistance by those groups which utilize the offices to advantage.

If the data reviewed here permit one to offer a tentative statement about the relationships between interests, party, and structure, it would appear that the interest group system is, as the Bentleyans argue it must be, basic. At the same time, however, the governmental structure affects in crucial ways the manner in which these interests will be articulated into political parties, and in so doing it plays an important role in determining the scope and intensity of political conflict in the community. It seems doubtful whether one could say that a particular structural form would in every case bring about a particular party system or give a particular shape to the conflict, since the structure and the interest configuration interact in each case. If the interest groups of St. Louis were more amorphous and diffuse and not joined in any bimodal pattern, even the most centralized structure of strong mayor control could not be expected to produce sharply competing parties. On the other hand, the present, somewhat diffuse structure would not appreciably moderate the conflict if St. Louis were divided into rigid class groupings of a quasi-feudal nature. Perhaps the study of the relationships of interests, parties, and structure in other cities will permit comparative analysis of a manageable range of data, and in turn lead us to more confident generalizations about the problem.

ISSUES AND PRESSURE GROUPS
IN THE STATE OF WASHINGTON

Daniel M. Ogden, Jr., and Hugh A. Bone

Daniel M. Ogden, Jr., is a member of the Technical Review Staff, U.S. Department of the Interior. He is co-author of *Electing the President* (1964).
Hugh A. Bone is professor of political science, University of Washington. He
is the author of *American Politics and the Party System* (1965).

A formal reception by Governor Albert D. Rosellini in honor of the lobbyists at the 1959 session of the Washington state legislature recognized
officially, for the first time, the important role pressure groups play in
the formation of public policy in the state of Washington. Their role is
not confined to shaping legislation. Public opinion, the activities of the
parties, and the work of all branches of government are of concern to
the various interest groups.

Pressure groups do not directly seek political power as political
parties do. They run no candidates for office, although some endorse
or support candidates sponsored by the political parties. They offer no
platforms for public acceptance or rejection, although all take stands on
public issues which they urge upon officeholders and the public. They
do not accept responsibility for the conduct of government. Pressure
groups also differ from political parties in that the state does not attempt
to regulate their internal affairs. Pressure groups generally are more
homogeneous than political parties and possess some common need or
goal which sets them apart from the rest of society. Many pressure
groups are highly centralized and assign potent internal disciplinary
powers to their state or regional headquarters.

Washington has hundreds of pressure groups. No one knows how
many. Virtually any association which an individual joins can use its
organization to try to affect the formation or execution of public policy
at some level of government.

Like most states, Washington has at least three principal types of
pressure groups which are organized in every conceivable field of interest. Some groups may be called "service" groups, for they unite people
who share a common occupation, religious belief, or experience primarily to serve the economic, religious, or social interests of their members. For them, pressure politics are incidental, and political action
outside their immediate field or interest may create internal cohesion
problems. Business enterprises, labor unions, and farm associations are
service groups. A second type are the "political-action" groups, which

From Daniel M. Ogden, Jr., and Hugh A. Bone, *Washington Politics* (New York: New York University
Press, 1960), pp. 54-63. © 1960 by the Citizenship Clearing House, Reprinted by permission of the
publisher. [Footnotes omitted. Originally titled "Issues and Pressure Groups."]

similarly unite people who share a common attribute, occupation, or belief, but are organized primarily to influence the course of government.
Smaller and less well financed than service groups, they also display
greater political cohesion. Trade associations and the political-action
arms of unions and churches fall in this category. The third and least
stable of the types of groups are the "goal" groups, which unite people
of all walks of life who wish to achieve a special objective from government. Goal groups regularly appear to promote initiatives and referendums and many goal groups have been used in the field of resource
development and conservation.

Key Groups in Washington

Business Groups

Business groups long have been active in Washington politics. The
chambers of commerce and the Association of Washington Industries,
as federations of businesses, serve as general spokesmen, but there is
much activity by individual enterprises and by trade associations. In
1956 and 1958, for example, the larger businesses of the state promoted
"right-to-work" initiatives through a Citizens' Committee for Voluntary
Unionism. A leading figure in the drive was the president of the Boeing
Airplane Company.

Many individual companies have influence in their own right. The
large lumber companies are active both directly and through the West
Coast Lumbermen's Association in shaping state timber policies, preparing municipal building codes, and watching over the regulation of
freight rates by the Public Service Commission. Four major railroads
operate in the state: the Northern Pacific, Great Northern, Milwaukee,
and Union Pacific. All have participated actively in trade-promotion
work, have opposed the use of public funds to build airports and to
extend navigation on the Columbia River, and have backed various
schemes to keep property taxes low. Even the banks send lobbyists to
Olympia.

The Washington State Research Council and special-industry trade
associations also are active on behalf of business goals. Contractors, producers of highway equipment and construction materials, and local
chambers of commerce have developed "good roads" associations, and
even groups to promote improvement of particular highways, such as
the Highway 97 Association, or special objectives, such as the Cross-
Sound Bridge, the Washington pass highway, the Naches Tunnel, or
the North Lake Washington Bridge.

Most observers agree, however, that the power exercised by business is essentially negative. For example, business opposition to a graduated net-income tax has kept the state's tax structure regressive.

In 1933 the state Supreme Court ruled a graduated net income tax unconstitutional, and the people subsequently were induced to vote down constitutional authority for it. Business also defends the constitutional restriction which limits property taxation to 40 mills on half of the "true and fair value." Property taxes may be raised beyond this point in any jurisdiction only by a three-fifths majority vote, which must constitute 40 per cent of the total number of votes cast at the last general election. Apathy and business opposition often have defeated special local and school-district elections to raise the property tax rate temporarily. The absence of an income tax and the rather low taxes on property thus have made the 4 per-cent sales tax the basic source of state revenue and have led the legislature to seek added funds through increases in sales-tax rates and the imposition of "nuisance taxes" and a "business and occupation" tax based on gross business volume. Important segments of business and industry also ordinarily have been able to veto legislation or administrative interpretations which would be directly detrimental to their interests.

Positive legislation which business has promoted has been much more difficult to obtain. The liquor forces provide an excellent example. The state has a monopoly of the retail sale of packaged hard liquor. After winning an initiative fight in 1948, which permitted the granting of licenses to restaurants to sell hard liquor by the drink, the distilling and brewing forces tried repeatedly and unsuccessfully to ease the restrictions on the hours of sale and on the facilities which bars and taverns must provide for women.

The heaviest, most vociferous, and most continuous pressure activity by business enterprises, however, comes from the electric-power companies. A bitter struggle between advocates of public and private ownership of electric-distribution facilities has swirled in the state since the turn of the century. The interest of the electric companies in minimizing regulation by the Public Service Commission is but a minor phase of the continuing pressure campaign. Literally millions of dollars have been spent by the Washington Water Power Company, the Pacific Power and Light Company, and the Puget Sound Power and Light Company in propaganda campaigns against public power. Public-power supporters led by the Northwest Public Power Association, the Washington Public Utility Districts Association, the Seattle and Tacoma Departments of Lighting, and individual public-utility districts, have replied in kind.

The power and conservation conflicts have produced an enormous number of goal groups to promote or oppose particular projects. During the 1920's, the Columbia Basin Irrigation League, an adjunct of the Spokane Chamber of Commerce, promoted the ill-fated "gravity plan" to prevent construction of Grand Coulee Dam, which was being urged by the Columbia River Development League of Wenatchee. The Inland Empire Waterways Association was formed in the 1930's by combining a number of local navigation and development associations, such as the Umatilla Rapids Association, along the middle Columbia. The Washington State Reclamation Association, an outgrowth of the old Columbia Basin Irrigation League, and still dominated by the power companies and railroads, operates in the interests of its sponsors on conservation matters. Important support is given from the state to regional goal groups, such as the River Resource Association of the Pacific Northwest, which is backed by public power forces, and the Pacific Northwest Development Association, which fronts for private power companies.

Controversy in the electric-power field has centered both around local public ownership of distribution facilities and the role and policies of the federal government in power development. The need for multiple-purpose dams to assure comprehensive utilization of the resources of the Columbia River early led to demands that the federal government build navigation and power dams in the lower river, reclamation and power dams on the upper river, and storage dams for flood control and power on the key tributaries. A series of comprehensive studies by the Corps of Engineers and Bureau of Reclamation led to the construction of such a system. The federal government markets its own power through a unified wholesale agency, the Bonneville Power Administration, which operates its own backbone grid transmission system and sells power, with preference to public and co-operatively owned distributors at a uniform low rate to encourage widespread use. Private power companies have fought construction of federal dams, construction of federal transmission lines, the uniform low rate, and the public preference clause.

Farm Groups

The Washington State Grange has been a prime mover in the fight for local public distribution of electric power. The early Grange struggle for the farmer against the shipping interests on the Columbia, the railroads, the power companies, and the stockyards has stayed alive and vigorous. Beginning in the 1920's, the Grange promoted a law to permit county-wide public-utility districts to serve rural as well as urban dwellers with electric power and domestic water. An initiative to the legislature in 1929 was rejected, but the people approved it at the 1930 election. The Grange then joined hands with the groups promoting Grand Coulee Dam to get that tremendous power project built by the federal government. It since has been a vigorous exponent of comprehensive federal development of the Columbia River. Most Washingtonians are now served by public power distribution.

Other Grange achievements are the blanket primary and an initiative outlawing daylight saving time. In recent years, Grange leaders have been staunch defenders of parity and highly critical of the farm program advocated by Secretary of Agriculture Benson. Grange goals often have been closely linked with those of organized labor, and the two frequently co-operate in the promotion or prevention of legislation of interest to either group. Increasingly, local Granges, particularly on the west side, have become social clubs for part-time farmers who really earn their living in the cities or in the woods. This had led to overlapping Grange-union membership, which has helped confirm the liberal bias of the state's major farm group. The Grange remains officially nonpartisan.

Its militant attitude against monopoly and in support of the small farmer and workingman has made the Washington State Grange atypical in its own national organization. Its stand has virtually eliminated the nationally more liberal Farmers' Union as an important farm force in the state. Efforts by conservatives to create a state Farm Bureau Federation also have met with but modest success, for the large farmers have been more interested in promoting commodity groups such as the Wheat Growers Association and the Apple Growers Association to represent their specialized interests.

Organized Labor

A larger percentage of nonagricultural workers are members of labor unions in the state of Washington than in any other state in the Union. In 1955, 53.3 per cent carried union cards, compared to a national average of 32.6 per cent. Even Michigan had put 43 per cent and California only 35.7. Organized labor long has been well established in Washington and powerful in the state's politics. It has succeeded in obtaining favorable workmen's compensation and welfare laws and has been able to prevent punitive legislation against labor, particularly "right-to-work" laws. The union of the American Federation of Labor and Congress of Industrial Organizations in 1956 centralized labor activity to a degree, but the subsequent purge of the Teamsters Union and the downfall of Dave Beck have affected labor unity. Most Washington workers long had belonged to the A. F. of L. Thus labor in Washington did not experience the militant uphill organizing struggles of the 1930's to the extent their fellow workers did in the mass-production industries in the Middle West and East. Although labor has been principally friendly to the Democratic party, some labor unions in Washington, particularly the Teamsters, have inherited Republican leanings. In 1958 the Joint Council of Teamsters, representing 47 unions, recommended 22 Republican and 107 Democratic candidates for the state legislature. Nevertheless, labor generally has assisted Democratic candidates with support, money, and endorsements; has placed a few union officials in responsible posts in government and the Democratic party; but has not systematically tried to win control of Democratic party machinery. Six Democratic members of the 1959 legislature were union officials, and many legislators held union cards, but none of the top labor leaders also hold leading posts in the party.

Professional Groups

Among professional groups, the Washington Education Association is the most influential. Its strength rests in considerable part on the strategic dispersion and high quality of its members, but its participation in the Allied School Council, which includes the School Directors Association, the Parent-Teachers Association, the Superintendents Association, and even the superintendent of public instruction, adds a broad base of support. Because of the 40-mill property tax limit, the bulk of the funds for Washington's common schools comes from the state. Out of a 1959-1961 general fund budget of $826 million, the common schools received $352 million and higher education $84 million. Because salaries as well as school operating expenses are at the mercy of the state legislature, the "school lobby" swings into high gear during legislative sessions. The school forces rely principally on the school directors and on the direct efforts of the staff of the Washington Education Association to do the research and to conduct the necessary lobbying. In addition, local units of the association interview prospective candidates for the legislature and endorse those who support public education. Some members of the association are active politicians. In the 1959 session of the legislature, the chairman of the House Committee on Education was a high-school teacher and WEA member who had drafted the education plank for the Democratic party at its 1958 convention. The association's staff of very able and experienced lobbyists and its ability to generate tremendous overnight floods of letters and telegrams from its well-dispersed membership once led former Governor Arthur B. Langlie to label the "school lobby" the most "powerful" in the state.

Other professional groups have interested themselves primarily in licensing practices by the state. A number of special boards for optometrists, beauticians, sanitarians, and others have been created. Local fights over the fluoridation of city water supplies have flourished in the state because the nation's chief medical opponent of fluoridation resides in Seattle.

Recreation Groups

The exceptional recreational opportunities provided by the Sound, lakes, and mountains have made sportsmen's and conservation groups significant in the state. The Washington State Sportsmen's Council protects the interests of fishermen and hunters. Local councils exist in most cities and towns. Their particular fight has been against high dams which would block migratory fish such as salmon and steelhead, but they also have opposed commercial fishermen on the use of traps, nets, and purse seines. "Wilderness" societies attempt to protect primitive areas from the onslaught of loggers, motorists, and resort operations. The interests of less energetic pleasure seekers are just as enthusiastically protected. Metropolitan Seattle boasts the largest number of boats per capita in the world, and the producers of pleasure craft stand ready to protect the interests of their consumers. Vendors of camping equipment urge more and better state and national parks, with overnight camping facilities, and point to the sales taxes which out-of-state tourists pour into the treasury each year.

"Senior" Citizen Groups

The proportion of persons over sixty-five years of age is 9.4 per cent in Washington, compared to 8.8 in the nation. Medical care, welfare, and pensions for the "senior" citizens have been important problems in the state's politics for nearly a generation. The aged have been treated well by the legislature, and the major issue has centered around the amount or extent and not the principle of the welfare program. A leading force in the 1930's and 1940's was the Washington Pension Union, but charges that it had become Communist-infiltrated destroyed its effectiveness.

Other Associations

A wide variety of other associations display interest in government. The Association of Washington Cities, the County Commissioners' Association, and associations of the various types of local government officials all meet, take stands, and urge action in the public interest as they see it. In 1956, the League of Women Voters, after a study of legislative apportionment in the state, sponsored a reapportionment initiative.

Pressure Tactics

Pressure-group tactics are of a bewildering variety. Virtually all groups in the first instance resort to public-relations devices to try to create a "favorable climate of opinion." Stacks of propaganda pamphlets greet the customer when he enters his utility company office to pay the monthly bill. The Washington Water Power Company and Pacific Power and Light Company have been participants in the nationwide Electric Companies Advertising Program which in 1959 came under fire by the Internal Revenue Service as a non-deductible expense. The National Association of Manufacturers maintains an office in Portland, Oregon, which offers to supply speakers to other groups and classrooms to put across the business point of view. Labor has now countered with a similar offer. Several groups have produced movies. The timber companies flood the schools with "conservation" films which incidentally show what a good job private industry is doing. In the late 1950's four private utilities which were proposing to build Mountain Sheep Dam (which would have killed the proposed federal Nez Perce Dam) produced a dramatic colored movie of their struggle against the elements to survey the site. Phonograph records and pamphlets promoting racial and religious tolerance are available from the Seattle office of B'nai B'rith. News handouts, "information for employees," and "reports to stockholders" also are used to spread information. One subtle propaganda device is the non-copyright "canned" editorial sent free of charge to the weekly press. E. Hofer and Sons in Portland, Oregon, for a generation have produced canned editorials from the point of view of big business.

Interest groups also work inside the political parties and try to influence the outcome of political campaigns. Service groups, because of their nonpolitical orientation, are likely to have members in both political parties who serve as committee officers or as delegates to county and state conventions. To encourage greater participation in regular party work, the AFL-CIO has put its Committee on Political Education into high gear in the state. Lists of union members have been checked against registration books, and many members and especially their wives have been added to the list of eligible voters. Labor's participation in regular party politics recently has frightened business into similar efforts, most of it expected to aid the Republican cause. In the spring of 1959 the General Electric Company started a practical politics course for its top-management people at the Richland plant. Second-line management was served in the fall of 1959 by a revised and improved practical politics course. The company persuaded the Richland Chamber of Commerce to adopt a city-wide course to interest businessmen in precinct political activity. Similar activity was begun elsewhere.

Many groups are represented on convention platform committees. Public and private power groups, business, the Grange, the AFL-CIO, the Washington Education Association, veterans' groups, and many others thus write their own platform planks. If a major group has no leader on the platform committee, its leaders attend subcommittee hearings to suggest the wording of special planks.

Labor and the Washington Education Association openly endorse candidates and campaign for them at election time. The Grange, American Legion, and many others are prohibited by their constitutions from such action, but individual leaders of these groups often get involved in campaign activities.

Lobbying is, of course, a major activity for many pressure groups, because individual legislators are free to vote as they think best on policy questions. Lobbyists play an important role in state legislative activity, for they not only supply legislators with their point of view, but do research which legislators have no time to undertake; draft bills for introduction; work with the limited legislative professional staff available in Olympia; appear before committees to supply information and answer questions; and apply grass-roots pressure by generating floods of letters, phone calls, and telegrams from constituents back home. Perhaps most important of all, however, lobbyists develop a detailed understanding of the intricacies of the legislative process and, through personal friendships with individual legislators, can keep careful track of the course of legislation in which they are interested. A desired bill may be called out of a committee at just the right time by a judicious suggestion, or an unwanted bill may thus be killed in committee.

Pressure groups also watch the executive branch, for the enforcement of laws is of vital concern to them. Groups take an interest in the amount of money appropriated to executive departments, in the persons appointed to fill executive posts, in the composition of boards and commissions, and in the way executive agencies conduct their work. Groups may appear at executive agency hearings, especially those of regulatory commissions; make direct representations to executive officials; or co-operate with field representatives in the conduct of a governmental program.

Although pressure groups sometimes take an interest in the personnel selected or elected to the courts, their more common role in the judicial process is to provide the funds and the skilled attorneys to carry cases through the appeals system.

Because the state of Washington uses both the initiative and the referendum, pressure groups have a still further role. Political parties have no need to use these devices, and a private individual cannot circulate petitions to obtain nearly 100,000 signatures or disseminate propaganda throughout the state. Pressure groups make the initiative and referendum work. In recent years, Washington has seen labor legislation, school legislation, social security legislation, and even reapportionment of the state legislature accomplished by pressure groups using the initiative or referendum.

In Washington, pressure groups are not regulated by law. The House of Representatives, by rule, obliged lobbyists to register and carry name tags in the 1959 session.

THE "ENGINEERING OF CONSENT"—A CASE STUDY

ROBERT BENDINER

Robert Bendiner is a free-lance correspondent. In addition to many articles on politics, he has written *Obstacle Course on Capitol Hill* (1964).

Back in the days of Ralph Waldo Emerson it was thought, at least by Dr. Emerson, that if a man built a better mousetrap than his neighbor, the world would beat a path to his door. Today, thanks to public relations, we understand that the builder must first arrange for "the engineering of public consent" to mousetraps. Next he must acquire "earned recognition" for his particular model. And then, according to extreme practitioners, he must, if necessary, "create situations of reality" by setting up, for example, a National Citizens' Committee for the Urgent Capture of Mice.

As to the second of the three quoted phrases—all culled from the sober pronouncements of eminent publicists—there can hardly be any question of logic or propriety. To see recognition for the merits of a product or an idea is clearly as inevitable as it is blameless, Dr. Emerson's theory to the contrary notwithstanding. But when it comes to "engineering" people's minds, the question naturally arises as to the moral mileage we have covered from The Public Be Damned to The Public Be Maneuvered.

Edward L. Bernays, father of the "engineering" line and one of the most vociferously idealistic men in the business, undoubtedly had in mind only proper objectives for his approach, presumptuous as its phrasing may sound, but the case study we are about to make shows what can happen when "opinion engineers" are given their head. It is a short step, it turns out, from wangling public consent to kidding the public into imagining its consent has already been given—a thought that Carl Byoir & Associates, Inc., it would seem, daringly worked up to a whole creative system for manufacturing "situations of reality."

(P.R.) Men at Work

It is this system, with its overtones of modified Barnum, that underlies, colors, and gives public meaning to the $250-million anti-trust suit formally titled *Noerr Motor Freight, Inc. et al. v. Eastern Railroad Presidents Conference et all.*, but better known in the trade as the railroad-trucker brawl. Should this case ever come to trial in the United States District

From "The 'Engineering of Consent'—A Case Study," Robert Bendiner, *The Reporter*, August 11, 1955, pp. 14-23. © 1955 by The Reporter Magazine Company.

Court in Philadelphia, where it has long been at rest, it would doubtless sustain *Tide's* prediction of the "most hard-fought and bloody of the century's legal battles." But even in the event of a settlement, now strongly indicated, enough has spilled out in pre-trial skirmishes to afford a remarkably complete and lively panorama of public-relations men at work — at least one variety of the species.

There is no intent here to judge the case or to pass on the relative merits of hauling freight by rail or truck. Neither is it suggested that the "engineering" that went on in this celebrated battle is synonymous with public relations in general, though in varying degree its aspects are to be encountered elsewhere in the craft. To find them all together it was clearly necessary to pick an extreme case rather than describe a typical one.

Nonetheless, what gives the affair its special claim to attention is that the rival concerns — Byoir for the railroads and David Charnay's Allied Public Relations Associates for the truckers — are whirring dynamos in the business, that their clients are economic powers of the first rank, and that in their raucous clash not merely a public-relations firm is on trial but some of the commonly practiced techniques of public relations as well.

Victory at Harrisburg

On January 21, 1952, Pennsylvania's Governor John S. Fine faced a hard decision. Without his veto a measure called by its sponsors the "Fair Truck Bill" and by its opponents the "Big Truck Bill" would automatically become law. That outcome, the Governor knew, would not sit well with the railroads, traditionally a power in Pennsylvania politics roughly comparable to oil in Texas and sin in Nevada. On the other hand, both houses of the Legislature had passed the bill, which would have raised the weight limit for long-haul trucks allowed on the state's highways from forty-five thousand pounds to sixty thousand. Except for Kentucky, the Pennsylvania limit was the lowest in the country, far below that imposed by any of its neighboring states. The trucking business, smarting under the drastic curb, had itself become a force in the Pennsylvania capital, perhaps not as entrenched as exponents of the older form of transportation, but brasher, with considerable appeal to voters, and an ample supply of ready cash.

Caught in this crossfire of special interests, the Governor may well have acted on what he conceived to be the pure merits of the case when, six minutes before the deadline, he vetoed the weight-increase bill. If Governor Fine had been cross examined on the reasons for his action, he could certainly have made out an excellent case.

In the first place, the Maryland State Roads Commission was co-sponsoring a test of the relative damage done by various axle loads to concrete pavement, and with what appeared to be providential timing, an advance copy of an interim report had come to Governor Fine's attention. The tentative findings were hard on heavy trucks.

The Governor also understood that the Pennsylvania State Association of Township Supervisors, a quasi-official body, was all out against the "Big Truck" bill. Tens of thousands of postcards were pouring out under its imprimatur addressed to the car owners of the state, and it had produced a television program on the Maryland road test.

The Pennsylvania State Grange appeared to be equally aroused against the bill. Material had streamed out of its headquarters during the legislative battle, and the Governor must have known that the Grange had worked on state Senators, especially those from politically doubtful districts, to vote against the measure.

So insistent, in fact, was the opposition—even after passage of the bill—that the Governor felt obliged to hold public hearings two days before the deadline for his decision—and at those hearings the anti-big-truck witnesses had made an extremely impressive case.

How Spontaneous Can You Get?

The result of all this civic activity was the veto. *Vox populi* had been heard and heeded. Or so it seemed, for few persons outside the offices of Carl Byoir & Associates knew until much later:

■ That the public relations man of the Maryland State Roads Commission, which had co-sponsored the road test, had been advising the Byoir office, on an expense account, and was later to go on the payroll of Byoir's client, the Eastern Railroad Presidents Conference (E.R.P.C.), at $1,000 a month.

■ That those tens of thousands of postcards mailed out to motorists in the name of the Pennsylvania State Association of Township Supervisors had been prepared and mailed by the Byoir organization and billed to the E.R.P.C.

■ That during the fight for the bill, a Byoir lieutenant, according to his own subsequent testimony, made his headquarters in the Pennsylvania State Grange, whose literature was similarly drawn up by Byoir men and billed to the railroads.

■ Or, finally, that the impressive showing at the hearings was not the spontaneous plea of affected Pennsylvanians, but the carefully coached performance of Byoir-organized witnesses.

Allowing for a certain freedom from shyness essential to the profession, let Reynolds Girdler, then a Byoir executive, tell the story of the "CB&A team" in his own words:

When January, 1951, opened, there seemed every reason to believe that the truckers would get their bill through, increasing the allowable weight to 60,000 pounds. The 17 railroads of Pennsylvania then started fighting. . . . They fought the bill for four months and then threw up the sponge. They reported to their superiors that they were licked. Even so the lobbyists in control of the railroad activity continued to oppose allowing the CB&A people to operate in Pennsylvania. Their superiors then thrust us down their throats.

Recommending a special award for C. Colburn Hardy, who commanded the Byoir forces in the 'Battle of Harrisburg, the interoffice memorandum continued.

The team went to work in Pennsylvania beginning in June, 1951. Not only did they begin to generate publicity against the bill, but they were successful in getting a long list of organizations and individuals publicly to oppose the bill. Those organizations ranged from the CIO to the Pennsylvania State Grange. . . . Even after the bill was passed by both houses, clamor against the bill continued. . . . The CB&A team thereupon went out and organized twenty-one witnesses for twenty-one organizations against the bill. They prepared their statements and the publicity . . . Veto of this bill meant that some five million dollars worth of freight was retained on the Pennsylvania Railroad, because the trucking limit was not raised. This represented one of the most dramatic illustrations of the power of organized public opinion that anyone could hope to find. . . .

The opinion may have been more organized than public (Mr. Hardy, the award-nominee, modestly dismissed this description of his efforts as "overenthusiastic" — "a sales pitch"), but the illustration was certainly dramatic enough. According to Edward Gogolin, general manager and first vice-president of the Pennsylvania Motor Truck Association, the veto "triggered the industry" into action.

While the truckers had never been a retiring sort, it was clear now that massive retaliation was in order. It was not surprising, then, that in May, 1952, they engaged the services of David Charnay and his Allied Public Relations Associates. As the Pennsylvania truckers' president, Floyd B. Noerr, put it, "We were trying to find out who was stabbing us in the back, and then if we did find out, to pull out the dagger and bring suit."

The identity of the assailant could hardly have been as much of a mystery as all that. Certainly, Gogolin, Noerr's lieutenant, had a good notion since, as he was later to testify, "Practically every morning, to get to my office, I had to stumble over C. Colburn Hardy, the Byoir man, who was using the Grange office on the first floor of our building as his headquarters." Nevertheless, it was plain that Charnay's services were not being engaged merely to "engineer public consent" for the hauling of freight by truck. He was hired as well to do a detective job on a fellow publicist.

Enter Miss Saroyan

Long before the Governor's veto or Charnay's entry into the picture, the American Trucking Association was aware of the Byoir tactics against the long-haul truckers.

The reason for this was dramatic and simple. One day in July, 1951, a young lady named Sonya Saroyan, originally Sonya Jigarjian, walked into the American Trucking Association's Washington office to tell Walter Belson, its public-relations director, all about Life with Byoir.

After two years as secretary to the Byoir executive in charge of the Eastern Railroad account, Miss Saroyan—twenty-nine and variously described as "an attractive brunette" and "a very strange dish of tea"— had resigned or been fired, a point not easily determined. With her went a large packet of memos, reports, directives, letters, and releases, mostly carbons or copies she herself had made and which she therefore somewhat naïvely regarded as her "own property." All of it was intended to show how the art of public relations was practiced by her erstwhile employer. Belson accepted her offerings, along with two days of tape-recorded "testimony" at $50 a day, plus expenses. For nearly a year that seemed to be the end of Miss Saroyan's brush with adventure.

What her motives were cannot be pinned down with certainty, but, as often happens, they seem to have been a blend. Richardson Dilworth, chief of the truckers' legal battery when he was not engaged as Philadelphia's district attorney, explained that she "had become thoroughly disgusted with the methods being used in the handling of this account" and had therefore gone to the other side as a matter of conscience. Sonya herself takes a somewhat less lofty view, explaining that she "very impulsively" walked out with the papers when she was bypassed for a promised promotion to the Tintair account.

At any rate, the truckers appear to have been extraordinarily slow to see the value of Sonya's contribution to their cause. At one point in the Battle of Harrisburg, Belson telephoned Gogolin to report that some pertinent material had been delivered to headquarters by an ex-employee of the enemy and to ask whether the trucking executive was aware of "certain things" going on in the state, more significant even than Gogolin's tripping over Hardy every morning on his way to work. Soon after, the Pennsylvania truckers dispatched an agent to examine the material in Washington and take notes. But it appears that if the

Charnay organization had not taken over, the Saroyan dossier, in all its colorful detail, might have been left forever to gather dust.

Things Get Going

It was in April, 1952, that three officials of the Pennsylvania Motor Truck Association called on David Charnay, an enterprising young man whose favorable impression on John L. Lewis had made him a major publicist, putting him in a position to ask the truckers, and to get, $36,000 a year, plus expenses, for his services. The sum was modest enough compared with the $150,000 a year the railroads were paying Byoir, plus expenses running up to $250,000, but still rather impressive for a man who only a few years earlier had been reporting nightclub doings for the New York *Daily News.* Besides the United Mine Workers of America account and a colorful and rewarding stint for the Nationalist Bank of China, Charnay had lined up such notable clients as Ballantine Beer and Eversharp. A man of versatile talents, he has managed to promote the fortunes of such diverse figures as Franklin D. Roosevelt, Jr., Richard Nixon, Robert F. Wagner, Vincent Impellitteri, and Louis E. Wolfson, the man who tried to take over Montgomery Ward.

In its preliminary phase the truckers' account was put in the hands of a former newspaper man named Henry Paynter, whose first order of business was to get a private detective on the track of Sonya Saroyan. She was located in New York, in May, and throughout the summer and fall, she says, Paynter and Charnay pressed her to release the material she had turned over to the American truckers office (which apparently would not yield it up to the Pennsylvania group otherwise), and to tell them more about the workings of the Byoir enterprise.

She was offered a job, according to her testimony, but turned it down. Eventually, as she tells the tale, she succumbed, on the understanding that the documents and her testimony—she had added an additional $1,050 worth—were to be turned over to a Congressional committee for investigation. Next thing she knew, she says, was the announcement in the papers of January 18,1953, that the Pennsylvania Motor Truck Association and thirty-seven trucking companies were suing the Eastern Railroad Presidents Conference, thirty-one railroads, thirty-four individuals (mostly railroad presidents and ex-presidents) and the public-relations firm of Carl Byoir & Associates.

"I have every reason to believe," wrote Sonya Saroyan less than a month later, "that the suit was based, in great part, on my testimony." Dilworth seemed to agree. When a railroad attorney offered to produce without subpoena certain items of interest to the truckers in exchange for the Saroyan papers, Dilworth is reported to have answered, "This would be like swapping a ticket to South Pacific for a Minsky burlesque ticket."

Cloak-and-Dagger Stuff

The Dilworth evaluation was probably accurate, but the truckers had
other sources of information as well. In the fall of 1952, the Charnay
office enjoyed the services of John G. (Steve) Broady, a private investigator who has since then added to his fame and drawn an indictment as
the alleged "master ear" of a Manhattan wiretap ring. Paynter says that
Broady's contacts were solely with him, rather than with Charnay, and
the fruits of his efforts, whatever they were, were turned over directly
to Dilworth. Both sides have complained of rifled files, and Dilworth
charged that the Byoir firm had destroyed some of its own records
rather than have them subpoenaed—a charge vigorously denied by
Byoir.

Allowing for the natural exuberance of lawyers, especially in pretrial procedures, it seems reasonably clear that in a public-relations war
anything up to and including piracy may well be expected. In any
event, what emerged from the Charnay firm's preliminary labors, as
refined by the distinguished Philadelphia law firm of Dilworth, Paxson,
Kalish & Green, amounted to the following charge:

That the defendant railroads had conspired, through vilification,
slander, bribery, and assorted devices to drive the long-distance truckers
out of business, with the objective of "carving out exclusive, monopolistic
spheres of operation in the freight transportation business." To this
end, the complaint ran, the Byoir firm had been hired and it "immediately initiated a vicious, corrupt and fraudulent campaign" to "obstruct, hamper and impede interstate transportation by motor vehicle,"
all in willful violation of the Sherman Antitrust Act. In its reply, the
Byoir firm flatly denied these allegations.

Boiling down the charges as they related to Byoir, Dilworth at the
pre-trial hearings specified "misinformation . . . front organizations
. . . distorted photographs . . . planting of stories . . . 'boilerplate'
announcements . . . phony polls," and the like. To which Philip Price of
the defense staff replied that much of the case seemed to be that the
"defendants got together and called the plaintiff bad names."

Whether such activities as those alleged form a pattern that is
vulnerable under the Sherman Antitrust Act may safely be left to the
courts and the fullness of time, but the open discussion of these techniques, illegal or merely tricky, is of general interest to the public and
of special interest throughout the whole hypersensitive realm of public
relations.

Leagues and Foundations

If, there is one obvious lesson to be derived from the railroad-trucker
affair, it is that the fulsome interoffice memorandum is a luxury to be

resisted. A specimen of the sort that prompted Dilworth to say he would guard with his life the collection of Byoir papers carted off by Miss Saroyan is this gem that Reynolds Girdler, the former Byoir executive, composed in 1949 to set the tactical line for promoting the firm's new railroad client:

> *You can see from the foregoing that this account is utterly unlike the conventional one.* Here we do not have a client for attribution. [Italics (roman here) mine.] *Of course we will release some stories under client attribution, but they will be of lesser propaganda importance than those we can generate from motorists, property owners, tax payers, farmers or women's groups. In sum, we not only have to create publicity ideas; we also have to go out in the field and create the groups and occasions so that those publicity ideas will become realities.*

One of the groups they created, in the New York sector of the battle line, was the Empire State Transport League. When Girdler first testified about this organization, he modestly credited its formation to a small group of upstate New York businessmen. They were aided, he said, by Thomas Kiely, a Byoir man, but "only in the nicest kind of way," and besides the impetus was their own. Confronted, however, with a memorandum he had dashed off to his superior on the subject— another of the documents spirited out by the impulsive Miss Saroyan— Girdler freely admitted authorship. It read in part:

> *We formed the Empire State Transport League in New York because we needed an organization that could legitimately mail all types of propaganda on the general subject of trucks and highways.*

The League had an address, of course—11 North Pearl Street, Albany, it said on the letterheads—but no office that a Dun & Bradstreet investigator could locate. A public stenographer took the mail and, presumably, relayed it on to the Byoir office. But the organization did have a constitution and bylaws, and for reproducing copies of these, along with membership-application forms, the Byoir firm duly billed the Eastern Railroad Presidents Conference on December 9 and 12, 1949.

The League was then all set to send out releases, reprints, and other such material, none of which would have been quite so persuasive if it had had to bear some such imprint as "Carl Byoir & Associates, Public Relations Counsel to the Eastern Railroad Presidents Conference" instead of "Empire State Transport League."

David I. Mackie, chairman of the E.R.P.C., has insisted that " . . . the real issue is not between the heavy truck operators and the railroads, but between an informed and militant public and the highway freighters." The League, it seems, was just a slice of that informed and militant public boiled down to a letterhead.

Another slice apparently was called the "New Jersey Citizens Tax Study Foundation," which was launched just as the Byoir office was warming up the campaign against the truckers. Among its original incorporators was one G. Colburn Hardy, then commanding the Byoir railroad campaign on the Jersey front. As Hardy later testified, "This was a personal matter that I did as a citizen, similar to a great many other civic projects in which I happened to be interested."

It was odd, though, that at the pretrial proceedings fifteen canceled checks amounting to $3,700.58 were produced from the Byoir files, made out to Fred W. Goodwin, executive director of the Foundation. The E.R.P.C. was also billed for the Foundation's envelopes, letterheads, and releases, as well as for "contributions" by the Byoir firm.

Still harder to square with Hardy's purely civic role in the Foundation was the directive he addressed to his staff with all the characteristic candor of Byoir executives:

> *We are also assisting in the formation of a new group: New Jersey Citizens Tax Study Foundation . . . ALL LITERATURE, ETC. from this group must be on plain paper and mailed from New Jersey.*

Yet the Foundation solemnly turned out studies on highway finance and even conducted a poll that showed the public fairly panting for a mileage tax on heavy trucks. "As a fact-finding group," said the covering release, "the Foundation takes no position, merely reports the results." With equal solemnity the Foundation later released to the press a letter to the New Jersey Motor Truckers Association denying that it was a "front" for the railroads.

The New Jersey Automobile Owners, Inc., was clearly not started by Byoir, having been incorporated back in 1938. But, testified Hardy, "I helped in reactivating" it. The pattern was similar to the relationship between Byoir and the civic-minded tax students. Again checks were produced from the Byoir files. Again the E.R.P.C. was billed for material put out in the name of the do-good organization. And again there was the unfailing memorandum. This one, also from Hardy, said:

> *We are cooperating with an autoist group, New Jersey Automobile Owners, Inc. . . . This group sends out considerable literature. It MUST be mailed in New Jersey.*

There was a further injunction: "Whenever any letter goes from the N.J.A.O., a copy MUST be mailed to Robert A. Fox, New Jersey Automobile Owners, Inc., 155 Evergreen Place, East Orange, N.J. . . . " A sensitive touch, perhaps, but it probably seemed only right and proper for Mr. Fox, as executive secretary, to be informed of what his organization was up to.

What's a 'Front'?

Practically every public-relations firm makes use of citizens' committees of one sort or another — and generally legitimate use. But as elsewhere in this business the area is cloudy, with only a shadowy line separating the relatively pure from the purely bogus. Thomas J. Deegan, chairman of the E.R.P.C.'s subcommittee on public relations, plays the ambiguity for all it is worth. Pressed by Dilworth, he expounded his views on fronts — "noble and ignoble":

> *"Front" can be the very evil one that we both talked about a moment ago, the Commy. "Front" can be something as simple and genuine as Bing Crosby smoking a Chesterfield. "Front" can be someone else with a co-interest saying the story that you are interested in, too, which, to my humble knowledge, is a perfectly genuine, proper thing to do. "Front" has taken an even other connotations — Marilyn Monroe.*

Gerry Swinehart, president of the Byoir firm and evidently far more active in the railroad account than Byoir himself, shrugged off the implications of the "front" technique altogether. "There may have been one or two instances where we organized groups," he said, "but those groups knew what they were doing." No one was fooled but the public.

Going My Way?

While few public-relations men share Swinehart's openly indulgent attitude toward the synthetic front, practically all of them endorse a close working relationship with what the trade calls "co-interest groups." In truth there would seem to be no reason why they shouldn't hitch a client's public-relations activities to the parallel program of another organization — as long as the thing is done openly. The rub is that it is not always, or even generally, done openly. Certainly not in this case.

The Grange, a good example of a co-interest group, was certainly operating in Pennsylvania before Carl Byoir & Associates were, and it continued to function there long after Messrs. Girdler and Hardy pulled out their "team." It was real and legitimate, but how independent it was in this particular campaign against the truckers is something else again. We have already indicated that a good quantity of the Grange's propaganda in that fight created by Byoir men, though the Grange was not their client, and that printing, mailing, and other publicity charges were regularly paid for by their office. Weekly work reports from Hardy and his team, later cited at the hearings, indicate that the Grange's lobbying was supervised by, and even its letters written by, Byoir lieutenants:

> *June 28, 1951: "With Grange set up special program to contact Senators in doubtful counties . . . Wrote material for Grange News Letter."*
> *July 29, 1951: "Letters to editor from J. K. Mahood, Pennsylvania State Grange, to answer inaccurate charges of proponents of S 615 (the truck bill)."*
> *May 9, 1952: "Hardy wrote letter from Master, Pennsylvania Grange, to accompany reprint of National Grange Monthly reprint."*
> *June 27, 1952: "Mailing reprints over signature of Master of State Grange."*

The Pennsylvania State Association of Township Supervisors similarly enjoyed the talents of the Byoir establishment, courtesy of the E.R.P.C., not to mention financial assistance. So, it appears, did the Citizens Tax League of Rochester, New York, and the Citizens Public Expenditure Survey of Albany.

It often happens that a potential co-interest group has to be subtly persuaded of its co-interest. In such cases, there is no substitute for the services of an eloquent member, and like all professional services these are not performed gratis. Such a "pro" par excellence is Mrs. Bessie Q. Mott, a veteran clubwoman, pamphleteer, and grant-grandmother.

Questioning Swinehart at the pretrial hearings, Dilworth sardonically suggested that Mrs. Mott was "getting to be practically a regular" at profitable crusading. Yes, Swinehart agreed, "She works for a great many people. . . . She is a specialist in the field of reaching women's clubs, women's interests." Indeed she is, having given unstintingly not only to the railroads, but also to the Great Atlantic & Pacific Tea Company, when Byoir was fighting that chain's case in defense against the Justice Department, and, before that, to oleomargarine, which she served under the banner of Batten, Barton, Durstine & Osborne, Inc.

"But I don't take on a fight," says Mrs. Mott (Smith, '99), "unless it's something I believe in." However, the lines between her personal crusades and the interests of her organizations tend to get blurred. She is said to have allowed Byoir to pay for letterheads of the American Home Department of the New York State Federation of Women's Clubs which showed Bessie Q. Mott as vice-chairman and were used to invite ladies to a forum likewise paid for by the Byoir office. A pamphlet under her signature, called "Are We Being Railroaded into Socialism?" is alleged to have been printed and mailed at Byoir's expense, though the author was carefully identified only with the Public Affairs Department of the Federation.

When the truckers formally complained in their suit that the lady was using her position as a platform for Byoir and the railroads, the president of the Federation could only concede to the press that as chairman of the public-affairs committee, Mrs. Mott had in fact issued antitruck propaganda and that the Federation had felt obliged to tell her to stop.

Mrs. Mott had been receiving $500 a month and expenses from Byoir. Canceled checks were produced to show that the civic-minded lady had drawn more than $7,500 for work on the railroad account. Evidently she was worth it, however, because when her name bobbed up again on the Byoir work reports, after a quiet spell, Swinehart inquired about her new activities. The answer, from staff-man Horace Lyon, was as follows:

> *She is on retainer ($500 a month) for months of May and June ONLY — when the state and national Fed. of Women's Clubs and Bus. & Prof. Women's Clubs are holding their annual conventions, setting up next year's program plans, etc. — to do these things:*
> *1. Get our program guide on the need for a modernized national transportation policy published with the endorsement of the Nat. Fed. of Women's Clubs.*
> *2. Get transportation on the program agendas for next year. . . . We are getting results, and value, on both counts.*

Byoir's own comment, as quoted by *Fortune,* was: "Sure we hired a clubwoman to get the women's clubs. What are we supposed to do? Hire a veteran to speak for women's clubs, and a woman to speak for veterans' organizations?"

The Role of Clinton Johnson

Inevitably, the spectacle of a Bessie Q. Mott manipulating women's clubs to the greater glory of a group of railroads has in it something of high comedy. Unhappily this element is lacking in the alleged working arrangements between the Byoir establishment and Clinton H. Johnson, public-relations agent for the Maryland State Roads Commission. The truckers' complaint uses harsh words and charges that Governor Fine's last-minute veto of the truck bill had been influenced by Johnson, who was in a position to have advance knowledge of the road test and who, at the same time, it said, had been receiving payments from Carl Byoir & Associates.

Johnson denied these allegations, but he conceded certain points that at least raise the question of propriety. Johnson's basic case is a simple one: He was not an employee of the State of Maryland but an independent contractor engaged to handle the public relations of the Roads Commission. His contract did not prevent him from engaging in other public-relations work as long as he did not let it interfere with his labors for the commission. Yes, he did make twenty to thirty trips to the New York offices of Carl Byoir & Associates, but his motive was to get their help in doing his job for the Maryland highway program.

At the same time, he gave the Byoir organization factual information about highway construction costs, overweight violations, and the like. At no time was he paid for services. Certainly he never took bribes nor did he misrepresent data or have any idea how the Byoir office got hold of the report on the road tests so far in advance of the general release. And, finally, he intended to bring suit against the truckers for libel and slander.

From Girdler's deposition we get a somewhat different perspective. Johnson did "interpretative and research work" for the Byoir office, he recalled, and was paid largely on the basis of the number of hours he put in. Girdler couldn't recall exactly the rate, and the arrangement does seem to have been pretty hazy all around. He recalled that amounts were given Johnson for expenses—Johnson confirmed this—without written statements, without itemizing, and often in cash. Girdler thought the expenses ran to $50 or $75 for an afternoon, night, and following day.

Hotel bills—Johnson usually stayed at the Biltmore—were often sent direct to Byoir. One of these, introduced as plaintiff's Exhibit P-65, covered a Labor Day weekend for Johnson and his wife, and must have been something of a bonus. Including theater tickets and meals, it came to $190.38. Johnson said it was for writing a free article for the Byoir firm—an article that, as it happens, never quite got finished.

In spite of Johnson's failure to remember payment for "services," several memos from Hardy to the bookkeeping department and at least one check bear the words "for research" or "services rendered." The sums were not high, but on January 1, 1953, Johnson went on a part-time basis with the Roads Commission and signed up as a consultant to the Eastern Railroad Presidents Conference for $1,000 a month. When plaintiff's counsel asked him, rhetorically enough, whether he considered this a "pay-off," his lawyer advised him not to answer. But he admitted that the Maryland Attorney General's office was investigating his relationship with Byoir while he worked for the Roads Commission and that as far as his state job was concerned, he was then on leave without pay. In a report later issued by the Attorney General's office Johnson was given a clean bill of health, but considered to have shown "poor judgment."

Accentuating the Negative

In the first of its many memoranda, in which it agreed to take on the railroad account, Carl Byoir & Associates laid down a few operating principles, to wit: The basic appeal must be directed not only to friends of the railroads but to motorists, conscious of hazards on the highway, and to taxpayers. Motorists are "ripe for action of some sort; but as yet they have not found a way to make themselves vocal or to express their

resentment in legislation. . . . It is our task to accelerate these spontaneously generated currents."

Accordingly, the magazine department was ordered to start work
"on the long process of researching and writing major magazine pieces."
The radio department was "alerted to write scripts and create events
acceptable to networks and local stations." It is a subject, wrote Girdler,
that should "give us plenty of scope for the ingenuity that distinguishes
CB & A departments. . . . "

Excerpts from early work sheets show the turn that this ingenuity
took almost from the start:

> *Production Department: 10/4 . . . Selecting pictures . . . featuring
> worst truck tragedy within the past year. . . .*
> *10/14 . . . Making layouts, selecting pictures, writing captions
> for Central States News Views featuring spectacular wreck near Gary,
> Ind., of large van-type truck. . .*
> *Radio Department: 10/21 . . . Securing radio script with
> mention of 'nasty truck driver' . . .*

Not all the railroad people took kindly to this sort of thing. Walter J.
Tuohy, president of the Chesapeake & Ohio, was sharply critical of an
inter-office Byoir memorandum that read in part:

> *At belated last, this is confirmation of my understanding of our con-
> versations concerning the desire of the account . . . to portray
> truckers as evil, sinister wrongdoers. Actually, the proposed program
> fell into three categories. . . 1. An effort by me to create and sell
> scripts to existing dramatic programs with the trucking theme as basic
> plot, picturing the trucker as a law-breaker, etc. As we discussed,
> invariably to conform with network requirements the 'bad' truckers may
> have to be compensated for by 'good' truckers but the poison will still
> be there and the damage done. 2. We will make all possible efforts to
> enlist the aid of regular and free-lance writers to utilize the truckers as
> a 'heavy'. . . .*

William White, then president of the New York Central, testified
that he had criticized some of these Byoir effusions as being in "an eager-
beaver jargon that I didn't like."

On the other hand, Thomas J. Deegan, who besides being chairman
of the E.R.P.C.'s public-relations subcommittee was vice-president in
charge of the Chesapeake & Ohio's public relations, thought the stress
on horror pictures perfectly proper because of the danger to the public
from trucks carrying explosives. "Seeing the explosives truck photographed riding along the highway with nothing happening is interesting,
perhaps, but certainly not striking," he remarked, "but seeing it ex-

ploded and children and mothers lying on the ground torn to bits brings one up short."

Of course, life in the publicity departments was not all melodrama. There were serious articles to be worked out with reputable writers for reputable magazines. To judge from a memorandum written by Patricia Lochridge, head of Byoir's magazine department, the firm was sometimes able to go rather far in the molding of articles. Staking a claim to one of the monthly awards that provide incentive in the Byoir establishment, Miss Lochridge wrote to a superior:

> Still a third nomination from the magazine department for the article, "You CAN Have Better Roads," which appeared in the April issue of Country Gentlemen. This was a cooperative venture pulling together the work of the account and the department in a year-long endeavor. . . . This was a difficult job to put across, entailing two complete rewrites of the article to satisfy both a pixie author and a difficult editor. This was accomplished without too much pain and the underlying philosophy of the . . . account came through in the final draft. . . .

At the pretrial proceedings Dilworth was unkind enough to confront Miss Lochridge not only with her memorandum but also with a note assuring the writer of the article that "tomorrow John Connor will send you some additional money as a working fund." It was "purely expense money," Miss Lochridge explained, to pay the author for research expenses prior to the article's acceptance. On rereading the piece, she felt "it was very much of Emily [the 'difficult pixie'] and very little of me." As for the memo itself, she dismissed it as "flowery," especially the part about the underlying philosophy. Then she added, by way of explanation, "Well, gee, I wanted to get the prize that month."

In many other ways the firm of Carl Byoir & Associates lived up to the dictum allegedly laid down early in the game by Hardy that "all publicity and activity should come through third parties," that the firm would "provide a vast amount of information but, for the most part, its source should remain anonymous." Polls and surveys appeared under high-sounding names, but the financing and, in some measure, the phrasing of the questions, originated in the Byoir office.

A Byoir work report for May 29, 1952, includes such items as: "Hardy revised material for speech by H. A. Thomson, Township Supervisors" and "Hardy wrote editorial for Pennsylvania Association Township Supervisors Magazine, endorsing weight-distance tax." Sonya Saroyan swore that press releases issued in the names of prominent persons were written and distributed from the Byoir office, including one from the insurance commissioner of Pennsylvania, in which big trucks were blamed for an expected boost in automobile-insurance rates. And even the New Jersey Rural Letter Carriers Association, which had also been enlisted in the cause, complained that the Byoir office had framed a resolution for the country mailmen and then reworded it in the press release they prepared.

They work hard at Byoir's.

Resort to Law

Confronted with this feverish activity and broad assortment of strategems, the truckers, on Charnay's advice, fell back on the law. It is not for the observer to contend, as the defendants have repeatedly contended, that the suit was brought as a counterattack in a publicity war. Assuming the plaintiff's perfect good faith in going to court, however, we can still appreciate the considerable tactical advantages that have accrued to them as a result.

By the very nature of the action, the enemy was put on the defensive. The plaintiffs also had an opportunity to strike an injured but gallant air and, through a "situation of reality" of their own making, get some pretty colorful publicity.

Two months after the intermittent pretrial sessions got under way, Robert McCay Green, co-counsel for the truck operators, filed an affidavit richly summarizing the testimony given up to that time and replete with stories of false fronts, weighted polls, and the doings of such persons as the remarkable Mrs. Mott. Five thousand copies went out to members of the Pennsylvania Motor Truck Association, the press, and interested outsiders. "Absolutely inexcusable," protested Byoir attorney R. Sturgis Ingersoll. But Dilworth blandly suggested that this was "obviously a protest inspired by your client, one of its happy ideas." Otherwise, he pointed out, the complaint would have been made to the court. Co-counsel Green added that by publicizing the document in this way, they had merely "kept the plaintiffs properly informed." And when Ingersoll sharply asked "Are the politicians in Ohio plaintiffs?" Dilworth settled for "This is too nice and too quiet a morning and we refuse to be needled."

It is true, of course that the doings of the truck operators and their publicists likewise became a matter of record, but because they had never put on anything like as intricate a campaign as their opponents and were not victimized by the disclosure of interoffice memoranda, there was much less for the railroad lawyers to work on. The latter were forced to make do with such scoops as the allegation that the truck operators had a war chest of $600,000, that they kept a hotel room in Harrisburg for "entertainment" (just as the other side did), and that even-handedly they doled out money to both parties shortly before elections.

Edward Gogolin, the Pennsylvania Motor Truck Association's general manager, didn't seem quite sure of the reason for this last custom. When Byoir's lawyer pressed the point that "nobody but a damned fool would bet a thousand dollars on each team" at a ball game,

Gogolin agreed, but as to why the truckers did essentially the same thing, he could only explain, "Well, I've been told all big business did that." While the testimony may have rubbed some of the gloss from the truckers' shield, it was mild stuff when compared with the single admission from the other side that five members of the Pennsylvania Legislature at the time were on the payroll of the Pennsylvania Railroad, four of them on the Senate Highway Committee.

'The Best Iron Tonic'

The suit had, from the truckers' viewpoint, the further merit of providing another public review of the career of Carl Byoir, surely one of the gaudier records of the era. The slight, conservatively dressed man of sixty-four scarcely looked the part of one of the great press agents of history, patent-medicine entrepreneur extraordinary, publicist for such diverse clients as Machado, Masaryk, and the German Tourist Information Office of the Nazi era, and finally head of the largest public-relations firm in the world.

In perhaps needless detail, Dilworth dwelt on Byoir's medicine-man period in the 1920's, when he collaborated with one X. La Motte Sage, A.M., Ph.D., LL.D., in the manufacture of Nuxated Iron. "The valuable blood, nerve force, and tissue-building properties of this preparation are due to organic iron . . . in combination with nux vomica," the label read. But the American Medical Association found less than four cents' worth of iron in a dollar bottle. Reminded of this finding by Dilworth, Byoir said, "That may be accurate," but it was still the best iron tonic on the market at the time. The trouble was with the distribution system, which he thought made such products too expensive. Another of his products was brought up—Seedol ("Natural Seed Bowel Tonic Works Wonders"). And furthermore, he had to defend his campaign in behalf of the A & P, which in 1946 cost him a conviction for conspiring to violate the Sherman Antitrust Act and a fine of $5,000.

Much of this line of questioning may have been irrelevant, as Byoir strenuously pointed out. "Ever since these depositions started to secure evidence," he complained, "that material has been used in many other ways by the Pennsylvania Truck Association to smear Carl Byoir." He added, rather wistfully it seemed, that to attract greater publicity the truckers had gone so far as to spread a rumor that a "Jelke girl" was to figure as a key witness at the trial.

But the grilling did serve to put Byoir on the defensive, and that evidently was the purpose. He felt obligated to disavow some of the phrases attributed to his subordinates in the railroad-trucker fight. Explaining that he had not been very active on the account, he said, "I am not taking the position that nobody ever did anything they shouldn't have done." But he was not for firing anyone. "If someone you tried to train gets a little too bright, a little too smart or too ambitious, his education needs working on." Let the truckers say what they would, the fact remained that "integrity is the cement of our business."

Blessed Are the Peacemakers

In the nature of things, the suit so far has aided the fortunes of Carl Byoir & Associates considerably less than those of David Charnay. But ironically, a settlement would prove still better for the latter than an eventual trial in open court, even one that resulted in a smashing victory for the truckers. Charnay is in this enviable heads-I-win-tails-you-lose position for the simple reason that in spite of the suit he has for some time been publicly and privately promoting the notion that the two branches of the transportation business "must decide to live together competitively and at peace."

Tide reported some months ago that in certain quarters "he is being touted as an 'industrial statesman'" for having brought railroad men and truckers together in a Council of Eastern Rail & Truck Common Carriers (C.E.R.T. for short) which seems to have found a potential meeting ground in the development of "piggyback"—the transport of truck trailers on railroad flatcars.

Charnay claims to have made "overtures" for a get-together of this sort even before the suit was filed, and he told this reporter of having offered Walter S. Franklin, President of the Pennsylvania Railroad, the friendly tip that "While you two roll around in the mud, that drone you hear overhead is air cargo." Perhaps more eloquent are two simple facts concerning C.E.R.T. David Charnay is a member of the Council; Carl Byoir is not.

Meanwhile, it is hardly possible to overlook the significance of what has been happening in Harrisburg in recent weeks. Once again, a bill to increase the weight limit for big trucks was put into the hopper. But instead of calling the Byoir men back into action again, the railroads almost immediately ran up the white flag. Associated Railroads of Pennsylvania, otherwise known as the railroad lobby, quickly announced that it would not oppose the measure. Its chairman, long one of the most trenchant foes of "big-truck" bills, did not exactly go all out for the measure, but it was plain that sweet reasonableness was the order of the day. "After a thorough study of the bill," he said, "we feel that it is reasonable in view of the laws of surrounding states." The bill was passed by the legislature and signed by Governor George M. Leader, Fine's successor.

Should a settlement sprout in this altered climate, what will have been the net effect? Two firms will have demonstrated the power of public relations as it has rarely been demonstrated before—one almost single-handedly defeated an important piece of legislation; the other stepped in and the bill was passed. The railroads and long-haul truck operators, neither of which has been made to look any better to the public as a result of their costly public-relations war, will have come to an understanding—after an enormous outlay of time, money, energy, and talent—that they almost inevitably would have reached anyway without benefit of public relations.

'What's Our Business?'

Whatever impact the railroad-trucker affair may have had on the principals or on the public, the publicity seems to have sent tremors through a calling already jittery with self-doubt. For in spite of a surface brashness, the public-relations industry in general is surprisingly marked by self-searching, ambiguity as to function, and an almost pathetic yearning for recognition by the American public.

The public-relations firm of Dudley-Anderson-Yutzy, one of the oldest and most respected in the field, recently felt obliged to call on an educator and researcher to solve a problem that had been bothering a good many public-relations men: "What's our business, anyway?" William G. Werner of Procter & Gamble, President of the Public Relations Society of America, has put out a booklet entitled "Can We Measure Up?" And a recent convention of the American Public Relations Association featured a panel discussion on the topic "Can a PR man's job be defined and respected?"

Yet alongside this introspective anxiety—whether or not in a causal relationship had better be left to others—go a bland assumption that public-relations men know best what is good for you; that their techniques can provide solutions to most problems, industrial, national, and international; and that they should, of necessity, be high in the councils of the Republic.

It is hard to read the trade organs of the craft without being struck by this somewhat inflated view. Does industry contemplate the introduction of atomic power? "It will require the best PR planning," says one agency official, "to fit this new development into the modern world." Is a new man taking over at the Voice of America? *Public Relations News* offers to "recommend the most highly qualified people in the country—the public relations professionals. They are peculiarly equipped with the special talents, training, and experience needed . . . to help fight the cold war and win the battle for peace." And when a high government post goes to a man recruited from a public-relations office, the fraternity indulges in solemn approval and self-congratulation in a way that would not occur to lawyers, preachers, or chiropractors.

Public-relations men are fond of viewing their function by analogy to other professions. Many see themselves as lawyers pleading before the bar of public opinion. A political member of the profession once spoke of promoting a major address by the President of the United States as "merchandising-in-depth."

Obviously, these comparisons are far afield. A lawyer is bound by rules of evidence and the restraining hand of the judge. An individual can buy a "merchandised" product or leave it alone, but a public policy successfully "merchandised" governs him whether he buys it or spots it for a fraud.

Actually this elaborate self-justification is a little bewildering to the layman who does not doubt that public relations has a legitimate and constructive role to play, one required by modern society. At its best it is a compiler and disseminator of useful information. More than that, it is increasingly a molder of policy in business and industry.

The more complex the community and the more varied the interests of the individual citizen, the more essential public relations becomes. Not only must institutions convey their purposes and merits to particular sectors of the public, but they must in return have the needs and desires of those they seek to interest conveyed back to them. The public-relations man is the interpreter in this two-way traffic of ideas — not only for railroad presidents and processors of cheese, but for university chancellors and yo-yo manufacturers, for Federal agencies and private trade associations, for aspiring aldermen and the governments of foreign states.

Perhaps it is this impression of mounting importance that gives some of the best people in the business a feeling of uncertainty, a sense that considerably more responsibility is in order.

As *Tide* commented, "Understandably, the pre-trial desposition-taking in the truckers' suit . . . has quite a few PR men wondering about ethics and behavior of the business."

RESEARCH: AN INSTRUMENT OF POLITICAL POWER

EDWARD F. COOKE

Edward F. Cooke is professor of political science, University of Pittsburgh. He is the author of *Guide to Pennsylvania Politics* (1957).

The decisions of state and local governments often affect the citizen more deeply and more directly than those of the national government or of private enterprises. Yet relatively little is known of the process by which decisions are made by state and local authorities. There is far from complete agreement even as to the people who take part in this

From "Research: An Instrument of Political Power" by Edward F. Cooke. Reprinted with permission from *The Political Science Quarterly*, LXXVI:I (March 1961), 69-87. [Footnotes omitted.]

process. It is of course obvious that decision making is the same in many respects at all levels of authority. Yet further investigation might reveal significant differences between the process as it is carried on at the state and local levels and at the national level, if only because state and local agencies have at their disposal less complete and unbiased information on which to base their decisions.

It is the purpose of this paper to contribute to this discussion by making a case study of one interest group in Pennsylvania, the Pennsylvania Economy League (PEL), that has come to wield great influence over the making of public policy instead of being only a research agency.

I

Essentially a taxpayers' association, the League enjoys a status and power that must surpass the fondest hopes of similar groups in other states. It manages to be handsomely financed by big business, respected by politicians in both parties, commended by the press and coöperated with by groups that might be considered natural enemies. It is able to perform this political miracle because it pursues its objective ("better government at less cost") by making available to public officials competent "research and professional consultation."

Apparently no problem is too small and none too great for the League's investigation and recommendation. Either by official request or on its own initiative, it has delved into matters as diverse as state tax policies, county sanitation authorities, municipal parking, county capital improvement programs and salary schedules. It has even made surveys of private and business associations. Its activities are limited only by the availability of funds and personnel. Its influence is felt by everyone, but its responsibility is to those who give financial support to its undertakings.

The Pennsylvania Economy League was established in 1932 and became a privately financed corporation in 1936. It claims to be the largest statewide governmental research organization in the country. The PEL operates in Pennsylvania through a number of offices divided administratively into three parts: (1) The State Office, located at the state capitol in Harrisburg, and concerned with general state policy, especially with administrative aspects of state government; (2) Regional offices located in Philadelphia (Eastern Division), Wilkes-Barre (Central Division) and Pittsburgh (Western Division), and concerned with the county and local affairs within their respective jurisdictions; (3) County Branches, established in over thirty of the state's most populous and wealthiest counties, dealing primarily with local government operations. Technically, each unit is an autonomous agency, but it is usually linked with the others by uniform objectives, joint financing and use of the same personnel.

Both in objectives and in methods the business orientation of the

League is abundantly clear. Its goals are those of other taxpayers' associations: sound fiscal management; improved administrative methods; and the elimination of waste and extravagance in government. Rarely stated in the literature but implicit in the discussions and the acts of the League is another important aim: a re-distribution of the tax basis to the advantage of the membership of the League. These objectives are to be reached by "continual surveillance of governmental operations and programs at all levels" through "techniques . . . used in successful private business."

The League is financed by the key industrial and commercial enterprises in the state. As a non-profit, tax-exempt organization, it has an advantage over some other groups such as labor unions and chambers of commerce. In 1951 Beverly Smith estimated its annual income at $500,000. Given the expansion in staff and operations, as well as the general rise in costs, since that time, it is not unreasonable to conclude that over $1,000,000 is required today to keep the League going. Smith's statement that "the biggest contributions come from the largest taxpayers, which means the giant corporations" would also hold true for 1960. In 1959-60 leading officers of many corporations were listed as board members.

This leadership at the state and divisional levels is strengthened at the county level by the presence of local representatives of big companies on governing boards. Thus a plant superintendent of United States Steel or a plant personnel manager of Alcoa may be on the governing board of a local unit of the League. However, county boards are not overwhelmingly composed of representatives of big business. Small manufacturers, merchants, real estate operators and professional people are so numerous in some places that the League competes for membership with local chambers of commerce. The League and the chambers of commerce hold similar views and draw support from some common sources, but relations between them, especially at the divisional level, are neither close nor constant.

The Pennsylvania Economy League claims that it is not a pressure organization but a non-political, non-partisan, fact-finding research agency. In its early years the newspapers usually identified the PEL as a business-supported research agency concerned with taxes; in the 1940's, the terms "non-partisan" and "fact-finding" began to creep into stories about the League; and finally in contemporary accounts we find the additional adjectives "non-political" and "non-profit" prefaced to the League's name. This gradual accretion of neutrality went parallel with the League's rise to key importance in the state's power structure. In fact, however, the Economy League appears to meet almost every test by which pressure groups are identified.

The PEL differs from other pressure groups, however, in the techniques it employs. It spends little time in buttonholing individuals or in campaigning for contributions. It does not play the rôle of ghost writer for business. It works chiefly by doing research, of all types and at any level of government, for whichever party requests its services.

Since the League is so well supported financially it is able to conduct research into almost every aspect of state and local government. Regional and county branches make regular surveys of state, county, municipal and school district finances. Periodically they do detailed studies of specific aspects of local government such as tax collection, purchasing or comparative tax burdens. The results of these studies and surveys are distributed to the League members and to a limited number of public officials and research agencies. In this way, influential community members are kept informed.

During the past five years the Eastern Division in Philadelphia published the results of over 75 investigations dealing with the problems of that city and of the four neighboring counties in southeastern Pennsylvania. The Central and Western Divisions have been equally active in the number and scope of their studies while the State Office has made management and budgetary recommendations at the state level. Many of these contributions were narrow managerial reports about matters like zoning or building code revisions, but a significant number dealt with broader matters such as the reorganization of the Philadelphia Controller's Office and the drafting of a personnel classification program for Allegheny County.

The League's services to governmental agencies are free, the only requirement being a written invitation and a clear definition of the scope of the investigation. The League makes it a practice to operate without fanfare and to show great deference to public officials. "It works so quietly that the majority of citizens right in its own state have never heard of it," said Smith in 1951. The public is no more aware of League activities in 1961. It is meticulous in its public relations so as to avoid the appearance of interfering in local affairs. It studiously avoids action which might give it the label of a "muckraker" or reform group; for example, it will not conduct a study for a private organization that may seek to embarrass or smear an administration. And though the word "Economy" appears in its title, the League tries to escape the negative reputation so often applied to taxpayers associations.

In undertaking a special project, the PEL stipulates that its report will be made only to the contracting agency which will then have the sole responsibility for making the findings public. As another way of securing the coöperation of officials, the League usually refrains from condemning individuals. In most cases, therefore, especially where narrow managerial functions are in question, the League's recommendations are accepted intact and without controversy. It is seen that they have been reached objectively and on the basis of the best available evidence. There may be a question about the League's objectivity in the areas of taxation, appropriations and personnel. Yet the reputation established by high quality work in such matters as managerial studies carries over to these other areas in which there is more room for controversy and where decisions are largely matters of policy. In all areas, after all, getting the facts upon which to make decisions is extremely important. Whoever is in a position to supply these facts is in a key rôle.

In the minds of most citizens, and of many politicians, the League is just an impartial research organization: "when the League has put its imprimatur on a budget or some public project, the taxpayer feels that he has an impartial and competent judgment on the proposal." Acceptance of League proposals is made especially desirable, or even necessary, when they are given almost universal newspaper support.

The impact of League research is made greater by the constant use of follow-up techniques. In fact, this is a major reason for PEL success. From its thirty bases in Pennsylvania's wealthiest and most populous counties, the League can muster an impressive array of economic and professional leaders to its support. The prestige and power of the men who sit on its boards add strength to the recommendations of its researchers. The members of its boards are not only community leaders but often personal and political friends of government officials. Their prestige can sometimes lead to acceptance of League recommendations even over the objections of those who will be affected most by the recommendations. More often, no pressure is necessary because there has developed an informal, but close and effective, relationship between the League's staff and government officials. In such cases decisions of community policy may be made without any clear indication of who has made them. The Western Division summed up the transition from watch-dog to confidant as follows:

> The traditional pattern of the League's operations has been the study and report rendered a distinct unit of government . . . the better understanding that comes with time has very often made our work less formal; there are more consultations and fewer documents, but the League's advisory work with the local officers continues and increases.

The follow-up process employed by the League is used at all levels and in all hierarchies within the Commonwealth. It illustrates the advantages that accrue from common objectives and a permanency of operation:

> We are in no danger of developing a split personality. On the contrary, it is fortunate that our structure permits a sense of detachment from any special interest or partisanship, and makes us equally at home at the State Capitol at Harrisburg or in hundreds of municipal buildings and courthouses throughout the State.

In this quotation the words, "at home," can be interpreted literally because "the League has furnished from time to time men from its own staff for important public assignments." Two recent instances of lend-lease occurred in 1959 when Dr. David Kurtzman, long-time Research Director of the Western Division, was appointed Secretary of Administration in Governor Lawrence's cabinet. Earlier in the year, David M. Baldwin, another long-term League employee, had been appointed Budget Secretary for the Commonwealth. Neither Kurtzman nor Baldwin has severed his League connection and both are listed as being on leave of absence.

The same pattern of relationships appears at the regional and county levels. For example, Lennox L. Moak, Director of the Eastern Branch, served as Finance Director for the City of Philadelphia during the first two years of Mayor Joseph S. Clark's administration. Another example was that of Milton Lavine who was brought to the Western Division at Pittsburgh to direct a personnel study for Allegheny County. The commissioners adopted Lavine's plan without change and two weeks later installed him as head of the agency created to carry it out.

The League, therefore, is able to work both from the outside and from the inside. Informal ties are strengthened by the periodic employment of League personnel in public posts. A case in point, a reversal of the usual practice but illustrative of the potential of the inside approach, is the appointment of Howard B. Stewart as Director of the Western Division of PEL. Stewart, a protégé of Governor Lawrence, had been Democratic County Commissioner in Allegheny County. He turned down his party's offer of renomination (tantamount to re-election to a $19,500 post, chairmanship of the Board and supervision of 7,000 employees) to accept the League position. It is not unreasonable to suppose that he has ready access to and a good deal of influence on key county officials, many of whom, including Lavine, were appointed to office during his term.

II

It is clear that the PEL has become an effective force in the shaping of state and local policies. It is probable that its influence will grow in the years ahead. But this impact on policy varies among the different sections that compose the League. Most influential of all, probably, is the Western Division.

The Western Division of the Economy League is one of a group of Mellon-supported enterprises that touch all aspects of life in Western Pennsylvania. The two main ones, of course, are the Mellon National Bank and Trust Company, and T. Mellon and Sons, but in addition to these purely economic enterprises, there are in Western Pennsylvania numerous community organizations receiving financial support from the Mellon family. In these organizations, it is usually possible to identify key persons as what may be called "Mellon men." For example, in 1958-59, the presidents or vice-presidents of the two Mellon companies named above held top posts in the following agencies: Allegheny Conference, PEL, Regional Industrial Development Corporation, United Fund, Pittsburgh Regional Planning Association, ACTION-Housing, Community Chest, Health Research Services Foundation, and Urban Redevelopment Corporation. Executives in the Mellon empire also hold high positions in colleges, universities, opera and symphony associations, scouts, foundations, chambers of commerce, playhouses, conservation groups, museums, libraries and welfare agencies.

The Western Division of the Economy League provides a central point at which persons from the various power groups in the Pittsburgh area can come together to make decisions for the region and the state. A striking example of the way in which the League and other élite elements coöperate can be found in a quotation from the *Pittsburgh Sun-Telegraph* for February 2, 1947: "City leaders and legislators of both political parties have agreed to support a 10-point legislative program for Pittsburgh and Allegheny County, including broader taxing powers. . . . The program was drawn by representatives of the Allegheny Conference on Community Development and the Pennsylvania Economy League." Incidentally, it should be pointed out that League recommendations carry so much weight in the community that in 1958 one of its reports had the effect of forcing the Pittsburgh Chamber of Commerce to divest itself of various functions and reorganize completely.

At the state level, the Western Division staff and directors often initiate legislative measures, especially in taxation and related matters. In addition, it is frequently called in by executive leaders either to advise on policy, or to participate in or to conduct special studies. For example, it joined with the State Office in supplying research help to the recent "Hoover Commission" study of the state government. It also joined in the State Tax Study Commissions in 1956 and 1958.

The accomplishments of the State Office are perhaps fewer than those of the Western Division, but they are considerable nevertheless. During the past twenty years, but especially since 1950, the State Office has been consulted regularly by administrative officers. It has also worked closely with legislative leaders, especially in making studies preceding legislative action. On some occasions, in fact, the entire responsibility for this work has been delegated to it by the legislature.

The Western Division and the State Office sometimes work together in advising the government. But relations between these two parts of PEL have not always been harmonious. In 1955 there was even something like civil war because the Western Division sought to dominate the central office in Harrisburg. As a result of this power struggle, the state director was forced out of office and John Ingram, formerly in the Western Division, was promoted to the directorship. We do not know all the reasons for this upheaval, but one prominent politician said: "The Harrisburg office had taken on too much of an independent air and had been too much the purist in terms of their research to satisfy certain elements in the Western Division."

In Philadelphia, the development of the Eastern branch of the League has been handicapped by a combination of factors. There it is known as the Bureau of Municipal Research, a name which indicates a somewhat narrower range of interests than that of the other parts of the PEL. Moreover, in Philadelphia, the League is only one among several research agencies that are consulted by the city government. In the city power structure, the League is in competition for influence with several other groups among which are the Committee of Seventy, the Greater Philadelphia Movement and the Chamber of Commerce. It is not likely to become the main vehicle for decision making unless the leaders of the community decide that they need one spokesman and select the League for the rôle.

The Central Division at Wilkes-Barre is like the Eastern Division at Philadelphia in that it has never achieved the same measure of success as that reached by the Western Division at Pittsburgh or the Central Office in Harrisburg. It has, however, taken part in scores of studies for the authorities in counties, municipalities and school districts included in its area. Moreover, its activity and influence have been increasing for some time past and are likely to increase still more in the future. It has not yet been completely accepted by the public and the officials in its area, but its usefulness is likely to become clearer to them as time passes, especially if the division is staffed adequately.

III

The position of the Economy League is made more secure by the insufficiency of public research facilities. Neither of the two existing state agencies is geared to satisfy today's demands. The Legislative Reference Bureau is primarily a bill-drafting organ for the General Assembly and secondarily a consultant on statute revision. The Joint State Government Commission, to which every member of the legislature belongs, is the research and planning arm of the General Assembly. It has a small research staff to carry out investigations, but is not an effective research agency because of its composition, the smallness of its staff and the meagerness of the funds placed at its disposal. As the Economy League pointed out in one of its publications, "these legislative commissions, valuable as they are, are limited in the subjects which they study, in the time which members are free to give between sessions and by their separation from each other and from the administrative offices of the Commonwealth."

Nor do academic institutions provide much help in this regard. As individuals, faculty members participate in state and local government study commissions, as well as carrying on their private research, but in spite of these efforts, academic research is a negligible factor in the conduct of public affairs in Pennsylvania.

The same statement can be made of the political parties, neither of which does any significant research or has a research agency worthy of the name. In Pennsylvania, politics is played "by ear" in much the same manner as that of the old time bosses Quay and Penrose.

Interest groups, including labor, are equally unproductive. At best their efforts are second rate because they lack skilled researchers and have only narrow interests. Pressure groups, such as the liquor and billboard lobbies, show great skill at political infighting when their interests are affected. But when it comes to the consideration of broad questions of public policy the Economy League is in a special class. It has the research field pretty much to itself and is quite willing to admit or assert its superiority to other organizations for performing the task to which it has set itself:

To the League, the interaction of State policies and local administration is one of the continuous processes which we clock and test and predict. We are able, as few others are, to see it through its whole development — in legislation, in state administration, and in local government. . . . We are also able to take our time. The elected official is a crowded man, racing against the calendar, the next election, and the momentary pressure. The League has permanence. . . .

IV

Pennsylvania is noted for the intensity of its politics. From the office of alderman to the office of governor, the game is played for keeps. Pennsylvania is also noted for the fact that in it labor and management have been more active politically than in any other state, with the possible exception of Michigan. It therefore seems strange that an organization like the PEL has been able to operate so effectively and with relative freedom from political attack.

There have been occasional protests from groups adversely affected by League recommendations, but no group or other individual has gone so far as Anthony J. Federoff, President of the Steel City Industrial Union Council (CIO), when he sarcastically proposed that city and county office holders abdicate in favor of government by the Economy League. "What is the use," he asked, "of elective officials if they are going to turn over their duties to the Pennsylvania Economy League? We can save the taxpayers a lot of money in salaries and election costs by getting rid of the office holders."

In spite of such adverse remarks, the League continues to enjoy great prestige. As Beverly Smith said in 1951, the League is "a freak, a none-such, a what is it,—it is backed primarily by Republican money but is consulted and trusted by many Democratic communities."

This bipartisan influence deserves further illustration. For some years the League has been a principal source for measures introduced by Republican legislators, even when the proposals disagreed with the programs advocated by Republican governors. It continued to render this service to legislators after the Democratic administration took over in 1955. Its political orientation broadened when it was called in to offer tax recommendations, on the basis of objective study, that would break an executive-legislative stalemate of seventeen months' duration. But the League acquired its greatest influence in the administration of the Democratic Governor, David L. Lawrence. At that time, in effect, the Pittsburgh alliance which was referred to earlier in this article was transferred to Harrisburg.

During the thirteen years that Lawrence had been Mayor of Pittsburgh, his chief advisers on management problems and the principal architects of the city's fiscal program had been the staff of the League's Western Division, especially its research director, David Kurtzman. After he became Governor, one of Lawrence's first acts was to appoint a bipartisan tax commission staffed by League experts. He also chose David M. Baldwin, a long time research associate with the League, as his Budget Secretary. The League and Lawrence were brought even closer by constant consultations between David Kurtzman and the Governor's staff. Just how close this association was can be seen from a Pittsburgh paper's report on a press conference held shortly after Lawrence assumed office: "The Governor presented the state's financial picture at a press conference yesterday. He was assisted in negotiating the more intricate phases of the complex situation by David H. Kurtzman, research director of the Pennsylvania Economy League." Some months later, in September, 1959, Kurtzman was appointed Secretary of Administration. As the Harrisburg bureau of the *Post-Gazette* reported: "Dr. Kurtzman, of Pittsburgh, will go on a leave of absence from the Pennsylvania Economy League to assume the $20,000-a-year state job which he has directed unofficially since the outset of the administration."

There is irony in the present situation. A major issue in recent campaigns has been Republican charges that Democratic administrations have produced a bad "tax climate" in Pennsylvania and that the state is losing industries. These charges were based on studies published by the Western Division of the Economy League. When David Lawrence became Governor he drew up a tax program under League guidance and used every device at his command to secure its adoption. He was opposed by a small group of Democrats, but the main obstacle in his path was a united front of Republican assemblymen, erstwhile allies of David Kurtzman and the PEL.

V

The tax controversy emphasizes what has become the main objective of the PEL. In early years it sought to reduce governmental expenses and to improve the machinery of administration. More recently, it appears to have switched to the promotion of state and local tax measures which would reduce the burden on corporations. Its concern with taxes is often obscured by the League's work in the managerial and personnel fields. But it is shown clearly by the part the League played in eliminating the machinery tax and instituting the wage tax, in servicing tax advisory commissions and legislative committees, and in preparing the budgets for state and local governments. For example, in 1959 PEL told its members that a change in the tax laws to permit pro-rata exemption of foreign manufacturing corporations was "the result of League suggestions and follow through."

Most of the time, however, the League is silent about its successes in the tax field. Only occasionally does a definite evaluation of its efforts creep into publication. A speech before the Washington County Branch of the PEL by Mr. D. C. Duvall, Assistant to the President of Pittsburgh Steel Company, is an example:

> *Under Pennsylvania law, there is no state tax on a manufacturer's personal income. A manufacturer cannot be taxed on his machinery and inventory, nor under the sales tax, on the materials and components he buys for manufacturing. Beginning next January, he will enjoy the state-wide manufacturer's exemption from the capital stock and franchise tax. Two years from now, the manufacturers state capital net income tax is slated by statute to drop from 6% to 5%. . . . Using a broad-based tax structure at both state and local levels in Pennsylvania will tend to reduce proportionate share of government expenditures paid by corporations, particularly those engaged in manufacturing activities. Dramatic evidence of this is the fact that although corporation taxes accounted for almost one-half of the state's general purpose income in the biennial fiscal period in May, 1957, the corporate share will drop to approximately one-third of the total anticipated income for the succeeding two year period.*
>
> *Much — if not all the credit for this can be laid at the door of the Pennsylvania Economy League. . . .*

The successes of the League have not gone entirely unnoticed. Observers of Pennsylvania politics like union leader Federoff regard it as a pressure group concerned particularly with the reducing of the tax obligations of its corporate members. Although the professional staffs of the PEL would not answer to the name lobbyist, their actions in Harrisburg, Philadelphia, Pittsburgh and in scores of county courthouses and city halls throughout the Commonwealth clearly reveal their calling.

VI

Many politicians are aware of the power exercised by the PEL, but feel that they are in no position to do anything about it. Democratic politicians, though critical of the League in private, are often among the first to seek its advice publicly. The gratuitous offer of high priced talent is difficult to reject, especially since the offer is sweetened by the knowledge that neither the public official nor his party will be singled out for condemnation by the League report. Coöperation with the League has been "good politics" for Democratic officials in a number of communities. Conversely, in these very same areas, League activity has placed Republican candidates in a form of political strait jacket. Since financial support of both the League and the Republican party comes from the same source, the money men are in a position to scuttle the campaign of a Republican candidate who becomes too critical of Democratically administered programs initiated and pushed by the League. Moreover, the incentive to finance the local party deteriorates as objectives are realized through the coöperation of Democratic incumbents. It is common knowledge that the Allegheny County Republican Finance Committee which contributes substantially to the national party committees, has practically starved the local Republican party and in recent elections has put the state committee on short rations.

Fortunately for the Republican party this situation is not universal since more than half of the state's 67 counties contain no League organization. Interestingly, these non-League counties include the highest percentage of registered and voting Republicans. An educated guess would probably show a high correlation between the money resources, staff and activity of the League and the Democratic rankings of the thirty counties having PEL affiliates. Of course, some politicians are scarcely aware of the importance of the League. They dismiss it, as one Republican county chairman did when he called it "just another one of those business groups," although, in fact, the League has made several significant studies in his own district.

Political leaders have been prone to take the easy way out of prickly problems by abdicating their responsibilities to the League. Many do it from the best motivations, sincerely believing that the League will render a truly public service. The alternatives of unwieldy, amateurish study commissions or expensive consultants from outside agencies are quickly dismissed by the financially embarrassed, research-starved municipalities in favor of expert advice, at no cost, from the Economy League. A trend has developed in numerous communities, where controversial issues have been avoided or evaded, to call in the appropriate League unit to conduct a study and make recommendations. Leslie J. Reese, former Executive Director of the Western Division, wrote in 1958: "Everywhere in the Western Pennsylvania community there is the growing feeling that when a serious problem exists, if it requires extensive research, or involves more efficient use of the community dollar . . . then 'Let's ask the League to study it.'"

The public image that the Economy League has fostered can best be illustrated by the experience of former Governor George M. Leader (D) who used about 150 consultants, both agencies and individuals, during his administration. Republicans, Democrats and most of the Pennsylvania press attacked the Governor for hiring "outsiders," for paying "high" consultant fees, and for not using the League to more advantage, even though Leader did call in the PEL for a number of studies. However, since the state government was not adequately staffed with experts, Governor Leader deemed it advisable to employ outsiders as a check on the recommendations that were submitted by the League and other research consultants. It is not unreasonable to say that one of the worst beatings Leader took politically stemmed from his use of these outside agencies.

VII

The implications of this analysis of the PEL go beyond the identification and evaluation of its rôle in the decision-making process to the serious issues of the form and operations of our representative system of government. A continuation of the present trend whereby public authorities are dependent upon the services of a private organization bodes ill for our democratic processes. The evidence presented above shows that the research weapon has brought the League, in its capacity as fact-gatherer, into the inner circle of decision makers. The evidence shows that the PEL has been a formulator of public policy; in some instances it has been responsible also for the administration of its own proposals.

Although it may be claimed that the League's functions are merely advisory, managerial and routine, enough data exist to show that many really crucial decisions may be made at these stages. The innocuous statement that the League "provided staff assistance to the new administration in putting the Governor's budget together . . ." may, in time, mean that "the League, by virtue of its parallel operations at the state and local government levels, enjoys a unique capacity to render objective assistance in the formulation of state policies and programs affecting its local subdivisions." If the League has a hand in drafting budgets and recommending personnel, it automatically plays a significant rôle in the kind of government a community, a county or a state will have.

The argument that the League is only one of a number of groups concerned with state and local problems does not give adequate weight to the organization's position in the power structure or to its record of accomplishments. Other groups engage in research, but the "countervailing force" theory has little application in Pennsylvania where most organizations do not have the resources, staff, or opportunity to present effectively their claims. The League is privy to governmental needs and designs, and often has supplied its findings and recommendations before other groups are aware that their interests are being affected. Moreover, the scope and quality of the services provided by the League are far superior to those any other single group could render. Even professional outside consultants are at a disadvantage when competing against the League's free service. This fact alone produces, or should produce, reservations about the "impartiality" of the League. In a materialistic society wherein taxpayers' associations and corporations preach against "creeping socialism" by constantly reminding the taxpayer that nothing is free, it appears contradictory that the League exacts no payment for its services.

The increasing scope and complexity of government have led many observers to believe that "there must be no important policy determinations unless they are supported by thoughtful analysis and research." In the current literature on policy making, research activity is usually presented as a mere question of fact-gathering and given a neutral connotation. Usually underemphasized is the selectivity factor, that is the ordering, evaluating and weighting elements. Almost completely ignored is the follow-up or action-taking aspect. Norman Meller discussed these aspects in his incisive analysis of policy formulation by legislative service agencies and concluded that government research or reference bureaus were really active participants in the decision-making process.

In effect, the Economy League performs the functions ascribed to legislative service agencies and the sampling of examples presented above provides supporting evidence for Meller's thesis. However, Meller, Harrell and others who have stressed the need and desirability of research-oriented decision-making assumed that some public or semi-public agency would be charged with the responsibility of supplying data. There is no such agency in Pennsylvania where a pressure group, vitally concerned with the content and course of public policy, is a principal in the decision-making process.

In an era when science and research have a public acceptance that exceeds public understanding, government by research is gaining constant adherents. Efforts are made to seek the solutions of governmental problems by objective inquiry into facts and then to make the application of these solutions a matter of routine administration. Partisan politics becomes sterile and superfluous. As the area of assured knowledge expands, the area of decision-making by purely political processes is contracted. There are fewer and fewer alternative courses of action open to legislative bodies. If contemporary trends continue long enough, public assemblies, once the rubber stamps for political bosses, could become merely ratifying agencies for research organizations. This prospect is not wholly pleasing even if we assume that these research agencies would be public and responsible bodies. To lodge so much power in the hands of a special interest group is certainly a travesty on representative government.

Chapter IV

The
Legislature

Most state constitutions grant the legislatures vast powers to determine the policies of the state. This traditional position is carried over from the early period in the nation's history when the legislature was made the vital center of government as a result of reaction against royal governors. The prominent position of the legislature in our early history was emphasized by the fact that a majority of leaders at the state and national level had served in the state legislature, a fact in which men like Jefferson took great pride. In practice, this position of the legislature eroded during the latter part of the nineteenth century, with greater emphasis being placed on the role of the governor.

Although the loss of power and position by the legislature resulted, in part, from a popular loss of confidence, other factors, too, contributed to the loss. For instance, the change from an agricultural to an industrial economy gave rise to problems with which rurally oriented legislatures were unable or unwilling to grapple. The lack of legislative leadership weakened the position of the legislature, and the increased demands for services resulting from industrialization and urbanization complicated the situation in which rurally oriented legislatures failed either to face social and economic problems or to concern themselves with organizational problems that hindered their ability to function properly. The selections in this chapter illuminate the causes of legislative failure as well as the hope for legislative resurgence. They will familiarize the reader with a wide range of legislative problems and illustrate current legislative politics of state government.

Legislatures need to update their procedures and practices if they are to function effectively in a modern, industrial society. James Nathan Miller's article "Our Horse-and-Buggy State Legislatures" points out that the archaic conditions and attitudes found in many state legislatures are visible symptoms of an illness which is sapping the strength of state legislatures and making it difficult or impossible for the legislatures to face modern needs with vigor and realism. Mr. Miller emphasizes that the lack of adequate pay and expert help make it difficult for the modern legislator to perform his legislative function efficiently. Furthermore, underpaid legislators find it easy to accept entertainment and minor favors and to depend upon interest groups for expert advice on legislative matters. The independence and the effectiveness of the legislator is thus compromised to the extent that these favors and advice color his actions on legislative matters.

Few people understand the political limitations and frustrations facing the legislator. Richard Neuberger, in the article "I Go to the Legislature," describes his experience as a member of the Oregon legislature. The article gives an excellent account of the problems faced by a legislator in his attempt to represent his constituents. Emphasis is placed on the varied constituent interests and problems which complicate the legislator's effort.

A first-hand account of the problems faced by a legislator is presented by Duane Lockard in "The Tribulations of a State Senator," an article based on his own experience in the Connecticut senate. The positive role of the legislature in the governing process is emphasized, but the weaknesses of the state legislatures are also discussed. In many states the inexperience of most legislators has led to stringent controls by outside political leaders and has reduced the effectiveness of the legislature as a truly representative body. Lockard considers rural over-representation and its impact on state politics and points out that low pay produces part-time legislators.

In his second selection, "Legislative Politics in Connecticut," Professor Lockard shows that parties dominate legislative politics in that state. He analyzes the role of the party leadership and the voting behavior of the party membership.

The internal organization of state legislatures is of prime importance in determining their political control. Legislative committees are the essence of the internal structure of legislatures and, because of the nature of American legislatures, always assume a major role in the exercise of the legislative function. The significance of the legislative committee and the relevance of committee composition to political power is discussed by Professors Beth and Havard in their article "Committee Stacking and Political Power in Florida." The authors find that malapportionment of the legislature and a weak executive lead to the control of state policies by factions of key committees, which, in turn, have a vital effect upon state politics.

State legislatures have not been immune to corruption, but few cases have been documented by a member as is done in Paul Simon's article "The Illinois Legislature." This article, written by Mr. Simon with information furnished by a state representative, Alfred Balk, clearly demonstrates the effect of pay-offs on legislation. Mr. Balk contends that the modernization of state legislatures is one of the most critical areas of unfinished business in state government, and that such modernization of the legislatures would lessen corruption. Although the situation described in this article is not necessarily widespread, corruption in the legislative branch does exist, and it is encouraged in many cases by outmoded legislative organization.

A recurrence of interest in unicameralism has been apparent since the Supreme Court's ruling in *Baker* v. *Carr* and other reapportionment cases. Though state legislatures have not seriously considered unicameralism as a remedy for the weaknesses of state legislatures, interest has been shown in unicameralism as a solution to reapportionment. Some argue that under the one-man-one-vote rule a bicameral legislature based strictly on population is an unnecessary duplication. Unicameralism has had only minor success in the United States since the Revolutionary War, but Nebraska, the only state to use the system in the twentieth century, has been a staunch advocate since adopting unicameralism by constitutional amendment in 1934. "The House Nebraska Built," by Donald Janson, is not only an excellent account of Nebraska's experience, but it is also a study in the politics of change in state government when road blocks to change are effectively surmounted.

The Supreme Court's new-found interest in apportionment has focused both popular and expert attention on the reapportionment of state legislatures. Malapportionment of state legislatures has been a serious problem throughout most of the twentieth century, but it has grown more acute as the pace of urbanization has quickened. Prior to *Baker* v. *Carr* only spasmodic attempts were made to apportion legislatures on an equitable basis. Examples of malapportionment could be found in almost every state, and attempts to reapportion were frustrated by rurally dominated legislatures. In addition to the reluctance of rural representatives, many business and suburban interests opposed change on the grounds that rural legislators were likely to be more conservative than urban legislators.

The results of malapportionment were obvious and city people contended that rural legislators were unsympathetic to the interests and needs of the city. It was pointed out that rurally dominated legislatures voted against legislation desired by cities such as governmental reorganization, increased taxing power, daylight saving time, welfare legislation, and urban-type regulatory authority. The greatest neglect came in the refusal of state legislatures to allow cities to solve their own problems. In addition, friction occurred in the division of the state tax money, in the control of streets and highways, and in education, welfare, and other major services essential to the city. The failure of state legislatures to act on matters affecting cities caused the cities to turn increasingly to the federal government for funds available under many of the grants-in-aid programs. This, in turn, started a significant trend toward increased centralization.

The Tennessee legislature, which had not been reapportioned in sixty years, met in 1961 under the threat of United States Supreme Court action.

A suit had been filed to compel the legislature to reapportion, and by its refusal to act it brought on the historic reversal of *Colegrove* v. *Green.* In *Baker* v. *Carr* the Supreme Court left to the lower federal courts the task of deciding whether the apportionment in the state was discrimination in violation of the Fourteenth Amendment. The case recognized that voters may sue for relief from any unconstitutional interference with their vote, that a complaint of discrimination in violation of the Fourteenth Amendment falls within the jurisdiction of the federal courts, and that the claim that such a case raises a political question is not sufficient cause for a dismissal. The decision in *Baker* v. *Carr* has had greater impact on state legislative reapportionment than any other action in this century. Action has been taken by legislatures, although reluctantly and often under the threat of court action; however, some change has occurred or is occurring in almost all of the fifty states.

Malapportionment is well documented as a major problem in state government, but Robert G. Dixon's "Reapportionment: What the Court Didn't Do" is a refreshing approach to the reapportionment problem. Dixon suggests that the Court's reapportionment decisions left a number of questions unanswered. Because of the Court's emphasis on population and the sweeping nature of its opinions, Dixon points out that it will be more difficult "to achieve fair representation of the many interests and groupings and shades of opinion in a multimembered body chosen from geographic districts. . . . As the courts go forward in this new era of 'one man, one vote,' the task will be to assure both majority rule and equitable minority representation."

OUR HORSE-AND-BUGGY STATE LEGISLATURES

James Nathan Miller

James Nathan Miller is a specialist in public relations. He has contributed articles to the *National Civic Review, Harper's Magazine,* and *The Reader's Digest.*

Visitors to the Massachusetts State House on the Boston Common invariably come away impressed by its architectural beauty. The more observant also note a strong and significant omission: in the building's 170 years—from the cornerstone-laying by Gov. Samuel Adams (assisted by Paul Revere) through five subsequent additions—nobody thought to provide offices for the 280 legislators who are its major tenants.

As a result, working conditions for the lawmakers, who must act as

Reprinted from James Nathan Miller, "Our Horse-and-Buggy State Legislatures," *The Reader's Digest,* May 1965, pp. 49–54. Copyright 1965 by The Reader's Digest Assn., Inc. [Footnotes omitted.]

overseers of a 750-million-dollar annual budget and the operations of 50,000 state employes, are incredibly poor. Important private discussions are held on green-leather couches in public corridors. The secretarial pool for the 240-man Assembly consists of five stenographers. The message center is a honeycomb of alphabetical pigeonholes reminiscent of a fraternity-house mailbox. "My real office is a telephone booth," says Thomas McGee, representative from Lynn — and sometimes he has to wait in line 15 minutes to use it.

Archaic conditions such as these, duplicated in state capitols from coast to coast, are merely the visible symptoms of a deep and dangerous illness that is sapping the strength of our state legislatures and undermining the very basis of state government. Although we hear much about the federal government's push to take over state functions, there is also a tremendous *pull: the inability of the state legislatures to keep up with the racing demands of the 20th century.* Charles S. Rhyne, past president of the American Bar Association and a longtime leader in efforts to modernize state government, sums it up: "Our legislatures try to solve jet-age problems with horse-and-buggy methods, and in their failure they're *inviting* federal intervention."

These horse-and-buggy methods are clearly identifiable — and can be remedied. Ironically, the remedy involves divorcing ourselves from the theories of one of our greatest political philosophers, Thomas Jefferson. For it is Jefferson's dream of a simple agrarian society that today haunts the operations of our state legislatures. Jesse Unruh, Speaker of the California Assembly and a leading legislative reformer, describes it thus: "Jefferson's model American would till the fields by day, improve his mind by study and learned discourse in the evening, and for a few weeks during the winter, when it was too cold to plow, would travel to the seat of government, there to meet with his peers and enact just laws."

It is incredible how closely our legislatures are still geared to this image of 150 years ago. It is why nearly all of them convene shortly after New Year's Day, in the dead of winter. But, far more important, it is the reason for their worst internal inefficiencies.

To appreciate the gravity of these inefficiencies, observe the massive demands that society has put on our state lawmakers in just the last generation. California's 120 legislators, for instance, voting on the state's projected four-billion-dollar 1965-66 budget, are responsible for more money than was spent by *all 48 states* in 1938. Even tiny Maryland, which spent 67 million dollars in 1946, has budgeted almost 800 million for the coming year. Indeed, this year, for the first time in our history, the states may well spend more for goods and services (an estimated 70 billion dollars) than the federal government.

But the legislators' problems are not only far bigger in financial and budgetary terms than they were a few decades ago; they are incredibly more complex. William Nelson, director of research for the Missouri legislature, explains: "When I was elected a representative in 1943, the legislature had no interest in the mentally retarded, in civil rights, in the growth problems of the cities, in air or river pollution." Hugh Sandlin, an Oklahoma representative, adds ruefully: "I'm supposed to be an expert on everything!"

Yet most of our legislators are *not* experts. In our complicated and urban society, they remain geared to face the problems of a simpler day. And in three key areas the failure of legislature to adjust to modern realities is causing basic damage to state government.

Not Enough Pay

The very basis of Jefferson's citizen-legislator concept was that the law-maker should not earn his living by making laws. Today's voters seem to concur. For years, in state after state, blue-ribbon commissions have been recommending more pay for legislators; but when the matter has been put to the voters, in more cases than not the raises have been refused. The result: by conservative estimate, *at least 75 percent of our voters can't possibly afford to serve.*

How many people, for instance, do *you* know who could afford to devote most of their weekends and evenings to campaigning and "servicing the electorate"; quit their jobs for an average of two to four months a year; support themselves during these months in a hotel at the capital; spend anywhere from $1000 to $15,000 every two years for campaign expenses—and do all this on a salary and expense allowance of $4000 or $5000 a year? Yet this is what our state legislators, whose annual pay ranges from a high of $10,000 in New York to a low of $100 in New Hampshire, must do.

Who *can* afford it? Three groups, mainly: retired people, men with independent incomes and professional people. The last group is the largest—lawyers, insurance men, real-estate agents, well-to-do farmers, all with partners or families back home to keep the business running. Many of them are fine people, but they represent a very thin slice of America.

The solution is obvious. Pay must be raised to the point where it won't cost a man money to serve in the legislature. And what about the danger of creating "professional legislators"? Says Robert Crown, chairman of California's Assembly Ways and Means Committee, "This is the 20th century. The California legislature, for example, is the board of directors for a four-billion-dollar corporation. The average Assembly-man services an electorate of 200,000 people. It's a full-time job. We *need* professionals. In fact, I like to think I *am* a professional. Yet I'm paid less than my secretary."

Not Enough Time

In the simple agrarian days, the idea of requiring the part-time legislator to get on his horse and travel to the state capital *every* year seemed absurd. Every *other* year was plenty. Moreover, in order to guarantee that the legislatures would work expeditiously, strict limits were placed on the time they could stay in session.

Today in most states the regular legislative sessions, still held every other year, consist of three to six months of Monday-through-Thursday workweeks that give the lawmakers long weekends for handling affairs at home. Though a stopgap patchwork of off-year "special" and "fiscal" sessions has been developed in an attempt to handle the growing volume of business, the overwhelming bulk of the work is still concentrated at the every-other-year regular sessions. This attempt to serve 20th-century needs on a 19th-century timetable makes for pure chaos.

Charles Rhyne kept a record of the 1963 spasm of the Connecticut legislature. It lasted five months. In the first two months only five bills were passed. Then bills began to pour through—4000 of them in all. During the final few days they whizzed by so fast that many members had no idea what they were voting on, and the legislature actually adjourned while forgetting to pass an essential $6,400,000 education bill. A special session had to be called to remedy the oversight.

In West Virginia, a lobbyist cited his rule of thumb for gauging the quality of a legislature: "If they understand 20 percent of the bills they vote on, they're a fine bunch."

The solution: Legislatures should meet every year and stay in session as long as necessary to do the work.

Not Enough Help

Probably the sickest aspect of our sick legislatures is their failure to provide themselves with adequate staffs and fact-finding facilities for keeping informed. Laws can be no better than the information on which they're based, yet most legislatures are miserably equipped to gather information. This leads to the domination of the legislature by the governor and his executive departments. It is responsible also for the legislators' dependence on lobbyists. "We are forced to rely primarily upon the lobbyists for information," says Thomas Graham, Speaker of the Missouri House. And this can lead to domination by pressure groups.

Winton Hunt, chief clerk of the Oregon House and a former legislator, cites an example: "A highway was being built through my district, and I started receiving complaints from farmers that they weren't being adequately paid for damage to their land. To get a law correcting this, I needed more evidence; but I had no way of obtaining it myself. So I asked the Farm Bureau, a lobby group, to go out and interview farmers along the route. They came up with a fine report, and the law got passed—but I never did feel comfortable about having to depend on a farmers' lobby for the facts in this kind of bill."

Such help is perfectly legal. Most lobbyists work publicly and straight forwardly. For a legislature equipped to evaluate prejudices and special interests, the lobbyists' role is constructive. But *few legislatures are so equipped.* As a result, in a majority of states the lobbyist— well-paid, well-staffed, well-informed and working full time—has become the tail that wags the dog of the underpaid, overworked, ill-informed, part-time legislator.

Such subservience to outside forces can be greatly reduced. California's legislature, infamous a dozen years ago for its domination by lobbies, has shown how. In its fight for independence, the legislature used as a major weapon the development of its own fact-gathering facilities. Today it is superbly staffed and informed. Every legislator has his own office and secretary in Sacramento, plus an office and administrative assistant in his home district. A six-man reference service digs into questions submitted by Assemblymen. A legislative-counsel bureau of some 20 attorneys drafts all bills, and there are other specialized staffs to examine the governor's budget in detail and to conduct "post-audits" of executive-department operations. All important committees are staffed with full-time researchers, who spend months gathering background on important bills. For special studies the legislature calls on the universities for experts, sometimes hires outside consulting firms. As a result, the power of the lobbyists—who still outnumber the legislators four to one—has distinctly shrunk.

The Vicious Circle

The failure of most state legislatures to reform themselves works in a self-perpetuating cycle. It goes like this.

First, underpaid legislators begin to find it easy to accept entertainment and minor favors—office space, secretarial help—from lobbyists. No specific favors are asked in return, and it seems innocent enough. Even more elaborate favors—the use of an oil company's private plane by a legislative official, a Caribbean cruise for legislators paid for by a savings-bank association—can be explained away as deserved perquisites.

Last winter I learned how pleasant these perquisites can be when I was a guest at a party given by Harrah's Lake Tahoe gambling casino to welcome the Nevada legislature into session. I was treated—along with about 250 legislators, their wives and secretaries and secretaries' boy friends—to an evening on the house, complete with dinner, champagne and entertainment. Nobody seemed to question the extending of such hospitality by a regulated industry to its regulators.

Such relatively minor favors blend imperceptibly into the vast gray area known as "conflict of interest." Though every year brings to light a few cases of outright bribery, the most pervasive method of "getting to" a lawmaker is far subtler and less easily combated. Bryce Baggett in Oklahoma, himself scrupulously honest, describes what happens. "You start getting indirect approaches — offers to retain you as a lawyer, hints that the members of a trade association would like to place their insurance through your firm. Nothing criminal, nothing you can really put your finger on. It's there, but I'd hate to be the district attorney who had to prove that any bribery was involved."

While the great majority of legislators are honest, the cloud of suspicion created by continual conflict-of-interest revelations colors them all in the public mind. Thus the circle is complete: low salaries and poor facilities, causing low standards and poor performance, causing public disgust, causing refusal by the public to raise salaries and improve facilities — and around and around.

Enter, the Federal Government

When state legislatures, slow-moving and bewildered, resist reform, they create a vacuum that pulls hard at the federal government. The Baker v. Carr reapportionment decision, in which the U.S. Supreme Court decreed that the representation in both branches of state legislatures must be based on population alone, is a case in point. At the time the case was argued, 20 legislatures were violating their own state constitutions by refusing to reapportion their voting districts. Yet only 16 years before Baker-Carr the Supreme Court had said it did not want to get involved in the "political thicket" of reapportionment. If the legislators had done the job themselves, the Court would never have had to change its mind.

To appreciate the real tragedy of what has happened in our state governments, contrast their performance in the last 30 years with their once bright promise. Supreme Court Justice Louis Brandeis wrote in 1932. "It is one of the happy incidents of the federal system that a single courageous state may serve as a laboratory and try novel social and economic experiments without risk to the rest of the country."

In the last century and the beginning of this one it was the *states* that pioneered legislation in such fields as female suffrage, child labor, railroad and utility regulation, unemployment and old-age compensation, and factory inspection. But today the states — with a few honorable exceptions such as California in higher education, New York in support of the arts, Wisconsin in conservation — have become the citadels of status quo and the federal government has become the laboratory of change.

Why, for instance, is President Johnson requesting a federal law to clean the junkyards from our highways? Because the states, which could have long since abolished them, have allowed them to fester and grow. Why is the federal government moving into such areas as education, housing, mass transportation for the cities? A major cause is the failure of the states to do what needs doing.

"People have needs," comments Gov. George Romney, of Michigan, "and if state and local governments are unwilling or unable to meet those needs we have only ourselves to blame."

That is why we must drag our state legislatures into the 20th century.

I GO TO THE LEGISLATURE

RICHARD L. NEUBERGER

The late Richard L. Neuberger served in the Oregon legislature and the United States Senate. He wrote *Adventures in Politics: We Go to the Legislature* (1954).

If, in this hour of crisis for democracy throughout the world, you seek direct contact with democracy in action I recommend service in the legislature of your home state. There you will become acquainted with the problems and aspirations and pet schemes of your neighbors, and you will find out all you want to know about their virtues and their peculiarities. You will be told their intimate opinions on the ridiculous and the sublime—what they think haircuts should cost and how we can avoid inflation.

In the six months I have been a member of Oregon's House of Representatives, I have learned more about the people and government of my native state than in four years at its university. I am taking a practical course in American democracy. A meeting of the Utilities Committee, at which we stormily try to arbitrate the conflicting proposals of power companies and public ownership groups, offers a perspective on democracy never gained from textbooks.

Charles A. Beard and James Truslow Adams cannot tell me as much about representative government as a delegation of angry taxpayers from my district, demanding to know why I have introduced a bill providing pensions for firemen. And after I have defended the bill and listened to their rebuttals, some of the taxpayers still indignant, a

From "I Go to the Legislature," Richard L. Neuberger, *Survey Graphic*, July 1941, pp. 373-376, 410-412, Reprinted by permission of Mrs. Maurine Neuberger.

few halfway mollified, I somehow feel that I have acquired additional knowledge about my fellow citizens and what makes them tick.

At the desk ahead of mine in the fir-paneled legislative chamber sits a piano salesman. Next to him is a haberdasher. To my right is a prominent lawyer, to my left a longshoreman. I can turn around and talk to a Ford dealer who was born in the Scottish highlands. We are a cross-section of our state, and the issues we decide upon, ranging from the length of passenger trains to the test for pure milk, touch the personal lives of every man, woman, and child in Oregon.

Any American who is free and twenty-one may do what we are doing. Without fiat or permission from high authority he can submit to other Americans like himself his candidacy for public office. In these troubled times we hold this privilege in common with the people of few other lands. Cattle rancher or accountant, banker or freight brakeman, any citizen of the United States may put his name on the ballot. In our ranks we have all four of these occupations and many more besides.

It is part of the American tradition for political careers, whether destined for fame or obscurity, to begin in state legislatures. Jefferson, Clay, Lincoln, and T. R. started that way. So have many of our present leaders—President Roosevelt, Senator Wagner, Cordell Hull, Speaker Rayburn. This training ground of American politics is open also to those marked for the commonplace, and one of the pastimes of the public is to wonder who among us will become United States Senators and who will fade into oblivion.

I ran for the legislature as an amateur. It was an end in itself rather than a means to higher position. I wanted to see at first hand what made the wheels of government go around. Yet I am afraid there is something contagious about the ambitions which hang like clouds in our chamber. I am going to exert all my will power in an effort to retain my nonprofessional political status. I have no desire to straighten up pompously and think I am confronting a future governor each time I look in the bathroom mirror.

West Point trains our generals and Annapolis prepares men to command the fleet. For half a century Americans have proposed an academy which would equip citizens for careers in public life. To date membership in the various legislatures has been most nearly the equivalent of this. There takes place the sifting and winnowing that matches the weeding-out process at our military institutions; there men discover whether they are temperamentally suited to the great game of politics. A few win their epaulets and go on to Congress or the governorship, and the rest gradually fall by the wayside.

What is membership like in one of these forty-eight academies that offer embryo American politicians their first practical experience?

I arrived at our new marble Capitol expecting to spend most of my time considering momentous issues – social security, taxes, conservation, civil liberties. Instead we have devoted long hours to the discussion of regulations for the labeling of eggs. We have argued about the alignment of irrigation ditches, the speed of motorboats on mountain lakes, the salaries of justices of the peace, and whether or not barbers and beauty parlor attendants should be high school graduates. For two days we wrangled about a bill specifying the proper scales for weighing logs and lumber.

None of these questions concerns large numbers of people. Yet each question concerns a few people vitally. Two or three poultry raisers told me that a change in the labeling of fresh and cold-storage eggs would put them out of business. I have received several dozen letters from merchants in my district complaining that parking meters along the curb are destroying their trade. More mail has come to my desk about what high-powered speedboats would do to the tranquility of Diamond Lake than about a series of anti-sabotage bills in which the issue of free speech is said to be involved. The solitary "old grad" letter from a fellow alumnus of the State University has asked not for lower taxes or improved law enforcement, but for action to control Bang's disease which afflicts goats and cattle.

In common with most other states Oregon has antiquated county governments. The state must undertake innumerable functions that are purely local. These things may be fundamentally unimportant, but the people directly concerned do not think so. A farmer cares whether his livestock can cross a state highway. Jewelers are deeply interested in regulations governing the sale of watches. Residents quickly protest an unreasonable speed limit in their suburb. After five months in the legislature I am convinced that the position taken on these many questions of comparatively slight significance has a lasting effect on a political career.

A few doors from me lives a prominent manufacturer. Going home on the streetcar we have argued violently about free trade *vs.* tariffs, Roosevelt *vs.* Willkie, the New Deal *vs.* rugged individualism. Not long ago I received a letter from him. Looking at the envelope I was sure another clash of political philosophies was impending. But he was writing me, as his representative in the legislature, seeking support of a bill to prevent canneries from gutting Oregon's streams of trout and salmon. If I voted for the bill my neighbor's devotion to fishing would overcome his Republicanism and "all would be forgiven."

Here my neighbor and I were in ready agreement. I not only voted for the bill but made a speech for it. My anti-New Deal neighbor is one of my backers now.

A member of the legislature, I think, assumes reality in the eyes of a constituent when he does something which touches that constituent personally. In preparation for my political debut I diligently read Marquis James' "Andrew Jackson," Beard's "Rise of American Civilization," White's "The Changing West" and "History of the Pacific Northwest" by Fuller. Into debates on the general conduct of the state government I have injected facts and quotations from these books. My colleagues, I fear, grow a little weary of hearing me tell what Old Hickory or the founding fathers of Oregon would say and do were they in our places.

To these oratorical efforts I have had no reaction whatsoever—no mail, no approval, no condemnation. I have drawn a blank. As far as I can determine, my best speech (*sic*) has not won me as much political support as my mailing copies of the official legislative calendar each day to schools, labor unions, and commercial clubs in my districts. Nor do I believe that my worse speech has cost me as many votes as endorsement of a "no-first bite" bill which has offended some of the dog owners in my part of the city of Portland.

"Many small make a great," said Chaucer and in that light our constituents seem to appraise our performance. I received a letter from an elderly man, obviously in difficult circumstances. He was confronted with loss of his small house. For some reason he had been denied an old age pension. He recited the details of his problem. Did I know his rights in the case? I spent a few minutes looking up the Social Security law. Then I wrote the old man about his legal claim to a pension. I also wrote state relief officials in his behalf.

The old man gratefully showed the letter to several of his neighbors. It was read at a pension club. Speakers commented on it at the meetings of other pension clubs. Members of these groups began thanking me for taking a personal interest in the old man's troubles. People seem to feel more intently about an episode such as this, with its human aspects, than about broad general principles which apparently have no direct application to their own problems. I came to the legislature expecting to be judged exclusively by my attitude on a few basic questions. This, however, is only about a dozen inches on the yardstick by which the voters measure their officials.

Mail is highly important. Letters unanswered are votes thrown away. This is particularly true of personal mail which some man or woman has taken the bother to write in longhand. There are stock letters sent to every member of the legislature; these we disregard or reply to with a perfunctory "I will give your views all possible consideration." But a personal letter from a constituent, a letter which has come to us alone— that is a totally different proposition. A citizen interested enough to write his legislator is also interested enough to tell his neighbors and friends and relatives his estimate of that legislator. This is why, if necessary, we miss a session of the House to turn out the morning mail.

I am a newspaperman. Before going to the legislature I heard my fellow newspapermen criticizing the trades and compromises customary in lawmaking. I resolved to have no part of this. Through thick and thin

I would stick to every original promise. I would not yield an inch. My strength would be as the strength of ten because my heart was pure.

I am old and wiser now. My newspaper friends were partially correct, but they also were downright wrong. The legislature is as full of compromises as the Pacific Ocean is of water. Yet I wonder how else laws could be enacted at all. There are 60 of us in the House of Representatives. Thirty-eight are Republicans, 22 are Democrats. Some of us think Franklin D. Roosevelt is the greatest President since Lincoln; others are sure he is the worst. A few blame the world crisis on labor; a few others attribute it to big business. Some of us are from metropolitan Portland; others are from the wilderness of the Cascade Mountains. On a multitude of issues the area of disagreement among us seems as vast as the universe.

We include many professions and occupations. Among us are lawyers, real estate agents, editors, prune growers, school teachers, storekeepers, mechanics, and men who are out of jobs. Each of us has prejudices and predilections which others consider unreasonable. Some members hate and fear doctors. Two members are doctors. Three or four legislators belong to the Associated Farmers, an organization bitterly fighting labor unions. One legislator is president of the largest labor union in the state. A member from Portland is proud of his pet police dogs which he rents to movie companies. A member from a woodland district forty miles from Portland insists that police dogs have been killing his sheep.

Yet all of us represent the people of Oregon. They have sent us to their Capitol to make laws regarding medicine, agriculture, roads, taxation, schools, and a huge variety of other subjects. We have to agree somewhere or government will break down. We must be able to give and take. This was impressed upon me early in the session. I sponsored a bill proposing a State Resources Council. I wanted to provide for an appropriation of $60,000. The Ways and Means Committee informed me that unless the appropriation were half that, the bill would not even be considered. I swallowed hard—and asked for an appropriation of $30,000.

Democracy is the fusing together of many ideas and that is what we are doing in the legislature. I introduced a measure making it mandatory for Public Power Districts to recognize the collective bargaining rights of their employes. The bill also gave the state commissioner of labor the right to fix the wages paid by those districts. Republicans on the Utilities Committee were against the bill entirely. They wanted to table it. The Democrats sought its passage unchanged. At last both sides gave in. The Republicans agreed to allow the bill to come out on the floor. We agreed to eliminate the provision permitting the labor commissioner to stipulate wages.

Was this a compromise with principle? I do not think so. The wage clause in the bill was important, to be sure. Yet insistence on it would have meant adoption of no bill at all. Now, at least, an act is on the statute books calling for the recognition of collective bargaining. Perhaps a future session of the legislature will add the clause which we had to abandon. After the settlement one of the Republicans wryly said to me, "Well, neither of us seems very satisfied. I guess that means we've got a pretty fair bill, huh?"

"Politicians are as compromised as a kept woman," say my cynical friends. Yet the concessions we have made in the legislature typify the way democracy works, and by and large they have done considerably more good than harm. Representative Herman Chindgren, a farmer from Clackamas County, will support my bill to guarantee school teachers adequate notice of reemployment or dismissal, provided I reduce the required time from nine weeks to six weeks. I will vote for the bill of Representative Jim Rodman, a real estate man from Lane County, to waive the penalties on delinquent property taxes if he will limit the tenure of the bill to two years.

My political science professor in college never said anything about this, but I am sure that in this fashion laws were passed in Thomas Jefferson's time—and in this fashion will be passed one hundred years from now, if only we can hang on to democracy.

Our angriest battle so far has been over unemployment insurance. The lumber industry, dominant among businesses in Oregon, contended that any increase in the payroll tax would push it into bankruptcy. With equal emphasis both AFL and CIO maintained that a boost in the tax was absolutely essential to the security of the unemployment compensation fund. I entered the legislature a confirmed champion of labor's viewpoint. The controversy bogged into a stalemate. Neither side would budge. After weeks of pulling and hauling the question finally was compromised midway between the demands of each group.

That night the head of one of the state's biggest sawmills told me in a Capitol building elevator, "Well, you fellows didn't do so bad. That agreement is pretty good. I think it will work out all right." And the next morning over coffee and butterhorns at breakfast the secretary of the Oregon Federation of Labor observed, "We've got no kick coming. Labor will get along O. K. under the new arrangement. The compromise bill is fair to everyone concerned."

That democracy in Oregon—and very likely in other states—has been operating like this for a long time is demonstrated by the fact that at least half the bills we consider are amendments to earlier laws. Some of the acts thus amended are extremely old, going back to the days before the railroads were thrust into the Northwest. Quite conceivably the frontiersmen who carved Oregon out of the forest fastnesses were of the same mortal clay as ourselves. Probably they had to make concessions to the other fellow and the other fellow had to make concessions to them, and all the time they hoped that the legislators who came along in the future would patch things up.

Despite the chasms of disagreement there is a certain comradery among us which not the most savage debate can stifle or discourage. I think this stems largely from the fact that we in the legislature are not responsible to each other. Our only masters are those unseen folks back home, those folks whose letters are piled on our desks in neat stacks every morning. If Representative French assails my resolution for the construction of the Umatilla reclamation project, I tell myself that irrigation farmers in the 22nd district will take care of him at the next election. He, I am sure, is equally positive that taxpayers in the 5th district will deal sternly with me.

No matter how contentiously we may argue, we invariably refer to each other as "My illustrious colleague from the picturesque Willamette Valley" or as "The worthy and honored member whose historic district occupies so warm a spot in the hearts of our people." We can be locked in desperate verbal combat one hour, and then eat lunch at the same table in the Capitol restaurant the next. Not only are we independent of our fellow members but also of the executive department officials and functionaries who swarm through the Statehouse. We have only to make our peace with God and the voters back home who elect us.

Many of my acquaintances speak of "politicians" with amused contempt. The word to them connotes venality, bribes and a fat man in a checked suit doling out payment contracts. Perhaps I need stronger spectacles, but I have seen no more evidence of corruption or dishonor among my colleagues than among any other similar group of citizens. The majority of the legislators work hard. They want to do a good job. One of the reasons for this is not without its humor. We are addressed as "Honorable." Lobbyists flatter us like prima donnas. We are provided with imposing stationery. Suppliants seek favors and audiences. Pages fetch and carry at our bidding. As a result of all this we probably harbor certain modified Napoleonic tendencies.

Yet I think the very fact that we are overly impressed with our own importance assures the state zealous and conscientious service. No man shirks a task he considers vitally essential. We take ourselves seriously. Almost half of us are just getting started in politics. We have none of the sophistication of men who have been to the political wars many times. And always lurking in subconscious minds is the lingering hope of outdistancing the crowd and reaching the governor's chair.

The outstanding human shortcoming in the legislature is timidity. In front of most of the members, tantalizingly near, is the will-o'-the-wisp lure of higher office. The temptation is strong to avoid taking a position on red-hair issues. Why court disaster? One particular legislator can be depended upon to develop a stomach attack the night before a bristling question is scheduled for debate. We never learned the truth of the report that on the evening of one of these convenient "attacks" a well-tipped bellboy smuggled a sirloin steak and hashed-browns into his hotel room.

Men who are neither venal nor dishonest will try to dodge a controversial vote. Bills which arouse both bitter opposition and strong backing give these members some difficult moments. Caught in a pincer movement, they do not know where to turn.

Along with a Republican colleague, I put in a measure to raise the shamefully low minimum salary paid school teachers in Oregon from $701 annually to $1,020. A number of legislators moved Heaven and earth to have the bill smothered in the Education Committee. They hesitated to antagonize powerful economy groups, yet at the same time feared the displeasure of the teachers. I may have whittled a few years off these gentlemen's lives when I introduced a motion to discharge the committee from consideration of the bill and then demanded a roll call vote upon the motion.

But despite these examples of pusillanimity, I am not convinced that politicians as a whole are more timid or spineless than anyone else. I remember an article which appeared some years ago in *Harper's* by Charles Willis Thompson. Its title was "Wanted: Political Courage." He mourned the lack of valor in public life. Politicians, he claimed, were straddlers and trimmers. At the time of reading I heartily concurred in these accusations. I am not so sure now. I am sure, however, that Mr. Thompson himself never occupied any political position.

Among us are men from every possible level and class of Oregon's people—owners of dairies, a former president of the State Bar Association, the leader of the CIO loggers and lumberjacks. Are these men any less valiant as legislators than in their other capacities? I think not. What I do think is that no chance ever is overlooked to embarrass politicians or box them in tight places. Pressure groups demand commitments and will take nothing short of Yes or No for an answer. Newspapers seek statements on all conceivable issues. The privilege of inconsistency, vouchsafed to others at will, is rigidly denied us.

What would anyone else—your butcher, your seamstress, your dentist, yourself—do if projected into similar circumstances? "Politicians are just people," William Allen White once remarked. I am afraid that the voters occasionally forget this. Frailties allowed us at home are taboo at the Capitol. We can change our minds about how to run our business or which house to buy, but if we switch on a political question we are cowards and trimmers.

Pressure groups alternately cater to our fears and hopes, threatening us with political doom one minute and promising us unlimited support for the United States Senate the next. We are constantly besieged for jobs and favors. If we cannot deliver a clerkship or a state police sergeancy, we are regarded as political washouts. Even our personal effects and habits are subject to goldfish-bowl scrutiny. I was severely criticized during the campaign for attending a luncheon wearing a sweater. And, conversely, a suspicious farmer said he would not vote for me because I drove to a meeting in a large Buick sedan.

Yet despite all this — and it may be heresy to say so — I believe politics frequently brings forth the best rather than the worst characteristics of an individual. Our colleague who had been a rather drab president of the Bar excited our admiration when he led a long fight to obtain representation on County Welfare Boards for the men and women on relief. "I am successful financially now," he said, "yet who knows what tomorrow will bring? For the first time I fully realize the problems confronting people who must rely on public charity for food and shelter."

Later this legislator told me that his efforts in behalf of the reliefers had given him greater satisfaction than a dozen legal victories. Here, I submit, is one of the real reasons Americans seek political office. In all of us the crusader spark flickers. We no longer can be Sir Launcelot or Robin Hood pursuing the wicked Sheriff of Nottingham, but public service presents a chance to express these suppressed tendencies. Listless indeed the member among us who has not some underprivileged group he is forever championing.

Near me sits a dull and asthmatic insurance agent. His political views antedate the McKinley era. Little or nothing stirs his interest. Yet he has a cause. He has struggled for many years to get state appropriations for crippled and handicapped children. Inert and lackadaisical though he may be when any other question is under discussion, let the Ways and Means Committee fail to do something for crippled youngsters and he can leap to his feet in wrath and hold the attention of the chamber. In this, I am sure, all his long-distant boyhood desires to be a Canadian Mountie or a U.S. Marine and save the weak and lowly find bold expression.

A group of elderly women, advocating beautification of Oregon's highways and roadsides, came to the Statehouse with a bill to regulate and control signboards. By giving free billboard space to commercial groups and patriotic societies, the sign companies had built up a powerful lobby. No one would introduce the measure. The discouraged ladies finally came to me with tears in their eyes. They were ready to go home — beaten. I took the bill, gulped as I thought of the possible political consequences, scrawled my name on it and shoved it into the hopper. As they poured out their gratitude I could not have felt more heroic had I rescued Loretta Young or held the Tiber bridge.

The fate of this anti-signboard bill demonstrated vividly just how clever lobbies can gang up on politicians. The sign companies first got the Signpainters' Union to denounce the measure in general and me in particular. Then people renting their land to the companies wrote tearful letters implying that passage of the bill might put them in the poorhouse. I am convinced that a vast majority of Oregon's citizens, proud of the state's scenery and anxious to tear away the billboards in front of it, favored the measure. Yet to the legislature it seemed as if the public was in arms against the bill and it failed decisively.

In the time I have been a member of the Oregon House of Representatives I have not enjoyed conspicuous success in sponsoring proposals. I am a New Deal Democrat in a chamber where Republicans hold a tenuous but working majority. Although they have dealt me some hard blows my faith in democracy is undiminished. In most instances my colleagues, either in their personalities or attitudes, pretty much symbolize the districts from which they come. "If you send a rogue to Albany to represent you," Henry Ward Beecher once told the voters of New York, "then indeed he represents you." That applies to every state. Whomever the men and women of Oregon want as their legislators they can have.

If the other members do not share my views, my disagreement is not primarily with them. It is with the voters in their districts. I am certain that indiscriminate logging imperils the economic security of Douglas County. Yet if the people of that great fir belt want to be spoken for in the legislature by Representatives Gile and Hill, who are dead-set against my resolution for selective cutting of timber under the supervision of the Forest Service, that is their inalienable right. Patriots died at Valley Forge to enable the electorate of Douglas County to make that mistake, if mistake it be.

Some men and women despair of democracy because it is cumbersome and works slowly. In the legislature I have had the experience of sitting with men of many faiths, of many political creeds. Somehow, out of all our quarrels and differences, we have produced the laws under which the people of a great Pacific Coast state will live. Some of those laws I voted against; others I supported. Yet only a few of them are very bad and a lot of them are pretty good. Whatever failure there has been in the legislature has been the failure of the human machine, and that failure, I suppose, occurs in armies, factories, chancelleries, and everywhere else on earth.

Skulduggery has not gotten very far. A bill before us exempted parsonages from taxation. In committee a utility lobbyist sneaked into the bill an extra sentence. The sentence would have lightened the tax load of power companies. Leaders of the public ownership forces rose and pointed out what had been attempted, how the companies were using the clergy for protective coloration. The legislators hooted the contraband sentence out of the bill, although had it been presented to the House in bona fide fashion I am sure that many members would have favored it. So even though democracy may not be a perfect method of government, at least it is basically a decent one.

For the next century to come legislators may improve and revise the laws we are now enacting, just as we are patching and remodeling the laws which those early settlers adopted long ago. This is the legislative system, the democratic way of shaping policy. Faults and defects the system assuredly has, and yet after six months of active participation in it I am more convinced than ever that it is a system worth defending.

THE TRIBULATIONS OF A STATE SENATOR

W. DUANE LOCKARD

W. Duane Lockard is professor of political science, Princeton University. He served as a senator in the Connecticut general assembly, 1954-1957. He has written *New England State Politics* (1959), *The Politics of State and Local Government* (1963), and *The New Jersey Governor: A Study in Political Power* (1964).

In forty-two of the forty-eight states this year some six thousand state legislators will be chosen, and the odds are that you will hardly know the names of the ones you vote for, much less the relative merits of the candidates. You will be voting on faith because state legislators are not big news. Their records are little publicized; their campaign pronouncements rank with want ads for newspaper prominence.

Having gone through the process of trying to attract the attention of the voters in a campaign for the Connecticut senate, I am certain that most people are unaware of their state legislators. I campaigned in a district of some fifty-five thousand people in the eastern part of my state, and although the area is small it was impossible to meet and talk with more than a small fraction of the voters.

My qualifications for the job — that I had studied and taught and written on state government — were never very widely known, in spite of newspaper advertising, speeches, posters, and even one costly TV appearance. My political mentors, incidentally, were rather concerned over the fact that I am a professor. They were careful to emphasize that I had once been a coal miner.

Early in the campaign my party's candidate for governor spoke at a dinner meeting and I followed him on the rostrum. One man in the rear of the room said to the ladies at his table, who included, as it happened, my wife: "Who's this guy? Nobody ever heard of him; they sure were stupid to nominate him." My wife, without identifying herself, argued my merits but left him unimpressed. "You gotta be well known to win that job," he asserted with assurance.

From "The Tribulations of a State Senator," W. Duane Lockard, *The Reporter*, May 17, 1956, pp. 24-28.

How wrong he was! I won as an unknown, and largely, I am forced to admit, because the Democratic Party was doing well, for most of my votes were certainly cast by people who had hardly even heard of me. Campaigning and publicity helped me, no doubt, but the margin of victory must have come from those who knew next to nothing about me. Even now most of my constituents do not know me. On one occasion when I was introduced to someone as a senator, he asked me how things were in Washington.

What if you do vote for a name? What does state government matter today? With the hue and cry that has been raised about transfer of functions to Washington, surely the important decisions are made by Congressmen rather than by state legislators. I might have agreed with this at one time, but not now. You grant more power than you probably realize when you vote for a state legislator.

For one thing the Eisenhower Administration came to power pledged to return more powers to the states and stop the "usurpation of our liberties" through growth of "bureaucracy in Washington." It has turned back a few of those powers, notably the control over tidelands oil, and its program of "partnership" on water and land resources promises more in that direction. Eisenhower's Commission on Intergovernmental Relations made a strong appeal not so much for the return of powers to the states as for retaining powers there and for placing as much responsibility as possible for future problems at the states' doors.

Even if these current developments had never taken place, the role of state government would still be significant. We can confidently expect the state legislators chosen this fall to pass about twenty-five thousand bills, to spend perhaps $20 billion, and to make some crucial decisions on such matters as highways, education, public welfare, mental health, transportation, labor relations, civil rights, and control over local governments.

Musical Chairs

Roughly half of the six thousand legislators you are going to elect will be entering the legislatures for the first time. Most legislators cannot afford to serve more than one term. In Connecticut we are paid a handsome $300 a year for the months of work we put in at Hartford. You have to be rich, retired, or crooked not to suffer financially in most state legislatures.

The game of musical chairs at the state capital cuts the efficiency of the legislature. It is a rare first-termer who can contribute much. A handful of veteran legislators and in many, if not most, states a few party leaders make the important decisions. Even the conscientious newcomer can be misled into playing the game of the crafty few. I once voted unknowingly for a bill containing a rider exempting legislators from highway tolls while increasing them for other motorists. It was weeks after the close of the session before most of us realized that the rider had been stuck in by the chairman of the house's finance committee. Although the bill has since been repealed, few actions of the Connecticut General Assembly have done more to lower its prestige, and it illustrates the power the well-placed few can exercise.

Not even committee chairmen in Connecticut wield more power than the party leaders, however, and by party leaders I do not mean the majority and minority leaders but persons outside the legislature. State party chairman and important city and county leaders are often the ones who decide a bill's fate. Caucuses are held frequently—in the senate daily and in the house once or twice a week—and there the party position is decided. Once the decision is made it is unusual for a legislator to vote independently.

At times I refused to go along with my Democratic colleagues, but in general I did not find it impossible to agree with the group decisions.

One advantage of the caucus, whatever its drawbacks, is that the party in the legislature takes a stand as a unit so that the public may judge the party's policy. To have every man go his own way often is tantamount to elimination of responsibility, for, if my argument about the relative anonymity of state legislators is correct, the records of individuals are simply not scrutinized. The record of a party as a whole cannot easily be hidden.

Rule by the Black Box

In Connecticut the caucus combines with strong party leadership to provide a tightly controlled system. State party chairmen traditionally are strong in Connecticut. J. Henry Roraback typified the old-time state party boss; John Bailey is a perfect example of the more modern type.

Roraback ruled Connecticut's Republican Party (and it is said he ran the Democratic Party too at times) from 1912 until his death in 1937. Connecticut was a strictly one-party state for most of that time, and by ruling the Republican Party Roraback ruled the state. By judicious combination of rural Yankee voting strength and rising industrial, banking, insurance, and power interests, Roraback made the state safe for the well-heeled interests that backed him. To accomplish his end he exercised iron-fisted control over governors and legislators alike.

In the early 1920's, Roraback became displeased with one of "his" governors, so when Calvin Coolidge, then Vice-President, came to Hartford to make a speech, the governor was "disciplined." Every nabob of any standing in the party was invited to sit on the platform with the illustrious speaker. But where was the governor? Up in the remotest balcony, in the only seat he could find! The unfortunate governor in due course was denied renomination.

During legislative sessions, so the story goes, Roraback had delivered to him after every day's session a black box containing all the following day's bills. After examining the bills, he cleared, rejected, or suggested revision of them as he personally saw fit.

The 'Messenger Boy'

The day is probably gone when any one man can exert that kind of power from outside state legislatures (at least, one hopes so), but lesser approximations of Roraback remain in vogue in more than one state. Connecticut's contemporary parallel is John Bailey, Democratic state chairman. If you want to get a bill through the senate when it is Democratically controlled, you would be well advised to consult with Bailey. A Harvard Law School contemporary of former Governor John Lodge, a Republican, Bailey is independently wealthy, intelligent and incomparably well versed in the political and legislative history of Connecticut. He sits in on and influences Democratic caucuses, even though his power to discipline is virtually nonexistent, at least when compared with Roraback's. Although he refers to himself as "nothing more than a messenger boy for the governor," his actual authority in many policy matters is great.

Right now, Connecticut Republicans have no leader comparable to Bailey. Since Lodge's defeat for re-election in 1954, the Republicans have been unusually disorganized. His defeat was the signal for the beginning of an all-out fight for control of the party. The lobbyist therefore has to deal with at least three Republican leaders nowadays: the state chairman and the G.O.P. leaders of Fairfield and Hartford Counties.

Although divided, the Republican Party leadership still has considerable power in the legislature. For example, during the 1955 session the House (Republican) and the Senate (Democratic) took opposite positions on two education bills, and it appeared that both might fail, although there was some sentiment for a swap—each chamber agreeing to pass the other's bill in return for safe passage of its own. In discussing this problem with Bailey, I was advised to talk to a Republican house member who would in turn get in touch with Meade Alcorn, Hartford County G.O.P. leader, who would arrange the swap. Bailey told me: "If Alcorn agrees to go for this, there won't be any trouble. His word is good." Bailey was right. I made the suggestion to the House Republican, who talked to Alcorn. In short order both bills were passed without further difficulty.

'Improve It to Death'

It would be wrong, however, to assume that these political leaders are omnipotent. They are utterly unable to get some bills through and they cannot stop others. The primary-election law is a good example. Nearly every party leader around Hartford in 1955 was opposed to the idea of a primary. Why should they want one? As things stood, Connecticut was the only state without a primary in any form, which simply meant that it was easier for the bosses to choose their candidates in a convention without outside interference. Yet by luck, maneuvering, and the misfiring of one of the time-tested methods for killing a bill, the primary bill did become law.

Some Republicans were won over to the primary when they realized it might be a weapon to use against Bill Brennan, the G.O.P. boss of Fairfield County, who, they feared, might win party control in a convention. Probably the law would never have passed, however, had it not been for the misfiring of the "improve-it-to-death" weapon. This technique involves the amendment of a bill in one chamber so as to "improve" it (by making its restrictions more rigorous or its terms more inclusive), always in the hope that the other chamber will not accept the changes. Then you can piously point to your "record" of having passed the "best" bill, which the other chamber defeated. The primary bill made five trips between the two houses in this manner before both passed it.

In the final stages there was no place to hide; further amendment would have made it obvious to everyone that the leaders were trying to kill the bill. Thanks to the identification of the party with its legislative record—not that of scattered individuals—the political leaders' fears of the primary were overcome by their greater fear of retribution at the polls.

Rural Over-representation

The potential of our state legislatures to meet the problems of the people —by which means alone can the drift to Washington be stopped—depends on the legislature's becoming more representative and more efficient. In Connecticut, as in most states, the legislature is neither representative nor efficient.

It is not representative because the smallest hamlets have the same representation in the House of Representatives as the largest cities. One town with 261 residents has two members. Hartford, with nearly two hundred thousand, also has two. Indeed, the towns with fewer than five thousand—whose aggregate population is just over ten per cent of the total state population—have a majority of the house. (The population of the United States is two-thirds urban and one-third rural, but the rural one-third has about three-fourths of the representation of the state legislatures.) The Connecticut house is not representative of the urban population of the state—about seventy per cent of the whole—and in consequence urban problems are often ignored. Even though the largest cities are somewhat over-represented in the senate, the veto power in the house remains one of the most important facts about the politics of Connecticut. Rural voting strength in the house (which has been Republican since the Civil War except for three years in the 1870's) is allied with industrial and moneyed interests in the state to cut off such legislation as that aimed at raising the minimum wage for persons not covered by the Federal minimum-wage law.

Part Time in a Flood Tide

To be efficient, a legislative body must have adequate time for the lawmakers to give some consideration to the questions they must decide. In Connecticut, legislators feel lucky when they know what's going on.

Before you conclude that we are a bunch of dolts to get into such a position, look first at the demands placed upon a member's time. He is a part-time legislator to begin with. At $300 a year how can he be anything else? Time that he might spend studying bills has to be spent making a living. Nearly all the legislators commute to and from Hartford while the session is in progress. I spent more than two hours a day driving fifty miles each way from home to legislative hall. There are, in addition to strictly legislative chores, hundreds of minor errands to be run for constituents. I do not object to the task of acting as liaison man between the citizen and the bureaucracy—over unemployment compensation or eligibility for old-age relief and the like—but such chores take up time.

In the 1955 session of the Connecticut General Assembly we considered no fewer than 3,600 bills. I undertook to read every one of them as they came from the printers but soon had to give up. Later I tried to read the bills with favorable committee reports. Finally, in the end-of-session rush, not even that was always possible. All this work has to be done within five months. Constitutionally, the session must end when five months have elapsed.

Nor does the state legislator have a staff to assist him in research on bills or in handling constituents' problems. These jobs are his alone. One constituent, writing in to request a minor but time-consuming chore of me, said he knew I was busy and he did not want to waste my time, but could my office do it for him? My office! I had no office staff and indeed no office except for a corner in my hallway at home, where unsorted and unfiled letters, brochures, notes, and thousands of bills constantly threatened to bury my children under a paper cascade. It is the same way with most other state legislators. We are on our own, and you get worse laws as a result.

Patronage questions also eat away at one's time. In one sense this may be the most useless use of legislative hours, but by the mores of American politics it appears unavoidable. The staffs of Connecticut's local courts are politically appointed, and with each change of administration there is a turnover of court personnel. When I had originally been asked to run for the senate, I had warned my backers that I would insist on a veto on court personnel recommended to the governor. I did not want to control the process or to appoint my own slate, but I did insist on a veto.

Making this veto stick for one of the towns in my district was a touchy job. Those whom I did not deem fit to be judges were outraged when I objected to their nomination. Meeting after meeting, often lasting until two or three o'clock in the morning, was called to iron out the matter. The rejectees pleaded with me in hurt tones: "Haven't we served the party well for years? Why kick us in the face like this?" My argument that professional competence as well as party service was a relevant consideration for appointment made little impression. I finally got my way, but malcontents told me to my face that I would be denied renomination and that "some old jerk without your smart-aleck ideas" would be nominated.

Dogcatchers . . .

The number of utterly insignificant bills is downright incredible. These trivia are of three kinds: local bills for specific municipalities, insignificant administrative matters, and minor economic-interest conflicts.

In Connecticut a high proportion of the proposals we consider are strictly local. We deliberate bills to decide whether clerks can be transferred from one municipal office to another in a given town. We approve the number of dogcatchers a small town should have. I spent considerable time getting a bill passed to permit a change in the title of the chief of police in New London.

To these local bills must be added a great number of proposals that are of no general importance. Why should the Connecticut legislature have to decide, for example, whether cuspidors should be permitted in barbershops? To let such trivia be decided by administrative agencies makes far more sense than to ask legislatures to decide them. And where the local bills are concerned, it is foolish, not to say destructive of local government initiative, to turn over such questions to the state legislature.

. . . and Cat Fights

State laws regulate many professions and most businesses in considerable detail, and it is not uncommon for a business or professional group to try to rig the laws so as to trim down or eliminate competition. Insurance agents try to deprive automobile dealers of the sale of auto insurance. Civil-engineering firms fight individually licensed engineers.

Large garages try to keep gas stations out of the repair business. Liquor distributors oppose liquor distillers; one type of oysterman is against another; dentists argue with dental laboratorists over rights to dispense false teeth. An endless array of economic interests combat each other, all fighting in the name of free enterprise, public health and safety, or fair trade.

These conflicts come to the legislator. Often he doesn't know anything about the particular interest involved and would prefer to ignore the matter, but he can't. A drumfire of propaganda and pleading is his lot on each of these questions. I was deluged with material on the matter of the sale of insurance by auto dealers. Dozens of letters and telegrams poured in. Local dealers telephoned to plead with me — this in response to urging by their paid lobbyists to get after their local legislators. (I certainly got more than my money's worth out of the telephone company during that period. At times we had to take the phone off the hook to eat dinner without interruption.)

This sort of legislation brings out the least noble traits of legislators. The lawyer, insurance man, druggist, real-estate dealer, or automobile dealer who is a part-time legislator is not always scrupulously careful to separate his two roles.

One question often put me about my legislative experience is: Did you find that state legislators were crooked? Speaking of Connecticut, I must say that they are not crooked. Bribery is almost unheard of in my state. A few years ago a legislator was convicted of bribery in connection with a fireworks-regulation bill, but he was an exception. On the whole, there is probably less unethical behavior among legislators than among businessmen. Indeed, some more or less accepted business practices would be a ticket to political defeat or prosecution if legislators tried them. Whatever the reason — and I am inclined to think it is partly because of the absence of horse racing in the state — Connecticut legislators have a pretty clean record.

Another question I am frequently asked is: "With all the pulling, hauling, deceit, and backstage maneuvering that goes on in the legislature, weren't you disgusted and disillusioned?" I answer that I was not particularly disillusioned because I had watched the Connecticut legislature enough from the outside to see how the game was played, and therefore I have no illusions to be shattered. I admit that at times I was disgusted with the way in which my fellow legislators — and even I, for that matter — behaved. I sometimes made blindfold decisions and went along with propositions that I doubted, and I knew others were doing the same.

However, I have no feeling of revulsion about politics or about my membership in the legislature. Since the interests behind some proposals involved the pursuit of thousands or even millions of dollars, I did not expect the legislature to be a Sunday-school picnic. The stakes are high not only for those who seek monetary gain but also for those interested in court reform, mental health, or indeed the improvement of legislative practices. In the process of working for goals compromises are inevitable, even though it is often distasteful to have to make some of the compromises demanded.

Far from shrinking from political participation, though, I hope to continue it and I highly recommend it to my friends. Some fourteen thousand places are open on the ballot for state legislatures this fall. Are there any takers?

LEGISLATIVE POLITICS IN CONNECTICUT

W. Duane Lockard

W. Duane Lockard is professor of political science, Princeton University. He served as a senator in the Connecticut general assembly, 1954-1957. He has written *New England State Politics* (1959), *The Politics of State and Local Government* (1963), and *The New Jersey Governor: A Study in Political Power* (1964).

Although there is a voluminous literature on the organization and procedure of state legislatures, material on their politics is relatively sparse. The classic work of A. Lawrence Lowell, now more than a half-century old, still appears to be the chief reliance of scholars in the field. Lowell's thesis was that parties were relatively insignificant in state legislatures; virtually the whole of the subsequent literature agrees with this. In the case of the Connecticut legislature, it would seem that parties, far from being relatively insignificant, play a dominating role.

The Extent of Party Power in the Connecticut General Assembly

The study of party influence in a legislature necessitates a two-level approach: analysis of the role of the party leadership and of the voting behavior of the party membership. Several questions must be answered with regard to the party leadership. Are the party leaders an identifiable and cohesive group? Do they develop a definite program for legislative consideration? Is their authority shared with factional leaders capable of frequent disruption of the party program? Are committee chairmen or party leaders in the stronger position for actually forming legislative policy? Do pressure group leaders work through the formal party leaders or do they attempt to build *ad hoc* legislative majorities for their

From "Legislative Politics in Connecticut," W. Duane Lockard, *The American Political Science Review*, XLVIII (March 1954), 166-173. Reprinted by permission of the author and the American Political Science Association. [Footnotes omitted.]

bills through independent action? Can the majority party leaders put desired legislation through the legislature with reasonable certainty?

Objective answers to each of these questions indicate great strength in the Connecticut General Assembly party leadership. Leadership on both sides of the aisle in both houses tends to be highly unified and cohesive. Normally this leadership consists of the state chairman of the party, the governor, a few chosen but powerful outside party leaders (e.g., heads of large city machines and heads of county organizations), and intra-legislative leaders such as the speaker of the House, the president pro tempore of the Senate, the majority and minority leaders, and the chairmen of the most important committees. Choices of these intra-legislative leaders, while formally made through election by the representatives and senators of the party in question, are in reality made by the state chairman and the governor. Assuming equal ability and backing, the chairman of the party *not* holding the governorship is *relatively* more powerful than his opposite number in the other party (by reason, of course, of the absence of gubernatorial competition), although his *real* power is obviously less, since he does not have the patronage and authority of the governorship to back him up. Ordinarily, however, his "suggestions" are enough to assure the selection of approved intra-legislative leaders.

During sessions of the General Assembly the "outside" party leaders are in daily attendance at the capitol and can be seen in corridor conferences with the great and small alike. Each party chairman sits in on his respective party policy conferences and not infrequently he is the real leader of the conference. With few exceptions the men who reach the party pinnacle of the state chairmanship can expect (and they certainly receive) proper deference from their fellows in the legislature, and, significantly, most party chairmen in recent years have been men of considerable experience in the General Assembly. Since about half the legislators of any given session are serving their first terms — with all the confusion that this usually implies — the experience and prestige of the party chairmen are important factors.

The leaders of both parties develop definite party legislative programs covering almost every important issue of state-wide significance, although this does not cover the whole area of potential policy enactments by any means. There is some competition in the formulation and carrying out of this program, of course, as factional leaders in both parties do not always share the relatively uniform views of the leadership on all matters, but these factional leaders are definitely of secondary importance to the party leaders. On occasion factional leaders can effect compromises on certain issues, but instances of outright rebellion are rare and cases of successful rebellion rarer still. Committee chairmen, carefully chosen by the leaders (and not on the basis of a seniority rule), are in a subordinate position; they are contributors to the party program,

TABLE 1.   AVERAGE INDICES OF COHESION* ON ROLL CALLS IN THE CONNECTICUT GENERAL ASSEMBLY: 1931-1951

Year	No. of Votes		Senate Indices		House Indices	
	Senate	House	Dem.	Repub.	Dem.	Repub.
1931	21	18	95.0	98.6	80.8	90.8
1933	88	17	75.1	96.9	91.5	76.1
1935	53	22	81.7	89.8	89.4	81.5
1937	18	13	83.0	81.0	88.0	80.2
1939	49	11	78.6	64.3	91.8	84.3
1941	14	10	66.0	78.2	80.9	76.6
1943	30	17	88.4	88.6	86.8	80.0
1945	10	14	89.9	79.2	87.3	84.0
1947	22	8	90.3	86.2	83.9	77.3
1949	35	14	88.4	79.2	99.7	99.0
1951	8	4	100.0	96.0	52.1	74.5

*The index of cohesion is a measure of the degree of party unity devised by Stuart Rice. See his *Quantitative Methods in Politics* (New York, 1928), p. 209. Rice's formula indicates not only that a certain proportion of the party voted together but also the exact degree to which the party was effectively unified. By first determining the percentage of the party which voted either way on a roll call it is possible to calculate the deviation between absolute cohesion (or unanimity) for an index of 100, and complete disunity (with a 50-50 split) for an index of 0. In other words, a group of 100 persons who voted 75-25 on an issue would have an index of 50, not 75, since their deviation from complete unity is not one-quarter but one-half. The figures used in the table are averages of the several indices of the votes of the session, and therefore provide a fair test of the overall degree of party effectiveness during the session. All record votes for the eleven sessions were used with the exception of 116 marathon votes in the Senate at the opening of the 1935 session, when the major parties were seeking the support of the Socialists who held the balance of power. To have included these would have needlessly inflated the overall percentages for regularity. Unanimous votes are included, though they are infrequent. Special sessions are excluded.

not successful competitors of the leaders in policy formation. Virtually without exception, pressure group leaders endeavor to win over the party leaders rather than the membership at large. There is some pressure group effort to "educate" General Assembly members through letters and circulars and conversation, but usually this is an effort more to get to the party leaders by indirect means than to build up a majority from the membership contrary to the wishes of the leadership.

Does the voting on roll calls in the General Assembly reflect the attitudes and activities of the leadership? Do the party members vote as a unit when the chips are down and important issues come up for a vote? Or do they freely cross party lines and form factional groups voting with the leadership today and against it tomorrow? As the data in Table 1 indicate, each party sticks together with a high degree of consistency.

Unlike several other states (e.g., New York and Illinois), Connecticut has no constitutional requirement that every bill be passed by roll-call vote. As a result, there are fewer roll calls than is the case under the mandatory system, but roll calls when used are less likely to be perfunctory gestures and more apt to be tests of strength either within or between the parties. Consequently the high indices of cohesion of Table 1 are all the more striking. Note that at the very lowest point for the

Senate the average index of cohesion was 64.3 and for the House 52.1 — in other words over 75 per cent of the party voted together during their "worst" sessions. The rule, however, is very different from these exceptions, as these averages of all annual indices show:

	Senate	House
Republicans	86.2	82.9
Democrats	82.5	86.7

During one session (1951) no Democratic senator cast a single vote in opposition to his party colleagues.

Unanimous roll calls yield an index of cohesion of 100 for each party. If the average indices included a large number of unanimous roll calls, the high indices would merely indicate concurrence among all legislators rather than the existence of highly disciplined party groups. In fact, only 7.3 per cent of the Senate votes and only 3.3 per cent of the House votes were unanimous. In the Senate, majorities of the two parties were on opposite sides of the question 83.5 per cent of the time and in the House 80.7 per cent. The data in Table 2, showing the frequency distribution of the indices of cohesion, further illustrate the consistency of party solidarity.

Unfortunately there are few similar studies with which the Connecticut data can be compared, but where data are available the contrast is striking. A recent analysis of the Illinois General Assembly, for example, which used a different method for computing party cohesion, presents a sharply contrasting picture of the role of party. In his Illinois study, William Keefe employs a variation of the "party vote" formula used by Lowell; that is, he calculates the number of roll-call votes "in which 80 per cent or more of one party voted on one side of the question while 80 per cent or more of the other party voted the opposite posi-

TABLE 2. DISTRIBUTION OF ROLL CALLS, CONNECTICUT GENERAL ASSEMBLY, 1931-1951, ACCORDING TO INDEX OF COHESION OF PARTY GROUPS IN SENATE AND HOUSE

	House				Senate			
Index of Cohesion	Democratic No.	%	Republican No.	%	Democratic No.	%	Republican No.	%
90-100	112	75.6	83	56.0	190	54.5	234	67.2
80-89.9	12	8.1	25	16.9	25	7.2	39	11.1
70-79.9	4	2.7	11	7.4	22	6.3	22	6.3
60-69.9	8	5.4	8	5.4	54	15.5	9	2.6
50-59.9	4	2.7	5	3.4	15	4.3	9	2.6
40-49.9	4	2.7	2	1.3	11	3.2	7	2.1
30-39.9	0	.0	3	2.1	6	1.8	14	4.0
20-29.9	1	.7	10	6.8	15	4.3	5	1.4
10-19.9	3	2.1	0	.0	3	.9	7	2.1
0-09.9	0	.0	1	.7	7	2.1	2	.6
	148	100.0	148	100.0	348	100.0	348	100.0

tion." By this means he found that during the two sessions the percentage of party voting never exceeded 4.4 per cent, whereas similar calculations for Connecticut show that party voting percentages often went as high as 90 per cent and rarely below 50 per cent.

A caveat must be entered, however, about these data. The index of cohesion is a more reliable indicator of party unity than the "party vote" method, and yet either can be misleading. Such statistics conceal the issue behind the roll call; in one sense lumping all votes together is like discussing units of variable volume. One does not speak of a thousand units of wheat where a mixture of grains, bushels, and carloads is involved. In the case of roll-call voting, some votes will be on matters of no consequence to the party; on these the party leaders make no effort to line up their forces. On other votes, highly important matters of policy may be involved, and the leaders may be pushing every member to conform. A party split in the latter type of vote is by no means equivalent to a split in the former type.

Still, corroborating evidence indicates strongly that these average indices for Connecticut do not greatly exaggerate the level of party consistency in matters of general significance to the state. Indeed, for some years the average *understates* the case, since the leadership during these years never lost control on any significant roll call, although some members may have voted contrary to the party position, either because they were given permission to do so (for local constituency reasons) or because (in a very few cases) they were independent enough not to care about the attitudes of their leaders. The effectiveness of the House majority leadership (which except for three sessions in the 1870's has been Republican since the Civil War) demonstrates the point. In the period 1931-1951 there were four sessions (1931, 1939, 1945, 1949) when the Republican leadership never once failed to push through any bill put to a record-vote test; yet the average indices of cohesion in these four sessions show something less than perfect consistency. During these years the will of the leadership prevailed on every single vote of significance to the party, and this does not mean party and patronage matters alone, but matters of general social and economic policy as well.

The effectiveness of the Republican leadership in the House is also shown by examination of the bills which they *could not* get through the House. Between 1931 and 1951 there were 148 roll-call votes in the House, and of all these (if we exclude for the moment bills on which the party did not exert pressure — women jury service, birth control, gambling and horse racing) there were only seven bills on which the Republican leaders either needed Democratic help (one bill) or failed to carry enough Republican votes to win. One of these losses was erased after a day's effort by the leaders to bring their people into line. There was then a net total of 6 losses out of 148 possibilities. Equally indicative is this fact: of these 148 roll calls there were but 26 on which there was a divergence of more than 10 per cent of the Republican membership from the position taken by their leaders.

We are often assured that in the state legislatures the party's influence in matters of purely party concern—e.g., patronage—may be high, but that the party only infrequently musters its strength on matters of broad governmental policy. During the two decades under study, however, the greatest dissension was caused not by broad policy issues but by matters of concern to the party organization *qua* organization. At least 9 of the 26 issues noted above (on which there was significant party cleavage among House Republicans) were concerned with general patronage matters, specific appointments, or other intra-party squabbles. The remaining bills were labor and agriculture bills and two proposals to change the state legislature—all issues which caused friction between the component segments of the party.

The evidence leads inescapably to the conclusion that the membership of the General Assembly has relinquished to the leadership the power to formulate substantive policy decisions. Yet the formulation of these policies is inevitably a compromise reflecting the different components of the parties. At times, when contentious issues threaten to pull the party apart, the leaders will refrain from pressing the matter to a vote. Groups within the party are thus not powerless when matters of importance to them or their constituencies arise, and yet with all the compromising within and between the parties, the final and almost invariably binding decisions are made by the party leaders themselves, not by isolated leaders of blocs, whether regional, social, or economic.

The Bases of Party Control

Why does party leadership dominate the scene in Connecticut? How have the leaders arrogated to themselves this measure of authority over policy enactments? These are questions not easily answered; however, the following are all contributing factors even though they may fall short of complete explanation.

Party Strength

Organizationally speaking, Connecticut parties are strong. As the only state which has not yet adopted the party primary election, Connecticut finds that the convention method of nomination of state and local officers has helped maintain leadership control of the party organization. While it is true that a primary does not give the voters "control" over a political organization, still the primary introduces an "outside" influence so far as the inner organization is concerned—it establishes a permanent *modus operandi* for factional rebellion, something not readily available under the convention system. As a consequence Connecticut parties tend to be strong at the apex, and, needless to say, the top management of the party concentrates upon the activities of the General Assembly.

Party Competition

In social group behavior it is common for sharp competition between groups to stimulate high levels of cohesion within the groups. The very struggle for power tends to emphasize the need for internal unity. In part, however, this depends upon whether there is a real opportunity for gaining power, and in Connecticut the battle between the two parties is remarkably even. Nearly all state elections over the last two decades have been decided by very small margins. (Of the last 11 gubernatorial elections, 9 have been won by margins no greater than 2 per cent of the total vole cast.) Winning these elections — especially those for the governorship — is important to the party since it means patronage, prestige, and political initiative. General Assembly members — who are, after all, politicians — are anxious for victory at the polls and thus during legislative sessions much corridor talk is concerned with the possible public impact of the party program. In regular caucus meetings (toward the end of the session caucuses meet almost daily), appeals to the members in terms of the next election are not uncommon. Other things being equal, this can have a considerable effect.

Ideological Similarities

There are broad areas of ideological agreement within each of the major parties in Connecticut. This is an important consideration, since obviously the degree to which any group can be held together in their actions will depend upon the area of agreement prevailing within the group. Sharp differences of opinion — such as the existence of conservative Democrats in the congressional Democratic party — naturally make it difficult to present a united front. But in Connecticut there is no group to compare with the Dixiecrats in the Democratic party and no La Follette, Norris, or Morse among the Republicans. The general division of the two parties along urban-rural and -suburban lines (Democrats, urban; Republicans, rural and suburban) has tended to produce a cleavage along liberal-conservative lines, which, of course, facilitates the task of the party leaders in getting party unity.

Party Discipline

As a final resort, party leaders in Connecticut will at times discipline legislators either because of factional shifts which cut the ground from under the individual or because of disloyalty to the party program. Discipline can extend to a denial of renomination for the General Assembly and, of course, denial of higher offices on the state level, but in more subtle ways it can make the individual very ill at ease while in the legislature, both through social pressures and through refusal to grant legislative time for pet projects which the legislator wants to enact for his home town. Disciplinary action is not brought against every legislator who happens to step out of line (for some, refusal of renomination would be impossible, since they control the local nominating caucus), but for a good many legislators, and especially the ambitious ones, it remains a fearsome weapon and its ominous existence in the party armory is not easily forgotten.

In view of the widely held notion that parties are of minor influence in the state legislatures, what is the significance of the Connecticut situation? Is it only the exception which proves the rule? Perhaps this is the case, but the writer is not convinced. Even assuming the accuracy of Lowell's description of the legislature *circa* 1900, half a century's political change must be accounted for. The extraordinary degree of party influence in Connecticut suggests the need for further empirical analysis, since what little evidence we have on the contemporary situation is conflicting.

COMMITTEE STACKING AND POLITICAL POWER IN FLORIDA

LOREN P. BETH AND WILLIAM C. HAVARD

Loren P. Beth is professor of government, University of Massachusetts. In addition to writing several works on constitutional law, he is co-author of *The Politics of Mis-representation: Rural-Urban Conflict in the Florida Legislature* (1962). William C. Havard is professor of political science, University of Massachusetts. He has written extensively in the field of state and local government.

Almost all students of American politics recognize that legislative committees play an important—perhaps a transcendent—role in the operation of the legislature. As Woodrow Wilson long ago remarked, power is divided into so many "seignories, in each of which a Standing Committee is the court-baron and its chairman lord-proprietor." Committees assume such importance because of some peculiarities of American legislatures. Perhaps the key factors are the free introduction of bills by legislators and the relative lack of a party agency such as the British Cabinet provides to screen proposed legislation and keep the bills actu-

From "Committee Stacking and Political Power in Florida," Loren P. Beth and William C. Havard, *The Journal of Politics*, XXIII:1 (February 1961), 57-83. Reprinted by permission of the authors and *The Journal of Politics*. [Footnotes omitted.]

ally being processed down to a number which can be reasonably considered by a numerous legislative body.

The American committee thus acts as a sort of surrogate for a party cabinet, and it performs two of the major legislative tasks which the British Cabinet accomplishes. In the first place, the committee acts to cut down the number of bills, either by pigeonholing (as in Congress) or by unfavorable recommendation (as in many state legislatures). The effect—so long as the system works efficiently enough to achieve its purpose—is to allow the full legislature to concentrate its attention on a relatively few important pieces of legislation. In the second place, the committee holds hearings and debates the desirability of legislation (as does the Cabinet in a different way); this committee discussion, as many writers have pointed out, has more and more taken the place of meaningful floor debate, and committee recommendations are handled on the floor almost as respectfully as the majority party handles Cabinet proposals in England. Wilson appropriately said that "the House sits, not for serious discussion, but to sanction the conclusions of its committees as rapidly as possible." Thus the committee screens legislative proposals both quantitatively and qualitatively, acting as both judge and jury for bills which, Lord Bryce wrote, come to it "as a shivering ghost stands before Minos in the nether world."

For these reasons the committee system of many American legislatures is likely to be the focal point of political power and pressure, and the selection and membership of committees will determine to a great extend the kind of legislature which exists. The present study is an attempt to look at the method of selecting the personnel of the committee system of one state legislature, that of Florida, and to assess its relation to the total political process.

I

The committee system in any particular legislative body is conditioned only partially by the dominant motifs of the American constitutional structure. The overall political style of a given polity will affect all of its important institutional arrangements. And while many of the aspects of a particular style will be shared with similar political units that have a common tradition (*e.g.*, the Southern states), certain features will be unique. In order to comprehend the role of a single aspect of the Florida committee system, then, a preliminary adumbration of the main characteristics of Florida politics in general and of its legislative committees in particular is required. The sketch which follows is necessarily foreshortened.

Florida is often cited as the prime example of a disintegrated or atomistic political structure. There are no party or factional alignments organized on a permanent or semi-permanent basis for the attraction of voter support. In his campaign for office practically every Florida politician harps on his independence; in the folklore of Florida politics, "machine man" is the worst label that can be attached to a candidate. The personalism and extreme localism which became identified in a somewhat primitive manner with democracy at an early period in the United States were sharpened in the Southern states by the experiences of the Civil War and Reconstruction. The lag in urbanization, and the attendant concentration on "county-seat" or "courthouse" politics further strengthened this tendency in the South. A suspicion of political organizations other than those based on personal loyalties, a fear of institutionalization of the points of contact between the citizen and government (with its reduction in the effectiveness of personal political intercession), and the persistence of the idea of direct and instructed representation of county units are reflected in the political practice of the region. These ideas and the practices which result from them have produced a politics which ignores the possibilities of adapting democratic ideology to the socio-economic conditions of an urban-industrial society. The function of institutionalized political activity in creating the conditions for popular influence on government in the form of alternative policy choices, the coalescence of amorphous opinion into a rough majoritarianism, and the maintenance of accountability has been disregarded or inverted into a mythical threat to "constitutional" government. Such habits of mind have commonly been interpreted by political observers as contributing to a lack of popular responsibility which, in the absence of some immediately obvious focal point of political power, is the basis for characterizing the political unit as a conservative anarchy whose focus is on extraneous issues. But the filling of a political power vacuum is usually far too subtle for such an interpretation.

Considerable evidence can be adduced to support the idea that effective political power at the state level in Florida is exercised by a coalition of legislators who operate largely on an interpersonal basis. Although the membership of these groups in each house is somewhat indefinite (especially on the fringes) and their activities are largely *sub rosa*, the leadership and hard-core adherents are fairly easy to identify. The group is united through the catalyzing influence of a set of political attitudes which its members hold in common. Characteristically, these attitudes may be said to consist of an identification with the rural or semi-rural areas of Florida, a propensity toward nineteenth-century agrarian conservatism and a belief in the efficacy of interpersonal contacts as the means of settling political problems. Such viewpoints are reflected in policy orientation on crucial issues of contemporary Florida politics: the dominant clique in the Florida legislature is likely to be militantly segregationist, opposed to the institutionalization of legislative and administrative practices, predisposed to extreme decentralization, partial to the idea of earmarking the use of revenue prior to its collection and an advocate of special as opposed to general legislation for local government. The leadership of this group may have personal economic interests which it serves through diversionary appeals to these issues; the followers, on the other hand, are more likely to accept these attitudes and practices at face value since they seem to reflect the political habits of their constituencies.

The power of the dominant bloc is sustained by a variety of institutional factors in Florida politics, some of which are longstanding traditions of the state. The absence of a party or factional system contributes to the dispersion of political influence and to the subordination of issue politics to office politics. The Florida legislator usually takes his seat without commitments other than on local matters; the big questions are settled within the privacy of the legislative family, often without the embarrassment of a clear-cut record vote. A premium is thus placed on horse-trading and personal influence. Admission to the inner circle of the coalition is by cooptation; an ambitious young legislator must demonstrate ability in minor matters and conform to a well-understood set of legislative mores if he wishes to wield influence, for the positions from which influence is dispersed are within the power of bequest of the in-group. Attachment to a senior "advisor," a facility for remaining inconspicuous but useful during his early terms and adherence to a line that demonstrates his "soundness" on basic questions are indispensable markers of the route to legislative power in Florida.

Naturally, control by this informally organized group could not be continued without the support of a legislative majority, a condition that is assured by the self-perpetuating system of malapportionment of the Florida legislature. The automatic House formula is extremely inflexible; each county is guaranteed at least one representative and no county may have more than three representatives. The five most populous counties are assigned three representatives each, the next eighteen counties in terms of population have two representatives each. As of 1958 the largest county in Florida contained 846,800 people and the two smallest counties each contained 2,800 residents. The forty-six smallest counties elect a majority of the ninety-five-member House, yet they contain only 17.2 per cent of the population of the state. The thirty-eight Senate seats are filled from single-member districts and no county may be divided in apportioning the Senate. The largest district (Dade County) has a population of 846,800; the smallest (Jefferson County) has 9,500 residents. The twenty smallest districts elect a majority of the Senate but contain only 13 per cent of the population. When it is considered that about three-quarters of the Florida population are urban and nearly two-thirds of the inhabitants reside in the ten counties whose population exceed 100,000 each, it may be seen that Florida is an exaggerated example of the rural-urban imbalance characteristic of a number of state legislatures.

Some lag in the adaptation of the political machinery is to be expected in states with rapidly changing sociological patterns. Florida, for example, underwent a shift from a population that was two-thirds rural to one that was two-thirds urban between 1920 and 1950. However, resistance to political accommodation of these developments has been intensified by the fact that much of the urban development took place in coastal south Florida, in areas that were undeveloped before this century and had no experience of the political influences which dominated the counties that are now so heavily over-represented. Today, well over 70 per cent of Florida's population live in sectors of the state into which slavery did not penetrate. The state's net population gain from interstate migration between 1950 and 1957 was over one million; the overwhelming proportion of these newcomers settled in the coastal cities of south Florida, and a high proportion of them came from non-Southern states.

The contrast between these new, urbanized areas of south Florida and the sector between the Apalachicola and Suwanee Rivers (which was the heart of Florida in the nineteenth century) is acute. There are eleven counties in the latter area, of which only Leon (Tallahassee) may be classified as urban. Six of the fourteen Florida counties which declined in population between 1950 and 1958 are in this area and the remaining eight are on its periphery. Whereas urban south Florida fans out from key cities along the coast and makes its impact felt in the entire peninsular region of the state, the influence of Southern ruralism has a strong hold on the ethos of the whole of continental (or north) Florida, even in the counties with a high degree of urbanization. These north Florida counties are heavily favored by the malapportionment described above. Even though the rural-urban split cuts across this regional division to some extent, the small-county bloc in the House and the pork-chop gang in the Senate have built their positions of power on the political geography just described and have as their *raison d'être* the perpetuation of the *status quo*.

The power élite in the legislature have additional natural advantages in the struggle to maintain their dominance. They are the residual beneficiaries not only of an antiquated system of apportionment that gives more weight to area than to population, but of other institutional anachronisms as well. The Florida constitution dates from 1885 and reflects the political outlook of that time, with its exaggerated emphasis on checks and balances and its narrow confinement of policy. The office of governor, for example, is a weak one. The executive power is checked by a cabinet system in which six elective constitutional officers cut into the governor's powers not only as independent heads of departments, but also through their collegial functions as budget commission and administrative head of several key agencies of the state. Florida governors may not become their own immediate successors and no governor has been able to maintain a factional organization beyond his term in office. The cabinet officers, on the other hand, can be re-elected, are virtually impregnable at the polls and are supported by their own clienteles; as a result their political *modus operandi* has more in common with the legislature than with the governor. Lacking both a disciplined political organization and integrated administrative control, the governor is in a difficult position with respect to the exercise of legislative leadership. The dominant groups in the legislature concede the fact that the governor is elected by the urban areas (thus tacitly admitting his unique role as statewide representative), but they insist that this makes it even more imperative that the legislature retain its characteristic features: the locally instructed mandate and a collective rural majoritarianism. The governor is thus forced to deal with the legislature on its own terms in order to secure passage of part of his general program. This means that local advantages must be forthcoming in exchange for support on statewide legislation. And the concessions to legislative power that have to be made on larger issues such as constitutional revision, taxation and the support of public institutions are so broad that they are likely to nullify the intended effect of the program and to strengthen the legislature's capacity for resistance to executive leadership in the future.

A constitutional system which greatly restricts the powers of the governor under conditions which make that office the most important initiator of proposals for social change is of great advantage to a power group more interested in negative than in positive government. By the same token, a constitution which limits legislative discretion severely in most fields and naturally favors the counties from which the dominant legislative group is drawn is a great boon to the type of politics described here. By minimizing the necessity for direct action these features of the system allow broad scope for service to local areas and for political brokerage on behalf of economic pressure groups. Given the complexities of the legislative process, it is usually far easier to defeat legislation than to pass it; passage of a piece of legislation requires a victory at every one of a long series of hazardous stages, whereas an apparently minor setback at any point may deny a bill any further consideration during the session.

Under appropriate circumstances power may not only be used negatively to achieve a consistent public policy, but may lend itself to subtleties of indirection that are denied to those seeking positive action. Among the circumstances most appropriate to the negative use of power is control of the procedures by which legislation may be forestalled without forcing a public commitment on an issue. Naturally, the positions of leadership and the influence that may be exerted through them (by way of either formal or informal investitures) are important determinants of legislative performance. In the Florida legislature the presiding officers of the two houses and the committees are the most important repositories of procedural power.

The presiding officers are elected by the members of their respective chambers and they serve during only one regular sixty-day biennial session. The techniques by which the speakers of the House and the president of the Senate are selected serve as substitutes for party or fractional nomination in allowing loose coalitions to form around various candidates. In the House of Representatives, the speaker-designate is usually elected by Democratic caucus (comprising over 90 per cent of the House) early in the session preceding the one in which he will hold office. An aspirant for the position, however, must begin to line up "pledges" from the House membership in the session prior to the one at which he is named speaker-designate. Thus the campaign for the speakership usually begins four years in advance of the assumption of office, a factor which makes for numerous long-range commitments and gives the successful candidate a span of influence that is far longer than his period in office. In the Senate the president has recently been designated one session in advance of his assumption of office, too. Senators are elected for four-year terms, but the membership is rotated for each session by having half of them elected at each biennial election. For a number of years it was customary for the selection of the president to be made by the nineteen holdover senators and for these members to choose as president-designate one of the senators who was up for election in the interval between his selection and assumption of office. Events of the past three sessions raise doubts as to the future of this practice; the last two selections were made after the candidate had been re-elected to a Senate seat, and the 1961 president has not been designated as yet.

Both presiding officers have extensive powers within their chambers. The appointment of committees and the authority to refer bills to them are foremost among these powers. In making committee appointments the speaker and president are not limited by the demands of a party organization or by usages such as a seniority system. They are, therefore, free to use this power as they will in making commitments in advance of their selection, in bargaining for their own political future and in creating influence blocs.

The power of reference complements the power of committee appointment. References in both houses are practically always final, although there are possibilities for the House of Representatives to override a speaker's referral by majority vote and for the Senate to change the president's reference by a two-thirds vote. There is one important difference between the powers of the president of the Senate and the speaker of the House in this connection. The Senate president is permitted to refer any bill to more than one committee. In such cases the bill is considered by the committees in the order in which reference was made, rather than simultaneously. Since an unfavorable report by any one committee has the effect of tabling a bill unless a two-thirds vote can be attained in favor of placing it on the calendar, and since the regular session lasts only sixty days, a bill referred to two or more committees may be considered safely buried. The House speaker is not allowed to make multiple references except for bills involving taxes or appropriations, which *must* be referred to the appropriations or finance and taxation committee and *may* be assigned to another committee as well. The House may, by majority vote, approve other multiple references. In both chambers reference to more than one committee (except for the aforementioned fiscal bills) is usually considered a kiss of death for the measure.

The Florida committee system exhibits certain faults that are generally characteristic of state committee organization—there are too many committees, their responsibilities are not clearly defined in terms of the legislation they are to consider and a few of them are of paramount importance while the others are insignificant in the total legislative process. In recent sessions the House has used as many as fifty-four committees and the Senate thirty-nine (every senator except the president chairs a committee). Technically, the committees may not kill bills by pigeonholing them since the rules require that House bills be reported back within fourteen days and Senate bills within ten days after reference. However, committees can and do ask for extensions of time on individual bills and blocs of bills, and these are disposed of in committee through repeated requests for additional time. In addition, some bills are pigeonholed when they are introduced too late in the session to come under the time-limit rule. The most formidable direct power of legislative committees in Florida, however, is the power to report a bill unfavorably, which has the effect, as noted earlier, of automatically tabling the bill. Given the prestige of the committee system, it would be a rare occasion indeed if a proponent of an unfavorably reported bill should muster the two-thirds vote necessary to bring the bill before the chamber.

The committees on rules and calendar of the respective houses are in especially influential positions. In the House of Representatives this committee is permitted to take charge of the calendar during the last thirty days of a regular session by bringing in a special order of business for each succeeding day. The order so prescribed can be altered only by a two-thirds vote. In the Senate, with its more leisurely pace, the rules committee has this power only in the last ten days of the regular session; again a two-thirds vote is required either to remove a bill from the special order calendar or to consider a bill not included in it. The short session of the legislature results in a typical end-of-session crowding of the calendar, so the rules committees have virtually life-or-death control over much of the major legislation of any session.

Committee chairmanships in Florida do not carry much in the way of prerogatives that would permit direct control over legislation. There is some flexibility in the number and length of committee sessions which the chairman may utilize for tactical purposes, and he can control the agenda of meetings within the time limits for reporting bills. On the whole, however, his influence derives mainly from undefined increments of power that relate to prestige, specialization and personal relationships with House or Senate leaders. Appointment to the chairmanship of one of the more important committees is sufficient indication of influence in itself. Most chairmen utilize this initial advantage to maintain personal predominance on the committee and can extend their spheres of influence by acting as spokesman for their committees both publicly and in informal conference with other leaders.

In sum, it may be said that the committee role in Florida politics is a most important one. Standing committees are charged with functions that are crucial to the legislative process and they are vested with the powers necessary to carry out these functions. The reluctance of Florida politicians to work through overt political organizations and the consequent obscurity in the location of political power further enhance their prestige as "independent" institutional devices. The skill with which the legislative leadership utilizes the committee system to maintain a dominant informal, and only partially acknowledged, organization is a major factor in the overall political system in Florida. These skills are manifested primarily in committee selection and in the interrelations of committee personnel who perform the leadership function for the majority bloc in the legislature.

II

The committees used for this study have been selected to illustrate three forms of "stacking." The first form is the stacking of those committees which are most important in the substantive work of each house. The second deals with certain committees which handle matters relating to specific economic interests. The third example is the so-called "dog-house" committee in the House, which is used by way of contrast. In addition, we have investigated the degree to which committee assignment is used as a device to create and perpetuate a ruling rural oligarchy in the legislature.

All American legislative committees are subject to the possibility of stacking, but not always is this as flagrantly the case as in Florida. For instance, one may compare the Agriculture Committees of the United States Congress with the Forestry and Citrus Committees of the Florida legislature. All of these are effectively stacked, but in Congress the stacking is in greater degree automatic and non-deliberate: it results in part from the large element of free choice of committee assignments by members of Congress. In Florida the control of committee assignments by the presiding officers is complete (subject, of course, to the normal necessities of politics, such as in the case of W. C. Herrell to be mentioned shortly); consequently stacking can only be a deliberate choice based on some sort of political calculation.

It is almost axiomatic in Florida that committees will be stacked, *i.e.*, over and above the inequities resulting from malapportionment. Two reasons appear predominant: the presiding officers hope to control the legislative output by stacking committees in the direction of their personal political policies (which are usually bloc-oriented); and for certain committees dealing with economic interests it is felt to be both "proper" and "wise" to make sure the committee represents the particular interest concerned, to the practical exclusion of the *public* interest.

Committees coming under the first of the above-mentioned criteria — that of importance — have been carefully selected. They handle, in an average session, more bills — and more *important* bills — than the rest. Positions on such committees are thus indices of personal position in the legislature, and control of them is a matter of prime political significance. If there is, as we have indicated, a rural-urban contest for legislative dominance, it should show up most clearly in the selection of members of these key committees. If the presiding officer is an urban man (as was Speaker "Ted" David in 1955) this fact should be reflected in urban control of these committees; while if he is a rural man (as is commonly the case), rural men should control them.

The speakership of "Ted" David can be viewed in several ways as a bench mark in the evolution of the rural-urban cleavage in the House. Prior to 1955 the conflict had been present, but muted and transformed by the character of legislative politics elaborated above. But David's role as the governor's leader led to his more or less open identification as a "big-county man." The speaker thus served, perhaps for the first time in Florida, as a partisan symbol of the desires of the urban population for certain types of governmental action and for more equitable representation. At the same time, David's fulfillment of this role brought about a sharp reaction on the part of the rural representatives, who felt that their exclusion from the positions of control constituted unfair treatment. Two factors seem to account for the open eruption in 1955 of the tension between the "ins" and the "outs" which we have identified as following a rather complicated geographical split along North-South and rural-urban lines. The first was the increasing awareness of the governor's role as a representative of the "new" urban (primarily southern) Florida. The second was the bitterness of the reapportionment fight in the 1955 session, which greatly sharpened the lines of cleavage in the House membership. Thus prior to 1955 it was possible, though rare even then, for a personable man such as Ted David, who played the legislative game of interpersonal relations extremely well, to get himself elected speaker even though his constituency was in urban south Florida. However, David's identification with Collins' programs for institutionalizing administrative practice, changing the bases of allocating highway construction projects and other policies that affected the rural-urban split and, above all, for reapportioning the legislature, solidified the ranks of rural members in opposition to the chief executive, his legislative lieutenants (including Speaker David) and the urban House bloc which supported the governor and his legislative leaders.

The formal organization of the small-county bloc was a result of the reaction of these conditions, and the small-county men vowed openly never again to allow an urban legislator to become speaker. So far they have made good their threat (into the 1961 session), and it is probable that the sessions after 1955, the wound having been laid open, reveal the rural-urban cleavage to be both deeper and broader than most observers had imagined. Committee assignment has thus probably become more significant than it was before 1955. Tables 1 and 2, based on the membership of the key committees in both houses in the three most recent sessions, indicate clearly that for important committees the presiding officer sees to it that the groups he represents — rural except for the House in 1955 — are heavily over-represented.

But several other considerations should be kept in mind. In the

TABLE 1. COMMITTEE STACKING IN KEY COMMITTEES OF FLORIDA HOUSE OF REPRESENTATIVES, 1955-1959*

	1955			1957			1959		
Committee	Rural	Mixed	Urban	Rural	Mixed	Urban	Rural	Mixed	Urban
Finances & Taxation	8	8	8	12	4	5	11	3	7
Rules & Calendar	6	11	10	11	7	7	13	3	5
Constitutional Amendments	3	6	7	12	5	4	8	6	7
General Legislation[a]	-	-	-	-	-	-	2	5	2
Apportionment	4	5	8	7	2	2	7	0	2
Public Schools	12	2	3	11	3	7	7	3	11
Appropriations	11	6	6	10	4	7	10	6	5
"Doghouse" Committee:[b] Aeronautics (1955, 1957), State Advertising (1959)	4	0	3	0	2	5	3	3	7
Total Seats in House	45	23	27	45	23	27	45	23	27

*Counties are classified as rural, urban or mixed on the basis of census data as to percentage of urban population, modified by the authors' personal evaluation (based on fairly thorough acquaintance with each county) of the type of population which dominates each county. Also, due to the rapid growth of many counties, some may no longer be in the status implied by 1950 census figures. An instance of the procedure used may be helpful: Polk County has no large urban centers and would classify, according to 1950 census data, as a non-urban county. However, we re-classified it as "mixed" because we felt that the contiguity of a number of smaller cities, containing a high proportion of retired people and having a tourist-oriented type of commercial development, deprive it of real rural dominance. Space precludes a breakdown of the detailed characteristics on which similar adjustments were made for other counties.
[a]Set up in 1959 to handle race discrimination legislation.
[b]Two members of this committee were Republicans in each session.

TABLE 2. COMMITTEE STACKING IN KEY COMMITTEES OF FLORIDA SENATE, 1955-1959*

Committee	1955			1957			1959		
	Rural	Mixed	Urban	Rural	Mixed	Urban	Rural	Mixed	Urban
Finance & Taxation	6	4	3	9	3	1	9	3	1
Rules & Calendar	10	2	1	10	1	2	9	1	3
Constitutional Amendments	8	1	2	10	0	3	8	2	3
General Legislation[a]	—	—	—	—	—	—	11	1	1
Education	4	2	5	2	3	6	5	4	2
Appropriations	8	4	1	5	2	2	10	2	3
Minor Committee:[b] Veterans, Aviation, Radio & Television	3	3	1	—	—	—	1	4	2
Total Seats in Senate	18	9	11	18	9	11	18	9	11

[a]Set up in 1959 to handle race discrimination legislation.
[b]Included for comparison only; this apparently not a real "doghouse" committee such as the House uses.
*See explanatory note to Table 1.

first place, a legislator must be viewed as a person as well as a representative (especially in a system in which so much emphasis is placed on independence of organizational ties), so that his actual attitudes and voting record do not necessarily reflect the type of district from which he comes. In the second place, many quantitatively urban districts, such as Pensacola, are experiencing a cultural lag: they have grown so fast that their objective urbanization has not yet been accompanied by the growth of urban attitudes. Thirdly, some urban districts (especially those in the "Old South" areas of northern Florida) show typical rural attitudes on race issues.

These factors mean that the actual rural predominance on committees is likely to be considerably greater than the figures given in Tables 1 and 2 suggest. Presiding officers know these facts, and often their appointment of one or another urban legislator to positions on key committees is made in the knowledge that their committee work will satisfy rural desires. When W. C. Herrell of Dade County (Miami), for instance, was chosen chairman of the House Appropriations Committee in 1959 by the rural Speaker (Tom Beasley of Walton County), one may suspect that Beasley believed Herrell's ideas on appropriations matters were suitable, and that a concession to urban demands for influence could be made without greatly disturbing the substantive policies followed by the committee. It was also rumored in the 1957 session, when Beasley was "designated" as 1959 Speaker, that he (though a rural man) had secured the support of the Dade County delegation in return for a promise of good committee posts for them in 1959. If so, Herrell alone reaped the payoff, for in addition to the Appropriations chairmanship he served on two of the six other "key" committees in 1959. This shows, incidentally, one way in which the rural counties maintain their slim control of the House: they manage by such favors or promises of favors, to keep the urban counties from solidifying as a bloc. It may also be significant that in 1959 Beasley was "running" for governor and needed to do something to try to gain urban support.

Such facts make a reliance on the quantitative method somewhat unsatisfactory unless it is complemented by close knowledge and used with some sophistication. Accordingly, we have attempted to correct the bias in the figures by making a much closer study of the 1957 legislature and presenting adjusted data (Tables 3 and 4) which have taken into account the factors adduced above. Although not sufficiently pertinent for reproduction here, the authors prepared for other purposes a scale showing the "conservative" rank-order of members of the 1957 Florida House of Representatives, based on six key issues on which social atti-

TABLE 3. COMMITTEE STACKING IN KEY COMMITTEES OF FLORIDA HOUSE OF REPRE-SENTATIVES, 1957 SESSION ONLY, ADJUSTED*

Committee	Rural	Mixed	Urban
Finance & Taxation	14	3	4
Rules & Calendar	16	4	5
Constitutional Amendments	16	2	3
Apportionment	7	2	2
Public Schools	14	2	5
Appropriations	14	2	5
"Doghouse" Committee:			
Aeronautics	1	1	5
Total Seats in House			
(Unadjusted)	45	23	27

*For this table the writers compiled a "dossier" on every legislator, consulting experienced political observers, other legislators past and present, and particularly the voting records on key issues during the session. Each committee member was then classified as to whether or not he stood with the rural bloc, regardless of the type of district he represented. The rural bloc is sufficiently well-defined to justify the assimilation of urban members to this bloc on the basis of the voting records of the latter on key issues relating to the attitudes which define the coalescence of the dominant rural group. Florida political observers commonly make statements such as the following: "He's from Pensacola, but he's really a pork-chopper." With the power structure in rural hands, some urban members clearly join them in order to get ahead in the legislature. That this tendency to join the rural bloc *generally* manifests itself among members who are from geographical sectors which are rural-urban transitional (mixed) or are in north Florida, was shown up most clearly when we scaled the legislators' responses to major issues.

TABLE 4. COMMITTEE STACKING IN KEY COMMITTEES OF FLORIDA SENATE, 1957 SESSION ONLY, ADJUSTED*

Committee	Rural	Mixed	Urban
Finance & Taxation	10	3	1
Rules & Calendar	12	0	1
Constitutional Amendments	10	0	3
Education	4	1	6
Appropriations	7	0	2
Total Seats in Senate			
(Unadjusted)	18	9	11

*See explanatory note to Table 3.

tudes could be readily identified. The pattern was remarkably clear: of the thirteen members who were identified as "least conservative," all were from urban counties and all but one were from south Florida. Of the twenty-one "most conservative" members, only two were from an urban county, and the county from which they were elected is in the transitional area of recently urbanized counties on the periphery of north Florida. The scale as a whole shows a strong tendency toward "conservatism" in the north Florida rural areas, a fairly heavy conservative bias in rural south Florida, a slightly less pronounced conservatism in the urbanized areas of north Florida and the transitional areas and a pronounced non-conservative bias in the urban south Florida vote. The issues concerned ranged from bills dealing with racial legislation to matters directly affecting the real or presumed urban-rural division, such as the distribution of funds for the purchase of highway rights-of-way. The same kind of study could doubtless be made for any rural-dominated session with much the same results. To a large extent our adjustment of the tables to reflect the personal attitudes of legislators regardless of the type of county from which they were elected is based on information of the type yielded by such studies of the voting patterns of the members.

Tables 1 through 4, then, indicate that (except for the 1955 House) the rural bloc dominates both houses of the Florida legislature. This dominance is obviously maintained through the selection of sympathetic presiding officers who will use their considerable powers to bolster rural power. The pattern is more obvious and more secure in the Senate than in the House, since malapportionment is more extreme in the former. In the House, members from urban or mixed counties actually hold a majority, but many of them (as noted above) do not always in reality represent urban interests, or at least they represent a combination of the rural and business-conservative elements in their respective counties. An additional factor is that in some mixed counties such as Alachua it seems to be more or less customary to "give" one seat (in attitude if not physically) to the out-county rural population. Even so, rural dominance of the House is rather shaky, depending as it does on rural-minded urban men to tip the balance. In the Senate, on the other hand, as the tables show, the rural districts have a clear margin of control. The rural bloc is usually said to contain twenty-one or possibly twenty-two members of the total of thirty-eight (in 1959); on many issues it is much larger. In view of these figures, it is apparent that the extent of the predominance of rural interests shown in Tables 1 through 4 cannot be explained by reference solely to malapportionment. The role played by the speaker and the president in making committee assignments is also of key importance.

It is also clear from the tables that rural interests consider some committees more important to control than others. The education committees especially (and to a lesser extent, the appropriations committees) have included a high proportion of big-county legislators. In the case of the education committees, this seems to be due to the fact that all counties, regardless of size, have a major and similar interest in the welfare of schools. The situation as to the appropriations committees is more obscure; it seems possible, however, that considerations like those mentioned above in the appointment of Representative Herrell may explain the matter. Since the big counties supply most of the state's revenues, it would be most unfair to discriminate against them as grossly as is the case with other committees; and with proper care they can be given the appearance of influence without its substance. Then again, fiscal conservatism (at least in Florida) seems as common among urban representatives as among their rural colleagues, so (as in Herrell's case) there is little to fear from allowing them substantial influence on this particular committee. The "economy bloc" cuts across other cleavage lines. The committees handling rules, taxation, constitutional amendment, apportionment and racial matters are, on the other hand, prime examples of areas in which rural dominance must be maintained because it makes so much difference to the whole political power structure and to the economic and social patterns of rural Florida.

The "doghouse" committee is of interest mainly because it shows the extent to which rural-urban rivalry can go on occasion. Its usefulness is largely symbolic: it indicates the determination of one side or the other to maintain its control. This shows up most clearly when the control of the chamber changes, as from 1955 to 1957 in the House. Since the "pork choppers" always control the Senate no doghouse is needed there. Although it is obvious from Table 1 that the House Aeronautics Committee was "reverse stacked" both in 1955 and 1957, the figures do not tell the whole story. The 1957 Speaker, Doyle Conner (a rural legislator from Bradford County), languished in the 1955 doghouse, while such 1955 urban movers-and-shakers as Henry Land (Orange County)

TABLE 5. COMMITTEE STACKING IN SELECTED "INTEREST" COMMITTEES, FLORIDA HOUSE OF REPRESENTATIVES AND SENATE, 1955-1959

	1955		1957		1959	
Committee	Interest	Non-Interest	Interest	Non-Interest	Interest	Non-Interest
House-Citrus	—	—	13	0	12	1
House-Forestry	—	—	11	0	8	(1?)
Senate-Citrus	13	0	—	—	13	0
Senate-Forestry & Parks*	7	4	—	—	8	3

*Evidently some of the members of the Senate Forestry and Parks Committee are selected to represent the "recreational interest" as distinct from the "forestry interest"; they are shown in the table as "non-interest." Obviously citrus and forestry interests are primarily rural, so there is a direct tie-in between interest stacking (at least on these two committees) and the predominance of rural interests.

TABLE 6. CONTINUITY OF LEADERSHIP IN THE FLORIDA SENATE, 1955-1959*

Senator	Type of District	Number of Key Committee Assignments		
		1955	1957	1959
Johns	Rural North	3	1	5
Pearce	Rural South	2	3	2
Connor	Rural South	3	2	4
Clarke	Rural North	4	4	4
Johnson	Rural North	3	2	Senate President
Hodges	Rural North	2	2	4
Stratton	Rural North	2	2	3
Edwards	Mixed South	2	3	3
Bronson	Rural South	1	2	4
Carraway	Mixed North	1	2	3
Davis	Rural North	Senate President	3	5
Rawls	Rural North	1	3	5
Shands	Mixed South	2	Senate President	-
Adams	Rural North	-	2	3
Beall	Urban North	-	2	4
Brackin	Rural North	-	2	2
Totals:	Rural, 12 North, 11			
	Mixed, 3 South, 5			
	Urban, 1			

*All senators serving in two of the three sessions and holding multiple assignments in two sessions are included.

and John Orr (Dade) were relegated to the doghouse for the 1957 session. It is also noteworthy that this committee serves as a repository for Republicans.

Table 5 reveals the extent of "interest packing" which can exist because of the influence over committee selection of the presiding officer, custom and (to a certain degree) political beliefs. It is obvious that there is a conscious effort to keep anyone off such committees as citrus and forestry who might conceivably represent consumer interests or even the interests of the state as a whole, as distinct from those of the clientele group served (literally) by the committee. Legislators with personal or representative stakes in the interest with which the committee deals make up all or almost all of its membership. The data in Table 5 confirm the aptness of James Madison's remark that legislators are often "but advocates and parties to the causes which they determine."

This type of stacking by interest is publicly acknowledged in Florida, and is so taken for granted that even those who might suffer from it seldom think to question it; no one, then, need bother to defend it. An incident in the 1957 session illustrates the confident acceptance of this practice. The Senate Committee on Forestry and Parks had before it a bill to impose a severance tax on pulpwood. When the bill came up for hearing, the lobbyists for the important paper industry were present to testify against it, but its legislative sponsor was unable to appear. As is customary, the hearings were postponed until the absent legislator could be present.

The pulpwood spokesmen were understandably not over-anxious to make the trip to Tallahassee again and were thus somewhat put out by the postponement. In order to placate them one senator pointed out that their presence was really not necessary anyway: "I think," he said, "if you will look at the membership of this committee you will realize you can all go home without saying anything." The committee chairman added, "I don't think you have anything to worry about," and the pulpwood lobby went home. Thus, regardless of the state's urgent need of new revenue sources, and the (admittedly arguable) objective merits of the severance tax, the membership base of the committee made impossible the consideration of the proposal from any viewpoint other than that of the woodpulp industry itself. The incident underscores the danger to the public inherent in the practice of "interest stacking" of legislative committees.

One would expect, in view of the discussion thus far, that there would be a high degree of continuity in legislative leadership. Table 6 indicates that this is the case, at least in the Senate: to a large extent the same men have held the positions of power for the last three sessions. It shows, in addition, that almost all of them are from rural districts, mostly in north Florida. Even the exceptions are more apparent than real, for Senator Beall of Escambia County (Pensacola) is widely regarded as a "pork chopper," which probably accounts for his success in obtaining influential positions in the Senate. Continuity of leadership has not been as pronounced in the House, partly due to the "urban breakthrough" of 1955. But even in the House, taking the two more recent sessions, a high degree of continuity exists, and again it is largely rural. Doyle Connor, 1957 Speaker, was Rules Committee chairman in 1959; Tom Beasley, Rules Committee chairman in 1957, was Speaker in 1959; and Bill Chappell, who is Speaker-Designate for 1961, served on three key committees in 1957 (chairing one) and on four in 1959.

It is also noteworthy that the key committee posts form a sort of interlocking directorate in each house, with the same men appearing on several such committees. There is thus a high degree of concentration in the leadership which, while not formally organized as a caucus or a party organization, nevertheless seems to function effectively to ensure rural control. The extent to which this is true is partially indicated by Tables 7 and 8, which show that Speaker Beasley and President Dewey Johnson used their committee appointment powers to construct or merely to recognize highly cohesive and homogeneous leadership groups. The pattern is much more extreme in the Senate, largely due to factors already mentioned. In the House, in addition to factors already cited, it should be repeated that Speaker Beasley's ambitions to become governor required him to seek urban support, and thus he was perhaps constrained to make a public show of fairness to the urban areas in committee assignments. Yet, as Table 1 indicated, he was careful enough to ensure that the small counties retained numerical control where it was deemed essential. Obviously some "pork-choppers" are more able and experienced than others; all of them may not be considered as legislative leaders. The important thing to note about Tables 7 and 8 is the almost complete absence of representatives from the large urban centers, particularly in the Senate.

It might be said, then, that each chamber is dominated by a rural-oriented oligarchy. This group is more readily identifiable, more cohesive and more secure in the Senate than in the House, but it exists in both.

III

Committee stacking in Florida deviates from orthodox models of representative democracy in two respects: it involves a calculated disregard for the general public will, substituting a set of local wills which do not add up to a majority; and it is an indication of the substitution of oligarchy for a popular, responsible exercise of political power. Yet stacking is a reflection of the nature of politics in Florida—fragmented,

TABLE 7. INTERLOCKING DIRECTORATES ON KEY COMMITTEES OF FLORIDA HOUSE OF REPRESENTATIVES, 1959*

		Combination of Committee Posts[a]						
Name	Type of County	1	2	3	4	5	6	7
Crews	Rural North		X	X			X	
Conner	Rural North		CH		X			
Herrell	Urban South		X				X	CH
Mathews	Urban South	X		X	X		X	
Inman	Rural North	X				X		X
G. W. Williams	Rural South		X			CH	X	
Livingston	Rural South	X	X	X				
Mann	Urban South	X	X	X				
Drummond	Rural North	X		X			X	
Shipp	Rural North		X				CH	X
Horne[b]	Mixed North			CH	X			X
Mitchell[b]	Mixed North	X	X				X	
Chappell[b]	Mixed South	X	X	X	X			
Stewart	Rural North	X	X	X	X			
J. J. Griffin	Rural South		X			X		X
B. H. Griffin[b]	Mixed South				CH			X
Cleveland[b]	Mixed South	X	X	X	X			
Sweeny[b]	Urban South	CH	X					
Totals:	Rural, 9	North, 8						
	Mixed, 5	South, 10						
	Urban, 4							

*All representatives serving on more than two of these committees, and their chairmen (CH), are included.
[a]1, Finance & Taxation; 2, Rules & Calendar; 3, Constitutional Amendments; 4, General Legislation; 5, Apportionment; 6, Public Schools; 7, Appropriations.
[b]Designates men from mixed or urban counties but who were largely rural in attitude.

TABLE 8. INTERLOCKING DIRECTORATES, KEY COMMITTEES OF FLORIDA SENATE, 1959*

Name	Type of District	Combination of Committee Posts[a]					
		1	2	3	4	5	6
Carraway[b]	Mixed North	CH		X	X		
Rawls	Rural North	X	CH	X	X		
Hodges	Rural North	X	X		X		X
Adams	Rural North	X		X	CH		
Connor	Rural South	X	X		X		X
Johns	Rural North	X	X		X	X	X
Davis	Rural North		X	X	X	X	CH
Stratton	Rural North	X				X	X
Clarke	Rural North	X	X			X	X
Bronson	Rural South		X	X	X	X	X
Edwards[b]	Mixed South			CH		X	X
Beall[b]	Urban North		X		X	X	X
Pearce	Rural South					X	CH
Totals:	Rural, 10	North, 9					
	Mixed, 2	South, 4					
	Urban, 1						

*All senators serving on at least three of these committees, or holding the chairmanship (CH) of one, are included.
[a]1, Appropriations; 2, Constitutional Amendments; 3, Education; 4, Finance & Taxation; 5, General Legislation; 6, Rules and Calendar.
[b]Designates men from mixed or urban districts but who were largely rural in attitude.

locally oriented, malapportioned—and one would not expect any great changes in the makeup of committees unless it were preceded by a pronounced transformation of the political system. This does not seem imminent.

Perhaps the logical conclusion is that in Florida, as elsewhere in the United States, the urban majorities will (because they must) turn increasingly to the national authorities; for, as has often been remarked, the drift of power from the state to the national level is at least as much a reflection of the inadequacies of state political systems as it is of the desires of either the national government or the people. Arthur Mac-Mahon has made this point in trenchant terms, speaking of civil liberties rather than urban needs, but his words are applicable to both:

> . . . a viable theory of modern federalism is based upon respect for personality. If federalism renounces this ideal in strained respect for territorial autonomy, its critics will be confirmed in their belief that protection is best afforded by the leverages of national politics and freedom mainly secured by the nationwide competition of broadly based, responsible parties.

To avoid this tendency Florida needs two specific basic changes: the development of a working party system, and the reduction of its excessive attachment to the county as a unit for determining legislative apportionment. Committee stacking, significant as it is in its own right, is symptomatic of these more basic problems of the Florida polity.

THE ILLINOIS LEGISLATURE: A STUDY IN CORRUPTION

PAUL SIMON AS TOLD TO ALFRED BALK

Paul Simon was an Illinois state senator at the time this article was written.

State legislatures are, historically, the fountainhead of representative government in this country.

So spoke the United States Supreme Court in the landmark reapportionment opinion of last June. The reforms that will follow are long overdue. For there is little doubt that these fountainheads of democracy are—as of this writing—polluted almost beyond belief.

This is my considered judgment after ten years of service in the body where Abraham Lincoln once sat. I did not expect moral perfection when I first went to Springfield. In my home district, in southwestern Illinois, criminal elements had seriously infiltrated both major party organizations until Governor Adlai Stevenson's courageous state police raids of 1950 slowed down their inroads. Illicit bookie joints and vice dens operated as freely as grocery stores in one town, and muggings, bombings, and gang killings were commonplace. However, this experience and a realistic attitude about society's shortcomings did not prepare me for the shock of seeing from the inside how the Illinois legislature—the lawmaker and "public conscience" of the nation's fourth-most-populous state—actually works. This is the legislature which last year enacted a redistricting plan so blatantly unrepresentative that the Illinois Supreme Court upheld Governor Otto Kerner's veto of it. As a result, this November all members of our House of Representatives will be elected at large—the first such election, I believe, in American history. At least 236 names will appear on a special ballot almost three feet long, out of which the voter must select all 177 members of the House.

This is only one of a series of breakdowns so frequent and so serious that I feel compelled to speak out about them.

My colleague, Republican Representative Noble W. Lee, who is Dean of the John Marshall Law School in Chicago and has served eleven terms in the House, estimates that one third of the members accept payoffs. In the light of my own observations, I agree. Most of these are recorded as legal fees, public-relations services, or "campaign contributions," though a campaign may be months away. If questioned, the recipient simply denies that the payment had anything to do with legislative activity. This makes it technically legal. A somewhat smaller number of payoffs are not veiled at all; cold cash passes directly from one hand to the other.

Recently, for example, the spokesman of a professional association visited a legislator, whom I will call Mr. X, to enlist his help with a bill. "Did you bring the money?" Mr. X asked.

"What money?" the visitor inquired.

"Money for the committee, of course," Mr. X replied. "It will cost two hundred to five hundred dollars a vote to get the bill out of committee." His caller dropped the subject and left.

Similarly jolted was a representative of the food industry when he sought a powerful Senator's support for a bill.

"Be glad to talk to you," the legislator told him. "For seventy-five hundred dollars I can get you nine votes."

A few legislators go so far as to introduce some bills that are deliberately designed to shake down groups which oppose them and which will pay to have them withdrawn. These bills are called "fetchers," and once their sponsors develop a lucrative field, they guard it jealously.

I learned this, quite by accident, four years ago in the House. I had found that some school districts and municipalities were paying needlessly high bond interest. So I introduced a bill requiring competitive bidding on public bond issues. Shortly afterward a colleague buttonholed me in the hall.

"What are you doing with my bill?" he demanded.

"What bill?"

"That bond bill. I always introduce it, and I do rather well with it." Seeing my surprise, he added, "Look, why don't you kill it? If you do, it could be a good thing for both of us."

I declined, and the bill was assigned for hearing to a committee whose members had never before shown any interest in this subject. Presently they were urging me to schedule a hearing, which is by custom the sponsor's prerogative. When I did so, the Taxpayers Federation, Farm Bureau, and other respected groups endorsed the bill. There was virtually no opposition. Whereupon the eager committee killed the bill by a vote of twenty to nothing, and I could only wonder why.

There are rumors—which obviously I cannot verify—that under-the-table transactions provide an income of $100,000 a session for one prominent Representative when his party is in power. Other leading legislators and their cliques reportedly collect profits well into five figures.

As in many state capitals, there are no controls on lobbyists in Springfield. A weak law requires them to register with the Secretary of State. But they can hand out any amount of money to influence legislators, without disclosing their expenditures. Legislators in turn need not account for campaign contributions or disclose their source. Nor are there any real safeguards against conflicts between the public's and the legislators' private interests.

Pampering the Ponies

Among the chief beneficiaries of these easygoing ways are our state's racetracks, which enjoy one of the lowest tax rates in the nation—while our tax on a loaf of bread and a pound of hamburger is the highest in the nation. There are no regular lobbyists representing racing and pari-mutuel betting interests in Springfield. But several influential legislators, or members of their families, are stockholders in racetracks. On special guest nights, busloads of sympathetic legislators are driven to the tracks, given a lavish cocktail party and dinner, then escorted to reserved seats and provided with tips on likely winners on the day's card. At one track, important races are named in honor of individual legislators on these gala occasions.

A notable racing enthusiast is the President Pro Tem of the Senate, a dapper, likable suburbanite named Arthur J. Bidwill, whose family has long been registered with the State Racing Commission as track stockholders. Bidwill distributes fistfuls of season passes in the Senate chambers, and when racing bills are heard in committee he testifies for the industry. At one recent hearing, he was the only witness to oppose increasing taxes on winnings. Yet he prevailed.

A few years ago, backers of Sportsman's Park in Cicero decided to stage trotting in addition to regular racing. To get legislative approval they sent ex-convict Irwin "Big Sam" Wiedrick to Springfield with authority to offer nine influential legislators large blocs of stock in an operating affiliate of the track, at the bargain price of ten cents a share. Among those who accepted was a long-time chairman of the legislature's budget-making commission; another was a shrewd, folksy downstate Representative who has served three terms as Speaker. He bought nearly 17,000 shares in his wife's name and was allowed more than a year to pay. Meanwhile, he received $16,900 in "dividends," enabling him to "buy" the stock without any capital outlay whatever.

The Chicago *Sun-Times* recently reported that his return on this investment amounted to $23,000 in 1963. When a reporter queried him about the transaction (he is now running for another office) he replied, "The only mistake I made was that I didn't get more."

Needless to say, Sportsman's Park got its trotting races despite a long history of hoodlum infiltrations. (The Capone syndicate helped found this track, and only last summer a multi-million-dollar bookie ring was uncovered there.)

The privileged position enjoyed by the state's racing interests was impressed on me during my first term when a bill was introduced to reduce by one third the taxes on two prosperous downstate tracks in which several legislators owned stock. At that time—in the 1950s—Illinois was starved for revenue, and was heading for the kind of financial crisis that soon was to plague Michigan. Though we were already borrowing against future tax receipts, revenue was still inadequate. To meet this crisis the House voted a 50 per cent increase in the sales tax, to a level of 3 per cent. (It now is 3.5 per cent in Illinois, plus an additional .5 per cent for municipalities, the second-highest combined total in the nation.) On the same day the leadership proposed a vote, without committee hearing, on the racetrack bonanza. I objected strenuously and several colleagues agreed. Richard Stengel, a highly respected Representative who later ran for the U.S. Senate, called the bill "the biggest steal since I've been in the legislature."

"You just call it a steal because you're not in on it!" a leading fellow Democrat retorted.

There was a motion for an immediate vote. The bill passed and was rushed to the then Governor, Republican William G. Stratton, for signature.

Stengel and I, suspecting skulduggery, filed a protest urging the Governor to veto the bill. The response was a unique experience—a resolution of censure against us filed by a House colleague, Carl Preihs. Stengel and I, he said, were "men who lacked integrity" and had "disgraced" the legislature. Legislative leaders who previously had been friendly suddenly became brusque. We were so ostracized that Stengel, in phoning me, quipped, "Hello, Measles. This is Smallpox."

Next day the Governor signed the bill—the only non-emergency measure to be acted upon so quickly in that session—and the censure resolution was dropped.

The Indestructible Syndicate

A bipartisan Chicago group known as the "West Side Bloc" consistently—and usually successfully—opposes periodic efforts to clean up elections, streamline Chicago government, and pass major anti-crime legislation. This coalition includes a few syndicate-backed Chicago aldermen, one State Senator, and several Representatives. Recently, it has been in the news because party leaders, for the coming campaign at least, have denied some Bloc members places on the at-large ballot on the grounds that they are "undesirables."

The Bloc crops up regularly in sinister headlines in Chicago. Just before my first term, for example, a State Representative named Clem Graver, a known associate of gangsters, was taken for a ride by unidentified men and was never seen again. The legislature, however, did not really investigate his disappearance.

Shortly afterward I witnessed firsthand the mysterious way in which legislation opposed by the syndicate is voted down even though it is favored by a vast majority of Illinois citizens. In session after session, proposals to create a State Crime Commission were defeated. Few legislators opposed the Commission publicly, though there were some who expressed sincere concern that it might be used for political purposes or would waste money. The majority of legislators either endorsed it or remained silent. Still, the measure repeatedly died while other commissions with less laudable objectives easily won approval. The main opposition pressure, without question, came from criminal elements.

Last spring Commission adherents tried again. Pressure from the press and civic organizations was intensified when a powerful alderman in Chicago, Benjamin Lewis, was found shot to death in his office on the city's West Side. The Chicago City Council chose not to investigate the case or the possible ties between the unknown killers and politics in Lewis' ward. The bill finally passed. But the legislature cut the new agency's proposed budget in half, to $100,000. Then House leaders went on to pick their representatives on the Commission. Breaking a long-standing tradition, they omitted the House sponsor of the bill, Representative Anthony Scariano—a courageous, honest suburban legislator who has aggressively fought organized crime. Instead, they chose one legislator who voted against the bill, another who had abstained (tantamount to a "no"), one who had voted against it in the previous session, and one who had been Chief Deputy Sheriff of populous St. Clair County at a time when it was so wide open that the Kefauver Crime Committee held a special investigation into its affairs. Reporters later asked Scariano whether he believed the West Side Bloc had kept him off his own Commission. "It wasn't the YMCA," he replied.

Almost every major anticrime measure proposed in Springfield in recent years has suffered similar sabotage. In the 1959 session, for example, a bill was introduced to ban a gambling-type pinball machine that had been outlawed in all states but Nevada, part of Maryland, and Illinois. Presently, one newspaperman reported seeing jukebox king Frank Zito (a delegate to the syndicate's famous Apalachin "Summit Conference") in a Capitol hallway, an unusual sight even in Springfield. The bill soon ran into trouble—a House committee tried to kill it quietly for lack of a quorum; the Speaker declined to schedule it for a full House vote until 3:00 A.M. on the last day of the session. When the bill nonetheless passed, Governor Stratton inexplicably vetoed it. In 1961, a similar measure was quietly amended to death. Last spring, another version passed—but, like the Crime Commission, only in watered-down form. It does not prevent the *manufacture* of these machines.

Around this time, Chicago Police Superintendent Orlando W. Wilson and other top law-enforcement officials were sponsoring another bill, patterned after a New York law, which would change syndicate gambling from a misdemeanor to a felony. The measure was killed. This time the Republican Majority Leader himself handled the main parliamentary maneuvers with the House Speaker, also a Republican, cooperating. The Chicago *Daily News* commented editorially under the headline, "Syndicate Rolls a Seven."

Bipartisan Gravy Train

Gambling and horse racing are not, of course, the only odd objects of legislators' benevolence. There is, for instance, the influential Republican Senator who owns a finance company. He routinely looks after the small-loan industry, which in Illinois is so loosely regulated that "easy payments" may carry interest charges as high as 36 per cent. Another Senator privately represents the state's largest highway-contracting association, according to a Chicago newspaper. Also among his clients was an engineering firm organized just in time to win a $600,000 state contract for a toll-road survey. Such conflicts of interest are common in both parties, which work together in ways that have little to commend them.

A bond between the parties is an interest in preserving patronage. Illinois has a spoils system second only to Pennsylvania's. There are nearly twenty thousand political state jobs; and local governments, especially Chicago, provide thousands more. "Never mind the issues, how many jobs can you get us?" is the theme song of hosts of precinct workers during campaigns. Legislators often collaborate to satisfy this hunger. The results are sometimes peculiar.

Occasionally, for instance, a Republican legislator turns up on a Democratic payroll. Thus, in 1961, two Republicans who held Democratic spoils jobs in Chicago announced that they were too ill to vote, and a third GOP member voted with the Democrats at our first organizing session. As a result, the Republicans failed to elect a Speaker though they held a one-vote majority in the House.

Cook County, which includes Chicago, elects the large majority of Democratic legislators. Whoever controls the political jobs in Cook County in effect controls the party. That man now is Chicago's Mayor Richard J. Daley. When a major bill is considered in the legislature, the floor leader, after getting instructions from Chicago or from the Governor's office, simply announces "We're for it," or, "We're against it." Only a few Democratic members from downstate—of whom I am one—and a handful of independent Cook County legislators dare to take a different position.

Budget-making in our legislature is handled by a self-perpetuating clique behind closed doors. Millions of dollars—approximately half the state's total revenue—now are frozen in "ear-marked" funds guarded by special-interest lobbies. There are right now huge, untouchable surpluses earmarked (but not being fully used) for highways, driver education, county fairs, and the like, while schools, mental health, welfare, and other vital programs lag for lack of money. But the legislature spends freely on certain highway programs. One pet project was a toll-road system costing hundreds of millions of dollars more than a comparable freeway.

The chairman of the Toll Highway Commission, Evan Howell, resigned a lifetime federal judgeship to accept the chairmanship at a lower salary. Subsequently it was revealed that he had founded a "contractors' club" with dues of a thousand dollars—allegedly to assure preferential treatment for members. His expense accounts in less than two years ran to $11,000, including such items as a Lake Shore Drive apartment in Chicago, and $18 one day for newspapers. Clearly an inquiry was in order. But Governor Stratton prevented an investigation with the help of most GOP legislators and two Democrats.

Near the end of the 1955 session this impregnable defense was broken by a weird incident—chairman Howell made a derogatory remark about a legislator in a Springfield bar. Like other legislators, Illinois lawmakers will overlook many things, but never an affront, real or fancied, to the legislature's "dignity."

The next day, amid indignant shouts, an inquiry into Howell's conduct was voted. Only six quick hearings were held, and the committee was not supplied with a lawyer or even a full-time clerk. Nonetheless some of the dismal facts I have cited here were brought out and published in a committee report. Howell was forced to resign, but there was no further probing.

Forgotten Headlines

Such speedy burial was to prove impossible in a situation that developed shortly afterward. This was the case of Orville E. Hodge, popular, playboyish, and apparently wealthy Republican State Auditor who had used up a two-year appropriation for operating his office in eighteen months. Now he was asking legislators for whom he had done many favors to bail him out by approving a half-million dollar deficiency appropriation to cover his shortage.

If ever a case called for legislative scrutiny, this seemed to be it. Two of us in the House said so, and opposed the appropriation. But, under prodding from Hodge, the request rolled through, plus a new appropriation almost $2 million larger than the previous one.

A few months later the Chicago *Daily News* revealed why Hodge had needed extra money: With the help of an assistant and a cooperative bank, he had stolen $2,500,000 in public funds. He had loaded his payroll with key legislators' friends, used public money for high living, associated closely with hoodlums and gamblers. According to the St. Louis *Post-Dispatch*, he even had entered a partnership in a motel with a rackets boss in the St. Louis area, Frank "Buster" Wortman, and slot-machine king Thomas J. Berry. Only masquerading as wealthy, Hodge actually was of fairly ordinary means. These revelations shocked the entire state, and many citizens elsewhere. A thorough investigation and major reforms seemed imminent. Hodge was quickly tried, and convicted of misappropriating a portion of the total funds. Then he was hurried off to prison without extensive public questioning. Only minor fiscal reforms were enacted, and proposals for a full-scale legislative probe were defeated. In 1963, Hodge was paroled without ever having told his full story.

The case refused to die, however. George Thiem, Pulitzer Prize-winning reporter who had broken the scandal in the newspapers, published a book, *The Hodge Scandal* (St. Martin's Press). In it he quoted a representative of a leading utility company, who described how it had succeeded in persuading the Illinois legislature to pass a bill saving the company $35,000 a year in franchise taxes. The price, said the utility man, was $35,000. And the money was paid to Hodge, whose friends in the legislature took care of the details. One former legislator, for example, admitted that Hodge gave him $2,000 for his "help" on this and other bills. The utility measure, naturally, passed easily.

"We didn't think the fee was excessive," a utility tax consultant told Thiem. "We got what we wanted. The fee was in line with what we were used to paying."

A major scandal like this, of course, makes front-page news. But, by and large, the press does not pay enough attention to the state legislature. Only a handful of papers — most of them in Chicago — even attempt full-scale legislative coverage. All too rarely is even a roll call published statewide showing how legislators vote. Nor is there a complete daily journal of proceedings beyond the mere disposition of bills. Clearly this lack of public scrutiny is an open invitation to mischief which, I fear, is equally present in many states.

Ten years ago, a report of the Committee on American Legislatures of the American Political Science Association said, "Modernization of American state legislatures is considered by many to be the most important piece of unfinished business in the area of government reorganization." From my experience in Illinois and my knowledge of other legislatures, I would consider that an understatement.

THE HOUSE NEBRASKA BUILT

DONALD JANSON

Donald Janson is a Midwest regional correspondent for the *New York Times* and has studied at Harvard University as a Neiman Fellow.

Though Vermonters may dispute the title, Nebraska is probably the thriftiest state in the union. For example, the state's bonded debt is limited to $100,000 and Nebraska stays well under that. It has no sales tax

From "The House Nebraska Built" by Donald Janson, Copyright © 1964 by Harper's Magazine, Inc. Reprinted from the November 1964 issue of *Harper's Magazine* (pp. 125-126, 129-130), by permission of the author.

or state income tax because so many Nebraskans feel the revenue would open the door to unnecessary spending.

If you are aware of this penny-pinching tradition it is a shock when you drive the arrow-straight road from Omaha to Lincoln to find a veritable architectural extravaganza looming up out of the surrounding plains.

This spectacular skyscraper is the State Capitol. It cost about ten million dollars and took ten years to build, being paid for by a special property tax which yielded a million dollars a year. "An innocent traveler from the East who thinks that Nebraska is a stick-in-the-mud state will get some surprises," John Gunther wrote in *Inside U.S.A.*, after his first glimpse of this startling building.

The surprises, however, are not merely architectural. Recent visitors are viewing with even more interest what goes on inside the Capitol. For this is the headquarters of the only one-chamber state legislature in the nation, an innovation which may, in the years ahead, be widely copied in other states. If this comes to pass, the full potential of a remarkable institution may be discovered — for Nebraskans, though generally pleased with their brainchild, have tended, in characteristic fashion, to maintain it on a starvation diet.

Senator George W. Norris — Nebraska's great innovator — was the chief architect of the "unicameral," as it is generally known. At the time it was created it seemed of no more than local significance to the rest of the country.

Now, thirty years later, it has become an object of national interest as a result of the Supreme Court's reapportionment decision on June 15. Despite the delaying tactics of the 88th Congress, district lines will inevitably be re-drawn and state legislatures are headed for a shake-up. Economy-minded citizens are pondering the possibility of shaking one house out of existence in the process. If this should happen, millions of tax dollars will be saved. More importantly, legislatures might be largely cleansed of the corruption and inefficiency that blight state governments across the country.

If nothing else, experience in Lincoln has proved that one house is cheaper than two. Specifically, the taxpayers' bill for the first unicameral that met in 1937 was approximately half that of the preceding chamber session. And when one body must do the work of two, there is little time to waste on the glut of meaningless bills commonly tossed in the hopper at the start of state legislative sessions. The number introduced was cut in half in the unicameral. Conspicuously absent are the hundreds of nuisance and special-interest bills annually proposed in one house on the assumption that they will be killed in the other.

"There's now no way for us to pass the buck," says State Senator Richard D. Marvel, who has served in the unicameral for ten years. "I can't say to a constituent, 'Okay, I'll introduce this for you,' and then run to the other house and say, 'Boys, kill this.' The lobbyist, too, doesn't dare talk out of both sides of his mouth and offer bribes. We are working in a goldfish bowl."

With only one house, there are, of course, none of those conference committees whose secret sessions have long been a convenient locale for lobbyists' less savory maneuvers. In Nebraska's unicameral, all committees are required to hold public hearings, to announce them far enough in advance so that all interested citizens can attend, and to conduct their deliberations in plain view of the electorate.

Senator Norris was particularly eager to eliminate the powerful conference committee, which he saw as the graveyard for much beneficial legislation as well as the focal point of lobbying manipulations. Traditionalists claim to fear that getting rid of one house would do violence to the governmental system of checks and balances, but Norris' response to that was curt: "After the legislative session comes to an end and we balance the books, we generally find that the politicians get the checks and the special interests get the balance."

Buck-passing, logrolling, and undercover pressure in matters of taxation, schools, utilities, public power, and transportation had long plagued Nebraska. These were the chief targets of Senator Norris' campaign for a unicameral legislature. But his arguments on these points had little impact for a decade. In the end it was a sure-fire Nebraska issue — economy — that proved his trump card.

This came about in the blistering summer of 1934, when temperatures steadily soared over the hundred-degree mark and only fourteen inches of rain — the least the state had ever had — fell all year on parched cornfields. In the third consecutive year of drought, hot prairie winds turned the plains into a dust bowl and the corn crop withered to a pitiful three bushels an acre, compared with the accustomed twenty-four. This agricultural calamity multiplied the miseries of the great depression, which had already swept the state with foreclosures, frozen credit, bankruptcies, and unemployment.

With his familiar black string tie hanging limp from his wilting collar, Norris stumped the state from Omaha to the western sandhills that searing summer pleading the cause of a one-house state legislature. He wore out two sets of automobile tires, crisscrossing the state. He had the aid of a small band of reform-minded allies. One of the most persuasive of these was former Congressman John N. "Nate" Norton (whose daughter, Mrs. Evelyn Lincoln, later became President Kennedy's secretary). "Save time, talk, and money," he urged.

Arrayed against the Norris-Norton forces was a formidable coalition of the state's power structure — major farm and professional organizations, railroads, utilities, and the press. Newspapers "forgot" to report Norris' speaking engagements; handbills posted to announce them were torn down.

"If I offered the Lord's Prayer as an amendment they would fight it," Norris said of his foes on election eve.

But in the end, Norris' dynamism and the appeal to frugality won out. Advocates of the unicameral were helped, too, by the fact that two popular proposals—one advocating repeal of prohibition, the other authorizing pari-mutuel betting—were also on the ballot. All three propositions were approved, the unicameral by a vote of 286,086 to 193,152.

The returns shocked Nebraska's newspapers and politicians. Most stunned of all were 90 of the state's 133 legislators who had been voted out of their jobs. The surviving 43 decided to call themselves senators and went to work as a single-chamber legislature in 1937. Norris skipped an opening of Congress to be there. "I congratulate you on being members of the first unicameral legislature," he told the new senators their first day. "Every professional lobbyist, every professional politician, and every representative of greed and monopoly is hoping and praying that your work will be a failure."

Lobbyists in the Open

Today the unicameral system is firmly entrenched in the state. Nebraskans deny that the money saved is the only reason. They claim that legislators have been made more responsive to the will of the electorate. Probably this is true. But in a tightfisted state, the result is not necessarily progressive.

For example, last year the revenue committee held public hearings on a bill to establish a state income tax. The American Farm Bureau Federation, the Farmers Union, and the Grange sent representatives to oppose it. So did the state teachers' association. Appearing in support was an Omaha taxpayers' group called the Nebraska State Improvement Association. Most witnesses opposed the bill and in the floor debate that followed it was killed.

Last year, similarly, the budget committee held public hearings for two weeks on a special appropriation for the state's university. Its backers, calling themselves Friends of the University, included prominent farmers and industrialists eager to see increased funds devoted to agricultural research. The owner of a television station and a former mayor of Lincoln favored increased university funds for other purposes. The principal officers of the university and its department heads explained their budget requirements to the committee. Individual taxpayers, however, spoke against parts of the proposal, as did representatives of more than 130 Omaha doctors who opposed a full-time faculty in an augmented medical school. Their testimony prevailed and a proposed $35 million program to improve medical-school facilities was drastically altered.

This was, of course, a victory for a special-interest group. In other states the AMA and the practicing doctors who have also been part-time teachers in medical schools have fought against salaried full-time faculties, although medical educators generally believe the trend is the inevitable consequence of the increased specialization and scientific intricacy of modern medicine.

The doctors' victory in Nebraska, however, was openly arrived at after public debate. This is a very different process from the backstairs operations of the lobbyists for the Union Pacific Railroad, the Burlington Railroad, the utilities and liquor interests in the old two-house legislature whose deliberations seldom saw the light of day.

Senator Norris hoped that the limelight shed on the unicameral legislature would attract more capable men to it. He assumed that they would be better paid for their work, since they were fewer in number. Nebraskans, however, don't believe in pampering their public servants. So for years, legislators' annual salaries remained at $872. Recently they were increased to $2,400, which is still not nearly enough to live on. (In other states legislators' pay ranges from New Hampshire's $200 per biennium to New York's $10,000 a year.) Inevitably the legislators' energies must be divided. Senator Marvel, for example, sold his insurance-and-loan business to serve in the legislature. But he will soon be back at a second job, teaching political science at the Municipal University of Omaha.

There are a number of competent, dedicated men in the Nebraska legislature, but there is a notable dearth of lawyers, and the overall caliber is not too different from that of the men I have watched in other state legislatures.

Unquestionably, however, they work harder and more effectively than in many states. For example, the senators assigned to appropriations serve on no other committees. They delve deeply into the specifics of all money measures and when a budget is finally passed there is no question that the legislators know, in detail, just what they are doing.

Between sessions, the legislature—which meets every two years—functions as a "legislative council" which works continually on the state's perennial problems. This valuable service would be considerably more effective if Nebraskans were less parsimonious. The council—along with the legislature generally—is short on research and clerical staff. No senator has a secretary or administrative assistant of his own—he must rely on a meager secretarial pool. Though the council studies and prepares some eight hundred bills on three hundred subjects for each session, its research staff consists only of a director, one assistant, and two secretaries. The budget committee has only two fiscal assistants. Some of these gaps could be filled by university graduate students serving as legislative interns. However, in 1961 Nebraska turned down a foundation grant offered for such a program because it required the state to match the foundation funds in part.

To cite such shortcomings is not to belittle the advantages of the unicameral system. The pattern of an agriculturally oriented state, which is in many respects unusually frugal, would not be duplicated in more urban, ethnically mixed, and liberal states. And those who have worked with the unicameral in Nebraska — from the Governor down — attest to its practicality, efficiency, and responsiveness.

"Ours is the best government on earth and the envy of a lot of people in other states," says Senator Leroy Bahensky. This may be hyperbole. But one cannot dispute him when he adds, "It isn't easy to acquire."

Not Ordained in Heaven

Probably the major roadblock for other states wishing to imitate Nebraska is tradition — the feeling that two houses were ordained by the Founding Fathers. Actually, the idea was borrowed from England. In the early days of the union, some states permitted only the wealthy to vote for members of the upper chamber.

In Maryland, for example, a net worth of at least a thousand pounds was required. Like the House of Lords, the upper chamber was intended to provide the propertied class with a check against impetuous action by the lower house representing the mass of freemen.

At one time some 40 per cent of the nation's cities also had bicameral legislative bodies. Only two now survive — in small New England towns. Britain, as a practical matter, long ago evolved a unicameral system, when the House of Lords was shorn of most of its power.

Apart from tradition, the odds against adoption of a unicameral are considerable. Though legislatures in all states but New Hampshire and Delaware may propose constitutional amendments, they are not inclined to propose eliminating half their membership. Nor is the idea likely to be popular with the politicians who dominate the constitutional conventions which could initiate such a change in all states.

The best prospects are in the dozen states, besides Nebraska, which permit the people themselves to initiate reform by petition leading to popular referendum. These states are Arizona, Arkansas, California, Colorado, Massachusetts, Michigan, Missouri, Nevada, North Dakota, Ohio, Oklahoma, and Oregon. There have been a few attempts, both before and since 1934, to eliminate one house. None has yet succeeded.

However, a major justification for two houses has been wiped out by the Supreme Court's decision that both houses must be apportioned on the basis of population alone, eliminating area as a consideration. "It doesn't make any sense," said W. Dale Hess, Democratic floor leader of the Maryland House of Delegates, after the ruling was handed down, "to have two houses, both based on equal population, since they'd only be duplicating each other."

While there are dissenters, the decided feeling from most quarters in Nebraska today is that Hess is absolutely right and so were Norton and Norris and the Nebraska voters of 1934.

REAPPORTIONMENT: WHAT THE COURT DIDN'T DO

ROBERT G. DIXON, JR.

Robert G. Dixon, Jr., is professor of law, George Washington University Law School. Recently he has devoted considerable study to reapportionment problems.

The Supreme Court's recent reapportionment decisions on the structure of state legislatures are a major event in America's long romance with the principle of egalitarianism. There is no doubt that much change was overdue in some states, and at least some change was overdue in most states. We are a democratic people and our institutions presuppose according population a dominant role in formulas of representation.

The court ruled that the members in both houses of state legislatures must be elected from districts of approximately equal population. At the same time, by its intensive focus on numbers, the court may have transformed one of the most intricate, fascinating, and elusive problems of democracy into a simple exercise of applying elementary arithmetic to census data.

Like so many of the Constitutional issues that have split the Supreme Court, the reapportionment decisions lend themselves to superficial characterization in simple, moral terms, but are devilishly difficult to assess in terms of political realism, political philosophy, and long-run implications. Chief Justice Warren's majority opinions in the reapportionment decisions find support in the oral argument, which the states, frankly, botched rather badly. But his opinions, and particularly the far-reaching opinion in the Colorado case, have not found universal support among legal writers. Among the general commentators there were many who hailed the decisions as a new charter of liberty, signaling a new majoritarianism that could yield fresh political force for more effective approaches to urbanism, civil rights, social welfare, and even international relations. They heard the death knell on a rule of rural virtue rooted in the mystique of the settler tradition, the log cabin, and the family farm. Several of the more perceptive columnists, however, such as Walter Lippmann and Max Freedman, have been sober and restrained in their praise, hesitating not so much over the need for

From "Reapportionment: What the Court Didn't Do," Robert G. Dixon, Jr., *The Reporter*, October 8, 1964, pp. 39-41. © by The Reporter Magazine Company 1964.

reapportionment as the sweep of the decisions, as Anthony Lewis reported in the New York *Times* a few days after the decisions. "Even some liberal-minded persons, admirers of the modern Supreme Court, found themselves stunned by last Monday."

Ideals and Reality

The difficulty lies not so much in the results of these cases as in the court's absolutistic approach. None of the apportionment opinions, except Justice Stewart's, showed an adequate awareness of the complexity of representative government in a pluralistic society. This complexity involves trying to achieve fair representation of the many interests and groupings and shades of opinion in a multimembered body chosen from geographic districts. In any election in any district system, there is a minority that is weighted at zero and a majority that elects its man or its slate and so is weighted, at least until the next election, at one hundred per cent. Some vote weighting necessarily is involved in any election system of a multimembered body from separate districts. To talk of "equal votes" in this context simply is not responsive to the issue. The important thing, in assessing the Constitutional fairness of the system, is how these "equal votes" producing one hundred per cent majorities and zero minorities add up across a state.

Actual examples of this complexity and the insufficiency of a simple "equal-population" formula are not hard to find. For example, a few days after the equal-population rule was announced for Congressional districts last February, in a Supreme Court case that preceded and foreshadowed the reapportionment decisions, Maryland's old-line legislative leaders demonstrated their resilience. They unveiled a plan for new arithmetically equal districts which actually would have worsened the position of the underrepresented suburbs that had brought the redistricting suit. The gerrymandering plan, which was narrowly defeated in the final days of the session, would have carved and regrouped the populous counties without regard to community of interest to yield equal-population districts that preserved the traditional power structure.

A second cause of the inequities even under an equal-population standard is the familiar balance-of-power factor. Significant interest-group overrepresentation can occur whenever a minority group—religious, racial, or other—holds the balance of power in a series of districts. The prohibitionists proved this by actually obtaining a Constitutional amendment. Fear of this balance-of-power factor may be one explanation for the outcome of the Colorado referendum that selected the apportionment plan subsequently nullified by the Supreme Court.

The Colorado case had attracted special attention and was thought to raise deeper philosophic issues than any others in the group of fifteen apportionment cases on the Supreme Court's calendar. It presented an apportionment plan placing the lower house on a straight population basis and the upper house on a modified population basis. This plan had been approved by every county in Colorado in a referendum. In the same statewide referendum, an alternative plan placing both houses on a straight population basis had been resoundingly rejected. Although Justices Clark and Stewart had given limited concurrence to Chief Justice Warren's basic opinion for the court in the Alabama case, they joined Justice Harlan in dissent in this case.

A third potential cause of gross inequities even under an equal-population standard is the possible operation of multimember districts. The South provides interesting examples of this in regard to two minorities in the populous urban-suburban centers: the Republicans and the Negroes. If single-member districts are used, the housing patterns in some populous areas will produce some Republican seats and some Negro seats. But if the legislators are chosen in large plural-member districts, the Negroes and the Republicans will be swamped, despite their substantial numbers.

In short, numbers are easy to play with so long as they remain mere numbers. If, as Aristotle said, "Law is reason unaffected by desire," the reapportionment opinions of Chief Justice Warren show up well as an ideal prescription for a theoretical society. But if what the Founding Fathers called "factionalism" rears its ugly head, and if, as Justice Holmes said, "The life of the law has not been logic; it has been experience," then the Warren opinions are inadequate. The basic difficulty seems to be that the court views all these cases as being simply civil-rights cases involving the personalized right of the individual voter to cast a vote that theoretically will have "equal weight" with the votes of all other voters. In one sense, of course, these cases do involve voting. But this simple characterization by the court misses the crucial point that in apportionment cases the personal civil right of the voter is intertwined with large, overriding questions concerning representation.

Unresolved Issues

Perhaps the first need is to perceive what these cases are all about, and the effect the court order unavoidably will have. In reapportionment, courts sit in judgment on the structure of political power, even effect a judicial transfer of political power. To speak thus in terms of distribution of political power is to talk not of legislative acts, and not of judicial acts in the previously accepted concept of judicial review, but of constitutive acts. Reapportionment restructures government at the core.

Although the judiciary is deeply immersed in reapportionment litigation that the various measures before Congress will not be able to halt, there is not nearly enough information available for intelligent decision. One recent study of the House of Representatives, in which congressmen's votes on four issues were weighted by the population of their districts and recomputed, rather surprisingly suggests that the liberals benefit from such Congressional maldistricting as now exists. A similar recomputation of twenty-two roll-call votes in two sessions of the Texas legislature indicates that the outcome would have differed on only one measure. This is an area where political science, unfortunately, has let us down rather badly. We are just beginning to compile studies of the actual operation of legislatures and the relationships between legislators and their constituencies.

Another critically important aspect, the matter of standards, will need perpetual refinement as legislators develop new patterns of apportionment under which some identifiable group has disproportionate representation. It is a problem of putting real meaning into Chief Justice Warren's admonition that "fair and effective representation for all citizens is concededly the basic aim of legislative apportionment."

To achieve this goal, the court will have to move forward in two directions beyond the equal-population principle. It will have to join Justice Stewart in his concern for "ultimate effective majority rule." And it will have to be disposed to act against gerrymandering devices whereby a minority political party spreads its voters over enough districts in a state to control a majority of seats. Conversely, it should be disposed also to act against gross and continued underrepresentation of a minority party or group which finds itself so distributed and "locked into" a district system that its votes, though substantial, always achieve zero representation.

On the latter point, two lower Federal courts already have suggested that the equal-protection clause, on which the reapportionment decisions rest, may require breaking up multimember districts into single-member districts. Under a statute voided by a lower Federal court in Georgia last March, some voters had their own state senator in a single-member district. Other voters in populous counties having more than one senator were under a system whereby each senator was chosen at large in the county even though assigned for representation purposes to a subdistrict in the county, where he also had to reside. The court found unconstitutional discrimination between the single-member-district voters who "owned their man," so to speak, and the voters in the subdistricts in the plural-member counties who might be represented by a man elected at large but not favored by the very subdistrict he represented. It does not take much imagination to see that this system could operate, and perhaps was designed to operate, to overcome subdistrict majorities that were contrary to the county-wide majority.

In Pennsylvania a lower Federal court last April held that both political philosophy and Constitutional law prohibited the use of multi-member districts along with single-member districts. "One man, one vote" means, the court said, that each voter must vote for the same number of legislators. Otherwise, some voters would have only one legislator looking out for their interests; others would have two, three, or four, although of course their districts might be two, three, or four times larger. The court added the more respectable rationale that "minority groups living in particular localities may well be submerged in elections at large but can often make their voting power much more effective in the smaller single-member district in which they may live." Both of these cases may be on the Supreme Court docket in the term starting this month.

In devising remedies for malapportionment, the courts also should guard against undue haste. How anomalous is the contrast between the "hell-bent for election" speed with which some courts approach reapportionment and the lengthy delay and procrastination in desegregation of public education! Desegregation is conceptually far more simple than legislative apportionment, and is a moral issue as well. It is almost exclusively a matter of vindicating a personalized civil right. And yet in desegregation we have had "all deliberate speed" over a ten-year period, whereas in reapportionment we have been treated to the spectacle of courts pressuring and threatening legislators and fixing exact deadlines measured in months or even weeks.

The "POLITICAL THICKET" that Justice Frankfurter warned the courts not to enter is no less political because the courts are in it. But the highest commitment is to the viability of the system and to maintenance of popular faith in it. With political avenues for redress of malapportionment blocked in many states, with protests mounting, the court has concluded that some judicial participation in the politics is a precondition to there being any effective politics.

Unfortunately, there are no simple formulas for making power just, and politics clean. An equal-population-district system will be no exception to the tendency of all district systems to exaggerate the strength of the dominant party, and may even heighten the tendency. As courts go forward in this new era of "one man, one vote," the task will be to assure both majority rule and equitable minority representation.

Chapter V

The Office
of
Governor

While governor of New Jersey, Woodrow Wilson once stated, "the governor is not the executive, he is but a single piece of the executive." The office of the governor today is, however, more than a piece of the executive; the governor today is a symbol of unity in the state. A powerful executive office was looked upon with suspicion by the framers of our early state governments, because of the experience of most of the colonies with royal governors. Royal governors, as agents of the Crown, wielded unusual powers which often came in conflict with the interests of the colonists, represented by local legislatures. Attempts were made, therefore, to limit the office in the new constitutions formed after the Revolutionary War.

The office of governor was of secondary importance during the early years of independence, and the legislative branch enjoyed a clear advantage. This was in line with the political thought of the era which tended to place great confidence in elected legislatures as protectors of the rights of the people and to distrust the concentration of power in the hands of an executive. The office of the governor was limited by the state constitutions in many ways. In the original constitutions of the late eighteenth century, only Massachusetts, New Hampshire, and New York provided popular election of the governor. By limiting the term of office and the number of terms a governor could serve, the office was further weakened. In addition, most states provided that many of the administrative officers be popularly elected, thus removing them from the administrative control of the governor. This practice led Wilson to comment that the governor was only a piece of the executive. Development during the nineteenth century established a trend to strengthen the office and bring about a more workable balance between the legislative and executive branches of government.

Demands for more effective political leadership, the popular election of governors, and the broadening of the base of suffrage all worked to strengthen the position of governor as the popular leader representing all the people. Although some constitutional changes did strengthen the office of governor, many restrictions or checks remain in a majority of state constitutions. It is impossible to summarize what the various constitutions say, so greatly do they vary. In spite of the difference in practices there has emerged a pattern which is discernible in most states, though the techniques used in achieving a pattern will vary from state to state depending upon the local circumstances.

The governor of the twentieth-century American state is basically concerned with three major facets of the executive function: formulation of policy, conduct of public relations, and administrative management. Professor Ransone emphasizes these three facets in his book *Office of Governor in the United States.* The chapter "The Executive Function," included in this book of readings, carefully details the nature of the three major areas of action and the techniques used to exercise them. The selection ably describes the modern concept of the role of governor in the various states.

As a policy maker, the governor is necessarily concerned with the legislative process. Today the governor does not wait for policy to be handed to him but is a prime mover in laying out a program which he considers essential for the development and well-being of the state. The governor is vitally concerned with the passage of legislation which will achieve these ends and uses a variety of methods to assure its passage. For example, he may vigorously wield such of his formal powers as the power to report to the legislature, the veto, the executive amendment, or the calling of special sessions of the legislature. Informal powers of persuasion are enhanced by the prestige of the popularly elected governor and the judicious use of appointive power. Although techniques, both formal and informal, vary somewhat from state to state, most governors have overcome the built-in restrictions on the office which tended to weaken their policy-making role.

The governor's power over administration is often more restricted than his influence as a policy leader because he must deal, in most states, with administrators who are elected or appointed for terms which may overlap his own. The power that permits him to meet his administrative responsibilities includes formal as well as informal devices. In order to achieve his goals the governor may be forced to use persuasion in cabinet meetings or personal conferences as well as budget and financial controls which may be available to him.

As a corollary to the Ransone interpretation of the governor's role, Samuel R. Solomon presents the governor as the chief legislator. His article discusses the governor of New York, but many analogies may be applied to other states. Three powers have been crucial in the development of the governor's legislative powers in New York: the veto, the item veto, and the executive budget. The uses of these powers are described in the Solomon article.

Sherrill D. Luke's article "The Need for a Strong Governor" points up the vital need for executive leadership in policy making in order to solve the ever growing and complex problems facing the modern American state. Professor Samuel K. Gove, on the other hand, bluntly asks the question, "Why Strong Governors?" As a close observer of state problems, he demands more evidence before accepting the arguments put forward to strengthen the governor's powers.

The transition from one state administration to another is a trying period which can be relieved to some extent if the incoming governor has access to information concerning the state administration. The article "Changing Governors — and Policies" by Clark D. Ahlberg and Daniel P. Moynihan is concerned with the politics of changing governors and administrations. It deals with the transition period following the victory of Averell Harriman in New York and contrasts his situation with that of his successor, Nelson Rockefeller. The problems involved in a change of administrations are emphasized and suggestions are made to lessen the strains of transition.

While the above articles deal with the various aspects of the role of the governor in state politics, the story would not be complete without some consideration of his role in national politics. The Louis Harris article "Why the Odds Are Against a Governor's Becoming President" states that during the first one hundred seventy years of our history a former governor held the Presidency eighty-two of those years. While Mr. Harris is discussing the 1960 elections, his observations are still pertinent. Their positions as state party leaders in a decentralized national party give the governors an obvious strength in nominating conventions. Mr. Harris, however, contends that the national scene has changed to such an extent that their power has been largely dissipated. The article notes the obstacles such as the lack of national appeal and lack of involvement in national and international issues that a governor must overcome in order to win the nomination and, subsequently, the presidency. While governors will continue to be contenders for the presidency, their road to election is much more difficult than it once was. There are others who view the experience gained as a governor to be the most valuable experience for Presidents, and certainly past history would support this view.

THE EXECUTIVE FUNCTION

COLEMAN B. RANSONE, JR.

Coleman B. Ransone, Jr., is professor of political science, University of Alabama. His writings on the office of the governor include *The Office of the Governor in the South* (1951) and *The Office of the Governor in Alabama* (1957).

The governor of the modern American state is concerned primarily with three broad areas of operations: policy formation, public relations, and management. Of these three, the governor's principal role seems to be that of policy formation, since the compelling force of policy considerations runs like a thread through all the governor's other functions. Most governors, sooner or later, find themselves enmeshed in the problem of formulating a legislative program and securing the acceptance of that program by the legislature. They also discover that they must be concerned with establishing the administrative policies which will govern the execution of this program and other programs which have been established on a continuing basis. Intertwined in both of these attempts are the governors' endeavors to exercise policy control over their party or over the faction of the party with which they are associated. This control may be either a direct control, as an adjunct to an attempt to establish legislative or administrative policy, or it may be more indirect in that the governors' concern with the control of the party organization may be based on a desire to influence the nominating process in connection with their renomination as governor or their nomination for some other office. Policy considerations also are an important force in the governors' role in public relations, since much of that effort is directed toward explaining or justifying their programs, either actual or proposed, to the people of the state. The American governor is deeply concerned with policy—legislative, administrative, and political—and while he is seldom conscious of the particular area in which he is operating and may be operating in all three areas simultaneously on a given problem, he is certainly active in the field of policy-making and decision-making.

Perhaps his most easily identified activity as a policy-maker takes place in the legislative policy field. The governor of the modern American state does not wait for policy to be handed to him by the legislature in the form of a legislative statute and then set about to carry out this policy. As numerous studies of the legislative process in the states have revealed, and as will be emphasized in a succeeding chapter on the

From *Office of Governor in the United States* by Coleman B. Ransone, Jr., copyright 1956 by the University of Alabama Press, pp. 146-156. Reprinted by permission of the University of Alabama Press. [Footnotes omitted.]

governor's role in policy formation, the majority of important legislative policies embodied in the major pieces of legislation passed by the average state legislature emanate from the governor's office or from the offices of his department heads. The separation of powers theory, which still·enjoys lip service among state legislators and constitution makers, is no great impediment to the governor in his role in the legislative process. In all states the governor is recognized by the constitution as having some part in the formation of legislative policy, and the development of the office has been such in most states that the governor has emerged as a powerful force in legislative affairs. The entering wedge in the governor's development as a leader in legislative policy is his power to report to the legislature on the condition of the state and to make such recommendations for legislation as he deems appropriate. Gradually over a period of time this power to recommend has been implemented by such powers as the veto, the executive amendment, and the power to call special sessions of the legislature. These formal powers have become more meaningful because the governor's popular election has greatly increased the prestige of the office. This prestige also has been increased through the example of forceful leadership presented by recent occupants of the office. The effectiveness of the governor's leadership in legislative matters also has increased with the development of informal arrangements to secure the passage of legislation. These arrangements seem to form an "influence cycle" which begins with the organization of the legislature, continues through such persuasive techniques as personal conferences with individual legislators and the judicious use of patronage, and finally ends with the veto, which generally is used as a last resort if other methods fail. All of these powers and techniques place the governor in a position to wield considerable influence in the legislative process. Whether he in fact assumes the role of legislative leader is another matter and depends on such factors as his party leadership, the customs and traditions of the state, and the governor's own view of his proper functions.

The southern governors tend to place more emphasis on this aspect of policy formation than do those from other sections of the country. In the South, legislative leadership probably would be ranked first in a listing of the governor's functions. In the rest of the nation, the governor's role in adminstrative policy formation probably would receive equal emphasis. However, the problem of legislative policy formation and the corollary problem of securing the enactment of a legislative program is one with which all governors are concerned. . . .

The governor's role in forming party policy or acting as party leader generally is not considered by the governors to be separate or distinct from their roles in legislative or administrative policy formation. In practice, the governor seldom acts as a party leader except with some specific objective in mind, such as using this power to insure the passage of a particular piece of legislation. Demands on the governor when acting in this role also generally take specific form, such as pressure by party leaders for recognition in the determination of the governor's appointments. Furthermore, party leadership in most states is apt to be split between the governor and some other leading political figure. This rival is likely to be the senior United States Senator of the state but may be another elected officer of the state or even a political boss who holds no elective office. The use of the term "party leader" is, therefore, somewhat restricted in a consideration of the governor's functions.

The term "party leader" is also not an entirely accurate description of the governor's status because of the nature of state political parties. The analysis . . . of the process by which governors are nominated and elected revealed that there are a great many states in which there are no effective opposition parties. . . . As was pointed out, there are some fourteen states which make up a one-party group. In addition, there are some twenty states which may be characterized as being normally Democratic or Republican. In these 34 states the governor is the leader of one faction of his party. He is not, therefore, a party leader in the generally accepted sense of the term. Within this normally Republican group, the governors of Nebraska and Minnesota are in a rather peculiar position in regard to party leadership. The governor is elected on a partisan ticket but the legislature in both cases is nominally non-partisan. It may be proper to regard the governor as a party leader in these states but again his leadership does not follow the accepted pattern at least as far as his legislative leadership is concerned.

In the remaining states, which generally are regarded as two-party states, there are some states which meet the specifications generally suggested for a two-party pattern. In these states, the governor is the party leader in fact as well as in name. He is the head of the dominant party and that party controls both the governorship and the legislature. The governor, therefore, is in a position to use his party leadership to implement the party program. However, . . . the states which fit this description are not as numerous as is sometimes thought. In a great many states, a pattern of party control has developed in which one party generally controls the governorship while the other party controls one or both houses of the legislature. In this case, the governor is still the leader of his party but that party does not have the control necessary to make a party program effective. Hence, the governor, if he desires to see his program enacted into law, must build a power base which must include at least some members of the opposite party.

The fact that the governor in the South and in the normally Democratic and Republican states is primarily a factional leader, coupled with the fact that many of the so-called two-party states fail to follow the prescribed pattern, leads to the conclusion that if the governor is a party leader, he acts in a fashion which does not follow the prescribed pattern.

In practice, it seems to the writer that the governor must build a bloc of votes from whatever source he can and that in only a few states are the members of his party alone a sufficient basis for such a bloc. Consequently, while the governor's effectiveness as a party leader should not be judged entirely in legislative terms, it seems clear that the term cannot be used in its generally accepted sense in referring to the governor of most states. While the governor may be a party leader in terms of the state party's relations to the national party, he is a factional leader in terms of the organization of the party within the state. The term "party leader" as used in this book in connection with the governor's role in policy formation should be understood to mean the governor's leadership of a faction of his party in most states and of the majority of his party in those states where a true two-party situation prevails. This function is so closely connected with the governor's functions in legislative and administrative policy formation that we will not attempt to consider it in a separate chapter in this book. This, however, is not intended to minimize its importance but merely to consider it at those points in the succeeding chapters where it has the most relevance.

The governor's role in management is also a policy role to a considerable extent, since the governor is concerned primarily with the establishment of the policies which will govern the operation of the executive branch during his administration. This aspect of policy formation has been distinguished from the governor's role in legislative and party policy formation primarily for the sake of emphasis, but it does have a different character because of the nature of the individuals with whom the governor deals. In attempting to establish administrative policy, the governor must deal with the heads of the agencies which make up the executive branch. In many ways the governor is in a weaker position *vis-a-vis* some of these agency heads than he is with the legislature. While the governor is supposed to be the state's chief executive, he is actually the chief executive only in the sense that he is the first among several executives. Because many of the other executive offices also are popularly elected, they are on the same level with the governor and draw their authority from the same source. Consequently, the governor is not in an ideal position to establish administrative policy because he does not control the department heads who will theoretically be bound by that policy and who will carry out the governor's programs. The position of the governor is further weakened by the fact that in many states he has only a two-year term and some of his department heads may have terms longer than that of the governor. This means that in addition to being confronted with other elected officers who share his executive power he also is faced with one or more department heads who have been appointed in previous administrations and who are probably of the opposite political party. These are only a few of the complicating factors which make the governor's role in management a very difficult one. . . . [I]t might be well to point out that the governor's central problem in management is the establishment and co-ordination of administrative policy in an administrative environment which is far from ideal. In attempting to achieve his goals, the governor is forced to depend primarily on such persuasive devices as cabinet meetings and personal conferences and on the executive budget and financial controls in those states where he is given these powers. In spite of the various state reorganizations which have been carried out in the last fifty years, it does not seem that the governor has yet become the state's chief executive. The governor's role in management is one of his most difficult functions and probably that in which he is least equipped in terms of powers and staff to do an adequate job. Curious as it may seem in many states, the governor is actually placed in the anomalous position of having far more influence with members of the legislature than with his own department heads. Under such conditions it is small wonder that his primary concern is with legislation rather than administration. . . .

The governor's function in the field of public relations is considered as separate in this formulation of his duties because so much of his time is devoted to public appearances, press conferences, correspondence, and interviews with the state's citizens on matters which have importance primarily in terms of the governor's relation to the public. It is perfectly true that in his major speeches he may be dealing with questions of policy or may be attempting to build up public support for his legislative program. It is true that his press conferences may be devoted to the announcement of appointments or to answering questions on some phase of administrative affairs. It is true also that the citizens of the state come to see him with personal problems in relation to state employment, old age assistance payments, highways, and a multitude of other matters which are directly related to administration. However, when the governor makes a public address explaining policy, or answers the questions of the press on a prison riot, or talks to a citizen about a job for a son-in-law, he is primarily engaged in explaining his program or the workings of one of the programs of the state government to the public, the press, or the individual citizen. The late James Forrestal put the matter very aptly in his diary when he said, "The difficulty of Government work is that it not only has to be well done, but the public has to be convinced that it is being well done. In other words, there is a necessity both for competence and exposition, and I hold it is extremely difficult to combine the two in the same person." The governor's position is such that he must be constantly engaged in exposition. He must not only prepare a legislative program and see that it is enacted and establish administrative policies and see that they are adhered to, but he must also constantly assure the citizens that these functions are being well done and that he is carrying out the promises which he made in the election. It is, indeed, extremely difficult to combine the talents for policy formation, management, and exposition in one person, but any governor must constantly attempt to perform this difficult feat.

Perhaps this need for constant exposition is the feature which most clearly distinguishes the occupant of a key government post whether it be legislator, cabinet member, or governor, from important positions in business. While public relations is now recognized in both fields, it reaches much further into the inner workings of the government than it does in business. The government's whole scheme of fiscal operations is an open public record. Every policy which is considered by the legislature, not just those which are successful, is put before the public for scrutiny. While the press occasionally complains of closed hearings of certain boards and commissions, the general tendency at the state level is for the operations of the executive as well as the legislative branch to be open to the press and the public. Pitiless publicity can be focused at any moment on any part of the whole governmental process and the office of governor is a favorite target of the spotlight.

The governor's every move is worthy of front page reporting. He has no private life and his day's work is not finished when he goes home from the office. One governor, who also had served several terms in Congress, said that he would rate the difficulties of the duties of the two offices about even but that the governorship was a much more strenuous position than that of a Congressman because the governor had no private life at all. "In Washington," the governor said, "a Congressman soon discovers what invitations he can refuse and what invitations he must accept. As a result, he has some time to spend with his family like other normal human beings. Such is not the case with the governor. When he goes home to the executive mansion, he discovers that he is still as close to the citizen as his telephone and that citizens think nothing of dropping in to see the governor at any time of the day or night." The governor lives in a goldfish bowl and cannot call his life his own until he leaves the office.

All of this emphasis on exposition means that the governor spends a tremendous amount of time on what has been called here the public relations aspects of his functions. It seems fair to say that the governor spends at least half of his time on such activities. This means that public relations is so time consuming that it limits the governor's other functions. The governor has only 24 hours in the day, and while it is not uncommon for him to devote twelve to fifteen of these to public business, there is a limit to what one man can accomplish.

The concept which we have developed in this country of a chief executive, whether he be President or governor, is that of a man who is expected to be simultaneously a legislative leader, a political chief, a general manager, and the ceremonial and public representative of the state. This concept places on any but the most exceptional individual an almost impossible burden. It seems abundantly clear that the average governor does not have the time to perform all of the functions which he is now called upon to carry out. The only way to give him sufficient time is to reduce the number of functions, reduce the time spent on certain of his functions, or to give him sufficient institutional aid to assist him in coping with these many responsibilities.

None of these approaches in itself is the entire answer, for none of them can be carried out completely enough to give the governor the additional time he needs. However, by a combined approach on all three fronts considerable progress can be made in this direction in most states. In many states it is also necessary to consider a closely related problem, that of giving the governor more power in those states where the office is still too weak for effective action.

It does not appear that the governor can abandon his major functions as policy maker, public relations man, and general manager, nor is it desirable that he give up any of these roles entirely. However, it is possible, as the experience of several states has shown, to reduce materially the minor duties of the governor, most of which have been saddled on him by legislative enactment, as for example, the commissioning of notaries public, appointment of justices of the peace, the approval in writing of all state contracts, and the like. This reduction in minor duties will save some time which can then be used for more important functions. In addition, better office management in the handling of correspondence and interviews should result in a reduction of the amount of time spent on these functions. This reduction in minor functions and the reduction of the time spent on those functions remaining is not a real frontal attack on the problem. What most governors need is some high-level assistance in performing their major functions, most of which cannot be completely delegated because of their very nature.

In the policy field, for example, the governor himself in the last analysis must make the policy decisions. Even in this role, however, he can be given some help. If the burden of decision-making cannot be transferred from his shoulders, much of the spade work preliminary to those decisions can be done by an able staff. Our experience with the Presidency and with developments in some of our states shows the desirability of what might be called a policy staff. . . .

Some progress can also be made through proper organization, scheduling, and staffing in reducing the governor's work load in the field of public relations. This is the most time-consuming of the governor's functions, but it is also one in which the people, particularly of the smaller states, are least likely to accept a substitute. Considerable public education as to the nature of the office will probably be necessary before substantial progress can be made in this field, but a beginning in the direction of a reduced work load is certainly in order. The primary complicating factor is that the governor's public-relations role is so closely affiliated with his role in partisan politics and with his future political aspirations that it will be exceedingly difficult as a practical matter to curtail.

The field in which the greatest progress has been made in delegation and staff assistance is in management. Here, we already have an example of what can be done in the Executive Office of the President, in the well-developed executive offices of several of our larger states, and in the recent development of the concept of a department of administration in some states. While none of these solutions has a complete transfer value, the experience at the federal level and in those states which have tried these devices should prove valuable to those states which have not yet explored such an approach. . . .

If we accept as a basic premise that the office of governor is an essentially political office, we have taken a step forward in a better understanding of the kind of staff the governor needs. If the three-fold nature of the governor's functions is recognized, then his staff may be organized in such a way as to assist him in policy-making and public-relations functions as well as in management.

THE GOVERNOR AS LEGISLATOR

Samuel R. Solomon

Samuel R. Solomon is associate professor of history and social sciences, Eastern Michigan University. He has published several articles on governorship in the *National Civic Review*.

New York has been the Empire State in lawmaking as well as in some of its more widely advertised products. Its legislature has enacted some 88,000 measures since 1777, and this total would have been considerably greater had it not been for the liberal use of the veto power by the governor. In the last 25 years alone, 1927-1951, the state executive has vetoed over 26 per cent, or 7,503, of the 28,740 bills submitted to him.

This extensive use of the veto and the emergence of the governor in the role of chief legislator have their beginnings in 1874, when the state constitution was revised to give the governor the power of item veto and the period allowed the governor for consideration of bills after legislative adjournment was fixed at 30 days. The vote required to override a veto was raised from two-thirds of the members present to two-thirds of the members elected to each house, and the agenda of special sessions was limited to those subjects recommended by the governor.

From "The Governor as Legislator," Samuel R. Solomon, *The National Municipal Review*, XL (November 1951), 515-520. Reprinted by permission of National Municipal League. [Footnotes omitted.]

The veto powers granted the governor in 1874 have remained virtually unchanged and have greatly affected the legislative process in New York. Reviewing these powers in 1917, Miss Margaret C. Alexander commented:

> *From that date [1874] the 30-day bill became a very important factor in New York State legislation. The frequent recesses of the legislature and the preponderance of special and local legislation resulted in the postponement of the great mass of business until the latter part of the session. The importance of the 30-day bill and the omnibus veto lies in the fact that they afford the governor an opportunity of passing judgment upon the work of the legislature. Since that body has adjourned, it cannot review the governor's disapproval. The governor thus ceases to be a mere restraining hand in legislation and becomes a positive force in dictating which of the hastily enacted measures shall be enrolled on the statute book.*

This picture is still accurate for 1951, for the legislature has not materially altered its practice of submitting the great bulk of its measures to the governor in the closing days of the session; the governor is thus allowed to sit as a "third house" with an absolute veto over most of the legislative product. Since 1927, more than 92 per cent of the governor's vetoes have been accomplished after the legislature adjourned; in 1948 and 1949, 99 per cent of Governor Dewey's vetoes were in the 30-day class. Even with the small percentage of bills vetoed during the session (i.e., ten-day bills—see Table 1), the governor's disapproval seems to have attained a quasi-absolute status, for no full veto has been overridden by the legislature since 1872 and attempted repassage of a veto is of almost equal rarity.

Of course, while the legislature is still in session the governor has opportunity to indicate his objections to the legislators concerned. Thus a bill may be recalled from the governor, amended and repassed, or it may never be resubmitted. It can be assumed that more of this type of executive-legislative agreement transpires when the governor and the legislative majority are of the same political party and it is significant that for the Dewey years the percentage of ten-day vetoes (i.e., those returned to the legislature) is considerably smaller than for that of his immediate predecessors.

It is significant that over half the 30-day vetoes are those without specific reasons or memoranda attached. Prior to 1931, disapprovals of this type were usually grouped together and vetoed in a bloc, or in several blocs, in an "omnibus veto," with a prefatory heading usually listing most of the reasons for which the governor had rejected other measures by specific memoranda. In 1931, however, Governor Roosevelt began using the term "vetoed without memoranda," for these bloc vetoes and this practice has been generally followed by his successors.

TABLE 1. NUMBER AND PERCENTAGE OF BILLS VETOED DURING SESSION (TEN-DAY BILLS)

Governor	Total Number Vetoed	Vetoed During Session	Percentage
Smith (1927-1928)	302	14	4.6
Roosevelt (1929-1932)	1,126	146	13.0
Lehman (1933-1942)	3,029	289	9.5
Dewey (1943-1948)	1,933	30	1.5
Total	6,390	479	7.5

The basis upon which the governor selects some bills to be vetoed "with memoranda" and others "without" is a matter of conjecture. Obviously, it would seem impossible for the governor and his counsel to prepare specific memoranda of approval or disapproval for each of the 800 or more bills that reach his desk in the 30 days allowed.

Former Governor Lehman, in reply to the author's question concerning his use of the veto without memoranda, indicated that many of the bills so vetoed were duplicate bills, special or local bills, private claim bills of long standing, poorly drafted bills, etc. Presumably a good share of such bills could be pocket-vetoed, as in some other states, and the governor could thus escape the onus of definite action. However, the pocket veto is not customarily used in New York and, as Governor Lehman expressed it, he felt a "personal responsibility" to affix his signature, in approval or disapproval, to every bill submitted to him by the legislature.

A popular conception regarding the executive veto is that a difference in political party between the governor and the legislature will result in a greater use of the veto than when the two are of the same party. This does not hold true for New York, although there is some difference between the exercise of the ten-day and the 30-day veto (see Tables 1 and 2) and the item veto. Republican governors with Republican legislatures have vetoed just as high or higher a percentage of bills as Democratic governors with Republican legislatures, or even Democratic governors with a Democratic legislature, a rare occurrence for New York. In 1935, when this situation existed, Governor Lehman vetoed 26 per cent of the bills submitted. In 1933, 1934, 1936, 1937 and 1938, when he was faced with Democratic Senates and Republican Assemblies, his vetoes averaged 27, 24, 19, 23 and 30 per cent, respectively.

Governor Dewey, with a Republican legislature for all his years in office, 1943-1951, has rejected 28 per cent of the legislative product, while Governor Smith, a Democrat with Republican legislatures, had a veto record of 14 per cent in 1927 and 17 per cent in 1928.

Governor Roosevelt, in 1931, believed he had attained the highest record of vetoes in the state's history when he disapproved 343 bills, representing 31 per cent. He achieved the same percentage in 1932, but the number of bills vetoed was only 283. However, his 1931 record was only second to that made by Governor Sulzer in 1913, when the latter vetoed 378 bills, 32.2 per cent of the bills submitted. Governor Sulzer's record remained intact until 1951, when Governor Dewey vetoed the unprecedented number of 426 bills, for an all-time high of 33.7 per cent.

The prime significance of the veto as exercised in New York lies not so much in the cold statistics of its extent as in the reasons justifying these vetoes delineated in veto messages and memoranda.

Veto Messages

The outstanding fact that emerges from a survey is that most of these bills have been rejected on grounds of policy. Only 4 per cent of the vetoes were based on constitutional grounds; drafting defects accounted for 10 per cent, while 12 per cent were bills considered "unnecessary," many being duplicates of bills already signed. Thus, 74 per cent of the vetoes were based on policy, a percentage that perhaps could be increased further if the governor's interpretation of some of the foregoing reasons could also be regarded as an expression of executive policy.

Of even greater significance, perhaps, is the prominence in this "policy" group of the large percentage of bills disapproved as being "contrary to the public interest." This seems to coincide with earlier studies of the veto power in Nebraska and Illinois, and more recent surveys in Pennsylvania and Alabama, depicting the executive veto as a weapon to protect the people, and the governor as a modern St. George slaying the dragon of "vicious legislation" with his veto sword.

According to the statements made by the executives, particularly Governors Smith and Roosevelt, the legislators would have "given the whole state away" time and again had it not been for the careful surveillance by the governor, the guardian of the people. Governor Lehman did not hesitate to take even his one Democratic legislature to task for legislation "not in the public interest." All three of these governors were able to capitalize on friction with the legislature by "going to the people"

TABLE 2. NUMBER AND PERCENTAGE OF BILLS VETOED AFTER ADJOURNMENT (30-DAY VETOES 1927-1948)

Governor	Number With Memo- randa	Number Without Memo- randa	Total 30-day Vetoes	Per Cent Without Memo- randa	Total 10-day + 30-day	Per Cent Vetoed During 30-day Period
Smith	160	128	288	44.4	302	95.3
Roosevelt	359	614	973	63.1	1,126	86.4
Lehman	1,364	1,375	2,739	50.2	3,029	90.4
Dewey	843	1,060	1,903	55.5	1,933	98.5
Totals	2,726	3,177	5,903	53.8	6,390	92.5

in the role of "protector" of the voters from the "evil influences" of their own legislative representatives.

Governor Dewey, having a majority of his own party in control of both houses for all of his terms in office, has not found it necessary to criticize the legislature in the same fashion. The percentage of bills vetoed by Mr. Dewey in the "public interest" class, however, ranks with that of his Democratic predecessors, though his language is more subdued and the term "contrary to public interest" is not employed as frequently. Governor Dewey did not have occasion to "go to the people" over a conflict with the legislature until the uprising—unprecedented for him—over his 1949 budget.

The story of the item veto during the 1927-1948 period is highlighted by the vigorous use made of it by Roosevelt and Lehman to resist what they considered to be legislative encroachments upon the principle of the executive budget added to the state constitution in 1927. It fell to Governor Roosevelt, a few weeks after his inauguration in 1929, to submit the first budget under this provision, one which contained some $56,000,000 in lump-sum appropriations which the governor proposed to itemize before the beginning of the fiscal year.

The Item Veto

The legislature passed this budget but added a provision that the "appropriations hereby made . . . shall be expended in accordance with a schedule to be approved by the governor, the chairman of the Senate Finance Committee and the chairman of the Assembly Ways and Means Committee." Governor Roosevelt vetoed the items segregated under this provision in order, he said, "to prevent an unconstitutional raid on the executive budget system," and his action was upheld by the Court of Appeals later that year.

In 1930, Governor Roosevelt and the legislature again clashed on the form of the executive budget, although not quite as seriously as in the 1929 session. The 1930 dispute reached its climax when the governor vetoed a number of items in the "revised version" of his budget bill. The legislature apparently did not wish to risk another court battle and most of the amount item-vetoed was finally returned to the budget on the basis stipulated by the governor. Mr. Roosevelt's success in maintaining what he felt to be the integrity of the executive budget principle, and his use of the item veto as an instrument in protecting that budget, seems to have been well crystallized by the end of these first two years.

Governor Lehman made use of the item veto in every one of his ten years in office except the last, 1942. Most of these vetoes were on grounds of economy.

Governor Dewey has used the item veto only twice—in 1947—and only to correct "inadvertencies" of $500 each in a salary schedule. With a legislative majority of his own party, there were no counterparts to the "battles of the budget" common to his Democratic predecessors until the uprising in 1949. Prior to that, Governor Dewey's budget had been enacted practically as submitted to the legislature.

It remains now to consider the role of the governor as chief legislator, a role which has been enhanced in New York during the last three decades by four successive strong governors. While the liberal use of the veto is a definite factor in this role, it is but one side of the coin; the other side, and the one the governor prefers to keep face up, is the success of his positive action in approving legislation, legislation which he has recommended. While administrative success is certainly not overlooked or underpublicized, it is to his legislative program that the governor points with particular pride. The veto memorandum says, "This measure is contrary to sound public policy." The approval memorandum says, "This is in line with what I recommended to your honorable bodies on such and such a date."

Governor Chief Legislator

While some commentators have expressed concern over this growing power of the executive in the legislative process, especially with regard to the veto exercised largely on the grounds of policy, it has also been emphasized that the governor is chief legislator because the legislature allows him to be; the New York governor's veto is absolute because the legislature makes it so; and his ability to capitalize on the dual role of chief protector of the public interest as well as of chief legislator is also made possible by the nature of much of the legislation that is introduced.

What apparently has happened in New York during the past 75 years, and has crystallized in the last 30, is that the governor has emerged as chief legislator because of the acclimatization of the electorate to the belief that the democratic tradition of representative government is best upheld when chief reliance is placed in the governor rather than in the legislature. A long line of vigorous governors has been largely responsible for this belief and the legislators themselves have not been able successfully to refute it. This is indeed a far cry from the status of the royal governors and the state governors who followed in the early years of the commonwealth's history.

This picture of the governor and his part in the legislative process is not new. More than 40 years ago it was drawn by Gamaliel Bradford:

> *In large affairs, affecting all the people, they [the legislators] have lost their initiative, because their time and strength are taken up with the petty interests of their constituents. For them they run errands, seek offices, work for local appropriations. Somebody else has to take the broad view, to look after the nation or the state, while they are absorbed*

with Buncombe County or Podunk. And this somebody is getting to be more and more the directly elect of all the people. To a president or governor thus chosen, all the people are coming to look increasingly, not merely for administration but for impulse and driving power in legislation.

The picture may have changed somewhat. It certainly would be criticized by today's legislator and he might argue, with some justification, that if he is an "errand boy" local pressures make him one. But the state executive in New York, as in other states, can still take comfort in the thought that "although the wisdom of a single veto might be questioned, the governors have not seriously abused the confidence of the people."

THE NEED FOR A STRONG GOVERNOR

SHERRILL D. LUKE

Sherrill D. Luke is a former secretary for urban affairs, office of the governor of California.

California's growth is the fastest in the nation at a rate of 1,600 persons a day, 600,000 per year. By July 1, 1980, a population of 27 and a half million is expected.

Some of the challenges of this mercurial growth are that California will have to build classrooms for 200,000 new youngsters every year; provide jobs for 200,000 new workers every year; construct freeways, highways, and streets to handle 250,000 new cars every year; and build 300,000 new homes every year.

Needless to say, meeting these and other challenges will require bold and imaginative leadership from the governor. He will have to use all of his powers as chief executive to meet the needs of a burgeoning population. He will have to find new solutions to complex problems, always weighing desirable goals against what is possible.

What are the requisites of a strong governor faced with challenges of this magnitude?

First: Constitutional Authority

It goes without saying that, in spite of the leadership abilities of the individual, a strong governor must have constitutional powers commensurate with his grave responsibilities.

From "The Need for Strength," Sherrill D. Luke, *The National Civic Review*, March 1964, pp. 126-130. Reprinted by permission of National Municipal League.

In California, the constitution—adopted in 1849 and revised in 1879—vests "supreme executive power" in the governor. He is required to see that all legislative enactments and constitutional provisions are faithfully executed.

Although there are other constitutional officers independently elected and deriving their powers from the same source—the governor may require them to report to him from time to time on matters within their respective jurisdiction. Of course, there is the possibility for conflict, especially where one or two of the incumbents are of a different party. But as a practical matter this has been minimized and there has been little public clamor to make any of the other elective offices appointive except in the case of the superintendent of public instruction where the suggestion came up recently.

In the legislative field, the governor has the all-important veto power, including the item veto with respect to appropriation bills. He also has the sole power to call the legislature into special session and to limit the subjects of the call to those specified in his proclamation convening the session.

Second: Adequate Personal Staff

To assist him in managing the affairs of state, a governor needs a personal staff of secretaries who are loyal to him, dedicated to the public service and experienced in the area of their staff specialties.

Governor Brown has ten such staff assistants. They include his executive secretary, legislative secretary, press secretary, cabinet secretary, extradition and clemency secretary, urban affairs secretary, research secretary, appointments secretary, travel secretary and private secretary.

They are "exempt" or non-civil service appointees who serve at the pleasure of the governor. Their salaries are paid out of the budget approved by the legislature for operation of the governor's office. Collectively, they relieve the governor of a myriad of administrative detail, freeing him to concentrate on matters of policy, ceremonial functions and executive leadership.

Third: Competent Department Directors

A governor should also surround himself with a group of departmental directors carefully selected on the basis of their loyalty, administrative skills and determination to carry out his and the legislature's policies and programs.

In California, the governor has the power to make approximately 40 such "pleasure" appointments. In addition, he appoints the members of some 300 boards and commissions which determine the policies under which various state agencies should be run.

But the bulk of the state's work force consists of more than 100,000 civil service employees. The governor's patronage appointments are limited to roughly two-tenths of one per cent of the total number employed.

Some have argued that the patronage positions should extend farther down the administrative hierarchy than the top level jobs. But California has actually moved in the other direction by creating a new class of "career executives" at the last session of the legislature.

Fourth: Modernized Administrative Organization

For maximum efficiency and economy, a governor must see to it that archaic forms of state organization are continuously streamlined.

Prior to 1961, California's more than 40 departments and 300 boards and commissions were autonomous entities whose heads reported directly to the governor. There had not been a major reorganization of state government since 1929, in spite of the fact that the state's population had almost tripled, its budget had grown from $125 million to $2.5 billion, and its employees had increased from 17,500 to over 100,000.

Under Governor Brown's reorganization plan, the state's major departments and boards and commissions were grouped into eight agencies. Four of them were created by legislative enactment and the other four by executive order. Administrators were appointed to coordinate the activities of departments within each agency. Together these agency heads comprise the governor's cabinet.

This plan brought the governor's span of control within reasonable limits and also improved the lines of communication from the governor's office down the chain of command. In the first year of operation, it produced savings of $174,000 from abolished positions and other operating economies.

Greater efficiency was achieved this year by creating a new General Services Department. This was accomplished by separating the "housekeeping" functions of the Department of Finance from its fiscal, planning and program responsibilities.

Fifth: Fiscal Responsibility

The key to a successful governor's administration is, of course, his ability to see that the state's income matches its expenditures, that its financial solvency is maintained, that a healthy business climate prevails.

To do these things, a governor must have control over the budget process. In California, that control is assured because under the state constitution the responsibility for preparing and administering the budget rests with the Department of Finance under the direction of a director appointed by the governor. After review and modification, the governor submits the budget as his own document to the legislature for adoption, which requires a two-thirds vote of both houses.

The importance of such control is illustrated by the fact that when Governor Brown first took office in 1959 he inherited an accumulated deficit of $68 million and was faced with the prospect of a $268 million deficit by the end of the first fiscal year. Through a broad tax adjustment program and efficient fiscal management, he eliminated that deficit in the first year and provided balanced budgets in every succeeding year.

As a result of tax reforms adopted this year, it is estimated that California can maintain its present level of services without new taxes through June 30, 1965.

Sixth: Legislative Majority

Nothing is more important to the success of a governor's legislative program than to have a working majority of his own party in both houses of the legislature.

In California's bicameral legislature, 52 of the 80 members of the lower house or Assembly are Democrats—two short of the two-thirds majority needed to pass the budget. On the other side, 27 of the 40 members of the upper house or Senate are Democrats—the exact number required for a two-thirds majority.

Assuming they are all healthy and all on the floor at all times and all in complete sympathy with all of the governor's program, he would have no trouble getting his program through. Needless to say, this is wishful thinking.

Not only do our Democratic legislators exercise a large measure of independence, but when the Republicans vote in a bloc—as they did on the budget last session—bills requiring a two-thirds vote are in serious jeopardy unless and until the deadlock is broken.

Seventh: Party Control

This, too, is a highly desirable ingredient in the formula for a strong governor.

It is a luxury which former California governors have seldom enjoyed because of the institution of crossfiling which was finally abolished in 1959. Since that time, the structure of both major parties has been greatly revitalized. And party responsibility has become something more than a cliché to which some pay lip service.

The dominant force in Democratic party politics is the California State Central Committee. It supplies the leadership, the platform and most of the campaign contributions. But its influence is being challenged by the California Democratic Council—a coalition of clubs having 70,000 volunteer members—which has become increasingly active in issue determination, fund raising and precinct work.

Since appointments to the State Central Committee are made by state legislators, the governor's control over that party organization depends on the election and perpetuation in office of assemblymen and senators who are friendly to him and his program.

Eighth: Good Press Relations

A governor's lifeline is tied to this requisite, for it determines his ability to be heard, his chances for achieving a public consensus in support of his plans and programs.

The techniques used in California are no different from those employed by governors of other states. They include weekly press conferences, television coverage, press releases, radio tapings, speeches, personal appearances, television panels, newsletters, letters to editors and photographs with people promoting good causes.

Ninth: Planning Program

A strong governor is acutely aware of the need for an effective program to guide the future growth and development of his state.

In California, the principal vehicle is the State Planning Office which was established in 1959 in the Department of Finance. In June of 1962, that office received a "701" grant of $376,000 from the federal government to expedite the preparation of a state development plan. This plan will provide the governor and the legislature with a set of reliable alternatives for meeting the growth needs of the state.

It will assist the state's decision-makers in planning the highways needed to accommodate thousands of new cars; the rapid transit systems needed to alleviate traffic congestion and smog conditions in metropolitan areas; the recreational facilities needed to satisfy our leisure-time interests; the dams, reservoirs, aqueducts and pumping stations needed to supply water for domestic, industrial and agricultural use; the educational institutions needed to prepare our youth for careers in business and industry; and the homes needed to house our teeming masses.

Tenth: Economic Development Program

This is closely related to physical development and hence should be considered an essential part of any governor's planning program.

The core of California's development plan is a series of population and economic studies designed to indicate the direction that our growth and development will take over the next fifteen to twenty years. From this data we are developing a "growth model" or economic forecasting device which will enable us to predict the level and composition of the state's economy in terms of jobs and income, and to test in advance the effect of possible changes in such critical factors as defense spending.

Electronic data processing techniques are being used to "feed in" proposed economic changes for evaluation and preparation of new estimates within moments. They will also be used for continuously "updating" data at periodic intervals. In other words, we will have an "early warning" system for compensatory state action in the economic field.

These vital statistics will be useful not only for public investment purposes; they will also be made available to private investors. They will have a marked effect on the joint efforts of our Economic Development Agency and State Chamber of Commerce to attract new industry to California.

Eleventh: Social Consciousness

In economic and other areas, a strong governor must demonstrate an awareness of the social implications of state action, especially as it affects the needs of persons disadvantaged by race, income or educational deficiencies.

In California this includes approximately one million Negro citizens and one and a half million Mexican-Americans. They make up a disproportionate share of the semiskilled and the unskilled, and the unemployment rate among them is twice or three times as high as that of the general population.

Under the leadership of Governor Brown, California is taking affirmative action to get at the root of the problem of minority unemployment which is the beginning of a vicious cycle of frustration and despair.

Among other things, the state is trying to increase training opportunities for the unemployed or marginal worker; it is working with private industry in an effort to involve more of their number in apprenticeship and on-the-job training programs; it is studying the re-training problems of those displaced by automation and technological change; it has established a pilot project to encourage culturally deprived children to stay in school, to develop job skills and careers, to become self-supporting and self-respecting.

Solving the unemployment problem will go a long way toward solving the problems of ghetto housing, de facto segregated schools, discrimination in public accommodations and other legitimate concerns of minority groups determined to take their rightful place in the mainstream of life in California and every other state.

States' rights carry with them the responsibility of looking out for the general welfare of all the people. This includes securing and protecting the human rights guaranteed by the federal constitution and reinforced by federal statutes.

As the chief executive, a governor has an imposing obligation to use all of the resources at his disposal to achieve the American ideal. If he

lives up to his responsibility, he need not be fearful that federal programs will infringe on his state's prerogatives or diminish the prestige
of his high office.

California governors have lived by this rule. As a result, many have
gained national prominence while the state stands out as a living symbol
of the strength of American democracy.

WHY STRONG GOVERNORS?

SAMUEL K. GOVE

Samuel K. Gove is professor of political science, Institute of Government and
Public Affairs, University of Illinois. He is the author of *Legislative Politics in
Illinois* (1960) and *Illinois Votes 1950-58* (1959).

The idea that our governors need to be strengthened, or at least that the
office does, is hardly new. It has been an accepted tenet of "reformers"
for many years.

It has been said that term limitations, the long ballot, earmarked
funds, inadequate appointive powers, as well as other factors have operated to "shackle" the governor. The "non-reformers" might well argue
that the civil service system, local government home rule and removing
some governmental services (such as education) from politics have all
worked to hinder the governor as head of state.

In trying to determine if our "weak" governors should be made
"strong" we need to consider many hard questions. One of the first is,
what are the consequences of strengthening the role of the governor?
Will this mean that our unshackled governor will behave properly and
use his newly won powers for the "public" good rather than for his own
advantage or, worse still, for political advantage? Will the newly freed
governor stay within bounds and not stray to such off-limit places as the
university gates?

There are many other important questions with far reaching implications that we should consider before creating our new "strong" governor. Does the establishment of a strong governor suggest that we then
must have a weak legislature? How can we have a strong legislature
without impeding our strong governor? What assurance do we have that
the individual who is elected to our reformed strong governor's office
will be capable of governing? Does the establishment of a strong governor automatically assure that capable people will be elected to the office?
In this connection, will the political system of a state automatically re-

From "Why Strong Governors?" by Samuel K. Gove, *The National Civic Review*, March 1964, pp. 131-
136. Reprinted by permission of National Municipal League.

form itself with the advent of the strong governor? Will the lobbies in the reformed state lie down and die as soon as they know they will have a strong governor to contend with?

We cannot, as has been the tendency in many circles, talk of a strong governor concept in the abstract, or in a vacuum. Maybe it would be easier if we could but unfortunately we have to contend with the real political world.

It is an obvious truism to say that the several states vary greatly and the greatest variations are found in the political systems of the states. As a result, for example, on a political basis we can hardly equate the governor of New York with the governor of Florida. Changing the structure of the governor's office in New York will not change the image of the New York governor as a potent force on the national political scene. The governor in New York, no matter who he is, what party he belongs to, or under what governmental structure he serves, will undoubtedly continue to speak out, and will be expected to, on national and international affairs. The governor of Florida, on the other hand, is not expected to play such a political role, and if he did speak out on national issues he probably would receive little attention outside his own state.

The Florida governor is handicapped, according to many observers in that state, by the unusual organization structure of that state's government, which includes a unique cabinet system. The Florida governor also is restricted by a one-term limit. But it is debatable whether a change from the cabinet system and one-term limitation would greatly change the Florida governor's role.

Many other examples as diverse as Florida and New York could be cited that raise questions about the wisdom of trying to implant a uniform governmental structure on all states and that indicate the great variations among states, especially in the political patterns or political cultures. Likewise, it is obvious that the role, and even the image, of the governor in each of the 50 states varies considerably. Should we then be aiming toward strengthening the office of governor in all states and making these offices identical in power and scope? Obviously this is unrealistic, and was well understood by the authors of the new *Model State Constitution*. In the first sentence of the introduction to the revised *Model*, the authors state that "strictly speaking there can be no such thing as a 'Model State Constitution' because there is no model state." If there is no model state, we can hardly talk about a model state governor. Each governor operates, and will continue to operate, in a distinct political world and, even within one of these worlds, governors, who after all are human beings, will operate quite differently.

We should not be trying to establish a strong governor in each state, for the case has not been made that the office of governor needs to be strengthened in each state. Perhaps, if we knew more in depth about the real world in which the governors of the fifty states live, we would be talking about weakening the office of governor in some states. This raises the point that, when we talk about the real world of state government in each of the 50 states, we are talking on the basis of some thin evidence, indeed. We can count the states which limit the term of governor, or the states with a statewide civil service system, but we know little more on a state-by-state basis. Even in regard to civil service systems, the existence of a statewide system is no assurance that the letter of the law or general intent of the law is being followed.

Let us now turn our attention to some of the organizational difficulties that have been said to hinder the development of strong governors. Probably the most obvious is the limitation found in several states of not permitting the governor to succeed himself in office. This limitation, it would seem, should make it difficult for a governor to get favorable responses for his programs from the legislature and the bureaucracy. Is this, in fact, the case? Are the governors under this limitation able to accomplish their programs by the development of public opinion or otherwise? If the legislature is not responsive, is this due to the one-term limitation or are there other causes? There are many other states, such as Massachusetts, where governors have trouble getting their legislative programs adopted. Massachusetts has no one-term limitation and one would guess that the governor's failures there have something to do with the political climate and the political divisions found in that state. In other states with a term limitation might the reason for a nonreceptive legislature be based on other factors such as a malapportioned legislature? All we can say is that we do not know much about the consequences of the term limitation. We do know that it makes it impossible for an incumbent to run on his record and to establish a record for that purpose. Probably most of us, using our intuition, would say the term limitation is undesirable, but are we on really tenable ground?

Another claimed handicap to effective gubernatorial control in some states, such as Massachusetts, is the existence of dominating legislatures. It is said that in these states the legislature in many ways ties the governor's hands and is unresponsive to his programs. Some of the states where there are remnants of a legislative budget illustrate this. Is the answer to this situation the strengthening of the office of governor while at the same time weakening the legislature? If we do make this change in balance of power, will there be adequate review of the governor's program? And is there an underlying assumption that "good" men will be elected to the office of governor? And, more realistically, are we having a semantic argument with ourselves when we talk about strong or weak governors and strong or weak legislatures?

The practice of earmarking tax revenue by either constitutional or statutory authority for specialized purposes has been said to be in some states a severe handicap to the effective administration of a state government. Is this valid? Probably in some states it is; in others it is not. In my own state, the legislature has somewhat reluctantly in recent years diverted road funds for other purposes. Earmarking is probably a more significant hindrance where there is a constitutional basis rather than a statutory basis, as is the Illinois case.

What about the long ballot? Does the existence of these separately elected officials tie the hands of the governor? We are told that these other elective officials diffuse responsibility. But in reality are these other officials so minor as to be only a slight hindrance? In some states the incumbents to these elective offices are returned to office without opposition year after year and, when a vacancy occurs, it is filled by appointment. In these states, the voter is not seriously inconvenienced by the long ballot at the state level. But for our purposes does the multiplicity of offices hinder the establishment of a strong governor? In Florida, the existence of the elected officials serving together as a cabinet, and with the governor having only one vote, establishes the potential for an intrusion on the executive power. Again, nationwide, there is a great deal we do not know about the consequences of the long ballot at the state level.

Another suggested hindrance to our strong governor is his limited appointive power. In some cases he faces a state government organization with agencies administered by departments with multi-headed bodies. Sometimes a majority of the members of these boards and commissions have been appointed by a predecessor and may be members of the party opposite to that of the governor. The single-headed agency is the ideal of most reformers but, when it comes to certain functions, they argue that this function needs to be kept out of politics and therefore the multi-member board or commission is justified. The reformers are in a dilemma, however, on which functions should be put "outside of politics" and which should not. Generally the regulatory agencies are under a multi-member commission but here there are many inconsistencies. In my own state, we feel that one man can regulate the banks and another the insurance companies but we need five to regulate public utilities. In other states, the conservation people have "avoided" politics by creating commissions as their cover; elsewhere it is the public assistance programs which are cleansed in this manner.

Probably the functional area that has caused the most consternation in this regard is education, both secondary and higher. Almost unanimously we hear that this is one area that certainly must be outside politics—the intrusion of politics here will mean the "downfall" of our civilization. But, try as hard as we do, politics does seep into education and occasionally governors exert much influence in this costly and vital area. But should our conscientious governor whom we want to make stronger be excluded from participating in this vital budget consuming area? It seems a little inconsistent to argue that the governor should be strong, a real chief executive, but on the other hand he is not to stick his finger into this function or that.

If there is some inconsistency in prohibiting our strong governor from getting into nonpolitical affairs, the nonreformers would argue that the reformers have further weakened the governor's potential power by insisting on strong civil service systems and home rule for local government. Given the nature of civil service systems and the way they have been administered, it is not unexpected that governors feel that civil service generally ties their hands. The governors feel, sometimes justifiably and other times not, that they are unable to get rid of incompetents and that they are not able to hire persons loyal to them. These criticisms would, of course, vary depending on the details of a particular state's civil service system.

Home rule theoretically would mean that all functions of local governments are beyond the power and authority of the state government. If we really wanted to make a governor "strong," shouldn't we give him authority over these local bodies that in many cases spend state money and in other cases enforce state laws or at least state administrative regulations? Does not a governor have the right and the duty to see that state public health standards are met?

We simply do not know enough about the real world of state government. We know little pieces here and there but political scientists have not given us enough information on which to base our conclusions. In fact, the urging for a strong governor seems to be based on "these are the findings on which I base my facts."

Until we do know more about the real world, we should concentrate on the few states we do know and perhaps use the experiences gathered there for consideration elsewhere. In December 1962 the Institute of Government and Public Affairs at the University of Illinois gathered some 40 knowledgeable Illinois citizens from various backgrounds in a seminar on our office of governor. After two days of talking, digesting background material and listening to past and present governors, the Assembly came to several conclusions.

The first finding was: "The prestige and importance that attach to the office of governor of Illinois well merit the continuing attention and concern of the leadership of all segments of the state's society. Illinois is fortunate in not having many of the organizational and constitutional deficiencies associated with the office of governor in some other states." (They were referring to one-term limitations and structural problems.) They then went on to urge that the governor be provided with more staff to help him develop his executive budget. They did not point out that hardly any governor had made a strong effort to get such staff or that Illinois statutes clearly provide for an executive budget. The outsider reviewing the Illinois statutes and procedure would have assumed that

Illinois was following the book in the development of an executive budget.

The next recommendation was: "The civil service system as presently constituted often limits the governor's ability to secure effective administrative action. . . . Salaries in the executive departments are in need of selective upward revision in order to obtain and retain the services of the best public servants. . . ."

Another recommendation was that "the authority of the office can appropriately be increased by granting the power to the governor to designate the chairman of all independent boards and commissions at any time during the governor's term of office" and "it would be desirable to strengthen the office of governor by providing that some of the presently elected state officials be subject to gubernatorial appointment." Here the participants were unable to be specific because several of them were close to one or more of the present incumbents or, as it later developed, were actually candidates for one of the lesser offices. The participants also thought gubernatorial elections should be held in off-years "to focus more attention by the citizenry on gubernatorial contests." They went on record against earmarking of state taxes as being "wrong as a matter of principle."

In regard to the legislature, the participants wanted the governor to take a positive role. They said, "The governor's role as a molder of public opinion is inseparable from his role as legislative leader. The likelihood of legislative success is enhanced by documenting to the public the desirability of policy proposals. The more complex the issue and the more controversial its history, the greater the responsibility on the office of governor to prepare the public, the non-legislative leadership of the state, and the legislature for his proposals."

And, to indicate that their concern was not restricted to organizational matters of the office of governor, the participants said, "The Assembly recognizes the basic responsibility of the state government for the economic development of the state. Leadership in this effort has and should continue to come from the office of governor."

These are the conclusions of knowledgeable persons of one state about the office of governor in their state. Are they the answers to the suggested problems of the Illinois office of governor? Probably yes, maybe no. Do they have wider application in other states? In part, probably yes, but in total, probably no. But the most important point is that we don't know. The obvious question is, how are we to find out?

It seems to me that what is needed is a major effort by political scientists across the country to learn about their office of governor and their state and local governments. When the evidence is in and they can accurately tell us how it is in the real political world of their state, this information can be turned over to the decision makers—the legislators, the governors, public minded citizens, or others—and these decision makers should be able to make more defensible recommendations than in the past.

Finally, we should declare a moratorium on suggestions for uniformly strengthening the governors until this evidence is in. We must keep an open mind until such evidence is in and realize that in some states we may even want to weaken the governor. In the meantime, perhaps we should stop concerning ourselves with structures of state government and start paying more attention to the substantive state problems.

CHANGING GOVERNORS — AND POLICIES

Clark D. Ahlberg and Daniel P. Moynihan

Clark D. Ahlberg is professor of political science, Syracuse University. He was a member of the Harriman administration in New York State. Daniel P. Moynihan is director of the Joint Center for Urban Studies of the Massachusetts Institute of Technology and Harvard University. He was a member of the Harriman administration in New York.

While it appears mankind has ever lived in a time of transition, the problem occurs in state government but every two or four years. Doubtless its onset varies with each occurrence: for some administrations it comes quietly, an awakening of powers; for others it is a troubled, foreboding period, reflecting the darkening winter skies that accompany it.

For still others it begins with a crash of understanding. That is the way it began for the Harriman administration in New York State. The scene took place in a New York City hotel, five weeks after the election of 1954. For a month Harriman and his advisers had been furiously at work drawing up a "bold and adventurous" legislative program designed to alert the country that a resurgent Democratic party was back in power in New York if not yet in the nation. In Albany, the new Governor's budget director designate and his aides had spent the same period going over the state's finances, intent on getting a picture of the financial situation and a view of ongoing state programs. On the Saturday in question the two groups met. The budget director reported there were no surplus funds for new programs nor would existing taxes produce sufficient revenues to meet even the ongoing program costs. There was in fact a deficit; there had been one for nearly every year since the end of the war. The discussion of new programs would have to be recessed while they talked of new taxes.

From "Changing Governors — and Policies" by Clark D. Ahlberg and Daniel P. Moynihan. Reprinted from *Public Administration Review*, XX (Autumn 1960), 195-204, quarterly journal of the American Society for Public Administration.

Harriman's program advisers reacted with open incredulity if not hostility. The meeting broke up in an impasse. The revenue problems that preoccupied the budget staff had hardly occurred to the program staff. The two points of view met head on and for the moment the work of the incoming administration came to a standstill. But its transition period had begun.

Popularly the period of transition is viewed as the time of the new broom sweeping out the old mess, refurbishing the executive mansion with fresh ideas and new men. In reality it is frequently a time of disadvantage and difficulty for the new governor in his relations with the legislature and within his own branch of government. The danger, from the point of view of effective government at the state level is that these disabilities will become permanent, that the new governor will lose entirely his opportunity to gain leadership over the government at just that moment when he is commonly thought to be enjoying the "honeymoon" phase of his administration.

In New York State two changes in government have recently taken place in comparatively rapid succession. In 1954, after twelve years of Republican governor Thomas E. Dewey, the Democrat, Averell Harriman, was elected. Four years later he was in turn succeeded by a Republican, Nelson Rockefeller. The events of these transitions, occurring in the context of relatively constant political conditions elsewhere, reveal a number of the factors at work during such a period in New York.

The theme running through each of the events that follow is the difficulty of change: the difficulty of devising new programs, of financing them, of winning support for them, of implementing them. Concern with political transition has long been directed to the task of providing stability and continuity to the processes of government. Clearly the newer task is to provide, as it were, an innovative element that will correspond to the function of government as an instrument of change and adaptation in a society constantly demanding both.

The Problem of the Out Party

The Republicans in the New York State legislature have more or less a permanent majority: Al Smith declared it unconstitutional for the Democrats to control the legislature and they have in fact done so for but three years of the twentieth century and then by accidents of national politics. Since 1942, however, the party division has been more geographic than ideological. Both the Democrats and Republicans are more or less impregnable in their respective strongholds. Their legislators generally represent the largely similar constellation of interests of the political establishments of large metropolitan areas. Notably since the ascendancy of the "modern" Republicans, brought about by Governor Dewey, there has been little sharp ideological conflict between the two groups in the legislature.

The Republicans, however, retain exclusive control of legislative business, allowing the Democrats little more than token participation and, to some minds, receiving only token opposition. (It is common for the budget to emerge from the finance committees without the minority members ever being given the opportunity to vote on reporting it out.) Having few strong ideological conflicts, the Democratic legislators generally acquiesce in their impotence. What little legislative patronage they get is used for local party purposes and the appointees generally offer little technical competence.

Given this situation, during periods of Republican governors the Democratic party almost completely loses touch with the affairs of the state government. By contrast the Republicans have available at all times a large legislative staff which serves the Republican state committee as well as the majority in the legislature. A Democratic gubernatorial candidate is left almost entirely on his own in developing campaign issues and, if elected, administrative programs. Except for the minority leaders and their counsel, no Democrat associated with the legislature provided Harriman assistance of any significance during the 1954 campaign or its immediate aftermath. The Democratic platform and campaign statements were drawn up principally by returnees from the Democratic administration in Washington using what information they could glean from the New York City government and the various interest groups. Apart from the traditional charges of economic decline and government corruption, the platform followed closely the pattern and subject matter of the Republican program: where the Republicans tended to take credit for having implemented the most recent increments in the various ongoing programs, such as unemployment insurance and civil rights, the Democrats tended to propose the next.

In only three instances were major new proposals made in the Democratic platform: "Assumption of responsibility by the State for the care of the chronically ill, as now done in the case of tuberculosis and mental illness"; a state minimum wage of $1.25; and a referendum on direct state aid for school construction. Whatever the merits of these proposals, they would have raised so many difficulties—the first would have required a vast increase in state expenditures—that once in office the Harriman administration changed them so completely as to constitute new approaches. Where the Democratic policy-makers had struck out on their own they completely lost touch with what they came to regard as reality once in office.

In contrast to Harriman in 1954, Rockefeller in 1958 had access to abundant sources of program information and ideas as a result of his party's position in the legislature. The Republican legislative leaders, supported by expert and experienced staff, had maintained a vigorous opposition to Harriman, accumulating in the process an impressive stockpile of information and some issues. Midway through the Democratic administration Rockefeller was made head of a state commission concerned with revision of the constitution. This provided him a year-and-a-half to assemble a staff, to inform himself on state problems and proposals for correcting them, and to appear before the voters in a responsible and non-partisan manner. When Harriman tried to put an end to this in 1958 by refusing to approve the continuation of the commission, it was re-established as a legislative body.

When the campaign arrived Rockefeller's top commission staff became his top campaign staff (as it later became his official staff). In rapid succession he issued a series of policy statements and speeches covering every major issue in state government, even discussing the need for a new state social insurance program to protect every wage earner against the danger of catastrophic medical expense. As events had it, a sharp economic recession and a development within the Democratic party led Rockefeller to concentrate on the issues of economic decline and political bossism — much the issues that had dominated Harriman's 1954 campaign — but at the same time Republican Rockefeller easily outdistanced Democrat Harriman as a proponent of more government action to the point of winning the last-minute support of the state's most "liberal" newspaper.

Rockefeller's election by 573,000 votes was a startling upset in the year of a historic Democratic sweep. It was brought about in measure by a heavy defection of voters from the liberal wing of the Democratic party — a movement certainly encouraged by the impression of vigor which Rockefeller was able to give as a result of the information and staff support he received from the legislature.

Clearly, a party lacking a vigorous legislative wing is handicapped in a gubernatorial campaign. If successful withal, it is likely to enter the transition period with little hard information concerning the task ahead.

By contrast, a party with too powerful a legislative wing will incline to be too little responsive to the policy objectives of even their own governor. Here the difficulty of changing policies arises from the absence of political necessity rather than from the shortage of technical ability and information.

Facing the Legislature

The new governor takes office only to find he must share power. The legislature, experienced, entrenched, indispensable, is there waiting for him. Having won the mandate of the people for his program, the governor now finds he must ask permission of the legislature to enact it. Conflict is inevitable: if there is a difference of party, the conflict is public and pronounced; if the parties are the same, a kind of family quarrel ensues, no less bitter for being more private.

With Harriman's election the Republican legislative leaders assumed a new importance and independence; both promptly became candidates for the 1958 gubernatorial nomination. Reinforced by a number of Dewey officials who took staff posts in the legislature, they commanded unusual, perhaps unequaled, knowledge of the New York State government processes. After announcing their own legislative program a day before the Governor's Annual Message, they promptly moved to dispute his gloomy view of state finances.

Finances: The Challenge to Harriman

For his part, Harriman challenged the powerful and widely accepted image of his predecessor, Thomas E. Dewey, as a prudent, pay-as-you-go fiscal manager. Although the Democratic platform had challenged this image, asserting "for the last nine years the State has been spending far in excess of its income," it is doubtful that even those who wrote the plank really believed it—as witnessed by their first reaction to the report of their own budget director which confirmed it. During the campaign, Harriman declared there would be no need to increase income or business taxes in order to meet the needs of the state and its communities. His running mate even proposed reducing income taxes.

On recognizing the true fiscal condition, the new Governor declared in his opening budget message that the state had been operating at a deficit for all but two years of the postwar period. To restore the balance of state finances, Harriman called for a general tax increase of $127.6 million, including the ending of the year-to-year tax forgiveness which amounted to some $48 million. He declared this necessary to avoid an approaching deficit in the capital construction fund and to provide for "mandated" increases in state services. The Republican leaders, appropriately shocked, charged revenues were underestimated.

Almost immediately Harriman began to soften his stand. He had been elected during the 1953-54 recession; unemployment, which reached almost 6 per cent of the work force in the fall of 1954, dropped off to just over 4 per cent by mid-1955. As the session progressed, revenue estimates were revised upwards $31 million, a development of little significance in terms of the state needs or its fiscal problems but nonetheless the subject of widespread Republican comment. This contributed, late in February, to Harriman's decision to postpone the effective date of his proposed motor fuel tax increase until the beginning of the following calendar year. This cut out for 1955-56 one half his tax package. At the same time the "freeze" on new construction was withdrawn. A month later he agreed to a modified series of Republican-sponsored income tax reductions for "hardship cases" which he had earlier indicated would be vetoed unless accompanied by measures to replace the revenue loss.

In the end Harriman got not quite 30 per cent of the new tax revenues he proposed and then only by use of his veto power to end tax forgiveness legislation. However, as a result of the economic upswing, the revenue yield from the state tax structure was $17.5 million more than he had predicted would result from the adoption of his entire new tax program. The revenue estimates approved by the new budget officials had failed badly to gauge the dimensions and significance of the economic recovery. The next year Harriman proposed a new type of personal income tax forgiveness and a reduction in the unincorporated business tax, thus ending even the tax gains he obtained in 1955 by means of his veto.

Finances: The Challenge to Rockefeller

Rockefeller's campaign in 1958 was marked by the number of new programs and projects which he proposed. Although Harriman's staff privately estimated they would cost $2,468,150,000 over a four-year period, he, like Harriman in 1954, indicated there would be no need for tax increases to pay for them. Early in the campaign he stated there would be no need even for Harriman's gas tax increase which by then the GOP legislative leaders and state chairman had agreed would be necessary. Rockefeller declared he would expand "needed social services" by pursuing policies of economic growth which would increase state revenues "without increasing the burden on the individual taxpayer." However, a national recession had once again reduced state revenues and new taxes were needed when Rockefeller took office. Most new programs had to be set aside.

Echoing Harriman, Rockefeller began his first budget message with the announcement that "New York is faced with the most serious fiscal problem of more than a generation." Like Harriman he blamed his predecessor but, again in parallel, the legislature was not long in blaming him. Before the session was concluded, the governor's authority had been dramatically shaken by a legislative revolt as had not been seen for a generation.

Finding himself in a situation seemingly identical to Dewey's, with the same legislative leaders, finance committee chairman, budget director, *et al.*, Rockefeller promptly restored the quasi-parliamentary practice which Dewey had instituted of weekly meetings with the legislative leaders to agree on the course of action for the coming legislative meetings. In this way a budget was drawn up calling for $277 million in new taxes, including the gas and Diesel fuel taxes Harriman had sought four years earlier. Though a Draconic measure, there was clearly little expectation of difficulty: the Republicans had the votes; in twelve years Dewey's budget had been cut but once. As if to emphasize that it would be easy, the gas tax increase was put through on a straight party vote before the new budget was even submitted. Within weeks, however, this masterful procedure was reduced to shambles.

Three factors seem to account for this. First, the public reaction was very bad, ranging as one upstate paper put it, "from rage to resignation." This was the aftermath of a Republican campaign which talked of tax cuts and new programs, not tax increases. Harriman had had a similar reaction of disbelief, particularly from the press. Second, the Republican legislature, after four years of vigorous opposition to "High Tax Harriman," found it difficult to adopt so suddenly a new attitude to finances and, at the same time, to revert to its former subservience to the governor. Dewey had put an end to twenty years of Democratic rule in Albany; Rockefeller became the head of a party whose legislative leaders regarded the Republicans as the normal holder of executive authority and felt no unusual obligation to him as the current incumbent, particularly as he was ideologically far to the left of most of his party in the legislature. Third, in an unusual election development, the Democrats managed to retain the office of state comptroller. This gave them a center of informed opposition, much as would be provided by an active and well staffed legislative party.

Within a week of the budget message, *The New York Times* reported mounting opposition among Republican legislators to the Governor's proposals. The Democratic comptroller spearheaded the attack with the charge that the proposed revisions in the income tax were regressive and, further, would yield from $80 to $107 million more revenue than the Governor estimated. This charge, although promptly challenged, was supported by a detailed economic analysis and gained increasing acceptance. In time it was taken up by the Republican majority leader of the Senate and the leaders of what became known as "the Budget Revolt." On February 27th, *The New York Times* reported that the revolt had been joined by sufficient Republican assemblymen to defeat the Rockefeller budget.

Weeks later, but only after the elimination of the Governor's proposed forgiveness of the 1958 tax on capital gains, an increase of tax credit for individuals from $10 to $25 to counter the "soak-the-poor" charges of the Democrats, and a $40 million cut in the budget itself which the Governor had agreed to accept, the legislature finally passed the administration tax program—by a margin of two votes.

Pursuing the Harriman parallel to the point of destiny, Rockefeller's revenue estimates blew up on him as well. He, too, had been elected at the peak of a recession. The unemployed percentage of the work force dropped from 7.4 per cent in the autumn of 1958 to 5 per cent in the spring of 1959 and continued to drop. With the business recovery and the effectiveness of withholding taxes, money came rolling in. The state completed the 1959-60 fiscal year without using the $133 million in bond funds that had been programed and with an actual increase in its cash assets. In June 1960, within two months of the close of his first fiscal year, Rockefeller suddenly announced a $120 million increase in his second year revenue estimates and promised a $90 million tax cut on 1960 personal incomes. But already on the preceding day the Senate majority leader had announced that the Republican members of the Senate had unanimously pledged themselves to a 10 per cent tax cut in 1960-61, an objective they had sought in the legislative session just ended but which the Governor had blocked.

As a result of the Harriman and Rockefeller transitions, the balance of executive-legislative power in New York State had come to a more nearly even point than at any time since the establishment of the executive budget system by Alfred E. Smith in 1927.

Finances: The Limit on Innovation

This New York State experience suggests that the range of practical policy choices open to new governors is limited by the financial commitment of existing programs and the relative inflexibility of state revenues. This essentially determines the difference between state and national politics. Change costs money. In New York, where some 60 per cent of all noncapital state expenditure goes as aid to local government and 75 per cent of state operating funds are required to run institutions, not much money can be had by cutting back existing programs. Capital programs provide the best opportunity, but even here it takes twelve to eighteen months to slow down (or step up) a capital program. As matching federal capital grant programs increase, significant cuts in this area may become too "expensive" to contemplate.

During both the Harriman and Rockefeller transitions, such fiscal considerations were dominant. Both governors were elected during a recession and took office before the extent of the recovery was discernible. Both found new taxes required to finance the ongoing government, and both abandoned election objectives of stepped-up state programs to deal with a revenue crisis. The national economy, both on the downturn and the upsurge, fixed the limits of the real policy alternatives for these new governors as must be true in nearly all states.

This also points to the crucial importance in the New York State experience of a knowledge of the state's financial problem as a basis of policy planning in the campaign period. Harriman did not have the necessary staff, the legislative assistance, or a budget document which provided this information when he won in 1954. Rockefeller had this financial data but failed to use it or thought it unwise to do so. Hence neither winning candidate prepared the voters in advance of his election for the fiscal policy he eventually adopted. Instead, each campaigned on the basis of new programs and new services to be financed by a resurgent state economy which he promised to bring about.

Finally, this experience would support Balfour's dictum that whichever party is in office the conservatives are in power. This has rarely been more evident than in the transitional phase of the Harriman and Rockefeller administrations when the boldest innovators were reduced to "marginalistic incrementalism"—or whatever the Russians would call it—by the automatic and built-in increases in the cost of the ongoing government programs and the money shortage resulting from an economic downturn.

Challenge to the Chief

In New York as elsewhere a number of important activities are carried out by officials whose terms of office extend beyond that of the governor who appoints them. A new governor almost never starts with control over these activities and may for some time find himself dealing with executive agencies which are actively hostile.

The Dewey administration, which had known for some time that 1955 would bring a change of governor if not of party, took the precaution of ensuring that most of these agencies would remain Republican for some time. The terms of the Thruway Authority members, just taking over direction of the world's longest limited access highway, were staggered to ensure Republican control throughout the succeeding administration. The Power Authority, engaged in the enormous enterprise of harnessing the St. Lawrence and Niagara Rivers, was scheduled to remain Republican for three years; the Public Service Commission was tied up for four. In fact, Rockefeller found most of the commissions and authorities still in the hands Dewey had left them though this may not have been true had Harriman anticipated defeat. With a Republican legislature to support them, these agencies constituted an important opposition enclave within Harriman's executive branch.

This problem was acerbated for Harriman by uncertainties about the neutrality of the state civil service. In New York, as in Washington, the government had grown enormously during the 1940's. Harriman found a civil service greatly expanded by the Republicans, including large groups that had entered state service by special devices. Eisenhower was confronted with a similar situation in 1953. The Dewey civil servants had become accustomed to working with the Republican legislators and found the habit hard to break, which gave rise to further suspicions, as did the fact that many of the Democratic legislators regarded these civil servants as "Dewey men."

The situation was made still worse for the Democrats by the fact that the Republicans were scheduled to control the Civil Service Commission for the first half of Harriman's four years. This would have prevented the creation of exempt jobs at the high civil service level which enables a governor to underpin his commissioners with deputies and aides in whom they have confidence. The anomaly of this situation was such that the Republican chairman of the commission resigned in order to give the new Governor a freer hand in organizing his administration.

When Rockefeller succeeded Harriman he found a civil service but little changed from that which Dewey left, and correspondingly a source of less apprehension, but even so a Democratic member of the Civil Service Commission was persuaded to resign in order to give the new Governor control over his personnel department, thus repeating and perhaps establishing the sensible practice begun in 1955.

In the best of circumstances, power can easily slip away from a governor during the transition period, as in the case of Harriman and the State University. After much Democratic pressure (this was one of the rare issues on which the Democrats were active during the Dewey era) the University was begun somewhat tentatively in 1948; a permanent board of trustees was not authorized until 1954, and it had not been appointed by the time of Harriman's election. This gave him an opportunity to identify himself and his party with a new institution of great importance and increasing political significance in an area of crowded colleges. However, in the context of a rumor that Dewey would call a special legislative session to confirm the appointments, and as a courtesy to the outgoing Governor, Harriman agreed to accept the recess appointment of a board of fifteen permanent trustees, of whom only one was chosen by him. The board chairman, chosen by Dewey and redesignated by Harriman, was an active Republican political leader who had served as state comptroller and lieutenant governor under Dewey. The chairman seized the initiative in January by calling for a $250 million bond issue for the State University together with a program for student loans and increased state scholarships awarded on the basis of need. As the Governor's annual message had contained no proposals of any kind relating to the State University, and with the budget at the printers, this proposal filled a vacuum. In time the Harriman administration proposed and pushed for more state scholarships based on need and for the State University bond issue but it could not claim exclusive credit for them. Eventually the board chairman emerged as Rockefeller's chief supporter for the gubernatorial nomination and thereafter as one of his closest campaign advisers and one of his first appointees as Governor.

A New York governor has far less problems with overlapping term commissions than do most heads of states. He appoints nearly all department and agency heads. Even so, the State Power Authority, the

Public Service Commission, the State Education Department, the Department of Social Welfare, and the State Thruway Authority all remained outside Governor Harriman's direct control through most of his administration. The most visible and frequent consequences were minor political opposition, withholding of information, and nonresponsiveness, but seldom with respect to any real policy issue or program objective. There is admittedly too little data to justify a firm conclusion, but we would question the wisdom of this method of policy insulation on the state level.

Strange Bedfellows

Both Harriman and Rockefeller recruited and kept on personal staffs of pronounced liberal views. In each administration, policy formulation was or is in the hands of persons considerably to the left of their party's center. These ideological differences tend to be associated with more general group differences. Thus of Harriman's seven principal staff aides, five were Protestant, two Jewish. None was Catholic, although Catholics predominate in the New York Democratic party, and only one was a regular party man. By contrast, of the twelve department heads originally appointed by Harriman, seven were Catholic, four Jewish and only one, a "nonpartisan" holdover from Dewey, was Protestant. Five of the seven who were Catholics and two of the four who were Jewish were party regulars.

An instance, of small matter but considerable significance, of the type of misunderstanding that can arise in such circumstances occurred early in the Harriman administration. As liberal Democrats, personally and ideologically involved with the conduct of foreign affairs under Roosevelt and Truman, Harriman and his staff were perhaps more easily aroused by the loyalty issue as it emerged during the McCarthy period than by any other current political conflict. This sensitivity was sharpened when the legislature raised the issue with regard to two of the Governor's most trusted cabinet aides. One of the first orders of business in the new administration was to revise what were regarded as exaggerated state security regulations. Several months later the Governor and his staff learned in the newspapers that one of the new department heads, a regular Democrat, was requiring all applicants for licenses issued by his agency to fill out questionnaires regarding membership in subversive organizations, a practice never previously required and clearly contrived with the object of getting political "mileage" out of the communist issue. This was the type of measure which brought fire to the eyes of liberals at that time. The department head promptly withdrew his order, but the episode illuminated the gulf of understanding on certain issues which separated the two wings of the administration team.

Governor Rockefeller's personal staff is drawn principally from the liberal wing of his party, while his cabinet ranges across most of the Republican spectrum. In this situation, essentially identical to Harriman's, it would be no cause for surprise if similar tensions were to arise.

In line with their tendency to ideological differences, party regulars present the familiar problem of dual loyalty—to their political sponsors as well as to the administration. Quite apart from any substantive difficulties, such persons rarely have a highly developed sense of the importance of working for or through the governor—far less through the governor's pink-cheeked staff. The regulars frequently find themselves more easily working directly with the legislature, and are, of course, much more readily distracted by matters of importance to the locality from which they happen to come.

Difficulty in Grasping the Reins

With rare exceptions, the new cabinet appointees of the Harriman administration came to their posts with little knowledge of their program assignments. They were not well prepared to assist the new Governor in framing his first legislative program and appeared to have much difficulty with the notion that he would assess their performance more with regard to the new ideas they produced than the quality of their administration of ongoing programs. Lacking confidence in their own information, they tended to embrace the "policy view" of the career civil service, which was often sound but seldom sensitive to the Governor's view or that of his party. Nor was it responsive to the Governor's need for original proposals, tending rather to produce extensions of the programs of the previous administration.

It appears that the Rockefeller administration has attempted to avoid this difficulty by looking outside the government for new ideas. At least one Rockefeller cabinet member has commented that he spends more of his time discussing his programs with outside advisers to the Governor that in consultation within the government. This could be regarded as an extension of the existing practice in New York of relying heavily on temporary state commissions for new policy proposals. If it eliminates the problem of developing a creative career service, it may also tend to produce wild ideas on the one hand and decidedly dull civil servants on the other.

Contrary to frequently held opinion, a governor cannot always appoint men who will be loyal both to him and to some ideal of service beyond party. Nor is the number of party appointments necessarily a measure of political independence or lack of it. New York State government finds it difficult to attract first line talent to appointive posts. Although New York pays as good or better salaries than the federal government, Harriman was never able to attract to Albany an adequate supply of the type of persons who would willingly serve in Washington.

It became a recognized rule that a less-than-adequate party nominee need never be accepted unless there were no better candidates available, but frequently there was none. Asked what were the *de facto* qualifications for a particular class of legal patronage, one of Harriman's secretaries wistfully replied: "Five years' unsuccessful practice of the law." Alternatively, this situation encouraged the hiring of young persons with limited experience but considerable promise, often at comparatively high salaries.

One consequence of the difficulty of recruiting qualified officials, particularly in the seven or eight weeks between the election and inauguration, is that a number of the key personnel of the preceding administration are given the opportunity to stay on for varying periods under the new regime. New commissioners without prior experience are inclined to regard an incumbent deputy or counsel or other experienced appointive officials as indispensable to their own transition. The tendency was marked in the Harriman administration, much less so during the Rockefeller transition when many former Dewey officials reappeared at once and even larger numbers were available.

In the Harriman administration this practice appeared to impede the achievement of control by the Governor rather than to ease it. The very efficiency of holdover deputies and legal counsel served to postpone for many new officials the actual date of coming to grips with their duties. A career service such as New York's embodies more than enough competence needed for day to day affairs and inclines to place considerably more than enough emphasis on the value of continuity in policy and program. In these circumstances a "throw the rascals out" policy is likely to have long-term advantages for the new governor that outweigh the short-run value of avoiding early mistakes.

Proposals

The recent New York state experience with transitions points to the curiously decisive problems of this transition period. At least four suggestions may have value in other situations.

1. *The state fiscal situation can and should be made known to the new governor.*

The New York practice of inviting the new governor to have his budget director participate in the budget hearings that normally begin a week after election is clearly of value. It enabled both Harriman and Rockefeller to present major tax programs which were largely of their own making, for in both cases the incumbent director dropped out of the process once the hearings were completed.

A complete and comprehensive budget document and comparable financial reports can contribute to a responsible political campaign. In New York state, lack of these materials prior to Harriman made it difficult if not impossible to talk intelligently about the state's financial problem. Perhaps of greater interest is the fact that the data were available in 1958 but were not used until after the campaign.

In so far as this recent New York experience is relevant, it also points with great emphasis to the importance of revenue estimates. A professional civil service staff of quality, both in the state tax department and budget division, applied advanced techniques but failed badly to gauge the revenue significance of the 1954-55 and 1958-59 economic upturns on the yield of the state tax structure. A more accurate estimate might have transformed the character of the transition periods of both Harriman and Rockefeller. Here is a specific opportunity for improvement within the scope of professional public administration. Similarly, it points to the difficulty of constitutional procedures such as New York's which require that the budget be submitted to the legislature on or before the first day of February. Printing schedules mean that the budget must be completed by mid-January—too soon for the administration to master its details and, more importantly, too soon to make use of the all-important revenue indications that appear at the end of the calendar year. Much could be said for delaying the submission of a new administration's first budget for a period beyond the customary date, perhaps, in a case such as New York's, until the middle or end of February.

This further points to the importance of the pre-inaugural period as a time of preparation. Certainly this period should not be shortened. Rather, there is a need for developing practices that will assist the governor-elect to make the most of the fleeting weeks available to him. The informal practice in New York of engaging certain of the governor-elect's aides as paid budget consultants made available professional assistance on most satisfactory, noncommittal terms.

2. *The governor's role in routine government business, particularly legislative business, should be institutionalized to provide continuity without overwhelming the executive during his first months.*

As much as half the thousand and more bills passed by the New York legislature each year are departmental measures of a nonpolitical character. The necessity to act on these measures seriously burdened Harriman's staff during his first legislative session. This came at a time when the legislature (and perhaps some of the departments as well!) yielded to the familiar temptation to try to slip by the new Governor measures which would not pass the scrutiny of more experienced eyes. To alleviate this situation in the future the Harriman administration instituted the practice of pre-clearance by the Budget Division of all departmental legislation. Before any such measures were introduced, they were studied, approved and logged by the Division, acting as a staff unit for the Governor's counsel. This system provided the incoming Rockefeller administration with a complete record of all departmental legislation pre-filed for the forthcoming 1959 session, as well as a system for reviewing and coordinating all such measures throughout the legislative period. It gives the new governor at least a fighting chance in his opening duel with the legislature.

3. *Each party should have a vigorous legislative wing which fully participates in the legislative process.*

The only thing that corrupts more than power is lack of it. An effort should be made to avoid the continuous dominance of one party in legislatures. New York is roughly divided between New York City and the rest of the state. The legislature for the city is twenty-five to one Democratic; the legislature for the state is as permanently Republican; neither is as good as it could be, and the source of difficulty in both is the absence of a vigorous minority.

This situation almost certainly could be helped in New York State by the innovation of a bipartisan legislative council and staff which would ensure that minority as well as majority members would have access to information on government issues and programs and which would in that measure make an informed opposition at least possible. While the legislative council may not have lived up to its full potential, when you are in the basement so far as a bipartisan staff is concerned, as is the New York State legislature, the only way you can go is up.

4. *The career service shall be responsive to the problems of transition.*

The practice begun by the Republicans and continued by the Democrats of turning over the civil service commission to the new governor is a sound step. Nothing does greater harm to the career service than to wall it off, as against a natural enemy, from the influence of the chief executive. First impressions remain. If the first impression a governor has of his civil service is that of a hostile and vigilant garrison entrenched behind statutes which he must somehow breach, both are in for troubled careers. Direction of the civil service should be turned over to the new governor promptly as his greatest source of strength during the period of transition—and as one of his principal responsibilities throughout his administration.

Correspondingly, the time of transition is one of great opportunity for the civil servant who will come forward with ideas and proposals. The tendency is to stay out of sight. It is a rare bureau chief who is ready for his new commissioner with a summary of the laws affecting the department or a list of suggestions for new legislation or for implementing the more viable campaign commitments of the victorious party. Those who are ready rarely regret it. Their rewards are fully their due, for a civil servant is never more valuable, surely, than when he is abetting the processes by which the citizenry choose to have things done differently. The important role the civil servant plays in contributing to responsible social change should be emphasized in training for public service.

The professionalization of government service and the concept of "permanent status" are marks of a complex society. Yet there is wanting a greater awareness among civil service career staffs of the essentially conservative consequences of such arrangements, most particularly in areas of government not subject to the pressures of social conflict. This traditional strength of the career service is its greatest weakness when it results in the tendency to resist change and adjustment wherever the values of elected officials conflict even slightly with established professional and career service values. Engineers, educators, doctors, social workers, nurses, to mention but a few, were among the groups most resistant to suggestions for change and quickest to sense "politics" where the slightest adjustment or shift in emphasis was proposed. Thus the prospect emerges that the ease of transition in administration will be in inverse proportion to the professionalization of the bureaucracy: hardly the outcome sought by the merit system, but doubtless a commentary on American professional education as a preparation for public service.

WHY THE ODDS ARE AGAINST A GOVERNOR'S BECOMING PRESIDENT

LOUIS HARRIS

Louis Harris is a well-known political pollster and editor of the *Augusta* (Georgia) *Chronicle and Herald.*

The presidency in 1960 is a wide-open, glittering prize. For Democrats, there is no longer the discouraging prospect of running against a nonpartisan institution, Dwight D. Eisenhower. For the Republicans, there is the hope that the issue of peace and an extended halo of Eisenhower will prove enough.

These facts, plus the powerful magnetism the nation's top elective office has always held for Governors, Senators, and other assorted prominent men, has indeed crowded the ranks of aspirants in 1960. The Republicans have what might be considered a normal situation: a Nixon-Rockefeller contest, a two-man horse race. The Democratic stable, however, has been especially burgeoning, with Senator Kennedy the front-runner; Senators Symington, Humphrey, and Johnson active; Adlai Stevenson demurely in the background; and Governors Brown, Meyner, Tawes, DiSalle, Collins, and at least a half-dozen more hoping for a stalemate that would let the lightning strike them.

From "Why the Odds Are Against a Governor's Becoming President," Louis Harris, *The Public Opinion Quarterly*, Fall 1959, pp. 361-370. Reprinted by permission.

Under such conditions, it is possible that by August of next year two men not now considered likely candidates will be heading up their respective party tickets. This is possible, but not likely.

At this writing, Vice President Richard Nixon is given a long head start over Governor Nelson Rockefeller. Nixon is better-known, has extremely good and active Republican organization support, is running better than Rockefeller in the polls, and has successfully managed to keep himself continuously in the public notice. Rockefeller's only chance is that the high-flying Nixon will stumble, and when he does, the New York Governor will move swiftly and surely into the breach—even if he has to undertake the ultimate in ironic strokes to do it, to enter the California Presidential primary against native son Nixon.

On the Democratic side, Senator Kennedy, also off to a flying start, has a lead, both with rank-and-file Democrats and with individual delegates. His chief rivals are thought to be Senator Symington, who hopes to be the man nobody is against; Senator Humphrey, who hopes to stop Kennedy in the primaries; and Senator Johnson, who hopes that the prestige he obviously has in the nation's capital will spread as far as Los Angeles when the Democrats meet there next July.

Certainly, as 1960 comes round the bend, very few people are taking seriously for the number one spot the multitude of Governors in the Democratic ranks. As a matter of fact, of the six Presidential candidates most talked about, there is only one who occupies a Governor's chair. And that is a Republican Rockefeller, who has an uphill struggle at best.

Thus, we have a Presidential election we are all but formally in the midst of, and there is every prospect that the best a Governor will do is to be nominated for Vice President. This is a vast shift from what has been the case in the past. Since 1900, with the exception of Warren G. Harding, who came out of the smokiest room this century has witnessed, and Harry Truman, who succeeded to the Presidency through the death of Roosevelt, our parties have simply not turned to candidates whose major records had been written in the legislative chambers of this country.

It seemed that Governors always had their own way when convention time rolled around. Somehow, the up-and-coming Governor seemed to be the President standing in the wings. Senators too often tended to conjure up an image of stentorian windbags whose clubbishness was born of a capacity to compromise any and all issues away, including more often than not principle itself.

Thus, Governors usually walked off with the top prize at convention, and Senators served the inglorious role of balancing out the ticket—in that mystical process of American politics that assumes a southerner as a running mate will automatically bring strength where weakness has been showing, or that a farm nominee for Vice President will cause recalcitrant farmers to forget their grievances. The fact is that Vice Presidents, even if they win, almost always tend to be also-rans. And Senators have always been thought to be prime Vice Presidential timber.

But today the ground rules appear to have changed. There is every likelihood that a Senator will run for President on the Democratic ticket and that one of the many Democratic Governors will bring up the number two spot. However, there is always the possibility that two of the front-running Democratic Senators will conveniently get together and make up the ticket all by themselves. On the Republican side, Vice President Nixon is rumored to prefer as his running mate a man who doesn't hold elective office at all, Secretary of Labor James Mitchell. So it's entirely possible that a present Governor might not even be running for any one of the four top places in next year's election.

A real question is whether this prospect is a temporary phenomenon that just happened as 1960 came up, or whether it is the beginning of a profound change in the way Presidential candidates are selected.

The Traditional Pattern

It used to be that a bright young man in politics would set his sights on the statehouse if he had Presidential ambitions. Fundamentally, these were the reasons why getting elected Governor of nearly any pivotal state could catapult a man into a position where the White House lightning could strike:

1. *Being Governor is like being President in miniature.* It was always reasoned that what a President has to do administratively, a Governor also has to do—except in smaller dimensions. A Governor appoints department heads who become his cabinet; he has to see that the work of the state is carried out; and he has to find the tax money to furnish the wherewithal for his budget.

2. *A Governor learns how to live with his legislature.* One of the perils of the Presidency is what can happen to his program on Capitol Hill. Presumably Governors are up against the same sort of conflict between the executive and legislative branches. A wise Governor is supposed to have received ideal training for the Presidency in licking this problem.

3. *A Governor can duck most of the controversial national issues.* Governors can avoid sticking their necks out too far for their own good by reciting the time-honored hedge of "I'm too busy running my own state to get involved in that," when queried about those issues that sharply divide the nation. By ducking behind the façade of "too busy" or states' rights propriety, many a Governor has been able to avoid taking stands for which people never forgive a man. Thus Governors have come up for national contention with unblemished records on national affairs,

records that didn't have to be soiled until the Presidential nomination was safely tucked away. Ironically, this was most dramatically the case with perhaps our most controversial President, Franklin D. Roosevelt.

4. *A Governor, through appointment plums, is also a political power.* Because most state governments have been bursting with non-civil service jobs, and because press monitoring of state government appointments is comparatively low-keyed, many a shrewd Governor has become a potent political power within his own party. When this fact was combined with the additional fact that national conventions find their real source of power rooted in the respective states, Governors have been (and, as any aspiring Senator will willingly concede, still are) key wielders of political strength in naming a President. The beauty of being a Governor, however, always was that it afforded a man a chance to be a political boss *and* a candidate at the same time. He could make or break someone else, or he could turn around and become a potential nominee himself.

By the same token, Senators and Vice Presidents were always thought to be foredoomed as Presidential candidates. These were the chief reasons:

1. *Senators and Vice Presidents get lost in the shuffle.* There is only one Governor of any given state. But there are 100 Senators in the upper chamber of Congress. And while there is only one Vice President, until Nixon he has always lived in the thick, black shadow cast by the President. What is more, United States Senators live by legislative privilege, seniority, and committee jurisdiction—a system that has made it well-nigh impossible for any one Senator to dominate Congress for any sustained period of time. (Again, in recent years, Taft and Johnson have belied this rule, but only partially.)

2. *Legislators ruin themselves by going on record on almost all controversial measures.* In the course of a six-year term, a man has to stand up and be counted on legislation affecting nearly every corner of American life. Traditionally, being *for* something automatically means gaining the enmity of another group which is *against* it. And the unfortunate experience of many a defeated legislator is that the people for whom he stands up somehow ˙orget his positive vote, while the "aginners" never forget and tend to turn up on that inevitable re-election day. What is more, the Senator who tries to switch his course in midstream is more likely than not to find both sides invoking a plague against him.

3. *Senators are not usually real political powers back home.* Many a local politician will comment sagely that when a man gets elected to the Senate he "goes national." Others back home tend to take over the running of the party machinery. To be sure, the Senator will be "consulted" on nominations and appointments, but it is a rare Senator who is able to head up a functioning political organization back in his home state. (Bridges, Byrd, and Talmadge again are exceptions.) Thus, when Presidential nominations take place, Senators are given honored places

on the platforms, but Governors head the delegations. And possession of power is nine-tenths of the law of convention.

4. *Senators by nature are compromisers, often with feet of clay.* While Governors can strike poses of morality and uncompromising stands on principle, Senators are, by their very process of legislating, compromised. The give and take of making laws requires logrolling and swapping. After a while, a United States Senator has backed and filled so often over such a wide range that he is more apt to have the image of a shrewd manipulator than of a white knight. The former is disastrous to Presidential aspirations, as everybody knows.

In fact, when all the things working *for* Governors and *against* United States Senators are added up, one is tempted to conclude that all the present Senate-reared candidates are veritable miracle men, or the political pundits have had their eyes on the wrong springboards, or, indeed, something profound is happening to Governors and the Presidential nominating process.

At any rate, it is worthy of a closer look.

The Plight of the Governors

Here are some of the underlying reasons Governors seem to be fading as ideal Presidential candidates in general, and in 1960 in particular.

It used to be that a relatively unknown Governor could be pulled out of a hat with a build-up that began around the turn of an election year, put on a whistle-stop train from coast to coast, and then put across on election day. Now things are different. In 1952, Adlai Stevenson suffered mightily from the fact that he was a Governor chosen in the traditional pattern. Even by election day he was not known by over 40 per cent of the electorate. General Eisenhower, by contrast, had long been a household word.

Part of the problem is simply that of being known. Today, for example, Governor Meyner of New Jersey is well-known and respected in his home state and in the important political areas of eastern Pennsylvania and southern New York State. But when one gets out to western Pennsylvania or up to Connecticut or down into Maryland, Meyner just isn't known by numbers of voters running into the 70 and 80 per cent ranges. Yet Meyner is one of the better-known Governors. Similarly, Governor Brown of California is well-known in his own state, but when he moves across the border into Oregon, an important primary state, he is known by no more than 10 voters out of every 100.

This problem of being known would not be disastrous if there were not likely candidates who *are* well-known. Vice President Nixon, the best-known of the possibilities for 1960, is a familiar figure now to 87 per cent of the electorate in this country. Not all, or even much more than half, that number might be especially fond of the Vice President, but he is a known quantity, not simply a faceless name or a nameless nominee. Similarly, Senator Kennedy is known by close to 70 per cent of the electorate across the country. And Senator Lyndon Johnson is known by nearly 60 per cent. (It is curious that neither Senator Symington nor Senator Humphrey is known by more than 35 per cent of the voters, and yet they are taken seriously as Presidential candidates. One might express doubt that they would figure prominently at all were it not for the example of the other Senators Kennedy and Johnson. It could be that there are other reasons why in 1960 a United States Senator, rather than a Governor, is a far more propitious title to possess).

But being known is not the entire story. A man must also have about him what can be called a "Presidential smell." To be sure, there have been men nominated who didn't seem to be likely Presidents, and some have even been elected. But all too often now, one hears a criticism of a Governor that "he is fine where he's serving, but he isn't big enough for the Presidency." Somehow in a cosmic, atomic, mass-media age, Governors have shrunk to being thought of all too often as local figures.

The answer, of course, is that Senators and even Vice Presidents have national and world forums to perform upon. Governors are being hoisted on their own traditional hedge, "I'm too busy running the affairs of my state." Part of what convinces people today that a Senator Kennedy or a Senator Johnson might be Presidential timber is the fact that they have been performing on the same wave lengths as the President himself.

In contrast, the Governors have had to contrive such excursions as the recent Governors' trip to Russia, which in the end was almost totally dwarfed by the Vice President's dramatic tour. Quite clearly, the Governors have felt the lack of a foreign affairs dimension, which is a "must" today for someone with Presidential aspirations.

But it is more than simply foreign policy which besets the Governors. To a degree it is also the active campaigning that has taken place on the part of men who have the platforms from which to wage a continuous bid for the Presidency. Thus, Nixon has performed functions far beyond the normal duties of a Vice President. But in so doing, while beyond criticism of misusing his office, he has also waged a four-year or better campaign for the 1960 nomination and election. Senator Johnson has made the most of his position as the top-ranking Democrat in the national legislature. Senator Kennedy has dominated the investigations of racketeering in labor and management and has taken journeys far and wide in speaking engagements well beyond those of a man whose sole interest is in continuing as Senator from Massachusetts. Senator Symington has an equally stepped-up schedule, interlarded with charges of defense negligence on the part of the Republican Administration. Senator Humphrey has perhaps traveled the longest and hardest, especially in behalf of his national agricultural interests.

The point is that these Senators have had a mobility and a far-reaching range that has been difficult for any Governor to match. In short, they have found means and ways of conducting four-year campaigns for the Presidency.

In contrast, the natural forum of Governors tends to be regional at best. And when they do campaign, they are hard put to find national issues to which people in other regions will respond. It is as if the built-in avoidance of national issues — which used to be thought of as an enormous advantage — suddenly has become an enormous handicap for Governors. Nobody in Oregon cares to know about the tax troubles of the state of Ohio or Pennsylvania. They have enough local problems of their own.

Part of the difficulty, however, rests right within the Governors' own bailiwicks. With rare exceptions, they have deep tax troubles, spending problems, and difficulties in making records for themselves within their own home states.

In recent months, our organization, Louis Harris and Associates, Inc., has completed surveys in Massachusetts, Connecticut, New Jersey, Pennsylvania, Ohio, Indiana, West Virginia, Louisiana, Nebraska, South Dakota, Iowa, Oregon, Washington, and California. In nine of the fourteen states, we found the Governors in trouble of varying degrees. Instead of appearing to be men with a solid base from which to launch vigorous Presidential booms, they will be fortunate, in at least half the cases, to win re-election to their present posts.

Let us take up a few cases in point. First, out on the West Coast, Washington's Democratic Governor Albert Rosselini. Elected in 1956 after long rule by Republican Arthur Langlie, Rosselini is in deep trouble today. Here are a few of the typical comments we recently heard on Washington's Governor, who must face a re-election contest next year.

The wife of a young insurance underwriter in Spokane had this to say:

> *I just think Rosselini is taking it out of the taxpayers' pocket. He raised the sales tax, and the tax on food, too — the poor man just can't make it. I say he's done a bad job.*

Up in Northwestern Whatcom County, along the Canadian border, a young dairy farmer put his sentiments this way:

> *I don't like Rosselini's appointments. Business and occupation taxes include more than they did and probably will take the farmer in for another year.*

In Skaget, a young fisherman had this to say:

> *Rosselini hasn't lived up to his promises. He was going to help the commercial fisherman by keeping the sportsmen's clubs off our backs. He's done nothing — except raise the taxes unnecessarily.*

And in Seattle, a middle-aged widow told us:

> *Our Governor does nothing right. He spends too much money and he's an 'old rip.' He should cut spending in all phases. He also called for an extra session of the Legislature with a cost of $8,000 a day and they accomplished nothing, most of all no tax relief.*

When we added up all the answers we received, by a staggering 71 to 29 per cent count the electorate of the state of Washington had told us that Governor Rosselini was doing an only fair-to-poor job. He is in trouble in his bid for re-election, and he can trace his problems directly to the need to raise more revenue for the state of Washington.

In adjoining Oregon, only recently elected Republican Governor Mark Hatfield is in similar trouble. He gets an even division, roughly 50 per cent approving and the other 50 per cent disapproving of the job he has done in only eight months since he took over as Governor. This contrasts sharply with the 77 to 23 per cent favorable rating incumbent Democratic Senator Richard Neuberger, up for re-election next year, achieved in the same survey.

Moving eastward, along the plains states, newly elected Governor Brooks, a Democrat in traditionally Republican Nebraska, is in trouble paralleling that of Rosselini in Washington. He also strikes an unfavorable balance. His neighboring Democratic Governors, Herseth of South Dakota and Loveless of Iowa, have escaped similar fates for one fundamental reason: they have found ways to remain frugal in a time of deep tax bites. But in the Middle West and border states, we run into another crop of Governors faced with deteriorating situations at home. In Indiana, incumbent Republican Governor Harold Handley has a 2½ to 1 unfavorable rating. Next door to the East, newly elected Democratic Governor Michael DiSalle is in tax trouble, too. And down to the South, Republican Governor Cecil Underwood of West Virginia, up for election again in 1960, is trying to come out from under the crushing weight of a recession that continues despite national recovery and of deep blame that all he has done as Governor is to increase state spending and let unemployment run rampant. In Kentucky, Governor A. B. "Happy" Chandler was fortunate indeed to take refuge under the state's non-succession law for its chief executive. He would have been snowed under in an avalanche of protests about misspending, alleged graft, and increased taxes.

And so it went all the way back to the Eastern seaboard. There were exceptions, to be sure, such as Meyner of New Jersey and Ribicoff of Connecticut, both of whom have danced a merry jig to escape the inevitable press of mounting state expenditures.

In New York, we found even Presidential possibility Nelson Rockefeller in some trouble. Here are typical comments about Rockefeller since the election:

On Long Island, a prosperous businessman told us:

> *I don't like anything about Rockefeller. He's trying to change everything about state government. And too quickly. He's a millionaire with a millionaire's disregard for money. When I saw this tax program I was sorry I voted for him.*

In Brooklyn, a Negro woman of about forty put it this way:

> *There is nothing at all I like about him now. I don't even want to mention his name. He's too rich to know the meaning of a dollar spent and the working man's problems. He just has no idea of what it takes to run a city like New York on a decent level. He has never been poor and doesn't know what it's like.*

Up in Watervliet, a factory worker had this to say:

> *Rocky looked good last fall. But that was when he was running against Harriman who was weak and not in the saddle. Now he's soaking the poor with the taxes. Now they say he'll cut them back again. In the meantime, I've been paying every payday. It's not so much the amount. It's the withholding all the time that kills us.*

In the 1958 election, Rockefeller severely cut normal Democratic pluralities in New York City and rolled up heavy pluralities in Republican upstate counties. Three months ago, we found a staggering 63 per cent of the electorate in New York City thought he was doing a poor job, not even an "only fair" one. To win the state, a Democratic candidate needs to take 68 or 69 per cent of the city's vote. As of late spring, Rockefeller seemed, at least temporarily, to assure a Democrat of all but 5 or 6 per cent of that margin.

To be sure, public approval of Rockefeller as a man and as a personality remains high. And the magic he demonstrated last fall could be touched to life again. But rather than set forth to the rest of the country at a peak of popularity within his own home state, Rockefeller has a long, hard fence-mending job to do. What is more, the underlying reason Rockefeller has lagged behind Nixon as a Presidential candidate has been mainly the word spreading across the country that he is a "rich man soaking the poor." This has sullied the almost ideal image of November 1958 of a "rich man who would take off his coat, roll up his shirt sleeves, and act like a regular guy."

The plain fact is that more Governors than not are in deep trouble right in their home states and regions. The source of the trouble is principally fiscal. The burdens of state financing have become crushing in the past decade, with expenditures rising and sources of revenue not developed nearly so fully as in the Federal government.

Accompanying the shrinking income of 1958 and the upward push of the high cost of living in 1959, the tax bite is very real and is looked on in most personal terms. It is not uncommon for voters to wail bitterly that the extra $100 they are being taxed is just the margin needed to keep them from going precipitously in debt.

Conclusion

In short, the job of being Governor of a state has become one of the hottest spots of all elective offices. The chances are that a man moving into the number one post in a state will inherit a financial situation where capital funds have been heavily tapped for current operating expenses, where tax collection methods are far from efficient, but where demands for dollars, from both municipalities and state-sponsored projects, have reached record heights.

Thus, we are witnessing a massive squeeze on the hitherto politically invulnerable position of Governors. The Governors do not have a natural forum to become nationally known and to campaign on a round-the-clock, four-year basis for the Presidency. And right at home they are getting the daylights knocked out of them for simply trying to make ends meet.

In contrast, while Congress has its storms and still takes positions on most of the major issues of the day, the roster of Senatorial candidates for the Democrats and Vice President Nixon, the presiding officer of the Senate, for the Republicans continue to make hay at the Governors' expense.

There is only one area in which the Governors as a group have not slipped, and here they are likely to be tough, hard bargainers. They are still, for the most part, important political leaders of their own party organizations. And at the national conventions next year they will unquestionably be centers of very real power.

But for the moment at least, and perhaps for some years into the future, the road to the White House from a governorship will be a lot longer and rougher than it has been in the past. Someone such as Rockefeller might break through and go all the way, and he could conceivably run against a Democratic Governor who could emerge from a dead-locked convention. But the odds at this juncture are against it. It appears that a good part of the revolution in Presidential campaigning that has been developed in Washington, D.C., must spread to the statehouse level before the old law of gubernatorial succession will be restored.

Chapter VI

The Administration

Administration of state programs and services is a responsibility of the office of the governor, yet governors in many states are hampered by Constitutional or statutory provisions giving some departments varying degrees of independence of the governor's office. This may be done by providing for the election of the department head or by providing for a board or commission which is elected or only partially appointed by the governor. The problems raised by such constitutional and statutory provisions must be faced and solutions found if governors are to be effective supervisors of administration. The selections in the previous chapter placed great significance on the importance of the governor as an administrator, and the selections in this chapter illustrate the practical as well as the theoretical side of administration. As the American states have moved from a rather simple, rurally oriented society to a more complex, urban society, the problems of administration have increased as state programs and services have increased.

Since administration is crucial to effective government, it assumes a significant position in our political processes. It is impossible to separate effective policy formation from administration because administrators are involved in policy formation; effective government depends upon the proper administration of these policies. Great emphasis has been placed in recent years upon the study of ways and means to improve administration. Well-known studies such as the Little Hoover Commission studies of various state administrations make significant contributions to information concerning administrative reorganization.

It is impossible to overemphasize the importance of administration in the development of effective state governments. The final test of leadership of the governor in developing a sound program may well be the effective administration of the program. The waste and inefficiency so often typical of state administrations may be minimized by sound administrative organization. In addition, the problems of developing responsible government are alleviated by effective administrative organization which pinpoints responsibility. The selections in this chapter illustrate some of the problems in developing sound administrative organizations and policies.

Effective administrative reorganization usually requires constitutional revision because state constitutions frequently spell o it in some detail the administrative organization. It is not unusual for a state constitution to provide for the number of departments, define the scope of their functions, and describe the method of selecting those who head the departments. The Texas constitution is a typical example of this practice. Not only are departments and regulatory boards and commissions provided for in the constitution, the heads of many of these are elected. Because of provisions concerning administration found in most state constitutions, constitutional revision is usually the only method available for effective administrative reorganization and modernization. Administrative reorganization may be achieved by either partial or complete constitutional revision.

A single amendment may be used to reorganize one department such as the Department of Education. An amendment of the Texas constitution abolished an elective state superintendent of education and substituted an appointive board which, in turn, selected an administrator to head a professional staff. Such reorganization is effective, although limited; a complete constitutional revision such as the New Jersey case provides a more thorough groundwork for administrative reorganization. Bennett M. Rich in "Administrative Reorganization in New Jersey" concerns himself with the process set in motion in that state by the revision of its constitution in 1947. The article is an evaluation of the progress of reorganization in New Jersey, and it evaluates the politics of reorganization.

Politics play a significant role in the administrative function in the fifty states. Ferrel Heady and Robert H. Pealy's selection "The Michigan Department of Administration" illustrates the role of politics in administration in Michigan. Michigan, in an attempt to provide effective housekeeping activities, established a Department of Administration in 1948 that was intended to be a central management agency. The department was designed as a staff agency to the governor and was organized with divisions of budget, accounting, purchasing, building, property management, motor transport, and office services. Through the selection of the department head who is subject to his direction, the governor can give direction to the agency's actions, thus strengthening the office of the governor in administrative management. Heady and Pealy discuss both the gulf which must be bridged between the establishment of an agency and its effective operation and the role of politics in converting a paper agency into an active force.

Another study in the politics of improving administration in the states is the article "The Politics of Management Improvement in the States" by Karl A. Bosworth. Bosworth analyzes in some depth the effort several states made to review the existing administrative structure and to reorganize where required. The state studies he analyzes are often referred to as the Little Hoover Commission reports, which have not had the impact on the states that the Hoover Commission study had on the national government. The article carefully evaluates the problems involved in reorganization.

ADMINISTRATIVE REORGANIZATION IN NEW JERSEY

BENNETT M. RICH

Bennett M. Rich is president of Waynesburg College. He is the author of *The Government and Administration of New Jersey* (1957) and *State Constitutions: The Governor* (1960).

Five years have passed since the people of New Jersey revised the state's century-old constitution. The year 1947 marks a major turning point; for many officials, governmental operations are described in terms of "before" or "after" the new constitution. The adoption of the constitution provided a stimulus to administrative reorganization and to an examination of operating programs which has resulted in substantial changes in policies and procedures. Not all that has been done can be classified as positive, nor has everything been done that should have been done. The millennium in New Jersey's state government has not yet arrived.

It is significant, however, that the adoption of the new constitution was merely the first step in a series of continuing acts of reorganization and adjustment. The constitution effected no instantaneous reform, adopting and freezing a new pattern. Rather, it has given the Legislature and the Executive opportunities to make a considerable number of changes. These changes have been much more sweeping and significant in some functional areas than in others owing, in part, to the realities of political life.

Woodrow Wilson observed in 1912 that the government of New Jersey had developed by "patchwork and mere accretion; by the multiplication of boards and commissions, by the addition of first this piece and then that piece to existing departments." Despite numerous attempts to gain some semblance of order, there were in 1947 over seventy

From "Administrative Reorganization in New Jersey" by Bennett M. Rich. Reprinted from *Public Administration Review*, XII (Autumn 1952), 251-257, quarterly journal of the American Society for Public Administration. [Footnotes omitted.]

agencies with varying degrees of autonomy. Fundamental reforms were impossible under the old constitution. Although the Governor was theoretically the chief executive officer—he was the only popularly elected administrative official—his ability to supply effective direction was seriously hampered by four constitutional defects: (1) the Governor could not succeed himself after his three-year term; (2) two principal officers, the state treasurer and the comptroller, were selected by the Legislature meeting in joint session; (3) the long terms of other officers, such as the attorney general, tended to destroy any feeling of personal responsibility to the Governor; and (4) the existence of two military officers, the adjutant general and the quartermaster general, compromised the Governor's position as commander in chief.

In view of the constitutional disabilities, the development of a fully integrated administration was impossible. Legislative enactments provided other obstacles. Laws had been passed providing for the selection of important administrative officers by the Legislature. Other heads of agencies were selected in a variety of ways. Terms of office were often fixed by law for periods longer than the term of the Governor, and each incoming Governor inherited literally dozens of top-level officials in whose appointments he had had no voice.

All of the constitutional and most of the legislative obstacles to effective control were swept away in 1947. The requirement of the new constitution that existing agencies be allocated among not more than twenty principal departments set the stage for a major reorganization of the administrative structure. A commission representing the Legislature and the Administration prepared plans for consolidating all executive agencies into fourteen departments. Individual reorganization bills were drafted for each department. All but one passed, the fourteenth failing because of a controversy over the procedure for selecting the commissioner of education. For some agencies, the reorganization meant simply a change in name and a change in status from one of seventy-odd to one of a select fourteen. For others, the five-year period has been one of constant activity as new functions have been added and old ones modified and occasionally eliminated.

I

In some instances, adminstrative reorganization was almost completely dependent upon constitutional revision. The state's military agencies are a singular illustration. In the constitution of 1844, two staff officers, an adjutant general and a quartermaster general, were given constitutional status, and no limits were placed upon their terms of service. Two separate departments evolved, each headed by an officer claiming life tenure. Conflict between the two departments was not uncommon, especially when divergent personalities occupied the two offices. The

Governor, though constitutional commander in chief, found his control of the military system extremely limited.

By legislation adopted in 1947, a new post, that of a chief of staff responsible directly to the Governor, was established. The department of Defense was created by executive order shortly afterward. During the constitutional convention, the problem of the incumbent generals was much discussed and extensive testimony was presented to the Committee on the Executive, Militia and Civil Officers. After a vigorous struggle, any reference to the adjutant general or to the quartermaster general was eliminated.

The State Department of Defense Act, passed in 1948, transferred all functions of the two old agencies to the Department of Defense. The chief of staff, who heads the department, is free to establish its internal organization and to assign personnel and functions. There is but one exception: the division of civil defense was attached by statute to the department in 1949. The director and his deputies are appointed by the Governor. Although the Civil Defense Plan states that the director "is responsible to the Governor through the Chief of Staff" there is doubt that the regulation would have much meaning in an emergency. The law ties the director closely to the Governor; indeed, in time of emergency, the director is authorized to exercise his powers "in the name of the Governor." Actually there is little relationship between the functions of the Department of Defense and the division of civil defense. The department is a military organization. The division is primarily concerned with the organization of voluntary protective forces, such as auxiliary police and firemen and rescue squads, and with recruiting personnel for the federal air raid warning system. Incidentally, both the department and the division are headed by unsalaried officials.

The department's internal organization follows the staff structure of the United States armed forces as closely as possible. The main function of the department is to perform the staff work incident to the recruitment, training, operation, and administrative and logistical support of the Army National Guard, the Air National Guard, and the Naval Militia. The peculiar status of the National Guard as a half-federal, half-state, institution requires extensive coordination and cooperation between these levels of government. The complete reorganization of the department, made possible by the revision of the constitution, unquestionably has resulted in a more effective military administration.

Constitutional revision also made possible radical changes in the functions performed by the attorney general. Reorganization, in this case, illustrates a pattern characteristic of the revision process. Several important new functions are placed under an officer subject to greatly increased control by the Governor. However, the head of the new "integrated" department is limited considerably by the fact that most of the added units are protected by a statutory divisional status. The rigidity resulting from separate legal status and the entrenched positions of certain agencies has retarded functional coordination.

Traditionally the legal adviser of the state and its representative in matters in which the state was a party, the attorney general is now the administrative head of the state's law enforcement machinery. Creation of a Department of Law and Public Safety would not have been feasible prior to 1947 because of the attorney general's long constitutional term. No Chief Executive would willingly have placed all machinery for law enforcement under an official who was virtually independent of executive control.

The department now comprises not only the legal staff of the attorney general but also four formerly independent enforcement agencies — state police, motor vehicles, alcoholic beverage control, and weights and measures. Each of these units has divisional status provided by statute. The traditional functions of the attorney general are concentrated in a division of law. A sixth statutory unit, the division of professional boards, brought eleven independent licensing agencies under the supervision of the attorney general. By executive order, a bureau of traffic safety was recently established.

Custom plays an important role in the functioning of the department. The practice continues of part-time service on the part of the attorney general and of his 30-odd deputies. Notwithstanding the importance and the varied character of departmental operations, the reorganization act did not require that the attorney general serve on a full-time basis. In an effort to meet the need for coordination of divisions, the office of administrative director was created last year.

Prior to the reorganization, at least three of the agencies — state police, motor vehicles, and alcoholic beverage control — were powerful, independent units. The process of integration requires time. Two illustrations will suffice to indicate the nature of the problem. The first concerns a curious anomaly in New Jersey namely, the presence on the highways of two uniformed state patrols. Historically, the Department of Motor Vehicles and the Department of State Police were each given power to enforce highway regulations. Each developed its own staff. When the agencies were allocated to the Department of Law and Public Safety, little effort was made to integrate them. To have done so would have been extremely difficult since their systems of operation were entirely different. For example, the motor vehicle inspector force is under civil service. The state police, on the other hand, operates as a semi-military organization with separate recruitment, training, pay, and retirement policies. In recent years, the staff of the state police has been increased considerably, from an average of 372 in 1947 to a present authorized strength of 643. It is possible that the road patrol activities of the approximately 125 motor vehicle inspectors may eventually be eliminated and that their major activity will be the examination of applicants for drivers' licenses.

A second illustration of the difficult administrative problems in the new department is the system of licensing and registering motor vehicles, established in 1906. The state does not perform the operations incident to the registration of vehicles and the issuance of license plates and drivers' licenses; private individuals are appointed on a fee basis in various communities to act for the director of motor vehicles. Despite attacks upon the system as uneconomical and subject to abuses, fundamental changes have not been acceptable to the Legislature. The system is a type of political patronage which the legislators are reluctant to discard. These illustrations indicate that effective administration is dependent not only upon constitutional revision or administrative reorganization but also upon a thorough overhauling of the state's general policies and procedures.

Executive control over fiscal matters was enhanced by eliminating the constitutional provision for election by the Legislature of the state treasurer and the comptroller. To provide the Chief Executive with at least the minimum financial controls, a State Department of Taxation and Finance was established in 1944 with budgeting, accounting, purchasing, and other functions. The reorganization act of 1948 combined this agency, the Office of State Treasurer, the Office of State Comptroller, the New Jersey Racing Commission, and a number of formerly independent retirement systems in the Department of the Treasury. The department is headed by the state treasurer, appointed by the Governor to serve at his pleasure.

Since the passage of the reorganization act, internal changes have been confined chiefly to a few areas. A division of investment was established in 1950, following severe criticism by a special study group of the state's procedures for purchasing securities. The state employees' retirement system, the police and firemen's retirement system, and others were brought together physically under one roof and now operate within a bureau of public employees' pensions. From a policy point of view, the importance of this last step can scarcely be exaggerated. For over a half century, pension legislation has been enacted with relative abandon. Now, for the first time, there exists an administrative agency to consider the many-sided aspects of this difficult problem.

II

For most agencies, constitutional revision in itself was comparatively unimportant. Reorganization was dependent upon executive leadership. In the Department of Health, for example, the adoption of the new constitution had nothing directly to do with the far-reaching statutory and administrative changes which have taken place, although the "reorganizing mood" of the period may have been influential.

Early in 1947 the twelve-member State Board of Health was abolished. Since 1915 the board had been the governing head of the department and had selected the director of health. Critics of the board contended that it was unwieldy and had a tendency to assume administrative duties. The members of the board sometimes assigned themselves to the various bureaus in the department and were looked upon as the unofficial heads of those bureaus. The department was criticized for the lack of coordination among the separate units.

The office of state commissioner of health replaced the board as head of the department. The commissioner was to be appointed by the Governor with the advice and consent of the Senate for a term of five years. A seven-member Public Health Council was created to advise the commissioner and to establish a state sanitary code. Following the adoption of the constitution, the 1947 act was amended. The department was classified as one of the principal departments and the commissioner's term of service was made dependent upon the pleasure of the Governor.

One of the striking features of the 1947 act was its authorization to the commissioner to prescribe the organization of the department, subject only to the approval of the Public Health Council. All appointments were to be under civil service. The amended act required that the State Crippled Children's Commission be placed within the department and that a bureau of examination, licensing, and registration be established. The structural position of these units was left to the discretion of the commissioner. A further limitation was introduced in 1952 with the passage of legislation establishing a division of chronic illness control.

The commissioner of health took full advantage of his freedom from statutory limitations. Previously, seven divisions, eight bureaus, and two miscellaneous units reported to the director of health. At present, there are six major divisions: constructive health, environmental sanitation, laboratories, local health services, preventable diseases, and vital statistics and administration. The recently created division of chronic illness control will constitute a seventh. Related functions have been placed under the same head. Laboratory services, for example, formerly were provided by at least six different units. Now a division of laboratories acts for the entire department. Personnel and housing changes were made with a view to bringing together appropriate units of each division. Unhappily, because of the lack of adequate office space in Trenton, the department is scattered among nine buildings.

The reorganization of this department, unlike some others, was much more than a reshuffling of the personnel and a regrouping of individual units. The decision was made to alter the character of the central office to provide consultative, advisory, educational, and promotional services rather than a variety of direct services. Formerly, for example, public health nurses were employed by the department to assist communities that did not have local health nurses. In theory, the nurse was to remain only until the community was willing and able to provide its own service. In practice, the community rarely acted. The state continued for years to pay and supervise nurses whose work was confined to one small area. Now the responsibility is being shifted. The money formerly applied to the salaries of nurses is made available to local governing bodies on a grant-in-aid basis. The community must take the initiative to hire the nurse. The department will assist her through its advisory services, but she is the employee of the municipality rather than the state.

Changes in the department's policy and organizational structure have been accompanied by a close examination of services performed. One illustration will suffice. After a survey of the use made of duplicate serologic examination reports, the duplication and filing of over 300,000 items annually was eliminated and the old files destroyed. Responsibility for retaining the original report was placed upon the doctor who had requested the examination. The original reports were returned in window envelopes, thus saving the typing of 300,000 addresses. Procedural economies and changes in departmental policy on the types of direct service to be provided have enabled the department to expand its overall activities without any increase in personnel.

In at least two agencies, assistance for internal reorganization has been obtained from management consultants. The Highway Department has had the benefit of a survey by Griffenhagen and Associates. The results of the survey have not been made public but, within the last few years, a number of organizational changes have taken place.

Representatives of the Council of State Governments in 1948 conducted a study for the Department of Institutions and Agencies of the varied systems of welfare administration. The report was critical of the categorical assistance programs, each of which was administered differently, involving "not only different staff relationships but also different financial relationships." Old age assistance and aid to the blind were administered locally by county welfare boards. Aid to dependent children operated through district offices of the department. General assistance was the responsibility of the municipalities with supervision from the Department of Conservation and Economic Development. As a result of the study, all welfare services at the state level were consolidated in a statutory division of welfare headed by a deputy commissioner within the Department of Institutions and Agencies. The county welfare boards now administer all programs at the local level except general assistance. The municipalities have been unwilling to surrender this responsibility.

III

Administrative reform in military affairs, law enforcement, finance, health, highways, and welfare, while varying in character and degree, may be contrasted with the lack of substantial change in other areas.

A number of departments have not been affected to any marked degree either by constitutional revision or by statutory reorganization. The major change in the Department of Agriculture was the allocation to it of the Office of Milk Industry. The Department of Banking and Insurance acquired the New Jersey Real Estate Commission as a statutory division. The Department of State was assigned the office of the state athletic commissioner. The former Board of Public Utility Commissioners—a part-time body—became the Department of Public Utilities.

The last structural change of consequence in the Department of Education occurred in 1945, before the adoption of the new constitution. An effort by educational groups to place the power of appointment of the commissioner of education in the State Board of Education rather than in the Governor has repeatedly been blocked in the Senate. The Senate's action has been due probably less to a concern for preserving the authority of the Chief Executive than to a natural reluctance to give up permanently every vestige of control over a patronage position of importance.

The redistribution of more than seventy agencies among fourteen departments resulted in instances of a greatly increased administrative burden upon the top-level departmental staff. For some departments, the large number of new units made impossible any rapid change in administrative practices. There was no choice but to keep the old agencies operating almost as they were prior to the reorganization. The department was, of necessity, little more than a legal framework within which numerous agencies were placed. The Department of Conservation and Economic Development is a case in point, consolidating under one head literally a host of formerly independent units bearing little functional relationship to each other. The Department of Labor and Industry combines the old Department of Labor with agencies in charge of unemployment compensation, rehabilitation, and mediation.

Rigid adherence to the number fourteen has resulted in a legal structure which sometimes does not reflect actual conditions. The New Jersey Turnpike Authority is the best, although by no means the only, illustration of an organizational fiction. By law, the Turnpike Authority was placed in the State Highway Department. Actually, it operates as an independent entity. The New Jersey Supreme Court has declared that the Authority is "in but not of" the State Highway Department. The state highway commissioner is not a member of the Turnpike Authority. His staff does not participate in its operations.

There are still many agencies which do not function as integral parts of the departments to which they have been allocated, but for most the condition is relatively temporary. Two powerful factors tend to support the continuing drive for integration. One is the problem of obtaining operating funds. Regardless of its former status, each unit's asking budget must have the approval of the department head. A second formidable budgetary hurdle is the hearing and determination by the Treasury Department's division of budget and accounting. Finally, on the executive side, there remains the problem of obtaining the Governor's approval. Financial control is a powerful means of inducing cooperation. The second unifying factor is personnel turnover. Retirements, deaths, and resignations create opportunities for new minds unfettered by outmoded practices. Time can be an able ally of a determined department head.

The Department of Civil Service, formerly the Civil Service Commission, continues to be headed by a five-member body. The leadership of a new president combined with the availability of additional state funds has produced promising developments for the approximately 23,000 state employees. Increased pay schedules, the adoption of a forty-hour week, a new effort at developing a sound merit rating plan—these and other efforts have done much to improve morale.

Among the obstacles to a fully integrated administrative organization are the reorganization acts themselves. Some are considerably more restrictive than the constitution requires. They hamper control by the department head, first by freezing the internal structure and second by compromising him with respect to the appointment of his divisional directors. In Health, Civil Service, Defense, and Highways the department head has wide discretion. He can create, consolidate, or eliminate divisions almost at will. In Treasury, Law and Public Safety, and others, the divisional structure is fixed. Whenever the department head desires to effect a change, he must seek enabling legislation. These variations stem in part from the nature of the functions performed and in part from the pre-1947 status of the agencies concerned. The more technical and specialized the function, the greater was the tendency to free the department head from statutory restrictions. However, where an agency of considerable importance was brought into a department, the reorganization acts nearly always accorded the unit divisional status.

Undoubtedly, there were also political reasons for the variations in the discretion given department heads by the reorganization acts. The specialized nature of the operations in some departments offered few opportunities for political appointments. As a consequence, the department head was permitted wide latitude. In agencies requiring administrators with less technical training, the department head was relieved of responsibility—or at least required to share his responsibility with the Governor and the Senate. Approximately twenty division heads are appointed by the Governor with Senate consent.

Inattention to the chain-of-command theory is evidenced further by the statutory term of many division heads. In some instances department heads who serve at the pleasure of the Governor have, as subordinates, division heads who are appointed by the Governor and serve during the Governor's term. Removal power is also vested in the Governor, not the department head. The department head may initiate each appointment or removal, but his freedom of selection and his ultimate control of the agency may be severely prejudiced.

In effect, many of the reorganization acts performed a twofold disservice to the department chief. His control over the department was appreciably reduced by the fact that he could not alter the fundamental structure without legislation. In the long run, this may tend to discourage organizational developments in keeping with changes in function. His control was lessened also by the provision for gubernatorial appointment of division heads. Much depends upon the attitude of the Governor and the political pressures of the moment. In the past, members of the Legislature have often looked upon the top-level positions in a number of agencies as avenues either for personal advancement or for discharging political obligations. Senate consent meant political selection. The reorganization acts do not alter the pattern.

Although the reorganization acts do not measure up fully to the standards established by the constitution, this failure should not obscure the substantial accomplishments of the last five years. Since the initial allocation of agencies to the principal departments, scores of less spectacular forward steps have been taken. Much remains to be done; but if events of the last five years are any guide, much more will be accomplished. Indeed, the most meaningful feature of the revision-reorganization movement has been the continuing nature of the efforts to improve the state's administrative structure and the efficiency of its operations.

THE MICHIGAN DEPARTMENT OF ADMINISTRATION; A CASE STUDY IN THE POLITICS OF ADMINISTRATION

FERREL HEADY AND ROBERT H. PEALY

Ferrel Heady is vice-president of the University of New Mexico and serves on the Governor's Commission on Reorganization of State Government. He is the author of *Administrative Procedure Legislation in the States* (1952) and co-author of *The Michigan Department of Administration* (1956). Robert H. Pealy is professor and director of the Bureau of Governmental Research and Services, University of Washington. He is co-author of *Field Organization of Michigan State Government Departments* (1956).

The Michigan Department of Administration, a central management agency which is responsible for most of the "housekeeping" activities of the state government, was created and began to function in 1948.

In commentaries on similar central management agencies and their work, references to the political environment of state government have been rare. The advocates of agencies like the Michigan department, together with the commentators on those which have been created, have seemed to assume that such agencies function in a "pure" administrative atmosphere, uncontaminated by political or policy considerations.

This assumption is certainly not justified in the case of the Michigan department. Although it is generally conceded, even by its severest critics, that the department has made considerable advances in the technical management aspects of state housekeeping activities, the department has been inextricably enmeshed in the complexities of "politics" in Michigan. Political forces presided over the birth of the department and have influenced it continuously since. Its future may well depend on its acceptability to dominant political groups, and their decision may not necessarily be based on an objective evaluation of its technical record. Consequently, its "political" life has perhaps been the most important and significant feature of the department's history. It is the purpose of this article, therefore, to attempt an assessment of the political ramifications of the department's activities.

The department is designed in theory, and functions in practice, as a staff agency to the Governor. It is organized with divisions of budget, accounting, purchasing, building, property management, motor transport, and office services. Through selection of the department head — the controller — who is subject to his direction, and who serves at his

From "The Michigan Department of Administration: A Case Study in the Politics of Administration" by Ferrel Heady and Robert H. Pealy. Reprinted from *Public Administration Review*, XVI (Spring 1956), 82-89, quarterly journal of the American Society for Public Administration. [Footnotes omitted.]

pleasure, the Governor is in a position to give direction to department actions. The agency is thus designed to strengthen the office of the Governor in administrative management.

Prior to the creation of the Department of Administration in 1948, the most notable attempt to centralize Michigan's housekeeping functions had been the creation in 1921 of the State Administrative Board. As we shall see, the relationships between this board and the department have been of very great significance. The board is composed of all of the elective officers of the executive branch: the Governor as chairman, the lieutenant governor, the secretary of state, the attorney-general, the auditor-general, the treasurer, the superintendent of public instruction, and the highway commissioner. Originally designed to have "general supervisory control over the functions and activities of all administrative departments, boards, commissions, and officers of the state, and all state institutions," the board gradually lost authority over specific functions such as budgeting, accounting, and purchasing; it operates today primarily as a body which is expected by law to approve or disapprove specific actions of other state agencies. It is in this "approval" area that board activities impinge significantly upon the functions of the Department of Administration. In no fewer than ten types of instance, the powers of the department can be exercised only with the approval of the board. In addition, the controller, whose superior is the Governor, is ex officio the secretary of the board.

The Department of Administration was almost the sole product of a broad campaign for administrative reorganization waged by Governor Kim Sigler during his single term in office from 1947 through 1948. The legislative history of the Department of Administration Act shows that the department was created reluctantly by an unenthusiastic Legislature as the price of avoiding a less acceptable kind of administrative reorganization through the constitutional initiative. Many legislators, particularly in the Senate, were firmly opposed to a central management agency responsible solely to the Governor. They succeeded in subordinating the department to the traditional Administrative Board by inserting numerous and ambiguous provisos calling for clearance or approval of department action by the board. The new agency thus had to begin functioning under a cloud of uncertainty about what it could or could not do, and where its responsibility lay.

State Political Climate

As an experiment in central management control, the department has inevitably been affected by the political climate in the state government. The political balance of power in the state has been unstable during the years of the department's existence. This indecisive political balance has conditioned both the external relations and internal operations of the department; hence, its place in the Michigan governmental setting can be depicted only against a background of political developments.

Briefly, the facts are these. In Michigan, the Legislature in recent years has been constantly dominated by the Republican party. Since shortly after the Department of Administration began functioning, the Governorship has been held by a Democrat. The Administrative Board has been divided between Democratic and Republican elected executive officials. Republicans dominated the board during the whole time from 1948 through 1954, the Governor being the lone Democratic member of the board during four years of this period. The pendulum swung in the 1954 general election, giving the Democrats a majority on the board for the first time, as of January 1, 1955.

In 1949, with the inauguration of Governor Williams and the other winning candidates for the offices on the Administrative Board, and the beginning of the legislative session, the department was drawn toward the center of the political stage. The Governor has the power to veto board actions, but may be overridden by five votes. During Governor Williams' first term, covering 1949 and 1950, a vital fact for the Governor and the Department of Administration was that the opposition party possessed exactly enough votes on the Administrative Board to override a Governor's veto of board action and was thus in a position to control the board's decisions, including the conduct of board supervision over the department. This close division of power on the board offered a temptation to make tests of strength out of issues involving the department.

The results of the 1950 general election intensified the political rivalry involving the board and the department. Democratic Governor Williams won reelection by the narrowest of margins. The Republicans recaptured the other two executive offices which had been occupied by Democrats, giving the Republican party possession of all offices on the Administrative Board with the exception of the Governorship itself. The Republicans also maintained top-heavy majorities in each chamber of the Legislature although the Democrats kept barely enough seats in the House of Representatives to sustain a Governor's veto.

In November, 1952, Democratic Governor Williams was reelected, again by a small margin. Republicans were elected to the offices of lieutenant governor, secretary of state, treasurer, attorney-general and auditor general. In the spring election of 1953, the incumbent Republican highway commissioner was reelected, and a Republican superintendent of public instruction was elected to succeed the former superintendent who was not a candidate. The Republicans, therefore, continued to hold all of the seats on the Administrative Board with the exception of the Governorship. The November, 1952, elections had continued the heavy Republican majority in the Legislature although by one vote in the house the Democrats could still sustain a gubernatorial veto.

The 1954 general election brought a drastic reversal to this Republican position of dominance on the Administrative Board. The Democrats swept the state ticket, electing Governor Williams for an unprecedented fourth consecutive two-year term, and displacing Republicans in the five other offices on the board which were filled in the election. In the 1955 spring election, this trend was arrested when the Republican incumbent as superintendent of public instruction defeated his Democratic opponent after a very close contest. The line-up on the board after this election stood at six Democrats and two Republicans. The Democrats thus moved swiftly from a minority of one on the eight-member board to a decisive majority, with the next election for officials who serve on the board scheduled for the fall of 1956. Meanwhile, the Republicans were still in control of both houses of the Legislature for the 1955 and 1956 sessions, although by reduced majorities.

Relations Between Department and Board

It is therefore plain that both statutory language and political considerations have made it inevitable that the affairs of the department should be closely interwoven with the attitudes and actions of the Administrative Board. The patchwork pattern of Administrative Board approvals over the conduct of functions basically assigned to the department would have presented thorny questions of exact division of authority in any event. When political rivalry and the search for partisan advantage intrude upon purely administrative considerations, the problem of board supervision over department operations becomes complicated and the results are not always in the interest of good administration.

The differences which have arisen in relations between the board and the department have for the most part appeared at three points which will be discussed below: (1) supervision of department activities by board committees; (2) the controller's relationships to the board as its secretary; and (3) disputes concerning the respective jurisdictions of the board and the department.

The Administrative Board prior to 1948 was accustomed to carry out much of its business through committees. When the department was created in 1948, the committee system was retained by the board and the board has continued to exercise its supervision of department activities through several committees.

The effect of the existence of the committees on relations between the department and the board is hard to measure. The retention of committees by the board disappointed some backers of the department, and it showed some reluctance on the part of the board to lean entirely on the department to do its staff work. Opinion concerning the effect of committees on the staff work of the department differs to some extent within the department. What is probably a minority opinion holds that a reasonable amount of scrutiny of the details of administration by the board and its committees has a good effect by keeping the department staff alert. Also, on difficult problems it is sometimes desirable from the department's point of view to have the board take some of the responsibility for a decision.

On the other hand, the majority opinion in the department is less favorable in judging the way board review works. Committee interest is said to show partisan bias and to depend a great deal on the political implications of the business at hand; board members show a tendency to send deputies to committee meetings to review operations of agencies headed by party colleagues of the board majority, but attend themselves when the business involving agencies controlled by the opposite party is under consideration. Committee scrutiny may require unnecessary delay in taking action in ordinary administrative matters and modification of the best administrative practice may have to be made because of committee and board desires. The paper work demanded for the conduct of the board business is irksome and expensive, with two secretaries spending full time in preparation of documents for approval, agenda, minutes, and other matters. Much of the time spent on board and committee matters by professional and secretarial staff of the department could be better used in other ways.

Some of the stresses and strains between the board and the department have arisen as a result of the controller's relationship to the board as its secretary and his policy and political relationship to the Governor. Three controllers have been appointed by Democratic Governor Williams, and, as is natural for a policy position of this nature, all three have been Democrats, although none of the three had been very active in party politics prior to appointment. The first of these Williams appointees served for nearly five years, the second for fourteen months, and the third, the present controller, has been serving since January, 1955. The controller appointed by Governor Sigler was a Republican and served for only four months in 1948.

Members of the Administrative Board seem to have accepted the logic of having the controller serve as secretary, and none has advocated removing him from the assignment. However, there has not been complete satisfaction by any means on the part of board members with the performance of the controller as secretary. The first Williams appointee, who served five years, was a favorite target for attack during his tenure. Some board members recognized that as a spokesman for the Governor the controller is inevitably in an awkward position when the board is controlled by officials politically antagonistic to the Governor. Nevertheless, a complaint frequently voiced was that he used his office "as a political weapon" or that he served in it "as a political aid to the Governor." It seems clear that he did not play a passive role as secretary or remain neutral about issues on which the board was divided. However, these rumblings must to some extent be regarded as a symptom of the split in the political composition of the board.

The two subsequent controllers have largely escaped this kind of criticism. In part, this must be due to their shorter tenure. However, to a greater extent it is probably due to their different concept of the controllership and to their conduct of the office. In their relations with the board, as elsewhere, they stressed the management aspects of the position rather than the political role. As a consequence, they appeared to be much less aggressive as secretary of the board.

Each of the numerous areas in which actions of the Department of Administration are subject to approval by the State Administrative Board offers a potential point for dissension between the two agencies. In several instances this smoldering jurisdictional friction has broken into flame; disputes over purchasing matters have been the most prominent. There have been several of these purchasing disputes, and usually voting on the board concerning the disputes has been along party lines.

The Department of Administration Act gives the department power to issue rules and regulations governing the operation of purchasing, subject to approval by the Administrative Board. A set of rules was formulated by the department and presented to the Administrative Board on May 17, 1949. After consideration, the board expressed dissatisfaction with the rules as submitted and sent them back to the department for certain indicated changes. The department made the desired changes and resubmitted the revised rules to the board, on August 2, 1949. However, a subsequent dispute between the Department of Administration and the Highway Department changed the atmosphere in which consideration of the rules took place. On a vote strictly along party lines, by a 5 to 3 margin, the board adopted significant amendments to the proposed rules.

The controller declined to accept Administrative Board amendments to the rules. He contended that the board had only the power of approval of the rules, and that this term should not be interpreted to mean revision. The approval power under this view permits only acceptance or rejection of the rules proposed by the department, and not revision and subsequent adoption of the revised rules. As a result, no purchasing rules were ever put into effect, and the matter reached a permanent stalemate, with the board being able to block rules drafted by the department which were not to the board's liking, but unable to promulgate rules of its own. As a substitute for formal purchasing rules, late in 1950 the Department of Administration issued a manual of purchasing procedures which serves to guide the agencies in their purchasing activities, so that the lack of formal rules has made little difference.

There has also been considerable difference of opinion between the department and the board about the proper procedure for control of agency allotments, the board having the statutory responsibility, through the Budget Division, to make allotments. Until 1950, allotment control was entirely a Budget Division function. Although the board had not formally delegated its responsibility to the Budget Division, the board had permitted the division to perform this function without interference.

Appropriations for the fiscal year 1950-51 were considerably lower than had been requested by the agencies and by the Governor. The Legislature, through appropriation language, and the Governor, through directives, attempted to prevent the agencies from exceeding their appropriations. The Administrative Board then issued a "Statement of Policy" which required that "all proposed periodic allotments of funds appropriated to the several departments, agencies, and institutions of the government of this state for the fiscal year 1950-51 will be submitted to this Board by the Controller through the Finance and Claims Committee, and no such allotments shall be effective until approved by this Board." This was apparently done to reassert actual control over allotments by the board.

The controller then in effect refused to assume responsibility for recommending allotments to the board, and merely transmitted agency requests to the board for action. The board and its Finance and Claims Committee, being ill-equipped to evaluate these requests, usually approved allotments as requested by the agencies. The results were not very satisfactory, and by the fiscal year 1951-52, the allotment procedure was back on substantially the same basis as before, with major reliance for consideration of agency requests and for the making of allotment decisions placed on the Budget Division.

The Budget Division and the board have differed on the period for which allotments should be made. Not until August 7, 1951, did the board consent to change allotments to a quarterly rather than a monthly basis. The board permitted the change to the quarterly system on condition that: (1) overruns of allotments in one quarter be made up in the next; (2) the controller submit a report to the board each quarter showing that the agencies have conformed to the allotment schedules; and (3) the controller report to the board each month on any "unusual" variations from monthly amounts shown on the schedules. The board's Finance and Claims Committee, which took the action on the quarterly procedure, stated that any agency which deviated from the quarterly procedure or from the monthly schedule within the quarterly allotments, would be subject to prompt return to monthly allotments. In practice this has not been enforced, however.

Evaluation

The review powers of the State Administrative Board make up the most serious obstacle to the effective operation of the Department of Administration as an aid to the Governor. This problem is intimately tied up

with the broader question of the multiple executive idea which underlies the board system. It is the consensus of a series of reorganization
reports, the latest being the 1951 staff report of the Joint Legislative
Committee on Reorganization of Michigan State Government, that the
Administrative Board should be abolished. This opinion has been shared
by several past Governors and other elective officeholders and is probably the correct view. But it is not the purpose here to deal extensively
with the broad question of board competency and usefulness.

The concern here is with the effect of the statutory review and
approval powers — both directly, on the operation of the department,
and indirectly, on the relationship of the department to the Governor.
The legislative history of the Department of Administration Act leaves
no doubt that these provisions were added as a means of curbing the new
department by diluting its powers and weakening its responsibilities to
the Governor. In practice, the review function has proved burdensome
but not unworkable. Ordinarily, approval of department actions is
forthcoming, and the main drawback is delay and repetitive paper work.
In the event of unreconcilable differences of opinion between the two
agencies, as in the dispute over purchasing rules, the department has
been able to prevail by simply avoiding action requiring board approval.
The work load of board business is considerable, requiring not only a
large share of the time of the controller as secretary to the board, but
the attention of division chiefs and subordinate officials as well, particularly in the Budget Division. This diversion of energies might be worth
while if there were reason to think board scrutiny and approval produced positive results. As a matter of fact, the board is ill equipped to do
this sort of supervision. Members, except for the lieutenant governor,
have full-time jobs as heads of executive departments and cannot concentrate attention on the problems of administrative management dealt
with by the department. Few board members have the technical skills
necessary in order to pass judgment on a multitude of technical matters.

The only kind of supervision that the board is really interested in,
or equipped to provide, is supervision which is political in purpose and
effect. The consequences of board intervention are much more apt to be
of political significance than of administrative assistance. The board provides an agency which can be used by one party against the Governor of
the opposite party. Even when the board majority is of the same party
as the Governor, there is no guarantee of harmony, because some of the
board members may be potential or actual rivals of the incumbent for
the office of Governor. In either case, the temptation is great to involve
Department of Administration business in political contests of power.

Inclusion of the approval and supervisory powers in the act has
created an unnecessary arena for partisan political warfare. The straight
party voting on the board on nearly every one of the jurisdictional disputes seems to indicate that the controversies were basically partisan in

nature. Alternative administrative techniques were not in question in most of the disputes. Whereas formerly the board as a group—prior to the creation of the department—was clearly responsible for certain state administrative affairs, the board now has a scapegoat in the department, which may be used as a political weapon against the Governor. On the other hand, there is every opportunity for the Governor to use any disputes between the board and the department as ammunition for political warfare. This particular political arena is not necessary to good government in Michigan. The best interests of the electorate and the Legislature are not served when it is possible for the board and the Governor to foment partisan disputes in this way. Abolition of the State Administrative Board would be a basic solution to this problem. If the board is retained, it should be removed from supervision over activities which are the primary responsibility, by statute, of the Department of Administration.

If the department is to be evaluated primarily as an aid to the Governor, the direct relationships between the Governor and the department are of utmost significance. The focus of interest here is on the Governor's attitudes and expectations concerning the controller and the Budget Division particularly, and concerning other units of the department to a lesser extent. Since the department is conceived of as a managerial agency, presumably it should be used by the Governor for management purposes rather than as an instrument of political action. The department in turn should regard itself as a management improvement agency rather than as a political agent of the incumbent Governor. That the line between "politics" and "administration" is no more clear cut here than elsewhere, however, is evident in the brief history of the department.

Governors must and should be politically oriented. Their main interest is in substantive matters of public policy—and the next election. Considerations of administrative management and improvement are secondary and peripheral. Much more important are issues of fiscal policy which have a direct bearing on the scope and content of policy programs. This scale of interests has been reflected in the record of relations between the department and the Governor. While regarding the department as a useful device and protecting its operating integrity, the Governor has shown most concern with departmental activities such as budgeting, which impinge most directly on policy matters. During campaigns and other periods of heavy political activity, even these activities must compete for his attention and often are put aside.

To sum up, the Governor is not only a chief administrative officer; he is also, and in the first instance, the elected political leader of the state. He will benefit as chief administrator from the help that he receives from the central management agency. Indirectly, his political reputation will be helped by a good record as an administrator. His political career is much more apt to depend, however, on his performance in other areas. The political scene is the Governor's abiding concern. Concentration on management problems tends to be spasmodic and irregular. The contribution which can be made by the Department of Administration is to provide continuous attention to state administrative management on behalf of the Governor when he is occupied elsewhere, and to respond promptly when the Governor needs help as the top-ranking administrator in state government.

In order to function effectively, it seems to us that the controller and the staff members of the department must endeavor to maintain loyalty to the policy positions and administrative directives of the Governor, while at the same time avoiding, as much as possible, embroilment in political controversies. We have already discussed the effect of Administrative Board clearances in pulling the department into the political arena unnecessarily. Another factor in the effective functioning of the department is the attitude of the controller toward his role in state government. If he identifies himself openly and ardently as an advocate of the Governor's program objectives and thus becomes himself a target of political attack, this may be to the detriment of the department as an effective management agency. There can be no hard and fast rules of conduct here, but our opinion is that the controller is well advised to refrain if possible from becoming a political symbol and to concentrate on his nonpartisan job of improving the standards of state administration. In the last analysis, it is the personal working relationship between the Governor and his controller that sets the tone for the department. Our view is that the Department of Administration will be most valuable to the Governor if both officials stress the housekeeping or management assignment of the department.

This does not mean that the controller and the department do not have important political roles to play. Depending somewhat upon the talents of the controller and the degree of intimacy of his knowledge of state politics, he may become one of the Governor's chief political advisers, and in this role may be bolstered by the staff services available in the department. His services can be of help to the Governor in policy formulation, in compilation of adequate data, through prevention of errors which might embarrass him, and also through discovering the fallacies in the arguments of his political opponents. The controller cannot reasonably aspire, however, to become an "assistant governor." He must be content with relative anonymity, and he must stress, at least overtly, the professional and business management aspects of his job rather than its political overtones.

In examining the legislative origins of the department, we found that it was created by a reluctant Legislature as the result of a political compromise with Governor Sigler. To an extent difficult to measure, the original reluctance to create the department has become a reluctance on the part of the Legislature to acknowledge fully that the department is a useful device. At the root of this attitude—it does not pervade the whole Legislature—is the political division between the Governorship and the Legislature.

Partly as a result of the division between the Governorship and the Legislature, there are strained relations between the Budget Division and the Legislature. The Legislature has kept an exceptionally tight rein on the operating funds and staff of the Budget Division. In part, this has resulted from personality differences, but the Legislature as a whole has, nevertheless, consented to stringent appropriations for the division. As much as anything else, the Legislature's tight rein on the division is the result of a general frustration in the process of budget enactment. The Legislature is unsure of its role in the process, yet extremely conscious of its power over the public purse and reluctant to give up any of its power.

The presentation of the Governor's program to the Legislature in the budget should be the signal for the most important political debate of the legislative session. The policy points of view presented in the Governor's budget should be fully debated in the Legislature on the basis of informed opinion. However, the Legislature does not have adequate technical staff to assist in analyzing the Governor's budget and this lack has contributed to the Legislature's frustration and its strained relations with the Budget Division.

The department has had to develop its technical housekeeping functions while adapting itself as well as possible to an indifferent or even hostile political environment. It has grown to maturity under conditions which have at times threatened its very existence. More than once, prominent legislators have castigated it vehemently, advocated its abolition, and introduced bills to terminate it or drastically curtail its scope of operations. Barring unforeseen developments, however, the department now seems to be secure against annihilation by statute, although it can expect continued harassment from the Legislature and other quarters.

Despite the tense political atmosphere in which it has had to operate, the Michigan Department of Administration has demonstrated the gains in state administrative practices which can be made, even under exceptionally trying conditions, by such a central management agency. In addition, the department has substantially succeeded in furnishing to the chief executive needed instruments of direction and control of the administrative machinery. The record of the Michigan department can be taken as an encouragement by other states which have created similar agencies or contemplate doing so.

THE POLITICS OF MANAGEMENT IMPROVEMENT IN THE STATES

Karl A. Bosworth

Karl A. Bosworth is professor of political science, University of Connecticut. Author of numerous articles, he is a contributor to *The Fifty States and Their Local Governments* (1967).

In the wake of the Hoover Commission reports, a great majority of the states authorized special inquiries into the organization and operation of their executive institutions. With very few exceptions, the numerous postwar movements for state reorganization appear to have resulted in only moderate or negligible legislative acceptance of the reorganization proposals. The spectacle of such meager accomplishment from so much effort invites reflection on the politics of management improvement in the states.

Through the generous cooperation of professional colleagues about the country, data were assembled on the successes and failures of these reorganization movements, upon the initiation, organization, and scope of the surveys, and upon the methods of presenting the survey reports to the legislatures and to the public. The data cover thirty states, in twenty-four of which the state legislature has had at least one chance to consider commission recommendations. In the remaining six states the reports are still in the process of preparation, or await legislative consideration. Included in the twenty-four are four states in which the study group has made some reports but continues in existence to make further reports, so that the success of the efforts in these states must be tentatively judged on the basis of legislative reception of reports so far received.

In only two of the twenty-four states — New Hampshire and New Jersey — was the legislative response pronouncedly positive. In New Hampshire, under the gubernatorial leadership of Sherman Adams, the legislature accepted all major proposals and all but one of an estimated 24 moderate-scale proposals. New Jersey is a special case in that this state was in a continual turmoil of constitutional revision and administrative reorganization efforts from 1941 into 1948, with five committees and commissions and a constitutional convention working on these problems and having among them some overlapping leadership. The commission created in 1944 to study administrative organization issued reports and recommendations serially over a period of years and received several positive legislative responses. In 1948, when the

From "The Politics of Management Improvement in the States," Karl A. Bosworth, *The American Political Science Review*, LXVII (March 1953), 84-99. Reprinted by permission of the author and the American Political Science Association. [Footnotes omitted.]

legislature met under a new constitution requiring all administrative agencies to be placed in no more than twenty departments, the legislature quickly completed a reorganization of the state's numerous agencies into fourteen statutory departments. This stage in New Jersey took place under the leadership of members of the commission created in 1944, including Governor Alfred E. Driscoll, and with the assistance of a joint legislative committee and strong, sympathetic party majorities in both houses.

In contrast, in nine of the states the legislative reception has either been completely negative or so slight as to be regarded as a soundly negative response. In thirteen states, the legislative response has been ambivalent with a score—according to my rough weighted scoring method—of between twenty-nine and fifty-two per cent adoption. In about half these states with ambivalent legislative responses, the classification would have been negative on the basis of the acceptance of major proposals, and was saved from that category only by greater legislative receptivity to moderate- and minor-scale proposals.

For those of us who have participated in these reorganization efforts, the question may be: What did we do wrong? From a more detached point of view, the inquiry could run either in the direction of a critique of the content of reorganization proposals and organization theory or toward an inquiry into the politics of state administrative reorganization. Following the latter course and the view that reorganization is as much a political as a scientific process, I propose in this paper to investigate the conditions affecting the likelihood of legislative acceptance of Little Hoover Commission or similarly sourced proposals for state administrative changes.

General Assumptions

It is appropriate to state certain general assumptions at this point. Legislatures tend generally to be negative toward proposals for either moderate-scale or major changes in the formal allocation of influence in their governments. The formal organization of the executive branch is, among other things, a distribution of political power and influence which reaches beyond the confines of the executive branch. There is a strong probability of alliances between legislators and officers and groups having a stake in the present organization, and there is some particular negativism toward building the influence position of the governor. These may be, in part, corollaries to a condition of general conservatism in the legislative consideration of any proposed major changes in public policy.

Certain general conditions in a setting may tend to reduce legislative negativism toward major proposals. Possibly situations of either deep despair or high optimism regarding the fate of individuals and institutions generally may reduce legislative negativism. When horizons are low because of despair, it is easy to reason that any change is unlikely to worsen conditions and may improve them (e.g., Nebraska's shift to unicameralism and other depression changes in important state policy). When horizons are wide with general optimism, the risks of any change seem lessened (e.g., the many changes in the period from the late 1890's to World War I).

If these assumptions have some validity, one may say that regardless of the immediate motivations of state reorganization activity, the excellence of surveys, the current political alignment or misalignment of the legislative houses and the governor's office, and the vigor and art of programs to interpret reorganization proposals to the public and to legislators, there is a good chance of failure in getting a positive legislative response. The existing institutions represent some sort of balance among existing forces. The usual negativism is such that a substantial share of the possible favorable conditions directly related to the reorganization effort will be needed in order to overcome what should be the expected negative legislative response. If one could time the starting of reorganization movements, probably periods of generally low personal expectations and—should they again occur in an area as large as a state—periods of high general optimism are most propitious.

The Motives for Reorganization Studies and Probable Success

The news that "good public administration is good politics" has obviously been getting around. There seem grounds for supposing that some political leaders have sought to reap some of the benefits of this proposition without paying the price.

If a reorganization study is undertaken for motives other than improved public management, it is quite probable that little will be accomplished. Motives of "getting into the act" by imitating other states and the national government, of diverting attention from other parts of the current scenery, or of creating supposed campaign advantages, seem to have been factors in the rash of Little Hoover Commission activity. Such motives may be exhausted in the study effort, leaving little or no motivation among the influential for the consideration and adoption of proposals. Further, if the mixed-objectives situation exists in the survey commission, the recommendations may be tailored for the accomplishment of public relations motives rather than with a view to making proposals having some chance for legislative adoption. Then too, if the motives of the proponents of a survey are suspected by the populace, the popular support generally necessary for legislative action may not be forthcoming. An administration survey undertaken halfheartedly and for devious reasons may nevertheless gather support and result in significant achievement. If I interpret accurately one of our participant's questionnaire responses, something like this may have happened in one state where the survey committee "brought temporary relief to a much harassed political organization" which was being harried in regard to services and taxes. The major problem of taxation was not resolved by the committee, but several of its reorganization proposals were adopted.

A nucleus of political leaders who clearly have good faith in seeking management improvement can quite likely find strong popular support for their proposals. This is a variant expression of the Brownlow-reported Wilsonian prescription to politico-administrators to "take high ground," for who can directly oppose improved administration? That private career motives may also be aided by this approach is generally not a detracting factor.

The muckrakers taught us that finding scandalous or notorious conditions is one way to provoke reform. Though one might question some of their methods and objectives, it does seem clear that the likelihood of positive action on administrative improvement is heightened if the inadequacy of existing administration has been publicly dramatized and if the motivation for reorganization activity arises out of protests at the dramatized inadequacies. It matters little that the breakdowns may have been personal moral lapses rather than the results of faulty administrative arrangements: the "ins" and their political allies are put on the defensive. They are vulnerable to an opposing political movement to reorganize the state government, or they may be persuaded to purify themselves in the public mind through measures for administration improvement.

Probably little planned help can be expected, however, from dramatized inadequacies. Crusading newspaper publishers and sophisticated reporters of state administration are seemingly scarce about state capitols. State government news seems to rank well behind national and local government news in the value systems of many publishers. With the best of will, the inadequacies of generally honest, but bumbling, public management are about as difficult to dramatize on a broad scale as is superior, professional public management. Those hopeful of a favorable moral and emotional climate for administrative reform probably must generally rely on the happenstances of defalcations, briberies, prison breaks, accidental patient and inmate deaths, failures of state structures, the discovery of fraudulent relief clients, and similar newsworthy calamities of life in the shadow of the dome.

It appears that the economy motive is still of relatively slight force in initiating administration improvement at the state level. In most states, the systems and levels of state taxation do not inflict sharp pains upon large, politically significant groups as do the local property tax and the national income tax. Although the lush state financial picture of 1943-45 is gone, it would appear that few, if any, states are making large numbers of taxpayers cry for professional state administration, as the taxpayers of hundreds of municipalities have sought relief from rising tax rates through council-manager government. Though this present judgment is, I believe, still correct, there is every indication that the economy motive may be heightened at the state level as a result of the rapidly growing state budgets and the trend toward shifting increasing amounts of the local government burden onto the payers of the state taxes.

State taxpayer organizations are, of course, present in many of our states, but their financial and political support seems to be limited largely to those particular elements of the business, financial, and industrial community having a direct economic concern with state taxes and state policy. Although such agencies are frequently vocal and active in the camp of administrative reform, the desire of the constituency to retain friendly state policy developers and enforcers can easily neutralize the taxpayer agencies in the political battles for legislative adoption of administrative changes which increase policy uncertainties. The utilities, banks, and insurance companies know where they stand with their current state regulatory agencies. Perhaps the present situation of state taxpayer pain as a motive for administrative reform can best be described as one in which the scattershot state tax systems provide substantial motivation for the consideration of change but frequently inadequate motivation for making changes.

Sponsorship and Reorganization Success

Hypothetically, it might be supposed that the opportunities for legislative enactment of reorganization proposals would be most favorable in a situation in which the survey is carried out under the leadership of the "outs," who thereupon become the "ins" and adopt their own recommendations before new vested interests are established in the offices to be eliminated. In 1948 Mr. Truman, with the cooperation of millions of voters, prevented the testing of this hypothesis at the national level, and, so far as has been learned, no state's reorganization activity falls exactly into this pattern.

Generally, we may agree that favorable auspices for reorganization activity would occur in the joint sponsorship of an administrative survey by a governor and legislative houses having majorities of the same political faith as the governor, with the recommendations received by the same alignment. One would also think that legislative council sponsorship would be auspicious in those states where the legislative council is well accepted as a source of legislative proposals; but in only one of the three such surveys was there significant achievement. In the South, gubernatorial sponsorship of administrative reform, with or without formal joint sponsorship by the legislature, appears to be generally auspicious. Sponsorship by a citizens' or taxpayers' organization may in some situations present feasibilities, especially if the private organization is given a temporary official connection or status by a co-sponsoring governor or legislature. The Colorado reorganization movement developed in this way. Sponsorship by the legislature through a special legislative committee or commission without formal sponsorship or participation by the governor is an alternative of rather dubious merit in most states.

In eight of the states in which there was no significant adoption of reorganization recommendations, the initiative came from the legislature in five instances. In three, the governor was the initiator or participated in the initiation. In one of these, the governor later withdrew his support, and the other two movements failed when "model" plans were rejected. In fifteen states where there was some significant adoption, governors participated in the initiation in ten, legislators were the apparent initiators in four, and a private agency sold the idea to legislators in the other one. Even more striking evidence of the significance of governors in these movements is seen in the fact that governors were active in the sponsorship of the movements in eight of the nine states adopting more than 40 per cent of the proposals, in my weighted measure.

As to party divisions between the legislature and the governor, or between one house and the governor, we know that in some sharply partisan situations the division has been fatal to reorganization proposals, while in other circumstances it has not. In these latter situations, the political risks of giving the governor something for which he could take credit have apparently seemed less than the risks of killing a popularly supported measure. In Illinois, Maryland, and Massachusetts governors lacked party majorities in their legislatures, yet significant accomplishments were attained.

We have had ample evidence that legislative sponsorship of surveys does not forecast receptivity to recommendations and that governor-sponsors sometimes lose their enthusiasm for administrative reform. However, the legislators and governors are the "powers that be" in the formal government; and unless they are willing to give consideration to administrative alterations, there is no basis for any expectation of legislative action for management improvement.

With regard to political party leaders, it would seem that one must adopt the view that professional politicians, of whatever party, are likely to be no more than reluctant allies in moves for administration improvement. They have learned how to operate in the situation as it is and should generally not be expected to be enthusiastic for changes in the rules of a game in which they have perfected some art, unless such changes would remove some inconvenient obstacle.

Changes which have the tendency of making the formal government *the* government—the gathering into a neat hierarchy of most of the decision points — may be particularly well understood by and likewise obnoxious to the professional politicians. To the extent that the non-office-holding professional politicians have confidence in their ability to operate through the official hierarchy, this conclusion may need modification. Thus, one might find the party leaders of a regularly dominant party somewhat more receptive to proposals for administrative integration than the party leaders of a state with relatively evenly divided party contests where the chance of losing all direct influence is a risk to both parties. Likewise, in situations in which the leaders of both parties think the trend in statewide elections is toward dominance by their party, the opportunities for action may be improved. Generally, it would seem that assistance from the professional politicians can be expected only as a short-run compromise of their long-run objectives in order to support a popular issue. Governors and others with large fractions of influence can sometimes compel the professional politicians to take a passive, or even reluctantly a cooperating, role in reorganization legislation.

To round out the consideration of the political bases for reorganization activity, one must cite the almost automatic resistance to being "reorganized" of the leaders and clienteles of most administrative agencies. The Mississippi Legislative Fact-Finding Committee on Reorganization of State Government interviewed the head of each state agency, quizzing him on his reaction to creating conditions for greater efficiency by a program of consolidation. In a letter of transmittal, the Mississippi committee synthesized the uniform agency head response in the following words:

> *I think this is one of the very best things that has ever been done in the State of Mississippi and I have long been of the opinion that this work should have been accomplished in the past. However, my department is of a type, character and kind that cannot be consolidated with any other agency, as its duties and functions are unique, and a reduction of personnel or a transfer of any duties of this department would work a hardship and prevent certain citizens from receiving benefits to which they are entitled.*

Such reactions are familiar to all of us, and one must recognize that these agreeing opponents of reorganization commonly have large resources of political influence which they have cultivated in their daily work of agency survival and growth. A clientele organization controlling the policy of the fragment of state government that specially affects it is a potent and sure source of opposition to reorganization and a ready ally in log-rolling to preserve realms undisturbed among organizations similarly situated. There are, of course, exceptions in which the case for independence is so weak as to be indefensible or where politically weak agencies become ready to seek a formal alliance with a politically strong agency. There are also the existing departments which may stand to gain by consolidations, but their enthusiasm and power potentials frequently do not match those of the agencies which have decided that "you can't reorganize us." The pluralistic character of our political organization at the state level is probably best illustrated when typical general reorganization proposals are announced.

Composition and Organization of Commission

In considering the probable fate of commission proposals in terms of commission composition, it is probably of greatest importance that the members be persons of high general prestige and of actual political influence. It is normally not enough that they be respected, able, personally successful citizens. To express it crudely: How many votes can they swing in the legislature, and how effectively can they rally popular support? It is probably of next importance that the commission be so composed that it cannot be identified as representing any limited elements in the political spectrum of the state. The first of these considerations is expressed with a view toward the positive organization of support for the recommendations. The second, although indirectly beneficial to that end through broad representation, is expressed primarily as a defensive and cautionary concept with a view to avoiding the effective and easy labelling of the commission's effort as a minority report from a limited segment of the polity. Most other considerations with regard to commission composition are subsidiary or corollary to these two seemingly basic ones.

As to the value of legislator memberships, there are the to-be-hoped-for positive considerations of having leading legislators both committed to the recommendations and prepared to explain the proposals to their colleagues. There are, at the same time, the risks that particular legislator members will choose to entertain specific or general reservations about the recommendations and become in the inner chambers trained opponents of the proposals. There is the further risk that if an election intervenes between the formation of the commission and the legislative session which considers the report, some of the legislator members may become lame ducks and lose their influence, while others succeed to posts which remove them from the legislative arena.

The occasional lukewarmness of governors to commission proposals suggest the desirability of attempting to get commissions constructed so as to avoid this contingency. Although other means may be designed, the arrangement which allows the governor to appoint at least some of the members serves to involve him and may make some member the governor's delegate who keeps the governor informed about and possibly privately committed to the commission's work, step by step.

It is, of course, desirable that commission members be well informed about a state's executive organization and about the feasibilities of political action in the state, and it would be presumed that persons of high prestige and influence in state affairs could generally fulfill these requirements. Former governors and others who have been near the center of the complex of executive-legislative forces, if they have escaped with their reputations fairly well intact, may have particularly valuable contributions to make to a commission's endeavors and may have an authority of personal knowledge of large weight. Even some unsuccessful candidates for governor may have thought more about the executive problems of the state than most citizens. All of these considerations have been evident in our data, and in states where it is appropriate the bipartisan theme has been emphasized. There are other important personal qualities, such as the disposition and ability to work with others towards agreement in the conference situation and ability in public expositions of the commission's work. But these are minor compared with the individual prestige and influence of the members and the invulnerability of the members collectively to easy attack.

Commission size in our data varied from four to forty-one members, with each extreme having some successes in adoptions. About three-quarters of the groups had from seven to thirteen members, and size, except for the risk of unrepresentativeness in smaller commissions, has no apparent relation to success.

Certain of the commissions have had advisory committees. The success in New Hampshire where this device was used suggests the desirability of giving careful consideration to adaptations of this arrangement. An advisory group of over thirty participated with the nine commission members in subcommittees, studying and making recommendations for particular areas. This group, along with the commission members, actively organized the public campaign for the adoption of proposals. The New Hampshire story suggests that the advisory committee was not a decisive factor in their success; rather, it was one of several important contributing factors.

The Oregon interim legislative committee on state organization, which had significant successes, created an advisory committee of six university professors. Although most of us might agree that this was a wise move, I have no information regarding the role played by these professional advisers, unless it is reflected in our respondent's comment that "the staff work, while quite limited, was of high quality. . . . " The Minnesota commission divided into committees to which approximately 150 citizens were added. In this case, it appears that the added members participated in the investigatory work and the committee deliberations.

Organization, Scope, and Method of Survey

In considering the scope of surveys, factors such as the terms of the authorization of the survey, the issues which precipitate the survey, the present condition of state administration, time, money, and the judgment of the commission or director may be determinative. It is with this exercise of judgment that we may be most appropriately concerned here. It has been the fashion to make the scope broad and to be expansive in the setting of objectives. Insofar as our professional craft has influenced these decisions, it is probably understandable that we have wanted to give the states the full benefit of our knowledge and wisdom. The state does not ask for our prescription every year. All too frequently, it would appear, commissions and advisers have not curbed these perfectionist inclinations; and where the authorization is broad and the time and funds are adequate, there may seem to be no alternative to the making of large plans.

Although in some states the conditions of state administration may almost compel the making of broad prescriptions, prudent judgment in the interest of securing some positive accomplishment may dictate the curbing of scope and the concentration of efforts on the areas of greatest vulnerability and the areas of greatest practicable gains. The device of being prescriptive on certain points and of being only educational on others, with suggestions of alternatives or of areas for further study, is frequently preferable. The generally limited results of the completed surveys suggest strongly that the planners of additional surveys give hard thought to the question: What are the feasible objectives of this survey?

The fact that constitutional proposals were made in all the states (with the possible exception of Delaware) in which the legislative response was negative is suggestive. Of the fifteen states in which there was significant legislative accomplishment, only six of the reorganization proposals included constitutional amendments. In most of the states where the scope of the survey was limited or the proposals have concentrated on a relatively few objectives, there has been some significant legislative acceptance of recommendations. The fact that the New Hampshire proposals were not perfectionist in any doctrinaire fashion seems relevant also.

Rather definitely to be avoided, at least on the basis of the Connecticut experience and perhaps that of other states, is the stretching of the scope beyond that understood by the authorizing body. Reorganization movements have sufficient hazards without raising the question of the legitimacy of the progeny.

In organizing general surveys, the commissions have apparently learned not to turn the whole job over to one of the national consulting firms. Monumental as the surveys and reports of these agencies have been, and useful as they may remain for various educational purposes, they have rarely been the means of producing directly positive legislative responses. Only Delaware and Virginia, among the states on which we have postwar data, turned the survey job over to one of the national consulting firms and in Delaware the accomplishment was nil. South Carolina, in a 1942-45 survey using a different national organization, had a similar experience, although a later attempt apparently using home grown talent was somewhat more successful. The outside firm arrangement creates several risks. There may not be enough participation by the commission and others for them to become parties to the conclusions and to gain an understanding of the proposals for purposes of communicating them persuasively. There is the risk that the surveyors may give too little attention to feasibilities, local values, and traditions. There is the ease of labelling the surveyors as foreign experts and thus as ignorant men so far as local conditions are concerned. With the best of will on the part of the consulting firms, continued consultation for the purpose of making explanations and modifications is likely to be difficult when the surveyors have to be pulled off new jobs and must travel back to the scene for necessarily limited periods. These observations relate solely to the use of consultant organizations for the whole survey job and not to their use on particular area surveys, as a task force, nor to their use as adviser consultants in planning surveys or reports where the survey work is done by the commission and other local agencies or consulting firms.

Although it is not a completely reliable touchstone, the engagement as survey director of a professional researcher already having some experience in the state and a favorable local reputation seems to be auspicious. Of fourteen states having some significant reorganization accomplishment for which this information is available, eleven had arrangements something like the above prescription. In several of the states with negative legislative results, the research direction seems as auspicious as in those above; but in more of them the research director had generally had less direct experience with the state government or very brief experience with the state. In one case, the director was apparently not a professional governmental researcher, although he had had state government experience.

If the governmental researcher skill group about state capitols and in nearby institutions is a superior hunting ground for survey directors, why is this so? Certainly these individuals have a head start in knowledge of state institutions. Also, they may already have in existence the nucleus of a research staff upon which to build. They are likely to continue available for the persuasion and modification stages. Finally, these individuals probably have a superior sensitivity to the feasible, the vulnerable, and the immobile and possess an authority based on the personal confidence of legislators and others in their abilities and trustworthiness. Some of them may also be able to give positive assistance in the political dynamics.

Whether task forces are used, whether specialists in functions survey the functions, whether "generalists" are used, whether the data collection on operations is heavy, moderate or slight—just so it doesn't seem to be altogether sketchy—appear to be of relatively little consequence in determining the fate of proposals for legislation on reorganization. Probably the heavy data collections are generally wasted effort, except where detailed legislation on procedures is being sought. Winners and losers have tried all methods. Perhaps the sales engineer needs to know only somewhat more about the products than do the customers. Having a few distinguished specialists may help lend authority to proposals and some of them may ease the gathering of the essential minimum of information in a field, but Connecticut, as well as other examples, illustrates the fact that having numbers of blue ribbon task force leaders does not sell the proposals. Giving attention to minor- and moderate-scale proposals seems to be somewhat controversial, some regarding it as likely to distract attention from the major proposals or otherwise disapproving of it. Most of the surveys have given attention to the lesser aspects of affairs and their successes have been largely in this area. This approach probably does distract attention, but it may also be a means of getting the legislature started in making positive responses so that the consideration of more moderate- and major-scale proposals may continue with possible favorable action. Some accomplishment, even though it is not of a first order, is a great solace to the participants and avoids the reputation of a fiasco, so that the start of future efforts may be easier. Where administration is generally good, details may be the appropriate objects of attention.

The plans in which committee consideration of reorganization is spread over a period of time, or indefinitely, with interim reports and recommendations from time to time, vary from the usual procedure. In some of these situations, as in New York, California and Massachusetts, the widespread use of legislative interim committees with vague deadlines seems to be habitual, and the prospect of results is probably closely related to the motives of the committee members and their influence in their houses, with governors possibly providing significant overtones. In Maryland, however, it is apparently the plan to complete the work before some not too distant date, but to report and recommend as studies of specific areas are completed. This approach may have the merits of concentrating attention on particular proposals and of avoiding having all the wolves howling at once. However, it risks a collapse of the movement following an adverse legislative response to the first recommendations.

Presentation of Survey Report and Recommendations

At least two related major considerations bear on the presentation of survey reports and recommendations. One concerns the attempts to influence the politically potent directly; the other has to do with attempts to interest the public widely so that there may be strong popular support nudging the politically potent toward action. As minimums in these two categories, one may expect the preparation of bills and appearances by the commission and its staff before legislative committees and the publication and distribution of a report with newspaper notice of the event. The varieties and variable intensities of additional efforts in the several state reorganization movements cannot all be catalogued and measured, but one can safely risk the proposition that it is the measures in addition to the minimum which generally produce the positive responses.

Measures to influence the more powerful include keeping the governor informed, interested and pleased so that he may be ready to use his influence on the legislature and the "wounded" agency heads, and the inclusion on the commission or advisory bodies of individuals with large direct political influence. In New Hampshire and Maryland explanation sessions on the proposals were held for groups of legislators about the state, presumably before the sessions at which the proposals were considered. In Utah the executives of private agencies which constitute the important lobbies about the legislature were cultivated, with efforts to neutralize them or to make them allies on the reorganization issues. In Kansas and other states some individuals representing these interests were on the commission. In states where the current configurations of political power are relatively simple, measures such as these may be adequate. In the more complex states, and anywhere in case of doubt, measures for inducing popular interest in reorganization are, of course, appropriate.

Some legislatures, in authorizing reorganization surveys, have restricted the press and public campaign opportunities by requiring a single report and directly, or in effect, extinguishing the commission upon the submission of its report. How strictly these directions are followed may depend upon the consciences and dexterities of the commission leaders. On the other hand, in Michigan there were three press releases on each of thirty reports over a two-year period, and one wonders if the human capacity for interest in reorganization may have been satiated. The device of releasing the report in chapters over a period of about two weeks has proved an effective way of getting large amounts of publicity and of producing public discussion of the report.

These considerations raise the question of secrecy for the proposals being considered and the trends of commission thought during the survey and report preparation stages. There is the quite natural tendency of commissions to attempt to minimize the pulling and hauling of contending forces about them which would be stimulated by news of commission thinking, and a like tendency to ease the altering of decisions by avoiding early tentative public commitments. There is possibly also some thought in this approach of giving the opponents less time to prepare their defenses. However, in most reorganization surveys the news gets around as to some of the commission views, and rumors and surmises based on inferences flow freely. If to these considerations are added the New Hampshire free press experience and the general tendency to involve larger numbers in the commission effort, one wonders if a nearly complete goldfish bowl policy isn't worthy of further trial. For the participants in the survey, it is undoubtedly a less comfortable, more tense situation than secret or semi-secret deliberations. The researchers should be stimulated to harder thought about the premises underlying their proposals and about the arguments and data which support these premises when their proposals and data formulations are to be opened quickly for public discussion. The injured may damage their case as much as they help it if the commission can maintain a mood of sweet reasonableness.

If a campaign for public support is to be conducted, there must be time for it as well as organization. Several of our surveys have had difficulties with their timing, getting their reports out just as legislative sessions were scheduled to meet or after sessions were well under way. All of us know some of the reasons why reports are late in appearing, but the difficulties encountered through late reporting suggest the desirability of curbing tendencies toward perfectionism and of leaving time in which public discussion of a completed report can be organized.

In the campaigns, newspapers, radio, and, in some areas, television, are media which have been used with some apparent success. Literature appropriate for mass distribution has been tried, particularly in Michigan. The device of the public forum has proved effective, particularly in New Hampshire, where over 300 such meetings were held before all sorts of organized groups. A one-day institute at the University of New Hampshire possibly helped train some of the people who participated in the forums.

The form of the commission report is, of course, significant in the campaign. If it is written and printed in a manner to stimulate wide reading, it can help. However, the generally limited success of reorganization efforts suggests the desirability of not keeping the report so simple that the substantial data relating to the proposals are omitted and are thus not readily available for later consideration of the original and alternative proposals.

In relation to the organization of mass campaigns, it seems in point to note that legislative council research directors and other similar types of persons who may direct surveys generally have disabilities for leading mass political action. For quite appropriate reasons, these researchers frequently cultivate political neutrality and the judicial habit of giving opinions only when properly requested. The university bureaus of governmental research also frequently have a cautious orientation toward political action. If these persons or agencies are leaders in the survey job, it may be appropriate for them to indicate clearly the limits within which they operate so that the commission, committee, or council can plan for and organize other leadership for a mass campaign. In contrast, survey directors who are heads of citizen or taxpayer organizations are generally in their element in the attempted organization of popular support. This has been the experience in Colorado and Michigan.

It is also to be noted that even legislative councils, which are accustomed to making legislative proposals, as well as many legislative interim committees, exercise restraint in organizing campaigns for popular support for their proposals. The courtesies among legislators, though somewhat indistinct, do not generally permit the indiscriminate building of fires under colleagues through mass political action.

The device embodied in the federal reorganization enabling acts of authorizing a chief executive to submit reorganization plans to the legislature, with the plans going into effect unless the legislature takes positive action to veto them, has had very slight use in the states. This attempt to put inertia and indecision on the side of change has been considered in a number of states but has been rejected, apparently generally in fear of adverse decisions on constitutionality. So far as has been learned, only in New Hampshire and South Carolina was legislation authorizing such plans adopted; and in New Hampshire this method was dropped when a request by Governor and Council to the Supreme Court for an opinion on the constitutionality of the procedure brought an adverse report. In South Carolina the device was provided for in their 1948 reorganization act (Act 621 of 1948), and, of nine plans submitted, three were allowed to become effective, one of the three being an alternative to one of the rejected plans.

In view of the usual result of partial or complete failure in reorganization movements, it is appropriate to consider how it may be possible to keep the movements in existence so that the proposals may have additional chances for consideration. Inside of government there are the possibilities that a governor may continue to press for action, that an interim committee to give further consideration may be formed, or that a legislative council may receive such an assignment, or, if it was the survey group, may continue the studies and resubmit proposals. In several states a legislative research agency is filling such a role. In Nevada, a legislative research agency is going this year into its third legislative session with its administrative survey proposals; some of its proposals were adopted in each of the first two sessions.

Outside of government are the existing private civic agencies and groups and newly formed citizens' committees to support the reorganization proposals in imitation of the national committee. Examples of the latter are to be found in Michigan and Minnesota. Some of these agencies and groups may have difficulty avoiding the label of special pleader and others may be amateurish at times; but when their actions are coordinated with similar moves inside government, action sometimes takes place. Even when a reorganization movement has been such a failure that no one wants to nourish it back into existence, the following years and even decades may see action on particular points treated or suggested in the survey. Although our frame of reference is legislative action following surveys, it is perhaps permissible to say that these reorganization studies and proposals have values in civic education regardless of the legislative accomplishments of the movements and that they sometimes stimulate agency-sponsored administrative improvement programs. The education of legislators and the stimulation of executive offices into thought about management may produce gains which in time justify the costs and efforts of the survey.

Legislators' View of the Proposals

Previous reference to the nature of the reorganization proposals themselves have been oblique. They will not be analyzed here in any detail. The Council of State Governments' *Reorganizing State Governments,* published in 1950, analyzes the recommendations of the state commissions as of that date. There seems to be little change in the later developments except perhaps for some new emphasis on legislative financial controls.

What is generally in controversy and what is in point here is executive - management - unity - of - command - single - head - departments centralized-auxiliary-services pattern. In the nineteen general surveys which have in some sense been completed and for which we have data on this point, fifteen embodied in their report some version of the theme of making administration responsible to executive political authority. It would thus seem that among the surveyors the executive-management-unity-of-command ideas still tend to prevail. When one looks at the adoption of *major* proposals in these fifteen states, he finds New Hampshire's and New Jersey's large successes and some fraction of adoption in Colorado, Nevada, Oregon, South Carolina, and Virginia, and almost no adoption of major proposals in the others. As the New Hampshire proposals tended to be very mild in their expression of the executive management concept, and as the enactment of major proposals has otherwise been quite slight, one can, I believe, assume a rather general resistance on the part of legislatures to the full acceptance of the executive management theme. There seems to be some willingness to give the governor added or enlarged tools for influencing management, but the unity-of-command-single-head administrative agency pattern seems to have limited attractiveness to the legislatures, perhaps less than in the 'twenties and 'thirties.

If these inferences are correct, we may, insofar as the content of proposals has influenced legislative reactions, have a situation of conflicting values and viewpoints. There is no way in logic to reconcile differences resulting from affinities for conflicting premises, and there is no point in attempting it. If some legislators want to think of reorganization proposals in terms of how they affect employees Mabel and Joe, the sportsmen and the dentists, and of how the likely officeholders they know about fit the gubernatorial and department head thrones prepared for them in a reorganization plan, these ways of thinking are to be expected. If other legislators, some governors, citizens, and students of state administration want to think in terms of countering the centrifugal tendencies toward governments for every group and region within a loose holding corporation state government and of creating conditions which are more favorable for the resolution of conflicts, for the co-ordination of those activities which may with economy be coordinated, for the location of responsibility for executive development and execution of policy, and for the development, preservation, and communication of the arts of professional management and professional performance of functions, these ways of thinking are also to be expected. Whatever one thinks of these varied expectations, there is for the professional participant in movements for administrative change no basis for being doctrinaire. There is rather an opportunity to try to find the accommodations to these various values which can be arrived at currently in enactable measures. What is arrived at in reorganization proposals may not be neat in pattern and may look both toward integration and particularism, but if the conditions for developing professional administration are bettered, that is much to be preferred than having copies of a rejected "model" report.

Certainly to be avoided is the highly vulnerable position of asserting that economy or better services will flow from the enactment of reorganization plans. Any legislator knows that the occupants of the governor's and commissioners' chairs may have as their better talents and primary interests other matters than the general management of large enterprises. What they may not know and can perhaps be taught by modest demonstrations is that better services and economies can be attained by creating the conditions in which many people in the administration search regularly and broadly for optimum methods and arrangements for performing public tasks.

Chapter VII

The
Judicial
System

A unique feature of American federalism is the dual court system, in which laws are made and enforced by two sets of governments. This dualism, coupled with a tradition of written constitutions and a fear of vesting governmental officials with discretionary power, has created a highly legalistic nation.

This legalism is reflected in the complicated structure of most state court systems. Most reformers agree with Arthur T. Vanderbilt, a former chief justice of the New Jersey Supreme Court, that the state court system should be composed of three levels: (1) a local court of limited civil and criminal juridiction, (2) a general trial court, and (3) an appellate court or courts. However, states have a wide variety of courts with limited or special jurisdiction. Even courts with identical names do not have the same jurisdiction. A small-claims court in one county may have jurisdiction over civil suits with amounts up to $3000, while in an adjoining county the small-claims court may be limited to cases of less than $1000.

Former Chief Justice Vanderbilt in his article "The Essentials of a Sound Judicial System" enumerates several other essential features of a good judicial system. He argues that there must be a corps of independent, professional judges and suggests that the best method of selection is executive appointment.

There is considerable controversy regarding the best method of judicial selection. In roughly three fourths of the states the law specifies that judges are to be chosen in either a partisan or nonpartisan election. The basic assumption underlying this method appears to be the belief that judges are decision makers, and decision makers in a democracy should be responsible to the people. Opponents of judicial election contend that justice should not be connected with the ballot box and that elected judges are too susceptible to public pressures.

The controversy over the selection of judges would appear to involve a very basic issue. However, Adolf A. Berle, Jr., in "Elected Judges — or Appointed?" suggests that the importance of the issue is exaggerated since most judges, even those in states that provide for election, acquire office originally by appointment. In those states where judges are nominally elected most incumbent judges resign, die, or become incapacitated while serving a term and a successor is appointed by the executive. The newly appointed judge will have little or no opposition at any ensuing election.

Regardless of the method of selecting judges, the essence of the judicial system must be a fair trial. Critics contend that several features of the present system inhibit a fair trial. Among the features most commonly criticized are the jury system, the fee system, and long delays caused by the heavy burden placed upon the courts.

The most common criticism of the jury system is that jurors are often not competent to learn the facts or to understand the legal concepts with which they deal. Quite often in civil cases jurors have to cope with highly complex or technical concepts in areas in which they have little or no knowledge. In other countries the jury is seldom used in civil cases, and its use in the United States is declining. However, Judge Bernard Botein vigorously defends the use of the jury and suggests in "A Judge Votes for the Jury" that the British experience with the abolition of jury trials in civil cases is not applicable to the American judicial system.

Although the justice of the peace and other minor courts seem to be unusually susceptible to corruption and prejudicial conduct, other courts are not blameless. Occasionally it is necessary to remove a judge from the bench for failure or inability to perform his duty properly. "Trouble on the Bench: Impeachment of a Judge" reports the impeachment and removal of a state supreme court justice.

In addition to impeachment, judges may be removed from office by failure of re-election, removal by the governor with or without legislative request or approval, recall, and removal by joint resolution of the legislature. Removal by any of these methods is quite uncommon, except in cases of physical incapacity. Most judges are competent and honest, and the case study reproduced here was chosen to demonstrate some of the potential problems of popular control of the judiciary.

In the final analysis, it is the people who are responsible for the quality of justice that is dispensed. The people, directly or indirectly, select the judges, make the laws, structure the court system, and serve on the jury. Although most Americans desire fair trials for the accused in the abstract, in practice it is difficult to apply the law evenly in highly publicized and controversial cases. One such case is "The Trial of 'Delay' Beckwith" described by Harold H. Martin. This may be an atypical example but it demonstrates the paradox in the American belief that ours should be "a government of laws, and not of men" when the system of laws must be interpreted and enforced by men.

THE ESSENTIALS OF A SOUND JUDICIAL SYSTEM

Arthur T. Vanderbilt

Arthur T. Vanderbilt is a former chief justice of the New Jersey supreme court. He is author of numerous books pertaining to law and the legal profession.

Men inevitably have disputes, and it is one of the great functions of the courts to adjudicate them according to law. This is termed the administration of civil justice. Men also commit offenses against the laws provided for the protection of all of us, and at the suit of the state the courts pass on the question of their guilt and enforce the law against any wrongdoers in an effort to protect society. This we call the administration of criminal justice. Of the two, although most people, including many lawyers who should know better, do not seem to realize it, the administration of criminal law is by far the more important. Of what value is a civil right under a contract or to a piece of property, or even the right to life itself, if its owner cannot enjoy it because of some breakdown in the enforcement of the criminal law? Going a step further and looking at both the civil and criminal law, of what real worth are the fundamental rights guaranteed by our federal and state constitutions if they cannot be enforced in a fair trial? In the last analysis, then, the right to a fair trial is the most fundamental of all rights, for without it all other rights are mere words, empty and meaningless.

From this point of view the judiciary, though the weakest of the three great departments of government—"It has no influence over either the sword or the purse," to quote the *Federalist*—is the most important of all to the citizen in distress and looking for a fair trial, either civil or criminal. Everything that is necessary to accord him a fair trial is an essential of a sound judicial system. Here at least is one point where there is no conflict between the needs of the individual and of the public.

Fortunately for us all the essentials of a sound judicial system are relatively few in number and are well known to the legal profession

From "The Essentials of a Sound Judicial System," Arthur T. Vanderbilt, *Northwestern University Law Review*, XLVIII (March-April 1953), 1-15. Reprinted by special permission from the Northwestern University Law Review, Copyright © 1953 by the Illinois Law Publishing Corporation, Vol. 48, No. 1. [Footnotes omitted.]

from centuries of experience (both good and bad, I hasten to add). All we have to do to attain a sound judicial establishment is to overcome our professional inertia and selfishness and adopt the standards of judicial administration that every intelligent and public-spirited lawyer (my adjectives, you will note, limit the class considerably) knows should long since have been adopted. Where thoroughgoing judicial reform has been achieved, as in England and in New Jersey, it has come, in spite of the bench and the bar generally, through the efforts of laymen led by a few brave lawyers. This is the darkest and most indelible spot on the escutcheon of our otherwise great profession. Perhaps (I wish I could be more confident) the great popular discontent that presently confronts government at all levels — national, state, and local — may inspire the bench and bar everywhere to undertake the task that is emphatically theirs, not only as a matter of professional duty but also as a matter of self-preservation, despite the inconvenience it will temporarily cause them until they become accustomed to the improved judicial system that they know the public is entitled to. I most earnestly hope so. Nothing else that they can do would contribute so much to restoring the faith in government and the respect for law so essential to the preservation of democratic, representative government.

Let me enumerate and comment briefly on the several essentials of a sound judicial system as I see them:

1. The first essential of a sound judicial establishment is a simple system of courts, for the work of the best bench and bar may be greatly handicapped by a multiplicity of courts with overlapping jurisdictions. Lord Coke lists 74 courts in his *Fourth Institute,* but three are all that are needed in a modern judicial establishment: (1) a local court of limited civil and criminal jurisdiction, (2) a trial court of general statewide jurisdiction, and (3) an appellate court or courts, depending on the needs of the particular state. Although only three courts are called for, instead of the many courts with special jurisdictions as we now have in many states there may well be — indeed there should be — considerable specialization by judges in the trial courts. Without limiting the general jurisdiction of each trial judge, he should be assigned to a division of his court specializing in the kind of work for which he is best qualified — criminal, civil (generally with a jury), equity, probate, juvenile, traffic, and the like. Some very good equity judges shrink from jury work and some very good law judges dislike equity. For sound judicial administration, therefore, someone should have the power to assign the judges where they are needed and to the work for which they are best fitted. Because this power of assignment is a delicate one to be exercised only on mature reflection for the best interest of the judicial establishment as a whole, it may best be committed to the chief judicial officer in the state and he, in turn, would do well to seek the advice of his colleagues, even though the ultimate responsibility for assignments must be solely his.

2. The second essential of a sound judicial system is, of course, a corps of judges, each of them utterly independent and beholden only to the law and to the Constitution, thoroughly grounded in his knowledge of the law and of human nature including its political manifestations, experienced at the bar in either trial or appellate work and preferably in both, of such a temperament that he can hear both sides of a case before making up his mind, devoted to the law and justice, industrious, and, above all, honest and believed to be honest. These standards necessarily exclude all judges who are not members of the bar and all part-time judges who are judges one minute and practicing lawyers the next. Relatively few judges have all these qualifications and yet are there any of them that you would dare to term superfluous? Of course, some good judges have learned their law after ascending the bench, and more have acquired courtroom experience as judges rather than as lawyers, but either process is an expensive and unsatisfactory one both for the litigants and the public and would not be tolerated in business. Some may question my insistence on a knowledge of man as a political animal, but politics plays so large a part in American life that a judge to be competent must know what it is all about. Understanding politics, however, is one thing; playing politics from the bench is something far different. It is utterly reprehensible.

How are we to recruit judges such as I have been describing? There is, it must be frankly admitted, no entirely foolproof way of selecting judges. The practice of executive appointment from among the leaders of the trial and appellate bar pursued in all common-law countries except our own produces the best results, but even so every now and then a distinguished barrister proves to be a mediocre judge. No system of selection could be worse, however, than popular elections on party tickets along with a host of other national, state, and local party candidates running for a wide variety of offices. There is not the remotest chance of a judge being elected on the basis of the traits we have enumerated as essential in a good judge. The qualities that make for judicial competence are not likely to be found impressive on the hustings, and the steps one has to take to get a party nomination are not likely to be quite compatible with the complete independence that is an indispensable requirement for a good judge. Nor do the drawbacks disappear following election: in many states the county judge is forced to act as the undisclosed—though actual—leader of his political party in the county if he wishes to have a chance for reelection, an intolerable situation known to all and sundry. No wonder that in a national poll held some years ago 28% of those queried stated that they did not believe their local judges were honest.

The plain truth is that popular, partisan judicial elections would have failed long since were it not for the fact that in state after state about one-third of the judges in office die or resign, giving the governor an opportunity to make ad interim appointments. These ad interim appointees as a class are much better than the judges elected in partisan elections. When they run for election at the end of their ad interim appointments, the prestige of their position generally insures their election. In this manner the calibre of the judiciary is improved, but not sufficiently to overcome the shortcomings of the elected two-thirds. This situation has led to the increasing approval of what has been variously known as the Missouri, California, or American Bar Association plan of judicial selection. The essence of each of these plans is the appointment of a judicial commission in part by the governor, in part by the bar; the recommendation by the judicial commission of several nominees to the governor for each judicial post; the appointment of one of these nominees by the governor for a fixed term, followed by a nonpartisan judicial election at which the appointee runs, not against the field but on his own record. If the people approve his work, he continues to hold office; if they do not, the process is repeated. It would be well to use a judicial commission even where the governor makes the appointments, for one politically-minded governor could undo the good work in judicial appointments of several governors who did not let politics influence their judicial appointments.

There is much to be said for requiring, even under the new plan, the appointment of all judges on a bipartisan basis. Justice, on principle, should be bipartisan. Its administration should not be vested in a single party. Bipartisan appointments are the best way of proving to the public that one party does not control the courts and that the courts are not in politics. The matter is of especial importance in the decision of highly controversial political issues. If all the judges in a bipartisan court, regardless of party affiliations, concur in the decision of such an issue, as they frequently do, their decision carries a weight with the public that an opinion from a partisan bench could not possibly do. I am speaking from experience because in New Jersey, without any constitutional or statutory requirement, we have had a bipartisan judiciary for nearly a hundred years.

3. Honest and intelligent juries, representing a cross-section of the honest and intelligent citizenry of a county, are as essential to the administration of justice as upright and learned judges. It is a mockery of justice to go through the form of a trial with a dishonest or unintelligent juror in the jury box. The jury is an integral part of the administration of justice and the selection of the panel from which juries are drawn should therefore be entrusted to the courts or to commissioners appointed by the courts. This has been done in thirty-three states, but in the remaining fifteen states the selection of the jury panel is in political hands, with the inevitable resultant dangers to the administration of justice.

4. In addition to good judges and good jurors, we must have

honorable, well educated lawyers, and an effective organization of the bar. It is too much to expect that the work of judges or of juries will often rise much above the level of the work of the lawyers appearing in the cases the judges and juries decide. Here I think we must appeal to our law schools for more help. By and large our law schools have done a splendid job of teaching the principles of substantive law and the art of legal reasoning—the "what" and the "why" of the law—but my experience as an educator, practitioner, and judge compels me to confess that the law schools have not kept pace with medical and engineering education in teaching the "how" of the law to the profession.

The complexities of our age call for more than individually good lawyers. We need a good organized bar. And how may we recognize a good bar? Without attempting a definition, I venture to say that a good bar will feel a very real sense of responsibility for the administration of justice, for the selection of judges and jurors, for legal aid to all in the state who need it, both in civil and criminal litigation (I am very proud that the bar of my state was the first to realize this), for legal education both before and after admission, for enforcing the canons of judicial and professional ethics, for eliminating the unauthorized practice of the law, for improving the substantive law, and for encouraging good government. A large order, you will say, but what may we omit without loss to both the profession and the public?

5. A simple court structure, good judges, jurors, and lawyers—what more do we need? We must have competent court clerks, stenographic reporters, and bailiffs, but above all we need an administrative judge and his *alter ego*, an administrative director of the courts working under him, to supervise the judicial system and to see that it functions effectively as a business organization. The Constitution of New Jersey was the first to declare that "The Chief Justice of the Supreme Court shall be the administrative head of all the courts in the state" and that "He shall appoint an administrative director of the courts to serve at his pleasure." I have found that my administrative work takes from a third to a half of my time and all the time, of course, of the administrative director and his staff. What other statewide business do you know of that attempts to operate without management, without supervision, without operating statistics, without periodic conferences of its key personnel, or without administrative rules? When you think of the lack of all these factors in most of our court systems, the wonder is that the judicial branch of our government has worked as well as it has.

With the right kind of courts, judges, jurors, lawyers, court officers, and administrative organization available, what else is needed for a sound judicial system suited to the needs of these troublesome times? Manifestly the next thing that is needed is a realization by all concerned of the defects of the judicial establishment, especially those defects which are so obvious that the people are complaining of them. These defects may be grouped under three heads: inexcusable delays, the lack of a fair trial on the merits of each case, and bad judicial manners. I will next discuss these defects in the order named.

6. Subordinate only to the complaint against dishonest judges is the popular resentment of the law's delays. The grievance is an ancient one. We find it mentioned in Magna Carta. Hamlet comments on it. Every step in the process of litigation, of course, takes time, but that is not what the public is complaining of. What the people object to is unnecessary delays. Often delays that are attributed to the courts should really be ascribed to the lawyers. I know of one New England state where the judges are unusually prompt in their decisions, but in which cases are often delayed by the bad habits of lawyers. The judges there owe the public and themselves the duty of placing the blame where it belongs.

Most of the delays of which complaint is made are quite avoidable. They fall into three classes:

First of all, litigants, witnesses, and jurors alike get very much annoyed when the judge fails to open court at the appointed hour. No single judicial fault, save lack of integrity, can do so much to create a bad impression. The failure of a judge to appear in court on time indicates to laymen his lack of interest in his judicial work and his unwillingness to conform to the rules of court, while insisting that others conform, as well as a failure to appreciate the value of other's time. It irritates the laymen's sense of equality, for with all their respect for the law and for judicial office as symbolizing the law, people regard a judge as a man. They have been taught, have they not, that all men are equal, and a judge should be wise enough to recognize their teaching. I have discovered that this bad judicial habit could be cured only by a positive rule requiring the opening of court at a fixed hour throughout the state. Here again a strong example has proved helpful; if the seven justices of our supreme court can get to the state house from all over the state in time to open court at ten o'clock, surely any judge can manage to get to his nearby county seat by the same hour. To some of you this may seem a small matter and unworthy even of mention here, but in actual practice it is an essential rule of judicial administration.

The second cause of complaint about the law's delays is the failure to get on to trial after all the necessary preliminaries of pleading and pretrial procedures have been disposed of. Here let me observe that a judge can never do his best work when he is asked to tackle a task which he knows is impossible of accomplishment, when he sees that for every case he tries two are being added to his list. Where arrearages have accumulated, the number of judges must be increased, either temporarily or permanently. It is a curious but nevertheless demonstrable judicial fact that two judges working on the same calendar can dispose of twice as many cases as they could working separately in different courthouses. The extent to which this principle may be applied depends upon the number of available courtrooms, the number of available trial judges, and the number of available trial lawyers. But subject to these limitations, an increase in the number of judges, either permanently or temporarily, at the congested spot is the first step in eliminating delays in bringing cases on to trial. This requires giving to someone, preferably to the chief justice, the power to assign the trial judges to those counties where they are most needed. Whatever success we have had in New Jersey in clearing our calendars—some cases in Chancery as much as ten or twenty years old—I think must be attributed in large measure to the power given by our Constitution to the chief justice to assign judges. In Chancery matters we cleared the decks within six months. On the law side within two years we disposed of all arrearages in sixteen of our twenty-one counties so that cases could be tried within three or four months after they were started, and in the remaining five counties we obtained a similar state of currency within the third court year—a striking contrast to the delays of the old system, in which one not infrequently had to wait two or three years for a jury trial.

In the work of clearing the dockets compulsory pretrial conferences, in all court cases except divorce cases, have also played a large part, for we have discovered that in county after county numerous cases have been settled before trial as a result of what has developed at the pretrial conference. The pretrial conference is an invaluable feature of adequate judicial administration and I shall refer to it again in dealing with trials on the merits where I deem it even more important.

There is one special cause of delay in getting cases on for trial that must be singled out for particular condemnation—the all too prevalent habit of sending matters to a reference. There is no more effective way of putting a case to sleep for an indefinite period than to permit it to go to a reference with a busy lawyer as referee. Only a drastic administrative rule, rigidly enforced, strictly limiting the matters in which a reference may be had and requiring weekly reports as to the progress of each such matter will put to rout this inveterate enemy of dispatch in the trial of cases.

The final cause of delay is the failure of the judge to promptly decide a case after he has heard the testimony, read the briefs (in advance of the arguments, of course), and heard the arguments of counsel. These delays in deciding matters are largely a matter of bad judicial habit. A judge can only decide one case at a time. No judge, moreover, will ever know more about a given case than he does when the testimony is fresh in his mind and while the arguments of counsel are still ringing in his ears. We in New Jersey have suffered much in the past from this bad judicial habit of delaying decisions. Some of our vice chancellors were truly judicial descendants of Lord Eldon. For them to delay a decision six, eight, ten, or even twelve years was not unknown. Four years ago when our new system started I had to assign three judges to work for several weeks on the arrears of one distinguished vice chancellor who had retired leaving a large number of cases undecided, some dating back more than six years. This bad habit of delaying decisions is not an easy one to break, but our administrative rule requiring all motions to be decided as a matter of routine within ten days, all cases to be disposed of within four weeks after trial, and all motions and cases heard but undecided to be reported in the judge's weekly report has completely eliminated the public's justifiable criticism of this phase of the law's delays. Most judges would rather decide a case than report it as undecided. The judge's weekly report is therefore an indispensable aid to sound judicial administration, and I shall have more to say of it in another connection.

7. The next great popular grievance against the courts is a failure in too many cases to get a decision on the merits. All too often the tendency is for a trial to become a battle between opposing counsel rather than an orderly, rational search for the truth on the merits of the controversy. There can be no doubt of the justice of this complaint. It is a complaint that is more difficult to overcome than the dishonesty—or the reputation therefor—of some judges or the law's delays. Three factors in particular contribute to this great evil. The first is the popular notion that a trial, and especially a criminal trial, is a sporting event rather than an orderly search for truth with justice as its great objective. In all too many communities counsel are still rated primarily for their histrionic ability. Secondly, this improper attitude toward litigation has been heightened by the fact that in the second quarter of the nineteenth century in many of the states the chief powers of the common-law trial judge were taken away from him by legislation as part of the equalitarian and antiprofessional revolt that culminated in the triumph of Jacksonian democracy. In many states the trial judge was deprived of the right to put questions to the witnesses even when they were necessary to bring out the truth. He was stripped of the right to organize the evidence into a systematic whole in his charge to the jury and to comment in his charge on the testimony of the witnesses. He was even shorn of his right to charge the jury in his own language, being obliged to charge in the technical language of the requests to charge submitted to him by counsel. Moreover, his charge so-called, but really his selection between the plaintiff's or the defendant's requests to charge, came before the summation to the jury by the defendant's and the plaintiff's counsel, so that whatever the judge said was quite forgotten by the jury after it had listened to the lawyers' barrage and counterbarrage of eloquence. The third cause of difficulty in the trial courts is the fact that the rules of pleading, practice, and procedure were prescribed by the legislature and in many states became increasingly complicated as a result of continuous legislative tinkering, with the result that the trial judge was often forced by statute to do things in the course of the trial that were

obviously unjust and contrary to common sense. The trial judge was thus reduced to the position of an umpire all but gagged and blindfolded.

The situation I am portraying is by no means fanciful. In this age of scientific inquiry, there are still twenty states in which the judge is not allowed to sum up the evidence, thirty-six states in which he is not allowed to comment on the evidence, twenty states where the instructions precede the final argument of counsel, and three states in which, believe it or not, the court must instruct the jury that his statements of the law are purely advisory and that it has the right in criminal cases to find the law as well as the facts! And yet with these odd notions of trial procedure we still expect judges and juries to do justice.

The first step in remedying the situation is, of course, to restore to the trial judge his common-law power to preside effectively at the trial. This is easier said than done. Many counsel cling tenaciously to their prerogative of surprise in the courtroom, to their concept of a trial as a battle of wits between two lawyers rather than a search for the truth, to the notion that the judge should be seen but not heard. Until these false notions are banished, justice will often be but a sham and a mockery.

The next step is to give the rule-making power to the highest court in each state. After what has been accomplished in the federal courts through the judicial exercise of the rule-making power, there should be no need of any argument to establish its advantage over legislative codes. The results of judicial rule-making speak for themselves. I doubt very much that strict judicial rule-making — and by that I mean the making of rules by the judges alone — would have been a great improvement on codes and statutes had not the methods pursued by the United States Supreme Court in drafting the Rules of Civil and Criminal Procedure insured the workability of its rules. Not only were the rules drafted by advisory committees of experts appointed by the court, but they were submitted and resubmitted to the criticism of the bench and bar throughout the country. After ten years of use the Civil Rules have again been reworked by the same process and over half of them have been amended. This method gives the court the benefit of the experience of both trial judges and practicing lawyers. The process of rule-making should be continuous. Judicial conferences or judicial councils in the several states should annually call for suggestions from the bench and bar and these suggestions should be carefully debated each year for the benefit of the supreme court in its rule-making capacity. Through such a continuous process, and through this process only, may we hope for a system of procedure that will be at all times adapted to its purpose and that will be at all times subordinate to establishing the substantive rights of the litigants.

A third step in obtaining a trial on the merits rather than a theatrical performance is the full use of modern pretrial procedures, such as interrogatories, depositions, examinations before trial, inspections and the like, culminating in a pretrial conference at which the pleadings are reviewed to see how they can be simplified and the issues are restated as preliminaries to seeing what facts may be stipulated and what documents may be admitted so as to shorten the trial. The pretrial conference gives counsel an opportunity, if they so desire, to canvass the possibilities of settlement, but the judge, of course, must never attempt to force a settlement. The most important aspect of pretrial conferences is not that many cases are customarily settled as a result of each party facing the facts on both sides for the first time under expert guidance, nor is it that the trial time of each case is greatly reduced. The great advantage of pretrial conferences is that the judge has a preview of what will be coming at the trial and he can, if he thinks it necessary in an unusual case, direct the filing of briefs in advance of the trial. No longer does he have to fumble through the pleadings to find out what the case is all about, while endeavoring to listen to the opening statements of counsel. No longer need he guess the answer to novel questions of law. He has a complete outline of the trial before him in the form of the pretrial conference order and he is master of the situation from the outset.

8. The third significant cause of public discontent with the courts springs from an occasional exhibition of judicial bad manners. There is less of it in the appellate courts than in the trial courts for the reason, among others, that the process of legal argument does not so often lead to the clashes that characterize the presentation of testimony. Judging from the number of complaints that come my way, judicial discourtesy is very much more prevalent in the criminal courts of limited jurisdiction than in either the general trial courts or the local civil courts. This may be accounted for in part by the fact that a large number of municipal magistrates are still laymen, in part by the difference in the mental attitude of the attorneys appearing in the local criminal courts, and in part by the volume of work in some of these courts. But whatever the cause there can be no excuse whatsoever for judicial discourtesy. A judge's bad manners can only serve to bring the administration of justice into disrepute. Establishing conditions under which a judge may work honestly and keep his self-respect will go a long way toward reducing complaints on this score. A judge who is not beholden to anyone and who is up to date with his work is less likely to be irritable than one who is under obligations and fears that others know it, or who is behind with his work. But whatever the cause, an irritable judge cannot be justified or tolerated in view of the disrespect for law which he inevitably creates. Requiring a judge, even of a local court, to wear a judicial robe has a marked tendency to increase decorum in the courtroom. It helps to keep court officers in their place. Every witness should stand and everyone in the room should remain silent while the oath is being administered to the witness by the judge himself. Applying to the local criminal courts the same rules of conduct as are applied in

other courts is equally essential. But the affirmative way of meeting any charges of discourtesy in the local criminal courts is for the judge to take the necessary minute or two to explain to each defendant just why he is being found guilty and why the particular sentence is being imposed on him. This can be done in a friendly manner so as to make clear the purpose of the sentence, whether it be intended as punishment for a violation of the law or as a deterrent for the purpose of saving life and limb. I know of one judge who by doing just this had eighty per cent of his "customers" thank him publicly for his courtesy, while at the same time he had increased the amount of his fines over sixty per cent. There is much to be said for the practice of the English chancellor who, when asked his formula for selecting judges, replied, "I pick a gentleman and if he knows a little law so much the better." We need gentlemen in our local courts quite as much as in our courts of general jurisdiction.

While we are awaiting the judicial millennium, perhaps the most effective way of counselling courtesy is for the chief justice to bring to the attention of the individual judge every charge of discourtesy by sending him a copy of any complaint against him and asking for his version of the facts. Sometimes the judicial alibis are so thin as to be almost transparent and they are often accompanied by a considerable show of indignation, but it is noticeable that following such correspondence complaints cease to come from the particular community again. Moreover, the news of such correspondence travels fast throughout a county by what is commonly known as "the grapevine" and serves as a deterrent to other judges. From my experience I arrive at another principle of judicial administration. Every complaint should promptly receive the chief justice's personal attention and should be pursued to a conclusion both with the complainant and with the judge against whom the complaint is made. Chief Justice Hughes often said he regarded judicial administration as more important than opinion writing, and even in regard to municipal court complaints I am prepared to agree with him, though the work is time-consuming. Here is a sphere in which the bar might be much more helpful than it has been in many places both with respect to the selection of the judge in the first instance and to his subsequent conduct on the bench.

9. Judges as well as litigants have their complaints. A principle of judicial administration, rarely discussed publicly but never out of the minds of the judges, is the fair division of work. Some judges are much more effective in their work than others; some judges are reversed less than others; some judges give more satisfaction to the bar and to the public than others; and some judges are more conscientious, more devoted to their work than others. These individual differences cannot be changed administratively, but there should and can be equality in the number of hours each judge of the same court spends in the courtroom. This may be accomplished by having each judge make a weekly report

of the number of hours he has spent on the bench each court day, the number of cases and motions he has heard but has not disposed of, with the reasons therefor. With this information available in summarized form the chief justice is in a position not only to make assignments of the judges to meet emergencies at the time they arise without waiting until a heavy list has been allowed to accumulate in a particular county, but also to prevent inequalities in work. You may ask, how will the making of a weekly report make an indolent judge work? The chief justice and his administrative director cannot hope to make a lazy judge work, and neither of them should be expected to be a policeman, but if summaries of these weekly reports are circularized among the judges in each court, it is truly remarkable how the relatively few laggards will mend their ways rather than incur the silent or occasionally vocal censure of their brother judges.

10. Statistics from the judges' weekly reports and from other data supplied by the court clerks are compiled in weekly and monthly reports by the administrative director, and these in turn are combined into quarterly and annual reports. In these reports there are comparative summaries of the work of the individual judges which disclose to every judge and to the public whether his record is above or below the average for his court. In the relatively few states where any judicial statistics at all are gathered, they have all too generally been compiled long after the event. I call these "dead" or historical statistics, because for the most part they are useless in affecting the work of the judicial establishment currently. After working with "live" statistics for four years, I am so impressed with their importance that I do not see how a judicial system can function effectively without them any more than a business could be run without current reports from its accounting department. By using "live" statistics and by assigning our judges on the basis of such statistics where they are most needed and to the kind of work they could best do, we not only increased the output of our general trial courts ninety-eight per cent in the first year and an additional twenty per cent in the second year—with twenty per cent fewer judges—but we have also improved the judges' working conditions and the quality of their work immeasurably. I am therefore rather emphatic in asserting that "live" statistics assembled into weekly, monthly, quarterly, and annual reports, both for the use of the chief justice and the judges themselves and for information of the public, are an essential of orderly judicial administration.

11. The examination of these weekly, monthly, quarterly, and annual reports, the assignment of judges and the general supervision of their work, the investigation of complaints from individuals or bar associations, conferences with individual judges concerning their work, attendance every few months at informal meetings of the judges of each court and each division thereof (I would list such meetings, which

generally are dinner meetings with their friendly personal contacts, as indispensable to sound judicial administration) all put a heavy burden on the chief justice of a state who is given broad powers of administration, even though he has the aid of a competent administrative director of the courts and staff. I am convinced from my experience, however, that all of these things are as indispensable to the functioning of an effective judicial establishment as they are to a business organization. Yet strangely enough those powers are rarely granted. Indeed, in twelve states the chief justice shifts every year or so and in two of these states, believe it or not, every six months. It is not without political significance that these short terms are so arranged that the title goes to a judge who is about to run for reelection. Clearly, it is essential for the proper administration of justice that there be a chief justice with a substantial term of office and with the power to call for reports, to collect "live" statistics, to assign the judges, to supervise the work of all the courts including the local criminal courts, to hold informal conferences with the judges, and to call judicial conferences in which the bar and the public are liberally represented to discuss the work of the judicial establishment.

12. The burden of this work necessitates giving the chief justice an administrative director of the courts to act as his *alter ego* in attending to the multitudinous details of running a great statewide business with branches in every county and in every community of the state. Time will not permit me to detail the wide variety of his activities. Such an officer must not only be a good lawyer and a diplomat versed in the ways of judges, but he must have executive ability and be skilled in the dispatch of business. Such an administrative director is, it goes almost without saying, a *sine qua non* of successful judicial administration.

13. The final essential of a sound judicial system is an abiding conviction, consistently acted upon by everyone in the judicial establishment, that the law and the courts exist not for the benefit of judges or lawyers or court officers who are merely the servants of the law, but for the benefit of the litigants and of the state.

There is nothing esoteric about these essentials of a sound judicial system. They are all quite obvious. They are not difficult to put into effect once there is the will to do so. They must be achieved in every state if we are to have an administration of justice worthy of the name. There can be no doubt as to the importance to us all of attaining such a goal if our kind of government is to function as it should. The only question is whether the judges and lawyers in each state will take the leadership in fulfilling the foremost obligation of the profession to society or whether they will abdicate to laymen. Once we become convinced of this self-evident truth, the law becomes our mission in the sense so eloquently described by Holmes:

*Law is the business to which my life is devoted, and I should show less
than devotion if I did not do what in me lies to improve it, and, when I
perceive what seems to me the ideal of its future, if I hesitated to point
it out and to press toward it with all my heart.*

ELECTED JUDGES – OR APPOINTED

Adolf A. Berle, Jr.

Adolf A. Berle, Jr., is professor of law, Columbia University. He served as a
member of F.D.R's Braintrust and was a consultant to the Secretary of
State, 1961-1962.

How should judges be chosen? The only honest answer is that the
method is less important than the true source of the appointment. Here
is one method now in use:

> *Dwight D. Eisenhower, President of the United States of America, to all
> to whom these presents shall come, GREETINGS:*
>
> *KNOW YE that, reposing special trust and confidence in the integrity,
> prudence and ability of John Doe, I " . . . etc. . . . . " do appoint him
> a Judge of the District Court of the Federal District Court for the
> Southern District of New York . . .*

John Doe, being fully confirmed by the Senate, thereupon holds his
judgeship for life. This is the appointive system; the Federal Government has it, and also a number of states, notably, Massachusetts.
Here is the second method:

> *We, the undersigned, the members of the Board of Election in The
> City of New York, having canvassed whole number of votes cast at the
> Election on (such-and-such a date) according to the original state-
> ments of said votes filed with us in the manner directed by law, do
> hereby certify that Richard Roe, of 10 West 76th Street, New York,
> N.Y., was duly elected a Justice of the Supreme Court . . . etc.*

This is a judgeship obtained by election in an open campaign. A majority of states uses this system for some, and New York uses it for all,
of its higher court judges. In New York the term is commonly for fourteen years. The judge was nominated by a political party or group, he
financed and carried on a campaign for election, and so got the job.

From "Elected Judges – Or Appointed." Adolf A. Berle, Jr., *The New York Times Magazine*, December
11, 1955, pp. 26, 34, 37-38. © 1955 by The New York Times Company. Reprinted by permission.

Both methods have had their advocates in a long-standing public debate, and both are now being considered by the Temporary Commission on the Courts which is preparing a report on judicial reform for submission to the 1956 Legislature.

Offhand, you might assume that the two systems are as different as possible. You would be wrong. The two systems are in ultimate analysis almost the same.

Factually, both the appointive and elective methods really mean that judges are chosen by the chieftains of the political parties involved. Your judge will be just as good as the political leadership of the area involved — state, judicial district, county, as the case may be. There seems to be no escape from this. Let us look behind the formal procedure and see what really happens.

Take the appointive system, prescribed by the Constitution of the United States with regard to all Federal Judges. The idea was that judges should be as far removed from political pressure as possible; so they are appointed by the President (in state systems like Massachusetts, by the Governor). Once appointed, they cannot be removed except by impeachment. Their salary cannot be cut; neither Legislature nor Executive can do anything to them. But behind the certificate of appointment, a quite different drama goes on.

A Federal judge is to be appointed, let us say, for the Southern District of New York. The President, unless he happens to come from that area, cannot possibly know the men who should hold judicial office. His principal law officer is the Attorney General of the United States. It is a recognized part of the Attorney General's job to recommend judicial appointments. Except in the case of his own district, he does not know the men either. So he expects, and the fact is, that the Republican state chairman of New York (assuming a Republican Administration) will make a recommendation, commonly in conjunction with the Republican Senator or Senators, if any, from the state. The Attorney General knows perfectly well that none of these men will recommend except after consultation with the county Republican leader who handles patronage in the district. That county leader has a group of hungry district leaders; they want credit for giving out the job (if they do not want the job themselves); indeed, they have been eying the particular vacancy for a good while. Probably several contesting leaders urge their pet candidates. The county leader has to resolve the question.

When, as in the case of the Federal judicial districts, the district covers more than one county, and even crosses state lines, he has to work it out with other leaders. Quite likely there has been a considerable ruckus — probably the continuation of ruckuses of previous years — resulting in a prior understanding about whose turn it is to get the next vacancy. The individuals who want the job have been busy as beavers lining up political support all the time.

County leaders, if they are any good, weed out the obviously impossible candidates. They finally arrive at an understanding that John Doe has the background necessary to be a judge, and decide that his appointment will satisfy the district leader who is entitled to it. All hands having been squared, a recommendation goes up. The local United States Attorney has probably been in on the discussion; he is likely to be asked by the Attorney General whether the man is all right. Not, you understand, whether he is the best possible man for judge, but whether his character, standing and so forth, are such that his appointment will not excite controversy.

The views of the state chairman have been ascertained. Consultation with the party United States Senator is usually essential; he is a political power himself; if the man is obnoxious to him, he can block confirmations by the Senate. (The most cruel Congressional prerogative is that of "courtesy of the Senate"—a polite way of saying that if a Senator objects to a Presidential appointment from his party in his state, all other Senators will vote against confirmation.)

By now, the "way is cleared," as politicians say. The recommendation goes forward to the Attorney General. He gets reports. The F.B.I. has investigated and discovers the man never joined the Communist party or murdered his mother-in-law. The local bar associations have reported him "qualified" for the job. The United States Attorney's Office has indicated that the man will do (not infrequently the United States Attorney is himself a candidate for the job). The party National Committee agrees because the party state chairman has agreed.

The Attorney General thereon takes or sends the whole dossier with favorable recommendation to the President, who sends up the name of the prospective judge to the United States Senate. The appointment goes promptly to the Committee on Judiciary; unless the man has made important enemies, this body after reviewing the file reports recommending confirmation; the Senate confirms; the Presidential certificate of appointment is issued; a new judge mounts the bench in the United States Courthouse in Foley Square.

On analysis, the real choice was made by the party leader or leaders in the unimpressive setting in which political parties act.

How about elective judges?

The power of choice is in the same hands, though the stages are somewhat different. The Constitution of the State of New York says that the justices of the Supreme Court (which in New York is not "supreme" but is a trial court) and the county judges shall be elected for a term of fourteen years. But, if an elective judge serves out his term with even moderate competence, the salutary and unbreakable custom in New York is that he shall have renomination by *all* parties, thus guaranteeing re-election.

For practical purposes, therefore, election is for life or until retirement age. He can only be displaced by a two-thirds vote of both houses of the Legislature on charges of misconduct. True, judges are nominated not by ordinary party convention, but by special judicial district conventions which are naively supposed to mean that the ugly hand of politics is somewhat removed from their choice. In practice, a judicial convention consists of a slate of delegates put up by the district leaders. Invariably they nominate the candidates arrived at by the county leader and his district leaders in the same way as are candidates recommended for appointment by the President.

But, at least, isn't there an election? A Republican does run against a Democrat, so that the people have something to say? No. Or at least, frequently not. There are few "doubtful" judicial districts in most states — very few, indeed, in New York. The Democrats know absolutely that they have control in most districts in the city; the Republicans have exactly the same control upstate. In the "safe" districts, the county leader's nod is equivalent to nomination and election.

When the election is in doubt, the practice increasingly has been for the leaders of both parties involved to get together. Not infrequently when three judges are to be elected, you find two Democrats and one Republican, or two Republicans and one Democrat, all nominated by *both* parties. The rival party leaders have sat down together, figured out the relative possibilities of the situation, agreed that one should nominate two judges and the other should have the third, canvassed their district leaders, decided on the deal and put through the nominations.

For practical purposes in that case, one of the judges has been picked by the Republican county leader; two have been picked by the Democratic county leader; as there is no contest, the election is a form. From time to time, of course, there are real contests. They are relatively rare.

So for practical purposes, ultimate power to choose every judge, elected or appointed, rests in the hands of the county machines of the two major political parties. There are exceptions, but so few that they rather prove the rule.

At this point one conjures up visions of a crooked, politically influenced bench. Has this been the fact? No, it has not. Surprisingly, the results in this strange and unpredictable working of the American political system have been good. The level of the New York elective bench rates as "good"; the level of the Federal appointive bench falls just short of continuous excellence.

If you examine the grimy surrounding circumstances, you would swear that it could not happen. Politics fairly burgeons in the selective process, frequently of the least savory kind. In nominating a man for the bench, a county leader frequently considers what kind of campaign contribution the candidate will make to the party war chest. At one time in New York City no one could expect a Democratic judicial nomination unless he was prepared to lay down $20,000 as a "contribution" to the campaign fund; frequently the quotation has been higher. When several men want the job (this is usually the case), they may even bid against each other.

One justice of the New York Supreme Court was widely known as the "$100,000 Judge" because he or his friends reportedly laid that contribution on the line. He got the job—and, having got it, did a remarkable piece of work. He was assigned to resolve the endless chaos resulting from the failure of the guaranteed mortgage companies in 1933; and he succeeded.

Powerful party figures often want judgeships for their relatives. The late Samuel Untermeyer had amassed a legal fortune. He was a thumping power in Tammany councils. He arranged to have two of his sons, Alvin Untermeyer and Irwin Untermeyer, named to the bench. Both turned in outstanding records.

The old Brooklyn boss, John McCooey, had his son put on the New York Supreme Court; a relative of the late Ed Flynn of the Bronx has quite recently got similar recognition. The old Manhattan Republican county leader, Sam Koenig, was represented on the Supreme Court bench by his brother, Morris Koenig.

Occasionally the nomination can be useful for other reasons: a party stalwart may have aspirations to be Mayor, and the organization can conveniently remove him from the situation by putting him on the bench. Yet the fact is that most of these men, once there, do an honest and effective job.

Politics does not quite end with appointment or election. A judge does have a considerable amount of patronage to distribute. In the Federal courts he can appoint trustees in bankruptcy, receivers, referees, and so forth. In the state courts he can appoint special guardians and other court officers. Both sets of judges have at least one very important appointment, namely, a law clerk or law secretary. It surprises almost no one to find that a Democrat invariably appoints Democrats to these jobs—not infrequently lists of suggestions are given him by the party which nominated him. His secretary is quite usually an aspiring lawyer with a good record for party fidelity.

But by now our judge is on, not off the bench, and he is thinking of his own reputation. If there is anything conspicuously wrong with the party follower he is asked to appoint as receiver, special guardian, referee, or the like, he knows the onus falls on him, and will find a way of appointing someone else. His law clerk on whom he must rely for continuous legal research has to be pretty competent, else the judge is in trouble.

Everything considered, the results have been paradoxically satisfactory. I have seen a Tammany judge, under the heaviest political pressure, decide squarely against his party organization in a proceeding to invalidate a nomination, the case involving construction of the election law. It did not hurt his career.

There have been scandals occasionally. They have been rare. One judge whose appointment was at least partly forwarded by the famous underworld character, Frank Costello (at all events, the judge thought so), has turned in an unexceptional record of judicial probity.

Still, one asks, is this rational? When choosing a judge we ought to be looking for the highest level of character and legal ability; we ought not to be dredging the party machines. Cannot better ways be found? Unquestionably, while the system has worked reasonably well, many men who should be on the bench never get there. Really first-rate lawyers rarely reach the bench. It looks like tempting Providence to expect figs from political thistles.

A number of possibilities have been suggested. One has been that all appointments to the state courts should be made by the Governor for life. This merely makes the Federal method of appointments general through the country. As we have seen, this merely means a political recommendation to him, instead of a political nomination for election.

A much discussed Western proposal has been that the bar association in each area shall make up a panel of names from which appointments or nominations for election, as the case may be, shall be drawn. In theory this is splendid: a bar association should be arbiter of legal ability, guardian of professional ethics, setting standards for the bench as well as for the bar.

In practice it is not so simple. Bar associations fulfill all these functions as long as, and only so long as, they stay out of politics. If at any time bar associations obtain power to name candidates for judgeships, would politics stay out of bar associations? Not probably. Most politicians are lawyers, and politics is one of the standard ways by which lawyers become known in their community. (On one occasion, even the Association of the Bar of the City of New York — blue ribbon organization of the county — was pressured into endorsing an individual for election. Its president, Harrison Tweed, a friend of the man in question, delivered a smashing rebuke, and in New York such an incident is not likely to be repeated.) What a bar association can do is to invite consultation with it before candidates are nominated for election or proposed for appointment, but only on a single issue: is the candidate of good character and professionally fit for the job?

Bar associations can — and do — issue reports to their members and to the public, stating that all of the candidates are of good character and are professionally fit to be judges — or the contrary, if any of them are not. Such verdicts have influence only. They may help to guide voters. In New York City, they frequently do not. Possibly such reports would have more influence on a Governor urged to appoint an unfit man.

But if the bar association ever is endowed with power to choose judges, or to make the panel from which judges are chosen, you can bet your last dollar that every political machine will suddenly take an enormous interest in seeing the bar association has the right president and picks the right committee on judiciary.

Political influence will be present in practically any system which can be devised. It will be there if judges are chosen by the Legislature instead of by the Governor, or by the Congress instead of the President. It will be there if they are chosen by a non-political council. It will get out of hand in every case where public opinion does not demand that judges be of good quality.

American public opinion is the reason why, in the main, American judges, Federal and state, have been good; it is the controlling reason; and it is the only safeguard. The American public unquestionably reveres its bench. A Governor or President who has appointed a bad judge hears from it in the newspapers, from his political opponents, and at the next election. He transmits his annoyance at once to the Attorney General and through him to the district leader who urged the appointment.

Next time around, recommendations from that source get bad treatment. Even county and district leaders dislike a bad reputation. Their other activities are likely to come in for more careful and wholly unwanted scrutiny if they have produced men who affront the desire of practically everyone for incorruptible and capable courts.

The crookedest politician knows that; and he can estimate very closely the extent of public interest. Public opinion, as a rule, has little interest in choosing who should be judges. But it is wholly clear that it wants good judges and someone's scalp if they are not. If that public opinion ever flags, the standards of acceptability used by political leaders and the quality of judges, however chosen, will promptly drop. Whenever the public and the press show interest in the subject, politicians will move up their standards and even "bosses" will request that the men proposed be top quality.

A JUDGE VOTES FOR THE JURY

Bernard Botein

Bernard Botein is a judge on the New York trial court, the supreme court. He is co-author of *The Trial of the Future*.

For centuries the debate has raged in England and this country as to whether the jury system should be abolished, but never with such intensity as in recent years. Some judges have delivered scathing denunciations of jurors, others have stirringly defended them; but many judges, I suspect, have resigned themselves to the weary conclusion that you can't live with them and you can't live without them.

Trial lawyers, who live and sometimes die by the jury, are the only other articulate group with a claim to actual courtroom experience with jurors. Jurors themselves, 1,000,000 of whom serve in 100,000 trials each year in this country, are usually heard from only when they seek to be excused from duty.

Few seriously advocate abolishing the jury in criminal cases. Even the most hard-bitten critic will either concede the unique value of the jury in criminal matters, or grudgingly admit that the public would never stand for its elimination where life and liberty are at stake. A powerful school believes that in a criminal case only the jury can bring the compassion of the community into the courtroom and soften for some particular defendant the harshness of laws designed to regulate human conduct in general.

Over the years the jury, primarily in the criminal case, has become, in the hearts and minds of many people, a bulwark against tyranny and oppression, the protector of the people against bureaucracy and against arbitrary, biased or corrupt action by judges.

But a campaign to eliminate the jury in civil cases—that is, all noncriminal lawsuits—has currently taken on fresh vigor. All men of law in this country are deeply concerned with the ever-increasing delays in the courts—sometimes as much as four or five years between a case's being placed on the calendar and reaching trial—and jury critics attribute much of this delayed justice and needless expense to time wasted by the jury process.

A reaction to this concern was manifested in California last year when Governor Brown invited study of a plan calculated to take automobile accident cases—representing one-half of all court business—out of the courts altogether. There is a closely watched development in England, which in 1933 virtually abolished the jury in the trial of civil cases. Opponents of the jury system here are encouraged by the fact that there is now general agreement that the change has proved eminently successful.

The average jury trial in the Supreme Court of New York County takes four days. It has been estimated that this is three times as long as the time required to try a similar case without a jury. While that statistic has been challenged, it is clear that the non-jury trial is much shorter. The hours spent in the selection of a jury, opening and closing statements to the jury, the judge's charge, all take time; and there are the time-consuming histrionics that lawyers fondly believe are so necessary before a jury.

It is claimed that jury trials waste not only time but also money. The cost to the taxpayers is $3,000 a trial in the Supreme Court of New York County, at the rate of $750 a day for the maintenance of one courtroom and its complement of judge and court officers. There is also an enormous loss of manpower. In the City of New York alone over half a million man days are devoted to jury service each year.

But the oldest and still most serious general criticism of the jury in civil cases is that it is less competent and less efficient than the judge as a fact-finder. (The traditional division of duties in a jury trial is that the jurors are the sole judges of the facts, but must follow the rules of law laid down by the judge.)

One familiar complaint is that lawyers sedulously exclude the most competent members of a panel from actual jury duty. Indeed, a well-known trial lawyer who represents plaintiffs in accident cases has written that married men and women favor plaintiffs; experts, professional people, nurses and wives of professionals are to be avoided, because they are indifferent to pain and suffering and inclined to rely on their own learning; and accountants are to be shunned, for they may inform their fellow jurors that a plaintiff does not pay an income tax on any money he may recover for his personal injuries.

A famous prosecutor once told me he would never select a man with a beard as a juror; he had found they were non-conformists and would, in an open-and-shut case, hold out and hang a jury out of sheer cussedness. And so, *ad infinitum*, lawyers have their pet notions and techniques for excusing jurors, irrespective of their competence—in fact, frequently because of such competence. Again, statutory exemptions from jury duty relieve millions of our best qualified citizens from serving.

A variation of this theme is that the average jury lacks the training and capacity to understand and determine a disputed set of complicated facts. Also, a judge sitting without a jury is usually required to make what are known as findings of facts—that is, to furnish a statement, in some detail, of every important fact upon which he bases his ultimate decision. But a jury almost always renders what is called a general verdict—an inscrutable "guilty" or "not guilty" verdict, or one for so many dollars in damages.

There can be no peering behind this verdict to ascertain how the jury decided the separately contested issues of fact, or whether it followed the judge's instructions on the applicable law.

There is the familiar contention that very often the judge's charge is unintelligible to the jury, or even when thoroughly understood is deliberately disregarded. "Lawless jurors," as Roscoe Pound terms them, will knowingly refuse to follow the judge's instructions because they believe the particular law to be unjust or silly or unfair.

Jurors are charged in this connection with being subject to a variety of prejudices and emotions. A somewhat related criticism is that they are easy prey to the arguments and histrionics of clever lawyers. Judges, as former lawyers, are presumed to be reasonably impervious to advocates' wiles; and through their discipline in neutrality, they are generally less susceptible to the emotional ingredients of a trial.

The really critical question, therefore, into which most of the complaints about the jury system funnel, is whether the judge or the jury is better qualified to determine where the truth lies in a trial and to make an appropriate decision on the basis of that determination.

The defenders of the jury have no hesitancy in locking horns with its critics on this question. They can quote many judges in praise of the composite acumen, conscientiousness, fairness and balance of juries. Profs. Harry Kalven Jr. and Hans Zeisel, directors of a number of massive surveys conducted by the Jury Project of the University of Chicago Law School, have written me that, on the basis of their varied research, their impression is that the jury understands and retains enough of the evidence to do its job.

They make the point that it is not necessary that every juror recall each item of evidence accurately. It is sufficient if a few jurors do so, as "the collective recall and intelligence of the jury is far higher than the average recall and intelligence of the individual juror."

It is pointed out that judges as well as jurors can be excessively emotional, biased, prejudiced or even stupid. The danger is that such a failing in a judge can be decisive, while in a juror its virulence will be diluted among all twelve members of the jury. Perhaps G. K. Chesterton had this in mind when he said: "I would trust twelve ordinary men, but I cannot trust one ordinary man."

The jury as a group, its champions also submit, may be entertained but will not be influenced by a lawyer's wiles. And while a lawyer may sometimes try to exclude an intelligent and competent juror, he cannot carry that practice very far. The number of peremptory challenges allowed each party to a lawsuit—a peremptory challenge is an outright exclusion of jurors for which no reason need be given—is limited. Usually a jury can be obtained that will fairly and faithfully reflect a cross section of the community, in intelligence as well as in other virtues and failings.

There are many who believe that the inability of a jury to understand a judge's instructions on the law is as much an indictment of the judges as of the jury. It often takes hard work on the part of a judge to reduce a charge on difficult questions of law to language understandable by laymen; but it can and should be done.

Defenders of the jury point out salient differences in practice and courtroom "climate" that made the elimination of juries more natural and smoother in England than it could be in America. In this country judges confine themselves pretty much to instructing the jury on the law only and remain remote from the fact-finding function. Judges in England, on the other hand, have always directed and participated forcefully in the fact-finding function of the jury, so yielding that function entirely to them did not come with quite so great a wrench as it would here.

Finally, rightly or wrongly, the man on the street usually feels safer in trying his case before a jury of his community than before a judge only. This is no whim of the moment. The Founding Fathers took great pains to spell out in the Constitution the absolute right to a grand jury and to a petit jury in criminal prosecutions and civil cases in Federal courts. Similar provisions are imbedded in state constitutions for state courts.

This was one way of insuring that the trial process would never be turned over to a bureaucracy that might become too subservient to governmental power, or too obsessed with the letter of the law at the expense of higher human values.

Underneath this there are still vestiges of the feeling that the little fellow opposed by powerful interests fares better at the hands of a jury of his peers.

Therefore, it is urged while jury trials may be more expensive and more protracted than non-jury cases, these are proper governmental costs of continuing and assuring to the public a sense of sure justice. There can be no risking the inferior administration of justice because of additional expense.

The jury champions also suggest the exploration of other remedies within our present procedure, such as broader and streamlined examinations before trial, elimination of the requirement for unanimity of the jury in rendering a verdict, perhaps the taxing of additional jury costs against the losing litigant to discourage the practice of demanding a jury as a tactical device, a six-man jury, the elimination of peremptory challenges or separate trials on the issues of liability and damages.

Speaking for myself, because of my concern with the administration of justice over the long range, I am opposed to the elimination of the jury or to any drastic tinkering with the system.

A good deal of the discontent with the jury system is due to the fact that jury trials do account for much of the delay in our courts. Critics see little hope that legislative purse strings will be loosened to furnish the courts with the vast additional facilities needed to keep up with the sharp rise in litigation bred by an exploding population. But this must be done. For the earnest, well-meaning persons who have turned to the elimination of the jury as a neat way of reducing delay, do not explore the consequences.

It has not yet been established that there is a more satisfactory way to decide the facts in contested trials. Moreover, the jury system has become a visible, close-at-hand symbol of democracy. In both civil and criminal cases it affords our citizens an opportunity to participate directly in the processes and responsibilities of government — participation that has been decreasing steadily in our highly complex and urban society.

We were reassured recently that, despite the economic and other hardships involved, citizens cherish and appreciate this opportunity to participate. In 1957 our court authorized the distribution of a questionnaire designed to obtain the reactions of a substantial number of persons who had recently served as jurors in the Supreme Court of New York County.

In answer to one question, 57 per cent termed their jury service a worth-while experience, 10 per cent a pleasant duty, 23 per cent a necessary but not too pleasant duty, 9 per cent pretty much a waste of time and 1 per cent a very unpleasant experience. In answer to what they liked about jury service, 38 per cent cited the participation in a civic duty and 35 per cent liked observing democracy in action.

I am gravely concerned that, if the jury is eliminated in the far more numerous civil cases, we may forget the significance of the jury in the defense of criminal charges. In one or two generations memories of the priceless heritage of trial by one's peers might be dimmed and the jury system consigned to the limbo of outworn expedients, like the trial by battle or ordeal of several centuries ago.

Sir Patrick Devlin has called the jury the "lamp of freedom." I, for one, would not want to risk the darkness of tyranny because of lack of oil for the lamps of freedom.

I suspect that no one can know whether the jury system would be missed, unless there came a time of crisis — when it would be most needed — and then there would be too little time to restore it. Trial by jury could be the most effective weapon in democracy's arsenal to combat tyranny. For tyranny cannot emerge until it has overridden the right of the individual to raise his voice — first in the legislature, and then in the courtroom.

TROUBLE ON THE BENCH:
THE IMPEACHMENT OF A JUSTICE

Napoleon Bonaparte Johnson sat, listening, in a brown, leather chair facing the Oklahoma Senate. Spectators packed the galleries, but there was little sound beside the droning of the clerk, calling the roll. As the votes came in, the 74-year-old, silver-haired Johnson glanced at a tally sheet his attorneys were keeping. A stunned look came into his face. A two-thirds majority — 32 votes — was needed to convict him; the total for conviction reached precisely that.

Presiding officer Roy Grantham solemnly made the official declaration of what the Senate, sitting as a Court of Impeachment, had determined: "It is the judgment of said court that you are removed from the office of justice of the Supreme Court of the state of Oklahoma."

Thus last week, for the first time in its history, the Oklahoma Senate removed a Supreme Court judge. In a week-long trial, the Senate heard charges that Mr. Johnson in 1957 and 1959 accepted bribes totalling $10,000. Throughout, Mr. Johnson insisted he was innocent. But the Senate voted 32 to 15 against him on each count.

Two Justices Convicted

Significant as the decision was historically in Oklahoma, it was but the latest development in a Supreme Court scandal that first shocked the state nearly a year ago. Then, a former Supreme Court justice, N. S. Corn, and one who recently resigned in the face of impeachment proceedings, Earl Welch, were convicted of Federal income-tax evasion. Mr. Welch, appealing the convictions, maintained that he was innocent.

But Mr. Corn confessed that he had received extra income from bribes. And he charged that he had shared the bribe money with Mr. Welch and Mr. Johnson. The Corn testimony was the basis of the case against Mr. Johnson, though much of the Senate trial involved accountants' figures on the earnings and expenditures of Mr. Johnson during the period when the bribes were supposed to have been given. The prosecution argued that Mr. Johnson overspent his income by approximately the amount of the bribes; the defense challenged the figures.

For some time there had been rumors, particularly among Oklahoma attorneys, that all might not be well on the state's highest court. But a Supreme Court justice, under the state constitution, can be removed only by the elaborate impeachment process.

From "Trouble on the Bench: The Impeachment of a Justice," *The National Observer*, May 17, 1965, p. 7. Reprinted by permission of the publisher.

Charged by the House

A State House of Representatives investigating committee first had to look into the matter. It recommended that the House impeach Mr. Johnson on two counts of bribery. The House voted 90 to 6 and 88 to 8 to do so. But to impeach is only to charge. The Senate then had to sit as judge and jury to decide if the charges warranted removing the accused. Members of the House conducted the prosecution.

Even before the court scandal broke, there was agitation among Oklahoma attorneys to change the system. They argued that the impeachment process was cumbersome, expensive, and politically difficult in that legislators would be hesitant to impeach or convict judges who might be members of their own political party. The Oklahoma Bar Association supported a state constitutional amendment to create a special "court on the judiciary" to have the power to remove or retire justices. But the public voted down the proposal in the 1964 general election.

The legislative action only removed Mr. Johnson from office; now it is expected that he will be prosecuted in regular court on the bribery charges. And the U.S. Internal Revenue Service declares it is looking closely into his financial records.

A Judge for 30 Years

The shock was intensified for the state's citizens because Mr. Johnson had been a prominent Oklahoman for so long. He had been on the Supreme Court some 16 years and a judge for 30. A Cherokee, he was educated at Indian missions, and in 1954 was chosen outstanding American Indian of the year.

THE TRIAL OF "DELAY" BECKWITH

HAROLD H. MARTIN

Harold H. Martin is an editor at large for *The Saturday Evening Post.*

Atop the massive granite-and-limestone Hinds County courthouse in tense Jackson, Miss., a gigantic statue of Moses holds aloft the ancient Tablets of the Law. Clearly visible in the streets below, as the morning sun falls on the weathered stone, is the admonition of the Sixth Commandment—THOU SHALT NOT KILL.

From "The Trial of 'Delay' Beckwith," Harold H. Martin, *The Saturday Evening Post,* March 14, 1964, pp. 77-81. Reprinted by permission of the author.

On the cold and blowing morning of last January 27, as Byron De La Beckwith went on trial in this courthouse for the murder of Medgar Evers, an old fat man in faded overalls set out his baskets of hot peanuts, parched and boiled, in front of the building's great bronzed doors. He stood there all morning, but his sales were few.

"They ain't coming to this trial like I expected," he said. "I guess they figure there's no use comin' to see a show when you know already how it's going to turn out."

The old man's words reflected the views of the majority of Mississippians. Byron De La Beckwith is a white man. Medgar Evers was a Negro—and an outspoken leader of the hated N.A.A.C.P. No Mississippi jury in the memory of living men has ever sent a white man to his death for the murder of a Negro.

"They'll acquit him in fifteen minutes," a florid man in a white jacket said. "The jury'll go back and play a few hands of Rook, just to make it look like they are studying the evidence. Then they'll walk back out and turn him aloose. That'll be all there is to it."

In the somber, dark-paneled courtroom the yellowish light from four huge chandeliers shone on the bearded, moustached and goateed portraits of famed Mississippi jurists of the past, and behind the judge's bench the tall carved scales of justice hung only slightly askew. All seemed normal. Yet from the moment the case was called, there were signs that this trial might not be just another sardonic charade.

On the bench Circuit Judge Leon Hendrick, 69, tall, lean, craggily handsome, with a mane of snow-white hair, ran his court with a gentle voice but a firm, unbending dignity. Son of a Jackson policeman, he was a Mississippian, and the customs and traditions of his birthplace were bred deeply in him. Admittedly he was a segregationist, but in his public acts and statements he had never demonstrated the slightest degree of racial bias or prejudice. Nondrinker, nonsmoker, noncusser, a quiet scholar of the law, no outside pressure could sway him except the dictates of a stern Calvinistic conscience. In his courtroom he recognized only one authority, and that was the law.

The atmosphere in the courthouse wasn't free and easy like it usually was, but solemn and somehow strained. They had set up a table outside the courtroom door, and every man who came to watch had to sign his name, and then a deputy sheriff felt him all over to see if he was toting a pistol. That was all right for the Negroes—no telling what they might do—but what white man was going to try to shoot "Delay" Beckwith?

In the courtroom itself things were even more unusual. The Negro spectators were being allowed to sit anywhere they wanted, instead of clustering all together in the back. If a man wanted to see and hear what was going on, he might have to sit down by a Negro. Or a Negro might come in and sit down by him. Worst of all was out in the halls during recess. A man might walk into a toilet with a big sign on it saying WHITE MEN ONLY, and a Negro could walk right in behind him, and the deputies standing around wouldn't do a thing about it. It was the judge's orders, they said, for the courthouse was a public place.

The young prosecutor was acting strangely too. William Waller, 37 years old, beginning his second term as district attorney, was a slow, soft-talking, brown-haired, full-faced man. Son of a Delta planter, graduate in law at Ole Miss, as a seventh-generation Mississippian he well knew the implications of this case. Ahead of him lay the prospect of one day sitting there on the bench as circuit judge—and the judge's bench could be a springboard to the State House, or a seat in the United States Senate. Trying this case, he must have known, could not help him in Mississippi politics, nor in the private law he practiced on the side. But murder was murder, and he had taken his oath.

When Waller was questioning the veniremen, trying to get a jury, he'd come right out and ask, "Do you believe it's a crime to kill a nigger in Mississippi?" And if the man hesitated over this question, he excused him from jury duty. For four days it went on like this before they finally got a jury.

"Call Myrlie Evers." There was a gentle stirring in the courtroom as the wife of the dead man took the stand. Calm, composed, quiet in dress and manner, she told what happened on the night her husband was killed. It was a little after midnight on the morning of June 12, 1963. She and the children had waited up for him. She heard the car come down Guynes Street and turn into the driveway. She heard the car door close. Then there came the crash of the rifle, and the children fell to the floor, as they had been taught. She ran out. Her husband, a red wound in his back, the front of his chest torn away, lay face down in the driveway. He was trying to crawl toward the door, trailing behind him a smear of blood. The children knelt beside him, crying, "Get up, Daddy." She began to scream, and that is all she could remember.

Hardy Lott of Greenwood, florid, heavyset, his thin hair rumpled, cross-examined for the defense. A White Citizens Council stalwart, he asked Mrs. Evers if it was not true that at the time of his death her husband had before the courts a suit to integrate the schools—on behalf of their son, Darrell Kenyatta Evers. He bore down on the "Kenyatta," the name of the Mau Mau chief. Mrs. Evers said, "Yes." That was all.

Leaning back languidly in his chair, his dark eyes roaming the courtroom, Byron De La Beckwith paid little attention to the story Mrs. Evers was telling on the stand. If he had the slightest fear that here was the beginning of a chain of evidence that might destroy him, he gave no sign of it. From the moment he sat down at the table with his defense counsel, his personality—jaunty, confident, sometimes even arrogant—dominated the room. Trim and erect at 43, his black hair slicked back over the faint suggestion of a bald spot, he had the air of a man come to receive the homage, not the judgment, of his peers. He would carefully adjust his red necktie, carefully lift his trouser leg to reveal his crimson socks, carefully thrust out the proper length of shirt sleeve so that his French cuffs would be revealed. Then one slim hand on the table, the other resting on the arm of his chair like a man posing for his portrait, he would sweep his eyes over the scattered spectators beyond the rail, nodding and smiling a thin, quick smile as he spotted a familiar face.

His was a history that Faulkner might have written—the story of a Sartoris whose views on race had made him a hero of the Snopeses. The names of his ancestors were honored in the Delta. His grandmother, Susan Southworth Yerger, came from an old plantation family that once had owned 10,000 acres of rich Delta land. She had been a friend of Mrs. Jefferson Davis, and he had inherited from her a china teacup and saucer and a gravy boat that Mrs. Davis once had owned. His grandfather, Lemuel P. Yerger, had gone off at 16 to ride with Nathan Bedford Forrest's cavalry, and had come home with a bullet in his leg, to live his life out as a lawyer, proudly wearing the honorary title of Colonel.

Beckwith himself remembered no great plantations, no summer homes on the gulf. He had been born in Colusa, Calif., where his mother, a gentle, pretty, brown-eyed woman, had gone to visit an aunt, feeling that a change of scenery would soothe her nerves. There she had married one Byron De La Beckwith, a convivial man who grew grapes and collected guns. The senior Beckwith died when their son was five, and his mother came back to the Delta town of Greenwood to live with her brother, "Mr. Will" Yerger, in a decaying old house their father, The Colonel, had built in 1900. When Beckwith was 12 his mother died, and he lived on with his Uncle Will, a dreamy-eyed old gentleman who liked to pass out toys and candy to small children in the street.

He grew up there in the old dark house with the gentle, addled old man, a lonely small boy with few companions of his age, leaving only for brief ventures at private schools. Then when he was 20 the war came along. He joined the Marines, fought at Guadalcanal, was wounded at Tarawa. He came home completely changed. Proud, cocky, affecting a black string tie, he would walk down the street jauntily wishing all he met a jovial "top of the morning." He married and got a job selling snuff, cigarettes and chewing tobacco to little crossroad stores. His acquaintances remember now, with some surprise, that he was pleasant and polite, almost deferential, to the Negro storekeepers who bought his wares. His virulent hatred for the Negro as a race, in fact, did not manifest itself until the Supreme Court's school decision in 1954. A Mississippi circuit court judge named Tom P. Brady delivered a vitriolic speech before the Sons of the American Revolution, in which he denounced the court and likened the Negro to a chimpanzee. Beckwith, a member of the Sons, was apparently much impressed by his speech.

"That speech," said a relative later, "changed Delay overnight. He became rabid on the race question. I do not say that lightly."

He warred with the rector of his Episcopal Church for his tolerance in racial matters, harassed his fellow members of the Sons of the American Revolution by demanding they pass resolutions denouncing the Supreme Court. His home life was affected. His wife, tall, dark-haired Mary Louise Beckwith, a former WAVE, was herself a strong segregationist. But Beckwith's moods made a travesty of their marriage. They were divorced, remarried, divorced and married again. At the time of his arrest they were separated, but as the trial began, she again took her place at his side.

As racial tension heightened in Mississippi, Beckwith began distributing his own diatribes in written form, bombarding newspapers with letters to the editor. In one of them, published by the conservative Jackson *News* in 1957, he said, "I believe in segregation like I believe in God. . . . I shall combat the evils of integration and shall bend every effort to rid the U.S.A. of the integrationist whoever and whatever he may be. . . ."

The integrationist leader in Jackson was Medgar Evers. Born and educated in Mississippi. Evers had fought in World War II and in many of his interests and activities he was the counterpart of thousands of white Mississippians. He was a Baptist, a Mason, an Elk, a member of the American Legion and of the Y.M.C.A. He was also field secretary of the N.A.A.C.P. in Mississippi. Evers had tried to persuade his people to register and vote. He had led them on street demonstrations and sit-ins in public places. Worst of all, he had brought suit to integrate the Jackson schools.

All through the balmy, flower-scented spring of 1963 tension had been building up between Jackson's 100,000 whites and 50,000 Negroes. Then on May 28 violence flared. At a ten-cent store four Negro students and a white professor from Tougaloo College had staged a sit-in at a lunch counter. A mob of whites attacked the five. Two were beaten, one severely. That night 2,000 people jammed into a church to hear Evers call upon the whole Negro community to take to the streets in protest. When he shouted, "Who's ready to march?" the entire audience rose.

The city struck back hard. Within the next few days over 500 demonstrators, many of them children, were thrown into paddy wagons and garbage trucks and hauled away to a temporary stockade.

"Hell," said a courthouse official, "our police have to be hard. If they showed any signs of weakness, thousands of white men would take to the streets, shooting every Negro they saw. The fact of the matter is, there are a lot of young, hot-headed Negroes here who are ready to die for what they believe in. And we've got a lot of white men who are ready to kill them."

White hatred focused on Evers. A fire bomb made of a beer bottle filled with gasoline exploded in the carport of his home. And though his telephone was unlisted, somehow the calls got through. Sometimes the hard voice threatened his life. And he answered, "Man, I don't want to kill you. Why should you want to kill me?"

But on June 12 someone did. The state claimed it was Beckwith.

Slowly, methodically, Bill Waller began to build up his case. Detective Sgt. O. M. Luke, heavyset, bald to the ears, with a black streak of hair in the middle of his skull, told of finding the ambush spot 200 feet away in a tangle of honeysuckle vines beneath a clump of sweet-gum trees on Missouri Street across from Medgar Evers's house. He described how the following morning he had found a .30/06 Enfield rifle, with a telescopic sight on it, hidden carefully in a tangle of vines, 50 feet away from the trampled spot where the killer had hidden.

I. Thorne McIntyre III, 26 years old, a Delta farmer, took the stand. Young, handsome, well-dressed, he wore dark glasses of a greenish tint, and the tension in him was palpable in the room. He told of trading an Enfield .30/06 rifle in 1960 to a man he knew well. He examined the murder gun.

"How does this compare with the gun you owned?" Bill Waller asked. "The type of weapon is identical," McIntyre replied.

"Who did you trade guns with?"

"A man from Greenwood named Delay Beckwith," McIntyre said slowly, his head turning briefly toward the table where Beckwith sat.

In the hall at recess a man said angrily, "I'd hate to sleep in McIntyre's bed tonight. I know those Delta folks. They won't even gin cotton for him this fall."

Waller tied the gun closer to Beckwith when FBI agents told of tracing the telescopic sight—a six-power Goldenhawk—from a Chicago supplier to a Mississippi gun dealer—and the dealer testified that a month before the killing he had traded this scope to Byron De La Beckwith.

Only one small chink appeared in the wall of evidence Waller was building. Agent Richard Poppleton could not swear under oath that the bullet which had killed Medgar Evers had come from the rifle that was found at the ambush scene. The bullet was too badly battered.

But he testified that it could have been fired from only one type of rifle in the world—a .30/06 American-made Enfield. "Didn't we manufacture about a million of these rifles back in 1917?" asked Hardy Lott, on cross-examination. "And haven't they been sold and traded all over the country ever since?" To both questions Poppleton answered, "Yes."

On this first faint note of "reasonable doubt" the first week of the trial ended.

Beckwith, still jaunty, strode between two bailiffs back to his fourth-floor cell. There on Sunday he worked on his memoirs, counted the checks and cash coming into his defense fund—nearly $16,000 by now—and pounded out on a typewriter long essays propounding his fiercely segregationist philosophy. The jurors filed out to their bullpen off the courtroom to loll on the prison-gray blanketed beds, read riddled newspapers from which all reference to the trial had been cut, and to watch TV while a bailiff sat poised to snap it off if a newscast of the trial came on. The three bridge players on the panel, unable to find a fourth, resignedly played Rook.

In her small, neat house on Guynes Street Mrs. Medgar Evers, tall, slender, soft-voiced, talked at length about her husband and his work. "I like to talk about him," she said. "It helps me. I want people to know what kind of man he was. He wasn't in this for money, for power, for prestige. He was in it to do what he could for his people, for their freedom and liberty and their happiness—and by so doing make this country itself stronger and happier and more free.

"For you see, he not only loved his race. He loved his country too."

On Monday morning at 8:30 the trial resumed. Capt. Ralph Hargrove, round-faced, high-voiced, turning slightly gray, limped to the witness stand and identified himself as head of the Jackson police department's Identification Office. On the morning after the killing, he said, he had dusted with gray powder the weapon found at the ambush site. There were smudges and smears on the rifle and stock but no identifiable prints. But on the painted black metal of the telescope sight a clear fingerprint had jumped up—a fresh print which by his estimate was no more than 12 hours old. He then photographed it and "lifted" it. Ten days afterward he had fingerprinted Byron De La Beckwith, and in 14 points of comparison the print from the murder weapon matched the print of Delay Beckwith's right index finger.

So far, so good. The rifle had been traced to Beckwith. The telescopic sight had been traced to him. The fingerprint on the scope had been identified as his. Now to put him as near as possible in time and place to the scene of the murder.

Here Waller began venturing out onto shaky ground—building his case on the fragile memory of human beings, of what they saw and heard at times that might be significant. Evers had been killed just after midnight Wednesday morning. Two white taxi drivers told the jury that a man had come to them on the previous Sunday afternoon as they sat talking in front of the Jackson bus station. He had asked if they knew where "Nigra Medgar Evers, the N.A.A.C.P. leader, lived." They told him they didn't. "I've got to find him in a couple of days," they swore the man had said. Later, in a police lineup, they had picked out Delay Beckwith as this man.

(Two days later a cabdriver said, "Them two fellers are through in this town. They tell me one of them already has quit driving. The other one is scared to death. The dispatcher gets calls from the bootleg joints across the river, asking for him by name to come make a pickup. He won't go. Serves them drivers right.")

Now to bring Beckwith closer to the murder spot. Pictures of the automobile he drove in his new job as a fertilizer salesman—a white Valiant with a trailer hitch and a long aerial for a two-way radio—were put in evidence. Robert Pittman, 17, the son of a grocer who lives on Missouri Street near Medgar Evers's home, remembered the car. He testified that on the Saturday night before the killing he had seen this car parked at the back of Joe's Drive-In, next to his father's grocery store. A man wearing dark glasses and white shoes was walking about near the tangle of vines from which the shot was fired. Then about 9 or 10 o'clock on the night of the murder, while Robert and a friend were playing outside his father's store, a white Valiant with a long aerial that made it look like a police car had driven slowly, four or five times, up and down Missouri Street across a vacant lot from Guynes Street and Medgar Evers's house.

"Call Jean O'Brien." Martha Jean O'Brien, 17, a carhop at Joe's Drive-In, whose parking area backed up to the tangled undergrowth on Missouri Street from which the shot was fired, came into court. Pretty, with slanting Oriental eyes and a little pussycat grin, she testified that on the night of the killing a white Valiant car had been parked in the shadows at the back of the lot. A man had gotten out of it and gone into the rest room. She was sure about the car. She couldn't identify the man.

Barbara Ann Holder, a chubby blonde wearing a bright pink dress, took the stand. She had gone by Joe's that night to see her friend, Jean O'Brien. She had seen the car parked in the shadows. She saw it first around 9:30. It was still there when she left at 11:45. The reason she had noticed it was she thought it was a police patrole car, because of the long aerial. She had seen a man get out of it and go in the rest room. In her opinion. . . .

The roaring objection of Hardy Lott stopped her short. The jury was dismissed while the attorneys argued. "Let's hear what she was going to say," the judge ordered. "In my opinion," she said, "according to the height and description and all, the man who went in the rest room was Beckwith. He walked straight, and people around here don't walk straight." (Beckwith, whose carriage is that of an old Marine, stared at her, his fingers drumming on the tabletop.) In the visitors' gallery back of the press seats there was an angry mutter. "Damn if I thought I'd ever hear a white woman in Mississippi testify against a white man in a case like this."

"Objection sustained," the judge ruled. "The jury cannot hear this testimony. It is an opinion."

Shortly after this the state rested. Hardy Lott moved for a dismissal. Judge Hendrick denied the motion.

The defense began perfunctorily. Employees of Joe's Drive-In said they had seen no car parked in the lot. One who had seen it swore it was not a Valiant but a Dodge.

Something stronger obviously was needed, and Beckwith's fellow citizens of Greenwood provided it. A neon-sign manufacturer, who was also an auxiliary policeman, swore that he saw Beckwith at a Billups filling station in Greenwood at 11:45 on the night that Evers was killed at 12:30 A.M. — in Jackson, 90 miles away. Two Greenwood car patrolmen, their uniform jackets unbuttoned, swore that they saw him at a Shell filling station at 1:05 on that same morning. Waller brought out on cross-examination that neither of the three could remember what other Greenwood residents they had seen that night at any hour. Then, as if fearful their alibi witnesses might not be believed, the defense attorneys took the gamble nobody expected them to take. They called Beckwith to the stand.

He came like an actor striding to center stage, sat down, adjusted his cuffs and beamed upon the jury.

"Yes *suh*. No *suh*," he answered Hardy Lott's preliminary questions, like a boot Marine snapping answers to a drill sergeant. He told of "getting the business" (his wound) at Tarawa. He spoke of his avid interest in guns. "I like guns. I like a man who likes a gun. I am a trader and collector of guns. I always carry guns with me in my car."

Then the crucial questions, with question and answer coming so fast they were almost one sentence: Did you shoot Medgar Evers No suh Were you in Jackson the night Medgar Evers was shot No suh Did you talk to those two taxi drivers who testified they saw you at the bus station No *suh* I don't even know where that bus station is in Jackson.

Once the dangerous questions were past, Beckwith relaxed. He examined the gun with the air of an expert, slammed the bolt back, sighted over the head of the jury and pulled the trigger. He would not say with certainty it was the gun he had owned. Very similar though. And what had happened to his gun? Oh, he had been target shooting on Sunday afternoon, and he had cleaned the gun and put it in the bathroom closet at his home. Monday night when he went to look for it, it had disappeared. "My house is an old house, gentlemen, a dime-store key would unlock its doors."

Slowly, heavily, Bill Waller rose to cross-examine. The courtroom tensed, for here, under heavy pressure, an unstable man might crack. Waller showed him the old letter the Jackson *News* had printed: "I believe in segregation like I believe in God. . . . I shall . . . bend every effort to rid the U.S.A. of the integrationists." Do you still feel that way? "Of course I still feel that way suh."

Waller read from another Beckwith letter written in January, 1963, to the National Rifle Association. "Gentlemen, For the next 15 years we here in Mississippi are going to have to do a lot of shooting to protect our wives, children and ourselves from bad niggers. . . ."

A third letter, written since the Evers killing, to the editor of *Outdoor Life:* "Sir, I have just finished an article on garfish hunting at night, which is sure to be of interest to the reader, along with several ideas I have on shooting at night in the summertime for varmints. . . ."

Waller: "Would you say an integration leader is a varmint?"

Beckwith: "Ohhh, that's a human bein'. I'm talking about crows, and things like that."

Waller changed the subject, questioning Beckwith on a book he was said to be writing in his cell. The title of the book, he drew from Beckwith, was *My Ass, Your Goat and the Republic.* Would Beckwith explain that title?

For the first time Beckwith seemed on the verge of losing control. His face grew taut, and officers in the courtroom near him saw a strange glitter come into his eyes. His voice lifted, and the words poured out. "It is thus explained: by the left-wing forces riding my donkey. They intend to aggravate the public and continue on their method of destroying states' rights, constitutional government and racial integrity." The words were innocuous enough, but to court observers the manner was that of a man on the verge of hysteria.

Sensing danger, Stanny Sanders, Beckwith's lawyer, jumped between his client and Waller. "If the court please, we are not here to discuss philosophy."

The judge overruled, but the interchange gave Beckwith time to regain control. Throughout the remainder of his testimony he was calm, even cocky.

All that remained were the closing arguments. John Fox III, Waller's crewcut assistant—looking more like a law student than a prosecutor—opened for the state. "Gentlemen," he said, "you have seen this man's demeanor in this courtroom. Has he in any act or utterance behaved like an innocent man? He sat in that witness chair as if he were on a throne of glory—and he reveled in it. He proudly demonstrated to you that he is a crack shot. He wanted the world to know that. Is it possible that he also wanted all the world to know that he killed Medgar Evers—but he didn't want it spelled out so plain you'd have to find him guilty? Gentlemen of the jury," Fox concluded, "Byron De La Beckwith is a fanatic pure and simple. He had not only the capacity and the capability and the power to kill, he had the deep compelling motives. And as calmly as he would kill a turtle on a log, as coolly as he would shoot a crow out of a tree, he did execute Medgar Evers, a human being—shot him like a varmint, in the driveway of his home, in the nighttime, in the summertime, in 1963. . . ."

Six of the 12 jurors apparently agreed with John Fox. After deliberating for nearly 11 hours, the jury was still hopelessly deadlocked, and a mistrial was declared. Sometime this spring or summer Byron De La Beckwith will be tried again for the murder of Medgar Evers.

In the light of Mississippi's history, and of the fears and hatreds which still haunt that troubled land, the fact that six white men held out for conviction was in itself a victory for the law.

Chapter VIII

Local
Government

The American attitude toward local government was expressed by the Advisory Committee on Local Government when it reported to the Commission on Intergovernmental Relations that:

> Local governments are to total government what basic tissues are to the human body. Without them, government would have no vitality.[1]

The same belief was echoed by the parent Commission in its final report which states that it is only at "the lowest level of government" that "every citizen has the opportunity to participate actively and directly."[2]

Faith in local government is an outgrowth of the frontier concept of democracy. The frontier, or Jacksonian, concept of democracy contained many values that still have vitality. The belief that small, local government is better than distant, big government still possesses propaganda value. Direct election of nearly all decision makers is preferred to any form of indirect selection on the assumption that officeholders will be more responsible and honest if directly elected. Major magazines still recall the glories of pre-

---

[1]*Local Government,* a report of the Advisory Committee on Local Government to the Commission on Intergovernmental Relations (Washington, D.C.: United States Government Printing Office, 1955), p. 9.

[2]The Commission on Intergovernmental Relations, *A Report to the President* (Washington, D.C.: United States Government Printing Office, 1955), p. 47.

industrial America and most Americans probably believe that rural government is more effective, efficient, and honest than its urban counterpart.

Roscoe C. Martin challenges these stereotypes of local government in "The Physiology of Little Government." He contends that even in the rural areas where the grass roots concepts should be most viable they are invalid. The government closest to the people is not necessarily the best government: it may be the most biased, inefficient, and corrupt government.

There is a wide variety of local governments in the United States, including 35,000 school districts and 18,000 special purposes districts, but the most important local governments are the 3043 counties and the 18,000 municipalities.[3] The cities and counties, unlike the special districts or the school districts, are general governments with jurisdiction over many aspects of the lives of the area's residents.

Counties exist in all states except Alaska, Connecticut, and Rhode Island. (In Louisiana the term *parish* is used.) The counties are the basic administrative subdivisions of the state; they maintain the legal and judicial systems, assume responsibility for the educational system, build and maintain the roads, etc.

The governmental structure of a typical rural county as described by Emmett G. Asseff in "The Government of Harrison County, Texas" is characterized by the long ballot. The voters normally choose a multimember governing county board, sheriff, coroner, county attorney, treasurer, tax collector, surveyor, recorder, clerk of court, judges, and a variety of special boards and commissions. Each of these officers is a county officer but many of them (i.e., the sheriff, coroner, and judge) are also representatives of the state.

Because the county is the major administrative subdivision of the state and because the state is increasing its functions, Bernard F. Hillenbrand argues that "County Government Is Reborn." While the rural county is declining in importance as an independent political unit, it will probably continue to grow in importance as an administrative subdivision of the state.

In some suburban areas the county is growing in political importance as suburban residents call upon it to perform functions which the core city can not, or will not, provide. An excellent example of this is Los Angeles County, which is discussed on page 495.

While counties, with the exception of a few suburban counties, are declining in importance as independent political units, cities are becoming more important. Roughly two thirds of the population is urban and an even greater portion of the population is affected by the decisions of the city, being dependent on it for jobs and services. As noted in the next chapter, the cities are losing population to the surrounding suburbs; however, the government of the core city is very important for the total community.

---

[3]Bureau of the Census, Department of Commerce, *Census of Governments: 1962* (Washington, D.C.: United States Government Printing Office), I, 1.

The major forms of city government are the strong mayor-council, weak mayor-council, commission, and council-manager forms. The council-manager form is a relative newcomer and is an attempt to provide a "businesslike" government by choosing a professional administrator to implement the policy decisions of the city council; the manager is a technician rather than a policy-maker. However, many scholars argue that it is not possible for a successful manager to completely avoid political involvement. In a pair of articles entitled "Is the Manager a Political Leader?" Gladys M. Kammerer argues that the manager must be a policy leader, whereas H.G. Pope contends that the manager is not a policy leader unless an extremely broad definition of politics is employed. Charles R. Adrian concludes from "A Study of Three Communities" that the manager and his administration have an important policy leadership role. The result is a different pattern of government than the one anticipated in the original theory of the council-manager plan.

The council-manager form of city government is most prevalent in cities of 5000 to 250,000. Most major cities have the strong major form, which is patterned on the American presidency. The basic assumptions underlying this form are that large cities require strong executive leadership and that city government is definitely political in nature. The strong mayor has full administrative responsibility and in the pure form is the only elective administrator. The mayor normally possesses the veto power over the decisions of the council, which is the legislative branch.

Chicago is one of the few large cities with highly decentralized formal power. However, Martin Meyerson and Edward C. Banfield have analyzed "The Weak Mayor System in Chicago" and discovered that the informal power is highly centralized. The relationship between formal governmental structure and the actual political power structure is often overlooked in discussion of the relative merits of the strong mayor and weak mayor systems.

Many reformers believe that politics and administration should be separate. Conversely, Seymour Freedgood in his essay "New Strength in City Hall" expresses a belief that the strong mayor must blend politics and administration in order to be effective. As a result he will arouse the advocates of "good government" who desire to shield city government from politics.

THE PHYSIOLOGY OF LITTLE GOVERNMENT

Roscoe C. Martin

Roscoe C. Martin is professor of political science, Syracuse University. He is the author of several volumes, including *The Cities and the Federal System* (1965).

Grass-roots government is held to be direct, personal, intimate, informal, face-to-face; the entire atmosphere makes for a spirit of democracy; the contacts of the administrator are with the client or customer direct; and there is a minimum of paperwork and of record-keeping, for democracy is not a thing to be written down but only to be experienced. The home rule movement for cities and counties gives tangible evidence of the widespread conviction that local governments can attend to their own affairs more successfully and with greater satisfaction than they can be attended to from the state capitol. By contrast, big government is held to represent the opposite of almost everything that little government stands for; it is indirect, impersonal, anonymous, distant, formal; the contacts between administrator and client-customer are long distance and customarily are handled by mail, often by exchange of form communications; big democracy emphasizes procedures and is a stickler for observance of regulations; there administration is in essence paperwork, with the administrator often coming to regard the record as the end product of a given transaction and the prime object of his concern. Thus do the easy, comfortable ways of government at the grass roots give way to the worship of forms under the watchful guidance of a jealous bureaucracy. The contest is a severe one, seeing that the American people must live the rest of their days with big government as well as little, but it is not more severe than the grass-roots rationale warrants.

The Physiology of Little Government

Here, then, is a complex structure for dealing with the public problems of rural America, and here are the interests which grass-roots government is expected to serve. It is in order now to examine the workings of rural government, not for its day-to-day operations but for its characteristic features. The purpose here is to describe, not to appraise. Criticism, even diagnosis, is forsworn for the present except as it may be inferred from a descriptive account.

Among the several characteristic features of little government is

From *Grass Roots* by Roscoe C. Martin, pp. 32-41, copyright 1957 by the University of Alabama Press. Reprinted by permission of the University of Alabama Press.

its part-time character. Of all the employees of municipalities of 5,000 inhabitants and less, only 37 per cent are full-time. This is suggestive of the nature of rural government, though it is necessary to add quickly that there are many thousands of local units which have no full-time employees at all. From the point of view of the employee, there are uncounted thousands of farmers, lawyers, mechanics, doctors, merchants, and housewives who devote one or two hours a day or one or two days a week (in some cases, five to ten days a year) to public employment. As an example, there is the Mayor of the small municipality (population 2,000) whose means of livelihood is his building materials business. Sought out at his shop (he rarely went to the one-room city hall), he chatted familiarly about municipal affairs. Presently the talk veered around to the Mayor's future plans, in particular reference to current street talk about a movement for the council-manager plan. "I won't run again," the Mayor said with finality, "but if they want a city manager, I'll take the job, and I won't charge 'em any $3,000, either." There are the three elected officials called listers (assessors) of the Vermont town, who work for only a few days each year except in the fourth year when real estate is re-assessed, when for a while they are quite busy. Secretaries, recorders, clerks, tax assessors, tax collectors, attorneys, engineers, treasurers, directors of recreation—here is an abbreviated list of the officers and employees who in rural government normally serve only part-time, when, indeed, they are found at all.

There is, of course, a way to make full-time work from these numerous part-time jobs, and that is by combining several kinds of duties under one office. The New England town clerk performs a great variety of chores, enough in a sizable town to warrant full-time employment. The clerk of a certain small southern municipality of record (population 1,800) serves as city clerk, treasurer, treasurer and purchasing agent for the water works board, tax collector, secretary to the city council, secretary to the mayor, clerk of the recorder's (mayor's) court, jailer, member of the volunteer fire department, member of the school board, member of the recreation board, city weigher, and notary public. On the side, by way of piecing out a living, he sells insurance and real estate, hires out as a public accountant, and buys and sells cotton. To complete his schedule, he teaches a Sunday School class and plays shortstop on the Lions' Club softball team. One is reminded of Pooh-Bah of *The Mikado*, who served as First Lord of the Treasury, Lord Chief Justice, Commander-in-Chief, Lord High Admiral, Master of the Buckhounds, Groom of the Back Stairs, Archbishop of Titipu, and Lord Mayor, both acting and elect. Here is a way to stop under-employment in its tracks!

A second feature of rural government is that it is almost wholly amateur, as indeed it must be in view of the foregoing. It is amateur in two senses. First, there are few of the tools of professional management now widely in use among the larger units; there is no regularized merit system, no budget system, no competitive purchasing, no double-entry accounting. To most rural administrators, these concepts remain in the realm of the far-away and the theoretical, for their equipment and procedures are rudimentary in the extreme. A small-town Mayor, hearing from a lecturer that the mayor's secretary should control the boss' telephone and appointment calendar, leaned over and whispered to the man in the next chair, "That's very interesting, but what do you do if you don't have a secretary?"

Little government is amateur in the further sense that its personnel is not professional. There is the clerk of a circuit court who by common consent knows nothing whatever about the duties of her office, but who manages to hold on because the local lawyers take turns at helping her with her work. There is the rural registrar who denied a Negro the right to vote because he could not "interrupt" the Constitution. In the same section, several registrars were found denying the right to vote to prospective voters (both Negro and white) because they could not interpret the Constitution, notwithstanding there was no such legal requirement. There is the case of the rural county which hired a retired railway express employee and gave him the title of "purchasing agent." After eight months in office, it was learned that the new person had participated in only two competitive purchase procedures. His salary as a part-time clerical person was $25 per month.

It is hardly necessary to emphasize that the part-time amateur government which is beginning to emerge is also quite casual in nature. A recent visitor to a rural county courthouse threaded his way up the steps through a group of six or eight men who were basking in the sunshine. His business carried him to the office of the tax collector, who, the sole clerk and attendant informed him, was out front. She fared forth to return presently with one of the men who had been sitting on the steps. When the visitor had finished his business with the tax collector, he inquired as to the county clerk. "Across the hall," said the official, nodding, "but he ain't there; he's out front." Then he stepped to the door of his office, aimed in the general direction of the front entrance, and called, "Hey, Ed, he wants you!" whereupon a second member of the group taking the sun pulled himself up and sauntered in. In another rural county, original county records were being copied at home by a housewife working part-time; when her employer's attention was called to the risk to his records through loss or damage, he required the typist to do her work in the office. In one of the smaller towns of Vermont, a representative of five successive generations of one family has served as town clerk, and the town's records have been kept in the clerk's family home for a century. A recent survey of town government in that state brought to light instances of official records kept on the backs of envelopes and on bits of scratch paper. Louis Brownlow tells a story of a local school board meeting held in Charlottesville, Virginia, in the early years of the last century. The board met on a street corner and transacted its business without fanfare, and also without reading of minutes, agenda, or other *Robert's Rules* items. The three members present were Thomas Jefferson, James Madison, and James Monroe.

Local government in rural America is (or may be) highly personal. A sheriff in a rural county some years ago learned that two communist votes had been cast in a local election. "I guess I broke every law there is trying to find out who cast those ballots," he confided. A visitor to a small municipality left his topcoat in the office of the city clerk while the two went out to lunch. Returning, he discovered that his coat had been taken. The city clerk was chagrined, but not defeated. "I'll just have the council appropriate money for a new coat," he said. In New England, the town overseer of the poor is expected to keep the poor of his town from leaving and descending upon other towns; he is also charged with the responsibility of protecting his town against the poor seeking entrance from the outside. In Kansas, a farmer complained that Johnson grass was spreading to his field from the neighboring county road right-of-way, and ultimately was successful in persuading the county commissioners to declare that grass a noxious weed, thus bringing it within the scope of the public weed eradication program. Here, by the way, is an excellent illustration of the way by which a function long considered private comes to be taken over by government. Here was no grasping bureaucracy seeking new worlds to conquer, but only a farmer seeking to keep his field free of Johnson grass.

Rural local government also has its private (or proprietary) aspects. A small-county judge complained that "the new law requiring a medical examination before a marriage license can be issued has cut my business $25 a month." Rural county officials habitually refer to the issuance of a license as a "sale." In one county, the clerk each month computes what is owed to the various state agencies for the licenses issued during the month and the judge remits checks for these amounts, transferring what is left to his personal account. (The state examiners regularly find his accounts in good order.) A rural legislator, in explanation of a proposed local bill, said, "Last session I raised my probate judge to $3,600 and my commissioners to $1,500, but their morale hasn't been too good so I'm giving them another little raise now."

There are occasions when grass-roots government takes on the character of an eleemosynary enterprise. A clerk is kept on because, though not satisfactory, she "needs the job." Another is retained because "he's crippled and can't do anything else." Many local office-holders run their own private systems of relief. One rural county judge, explaining his periodic disappearances into the vault room with constituents, observed that people requested him to step into the vault when they wanted to ask for help. "It costs me a couple of dollars every time I go into the vault," he said. A rural state legislature some years ago refused to switch to typewriters for enrolling bills because some of the copyists who wrote well enough by hand were not able to type. A certain grass-roots county judge will not allow a hard-pressed constituent to become delinquent for want of payment of a license fee. As a consequence, he has advanced some $4,000 in petty personal loans over the course of the last several years.

In many respects rural government is anachronistic, being closely wedded (as is all government, indeed) to the past. The New England towns, the oldest of local governments in America, generally have eliminated the culler of hoop poles, staves, and headings, in recognition of the passing of the barrel; and the rural schools have abolished the post of wood inspector, which was necessary in other days to ensure that each patron contributed his share to the winter's wood supply. In Vermont, however, each town still must appoint three fence viewers, who are charged to see that fences are kept in order and in the proper location. A tree warden likewise must be appointed to keep the public shade trees in good condition. The organization of grass-roots government is almost wholly outmoded, but that is a subject not appropriate for examination here.

Rural local government, for all its seeming simplicity, can become quite complicated. The average citizen lives within and has at least some dealings with not less than four units of government: the nation, the state, the county, and the municipality. He frequently finds himself resident within three or four units in addition—township, school district, soil conservation district, and so on. The result is that residence within seven or eight overlying units is not uncommon. These units normally were established with little or no thought for the convenience of the citizen, who often is not able to differentiate one government or one program from the other.

Little government, being personal, intimate, and informal, is supposed by some to be free of politics. In simple truth, no concept concerning local government has less merit. The image of politics as an evil art practiced somewhere else by somebody else is, of course, quite unrealistic; for politics is found wherever people debate issues of public import. Grass-roots politics frequently involves little of public policy; on the contrary, it may be largely of a personal character, and it may indeed be cast in terms of personal loyalty rather than in those usually held appropriate to the public arena. For all that the citizen, and more particularly the minor office-holder or employee, will discover quickly is in what direction the imperatives lie, and he will experience prompt and sure retribution if he does not hew to the established line. A rural county commissioner elected on a "reform" platform found the ground cut from under him in one deft move when the county board abolished the district system and brought the construction and maintenance of county roads under the direct supervision of the board. Here was as effective and as ruthless a political move as ever was engineered by a big city boss.

Last among the features of rural government to be examined here is the basic nature of the process of governance at the grass roots. The student of public affairs distinguishes broadly between government, politics, and administration; but in little government these distinctions are not valid, or if valid in principle, are not overly useful in practice. The smaller the unit or area is, the closer the government is to the grass roots, the less meaningful is the distinction between politics, government, and administration; the larger the unit or area, the sharper the distinction. Grass-roots government is therefore pre-eminently the domain of the generalist, big government that of the specialist. Big government needs the generalist, of course, and it is, indeed, one of the prime problems of public administration to develop managers with a general sense of government and administration. Little government by contrast has generalists in plenty; for there the lines separating politics from government and both from administration blur and grow dim, with the result that nothing more than a general impression of government remains. The differentiations in process common in big government are hardly known at the grass roots.

Rural local government, then, is different; it is so decidedly different from the "local government" of the textbooks as to be hardly recognizable from the generalizations found there. There is nothing whatever, beyond a legal fiction, in common between, say, Cleveland, Ohio, and Auburn, West Virginia. The action of the Mayor of a Kentucky village in adjourning a council meeting (with apologies to the visitor present) at 4:00 o'clock so that the council members could get home to do their milking before dark would prove utterly incomprehensible to the mayor and council members of any of the larger cities. Yet this incident did occur, and many others like it occur every day in the little governments of America. This is government at the grass roots. It is not important in terms of functions performed, personnel employed, or money spent, but it does stand as the guardian of the American tradition of rural democracy.

THE GOVERNMENT OF HARRISON COUNTY, TEXAS

EMMETT G. ASSEFF

Emmett G. Asseff is a former director of the Louisiana Legislative Research Council.

The Commissioners' Court

The local governing body in Harrison County, as in the other 253 counties, is the commissioners' court. In Harrison, as in the other counties, there are four commissioner precincts, and the voters within each elect a commissioner for a term of two years. The court is vested with discretion to change the precincts, but such changes must be "fair and reasonable." If there is excessive disparity in area, population, and property valuation, the district court will nullify the order. The four commissioners together with the county judge, who is elected at large for a term of two years, constitute the court. The county judge presides but votes only in case of a tie. The county clerk serves as secretary. A vacancy in the office of county judge is filled by the court whereas any other vacancy on the court is filled by the judge. Some of its functions, such as providing for the construction and maintenance of a courthouse and jail, are mandatory whereas others, as providing for a county hospital and a county library, are optional. The commissioners' court does not exercise "general police power" but only such functions as are specifically vested in it by the constitution and laws of the state. One of its main functions is the supervision and control of county roads and bridges. In some counties this function is administered by the county road department though in most counties the work is carried on by precincts, each commissioner being in charge of the roads within his district. The court serves as a board of equalization for county and state taxes and when acting in such a capacity it is authorized to increase or decrease assessments. Its decisions in this respect are final except in case of fraud. The court also serves as the county board of election commissioners and in this capacity performs various duties in respect to elections. If a county library exists, the court serves as its governing body and appoints a librarian from a list certified by the State Library Examining Board. The court approves the appointment of various personnel, among them being road and bridge personnel, deputy clerks, a health officer, and personnel in the county agent's office. In some instances the court fills vacancies in county offices. As a result of a con-

From "The Government of Harrison County, Texas" by Emmett G. Asseff, from *County Government Across the Nation* edited by Paul W. Wager (Durham: The University of North Carolina Press, 1954), condensed and adapted from pp. 562-567. Reprinted by permission of the publisher.

stitutional amendment adopted in 1891, the district court exercises general supervisory control over the commissioners' court and may nullify acts of the court which are an abuse of discretion. The court meets in regular session the second Monday in each month and in special session when called by the county judge or by three of the commissioners. Meetings usually last one day. If the court so desires, it may meet only once in each quarter. A quorum for ordinary business is three commissioners or two commissioners and the county judge. The entire court must be present when the tax levy is adopted. The tax rate is usually set in August or September and the budget adopted in December. The fiscal year is the calendar year. The budget is prepared by the county judge and approved by the court. A public hearing must be held before the budget is adopted. There are no committees. Members of the court are paid $250 per month.

Other Elective Officers

Harrison County has a county judge, a county clerk, a district clerk, a tax assessor-collector, a sheriff, a treasurer, a surveyor, and a county attorney, all elected by the qualified voters of the county for terms of two years. The county superintendent of education and the various school boards are discussed under education. Justices of the peace and constables are elected by precincts for terms of two years. The office of coroner has been abolished and the duties of that office are performed by justices of the peace.

One of the most important county officials is the *county judge*. He acts in an administrative as well as a judicial capacity and like the county clerk's office his office serves as the "dumping ground" for a variety of functions. He is elected at large for a term of two years, and if a vacancy exists in his office, it is filled by the commissioners' court. On the other hand he fills vacancies on the court. As judge of the county court, he exercises the judicial functions vested in that court in respect to civil and criminal matters. He presides over the commissioners' court but votes only in case of a tie. He prepares a county budget for submission to the court and works in conjunction with the court in performing various county functions. He may call the court into special session. He performs various duties in respect to elections and fiscal affairs and makes certain minor appointments. In counties with a scholastic population of less than 3,000, he is *ex officio* county superintendent of education. This is true in 85 counties.

There is a *county clerk* who is clerk of the county court, clerk of the commissioners' court, clerk of the board of equalization, clerk of the county board of election commissioners, county recorder, and register of deeds, mortgages, contracts, and other papers. Vital statistics records are kept in his office. He is required to keep the various record books for which he is responsible "properly indexed, arranged and preserved." In counties of less than 8,000 population (there are 78) he is also *clerk of the district court.* In most counties he is also *county auditor.* In Harrison County the county clerk does not act as district clerk or as auditor. Like the office of county judge, this office has served as the "dumping ground" for a variety of functions. As clerk of court he performs the usual judicial functions and maintains the court records. Various other records are filed in his office, for example, delinquent tax lists, a list of those paying their poll taxes, election ballots, and many others. He supervises absentee voting. The clerk together with the county judge and sheriff are responsible for election supplies. He has often been termed the "official county bookkeeper" because of the variety of records maintained in his office.

There is a *district court clerk* who is clerk of the Seventy-first District court when sitting in Harrison County. As clerk of court he performs the usual judicial functions and maintains the court records. There is one deputy who is appointed with the approval of the commissioners' court. A vacancy in this office is filled by the district court judge.

There is a *tax assessor-collector* who is responsible for the annual assessment and collection of county and state taxes. In counties, however, of less than 10,000 inhabitants (there are 91), the sheriff is *ex officio* tax assessor-collector. Cities and towns and independent school districts are authorized to have their own assessing, collecting, and equalization officials though they may use the tax assessor-collector. In Harrison County the city of Marshall and the three independent school districts have their own assessing and equalizing and collecting agencies. The assessor is required to visit each taxpayer and personally view and inspect his taxable property, real and personal. The owner is required to list his property subject to taxation. The assessor assesses real and personal property annually between January 1 and April 30. The commissioners' court determines the percentage of true value at which property shall be assessed for purposes of taxation and as a result the rate varies in the counties from 20 to 100 per cent. Property in Harrison County is reputed to be assessed at 50 per cent of true value. The commissioners' court sits as a board of equalization and has the final word on property valuation for state and county taxation. Railroads are required to list and report their property to the assessors of the counties and incorporated places in which located. It is to be treated as other property. The rolling stock of railroad corporations, however, is to be reported to the assessor of the county in which the principal office is located, and the commissioners' court thereof sits as a board of equalization in respect to such property. The value is then certified to the comptroller of public accounts who apportions the value among the counties in which said corporations are located. The value of the intangible assets of certain corporations (railroad, bridge, motor bus, and truck, etc.) is determined by the State Tax Board (comptroller, secretary of state, and attorney general) and apportioned among the counties affected. The value fixed is not subject to review by local boards of equalization. Homesteads up to $3,000 are exempt from state property taxes. The tax collector collects only state and county *ad valorem* taxes in Harrison County though he may be authorized and does in some counties collect taxes also for municipalities and independent school districts. He also collects poll taxes and automobile license fees. Taxes are payable on October 1 and become delinquent on February 1. Discounts are offered for taxes paid in advance. If sold for taxes, which is rare, the taxpayer has two years in which to redeem his property.

There is a *sheriff* elected in each county who is a peace officer, maintaining law and order and arresting criminals. He and his deputies also serve as officers of the various courts sitting in the county and execute their decrees. There are four permanent deputies in Harrison County and they are appointed by and subject to removal by the sheriff. In counties with a population of less than 10,000 (there are 91), the sheriff is *ex officio tax collector-assessor*. The Texas State Department of Public Safety is divided into two sections—the Texas Rangers and the Highway Patrol. The Highway Patrol enforces traffic laws. The Texas Rangers cooperate with local law enforcement agencies and in solving major crimes, and they also assist in restoring order in areas where riots and other major disturbances occur.

There is a *county treasurer* who is responsible for receiving and disbursing county funds. He submits financial statements to the commissioners' court and performs other duties of a fiscal nature.

There is a *county surveyor* who performs surveys when requested and for which he is paid by fees. Although the office is filled in Harrison County, there are 86 counties at the present time in which the office is vacant.

There is a *county attorney* in Harrison County, and he represents the state and county in criminal cases. He may appoint from one to three assistant prosecuting attorneys with the approval of the commissioners' court. There are two assistant county attorneys in Harrison. The county attorney acts for the county in civil cases only when authorized by the commissioners' court or by statute. In special cases the court may hire a special attorney to represent it. Harrison County does not have a district attorney.

Harrison County is divided into eight justice of the peace precincts. Each elects a justice of the peace except Marshall which elects two. Each of the precincts elects a constable who serves the justice of the peace court. Justices of the peace serve as *coroners* and as such perform inquests and other duties ordinarily required of that official.

Appointive Officers

Appointed officials include a county auditor, a county health officer, county agent personnel, deputy clerks, deputy county attorneys, clerical assistance, road personnel, and various other personnel as needed. Each is discussed under the appropriate heading except the office of auditor which will be explained at this point.

The district judge of the Seventy-first Judicial District appoints a *county auditor* for a term of two years. The office is mandatory in counties with a population of 35,000 or over (there are 39). The office may be established in other counties under certain circumstances. If the office is not established, the county clerk serves as auditor. The auditor is required to examine and audit the books, accounts, and reports of all county officials. He makes monthly as well as a yearly audit of the books. He has no relationship to the state. The state does not audit county books with the exception of the office of the tax assessor-collector. In this instance only state funds are audited. The salary of the auditor is set by the district judge and paid by the commissioners' court.

Education

Although the county serves as the unit for certain educational purposes, the basic unit of school administration in Texas is the school district. This has been so since the days of the Republic. There is a county board of education which is composed of five members, one of whom is elected at large and one from each of the four commissioner precincts, all for terms of two years. The board exercises the authority vested in it in respect to all the districts except independent school districts which are completely within a municipality. Some of the functions which may be exercised by the county board are: (1) classification of schools in respect to the number of grades to be taught; (2) establishing a transportation system for the county; and (3) altering of the boundary lines of school districts under certain conditions.

There is a county superintendent of education who is elected for a term of four years by the qualified voters of the county. In a few counties, however, the superintendent is appointed by the county board of education. In counties with a scholastic population of less than 3,000, the county judge is *ex officio* superintendent of education. This is true in 85 counties. In Harrison County there are three independent school districts (Marshall, Waskom, and Karnack), three rural high school districts, and 17 common school districts. The county superintendent exercises general supervisory powers over the rural high school and common school districts. Each of the three independent school districts has its own superintendent, and each is responsible for the schools within such district. The county superintendent performs a variety of duties, many of them on behalf of the State Department of Education. Among his many duties are the following: (1) to visit the schools and to make recommendations in respect to them; (2) to make various reports to the State Department of Education; (3) to approve teachers selected by the trustees in the school districts under his control; (4) to prepare the school budgets for the districts under his control subject to the approval of the trustees; (5) to approve the school census; (6) to apportion state and county school funds to the districts in conformity with state law; and (7) to hold teacher institutes and perform many other duties of like nature.

Each of the school districts has a board of trustees which is elected by the qualified voters of the district. All the 17 common school districts have boards of three, and they are elected for overlapping terms of three years. The rural high and independent school districts of Waskom and Karnack have boards of seven, and they are elected for overlapping terms of three years. The independent school district of Marshall has a board of seven members, all of whom are appointed by the city commission for overlapping terms of three years. The trustees are responsible for the construction and maintenance of school buildings and the purchase and sale of school property, the hiring and firing of teachers (subject to the approval of the superintendent in all but the independent districts) as well as the selection of other personnel, the approval of school budgets, determining the opening and closing dates of school, and many other matters pertaining to the administration of the schools. . . .

Public Welfare

Public assistance programs are administered by the state and financed from state and federal funds. The State Department of Public Welfare is authorized to determine the administrative unit for administering the public welfare program. The county has been designated as this unit, and each county has at least one worker assigned to it. However, in some of the sparsely settled areas, one worker serves two or more counties. The department is authorized to establish local advisory boards and to determine their size, membership, and qualifications, but such boards have not been established. There are six field workers, three junior stenographers, and one supervisor in Harrison County, all selected through the merit system. For purposes of state supervision and control, the state is divided into regions and the regions into areas. Child Welfare Services have their own supervisory force. The county has not established a county welfare department to administer local funds. The major welfare programs are administered by the State Department through its local office in Marshall. . . .

Public Health

Harrison County is not included in a health unit. The county board of health has been abolished. The organization of a board of health is discretionary with the commissioners' court, and the board does exist in many counties. The members are appointed by agreement among all appropriating units. The number of members on each board varies. All personnel in a health unit must meet the minimum requirements of the merit system.

There is a county health officer who is appointed by the commissioners' court for a term of one year. Funds for public health are appropriated by the commissioners' court from the county general fund. The state makes no direct appropriation to the health program in the county. . . .

Highways

The construction and maintenance of county roads and bridges is under the supervision of the commissioners' court as the policy determining body. It serves in this capacity much as the State Highway Commission does in respect to the State Department. Like the State Department, the county has its engineer, and he serves as the executive officer of the court. He is appointed by the commissioners' court and serves at its pleasure. The court also determines his salary. There are about 50 employees in the county road department, and they are selected by the county engineer with the approval of the court. The county engineer acting under the direction and supervision of the court is responsible for the maintenance and construction of county roads and bridges. This unified control of roads and bridges has been in effect for about 25 years. In most counties, however, roads and bridges are administered on a precinct basis, each commissioner (4) being responsible for his precinct. In 1947 the legislature enacted the Optional Road Law which authorized a county road department, a county engineer, and a county-wide control of roads and bridges for all the counties — much on the order of the Harrison County system. . . .

The automobile registration fee is collected by the tax assessor-collector. The first $50,000 of the fees collected and one-half of the balance collected until the total reached $175,000 is retained in the county in which it is collected and is earmarked for county roads and bridges. The present *ad valorem* levy is 50 cents. The commissioners' court is authorized to levy a 15 cents tax for roads and bridges. The qualified property tax paying voters may authorize an additional 15 cents. In a reallocation election the voters may authorize an increase in the levy for one fund and the decrease of others. This was recently done in the county, and the road and bridge levy was increased from 30 cents to 50 cents. In addition to the Road and Bridge Fund, Harrison County has a Special Road Bond and Interest Fund the revenue for which is derived from a property tax levy of one cent. Expenditures from this fund for 1948 are estimated at $12,047, mostly payable from an accumulated balance.

Elections

The county serves as the basic unit for political party organization and the conduct of general and primary elections. The county executive committee is responsible for administering party affairs. It is composed of a chairman elected at large and one member elected from each voting precinct. In August, 1947, there were 25 voting precincts in Harrison County. The committee is responsible for the conduct of primary elections, appointment of officials, preparation of ballots, certification of results to the county clerk, and a variety of other duties subject to party rules and regulations and state law. The county executive committee decides whether to have a second primary in purely county races. The commissioners' court in each county is *ex officio* the county board of election commissioners, and the county clerk serves as its secretary. The county election board is responsible for the conduct of general elections and divides the county into election districts, appoints election officials, and performs a variety of other duties similar to those of the county executive committee. A county board composed of the clerk, sheriff, and county judge is responsible for election supplies. The tax collector is required to file a list of those who have paid poll taxes with the commissioners' court. There is no provision for registration of voters, but the poll tax receipts serve this purpose. The voter in marking his ballot is required to scratch out all names except those for whom he intends to vote.

Agriculture

Harrison County has a county and an assistant county agricultural agent, a county and an assistant county home demonstration agent for white families, and a county agricultural agent and a home demonstration agent for the colored. All personnel are selected, trained, and placed under the direction of the vice director of extension (Texas A. & M.) in charge of county agent work in conjunction with district agents. The various district agents are responsible for recommending qualified personnel to the commissioners' court which may accept or reject those recommended. The commissioners' court is advised of all transfers of personnel and it may itself request a transfer. The court is advised of anticipated transfers in order that it may have the opportunity of increasing the agent's salary in order to retain him.

The counties contribute the following: part of the salaries of county extension personnel, office quarters, and some office supplies and expenses. In addition, a few counties appropriate funds for travel expenses and full- or part-time office and secretarial help. . . .

Sources of Revenue

The primary support of county government is the property tax. Harrison County has an assessed valuation (1946) of $22,832,005. The total value for state purposes is $16,389,475. The present valuation (for city taxes) of taxable property in the city of Marshall is $14,800,000. The constitution establishes four county funds and provides that the maximum levy for all these funds may be only 80 cents. The limits are a maximum of 25 cents for general purposes, 25 cents for permanent improvements, 15 cents for the jury fund, and 15 cents for roads and bridges. Tax-paying property owners may authorize an additional 15 cents for the last mentioned purpose. Moreover, in a reallocation election the voters may increase the tax levy for one fund and reduce it for others, and this was recently done in Harrison County. Again, the limitation of 80 cents does not apply to special funds that have been set up. The county *ad valorem* rate for 1948 is $1.00 distributed as follows: jury fund, 3 cents; road and bridge fund, 50 cents; general fund, 25 cents; permanent improvement, 3 cents; road bond and interest fund, 1 cent and airport bond and interest fund, 18 cents. The state property tax is 72 cents and the tax rate in the city of Marshall is $3.00. One-half of the Marshall tax levy is for the independent school district. The state levies a poll tax of $1.50 of which $1.00 goes into the available school fund of the state and 50 cents into the state general fund. Counties are authorized to levy an additional 25 cents poll tax, and this has been done in Harrison County. The city of Marshall levies a $1.00 poll tax. Marshall also receives 2 per cent of the gross revenue from taxicabs, city buses, telephone companies, and electric and gas companies. Taxes are also levied by the various school districts. There is no tax levy for the officers' salary fund. Fees and commissions which were paid to county officials when this method of compensation was used in the county now go into the salary fund.

COUNTY GOVERNMENT IS REBORN

BERNARD F. HILLENBRAND

Bernard F. Hillenbrand is executive director of the National Association of Counties. He has contributed numerous articles in professional journals.

Many people have mistaken ideas about county government. They have a mental picture of fat politicians sitting around a pot bellied stove, spraying tobacco juice into a copper spittoon, and plotting how to grease the political machine. Actually, have you been in a courthouse lately? One is more likely to find that it is a modern, air-conditioned building with automatic data-processing machines in the basement; an ultra efficient, two-way sheriff's radio on the roof; and everything in between just as modern—symbols of 20th Century progress.

County government will be the dominant unit of local government in the United States in the next decade. The following facts offer support for this belief:

1. In the six-year period from October 1951—October 1957, county government (as reflected by the number of full-time employees) increased an incredible 36 percent—an average increase of 6 percent per year, while municipal government and the general population increased only 3 percent per year.

2. Virtually every state in the union reports that its county governments have been authorized to undertake a host of new governmental responsibilities.

3. Our 3,047 county governments now employ 668,000 full-time people and spend about $6.5 billion per year.

4. One county (Los Angeles County), for example, employs 37,000 persons and has a payroll larger than 41 of the states. In these terms, many counties are larger than one or more states.

5. Some 133,360,000 Americans are served by county governments.

These facts seem to indicate that counties are growing like adolescents. A portion of the increase in the importance of county government is reflected in the expansion of traditional county government services, due both to the population increase and the traditional American demand for improvement and expansion of existing services. These demands have brought spectacular county improvements in election administration (automatic ballot-counting); penal administration (honor farms); administration of justice (streamlined court procedure and use of special service personnel, psychiatrists, etc.); roads and highways

From "County Government Is Reborn" by Bernard F. Hillenbrand. From *Public Administration Survey*. May 1960 (University, Miss.: Bureau of Public Administration, University of Mississippi), pp. 1-8. Reprinted with permission of the publisher.

(use of modern earthmoving equipment); record keeping (up-to-the-minute machines and techniques); education (student aptitude testing, special counseling, etc.); health and welfare (out-patient clinics for the mentally ill and spotless hospitals).

The really tremendous growth of county government, however, has come in urban areas where the existing units of government have demonstrated that they are not capable of solving area-wide problems. Here one finds counties assuming responsibility for police and fire protection, planning and zoning, water supply, sewage disposal, civil defense, industrial development, air pollution control, airports, traffic control, parks and recreation, urban renewal, and finance administration.

Rural and Urban Counties Today

Today, the life and needs of the rural citizen have changed. He drives an automobile and probably shops as often in the downtown area of the city as does the suburbanite. He sees the same programs on television and his general standard of living is not in any way inferior to that of his city cousin.

From the county government, this rural citizen demands very high and efficient levels of services. He wants good roads, the best of educational and recreational facilities, modern fire and police protection, public health and welfare facilities, and a host of other services.

County governments, moreover, have expanded to provide these services but this expansion has caused many problems, particularly the problem of how these services are to be financed. Counties to a very large extent depend upon the property tax for revenue. The inadequacy of property taxes in our present economy is well known and, as a result, our counties have been experimenting with sales taxes and state-collected, locally-shared taxes to augment the property tax. As long as counties are dependent upon the property tax as their principal source of revenue, county officials must appeal to both state and national governments for financial assistance, even though there is strong resistance on the part of these officials to increased state and Federal control.

The population shift from rural to urban areas is compounding rural problems. A county road, for example, is just about as expensive to maintain as a city road, even though there are fewer citizens to use it. In fact, most services increase greatly in cost per-citizen-serviced when there is a decrease in population. Many counties in Mississippi and in other parts of the South are struggling with areas that are de-populating, which has stimulated these counties to pursue vigorously new industry. Those familiar with the property tax know that in most cases residential property alone cannot support a high level of education and other services. A community, therefore, must have new or expanded business and industry. In a county that is depopulating, the need to attract new industry is more urgent than ever.

Here again we see the particular value of the county as a unit of government. A municipality usually cannot serve effectively as a unit to promote new industry. It is a costly activity; and after a great deal of effort, the industry sought may locate in the vicinity but outside the very municipality which attracted it in the first place. Since the industry is outside the municipal taxing jurisdiction, it would derive no immediate tax advantage. A county, by contrast, serves the entire area; and the business is taxable by the county no matter where it locates in its boundaries. Since all citizens in the area bear the cost of county government, a new industry eventually helps reduce the total tax liability of all the individual citizens of the county.

County government in the rural areas, by and large, seems to have satisfied its constituents. That the county is the most promising and virile unit of rural government is attested to by the tendency of rural citizens to dissolve their township governments, where they exist, and transfer their functions to the county.

In the urban areas, on the other hand, "the fat is in the fire." Substantially, there are two different arguments advocated as solutions to urban problems: one group argues that the only real solution is the creation of more municipalities or independent authorities while an opposing group argues that all existing units of government are ineffective and should be abolished giving way to new "super governments." But county officials find that neither position is a realistic solution to immediate problems. Instead, the county is being called upon to assume those responsibilities (one by one) that are of an area-wide nature, such functions as transportation, civil defense, water and sewage, planning and zoning, and others.

In a typical urban area we find these conditions. The central city is declining in population and the more well-to-do are moving to the suburbs. The central city is being populated by the less well-to-do; gradually it contains more older people and fewer business and professional people and those whom college professors like to call the "leader group." The tax base no longer is able to provide sufficiently high levels of services because new business industry continues to locate outside the city. Traffic congestion and deterioration of the downtown business districts set in.

The core city tries annexation as a means of increasing its tax base. Surrounding the core city are a host of smaller cities that do not want to lose their identity. In unincorporated areas there is equal resistance to annexation because the surburbanites would be required to pay city taxes but could not, in most cases, obtain the same level of services as those in the core city. Often when the core city taxpayer realizes how much it is going to cost initially to provide city services to annexed areas, he balks too!

The crisis usually comes in a single functional area. The airport, for example, needs to expand its runways to provide jet service, but airports are (contrary to fancy bookkeeping) usually money-losing propositions. Usually this airport is located physically outside the city. Always it serves the people of an entire area but is supported usually by city taxpayers only. The city fathers realize this fact, and the county is asked to take over their responsibility. Thus one finds that two of the most modern airports in the nation—Miami in Dade County, Florida, and Detroit in Wayne County, Michigan—draw upon the total resources of the county area.

Here it is important to burst the bubble of the popular fairy tale. County officials are not trying to take over anything. The reverse is true. Most county officials have plenty of problems to occupy their minds and are reluctant to seek new ones. Usually the idea starts with some study group or with municipal officials themselves. County officials have, of course, urged legislation to allow them to provide municipal-type services (at a fair price) to county residents not in incorporated areas, which is something quite different.

It might be well to dispel another fiction. The day of rip-roaring city-county fights is just about over. Cooperation is the new watchword. For every case of real or imagined city-county tension, there are a dozen cases of city-county cooperation. These range from something as simple as informal exchanges of equipment or services to something as complex as formal contracts for services. Sometimes the city provides services to the county and sometimes the county provides services to the city. In either event both sets of officials are working together far better than most people realize.

Advantages of County Government

As a solution to local problems, county governments offer many innate advantages that theoreticians sometimes overlook. In the first place, counties have a long and honorable history of service, dating from the earliest times in America and before that in Great Britain. Henrico County, Virginia, for example, was established in 1611. It will not be until 1967 that this county will have served the United States of America as long as it served as a unit of local government to the Virginia Colony. This county is, today, one of the most progressive in the nation; its advance in the area of automation is the envy of many larger communities.

Second, counties provide the territorial limits for the organization of many non-governmental as well as governmental activities. Medical Societies are nearly always county-wide, as are Bar Associations. Nearly all of the nation's agricultural and rural service programs are based upon the county as the primary unit. A large part of our educational systems are county-oriented. The national census uses the county as the basic accounting unit. Virtually all of the country's systems of courts and administration of justice are county-oriented. Conservation and soil conservation districts are usually coterminous with a single county.

Perhaps the greatest advantage of a county is that everyone in the state is served by a county government. Whether a voter lives in a city or in the rural portion of the county, he is represented on the county governing body. The notion that county functions are beyond the control of the city resident is, of course, false since the city resident is required to contribute to the financial support of the county since he participates in the election of representatives to the county governing body just as the rural resident does. It is true, however, that very often a rural resident has a stronger voice in county affairs because he has only one unit of government to keep an eye upon and therefore is more vigilant in county affairs. The city person has both his city and county governments to watch; and because his attention is divided, he may be less knowledgeable about his county government. This problem, however, can be remedied. In a democracy every citizen has the positive obligation to participate fully and intelligently in the affairs of his governments no matter how many there are. We certainly concede that actual participation in local affairs is increasingly difficult — particularly for that poor citizen who is served by a city, school district, multiple-service-district or authority, and by his state and Federal governments as well.

Finally, the county serves as the political base upon which our two-party system is built. The county is the fundamental organizational unit of both major parties and is their basic strength both state-wide and nationally. Because the parties are based on the county, they are controllable by the electorate. This political arena is the one place where all of the interests of the community are represented. Many decisions about local affairs are and should be made at this level because all interests are represented. The decision as to whether limited community funds are to be used to build a school or a bridge is, in this sense, political; and typically it is debated (or mutually endorsed) by the two parties in two-party areas and by opposing factions of the same party in one-party areas.

County Problems

To say that counties have a bright present and an even brighter future is not to say that they do not have problems. Chief among these is the absence of home rule (the right of local people to decide local affairs for themselves). Originally (and presently, for that matter) counties were established as local administrative districts of the state. Their responsibilities were quite simple in the beginning, enabling the state to establish a uniform system of county organization and to spell out in precise detail, in statute or constitution, exactly how the counties were to discharge these responsibilities. Most counties, however, are still forced to operate under these same rules in spite of changed circumstances which have brought on new responsibilities. As a result, counties now find themselves in a veritable strait jacket of state control.

The problems created by this rigid control are numerous. Most county officials are severely restricted in establishing local salary scales for county employees. In Massachusetts, for example, the state legislature has complete control over local county budgets, personnel and all. In order for a county official to purchase a typewriter, the item and the specific cost must be included in the county's budget and approved by the state legislature.

Increasingly the functions that counties are called upon to assume require endless special state statutes, and yet all but a handful of state legislatures meet only once every two years to consider substantive legislation. Many of the restrictions that are most disruptive of orderly, sensible local determination, moreover, are spelled out in the state constitution — an extremely difficult document to amend.

The Need for Executive Leadership

Of all the difficulties facing counties, perhaps the most complicated is the absence of an executive comparable to a municipal mayor, a state governor, or the President of the United States. As a matter of fact, in some states there is no real separation of legislative, judicial, and executive functions at the county level. Instead, we find single, elected officials discharging all three functions.

Opposition to a single chief executive runs very strong at the county level and apparently lies deep in the American concept of government — stemming from a fear of placing too much power in the hands of a single individual.

Two trends in the practices of American counties appear to be running contrary to this attitude, however. In some states — California, for example — the elected county supervisors (composing the county governing body) are turning to the professionally-trained, appointed county executive to discharge the mountains of detail incident to conducting the public business. Approximately 36 of the 57 counties in California have reported the creation of a position of this nature (under various names). Once adopted, the elected supervisors appear to have become the strongest supporters of the concept.

The other trend is in the direction of an elected county executive, undistinguishable from a strong mayor at the municipal level. The city and county of San Francisco and the city and county of Denver both have an elected mayor who also is, in varying degrees, responsible for county affairs. This is also true of the mayors of New Orleans and Baton Rouge and their parishes (counties) in Louisiana. Baltimore County in Maryland; Westchester, Erie, Nassau and Suffolk Counties, all in New York; and Milwaukee County in Wisconsin also have recently adopted the county-wide elected chief executive plan.

One of the most strenuous criticisms of county government has come from those who argue that there are too many elected executive positions at the county level, and indeed the list is long. Some 68,000 county positions are filled today by election. Chief among those attacked is the position of coroner. Lately, many statistics have indicated that there is a trend away from the election of many of these officials, but the National Association of County Officials has always taken the position that every community, in accord with home rule standards, should have the right to elect or appoint their officials as they see fit. If they want to elect the coroner, then they should have that right. It could very well be, as many of the defenders of the long ballot argue, that most of the officials who are elected to these positions now would probably be the ones who would hold them as appointees if the system were changed. Compared to the county problems caused by the crippling effect of almost exclusive reliance on the property tax, the election-appointment controversy pales into insignificance. This is not the problem over which to draw the battleline.

Relations Between Governments

Nowhere is the philosophy that "no man is an isle unto himself" more true than in county government. At no time in history have the relationships between Federal, state, and local governments been more complex; and, to quote an old infantry maxim, "they are bound to get worse before they get better." Take a single function—highways. The Federal government imposes a tax upon gasoline and other highway-user products and uses a portion of these funds to help finance certain highways that have been determined according to national defense or national economic need. The states in turn build and maintain all Federal-aid roads (with minor exceptions) and in addition levy gasoline and other highway-user taxes to finance a portion of the Federal-aid roads and all state highways. Counties, in turn, do not generally have access to highway-user fees (unless shared with them by the states) but do build and maintain an overwhelming proportion of the roads in the United States—largely with property taxes.

Why not, then, give one level of government the responsibility for all roads? Could the Federal government abandon the roads and the Federal gasoline taxes to the states and leave it to them to build all roads? No! States are all in competition one with the other for business and industry. Some would not levy the gasoline tax; many roads of national import would not be built in individual states. The same arguments would apply if the county were to build all roads. The opposition to having the Federal government build them is obvious.

This one case, therefore, illustrates why, for the forseeable future, most governmental functions must be on a partnership basis (including private enterprise) and why these interrelationships are so complex.

County and Metropolitan Problems

Metropolitan problems of today have grown so numerous and important to the welfare of our society that a whole new profession dedicated to their study has sprung up; but from the nearly 200 major studies produced by these professionals, less than half a dozen have realized the adoption of a substantial number of their recommendations. Because metropolitan problems often spill over the bounds of a single county, these studies have neglected the county as the potential core around which their solutions might have been built. But those studies which have shunted aside the county have done so in the face of evidence in practice of the adaptability of this unit of government to new conditions.

Counties have met metropolitan problems through the use of multi-county arrangements. Since 1924, Montgomery and Prince George's Counties in Maryland have had a bi-county Suburban Sanitary Commission (controlled by the counties) to provide water, sewage and refuse collection for hundreds of thousands of county residents in the area (there are few cities). Franklin County, Massachusetts, is the headquarters of a multi-county fire protection setup that brings fire protection to rural areas in Massachusetts, Vermont, and New Hampshire. And, there are literally hundreds of similar examples of two, three, or more counties joining to provide these or other area-wide services.

More recently the multi-county (and city, too) arrangements have flourished in great numbers. In the New York area, some 22 counties and their cities in Connecticut, New Jersey, and New York have banded together to start an area-wide approach to some of their metropolitan problems. The Supervisors' Inter-County Committee, composed of six counties in the Detroit-Wayne County area, are banding together voluntarily to solve their area-wide problems. The same is true of the four counties, two in Virginia and two in Maryland, who are banding together with the District of Columbia in the Washington area, and of the multi-county-city approach also being tried in the San Francisco Bay area.

If the county is proving that it can be placed in combination like building blocks, it is also showing that it is divisible, too! Counties everywhere are reporting great success in creating special districts to provide special services to selected parts of the county. All residents of the county pay a basic tax for county-wide services such as welfare, education and administration of justice. In addition any area that wants water and sewerage, for example, can have it provided by the county and can pay separately for the service. Thus the special service district under the control of the county governing body can provide municipal services to those that need them and who will pay for them without interfering with the farm resident who does not need them. Thus we have the farmer and the city dweller living happily side by side and serviced by the same county, and once again the county has shown its adaptability to the needs of its residents and their circumstances.

Is the County Obsolete?

Critics of county government have taken heart from the fact that the Connecticut Legislature, under Governor Abraham Ribicoff's leadership, has voted to abolish the state's eight counties on October 1, 1960. Does not this refute much of what has been said here? No. County government in Connecticut was not typical of county government in other parts of the United States. The county commissioners were not elected; they were appointed by the state legislature upon recommendation of the county representatives and senators elected to the General Assembly. Through years of centralization of power at the state level in Connecticut, the counties had been gradually stripped of all important functions and were left pretty much with the single major function of maintaining jails. This and the remaining minor functions performed by the counties, therefore, will not now be given to another unit of local government but will be taken over by the state.

How serious is the loss of Connecticut's counties to the county movement in the United States? While the nearly 300 county employees will now be absorbed by the State of Connecticut, the loss is insignificant in the stream of expanding county government. When this loss is weighed against an average daily increase of over 150 employees per working day, the loss of Connecticut's counties will stem the national tide of county progress by approximately two days.

In only a few other areas of the United States are there no counties to be found. Rhode Island is so small that it has never needed county political subdivisions and Alaska has created local units called Boroughs. There is now some consideration being given to creating counties. Hawaii, of course, has no separately organized cities. Honolulu is a city-county like San Francisco. With these few exceptions, therefore, county government can rightly claim to be the one universal and all-encompassing unit of local government. County government is not dead. Instead, it has just begun to live. It has proved that it is flexible, adjustable, resilient, and full of potential for meeting the needs of a new America. County government is, indeed, reborn.

IS THE MANAGER A POLITICAL LEADER?—YES

GLADYS M. KAMMERER

Gladys M. Kammerer is professor of political science, University of Florida. She is co-author of *Florida City Managers: Profile and Tenure* (1961).

A definition of terms is essential in debate in order that the frame of reference may be established and discussion may be to the point. It is the term "politics" that must be defined. A number of eminent political scientists, including Charles E. Merriam, George Catlin, Harold Lasswell, V. O. Key, Jr., and many others, have defined politics as the process of governance or the process and practice of ruling, thereby applying the term to the workings of governments generally, their impact on the governed, their manner of operation, and the means by which governors attain and retain authority. In much the same view David Easton defines politics as the authoritative allocation of values in a society.

The common conception of politics as merely a "dirty business" is unrealistic and nonoperational. It offers no explanation whatsoever for the process by which governmental improvements are effected in a democracy and only "explains" deviations from our values. Yet there are still many individuals, especially journalists, who choose to warp and twist the definition of politics to describe only the "bad" processes of government. The "good" processes are apparently "civic" activity, not politics. In this vein a leading Florida newspaper recently stated:

> The business of city government is to run a municipality efficiently and serve the people to the best of the establishment's ability. There is no "issue" in this. There is nothing "political" about drainage, sewers, street lights, police and fire protection and so on. On the contrary, if they are injected into the field of politics we are bound to lose efficiency and economy down the drain which runs through the pork barrel. . . .
>
> Certainly we want no "boss" rule, no partisanship in fundamental municipal affairs, no "spoils" system and no political approach to routine affairs.

Yet normal controversy in this very city did make issues out of proposals for financing storm sewers and for urban renewal and defeated both programs. Presumably such defeat was not "politics," according to the local newspaper, because that city had no politics. But one is thereby left without the foggiest notion of how to describe the behavior of this city.

The political process cannot be limited, as some would do, to election

From "Is the Manager a Political Leader?—Yes," Gladys M. Kammerer, *Public Management*, XLIV (February 1962), 26-29. Reprinted by permission of the publishers, The International City Managers' Association. [Footnotes omitted.]

and campaigns. Elections are only a single aspect of political behavior, which also includes discussion of public affairs, writing letters to public officials about policy, and acting in and through groups to influence public policy.

Role of the Manager

The city manager is a political leader for the following reasons: (1) he is a leader in proposing public policy for his city; (2) the role perceptions councilmen and citizens have of the manager are those of a political leader; and (3) long-term managers, in Florida at least, either have been major members of the political faction in control of the council or have possessed some independent base of political power, and they can be distinguished thereby from short-term managers who either were not included in the dominant political clique or had no base of political power of their own to provide policy support while they were forced to act as political leaders.

Public policy advocacy puts one into politics for the reason that the policies adopted in any jurisdiction embody the authoritative values of that polity. Public policy therefore is central to politics as the two words come from the same root—the Greek word *polis* for city. Easton says on this point, "We are said to be participating in political life when our activity relates in some way to the making and execution of policy for a society."

The political process is a continuous process centered around policy-making. At the heart of this process in a council-manager city are two institutional components: the council and the manager. The manager is expected under the terms of the *Model City Charter* to propose policy for the council to consider. In practice, some managers are delegated considerably more policy-making power than this statement would imply, and they are expected to establish and not merely propose policies on many matters. But even where the manager is expected to limit himself to proposal rather than final decision on policy, the public has learned over the years to assess the manager as an "influential" in making political decisions. He thereby becomes identified with certain policy positions in the eyes of the public to an even greater extent than are some councilmen who may shy away from issue or policy involvement out of a general sense of political insecurity.

Many city managers have themselves espoused the notion of the manager's role as one of policy leadership. For example, one of them was quoted in a recent study as declaring, "There is no question in my mind that the City Manager has an inescapable responsibility to his council and his city in participating and assuming proper leadership in shaping municipal policies."

In all but one of the study cities involved in our research into the tenure of Florida city managers we found that the manager played a significant part in proposing or killing policy proposals. He was indeed expected to play this role and was subjected to criticism in some cities if he was timid about coming forward with new policy concepts. The one city that was clearly an exception was a boss-controlled city where the boss brooked no ideas from others.

The word "leader" can of course give one some trouble. Definitions of "leader" or "leadership" are about as numerous as the political scientists and sociologists who grapple with this dimension of behavior. The examination of the making of major policy decisions on various issues to discover what persons were most influential is regarded by a number of political scientists as one of the operational measures of validating leadership. Political leadership is found to exist where the content of a public policy decision is influenced positively or negatively by an individual. It may well be that in a council-manager city neither the council members nor the manager is at the apex of the power structure. But whether the city manager is a major influence or a sub-leader in the final decisions on public policy, the fact that he makes policy proposals to the council and to the public on public matters places him in the political process willy-nilly.

In a democratic system of government it is just as important to discover the perceptions of the community with respect to a particular public office as it is to unearth the perceptions the incumbent has of his position. With respect to the city manager it is vital to identify the perceptions of community leaders, the press, other communications figures, and councilmen with respect to the role of the manager before one can start separating myth from reality.

Perceptions of Councilmen

We found in our Florida study that the councilmen in each of our cities, except the one boss-controlled city, identified managers as policy proposers or vetoers and hence as principal political figures in their cities. The identification of political leadership was particularly clear and explicit in the instance of managers they opposed because they found it easy, for one thing, to affiliate such a manager with the rival political clique and, secondly, even to attribute a leadership role in that political clique to the manager. Frequently he was the very embodiment of all they disliked in the opposition for the reason that politics was so unstructured in most of these cities that the councilmen who initially had suggested a policy themselves "turned tail" in the face of opposition and allowed the manager to become the focus for public opposition.

In contrast, councilmen who agreed with their manager politically did not at first assign him a major political leadership role. Rather they thought of the policies he espoused as their policies, with the leadership resting in their own hands. Only when they were questioned on specific issues of government, did they reveal that the manager actually played an important leadership role in bringing forward policy notions, clarifying their own ideas, or vetoing proposals. In the course of their discussion of the manager's role in policy formulation, they usually came to the conclusion expressed very clearly by one young councilman who described his manager as "knowing so much more about city government than any of us, he usually decides what we need to do and we go along with him." In one city the councilmen of both factions identified the manager as having a major base of political power in the form of a voter block which could affect their futures.

Both the press and civic leaders similarly identified managers whose policies they opposed as playing an avowedly political role and those they supported as merely having influence on policy. Naturally this identification did not always coincide with that of the councilmanic majority use of the terminology of "political" and "policy-making." But it did coincide in terms of identification of political ideology and alignment of the manager with the particular faction that shared that political ideology and also in terms of the degree of influence exercised by the manager within that faction.

Tenure of Managers

The reasons for agreement in perception of the basically political dimension of the manager's role on major issues may be that managers who achieved long tenure usually were "local boys" who either were major members of the majority clique or had been co-opted into that clique as they in time solidified their policy front with that of the council majority, which was itself well entrenched in control. In contrast, short-term managers were frequently professional managers recruited from outside who had a strong policy orientation that appealed to a clique which had suddenly gained power in an electoral overturn in a highly unstable town and which wished to push through a program expeditiously. However, such a clique in several instances tried to save themselves from defeat by trying to tie policies that proved politically unpopular in the town to the manager alone, and at times they even went so far as to fire a manager in a vain attempt to stave off defeat.

Some managers had refrained from taking a public posture on policies. But this avoidance of positive policy commitment was to no avail in preserving the manager when a change of factional control occurred. Electorate and councilmen alike who strongly favored certain policies equated the manager's neutrality as hostility to their own beliefs on municipal program. Thus it appeared to be impossible for the manager to avoid clique identification, for silence was held to be as indicative of political preference as public enunciation.

A manager dismissal is normally an occurrence of great political significance in a community. Because the manager is inevitably coupled with certain policy stands, his dismissal may articulate the issues in a way that the blurred lines of councilmanic elections frequently fail to do. For example, in one city last year the ruling clique of developer interests was compelled to admit that the then manager was being dismissed because he was "too zealous about planning and zoning." This public admission brought into the open the clash of interests in the community that overturned a councilman in the ensuing election and has boiled up into a first-class local power struggle.

The Parliamentary Approach

Both the theory of council-manager government and the learned response of the manager to repudiation by the council on a major policy proposal call for him to submit his resignation. This is the behavior required of the most political of governmental figures: the prime minister in a parliamentary system of government. It is a denial of reality to call a city manager non-political, yet structure his role to have him make policy proposals and then expect him to resign upon rejection of such proposals. This is a very different set of expectations and standards from those built up around the career administrator in a civil service system, for such an administrator, when asked to make policy proposals, is expected to continue in his employment regardless of whether his proposals are acted upon favorably or unfavorably by the highest policy-making organs of government. The civil servant is expected to exhibit a "dead-pan" *sang-froid* about policy and find it just as easy to work within the framework of one policy as another. But the manager, while accepting the notion of the elected councilmen as the highest policy-making organ, is assumed to be ready to resign when his own policy notions do not get majority support from the councilmen.

The city manager cannot allege to be nonpolitical and at the same time take a policy stand. The very nature of his work as chief administrator of his city requires him to have policy ideas and public positions on those policies. This role is inescapable. By the same token the requirements of his job as policy leader make him a political leader. Leonard D. White, in his classic study of early city managers, was correct in predicting that once the manager started taking policy stands, he would rise and fall in tune with acceptance of his political leadership.

This we found true in Florida, and the rise and fall of managers in this state has been especially rapid because population growth has added new economic and social interest groups to many Florida cities, unsettling their political equilibrium and causing power to fluctuate from one group to another with each municipal election. Many of our cities are now going through the throes of trying to decide what kind of a city they are to be—a question settled decades ago in older parts of the country—and this seminal question brings to the fore many significant issues of municipal government that must be fought and refought. The manager is inextricably caught in these stresses and is made a scapegoat for the pains of change.

We do not exercise an adverse judgment against the explicitly political role the manager is compelled to play. Even in our most unstable cities persons interested in public policy development will be impressed by the concrete achievements that can be attributed to manager leadership. Undoubtedly there has been lost motion, human waste, and sacrifice of good men as managers in all the turmoil of municipal instability in Florida. But most of our cities have been better cities because their city managers have been willing to assert political leadership when councilmen frequently have been unwilling or unable to do so.

IS THE MANAGER A POLITICAL LEADER?—NO

H. G. POPE

H. G. Pope has served as a city manager and is presently executive director of the Public Administration Service, Chicago.

Dr. Kammerer says the manager is a political leader but avoids a judgment as to whether he should be. I say he is *not* a political leader and freely offer the judgment that he *should not* be.

A subject such as this tempts one to use the available brief time to quibble over definitions of a political leader. Were I addressing people without official responsibility for government, or a direct personal stake in it, I might do so. Here, however, I am talking to people who have, in the course of their careers, repeatedly sweated out political campaigns and election nights. By this time you know what a political leader is and have become radar-equipped to detect him. Similarly, though less expert, the citizens in the small town where I live know who their leaders are and, at least biennially, are vigorously reminded of who their political leaders are.

The same situation prevails even in Chicago, a city almost a thousand times the size of the town where I live. Its three and one-half million people know what a political leader is, and, I might add, they even know who he is. As long as the voters, in whom the ultimate political power resides, have their own notions about what and who their political leaders are, any definitions we technicians and theoreti-

From "Is the Manager a Political Leader?—No," H. G. Pope, *Public Management*, XLIV (February 1962), 30-33. Reprinted by permission of the publishers, The International City Managers' Association.

cians may devise become relatively academic. I do not quarrel with Dr. Kammerer's classic definitions any more than I would quarrel with a philosopher's concept of the universe. I simply can't accept her definitions for this discussion any more than, were I an astronaut, I could use the philosopher's concept of the universe for interplanetary navigation.

Kinds of Leadership

I do say that, as commonly understood and practiced under the council-manager plan, administrative leadership, general community leadership, and political leadership are not one and the same.

Political leadership is invariably aimed at controlling governmental policy and often governmental patronage. Unlike general community and civic leadership, it cannot limit itself to influencing decisions on selected questions. It will be forced by circumstances to undertake more broadly based activities, including electioneering. Factional political structure and process are not confined to particular municipalities or particular subjects. Rather, these particulars are part of the whole fabric of political structure—city, county, state, and federal.

It would be naïve to theorize that effective political leadership, with its ambitions, obligations, and rewards, can be contained within a particular municipality, or limited to a specific issue, or turned on and off like a spigot. Effective political leaders must play for keeps on a court whose boundaries are not neatly outlined by specific issues, and always with an eye to the rewards and retributions that are part of the entire political process.

I am not among those who, as Dr. Kammerer says, define politics as merely "dirty business." I am well aware that the United States Constitution makes no provision for political parties, that so distinguished a person as George Washington admonished us against them, and that they are anathema to many reformers. Nevertheless I feel that our history demonstrates that political parties are a requisite of democratic government on a large scale.

Role of Political Parties

In the United States, parties are essential to the selection of alternate policies or alternate groups of leaders. Without them it would be difficult, perhaps impossible, to nominate candidates and conduct contests that insure that the most relevant, as well as many irrelevant, facts and views are presented to the voter for consideration and choice. Political parties also do much to give the citizen a sense of participating in the enormous complex of government. Again it may be argued that political parties contribute some needed coordination and cohesion to our federal system of a national establishment, 50 sovereign states, and innumerable local units, including home rule or otherwise partially autonomous entities. And last but not least, without organized partisan political parties, bureaucratic power might so extend itself that we would be governed by a bureaucracy rather than democratically.

Collectively these arguments persuade me that the practice of politics should be improved and enlarged and its leadership strengthened. It does not follow that, in municipalities, this political leadership can or should be furnished by the city managers.

I know that there are those who hint that the efficiency in municipal services attributed to the council-manager plan is ignoble and that a more important reason for the existence of municipal corporations is the strengthening of our state and national political machinery. Certainly a lively citizen interest and participation in local government will strengthen democracy generally and without regard to level of government. Admittedly federal and state action through grants in aid, regulatory measures, and otherwise have great impact on local government and with interlocking political implications. It does not follow that the political structures and processes we use for policy decision should be monolithic from bottom to top and that city managers should be the operators of the local units.

This particular standard of proprieties, developed to help make our democracy work, is not limited to government. Rather it is almost a part of our national manners. In most private corporations there would be an inclination to frown upon an appointed executive who bypasses his board of directors to indulge in factionalism among stockholders. The pastor who assumes leadership of a clique within his congregation may well find himself in an untenable position.

To take an example closer to home, I might note that my experience of more than 25 years of membership in this association leads me to believe that its members would frown if their director were to assume a leadership role in relation to factions that might, as sometimes happens in organizations, develop over important issues. These are roles for members of the governing boards to assume in our private institutions, just as they are appropriately roles of elective officials in our governments.

Role of the Manager

It may be worth while to remind ourselves that the council-manager plan was developed to eliminate the intermingling of administrative and political leadership. The stature and effectiveness of the manager depend in no small part on his earning and maintaining an image of integrity, competence, and objectivity. These qualities must of course be exercised with an awareness of and a sensitivity to the realities of political conflict, but without direct personal factional involvement.

Even those who are disappointed in the council-manager plan and propose the alternative of a chief administrative officer responsible to the mayor do not suggest that the chief administrative officer should exercise political leadership. Instead that officer is justified on the grounds that he will improve administrative performance without impairing the political leadership exercised by someone else.

A sound organization requires that everyone be responsible to someone. City managers commonly expect that department heads should recognize their responsibilities to the council and by established patterns of legislative and administrative practice resulting from a combination of law, habit, and practical requirements. This is, of course, among the reasons that effective municipal government is entirely practical in many communities without highly organized political factions.

Professional Administrators

I am fully aware of the importance of the municipality in our social and political scheme. Also, I would be the first to insist that the city manager is something special among the professional public administrators appointed to administer our governmental affairs. However, there are entities within our governmental structure that are *not* cities, and there are appointed professional public administrators who are *not* city managers. We can, in some measure, determine the propriety of political leadership by the manager by relating this concept to these other appointed professional officers. I shall choose only a few of the many examples from government to make this point.

For example, I expect top professional soldiers, educators, whether state university presidents or local superintendents of schools, health authorities, engineers, and others with important roles in the present-day scheme of things to exercise full executive leadership with respect to the men or functions under their direction. I expect these top professional people, who normally have devoted a lifetime to their respective professions, to plan for their programs and to present to policy makers considered views on what is needed and how it is to be employed. I expect them to be positive, even vigorous, in the presentation of judgments to the policy makers.

Otherwise, how can the average legislator know what he needs to know in order to make responsible policy determinations in these fields? Additionally, these administrators have general leadership obligations in the communities with which they are identified. This obligation for community leadership does not mean, however, that they should be partisan political leaders, and when they do so it is to the discomfort and even dismay of others in their professions.

I consider it unlikely that it will become fashionable for politicians to hire outsiders to do their political chores. Also, of the hundreds of managers that I have known, relatively few have had the equipment to deliver a political clout. And, if a manager has it, one could not expect it to be readily transportable from one community to another — any more than one would expect Mayor Daley, a highly effective administrative, legislative, and political leader, to get the same comfortable majority in another city that he gets in Chicago.

Most managers would shy away from extracurricular political activity, which would have to be personal rather than official, and most would expect that, if they made personal forays into the political arena, they could not enjoy the privilege of retreat into the sanctuary of professionalism when the going gets rough.

Policy and Administration

Discussion of political leadership must include a word of the distinctions between policy determination on the one hand and policy execution on the other. Clearly, the two require different kinds of judgments and actions, arrived at differently and employing different kinds of resources and considerations. Consequently a sensible case can be made for some reasonable measure of separation of policy determination from policy execution, with advantage to both. Yet, it is impossible to establish a sharply defined line between policy and administration. Instead there is an area in which the interdependence which typically characterizes the two becomes an intermingling that requires a close working relationship between the executive and legislative branches.

As a practical matter, an effective city manager has a significant influence on policy decision, and an effective council has a significant influence on administrative action. Also, argument about the line between policy and administration can easily be pursued past the point of diminishing returns since it is irrelevant to much of a city's business. Most municipal business is characterized by routine made possible by the mutual confidence between manager and manager. Similarly the manager must recognize his responsibility to the mayor and council. In doing so he foregoes the privilege of political leadership, which automatically implies involvement in factionalism among citizens to whom the mayor and councilmen are responsible.

To grant the manager a license to use his administrative resources for political partisanship would be intolerable. Since elections are related more often to candidates than to issues, there would quickly be created the deservedly unpopular picture of the manager selecting his own council. Once this notion, even though distorted, has been sold by enemies of the council-manager plan, the plan's greatest persuasion would be gone. This persuasion lies in the fact that the council-manager plan, while centralizing administrative authority, remains safely demo-cratic — since the manager serves only at the pleasure of a council elected by the people of the community without political leadership on the part of the manager. Should it become fashionable for the manager to assume political leadership responsibilities and prerogatives, it would, indeed, become hard to answer the cry of dictatorship now so popular with enemies of the plan.

This does not mean that the manager is free from politics. What he does will always be political news, and whether he is the man who should fill the position will often be the principal political issue in a municipal election campaign. He may create political issues through his work in preparing a budget or in recommending particular courses of action for decision by the community's policy makers. However, it is one thing for a manager to develop and present proposals, plans, and solutions to his council, sometimes with alternatives and projections of their probable effects, and to discuss and support his views. It is something else for him to assume political leadership among the voters and to be identified with and particularly responsive to selected special-interest groups.

Participation by the manager in partisanship, an essential to honest, effective political leadership, would not merely modify but would basically change and destroy the council-manager plan. This would be unfortunate because the proof of council-manager government lies not only in its theory but in its results, and these results have been good enough to warrant continued growth of the plan until a better one is devised. Such growth cannot be expected if the managers violate the proprieties our society has established for professional appointive executives.

A STUDY OF THREE COMMUNITIES

CHARLES R. ADRIAN

Charles R. Adrian is professor of political science, University of California, Riverside. His publications include *Governing Our Fifty States and Their Communities* (1963), *Governing Urban America: Structure, Politics and Administration,* (1955), and, with Oliver P. Williams, *Four Cities: A Study in Comparative Policy Making* (1963).

This is a report on a continuing study of policy leadership in three middle-sized council-manager cities. All three cities are in the 50,000 to 80,000 population range, are in Michigan, and have been council-manager cities for over twenty-five years. The study covers the period of the calendar years 1953 through 1957. The manager in each city had

From "A Study of Three Communities" by Charles R. Adrian. Reprinted from *Public Administration Review*, XVIII (Summer 1958), 208-213, quarterly journal of the American Society for Public Administration. [Footnotes omitted.]

been in office before the beginning of this period and remained in office throughout the period.

None of the cities is within the six counties of the Detroit metropolitan area. Cities A and B are manufacturing cities with a fairly slow population growth; city C, also predominantly a manufacturing city, has grown somewhat more rapidly. All have nonpartisan elections. Labor is organized in the three cities but has been of little influence in the selection of the council in cities A and B. City C had one AFL and CIO endorsee elected to the council during the period studied; two other councilmen were given limited labor endorsement.

Tentative conclusions reached in this preliminary report indicate that the manager and his administration are the principal sources of policy innovation and leadership in council-manager cities, even though the manager seeks to avoid a public posture of policy leadership; that the manager has resources and techniques that enable him to withstand even strong attempts by some councilmen to take policy leadership away from him; that nonofficial groups provide a greater amount of leadership in council-manager cities than is allowed for in the theory of the plan; and that this leadership is a result of councilmanic leadership falling short of the idealized role assigned to it by the theory. Councilmen who do seek to lead place their political careers in greater jeopardy than do other councilmen. It was also found that there were few important issues confronting city councils in middle-sized cities and that even some of these were settled with little conflict, particularly those where few solutions seemed to be available.

The Manager Plan

The basic idea of the council-manager plan is well known: an elective council of laymen is to make policy and a professional administration under a chief administrative officer selected by, and responsible to, the council is to carry out policy. It is not necessary to comment here on the fact that this approach to organization seems to imply the acceptance of the dichotomy which was held, some years ago, to exist between policy and administration. Practicing city managers quickly learned that they could not avoid taking leadership in policy-making. (The tempests created in academicians' teapots when the idea was presented that politics and administration cannot be separated were of little or no interest to managers and their subordinates who must have discovered the necessary interrelationship of the two about the time that the first manager was appointed in 1908.) Summarizing some studies which were made about twenty years ago, Stone, Price, and Stone noted that:

> *It is generally impossible for a city manager to escape being a leader in matters of policy, for it is an essential part of his administrative job to*

make recommendations. The most important municipal policy is embodied in the budget, and the city manager, of course, must prepare and propose the budget. The city manager's recommendation on an important policy, even if he makes it in an executive session of the council, is usually a matter of common knowledge.

Thus, while it is recognized no doubt almost at once that the manager would have to be a policy leader, he was also expected to do this in a discreet manner. The code of ethics of the International City Managers' Association enjoins each manager to further "positive decisions on policy by the council instead of passive acceptance of his recommendations," and to give formal credit for policy decisions to the council. (The code, with some modifications, dates from 1924.)

Thus, the role of the manager was conceived realistically decades ago and is well described in the study by Stone, Price, and Stone. On the other hand, neither that study nor other writings on the council-manager plan have paid very much attention to the role of other individuals and groups in the municipal policy-making process: the mayor, the council, and interest groups confronting the manager and the council between election campaigns. It is principally to these areas that this paper is addressed.

Scarcity of Issues

A study of the role of various groups and actors in the making of municipal public policy is handicapped to some extent by the relative scarcity of issues that could be classified as important. Most of the work of the council appears to consist of routine approval of recommendations from the city manager or his staff; these actions are routine because they fit within general policy already well established.

Judged on the basis of the amount of controversy engendered, the time required to achieve a policy decision by the council, and the amount of space devoted to the issue by the local press, the number of important issues coming before the councils of the three cities averaged about two per year. There was little variation among the cities on this point. It should be noted, however, that an issue may be divided into a number of parts and take many forms. A major conflict between the manager and one of the councilmen in City C, for example, was raised as a background issue in connection with almost every other councilmanic discussion during the period of the controversy.

The Role of the Manager

In all three cities studied, the manager played the social role expected of him by his professional organizations. In each case, he avoided taking a public role of policy innovator, except at the specific request of the council or in cases involving matters on which he could be considered a technical expert (e.g., on the effect of allowing a bank to install a drive-up window or of a proposed shuffling of administrative agencies).

If we assume, along with Herbert Simon, that major decisions are almost always made through a "composite process" involving many people, so that no single person is wholly responsible for the final product, it becomes advantageous to view the policy-making process as one in which individual roles are specialized. Since the leader, according to Simon, is a person "who is able to unite people in pursuit of a goal," alternative goals must first be perceived by someone. This is done through a precedent role of *policy innovation*, by which I mean the development of ideas, plans, or procedures that may be presented as alternative choices to the decision-makers. A decision might be said, for purposes of this article, to refer to the selection of an idea, plan, or procedure from among the perceived choices. Many decisions must be made in the development of a policy. To name only a few, the innovators of policy must decide whether their incipient suggestions are worthy of development and subsequent presentation for consideration by the leaders. Each leader must decide upon a policy from among what may be several proposals coming from a single individual or agency or from more than one agency. Once the manager or other leader has decided upon a proposal, he will seek to secure its acceptance. The governing body must then choose a proposal presented by one leader or must consolidate the proposals of two or more leaders. Final acceptance by the council gives the policy legitimacy. Of course, the council may veto all proposals, which would then force a reconsideration of the earlier decisions by other actors.

In the council-manager cities studied, the manager presented and sometimes strongly defended policy proposals that had originated largely from one of his own agencies (e.g., the police department on parking policies), from an advisory group (e.g., the planning commission which developed urban renewal plans), from study committees of lay citizens (e.g., citizens seeking to prevent the breakdown of public transportation), or private groups (e.g., downtown merchants interested in off-street parking). There appeared to be a psychological advantage to the manager if he could place himself in the position of defending a policy developed by these individuals or groups. He would take a strong stand, but would use the protective coloration of saying, "professional planners tell me. . . . " He would, in other words, take a public position of *leadership* in policy matters, but preferred to attribute policy *innovation* to technical experts or citizens groups.

Although managers in all cities appeared to exercise considerable skill in avoiding a public appearance of being the tail that wags the dog, in two cities they were accused of seeking to "control" the mayor or council. In City C, the manager had to overcome major opposition which, for a short while, actually held majority control of the council. The manager chose to wait out the opposition, almost succeeded in keeping from being quoted in the newspapers concerning his own views on the conflict, and eventually weaned the mayor from the opposition, thus making his supporters on the council a majority. In City B, two councilmen, elected to office late in the five-year period studied, accused the manager of policy domination and voted against proposals that had his blessing, but there appears to have been no support for the two from other councilmen. In an election toward the end of the period studied, a little-known candidate, seeking to join them, failed to secure nomination.

The Role of the Mayor

What of the mayor as a leader? In two of the cities studied, the mayor did not play a special leadership role. In one, he was elected by the council; in the other he was directly elected. In the third city, the mayor was the councilman receiving the largest number of votes. An individual of high prestige both among the public and on the council was regularly elected mayor through the period studied. Because of his high status, he appears to have been deferred to by other councilmen and his views were respected. His leadership was rather inconspicuous, however, and he did not play the role of policy innovator, or of a chaperon of legislation through the council.

In the thirty issues of importance during the five-year period, the mayor was a principal leader on only two, both of them in City B. The mayor in this case was an elderly man who had held his office for many years. He was chief spokesman on the council for an unsuccessful proposal for a metropolitan area hospital authority, although the plan had first been worked out by a citizen group which strongly supported it. A new city hall for the community was a matter close to his heart, but he was opposed by the chamber of commerce and the taxpayers groups which thought the plan extravagant and unnecessary. Although the mayor had the support of the manager and of the planning commission, the council finally accepted the plan of the economy groups.

It is impossible to conclude whether the manner by which the mayor was selected affected his role as a policy leader. In general, there was not much reason to believe that the office of mayor, as such, was prestigious enough to give the incumbent a significant advantage over other potential leaders.

The Role of the Council

Members of the council did not emerge as either general policy innovators or as general policy leaders. The individual councilman, rather, was likely to assume leadership in connection with a specific issue or function of government. He developed pet interests or came to know one area of municipal activity especially well and concentrated upon that.

There was one exception: a councilman who acted as a leader both in the general development of policy and in seeking support for policies first presented by some other individual or group (Councilman n in City A). To this case might be added another, somewhat similar. In City C, one councilman definitely acted as the leader of the opposition to the manager, regardless of the particular policy issue under discussion. His leadership, with a few exceptions, was of a negative sort, however. Since the conflict over the manager began almost at the outset of the period covered by this study, it is impossible to say if this councilman could also have served as a constructive policy leader under other conditions.

While a councilman might concentrate upon a particular aspect of municipal policy, it was found to be dangerous for him to seek to make some specific issue a *cause celebre*. If he chose to do so, he immediately subjected himself to greater public attention and scrutiny than was the case for the typical councilman, and he risked a defeat on the issue which could in turn have disastrous political consequences for him. There is danger in leadership, relative safety in conformity and anonymity. The study indicated that councilmen were aware of this.

In the five-year period covered, there were two incidents in which councilmen chose to make major controversies out of particular issues, and in each case the councilman was defeated in his try for re-election. In City A, Councilman m, who had served continuously for a quarter of a century and who came from one of the city's high prestige families, chose to take the lead in a full defense of municipal ownership of the light plant. The plant, long owned by the city, competed with a private utility. It served relatively few customers and costs were higher than those of the private company. As a result, patronage was falling and unit cost rising. Shortly after a new councilman took office, he began a campaign for the sale of the light plant to the private utility. His proposal was immediately and vigorously opposed by Councilman m. The issue was carried along at council meetings, through referendums and into court before it was finally settled in favor of sale to the private company. When Councilman m ran for re-election, he was defeated. He lost again two years later. (The referendums on the issue indicated that he was on the unpopular side of the controversy.)

Another case, in City C, involved the leader of a group opposing the city manager and his policies. Councilman y in this case was hostile to the manager at the beginning of the period studied. It took him some time, however, to organize a bloc. After an election, he picked up two new council members. When the mayor joined with him on two important issues, involving the dismissal of two employees and wage and salary policies, Councilman y had a 4-3 majority on the council. The local newspaper speculated on the possible resignation of the manager. The manager apparently decided to wait for further developments and for public opinion to become crystallized. He neither fought back nor made plans for resignation. Later, he became ill and the mayor acted in his stead for a few weeks. Shortly after, the mayor began to support the pro-manager group under Councilman z's leadership. This switch produced a new one-vote majority in support of the administration and talk of the manager's resignation stopped. A hard fought election campaign followed in which the issues included the question of wage and salary policy, support for the principle of the council-manager plan (all groups claimed to support it, but Councilman y was accused of seeking to sabotage it), and support for the incumbent manager. Councilman y was defeated for re-election by one of the city's leading industrialists, a supporter of the manager.

Leadership on Important Issues

Since in both policy innovation and leadership, the role of the councilmen was a relatively modest one, it is necessary to look elsewhere for the actors who played these parts. They were the manager, the members of his administration, and the leaders of interest groups.

Not all issues that were regarded in the community as being important involved intense controversy. In the case of some significant community problems, only one plausible solution was offered. In others, no councilman seemed to see any political advantage in presenting alternative solutions.

When the bus companies came to the councils from time to time asking for fare increases, each councilman would deplore the trend toward higher fares and poorer service, but since the only discernible alternative to refusing the rate increase was a discontinuance of service, almost all councilmen voted in favor of the request. In each of the cities, study committees of lay citizens were appointed to seek solutions to the bus problem. In two cities, they recommended that the city lease the lines and then hire the bus company to run them, thus avoiding certain taxes. In the third city, the committee found another bus company to operate in the city when the existing company sought to withdraw. In each case, the council gratefully, and with little discussion, accepted the proposed solutions. Although the operation of the bus lines was considered vital to each community, a crisis situation was solved in each of them with little or no conflict.

In cases where controversy did exist, as Table 1 indicates, leadership in favor of a proposal was most likely to come from the administration, with outside groups the second most likely source. In fact, nearly all the really significant issues derived their leadership from these

TABLE 1. LEADERSHIP ON MUNICIPAL ISSUES IN THREE MICHIGAN CITIES

Source of Leadership	In Favor	Opposed
Administration	15	—
Mayor	2	—
Councilmen	7	15
Outside Groups	10	7

Note: The table covers the 30 important municipal issues discussed during the years 1953-57. Because leadership was shared in several and lacking in others, the totals do not equal 30.

two sources. (The cases are too few to attempt to correlate the types of issues with the sources of leadership.) Councilmanic leadership came in annexation proposals, in seeking to make suburbs "pay their own way," and in revolts against the manager. Only in the proposal to sell City A's light plant and in a water supply revenue bond plan in City B did a councilman provide the leadership. In the second case, he had strong administration backing. Issues involving sharp conflict were rarely resolved as the result of leadership coming from the governing body.

In contrast to the leadership *for* proposals, councilmen did lead in opposition to proposals more often than did persons in any other category. Most of the opposition was aimed either against the manager or against expanded services or capital outlay. A good bit of it was non-constructive and perfunctory. The picture of the council, in summary, was one of a largely passive body granting or withholding its approval in the name of the community when presented with proposals from a leadership outside itself.

Nonofficial leadership was important in the case of two types of issues in addition to those that were regarded as "hot potatoes" and so treated gingerly by elected officials. The first type included those submitted by both neighborhood and downtown businessmen seeking municipal assistance in solving their problems. The second included the public transportation problems which, in all three cities, were turned over to citizens committees to bring in recommendations. The first is the kind of interest group activity commonplace before legislative bodies at all levels of government. The second offers something of a puzzle, however. It would seem likely that the solution to the bus problem in each city was one that might have been pushed by almost any councilman, and to his political advantage. Yet, this was not the pattern. Possibly councilmen feared that any solution would also involve increased rates or the necessity of the city buying the transportation system—a solution that seemed unpopular in each city. Possibly controversy was anticipated that never materialized.

It might be noted that the important policy and leadership role of the manager, of his administration, and of leaders of nonofficial groups differs from the pattern intended in the original theory of the council-manager plan. That theory assumed that able, respected leaders of the community would be willing to serve on councils and would take responsibility for policy decisions in government as they did in their businesses. While the typical councilman in the three cities studied gave the impression of being a sufficiently competent person, it seems clear enough that he was not willing to assume a public leadership role under circumstances where he might thereby be plunged into controversy. The politician in the council-manager city, though he may be an amateur, thus follows the traditional practice of American politicians and seeks to avoid taking sides in closely matched battles.

Suggested Areas for Further Study

A study covering a span of only five years in three cities is scarcely sufficient to serve as a basis for firm generalizations. It is, however, possible for certain tentative hypotheses to be offered from the work reported on here and these may properly provide a basis for further investigation. The following seven hypotheses appear to be most worthy of further inquiry:

1. There will be relatively few issues coming before the council that will be regarded by councilmen, the manager, or the press as involving important, nonroutine decisions.

2. A manager will avoid taking public positions as a policy innovator on items of major importance, but will serve as a leader in presenting and publicly defending policy recommendations developed within the administrative departments, the advisory boards and commissions, study committees of lay citizens, or private groups.

3. The mayor is not chosen on the basis of leadership ability or willingness to play a leadership role and he is, therefore, no more likely to serve as a policy leader than is any other councilman.

4. A councilman is likely to assume leadership in connection with a specific issue or a specific function of government, but not as a general policy leader.

5. A councilman who chooses to make some specific issue a *cause celebre* thereby becomes subject to greater public attention and scrutiny than is the case with the typical councilman and, if he fails in his objective, runs serious risk of defeat in the following election.

6. Important issues, measured by the consequences of failure to act, may involve little controversy if no alternative solutions are perceived, or if no political advantage is seen in the advancement of alternative solutions.

7. When issues are regarded as being important, but when possible

solutions are controversial, or many plausible solutions are discernible, the alternative finally selected is likely to come from the administration or from a group outside of the local government structure.

Further inquiry into these hypotheses should help to expand our areas of knowledge about local government and the characteristics of the public policy-making process.

THE WEAK MAYOR SYSTEM IN CHICAGO

EDWARD C. BANFIELD AND MARTIN MEYERSON

Edward C. Banfield is professor of urban government, Harvard University. He is the author of *Political Influence* (1961), *City Politics* (1963), and *Big City Politics* (1965). Martin Meyerson is professor of urban development, College of Environmental Design, University of California, Berkeley. He has served as director of the Joint Center for Urban Studies of the Massachusetts Institute of Technology and Harvard University.

"Chicago needs a city government which can govern," the editorial began. "Chicago needs a city government which will provide a just and workable balance between the local interests of its many neighborhoods and the general interests of the city as a whole. Chicago needs a city government which can plan, legislate, and administer public services for the common good of all of its two million citizens, rather than for the special interests of special groups."

With a city council consisting of 50 delegates from 50 localities, each elected by a small constituency, each owing nothing to the city at large, and with only the mayor elected by the citizens at large, it was inevitable, the editorial said, that local interests, narrow interests, sectional interests, factional interests should often prevail over the interest of the city as a whole. Chicago should have a council of 15 or 20 members. In order that local interests have fair representation, half of the council, perhaps, should be elected by districts. The rest of the members, together with the mayor, should be elected by and represent the city at large. "Such a city government," the editorial concluded, "would not always act wisely. But at least it could come to some decision on the vital problems of a vital metropolis. And when it acted unwisely, its members could be held responsible at the polls."

This view was widely accepted among students of municipal government in Chicago and elsewhere. Indeed, not many important cities still had governments like Chicago's. For many years the trend all over the country had been to reduce the number and powers of aldermen and to increase the powers of the executive. In several hundred cities (although not in any of the 20 largest) a small elected council hired a professional manager who administered the affairs of the city as unpolitically as if it were a business or a factory.

That Chicago's government was behind the times was unquestionable. But it was probably exaggerated to say, as the *Sun-Times* did, and as many liberals concerned with reform in Chicago did, that the struggle over public housing showed that the city could not act effectively because it was broken into 50 wards, each represented by an alderman. In fact, there rarely was a moment during the long struggle when Duffy and the other "Big Boys" could not have made a decision for the Council and for the city. Power was not divided among the 50 aldermen or even, as the *Sun-Times* suggested it should be, among 15 or 20 aldermen and a mayor: it was amply concentrated in the hands of two or three aldermen. These two or three, moreover, although particularly concerned with the interests of their wards and with the interest of the South Side, were also concerned very actively, if not with the interests of the city as a whole, at least with the maintenance of the Democratic organization in the city as a whole. In addition, Duffy, the most powerful of the "Big Boys," was running for a county office and so of course had to take account of the wishes of voters throughout the city.

Concentrated as it was, power was less concentrated in 1949 and 1950 than it had been for many years past. Mayor Kelly had ruled the city almost despotically. That Chicago had a weak mayor in 1949 and 1950 and that there were two factions within the Council was an unusual circumstance, one to be explained, perhaps, by the fact that some time would have to elapse before the power-vacuum created by Kelly's retirement could be filled. Certainly under Kelly's administration no one had ever complained that the city could not reach decisions regarding public housing or other matters. "Under Kelly," as Duffy once remarked, "the Housing Authority submitted a proposal and that was it."

In Chicago, political power was highly decentralized *formally* but highly centralized *informally*. The city had what textbooks in municipal government called a "weak-mayor" form of government to be sure, but it also had a powerful mayor, or, if not a powerful mayor, a powerful leader of the Council. This paradox of a "weak" government that was strong was to be explained by the presence of the Democratic machine, an organization parallel to the city government but outside of it, in which power sufficient to run the city was centralized. The weakness of the city government was offset by the strength of the party.

The "Big Boys" could get and keep power enough to run the city only by giving the favors, protection, and patronage which were essential for the maintenance of the machine. It is quite possible, of course, that they preferred to operate the city government in this way. But whether they preferred it or not, the "spoils system" and even to some extent the alliance between crime and politics were the price that had to be paid to overcome the extreme decentralization of formal power. If overnight the bosses became model administrators—if they put all of the city jobs on the merit system, destroyed the syndicate, and put an end to petty grafting, then the city government would really be as weak and ineffective as the *Sun-Times* said. Indeed, under Kennelly the government of Chicago became both a great deal cleaner and a great deal weaker than it had been for many years.

The people of Chicago probably did not fully realize the price that was being paid to assemble power enough to govern the city. But although it had never calculated the cost in deliberate ways, the public, it seems safe to say, had some awareness both that these costs were there and that there were some benefits in return—in fact, the disadvantages of a formal centralization of power, although different in kind, might possibly be even greater.

As they actually worked (but not as they were formally designed to work), Chicago's governmental institutions achieved a high degree of centralization *and* a high degree of decentralization: they put a great deal of power over some matters in the hands of the city administration while leaving a great deal of power over other matters in the hands of the neighborhood and ward leaders. The politically active people in the wards had their way in all matters which were not of first importance to the city administration. The voter who stood well with his precinct captain (and most voters could) could expect prompt action if he complained that the street in front of his house needed repairs, if he wanted a change in the zoning law so that his son-in-law could go in the pants-pressing business, or if the traffic cop was too free with his tickets. Having power like this close at hand was of great importance to many people: street repairs, zoning changes, traffic tickets and the like were the main business of city government from the standpoint of most citizens. Government so close to many people and so responsive to them was "grassroots democracy," although perhaps not the kind that those who most use the term would recognize as such.

Most of the matters that were decided locally were of local interest. Whether a street was to be repaved, the zoning law for a block changed, and the traffic cop transferred were questions which had direct and clearly ascertainable consequences mainly for the locality. It was true that they might have even more important indirect consequences for the city as a whole (for example, an exception to the zoning law may set in motion a series of changes which cause the decay of the neighborhood and ultimately affect the ecology of the whole city) but these consequences were usually so obscure and so involved in detail that a central authority would rarely have staff or time to take them into account. Some matters were on the border between being of local and of city-wide interest or were of both local and city-wide interest. In these matters there would be friction because of overlapping jurisdictions of the local and central powerholders, but this was not a very strong argument for eliminating local autonomy altogether.

Whether an issue to be regarded as primarily of local or primarily of city-wide interest may depend upon the observer's value premises and especially upon whether his model of the public interest is individualistic or unitary. One who takes what we call an organismic view of the view of the public interest subordinates all other interests to that of the social "organism." At the other extreme, the Utilitarian, granting that matters like housing have more than contingent or constructive importance to the whole population of the city, tries to compare utilities so as to arrive at the "greatest happiness."

Machine government (which, as its opponents have always recognized, depends for its existence upon ward organization and a formally weak executive) and its opposite, "honest and efficient administration in the public interest" (which implies a small council elected at large, often by proportional representation, and a strong mayor or city manager), are suitable to separate and distinct social and economic class interests.

Lower and lower-middle class people, especially members of ethnic minorities, have often favored machine government rather than its opposite, and not, we think, chiefly because, as Lord Bryce and many others have supposed, they have been ignorant of democratic traditions. Many of these people have found the ward and precinct organization an almost indispensable intermediary between them and the formal organs of government, especially the courts, and they have known that the machines, however corrupt they might be, are run by people of economic and ethnic origins similar to their own. The interests these people usually regard as most important are local, not city-wide, and their outlook is generally self- or family-regarding rather than community-regarding. Machine government seems to serve them best.

It is mainly upper and middle class people who have fought the machines and sought to establish a cleaner, more businesslike, and more respectable government. As a general rule people of these classes have little need of petty favors; many of them have business or other interests which are city-wide and which are facilitated by progressive, impartial, and low-cost administration; many of them act in representative rather than in personal roles (e.g., as officers of voluntary associations) and these roles are commonly community-regarding, and, of course, upper and middle class people, too, like to be ruled by their own kind.

In communities where middle and upper class people have an overwhelming preponderance of political power — despite their sizeable numbers, these groups, except for some businessmen, were typically bypassed by the Chicago machine — this model of local government, the apogee of which is the council-manager system, is likely to succeed very well. But where control is not firmly in the hands of the middle and upper classes or where there is an important ethnic or class minority — and therefore in all of the great polyglot metropolises of the United States — "honest, impartial, businesslike" government is not likely to be tolerated for long because it runs counter to the ends and to the class feeling of many citizens.

It was, we think, an advantage of the Chicago system of government that it conformed to the tastes and interests of the most numerous social group (no government which did not do this reasonably well could survive, of course, but foolish and costly and less successful attempts might have been made and might have persisted long enough to do great damage). But it was also an advantage of the Chicago system that, while keeping control over local matters within the voters' reach, it interposed the party between the voters and the most important city-wide (as well as state- and nation-wide) decisions. The heads of the machine could not ignore the voters on all issues, but they could ignore them on many issues and on almost any particular issue. The advantages of this were great. Chicago was not governed, as are some cities in which strong machines do not stand between the voter and the issue, by the pull and haul of a few irresponsible pressure groups which get the voter's ear at election time; instead, there were only two important political organizations, the Democratic and the Republican parties, both of which had to accept some responsibility for not one or a few interests but for all of the many conflicting interests that were important in the life of the city. And since they depended upon a highly disciplined organization built upon a system of material incentives, the leaders of the machine did not have to rely mainly upon ideological appeals to the voter. This meant that, although issues were often decided upon non-ideological grounds, they were not settled upon the basis of an anti-democratic ideology. The South Side of Chicago, it should be remembered, was Studs Lonigan's stamping ground, and Studs and his friends would have been happy to vote for a man like Senator McCarthy (who was a product of ideological, not of machine, politics); instead, they voted for Governor Adlai Stevenson and Senator Paul Douglas because Jacob Arvey, the man who ran the Democratic machine, could afford on behalf of its liberal wing the luxury of some "high class" candidates.

In our opinion, believers in traditional democracy, both the conservatives and the liberals among them, in their criticism have neglected the advantages of effective machines in Chicago. The machines not only give the mass of the people, with their limited interest in politics (what some would call their "apathy") the kind of government they seem to want — or least object to — but they also insulate traditional democratic values and institutions from the forces which unscrupulous demagogues using mass communications media can so easily unloose in a society deeply divided by ethnic, economic and other conflicts. Naively to destroy the political machines and to undertake to govern the city in the way its "best elements" think is impartial, businesslike and in the public interest is to run the risk of deepening the conflicts which already exist while at the same time discarding a social structure by which conflicts may be confined and managed.

If, as some of the reformers had suggested for years, the size of the Council were to be reduced to 15 or 20 members, half of them elected at large, and if the power of the machine were also reduced (as we suppose they intended), the result in our opinion would be to eliminate both the regulated local autonomy which many people so prize and the concentration of power in the hands of the city's leaders which makes effective city-wide action possible. Instead of making the government of the city stronger, such a change would make it weaker; while making it impossible to decide anything on a neighborhood basis, it would also make it impossible to decide anything centrally.

In order to centralize formally as much power as is now centralized informally, a governing body of not more than six persons, all elected for long, overlapping terms from a city-wide constituency and a mayor whose power is preponderant within the governing body might be required. Little short of such extreme centralization would yield power enough to govern the city in the absence of some kind — not necessarily the present kind — of a strong machine. The dangers of such a government we have already pointed to, but the more probable danger — the danger associated with a half-way proposal such as that proposed by the *Sun-Times* and the liberal reform groups — is of a government which would not have enough power, formal and informal, to enable it to rule effectively.

NEW STRENGTH IN CITY HALL

SEYMOUR FREEDGOOD

Seymour Freedgood is an associate editor of *Fortune* Magazine.

At the troubled core of the big city stands City Hall, a block-square, granite citadel heavily encrusted with myth. It was a half-century ago that Lincoln Steffens described the "shame of the cities" — the bosses, the boodlers, the job sellers, and the hopeless inefficiency of the city's house-keeping. The image persists. Most people are aware that the machines have fallen on parlous times — but they're not sure that what's left is

From *The Exploding Metropolis* by Seymour Freedgood (New York: Doubleday & Company, Inc., 1958), pp. 81-87, 92-99. Originally published in *Fortune* and reprinted with their permisssion.

much better. The dramatic corruption may have gone but the belief that the big city's government is a mess remains. When people look for models of municipal efficiency, it is outward, to the hinterland, that they are apt to turn; here, where "grass roots" are more visible, are the slumless smaller cities and the towns with city managers, and it is to them that most of the accolades for municipal success are directed.

The emphasis is misplaced. Where the problems are the toughest — in the big, crowded, noisy city — government has vitally transformed itself. Today the big city must rank as one of the most skillfully managed of American organizations — indeed, considering the problems it has to face, it is better managed than many U.S. corporations.

The suburbanization of the countryside has plunged America's big cities — specifically the twenty-three cities with population of 500,000 and over — into a time of crisis. Hemmed in by their hostile, booming suburbs, worried about the flight of their middle class, and hard pressed to maintain essential services for their own populations, they need, if they are to hold their own, let alone grow, top-notch leadership.

They have it. Since the 1930's, and at an accelerating rate after the second world war, the electorate in city after city has put into office as competent, hard-driving, and skillful a chief executive as ever sat in the high-backed chair behind the broad mahogany desk. At the same time they have strengthened the power of the office.

This has not been a victory for "good government." To most people, good government is primarily honest and efficient administration, and they believe that the sure way for the city to get it is to tighten civil service, eliminate patronage, and accept all the other artifacts of "scientific" government, including the council-city-manager plan. But today's big-city mayor is not a good-government man, at least in these terms, and if he ever was, he got over it a long time ago. He is a tough-minded, soft-spoken politician who often outrages good-government people, or, as the politicians have called them, the Goo-Goos.

One of the biggest threats to his leadership, indeed, is too much "good government." The big problem at City Hall is no longer honesty, or even simple efficiency. The fight for these virtues is a continuous one, of course, and Lucifer is always lurking in the hall, but most big-city governments have become reasonably honest and efficient. Today, the big problem is not good housekeeping: it is whether the mayor can provide the aggressive leadership and the positive programs without which no big city has a prayer. What is to get priority? Industrial redevelopment? More housing? (And for whom?) There is only so much money, and if hard policy decisions are not made, the city's energies will be diffused in programs "broad" but not bold.

The mayor is hemmed in. As he strives to exercise policy leadership, his power is challenged on all sides. In his own house the staff experts and the civil-service bureaucrats threaten to nibble him to death in their efforts to increase their own authority. Then there are the public "authorities." Some are single-purpose authorities — like the city housing authorities, and the sewer districts; some, like the Port of New York Authority, handle a whole range of functions. They are eminently useful institutions, but however efficient they may be, they are virtually laws unto themselves and they have severely limited the mayor's ability to rule in his own house and, more important, his ability to plan for long-range development.

The power struggle also goes on between the mayor and the state legislature, which has a controlling voice in the city's fiscal affairs, but whose membership is apportioned in favor of the rural areas. It is the rare mayor who need not make frequent trips to the state capital for additional funds, and the legislature is usually unsympathetic. Colorado's, for example, gives Denver a niggardly $2,300,000 a year in state aid for a school system of 90,000 children; right next to it, semi-rural Jefferson County, with 18,000 pupils, gets $2,400,000.

There is the continuing struggle between the mayor and the suburbs, whose people, the big city firmly believes, are welshing on their obligations to the city. The mayor must win the cooperation of his suburban counterparts if he is to do anything at all about the city's most pressing problems — e.g., the traffic mess — and the going is grim. No one is against "saving our cities," but in this seemingly antiseptic cause there are fierce conflicts of interests and the power struggle is getting more intense.

There has been a change in City Hall because there has been a change in the city itself. For the better part of a century, the core of big-city life was its immigrants — waves and waves of them, many illiterate, few English-speaking, all poor. Their grinding misery kept the machine in power at the hall. The machine fed on the immigrants, but it also helped them — with jobs, with welfare services and personal favors, with Christmas baskets and dippers of coal — and the immigrants, in turn, were generous with their votes. The 1924 Immigration Act put an end to this cycle. Reduced immigration gave the city time to absorb the earlier newcomers, reduce the language barriers, educate them and their children, and raise many of them into the middle class. This, along with federal social security and unemployment insurance, reduced the dependence of the big-city masses on the political machines. After World War II came the huge influx of southern Negroes and Puerto Ricans, but by this time the machine was beyond a real comeback.

A half-century's work by the National Municipal League, the Institute of Public Administration, and other government research groups was a big factor. They fought and in many places won the hard fight for the short ballot, which eliminates "blind" voting, and for better city charters, better budgeting, and more efficient management methods.

Better-qualified people came into government. During the unemployment of the 1930's governments could recruit talent they couldn't before. Most of the bright young men went off to Washington, but many of them went into city government too. Some now man its top administrative posts, and they have done much to raise civil-service standards.

Most important, the public began asking for more. It now demands as a natural right better-administered services — police and fire protection, water, sewerage, and all the rest — and it judges its public officials on how well they are able to satisfy this demand. It also demands services — psychiatric clinics, youth boards, air-pollution control — it never had before. City government, as a result, has been transformed into an enormous service machine, infinitely complicated to run.

To many an aspirant who wouldn't have thought of city politics a generation ago, the mayoralty is now eminently worth his mettle. This has been particularly true in cities where long-standing sloth and corruption had created the possibility of a dramatic reversal; in these places an able and ambitious man might well conclude that his opportunities for spectacular, visible achievement outran those of a governor or senator. But the new mayors are more than opportunists. They come from widely different social and economic backgrounds, and they differ as widely in temperament, but all share a sense of mission: while it also happens to be good politics, they feel deeply that they should make their decisions in terms of the community-wide interest rather than the interest of any one group.

The profile of today's big-city mayor — with one difference — is quite similar to that of the chief executive of a large corporation. Typically, the mayor is a college graduate, usually with a legal or business background, and is now in his late fifties. He puts in hard, grinding hours at his desk, sometimes six or seven days a week, and his wife suffers as much as his golf game. The difference is in salary: he usually makes $20,000 to $25,000. There is also a chauffeur-driven limousine and, in some cities, an expense allowance, ranging from $2,000 (Milwaukee) to $55,000 (Chicago).

"Public relations" take a big chunk of his time. He is aggressively press-conscious, holds frequent news conferences, often appears on TV-radio with his "Report to the People"; and from his office flows a flood of releases on civic improvements. About five nights a week there are civic receptions, banquets, policy meetings, and visits with neighborhood civic groups. In between he may serve as a labor negotiator, or a member of the Civil Defense Board.

The mayor is also seeing a lot more of the city's business leaders, whose interest in urban renewal is growing steadily. Despite the fact that His Honor is likely to be a Democrat, he gets along very well with the businessmen, though he is apt to feel that they have a lot to learn about political decision-making. A City Hall man recently summed up the feelings of his fellows: "These businessmen like everything to be nice and orderly—and nonpolitical. They're getting hot now on metropolitan planning. They think it's not political! Throw them into shifting situations where there are a lot of conflicts and no firm leadership and they're completely buffaloed. It's painful to watch them trying to operate. But once there's a firm program lined up and they've bought it, they're very effective."

Above all the mayor is a politician. True, he may have risen to office on the back of a reform movement. But he is not, as happened too often in the past, a "nonpolitical" civic leader who rallies the do-gooders, drives the rascals out of City Hall, serves for an undistinguished term or two, and then withdraws—or gets driven out—leaving the city to another cycle of corruption. Instead, he fits the qualifications of the mayors whom Lincoln Steffens called on the public to elect: "politicians working for the reform of the city with the methods of politics." His main interest is in government, not abstract virtue, and he knows that the art of government is politics.

DeLesseps Morrison of New Orleans is a notable example of a political leader who leaped into office on a reform ticket, then used the methods of politics to put his programs across. In the years since insurgents elected Mayor Morrison over opposition from the long-entrenched regulars who had run the town wide open, he has done more than demonstrate that hard-working and efficient management can change the face of a city. Morrison has consolidated the gains—in large part by his ability to turn the loose organization that first supported him into a thoroughly professional political organization, which regularly helps elect friendly councilmen. The Morrison organization, not surprisingly, is anathema to the old Democratic machine.

In Philadelphia, Richardson Dilworth and his predecessor, Mayor (now Senator) Joseph Clark, have followed the Morrison pattern up to a point. In 1952 Philadelphia civic groups wrested control of City Hall from a corrupt and contented Republican machine, and the Clark and Dilworth administrations have given the city vigorous and honest government ever since. Mayor Dilworth, in office since 1956, is making considerable headway with his programs; unlike Morrison, however, he has not yet chosen to organize his followers into a political organization that can regularly get out the vote on election day. The old-line Democrats and Republicans, as a result, have been increasingly successful in electing their own men to the council. . . .

The new mayor, of course, does not need a dragon to fight. Indeed, some of today's best mayors are in cities that have enjoyed reasonably honest government for quite some time. Detroit's late aggressive Mayor Albert Cobo was one of these. He believed that government should be run like a business: during his eight years in office he overhauled the city's government, department by department, replacing the old, wasteful ways of doing things with machines and management systems that would do credit to any corporation.

St. Louis, Cincinnati, and Milwaukee, all with long traditions of honest government, have a remarkable trio of mayors: each wears a distinctively scholarly air, and is a pretty good politician to boot. St. Louis, once an ailing city, has found one of the ablest leaders in its history in an engineering professor, Raymond Tucker. Enthusiastically backed by the city's business leaders and the St. Louis press, Mayor Tucker has persuaded the voters to approve new taxes and public-improvement bond issues with which he has pulled the city out of the red and away from the blight. Milwaukee, a well-governed city since 1910, now has professorial, mild-mannered Frank P. Zeidler as its mayor. He too has stimulated a conservative, frugal citizenry into approving needed physical improvements. Cincinnati, under council-city-manager government since 1926, has Charles Taft, a top mayor who has given the city's urban-renewal and highway programs a powerful boost.

The mayors of Pittsburgh and Chicago bridge the gap between the traditional machine-boss mayor and today's management-man mayor. Pittsburgh's David Lawrence and Chicago's Richard Daley are both powerful Democratic organization leaders as well as strong mayors: each has given his city increasingly good government—and a big push forward in meeting its problems—while at the same time maintaining his organization in viable if declining power. Of the two, Daley has been the bigger surprise. When he was elected many people believed he would sell City Hall to Cicero without a qualm. Instead, Daley went along to a remarkable extent in putting into effect reform legislation that tightened and improved the structure of Chicago's city government. Chicago, Senator Paul Douglas once observed, is a city with a Queen Anne front and a Mary Ann rear. That may still be the case with its government: it undoubtedly has much to do before its rear is as respectable as its front. But Daley, a man who has been known to do odd things with the queen's English, seems determined to close the gap. "We will go on," he once announced at a town-and-gown dinner of the city and the University of Chicago, "to a new high platitude of success."

In his drive for more power, the big-city mayor is in direct conflict with a strong trend in municipal government. This is the council-city-manager plan, which is the fastest spreading form of government among cities of 25,000 to 100,000. To many do-gooders, it is the ideal form of government for the American city, big or small. Basically, it is government by a board of directors: an elected committee decides on city policies, and the hired manager and his experts carry them out.

The system has been most successful in smaller cities—e.g., Watertown, New York (population, 35,000), whose inhabitants are for the most part homogeneous and native born, where ethnic and economic tensions are low, and where the future holds no big threats. Cities like Watertown may thrive under such government; most big cities cannot. Their electorates seem to sense this. When asked to vote on a new city charter, they have usually settled on one providing for a strong mayor rather than committee leadership. As a result, the trend to the strong chief executive, long evident in the federal government and the urban state capitals, is now running high in the cities. Of the twenty-three largest, fourteen have adopted some kind of "strong-mayor" charter, five still vest most power in the council, and four use the council-manager plan.

Philadelphia, which is symbolic of so much of the best and worst that can happen to a city, has indicated why the major cities are choosing the strong-mayor-council rather than the council-city-manager form of government. In 1949, civic dissatisfaction with the machine was picking up so much steam that Mayor Bernard Samuel consented to the appoint-ment of a fifteen-man bipartisan commission to draft a charter for the better government of the city. After months of study, the commissioners arrived at these alternatives:

New York: Under the 1938 charter, drafted by a commission appointed by Mayor La Guardia, New York's mayors were given strong statutory powers, and the city council, then called the board of alder-men — and sometimes the Boodle Board or the Forty Thieves — was cut in both size and authority. The charter gave the mayor two prime tools of the strong chief executive: the right (1) to hire and fire his key department heads and (2) to make his operating budget, which the council may cut but not increase. He may also veto council ordinances, and a two-thirds vote is needed to override him. But the mayor's fiscal powers were shackled from another direction: the city's "upper house," the board of estimate, may do almost as it pleases with his budget and the mayor has no veto there.

Cincinnati: In 1924, civic reformers, now called the Charter party, swept out the corrupt administration of Boss Rud K. Hynica and adopted a package of related reforms — the city-manager plan with a nine-man council elected at large on a nonpartisan ballot by proportional representation. Under the plan, the council elects the mayor, who, with the council's approval, appoints the city manager and the city's boards and commissions. The manager, in turn, picks his department heads and is responsible for administration.

The Philadelphia commissioners, at least half sold on the beauties of the council-manager plan, decided to visit Cincinnati to take a first-hand look at a successful city-manager city. They spent a day in the city, and consulted closely with Charles Taft and other Cincinnati officials. Finally, the Philadelphians asked Taft if he would recommend the manager plan for a city of two million people — i.e., as large as Phila-delphia. "No," he said flatly.

"When the Lord himself said he didn't want those ten command-ments spread elsewhere," an ex-commissioner observes, "that was the death knell."

One reason the manager plan has worked admirably in Cincinnati is that the Charter party—which first sponsored the system—is a fairly well-organized political party, and it has been helped considerably at the polls by proportional representation. The Charterites, a fusion of independent Republicans and Democrats, have been able to beat off the regular Republican machine at election time and thus maintain a majority—or at least a strong minority—on the council. (The city, although technically nonpartisan in municipal elections, has local political parties, and the voters generally know who the parties' can-didates are.)

In other cities, however, the council-manager form of government revealed a significant flaw: it failed to produce political leadership on which responsibility for the city government could be pinned. The very large cities, with all their complex needs and challenges, require an elected chief executive to serve as the center of political leadership and responsibility, and to provide policy guidance and planning.

The new Philadelphia charter, overwhelmingly approved in 1951, incorporated the elements of New York's "strong-mayor" plan with the significant omission of the board of estimate and with some very im-portant additions. Most notably, the mayor's office was strengthened by permitting him to appoint a managing director, who, with the mayor's approval, appoints most of the city's department heads and is respon-sible to the mayor for over-all administration. The idea was to relieve the chief executive of routine administrative chores, and thus give him more time for the important job of hammering out policy.

Presumably, the professionalization of his staff is a great help to the mayor in his efforts to provide leadership for the city. Increasingly, his appointed department heads are top specialists in their fields. The public-health commissioner, in vivid contrast even to twenty years ago, is a Doctor of Public Health, or at least an M.D. The public-works and sanitary commissioners are graduate engineers. Almost always, the men serving as division and bureau chiefs under the executive staff are career civil-service officers. The trend to professionalism is at high tide in Dallas, San Antonio, Cincinnati, and Kansas City—all manager cities. But it is also far advanced in the very big cities, where the need for ex-pertise is great. Mayor Wagner's first city administrator (New York's version of the general-manager idea) was Luther Gulick, perhaps the country's foremost specialist in municipal affairs. In Chicago, reformers were incredulous when Richard Daley announced on taking office: "I'm going to listen to the professors." He has done so, and he has also hired some of them. His city controller and guard of its moneybags, for example, is Carl Chatters, onetime executive director of the Municipal Finance Officers Association, and a distinguished public servant.

Almost everywhere, in fact, only one big soft spot seems to remain — the police department. There are some exceptions. One is Cincinnati. Another is Milwaukee: its police department is one of the few in the country where organized crime has never acquired a foothold, and the city's policemen, long free from political taint, are professional from the top down. But in most big cities the gambling fix is still a problem, and corruption appears to be endemic — in spite of many top-notch police commissioners.

On the whole, however, the mayor — and the city — has profited from this administration by specialists. To many a big-city government, hard pressed to find money to maintain essential services, much less to provide new ones, the presence of a band of top professionals at City Hall has probably meant the difference between success and failure in operating the big service machine.

But this aspect of "good government" has its drawbacks too. "The next big concern for the big city electorates," says Columbia University political scientist Wallace Sayre, "is how to curb the bureaucrats, how to keep the experts under control, how to keep them from making all the decisions."

The mayor can hire and fire his appointed experts. Controlling the civil servants beneath them, however, is something else again. In Newark, Mayor Leo Carlin was recently confronted with a typical case of a bureaucracy trying to extend its control over a city government. Carlin, under his city's "strong mayor" charter, adopted in 1954, has the right to hire and fire his aides with the council's consent. The New Jersey Civil Service Commission, which gives the examinations for and acts as the guardian of all "classified" city employees, challenged the mayor's right in the case of his deputy: it attempted to bring the deputy mayor's job under civil service, claiming the post was within its jurisdiction under the wording of the state law. The city rejected the claim, and the commission seems to have backed down. If the civil service is able to extend its authority to city officials as well as employees, many people feel, it will be able to hamper, if not control, city government and policy making in the same way that the French civil service controls much of the government of France.

The municipal civil-service system, ordinarily, is administered by a semi-independent commission whose members are appointed for fixed terms. Once in office, they have wide latitude in running their show. In addition to setting up and conducting the examinations, they see to it that employees are dismissed only for "cause," usually after trial by the commission. The system, as a result, is fairly "tight" in most big cities — i.e., the vast majority of city employees are hired through civil-service channels and enjoy full job security. But tightness, whatever merit it once had in discouraging politically motivated hirings and firings, can make for considerable inefficiency. The entrenched bureaucrats, protected by tenure, tend to develop a clique feeling among themselves, and the clique is opposed to all change—except in the direction of greater rigidity.

The mayor may try to solve this problem by exerting greater executive control over the civil-service commission, and by raising wage scales to attract higher-caliber civil servants. Each course is difficult, the first perhaps more than the second. The commissions were originally set up as semi-autonomous agencies to "take them out of politics." The do-gooders feared—with great justification a half-century ago, with much less justification now—that if the commission was made directly responsible to the chief executive, he might use his influence over the commissioners to get patronage jobs for his followers, and the fear persists. For the mayor intent on providing aggressive, efficient government, the net effect is to put him at a competitive disadvantage in hiring new, better-qualified people, and at an institutional disadvantage if he wishes to clear some of the tenured deadwood out of the hall.

Chapter IX

Metropolitan Problems

The United States has had three basic population patterns since its origins. At the time of its inception a large majority of the citizens lived in the rural areas. It was not until 1920 that a majority of the American people lived in urban areas and even then a significant portion lived in small towns of less than 5000. However, by 1950 over half of the population lived in metropolitan areas (generally defined as a central city of 50,000 and its outlying areas).

The transformation from an urban to a metropolitan society entailed more than a mere growth in size. The growth of metropolitan areas is a challenge to the traditional concepts and structures of government. Whereas cities are legal creations of state governments, metropolitan areas are not. The metropolitan area sprawls well beyond the boundaries of the central city and may include several cities, counties, or states. A few metropolitan areas such as Detroit and El Paso even extend into foreign countries.

The settlement pattern of many metropolitan areas is outlined by Raymond Vernon in "The Economics and Finances of the Large Metropolis." At the center is the core city, which contains the earlier mercantile section and is populated by the lower-income groups, the jobless, the destitute, and the older citizens. The core city faces an almost insurmountable problem created by the departure of its taxpaying, middle-income citizens to the suburbs which surround the city. Despite the loss of a significant portion of its major taxpayers, the core city must maintain its facilities and quite often it must build streets for the suburbanites commuting to work. It is also possible that the core city will lose some of its industry and business to the newer suburban areas.

The suburban areas are not without problems, however. Not all suburban areas are upper- or middle-income, and the lower-income areas can deteriorate into slum areas. Even in the middle-income suburban areas the problems are monumental. First, most suburban areas are poorly planned and poorly built. Built outside the protective zoning ordinances of the city, provisions for water, sewage, streets, and education are inadequate for the high population density that most areas acquire. After a few years the suburban area may be in the same financial plight as its core city.

Most proposed solutions to the metropolitan problem place major emphasis on the problems of the core city. For example, Bernard Weissbourd asks "Are Cities Obsolete?" and implies that they are unless they are able to get financial relief. He argues that the federal government has a responsibility to restore the core cities because federal loans are largely responsible for creating suburbia. (Without loans from the Veterans Administration and the Federal Housing Administration, the rapid development of suburbia and the concurrent degradation of the central city would not have been possible.) Therefore, federal planning and resources should be used to rebuild the cities.

The problems of a large metropolitan area are distinctly different from those of a small city or even a small metropolitan area. Daniel R. Grant's study of "Urban and Suburban Nashville" examines the structure and problems of a middle-sized metropolitan area. The Nashville metropolitan area has a comparatively simple jurisdictional problem since it is confined to one county. The problem is to establish an adequate governmental power for the area by combining the powers of the city and the county. One of the major factors in the solution of any metropolitan problem is the willingness of the state government to make the necessary changes in the governmental structure. Professor Grant highlights this problem by recounting the activities of city and county state legislators. In 1962 (after the article was written) Nashville was able to solve many of its jurisdictional problems by consolidating the city and county governments.

Consolidation may be achieved in many of the developing metropolitan areas but often is not possible in the larger, established areas. Many metropolitan areas contain several towns or cities that are determined to maintain their separate status, or the area may include several counties or even extend into other states. Because of the pattern of development the government of the core city cannot legally, politically, or economically provide the services needed by all of the citizens in the metropolitan area. One solution is the utilization of the powers of the county to solve the problems, as is being done in Los Angeles. Because of excessive fluidity and tremendous growth of population, Los Angeles county is having to face and solve major problems at a faster pace than most cities. Therefore, Richard A. Smith suggests Los Angeles may serve as a "prototype of supercity."

Robert C. Wood in "Metropolitan Government, 1975: An Extrapolation of Trends" suggests that the future of the metropolitan areas is not as bleak as it has appeared to many commentators. While it is true that the rapid growth of the suburbs has caused a population, industrial, and revenue drain for the core cities, these cities have survived. Several factors have contributed to reduce the effects of suburbanization. The rising level of income has made it possible to tax at a higher rate, since higher income levels can be taxed at an increased rate without intolerable effects of taxation at the subsistence level. Also, the increasing value of white-collar occupations has partially offset the loss of industry; income taxes collected at the place of employment have helped to defray the cost of providing services for commuters.

The state governments are assisting the cities in a variety of financial and jurisdictional ways. State governments have begun to create special governmental districts for entire metropolitan areas. In some cases this has allowed the cities to evade some of the legal limits on indebtedness. The states are also making financial contributions to the cities in the form of grants-in-aid or shared taxes.

Despite the progress that is being made, many problems remain for the metropolitan areas. Many states are unable or unwilling to make the necessary financial contributions to cities. Equally important, many of the jurisdictional problems of the metropolitan area cannot be solved by the states because the areas extend into other states. Robert H. Connery and Richard Leach argue forcefully in "The Case for Federal Action" that because of the interstate and international nature of many metropolitan areas, the federal government will have a major role in the future development of these areas.

THE ECONOMICS AND FINANCES
OF THE LARGE METROPOLIS

RAYMOND VERNON

Raymond Vernon is professor of international trade and investment, Harvard University, and has served as director of the New York Metropolitan Region Study. His books include *Anatomy of a Metropolis* (1959) and *Metropolis, 1985* (1960).

I take it for granted that my fellow contributors employed in this joint exploration of the life of the metropolis look for the continued growth of giant urban clusters in this country, expanding in population at rates at least as fast as — perhaps faster than — the nation's total population growth. I assume too that there is very little disagreement on the

George Braziller, Inc.—from *The Future Metropolis*, ed. Lloyd Rodwin, pp. 43-63; reprinted with the permission of the publisher. Copyright © 1960 by the American Academy of Arts and Sciences. Reprinted by permission of Constable Publishers, London.

general pattern of that growth. I envisage that the really big growth within these oversized metropolitan complexes will take place outside of the old cities which usually lie at the core of these clusters; that it will be primarily a suburban expansion, spreading thinly over the landscape and using up large quantities of land which not so long ago were cow pastures and cornfields. This general pattern of growth suggests that as a nation we are facing the exacerbation of some old problems, such as transportation, and some new ones as well. To get a more solid sense of what these problems are, however, one has to know a little more about the likely character of urban development.

Growth in the Urban Complex

No one needs to be told any longer that the great growth of population in the suburbs surrounding our crowded cities has been speeded by the passenger car and truck, coupled with rapidly rising living standards. Despite all the dicussion about the richness of city living and the rewards of propinquity, most of us who are a part of the western culture want to have our cake and eat it too; we want to be near the city, not in it. And we seem willing to pay the price of suburban living, including the cost of transporting ourselves to and from the city in order to partake of its economic and cultural opportunities.

Some drift into the city after a taste of suburban life; their suburban neighbors have proved dull and intrusive, or their lawns have proved a malevolent tyrant. But all the available statistics, such as they are, suggest that this is distinctly a minority reaction, more typical of the intellectuals who write about the metropolis than of their fellow mortals. Most people who have any choice in the matter seem to take to the suburbs with a minimum of grousing, enjoying the security of living among their peers and the insulation from such untouchable city dwellers as Negroes, Mexicans, hillbillies, and Puerto Ricans.

Nor does the future demographic pattern suggest a very different set of preferences in the future for those who have a choice. Over the next two or three decades, there will be more growth at the two tail ends of the demographic curve than in the middle — the greatest growth will be among the very young and the rather old. There has been consider-able wistful speculation that the increase among the aged will lay the basis for a revived city growth. The theory is, of course, that older people will find their suburban homes and their automobile-oriented travel patterns to be a heavy burden, and that they will react by moving to the city.

But it is chimerical to suppose that any such move could be the basis for a general city revival. For one thing, the numbers involved are not all that large. For another, the cost of capturing space near the part of the city that really matters — near the cultural and business centers —

is prohibitively high and promises to remain so; just why, we shall make clear a bit later on. Finally, many in the older group have obvious alternatives to a return to the city and seem already to be exploiting those alternatives. One is to migrate to more pastoral settings. Now that the airplane makes travel fast and easy, and the decision to migrate does not involve the final separation from children and grandchildren, this would seem to be an attractive alternative for older people. The scraps of evidence we have been able to collect show a net exodus of older people out of metropolitan areas since 1940, and an even larger net exodus out of the central city portions of these areas. The other alternative for the aging suburban dweller is to give up his house for a suburban apartment located in the neighborhood where he has lived. This, at least, keeps him closer to the social structure which he knows and often keeps him closer to his grown children and grandchildren as well. For most, these are much more tangible advantages than those which city life has to offer.

True, some will return to the city, drawn back by the increasing difficulty of finding an "exclusive" suburb within tolerable commuting distance from a job in the city center. But these will be an elite group, able to pay for precious space close by the central district or for some strategic and attractive location a few minutes away by car. For this group, the endless neighborhoods of deteriorating middle-rent and low-rent housing which ring large city centers in a belt many miles deep would not be an acceptable alternative to the remote suburb.

The demographic future of the big cities inside our growing metropolitan areas is affected by still another force. The phenomenon of slum crowding is much more complex than some of its popular descriptions would allow—and by some measures, much less extensive. Slum crowding can be thought of as a phase in the growth cycle of an aging city neighborhood. Just before it appears, the neighborhood commonly is going through a period of population decline; the middle-income inhabitants of the slums-to-be are growing old, are being left behind by their grown-up children, and are finding their dwelling places increasingly unsuited for the washing machines, automobiles, and other possessions which a rising income and changing technology have made possible. Accordingly, their row houses and apartments grow ripe for downgrading and for higher densities. As the newest untrained outlanders appear in the city to join the labor force—green, ignorant of housing conditions, uncertain of their job future—they fill the downgraded properties, crowding them far beyond the densities for which they were designed. Because these newly arrived outlanders are usually quite young, they quickly add to their numbers with the arrival of children.

The history of the older portions of our big cities, however, indicates that this overcrowding phase eventually comes to an end. In a repetition of the middle-income cycle preceding it, the low-income family ages; the children and the boarders depart for newer neighborhoods; the seed couple often remains behind in the old, worn quarters, spreading out in some of the space which once they shared with children and boarders. Population declines, therefore, have come to be endemic in the older portions of most large American cities. Soon, this will be the dominant demographic characteristic of many such cities.

Enough about population trends for the moment. What about jobs? We have already implied two things about the distribution of jobs, two things which seem to run at cross purposes. In the first place, the automobile and the truck have extended the radius of the metropolitan area, not only for homes, but also for jobs. A grocery distributor no longer needs to be located alongside a river dock or at a rail head in order to receive his supplies; and he can distribute to retailers within a forty-mile radius rather than a five-mile radius if he chooses. On similar lines, a mill no longer need locate within walking distance of a trolley line in order to recruit its labor; it can count on workers' driving twenty or thirty miles to their jobs. So most manufacturing and distributing activities have taken advantage of the new-found freedom by spreading out on the land, exploiting all of the cost advantage of spacious sites. The result has been that manufacturing and distributing jobs have been falling off in the older portions of the old cities, while growing at a rapid clip practically everywhere else in metropolitan areas, particularly in the open spaces.

There is a major slice of economic activity—several slices, in fact— which have responded rather differently to their new-found transportation freedom. Many of these have a need which speedy transportation does not really satisfy; this is the need for constant face-to-face communication with a variety of other entities outside the firm. Elite decision makers of the big central offices usually want to be near a complex of lawyers, bankers, advertising agencies, accountants, and management advisers in order to tap their expertise on short notice. Traders in the volatile money markets want to be near others like them, continuously to swap rumors, ferret out information, and provide mutual reassurance. Sellers of unstandardized products want to be near one another to share the attention of visiting buyers. And so on.

Groups such as these have preferred to remain tightly clustered in the central business districts of the old cities and to grow there. If they have changed their locational preferences at all, it has been a complex change. In some cases, enterprises have reorganized themselves to retain the functions with communication needs in the central business district while relocating the repetitive, routine, standardized functions elsewhere; the sales offices of the garment industries, for instance, have clung to the city sales districts, while the sewing of the garments has moved off. In other cases, offices located in the central business district of one city have moved to the office center of another city, as the growth of air travel or other considerations have changed the relative attractions of the competing cities.

The compulsion of activities of this sort has been to cluster with related enterprises, in order to minimize communication time and cost. It is true, therefore, that if clusters such as these began to develop afresh today, no one could be sure exactly where they would grow. But they began in the downtown portions of the old cities a century or more ago, pinned there by such anachronistic factors as the location of the railroad termini and the limited supply of literate clerks. Once located, their very existence was a powerful lodestone for added growth.

These communication-oriented activities are a fast-growing part of the nation's economy. Their growth—at least their growth as measured by employment and space-occupying criteria—could be stunted, of course. Technological advances in office equipment will hold down office growth somewhat. And some really startling advances in the media of communication—something better and cheaper than closed-circuit television—might change the need for clustering and cause the establishments to scatter. But we are inclined to believe that the largest cities of the country will continue to see modest growth in these activities in their downtown areas.

What of the city areas outside of "downtown"? What of the remaining 90 per cent or so of big-city space which falls outside the central business districts—in residential neighborhoods, industrial enclaves, and the like? The neighborhoods that are strait-jacketed by street grids laid out for an earlier era and encumbered by obsolescent structures have little to offer the private industrial developer which he could not acquire more readily in spaces farther out. Accordingly, such neighborhoods are showing the signs of prospective loss. Some are already losing. Nor are trends of this sort limited to neighborhoods in the older central cities. They are beginning to appear in suburban cities as well, wherever the settlement pattern was already fixed in the pre-automobile age.

One way of summing up the story is this: the new suburbs of the giant metropolitan areas are growing fast and promise to continue their growth in population and jobs, using the land lavishly as they develop. The central business districts at the very core of the large metropolitan areas have elements of vitality which could have the effect of increasing—or at any rate upgrading—their jobs and their resident populations. In between the central business districts and the new suburbs, however, the likely predominant pattern is one of a thinning out and aging of the populations, a continued deterioration of the physical plant, and a stagnation or decline of the job market.

Balancing Income with Outgo

The pattern of change we envisage suggests various things for the future of the old cities inside the urban mass. Holding transportation and housing needs aside for the moment—we shall discuss them later on—it seems evident that the current problems will probably grow more acute.

It is true that, as the residents of these cities grow older and as their numbers shrink, some of the cities' problems may ease off. The cost of opening up new neighborhoods, including the investment in streets, sewers, water mains, and schools, is unlikely to figure so prominently in future budgets. There will be the renewal of existing plants to deal with, of course, but this is a deferrable expense—deferrable in the sense that a failure to renew is unlikely to generate the same kind of acute political response among city voters that the total absence of a municipal facility might generate.

But as the shrinkage in city populations occurs, there may be limits on the extent to which the cities can cut back on their existing municipal facilities. If our prognosis is right, the population decline we foresee will be the result of a thinning-out process, that is, a decline in the size of the average family occupying a dwelling unit. We do not envisage the wholesale abandonment of neighborhoods and the rapid rise of vacancies in tenements and new houses. Instead, older people will simply use more space per head.

This pattern of population decline means that there will be obstacles in the way of reducing police or fire protection, closing off libraries or schools, shutting down water mains, or blocking off streets. Here and there, such measures may be possible. By and large, however, it may not be possible to reduce the facilities *pari passu* with the population they serve.

On top of this, as the city population ages, the proportion of the population which is unemployable or in poor health will probably rise a little; it may even be that the absolute number of such people, as well as the proportion, will rise. Accordingly, quite apart from the pressures produced by constantly rising professional and social standards in the welfare field, the demand for welfare services may go up in the old cities.

Pressures of this sort are hardly novel. The responses of the cities to these pressures have taken a number of forms. One, of course, has been to raise the real property tax rate or to stiffen assessment standards so that the tax yields could be increased. But the real property tax, as so many experts have observed, cannot be pushed forever upward. The tax is so brutally visible and hits the taxpayer with so direct an impact that any proposal for an increase almost automatically faces impassioned opposition. Besides, as the tax yields rise, problems of equity become more severe, and the city's fear of losing business to the suburbs grows apace. Accordingly, another response of the cities to the need for more revenue has been to impose new taxes in the form of sales and payroll levies.

This kind of response has made a good deal of sense, given the changing function of the old cities. As they have come to specialize in trade and office work and to lose ground in manufacturing, the amount of real property occupied by any enterprise has become a poorer index of its ability to pay. The shift from a real property tax to a levy on money flows such as a sales tax or a payroll tax, therefore, has probably established a somewhat closer correspondence between ability and liability among taxpayers in the cities.

Another factor probably supports the wisdom of the shift for the older cities. Good tax strategy demands that the city should avoid taxing economic entities which are in a position to respond by fleeing the jurisdiction; or to turn the proposition around, that the city concentrate its taxes on economic entities which have the least choice about remaining in the city. Of all the various types of economic activity, manufacturing establishments with heavy real property commitments typically rank among those with the weakest ties to the city; there are occasional exceptions, of course, such as newspaper plants and bakeries, but by and large the generalization seems valid. At the same time, wholesale and retail sales outlets appear to have the least choice in finding an alternative location outside the city. Once more, we must not overlook the seeming exceptions, such as department stores, but neither must we exaggerate the degree of locational choice of such outlets nor their relatively minor importance as a proportion of the total sales in most cities. We are inclined to suspect, therefore, that the disposition of big cities will be to make more and more urgent demands on state legislatures for the authority to impose sales taxes and payroll taxes and that the use of such taxes by big cities will increase with time.

The fiscal problems of the raw suburbs are quite different, of course, from those of the central cities. From a septic-tank and artesian-well civilization, sleepy semi-rural communities on the edge of an urban mass have suddenly been projected into the nightmare of financing water mains, sewage lines, new schools, professional fire companies, and so on—and all in the briefest span of time. Their problems in this regard have been worse than that which the older cities had experienced in the course of their growth. The older cities, by and large, covered much more territory than the little new communities; hence, while growth was occurring at the edges of the cities, there were settled neighborhoods inside the city boundaries to help finance their growth. Small suburban communities hit by the growth tornado, however, encompass no such variety of neighborhoods; when they are overrun by progress, they are often totally involved in the phenomenon.

These raw communities have other problems which make their lot especially hard. Once they are hit by urban growth, the facilities they are expected to provide are not the rough-and-ready makeshifts with which cities could satisfy their constituents half a century ago. All at once, they are expected to provide municipal facilities which are in accord with the expectations of an urban society in the mid-twentieth century. Worse still, they are expected to provide these urban facilities to a taxpaying group which persists in living in a dispersed pattern, 5,000 or so to the square mile instead of the 100,000 or so in the old cities. Roads, water mains, and fire-fighting apparatus must be provided to suit urban appetites in non-urban surroundings. Little wonder that the resulting fiscal needs are high.

But all the urban world is not divided simply between the old central cities and the new suburbs. There are two other sectors of the urban structure which need mentioning. One of these is the older suburban cities, like Camden, Evanston, and Newark. Demographically, many of these cities are going through a phase not unlike that of the central cities. Accordingly, the prospective fiscal problems of these older suburban cities bear many similarities to those of the central cities —but with some differences. The suburban cities have much less expectation of corralling and holding communication-oriented activities of the sort that cluster in the central cities; on the contrary, their competition for a place in the economic sun is principally with the shopping centers and highway stores of an automobile age, and their chance for success in the competition in general is quite low. As a result, unlike the central cities, these suburban cities dare not resort to such taxes as sales or payroll levies, except at the risk of driving out business. Even if they could impose such taxes with impunity, most of them are not large enough to administer these kinds of taxes with the sophisticated expertise that they demand.

We must not leave the impression, however, that the whole of the urban world is in desperate fiscal straits. For there is another sector still —our fourth and final one—which is suffering no particular fiscal pain. In most large metropolitan areas, we find a comparatively large group of mature, well-established suburban communities, growing moderately if at all, well equipped with schools and other municipal facilities, well able to meet their fiscal obligations. We hear little from this group, except for some occasional grousing as the tax rate goes up to match municipal salary increases. But the grousing is usually subdued, since in general the tax increases in communities of this sort probably have not been as large as the income growth of their inhabitants. Despite the comparatively unsung existence of this sector, there are indications that it is a not inconsiderable proportion of the larger metropolitan community.

It is not hard to foresee the nature of the tax struggle that is shaping up. By one device or another, the hard-pressed cities and raw suburban towns will be looking for ways to tap the tax resources of their comparatively prosperous neighbors. The devices will vary as they have in the past, depending in part on pure chance, local custom, and local law. But two popular devices will surely be used in increasing degree: the use of the special district, set up to merge the school system or other municipal service of hard-pressed areas with those of their less pressured neighbors; and the use of higher state taxes and larger state subsidies to localities, granted in support of some specific service. These devices may well miscarry at times, especially the state subsidy technique. That is to say, the system may in the end provide the largest subsidies to these areas that seem to need them least, as the interests of the rural areas and the well-to-do communities of the state struggle with those of the hard-pressed cities and raw suburbs over the division of the spoils. But more resort to the state approach seems altogether likely.

One is tempted at times to remove the lead weights of reality from his earthbound feet and to ask what other solution for local fiscal problems might be conceived. The obvious one, apart from leveling the differences in tax burdens and services through state-aid and special-district devices, is to create a new level of general government at the metropolitan level, with powers to tax and spend supplementary to or in lieu of the localities below. Pioneer efforts of this sort in the United States have run up against stony resistance. Whatever the expert may think of the desperate need for innovation in government, the failures of existing government are not so obvious, as seen through the eyes of the average urban dweller, as to justify major surgery. Besides, moves of this sort are conceived to fly in the face of the American tradition of local self-government; they raise specters for the well-placed communities of public services dragged down to mediocre levels; and so on. We see little future for this approach. But some of what it would accomplish will be achieved less obviously by other means.

Rails and Rubber

Our picture of the future development of the metropolis, if it should come to pass, carries with it some fairly explicit implications about the future of passenger transporation within the great metropolitan areas of the country.

No one needs to be told that the problem of moving people daily from their homes to their jobs constitutes one of the major headaches of many metropolitan areas. There are two distinguishable kinds of problems. One is that of physical facilities: though the number of jobs in central cities seems hardly to be growing, nevertheless the roads, bridges, tunnels, and parking areas—even the suburban trains and subway facilities—simply seem too limited for the traffic that they carry. The other is a problem of finances: though the mass transit suburban trains and subways seem well filled, somehow the companies that own them seem constantly on the verge of bankruptcy. These are some provoking paradoxes that demand understanding.

The reasons for the overburdening of the roads, highways, and parking areas are the most transparent part of the puzzle. As people have dispersed outward on the land, far from the suburban railway stations and the city subways, the relative attractiveness of commuting by automobile has grown. The first stage of the commuting journey, in any case, has demanded the use of a car; and once ensconced behind a wheel, one often thinks it sensible to make the whole journey by car. The propensity for car travel has been increased, of course, by the rise in car ownership—an inevitable concomitant of dispersed suburban living.

Another trend—a less obvious trend of the whole—has added to the peak flows of traffic between suburb and central city. This is the rise of "reverse commuting," that is, the increased use of daily car pools bearing the lower-income residents of the central cities outward to their jobs in warehouses, factories, and retail stores dispersed through the suburban areas. Here, too, the need to make the final leg of the journey by some form of automotive conveyance or on foot has often prodded the commuter into making the whole trip by automobile.

All this increased hauling of wage earners across the face of the metropolis, it should be noted, would take place even without any assumption about job increases in the central city. The dispersal of medium-income and high-income families from the city center and the dispersal of low-income jobs from the center are all that is needed to generate the increased flows.

While the suburban rail facilities have been losing some of their customers to the highways, at the same time they have been gaining others. The outward trek of homes from the central cities has carried many commuters outside of the range of central city trolley, subway, and bus systems into the orbit of the suburban rails. Most of the rails, therefore, have not lacked for rush-hour business.

What they have lost is the off-hour and week-end trade. The suburban housewife who takes the 10:45 into the central city for a day of shopping downtown and the suburban couple who take the 7:32 for an evening at the theater are a vanishing species. Off-hour and week-end traffic are now almost entirely in the province of the highway. For the railroads, this has been a cruel blow. Off-peak business had been the bread and butter of the rail system, since it could be accommodated without added manpower or equipment. The principal business left to the rails, therefore—the peak-hour business—has been of the kind which is least profitable.

At the same time, the suburban railroads have had other problems. Featherbedding practices plus pervasive government regulation have rocked these institutions into a state of technological moribundity. Few rail systems have had the will or the means to meet the challenge of changing transportation needs. The possibilities of pruning labor costs through mechanization have barely been scratched, partly because the rails have been unsure whether the unions would tolerate the necessary changes. The possibilities of devising coordinated mass transit systems which could capture some of the reverse commuting business or could serve the needs of commuters traveling circumferentially between different suburbs have also been neglected. If such innovations could be developed on paper, as they no doubt can, there is still the problem of obtaining the needed governmental action and the problem of gaining approval for a system of rates which would return the investment. Facing such problems, the long-run strategy of many suburban railroads has been to pull out of the passenger business as rapidly as possible.

The problems of subways and surface cars in the big cities have been of a somewhat different sort. Few of these systems have increased their business in recent years, as measured by paid trips; many have actually been losing ground by such a yardstick. In New York City, for instance, the decline has been in evidence for several decades. Once again, however, the lucrative off-peak business has fallen off faster than the rush-hour traffic. To add to the difficulties of these systems, the business that remains has consisted more and more of long-haul trips between the edges of the city and the very center, a fact which puts a particularly heavy strain on any system with a flat fare. Finally, the business at some termini in the central city—those located in the office district—has grown in some cases as the central city's jobs have tended to become more and more specialized in office work. To those using the subway system, therefore, the facilities sometimes seem progressively overcrowded and inadequate, even though the system as a whole may be operating well under capacity.

One line of remedial action suggested with increasing frequency by city planners has been to alter the relative prices of transportation services. It has been assumed that if somehow the use of the automobile could be made more expensive relative to the rail, this might check the shift from rail to rubber. To achieve this result, a variety of proposals have been made. One approach has been to introduce or increase public subsidies for mass transit facilities. Another has been to raise the tolls on bridges and tunnels and increase the fees on central city parking. Various difficulties have hobbled these approaches, however.

When subsidies were proposed, the first hurdle—not the only one, by any means—has been the problem of finding the money. Where raising the cost to the motorist has been proposed, it has evoked the fear that prospective commuters to the central city might respond, not by turning back to the use of the rail, but by avoiding the central city altogether. The response of some shoppers could well be to shop more in the suburbs and less in the central city. And other kinds of business might be lost to the central city as well.

Another difficulty is one which has arisen out of the institutional structure of the entities operating the subways, railroads, bridges, tunnels, and parking areas. In many metropolitan areas, the ownership of these competing or complementary facilities is vested in a maze of public and private bodies. The suburban railroads ordinarily are privately owned, though subject to federal, state, and local regulations. The subways, surface lines, and buses are sometimes private, sometimes public; when public they are sometimes run by a division of general government, sometimes by an independent authority. The tunnels and bridges are almost invariably public, usually under the control of a separate authority and insulated from the influence which the electorate might bring to bear. The notion of coordinating these systems has rarely been explicitly considered. Where it has, however, one obvious problem has arisen at once: those entities that are solvent want to avoid entangling alliances with those that are not. In some areas, this has meant that agencies which purvey services to the motorist are careful to steer clear of those responsible for the operation of mass transit facilities. What is more, their desire to do so is often supported by a public conviction that somehow this separation is "sound business."

The difficulties do not end here, however. Still another obstacle to a coordinated metropolitan transport policy derives from the fact that the central city and the suburban cities and towns see themselves—quite rightly—as rivals in the great game of attracting business and taxes. One may say that this is a short-sighted view—that the deterioration of a metropolitan area's means of internal circulation will eventually damage all its parts. But, unhappily, it is also true that the *improvement* of a metropolitan area's means of internal circulation may damage some of its parts as well. And where some area sees itself as the prospective victim of a metropolitan improvement, one can hardly expect it to participate in the change with demur. So it is that we find some suburban cities, wisely or otherwise, resisting the development of highways which bypass their downtown shopping districts.

There is no doubt that comprehensive regional approaches to the transportation problem could provide better transportation than the existing fragmented system. The facilities for commuter travel are so closely complementary that their pooled use opens up vistas now excluded by organizational and political boundaries. In some measure, such approaches will probably develop. It may not be difficult, for instance, to pool a number of rail lines in different jurisdictions if all of them are losing money. But the pooling of vehicular facilities with rail facilities will prove a harder nut to crack. Here, the built-in jurisdictional hurdles seem so high as to be nearly insurmountable.

What we envisage, therefore, is primarily a series of palliatives within the mass transit field. Some states show signs of getting into the problem, for instance, by providing help in meeting the capital needs of the mass transit facilities and by enacting measures to encourage local tax abatement for such facilities. It is not farfetched to suppose that the federal government will eventually get into mass transit as well, sucked in as an inexorable consequence of its present involvement in the financing and planning of the nation's highway system. One way or another, there will be efforts to redress the balance between mass transit and the automobile. But the results promise to be slow in coming and fragmentary in their application. In fact, before such results materialize, the most pressing transportation problem inside some metropolitan areas may have changed in character. Instead of wondering how to haul people to and from the central business district with comfort and dispatch, our prime question may well be how to move people from the dispersed homes in one suburb to the dispersed plants in another.

Obsolescence and Decay

According to our argument, the private demand for space in the central business districts of the old cities may well continue fairly strong. But the private demand for space in the grey areas beyond seems weak. Here populations promise to thin out; retail trade will decline; factory jobs should stabilize or fall off in number; and no private force seems at hand with sufficient incentive to recapture such space for other uses.

The central cities and the old suburban communities are unlikely to sit by, however, as they see the populations in their grey areas decline and the streets and structures grow old and outdated. They will try to arrest the rot as they have been trying in the past. And they will succeed in some measure, just as they have in the past. All told, these efforts at rejuvenation—many of them the efforts of private civic bodies rather than exclusively those of governments—have had a visible impact.

While acknowledging the impact of these efforts and the truly heroic contributions of some groups and individuals in bringing them about, however, one must also soberly recognize their limitations and appraise their future scope.

These efforts have produced their most spectacular successes in or near the central business districts of the old cities. This means two things: first, the impact of these successes upon our collective consciousness has been many times larger than the areas involved—many times larger than the impression we would glean as we observed the total urban mass from a helicopter, for instance. Second, the efforts at rehabilitation have been made precisely in those sections of the city where, as we indicated earlier, a real private demand for space has existed; these civic and governmental efforts have been floating with the currents of the private real estate market, not bucking them.

Every technique so far devised for recapturing the obsolete portions of old cities where no such private demand exists has been breathtakingly costly to the public purse. The cost of recapturing an acre of old buildings in the built-up grey areas of old cities of our metropolitan areas commonly runs over $500,000, though old suburban cities have sometimes been known to recapture such sites at a price as low as $100,000. Once the expenditure is made, all that society has is a leveled site. A new suburban site suitably supplied with roads and utilities and close enough for most purposes to an urban center usually can be had for $15,000 or $25,000 an acre. At a cost of, say, $160,000,000 per square mile, we are bound soberly to ask how many square miles of rotted urban streets and structures the public authorities are likely to raze.

The bulldozer is not the only means for reconverting an urban environment, however. There is always the possibility of urban renewal of other sorts. Old structures are sometimes sound enough to invite rebuilding; and if the rebuilding takes place all at once in an entire neighborhood, one sees hope of giving the neighborhood as a whole a new lease on life. But at what cost? Here again, the facts are a little disconcerting. The cost of remodeling, rewiring, replastering and repainting "sound" old city structures, according to some pilot projects, comes to about $3,000 per room — about as much as building a room from scratch in a modest one-family house in the suburbs. Add the cost of acquiring the city structure, and what we have is high-cost housing, not housing for middle- and low-income groups.

Cost considerations aside, however, there is another reason to doubt that urban renewal will take the form of a vast subsidized bull-dozing and rebuilding of cities in new dwelling units for medium-income and low-income families. As far as middle-income families are concerned, there is nothing in our analysis to support the notion that their demand for suitable housing in the grey areas is really very large; certainly, the prospective location of jobs in metropolitan areas and the present and prospective structure of social values in American life offer no promise on this score. And as for low-income families, if our analysis is right, their demand for dwelling units in the grey areas may actually decline. The families dependent on the relatively low-income jobs in retail trade and consumer services, in goods handling, and in unskilled factory operations will find declining opportunities in the city and increasing ones outside; their disposition will be — indeed, it already is — to follow the jobs by finding quarters in the older sections of suburban cities, even if this requires the overcrowding of such quarters.

Two *caveats* to these sweeping propositions must be made at once. One is the observation that a ready market does exist at this very moment for a considerable added amount of subsidized low-rent or medium-rent housing in the grey areas of many of our central cities. But we would guess that the size of this unsatisfied demand, at least for housing located in the grey areas well removed from the central business district, is not expanding but shrinking. Our second qualification has to do with the inevitability of the shrinkage. Symbols such as the home in the suburb can probably be changed by massive psychic and physical intervention. A giant garden city in the middle Bronx—so vast as to constitute a new neighborhood socially segregated from the denizens of the obsolescent structures about it—might conceivably find takers, especially if it were being reproduced with suitable fanfare many times over throughout America. But the intervention would have to be much larger in scope and far fresher in concept than anything so far seriously proposed.

It is safer to assume that the pattern of urban renewal will be shaped by events more than it will shape those events. In the great central cities, the thinning out of populations in the grey areas will create the possibility of recapturing some open space, and this will no doubt be done. The old suburban cities may find more need for added low-cost public housing than the central cities. But their ability to convert that need into an operating public program may not be as great as the central cities', simply because the size of a suburban city is sometimes not sufficient to allow it to acquire the skilled technical staff needed to plan and carry out such programs. It may be that, at this stage, the state and federal governments will assume more direct responsibility for such programs simply in order to fill the breach, or that regional authorities will be created to handle the housing problem for groups of municipalities. One way or another, the suburban cities may fill a part of their needs, but the institutional problem will be a very real one.

Of course, if urban land were to prove an acutely scarce resource at some point in the future, this picture might be very different. Then, the pressure to recapture the "underused" grey areas for living space might be so strong as to generate vast expenditures to that end. But it is one of the paradoxes of urban growth today that the increase in the supply of urban land is probably outstripping the demand. At the edges of most urban masses, farmers are shrinking their land use, on the whole, faster than developers are taking the land up. Part of the reason for this shrinkage is that farmers have been unwilling or unable to match the wage structure of the nearby urban labor market and have been encountering increasing difficulties in holding onto their hired hands. Part of it has been due to the swiftly increasing productivity of agriculture coupled with a relatively stable output. As a result, as geographers are pointing out, the amount of acreage covered with scrub forest on the edges of the great urban masses on the Eastern seaboard has been increasing in recent years, not shrinking. The deer are reappearing in large numbers, to nibble voraciously at the tender foundation plantings of the anxious suburbanite.

Eventually, of course, this will change. Urban land will become scarce again as sheer population growth fills up the empty spaces. But the land promises to grow more plentiful before it grows scarce again. And for several decades, we are likely to see suburban developments making more and more profligate use of the land.

The Total Pattern

What we foresee, on the whole, is a pattern of continued change in the large metropolitan complex not vastly different from the change recently in evidence. That we should have come to this general conclusion was perhaps inevitable. Man's favorite technique of projection has always been to extrapolate the recent past.

Seen from the viewpoint of the people who live in this urban setting of the future, the problems may not seem much more severe than they do today; indeed, some problems may seem to have been mitigated. The housing conditions of the low-income groups, if our prognosis is right, may seem no worse and may even appear to have been alleviated a little. The problem of hauling people to the central city and back will not grow so swiftly as inevitably to outrun the countermoves of the Robert Moseses of the urban world.

Still, the continued change will flush up incipient problems and exacerbate old ones to the point at which they may appear as new questions. The continued decline in the population of the old neighborhoods may appear as a fresh problem as it begins to reduce the total population of old cities. The growing financial problems of the old cities and the mass transit systems may acquire the crises label very soon, as well.

Crises commonly engender unpredictable reactions. As earthbound mortals, however, we have been bound to stress only what is predictable. On that basis, we see measures at the margin which will ease the problems to the point at which they are barely tolerable but not measures which will greatly change their character. It is on this score that the blinders with which all mortals are equipped may prove to have betrayed us.

ARE CITIES OBSOLETE?

BERNARD WEISSBOURD

Bernard Weissbourd is president of Metropolitan Structures, Inc., which specializes in the construction of apartments, hotels, and offices.

From 55,000,000 to 60,000,000 more people will be living in metropolitan areas in 1980 than were living there in 1960. How will we manage? Already our cities are decaying faster than they can be rebuilt. Parking is a universal problem. The tax base of the city is eroding as industry moves to the suburbs. A significant part of the white population is also moving to the suburbs, while the cores of our cities are filling with Negroes as the migration from the South steadily rises. The cost to the cities of trying to adjust the migrants to a new kind of existence imposes additional burdens upon the city's tax base.

Taxes are also rising in the suburbs to pay for the high cost of municipal services spread out over areas of low population density. Open space is being consumed at a terrifying rate, so that suburbs once in open country are now surrounded. Travel time to the city has multiplied as the expressways get clogged during rush hours.

Some experts do not find these problems of city decay and suburban sprawl unduly alarming. They maintain that the continuing dispersal that present trends indicate for the future is inevitable, and not necessarily undesirable. I believe the opposite.

Suburban sprawl and urban decay have not come about solely because people have made a free choice in a free enterprise market. That choice has been influenced by federal housing subsidies, which, purporting to be neutral, have in fact subsidized low-density middle-income living in the suburbs and have thereby financed the flight of white population from the city. Another factor affecting this dispersal has been our segregation practices within the city.

The lack of public discussion about the influence of housing segregation and federal housing subsidies upon urban growth patterns has been a barrier to understanding the problems of the city and suburbs and has created a feeling of hopelessness about the future of America's cities. It is my purpose here to show that it is possible to deal constructively with the problems of the metropolitan region if these important factors are not ignored.

Compared to the time span of Western civilization the modern urban complex, sometimes called megalopolis, is a new, young phenomenon. Some people are confident that a new technology of com-

From "Are Cities Obsolete?" by Bernard Weissbourd, *Saturday Review*, December 19, 1964, pp. 12-15, 66. Reprinted by permission of the author, *Saturday Review*, and the Center for Democratic Institutions.

munication and transportation will solve many of the most intractable problems of the metropolitan region and that, in time, the region of the future will emerge. One author envisions "continuous low-density urban belts stretching from Maine to Virginia, from Toronto and Pittsburgh to Milwaukee, and from Amsterdam to Frankfort and Mannheim. . . . However, there seems to be no reason why, properly organized and interlaced with greenbelts, freeways, natural reservations, and sites of historic interest, and accented vertically by occasional high-rise elements, these low-density urban regions of tomorrow should not be more livable and effective in satisfying the totality of human values than the transitional urban forms of today."

While no businessman whose offices must be located in the central business district, and no dweller in the city slums, can accept the decline of the city with equanimity, it is quite likely that if we do nothing to alter present trends the low-density urban region will be the pattern of the future. The New York metropolitan region, for example, has grown outward along major transportation arteries. Its axis of growth extended five miles in 1900, twenty-five miles in 1960, and may become fifty miles by 1985.

Acceptance of low-density regional growth implies, of course, a curtailment of mass transportation, for mass transportation works well only in highly concentrated areas where trip origins and destinations are clustered rather than widely dispersed. Conversely, the automobile, which functions so efficiently for decentralized traffic, becomes highly inefficient under conditions of intense demand. Suburban sprawl will thus bring about a further decline in mass transportation, as increasing reliance on the automobile brings further congestion to central business districts.

Each new expressway not only undercuts the market for mass transportation but accelerates the movement of industry away from the central cities. The truck and the car have given the manufacturer new opportunities to select sites in outlying areas. The movement of industry from central city locations to outlying suburban locations has created a new phenomenon — out-commuting.

Nor have the results of the federal programs for slum clearance, urban renewal, and public housing so far given any reason to expect that the trend toward city decline and low-density regional settlement will be reversed. Slums in the cities are growing faster than we can clear them. We should not expect urban renewal to work so long as there is no place for persons evacuated from the slums to live. People displaced by urban renewal and by the new expressways have created new slums.

Moreover, no one is satisfied with public housing. By rejecting all those whose incomes exceeded the prescribed limits, public housing has developed a concentration of those members of society who are not able to support themselves. Coupled with the fact that most cities have followed a deliberate program of segregation in public housing, the result has been to create in many places an environment lacking in all the positive attributes of urban life. The second generation of many public housing occupants is now coming to maturity and it is already clear that many of them will never become viable, self-supporting members of society.

Urban renewal programs aimed at aiding the central business district show greater promise of long-range success, probably because there is considerable strength in the central business district to begin with. New office buildings in the central areas of each of the metropolitan regions demonstrate that financial and commercial institutions, public utilities, newspapers and magazines, and government, together with the lawyers, accountants, stockbrokers, and others involved in serving these institutions, require a centralized location. Thus, although a sizable number of people and industries has moved out of the central city, there has been far less movement of office activities to outlying areas than speculative reports would lead us to believe.

The movement of white population to suburban areas and the concentration of Negro population in the central city will be intensified during the next fifteen years if present trends continue. Since the end of World War II the Negro population has been increasing even faster than the white population. Philip Hauser points out that the decline of the non-white death rate together with the increase in their birth rate has resulted in a rate of growth for non-whites 60 per cent higher than for whites. This great national rise is dwarfed by an even more explosive increase of non-whites in metropolitan areas. By 1990 about 2,500,000 Negroes are expected to be living in the Chicago metropolitan area, about 1,500,000 more than in 1960. The migration to the cities of rural Negroes and Southern whites and Puerto Ricans has already imposed heavy tax burdens on the city. In 1959, for example, New York City spent $50,000,000 for remedial programs for its Puerto Rican newcomers, more than it spent on all its parks, libraries, zoos, and museums in that year. In its 1959-60 budget New York City assigned 23 per cent to public hospitalization, health, and welfare and 20 per cent to education. The great growth rate of the Negro population in New York, through continued migration as well as natural increase during the next fifteen years, will tend to increase even further the city's costs for welfare, health, and education.

The picture that emerges from these forecasts is far from salutary. Low-density regional settlements in which industry and the white populations spread out over the countryside without adequate mass transportation contrast with the concentrated Negro occupancy of the center city, whose tax base has diminished by the flight of industry and whose expenses have increased for the care of its immigrants. Moreover, a growing number of the center-city population will be commuting to jobs in the suburbs while many of the suburban whites will continue to travel to jobs in a still strong central business district.

The waste of human resources and money in this increased commuting, the inability of the automobile and the expressways to handle the traffic, the changing character of the city largely occupied by a financial and business community and a segregated Negro population, the financing of public services for a migrant population in the face of disappearing industry and lost taxes, the interdependence of the financial and commercial life of the suburbs and the city—these are all reasons for not allowing present trends to continue.

But are there alternatives? As we have noted, there are many who doubt whether the trends are reversible. I believe the pattern can be changed, but first it is necessary to say something about the federal housing subsidies, because they are both one of the causes of the current suburban growth and one of the possible tools for creating a different picture for the future.

It is important to understand that dispersal of the urban population in the United States has not come about solely as a result of a free and open market. Government inducements to buy in the suburbs have been substantial and have brought about a remarkable increase in home ownership since the war. In 1957, of the total mortgage debt of $107 billion on one- to four-family non-farm homes, $47.2 billion was FHA-insured or V.A.-guaranteed. Of the balance, so-called conventional loans, a substantial portion was held by savings and loan associations. The funds involved in the federal encouragement of home ownership are thus enormous compared to the amounts involved for rental housing in the city.

The success of the federal housing program in suburbia results from the availability of mortgage funds that have not had to measure up to the usual free-market considerations of risk and competitive yield of other investments. Guarantees and insurance by the United States provide money for suburban home ownership at interest rates lower than the market over longer periods of time.

A subsidy is also involved in the activities of federal and state savings and loan associations. Because law restricts the investments of these associations largely to home mortgages, the flow of capital has been directed artificially to suburbia, and money has been made available for houses at rates lower than those that would have been available if the home owner had had to compete for the funds with other sources of investment of comparable risk. To the extent that deposits in savings and loan associations are insured by the federal government under the Federal Home Loan Bank System, capital is attracted that *must* be invested in home mortgages. The federal insurance, therefore, constitutes an indirect subsidy.

Another heavily subsidized federal housing program—public

housing—has also contributed to the condition of our cities. Public housing has been the prisoner of its opponents, who have largely determined its character. Locating public housing projects in the inner city has contributed to keeping lower-income people in the city and has strengthened the patterns of segregation, except in a few cases where careful planning has been able to achieve successfully integrated projects. One arm of the federal housing program has financed housing for middle-income families in the suburbs. The question may well be asked: "Why should not the opposite program have been adopted?"

Other federal subsidies have also had their influence. The disproportionate amount of the federal budget allotted to agriculture has helped bring about the mechanization of the farm and speeded up the migration of both Negro and white farm labor to the city. Similarly, the federal defense highway program has represented an enormous subsidy to the automobile at the expense of mass transportation. Whether these subsidies have been beneficial or detrimental is not pertinent here; what they indicate is that the conditions of our metropolitan regions is not the result of "natural" forces alone. The federal government has played a major role in contributing to the shape and character of urban America.

The forces at work in the city and region are cumulative. They all move together toward making the city a more desirable or less desirable place to live. The federal subsidies that have encouraged highway construction instead of mass commuter transportation and thus drawn industry out of the city have reduced the city's tax base. A lower tax base means less money for education and for the adjustment of rural migrants to urban life. Poor schools and changing neighborhoods encourage middle-class white families to move to the suburbs. Higher welfare costs increase the tax rate and thus encourage industry to relocate in outlying areas. All these factors are interrelated. If they can be altered, it might be possible to reverse the cycle of urban decay and deterioration and move the forces of the market place toward renewal and reconstruction.

A total program that recognizes the interdependence of city and suburbs is needed. The creation of new communities on the outskirts of suburbia is a necessary element in the restoration of the inner city. The vitality of the city is, in turn, important for all of the inhabitants of the region. A total program must be able to differentiate between which of the forces at work in the region must be shaped by government action in a private enterprise system and which do not lend themselves to it.

We cannot, for example, prevent those industries that do not require a central location from moving to less expensive land in outlying areas. However, through a regional open-space plan, we can limit the areas in which these industries may choose to locate. We cannot prevent middle-class white families from leaving the cities because their children are not being educated in accordance with middle-class standards. But we can induce middle-class families to live within the city if we can create areas large enough to establish a genuine community with good schools. We can find the land for these communities by clearing industrial as well as residential slum property, provided that we undertake to relieve the city of part of its tax burden or change the methods by which it collects taxes.

"New towns" are already being created in areas beyond suburbia to accommodate an exploding population, but these "new towns" may become exclusive suburbs, which in time will be engulfed by suburban sprawl.

I am suggesting a different kind of "new town" program. We should attempt to create "new towns" pursuant to regional open space and transportation plans. These towns will also accommodate industrial workers and industries displaced by an intensified residential and industrial slum clearance program in the core areas of our major cities. At the same time, on the land within the cities made available by slum clearance, new communities can be established for middle-income families.

This program would make both the central city and the "new towns" more heterogeneous in social composition, reduce travel distances to work and thus diminish the urban transportation problem, and, finally, bring suburban sprawl under control through regional planning of open spaces and mass transportation.

Present segregation practices are a serious obstacle to this kind of program; at the same time they provide an additional reason why a program designed to create heterogeneous communities both within the city and beyond the suburbs has become imperative. Not only is the Negro population of our cities increasing in numbers but housing for Negroes is becoming increasingly segregated. The question of segregation is always present when the character and location of public housing and urban renewal projects are being determined. An unwillingness to face up to it has paralyzed city planning. It is necessary to deal with the question not only for the sake of civil rights for Negroes but in order to free city planning from some unspoken assumptions that underlie almost everything that happens about housing in our cities.

Juvenile delinquency and adult crime, school drop-outs and unemployment, the spread of slums and the cost of welfare are all related to segregation in the cores of our cities. The social and economic costs of these problem areas both to the Negro and to the community as a whole are enormous.

The Negro ghettos will not dissolve of themselves. The middle-class Negro family has had great difficulty in finding suitable housing outside of the segregated lower-income neighborhoods; only very recently has housing for these and higher-income Negroes begun to open up. A policy of nondiscrimination in rentals or sales can help, but the ghettos are still so large that only a major plan to induce a substantial part of the Negro working population to live in outlying "new towns" can bring about a more uniform and just distribution of these people among the population as a whole.

We should not underestimate the difficulties of creating interracial communities. Experience shows, however, that it is possible to create interracial housing in stable communities where the housing is sufficiently subsidized. The existence of heterogeneous communities in outlying areas will make it more possible for the Negro to relate to the urban culture. Schools in a smaller community, for example, can be so located that even if there are neighborhoods within the community that are predominantly white or predominantly Negro all of the children can attend the same schools. So many industrial workers are Negro that any problem for creating outlying "new towns" for industry and industrial workers must aim for heterogeneity. As for the cities, where Negroes are already established, a program to bring back middle-income white families must encompass the creation of interracial middle-income neighborhoods. If America is not prepared to accept interracial communities, there is little hope of arresting the decline of the city.

Only a slight extension of the tools already in hand is needed to foster the development of middle-income communities within the city and of "new towns" on the outskirts of suburbia. The Housing Community Development Act of 1964 (which was not enacted into law) proposed for the first time that the Federal Housing Administration insure mortgages for the purchase of land leading to the development of new communities. The Administration thus proposed to finance "new town" developments, although the result may well have been that under such a program the "new towns" would have become exclusive suburbs like many "new towns" now being built with private financing.

Assume, however, that FHA and V.A. financing were abandoned except in urban renewal areas in the city and in "new town" developments. In addition, assume that a regional open space and transportation plan were required before this financing is made available. Assume, further, that the regulations governing savings and loan associations were amended to allow them to allocate a substantial portion of their funds to financing mortgages for multiple dwellings, and to limit financing of either homes or multiple dwellings to established suburban areas, to the cities, or to "new towns" in regions where an open space and transportation plan exists. Moreover, suppose that the V.A. and FHA regulations prohibiting discrimination because of race were also applied to savings and loan associations. Suppose, in addition, that the FHA programs for middle-income housing were made available in the "new towns," so that the goal of an economically heterogeneous community would be vigorously pursued. Suppose, finally, that each "new town" were required to provide some minimum of public housing and housing for the elderly in order to be eligible for federal financing.

These federal tools, almost all of them readily adaptable, would be powerful inducements for the creation of heterogeneous "new towns" in which individuals and industry displaced from the city, together with some of the 80,000,000 new people to be housed between now and 1980, could be accommodated. Moreover, federal incentives could be geared to the creation of "new towns" of higher density so that effective mass transportation between them and the center city could be developed.

Assume that the federal urban renewal programs for clearing residential slums and renewing central business districts were extended to permit the clearance of industrial slums. And assume that the federal government were prepared to finance the construction of industrial facilities in "new town" industrial parks. Can there be any doubt that such a program would have enormous impact in hastening the creation of "new town" developments and in clearing land within the city for the construction of middle-income communities?

It should be clear by now that I am proposing regional planning only in a most restricted sense. It is not necessary for public agencies to provide comprehensive master plans for each region, leaving no room for diversity created by private choices. Some planning, however, is necessary, particularly by the agencies responsible for water, sewer, and transportation because they must be able to project the future needs for public services of an ever-expanding population. In many places these agencies plan independently of each other, and the federal agencies that subsidize housing do no planning at all. What each region now needs is a plan covering all of the agencies already involved in the expenditure of public funds, stating where and when the public will spend its money for water systems, sanitary and storm sewers, highways, and rapid mass transportation, and in what areas subsidies will be available for housing. Regional growth can thus be controlled, with private enterprise left to develop variety within the over-all framework of the plan.

An essential part of the program I am describing is the clearance of industrial slums at the cores of most of America's cities. One of the major obstacles to this has been the reluctance of cities to lose industry for fear of further jeopardizing their real estate tax base. But industry is moving to the suburbs anyway, and the real estate tax structure of the city will have to be revised in any event. Real estate taxes in most places have already reached the limits of economic feasibility. Assessments against property are still the major means by which cities collect taxes, and they have fallen behind in their share of the total tax dollar.

A case can be made that the wealth produced by the cities has been drained out by federal taxes and redistributed first to agriculture, second to suburbia, and third to the cities. At the same time the welfare costs of the cities have increased their tax rates, so that what the federal government has contributed in the form of urban renewal has been taken away by the costs of municipal services. The cities must revise the methods by which they raise revenues, and a greater share of the cost of health, welfare, and education must be allocated to the federal government. The migration to the cities of rural Negroes, Southern whites, and Puerto Ricans is a national problem; the federal government should bear the tax burdens this has created.

Before state as well as federal power becomes available to solve the problems of real estate tax revision and regional planning, the now rural-dominated state legislatures must develop greater sympathy than they have exhibited for the problems of the city and region. The recent decisions of the United States Supreme Court on reapportionment give some hope that city and suburb may soon have more influence upon state legislatures in their dealings with urban problems.

Obviously, each city or each region has unique problems that require more specific solutions than have been suggested here. Nevertheless, these proposals are not offered just as a panacea. We should bring suburban sprawl under control so that we can get better transportation, water and sewer control, and more open space, but a regional plan will not necessarily produce a beautiful region. There is still much to learn about "new town" development, about the creation of communities in which the citizens can govern themselves and in which life is pleasant and interesting. Similarly, the restoration of middle-income families to the city does not automatically solve the financial problems of the city, nor will troubles in race relations disappear even if all communities are racially heterogeneous. We should not try to control too much. At best, we can give direction to economic and social forces already at work and seek to provide better communities in which people can create a variety of environments appropriate to their way of life.

It is possible to shape the character of our urban environment. The population explosion provides the opportunity and existing federal subsidies provide a means. If we deal realistically with segregation and with the sources of city revenues, we can create a more livable community. Public thinking and discussion can clarify what we value about urban life. If we know what kind of urban environment we want, the power and the tools to create it are at our disposal.

URBAN AND SUBURBAN NASHVILLE:
A CASE STUDY IN METROPOLITANISM

DANIEL R. GRANT

Daniel R. Grant is professor of political science, Vanderbilt University. He is the co-author of *State and Local Government in America* (1963).

One of the greatest tragedies related to the unsolved problems of metropolitan areas is the fact that most of the work being done on these problems is curative rather than preventive. Metropolitan growth brings conditions similar in many respects to a disease which can be prevented with comparative ease if properly anticipated, or easily arrested if properly diagnosed and treated in the early stages. Almost without exception, however, the town fathers either do not recognize the symptoms in the early stages or do not become seriously concerned about them until it is too late for simple or easy measures. An effective remedy then becomes exceedingly difficult, if not impossible, to achieve.

Charles E. Merriam's oft-quoted statement that "the adequate organization of modern metropolitan areas is one of the great unsolved problems of modern politics" is no less true today. Such cities as New York, Chicago, Pittsburgh, St. Louis, and Philadelphia, each of which has over five hundred units of government within the metropolitan area, have long ago passed the stage in which relatively quick and easy solutions for governmental headaches are possible. In these and many other large cities local government seems to have become almost hopelessly fractionalized. The result has been unequal governmental services in different parts of what is essentially one urban community, uneven distribution of tax resources throughout the area, and dispersion and dissipation of citizen control of local government. Virtually all of these metropolitan headaches can be traced directly to lack of foresight or failure to act in time.

Metropolitan Nashville, with its some 320,000 persons, provides an interesting case study of a city in the early stages of metropolitanism. While the problem Nashville faces in achieving integrated government for the whole community may seem to be an exceedingly difficult one in the eyes of Nashvillians, it cannot be compared in complexity to the problem of most of the larger cities. Even in the case of Nashville, however, no assurance can be provided of a prolonged period of

From "Urban and Suburban Nashville: A Case Study in Metropolitanism," Daniel R. Grant, *The Journal of Politics*, XVII:I (February 1955), 82-99. Reprinted by permission of the author and *The Journal of Politics*. [Footnotes omitted.]

dormancy before the problems of metropolitan government change to the stage of malignant growth and apparent hopelessness.

This article undertakes to describe the extent of the suburban movement in Nashville and Davidson County and its effects upon local government in the area. It further undertakes to examine the prospects for solution of Nashville's metropolitan problems with special reference to the recommendations of the Community Services Commission, a joint city-county survey agency which made its report on June 1, 1952. It is not the purpose of this article to re-explore the traditional problems and alternative solutions of the older metropolitan areas. These are familiar to most political scientists. It is intended, rather, to present Nashville as a case study of a city which has not yet taken the fateful steps that so many other cities have, but which is nevertheless standing on the brink of metropolitan disintegration.

A Tale of Two Cities

Since the last annexation of appreciable extent (in 1929), Nashville has been two cities. One is the economic and social community of over 300, 000 persons living in an area of some 125 square miles. The other is the legal city of Nashville, which includes within its boundaries slightly more than one-half of these persons and only one-sixth of the metropolitan area. The outer parts of the metropolitan community are growing in steamroller fashion both in population and in assessed property valuation. The development of the central core city is slowing down to a snail's pace, its population growth virtually ended and its total property valuation increasing more slowly in the face of actual decreases in many blighted areas.

The great contrast between the population growth inside and outside Nashville's city limits is shown in the tabulation below. The 1950 census indicates that the suburban movement of previous decades became a virtual avalanche between 1940 and 1950. During that period the city of Nashville had an increase in population of 6,905, which brought its total population to 174,307, or an increase of only 4.1 per cent during the ten-year period. In contrast to these figures is the tremendous growth of the county area outside the city limits of Nashville, which showed an increase of 57,586, representing a 64.1 per cent increase over 1940, and bringing the total population outside the city to 147,451. The rate of increase for the entire metropolitan area, as expressed in the Davidson County figures, was 25.1 per cent and the population was 321,758.

An examination of the population trends in the Nashville metropolitan area since 1900 reveals that the external city has exceeded the internal city in rate of increase in five of the past six census reports. Not

POPULATION GROWTH IN THE NASHVILLE METROPOLITAN AREA, 1900-1950

	City of Nashville		Davidson County Outside City		Davidson County As a whole	
	Popula-tion	Rate of Increase	Popula-tion	Rate of Increase	Popula-tion	Rate of Increase
1900	80,865	6.2%	41,950	30.4%	122,815	13.4%
1910	110,364	36.5	39,114	-6.8	149,478	21.7
1920	118,342	7.2	49,473	24.2	167,815	12.3
1930	153,866	30.2	68,988	39.4	222,854	32.8
1940	167.402	8.1	89,865	30.3	257.267	15.4
1950	174,307	4.1	147.451	64.1	321,758	25.1

Source: Adapted from reports of the United States Bureau of the Census.

since 1910, when the census reflected large annexations to the city, has Nashville shown a greater rate of increase than the county area beyond its city limits. The suburban movement was stronger in the 1940-50 period than it was during the decade of the thirties. From 1930 to 1940 the average yearly increase approximated 2,000 persons outside the city, compared to 1,300 yearly additions in the city. During the 1940-50 period almost 6,000 persons were added to the suburbs each year, while the average annual increase in the city dropped to a mere 700 persons.

This exodus of population from the central city to the outer fringe areas is the result of many factors. The seriousness of Nashville's winter smoke problem makes this a more important cause of the suburban movement than in most metropolitan areas. Lack of room inside the city, either for residential or industrial purposes, is an important factor. In addition, motivating forces such as the desire to "keep up with the Joneses" who have moved out where the more well-to-do live, the desire to avoid the city's congestion and noise as well as its taxes, and the desire of retail merchants, craftsmen, restaurants, and theaters to locate near these new suburban centers of population all play parts in the flight to the suburbs. In Nashville, as in most of the metropolitan areas, both a push and a pull toward the periphery are evident. Many things within the central city tend to push the residents outward, and the magnetism of the desirable features of the suburbs gives a strong pull in the same direction. It is almost as if the central city and the suburbs are cooperating beautifully to rob the central city of its resident population.

What is the governmental picture in this metropolitan community? Logic may dictate a single unit of government for the whole urban area, but this the area does not have. But neither is there a seemingly hopeless proliferation of incorporated cities, towns, counties, special districts and other units of government such as exists in so many other cities in the United States. Nine separate units of local government operate within the Nashville metropolitan area, including the two major units, Davidson

County and the City of Nashville. In addition to Nashville, three other incorporated cities, Belle Meade, Berry Hill, and Oak Hill have been created. The remaining four units of government are suburban utility districts devoted almost exclusively to supplying water.

Nashville is considerably better off than most other metropolitan areas in the United States in the matter of incorporated satellite cities which tend to make annexation impossible. For example, in 1952 the Birmingham metropolitan area contained 23 separately incorporated cities in addition to the central core city, the Atlanta area also had 23, Cincinnati had 60, and the largest metropolitan area (New York-Northeastern New Jersey) contained 291 incorporated satellite cities. Prior to 1938 there were no incorporated cities at all other than Nashville in Davidson County, but in that year one of the most fashionable residential sections was incorporated as the city of Belle Meade, primarily to zone the area exclusively for residential use. Its population in 1950 was 2,831. More recently two other cities have been incorporated, Berry Hill in 1950 with a population of 1,238, and Oak Hill in 1952 with 3,031 persons. Belle Meade and Berry Hill are, in effect, pseudo-municipalities since their activities are limited for the most part to zoning, street maintenance, and garbage collection. Oak Hill activities were even more limited during the first year after its creation as a result of a court contest over the legality of its existence. All three are located south of corporate Nashville.

For the student of metropolitan government, it is encouraging that out of the 147,451 total population in the county outside of Nashville only about 7,000 persons live in separately incorporated cities. However, the urban area of Davidson County contains several unincorporated cities which show considerable community spirit and local pride closely akin to isolationist sentiment. Such communities as Inglewood, Madison, Bordeaux, Richland, West Meade, Woodbine, Hillsboro, and the Granny White-Belmont communities are all thickly populated and a part of the economic community of Nashville, but they have traditionally given very little encouragement to annexation movements. The unincorporated communities of Donelson, Old Hickory, and Goodlettsville are more separated geographically from Nashville than the other suburbs, but are still a part of metropolitan Nashville. Although none of these communities has a municipal government of its own, each one has a civic club or improvement association of some kind which purports to look after the best interest of the community.

Suburban Nashville presents a picture, therefore, of more than 100,000 persons living under conditions calling for urban-type services similar to those required inside the city, but without municipal government to provide these services. What, then, have been the various makeshift substitutes for municipal government sought by the suburban areas?

Some Symptoms of Maladjustment

Sewage Disposal

Suburban Nashville is a city of 100,000 population without a sanitary sewer system. The so-called "septic tank problem" is considered by many, particularly by public health authorities, to be Nashville's number one metropolitan problem. The county's sanitary engineer has estimated that at least 10 per cent of these septic tanks could be found discharging sewage to the surface of the ground at any given time, and that 25 per cent of the septic tanks operate dangerously, if at all. The subsoil of Davidson County, underlaid with limestone, is shallow and marked by frequent outcroppings of rock, all of which makes it very poorly suited for absorption of sewage. The disease menace of thousands of closely-built septic tanks beyond the city limits also threatens the homes in the well-sewered areas within the city limits.

The economic problems resulting from inadequate suburban sewage disposal are undoubtedly more evident to Nashvillians—certainly to the Chamber of Commerce—than the danger to public health. Prospective new industries are discouraged because most of the undeveloped ground in larger tracts, usually available only outside the city limits, is completely unsewered. In addition, the range of choice for the prospective homebuilder is narrowly limited because suburban subdivisions of small and medium size lots are allowed to be located only in deep soil areas, which are exceedingly scarce. This one factor has strongly influenced the direction of suburban residential development and growth in Davidson County.

Police Protection

Metropolitan Nashville receives police protection from several different sources, but police protection is virtually non-existent in large parts of the suburban area. In addition to the Nashville Police Department the police agencies consist of the County Sheriff, who has a salaried highway patrol and fee-paid deputies, three private subscription "police departments" deputized by the sheriff, 15 constables who are virtually useless, and a portion of the State Highway Patrol.

The result of the rapid growth of the urban area outside the city has been a series of makeshift efforts to provide adequate police protection, none of which is calculated to provide integrated metropolitan police protection for the whole area. Probably the device most open to criticism is the private subscription "police departments" which are, in effect, private enterprises depending upon the good graces of the sheriff, who may refuse—and has refused on at least one occasion—to deputize their men. Furthermore, such organizations, providing protection for all who pay a subscription fee, face the possibility of being called on to raid a commercial establishment which is a subscriber.

One of the most evident shortcomings in law enforcement in the area is the sharp difference which exists in the amount and quality of protection provided in various parts of the county. The number of police employees per 1,000 persons inside the city of Nashville is more than twice the corresponding number in the suburban area. Both the city and county operate separately a jail and workhouse. The division of responsibility between State, county, and private agencies for patrol activities is vague and indefinite.

Fire Protection

Residents of suburban Nashville probably pay more for less in the field of fire protection than in the case of any other urban service. Except for about 2,000 persons who have made financial arrangements for the Nashville Fire Department to respond to fire calls, the area outside the city limits is protected, if at all, by one of the eight private subscription fire "departments." In addition to the eight private companies in the suburban area, one special district provides fire protection.

Several factors combine to make suburban fire protection shamefully inadequate for the 100,000 residents located outside the city. In the first place, fire hydrants are almost non-existent outside Nashville's city limits. This could be corrected without great expense if it were not for the fact that over 200 miles of suburban pipelines are either 2-inch or 4-inch lines—inadequate to serve fire hydrants. In most instances these lines will have to be replaced with 6-inch lines in order to serve fire hydrants.

The absence of public fire departments or adequate water supply has caused a very high "birth rate" for private subscription fire companies which carry their own water and use high-pressure fog equipment that conserves the water supply. As in the case of private police agencies, the private fire companies are open to severe criticism on several scores. Almost all of them are under-manned and under-trained, and by their very nature do not possess the governmental authority necessary for an effective fire prevention program. Furthermore, relations between suburban fire "departments" are not conducive to co-operation and teamwork. In three instances a private fire company has located a new fire hall near a competitor and has proceeded to solicit subscribers in the identical area served by the competitor. Two other companies recently engaged in a prolonged court battle over possession of a fire engine.

An indication of the relative quality of fire protection inside and outside the City of Nashville is given by comparing the fire insurance ratings. Within Nashville the rating is third class, while the lowest possible rating, tenth class, is given to all sections outside the city except Old Hickory. This makes the cost of fire insurance on residential property almost two and one-half times as great outside the city as inside. The Community Services Commission estimated that suburban dwellers paid $250,000 in subscriptions to private fire companies in 1951 and $412,000 in fire insurance premiums in excess of the City of Nashville rate. This means the suburban dweller actually pays more, per capita, for tenth-class fire protection than residents of the City of Nashville pay for third-class fire protection.

Water Supply

The chief source of water in the metropolitan area is the City of Nashville's municipally owned and operated system, but the suburban consumers receive and pay for the water in such a strange variety of ways that a member of the State Railroad and Public Utilities Commission was inspired a few years ago to describe the Nashville suburban water situation as "scrambled eggs." A part of the suburbs receive water directly from the City of Nashville, either through private or city pipelines at a rate almost three times the rate inside the city. Others are served by special utility districts which buy the water from the city at a wholesale rate and retail it to the consumers. Other parts of the suburban population are served by special utility districts which have their sources of water and distribution systems independent of the city. Finally, there are a few private water companies which have sources of water separate from the city and which serve a small portion of suburban consumers.

The suburban utility districts are strange governmental creatures which have crept into the metropolitan scene in Tennessee without any thorough examination of their political and administrative implications. Space does not permit such an examination in this article, but some of their characteristics at least should be described. Davidson County's four utility districts were formed under the authority of the State Utility District Act of 1937, which, with subsequent amendments, permits the operation of water, sewer, and fire protection systems and certain other limited functions. Each district is operated by a board which, once appointed, is self-perpetuating, and which is not responsible to the people of the districts or subject to public regulation by any responsible regulatory body. Neither policies nor personnel are made subject to popular vote, and the property, income, and bonds of the districts are exempt from taxation. They are denied the power to levy or collect taxes, a fact which tends to make the larger property owners prefer the utility district over annexation or separate incorporation as a means of securing urgently needed services for the suburbs.

The existing arrangement for metropolitan water supply discloses serious weaknesses. The suburban water supply systems are substantially uncontrolled monopolies; six different water rates exist within one metropolitan area, with suburban rates averaging more than double the rates inside the city; suburban pipe lines are completely inadequate for fire protection; and each of the suburban water systems represents a piecemeal and essentially isolationist approach to a single metropolitan problem.

Public Health and Hospitals

Prior to 1952 public health authorities were compelled to draw an artificial boundary line within the urban area to separate the work of two health departments, one for the City of Nashville and one for Davidson County. Each department duplicated the personnel, training, and equipment of the other and the whole community was being denied many advantages which may accrue from a single county-wide health department. Following the recommendation of the Community Services Commission, the City of Nashville abandoned its own health department in November, 1952, and since that time there has been only the one health department responsible for the entire county.

Hospital care for indigents is divided between the City of Nashville and Davidson County, and three public hospitals and two private ones are involved in several complex and highly controversial arrangements to provide and finance hospitalization for the poor. The transformation of Davidson County into essentially one metropolitan area has made it illogical to have more than one governmental unit responsible for this function but the transfer of the public health department to the county has not yet been followed by a total transfer of hospitals.

Public Schools

The growing pains of metropolitanism are perhaps more easily recognized in the public school systems of Nashville and Davidson County than in any other area of governmental activity. Two public school systems exist side by side in the Nashville metropolitan area. The city system, always the largest until recently, has declined in enrollment with a resulting increase in vacant classrooms. The county school system, until recently distinctly a rural system, has experienced such phenomenal increases in enrollment that increases in budgets, buildings, and teachers persistently lag behind minimum adequacy year after year. By 1951 the county school system served more than one-half of the 50,000 school children in the total city-county area.

The results of this divided responsibility for schools between the city and county have been on the whole undesirable. Distribution of city and county school tax money has become a constant source of irritation, dispute, and charges of injustice. Vocational and other specialized education is much more costly, and in some cases economically unfeasible, under the dual school systems. One of the most serious consequences is the reluctance of the county school board to spend large sums of money constructing suburban school buildings which might be annexed by the city. This tends to result in stop-gap measures not in harmony with the best planning of the over-all physical plant for a metropolitan school system. Other weaknesses of the existing arrangement for schools include the duplication of administrative personnel, the variance of educational standards in different parts of a single urban area, an unhealthy proselyting of teachers between the two systems, and problems of interchange of students between the two systems. Some progress has been made in recent years by means of city-county cooperative arrangements, particularly to permit county residents to attend the city's vocational high schools.

Welfare

The traditional welfare activities known as "public assistance" are administered on a county-wide basis by the Davidson County office of the State Department of Public Welfare. Prior to 1953 the city of Nashville supported additional welfare activities, consisting primarily of a Juvenile and Domestic Relations Court and two homes for the care and protection of children who are committed under order of this court. Although financed by the city, both the court and the children's homes served the county area outside the city. The Community Services Commission recommended that the city get out of the welfare field and turn these functions over to the county. This was actually done in 1953, when the General Assembly passed a local bill making the Juvenile and Domestic Relations Court a county agency, and the city has indicated that it will no longer operate the children's homes. The reasons for this action were varied, including the doubtful constitutional status of the city court, but the result has been to implement the Commission's recommendations.

Other Metropolitan Headaches

Many other examples could be cited of governmental maladjustment arising from the political lag behind the expanding suburban movement. In the case of parks and recreation, for example, the county government operates no park system and the City of Nashville is actually furnishing free park facilities for over 100,000 non-taxpaying residents of the county who have access to the various parks. Suburbanites must pay for their refuse collection and disposal on a service-charge basis, even in the incorporated cities of Berry Hill and Oak Hill, which do not provide free collection out of city funds. Street lighting is almost totally absent from the suburban areas although a few of the commercial areas outside the City of Nashville have street lights as a result of suburban civic club projects. The darkness of the suburban areas is made even more serious because of the absence of sidewalks for pedestrians. In addition, there are many complex metropolitan problems concerned with public transportation, street construction and maintenance, and library service, as well as the over-all problem of urban planning and zoning.

The foregoing examples of governmental functions in the setting of a surging suburban tide each illustrate in one way or another the makeshift efforts of people just beginning to feel themselves caught in the grips of metropolitanism in its early stages.

Tugs on the Purse-strings

Metropolitan Nashville's split personality is more acute in the field of public finance than in any other field. The maze of public and private bill collectors for urban services in Nashville and Davidson County has become both complex and unjust. It has become confusing for suburbanites to pay the four incorporated cities, four utility districts, the county, and a multiplicity of private enterprises in various combinations for the municipal-type services which they provide outside Nashville's city limits. Not only has it become complex and needlessly confusing for the suburbanite, but it has in many instances placed an unfair tax burden on the city dweller, particularly in the case of "free services" which he finances for the non-taxpaying suburban dweller. In still other cases, as with the sharing of state taxes with cities on the basis of population, Nashville suffers serious losses because failure to annex outlying areas has resulted in bringing the city's population growth to a virtual standstill. The major financial problems resulting from the dispersed political structure in the Nashville metropolitan area may be summarized into five categories. The city has opened a frontal assault on many of these problems in recent years.

"Free Services" to Suburbs

Growing resentment has arisen in recent years on the part of Nashville home owners against what they consider to be the "free ride" given to suburban home owners out of the city taxes. For example, the Nashville Department of Public Works must spend more for street construction and maintenance in terms of a metropolitan population of some 300,000 persons who come and go without regard to corporate boundary lines. However, the city collects taxes to pay for such expenditures only from a population of 174,000. Similarly, the costs of traffic regulation are obviously more related to the volume of traffic than to the proportion of the urban area's population which happens to be within Nashville's city limits. Another example of free service to the suburbs is the Nashville park system, previously mentioned. City dwellers who want to complain are provided with a "natural" here, because over 70 per cent of the park acreage is located outside the city limits in areas more convenient to the suburban residents than to city residents. Another case of the city's "footing the bill" for a service to the entire urban area is the proposed municipal auditorium, to be constructed from a city bond issue of $5,000,000. Until recently such activities as library service, fire protection, sewage disposal, and water supply were included in the category of city subsidies to suburban dwellers, but these have been placed either on a service charge or county payment basis. All these arrangements are the subject of periodic disputes on the equity of the terms or their application.

Inequitable City Share of County and State Taxes

For many years the most serious case of discrimination against the city taxpayer has been the county high school tax, levied both inside and outside the City of Nashville, but spent only outside the city. Under this arrangement Nashville residents have been taxed to support two school systems while county residents outside the city supported only one. The proceeds of this tax amounted to almost $1,000,000 for the year 1951-52, over one-half of which came from city taxpayers. The 1953 legislature enacted a measure requiring the county to share the high school tax with the city on the basis of school attendance, so this inequity has been eliminated. However, grounds exist for similar charges of inequity in the case of other county-wide tax levies which are spent exclusively outside the city of Nashville for such purposes as the Sheriff's Patrol and streets and roads.

Nashville is not getting an equitable share of the Tennessee sales tax, part of which is returned to cities on the basis of population and other factors. To term it an inequitable share is not to blame the State of Tennessee, however, for the distribution formula is not unreasonable. Nashville can only blame itself — or rather itself and its suburban fringe — for having permitted stagnant city limits to conceal the actual growth of the community. Metropolitan Nashville had actually grown enough to get a larger share of the sales tax in 1950 than in 1940, but use of the 1950 census figures caused a $100,000 reduction in the city's annual share of the sales tax. The same is true in the case of state liquor and beer taxes which are distributed under formulas that employ population as a factor.

Uneven Distribution of Taxable Resources Throughout the Metropolitan Area

The familiar problem of the larger metropolitan areas in the United States which constitute a patchwork quilt of very rich patches, very poor patches, and varying degrees in between, is also present in metropolitan Nashville. However, the ill-effects are not nearly so serious in Nashville because the great majority of patches, whether rich or poor, are not separately incorporated into satellite cities as they are in most of the other metropolitan areas. The problem of poor cities and wealthy cities within a single metropolitan area, each isolated in taxing power from the other, is an extremely serious one, but Nashville does not have this as a present problem; it is a potential one which would arise upon encirclement by incorporated cities.

County Expenditures Benefitting Primarily the Urban Area

The county's side of the picture of metropolitan finance must be given to make the picture complete. Certain Davidson County expenditures, financed in part by rural taxpayers, benefit the City of Nashville primarily. Over two-thirds of the patients in the county hospital and asylum, as well as in the county tuberculosis hospital, are residents of the City of Nashville. County contributions to the three bridges across the Cumberland River, and a fourth now under construction, must be considered as primarily benefitting the city. It was said, in opposition to transferring the city's juvenile court to the county, that the court primarily benefitted the city and that the rural people of the county should not be compelled to support it.

Duplicate Expenditures by City and County Government

One problem of metropolitan finance is not related to discrimination against either the city or the county, or against any particular section of the metropolitan area. This is simply the duplicate performance, by the city and county governments operating in a single urban community, of many of the same financial operations, and of many of the same service operations as well. Some of the more ridiculous examples of duplication of effort are the separate city and county staffs performing the functions of tax assessing, tax collecting, custody of funds, purchasing and accounting. Both the city and the county undertake to secure trained personnel for two police departments, two school systems, two public works departments, and two civil service agencies, to name only a few. Some unification has occurred in the field of planning where a single staff serves separate city and county agencies. The duplication in public health was eliminated in 1952, as previously noted.

Nashville's Future

From the standpoint of the central core city and its financial self-interest in the narrow sense, Nashville is making considerable progress in the elimination of free services to the suburban area and the correction of tax inequities. However, the fact that suburban dwellers find themselves still without certain services or with a price-tag considerably higher on the existing services by no means guarantees eventual metropolitan integration under one government. The critical question now in the Nashville metropolitan area is whether the suburbs will choose to follow the path of annexation as a means of securing additional and improved services at a fairer price, or one of several other paths which reject annexation to the central city. The great majority of those metropolitan areas in the United States which are in a more advanced stage of their "time of troubles" have chosen the "several other paths," especially the paths of separate incorporation and special districts. Both involve a block to the growth of the central core city.

Three views of the metropolitan problem may be noted. One is the viewpoint of the insider who considers the most serious problem to be the inequity of providing services for the non-taxpaying suburbanite and the injustice of his being permitted to reside beyond the reach of the city tax collector, while enjoying all the social, cultural, and economic benefits of the city. The outsider is not only concerned with the seriousness of the inadequacy or absence of such services as sewage disposal, fire and police protection, water supply, and street lighting, but is also fearful of being annexed by the city of Nashville and taxed for many years without receiving services. He may also wish to remain aloof from what is vaguely referred to as "city politics." A third viewpoint is that of the citizen of the whole metropolitan community without regard to "insider vs. outsider" conflicts. The most serious problem from his standpoint is the absence of effective, integrated, over-all metropolitan government with authority to guide the progress of the whole urban region of Nashville and Davidson County. A unified public policy is important for a rapidly growing urban community, but the existing structure of local government—city government, county government, half-governments, and no government—makes it virtually impossible to secure such unity of direction.

It was in this general setting that the Tennessee General Assembly of 1951 created the Community Services Commission for Davidson County and the City of Nashville and authorized appropriations of up to $35,000 each by the city and county for a study of the whole problem. Of the fifteen members of the Commission, eleven were named in the act and four were subsequently named by the eleven. An equal number of members resided inside the city of Nashville and outside, not counting the chairman, and all members served without pay. A staff was employed in August, 1951, and the report with recommendations was made, as required by the act, on June 1, 1952, under the title, *A Future for Nashville*. Although the Commission made detailed recommendations concerning each governmental activity in the metropolitan area, the over-all recommendations may be summarized as follows:

1. *Annexation of Suburban Nashville.* The Commission recommended the annexation of approximately 90,000 persons and 69 square miles of suburban territory surrounding Nashville, including the incorporated cities of Belle Meade and Berry Hill. It recommended a single area-wide advisory referendum and annexation by special act of the state legislature upon the affirmative vote of a majority of those voting in the proposed enlarged city.

2. *County Responsibility for County-wide Functions.* Four governmental functions being performed by the city, which were clearly county-wide in character, were recommended to be transferred to the county: public health, hospital care for indigents, public schools, and public welfare. In each case the method recommended was simply for the City of Nashville to get out of the field and leave it to the county government.

3. *City and County Home Rule.* The Commission recommended amending Tennessee's constitution to provide for city and county home rule.

4. *Redistricting of Davidson County.* The urban sections of Davidson County are seriously under-represented in the county governing body (the County Quarterly Court), which has not been reapportioned since 1905. The Commission considered the correction of this by redistricting the county to be an essential corollary of the proposal to transfer the four city functions to the county.

During the period of study the Community Services Commission considered and rejected such proposals as special metropolitan districts and complete city-county consolidation or separation. In effect, the Commission proposed annexation and "functional consolidation" as the most feasible solution. The use of special districts was considered to be a piecemeal approach and therefore undesirable. City-county consolidation faced certain constitutional obstacles, and city-county separation was considered unfeasible for such a historic county as Davidson County.

The annexation proposal was made dependent upon Davidson County's nine-man delegation to the state legislature (two senators and seven representatives), which, under the state's "local bill" system, could secure passage of the necessary legislation for annexation simply by their own agreement. Only about two months expired between the release of the Commission's report and the primary election at which the county legislative delegation was chosen. During this interval Nashville's two daily newspapers, the *Banner* and the *Tennessean*, which tend to take opposite sides on political issues, both gave generous endorsement and publicity to the report. The nearly fifty candidates for the nine legislative positions took very similar stands concerning the

Commission's recommendations, usually commending the Commission members and staff very highly on its labors, and stating that they favored "most of the recommendations" but opposing any annexation without a vote of the persons affected. The result was the election of a delegation uncommitted in any concrete way to the over-all recommendations of the Commission. When the legislature met early in 1953 the proposed advisory referendum was not passed, the principal reason being the announced opposition by one of the senators to annexing by legislative act. The same senator opposed any redistricting of Davidson County to provide equitable urban representation in the county governing body. The two major recommendations which have been carried out are the transfer of the city's health department and juvenile court to the county. Certain other recommendations were partially carried through.

This, in brief outline, is the case history of urban Nashville up to date. Compared with most of the other metropolitan areas Nashville is still in the early stages of the metropolitan malady and in a condition where annexation is still possible. It is impossible to predict, however, how long it will be before Nashville is surrounded by a host of incorporated suburban cities. There is no way of knowing whether the incorporation of Berry Hill in 1950 and Oak Hill in 1952, both by narrow vote margins, were exceptional incidents, or whether they indicate a pattern soon to be followed in other suburban areas, particularly if the annexation drums should beat too loudly.

City planning authorities in other areas, who are struggling with their problem of metropolitan dispersion and disintegration tend to look with jealousy at the comparative simplicity of Nashville's metropolitan problem, particularly the small number of incorporated satellite cities and special districts. The feeling of "It's too late for us but not too late for Nashville," seems to be general — except in Nashville. Probably the most serious threat to Nashville's future well-being is the clear trend in the direction of the establishment of many separately incorporated suburban cities, the creation of small suburban utility districts, and the establishment of numerous independent private agencies to perform municipal-type activities. If such a trend is allowed to continue uninterrupted for even a few more years, all hope of checking in their early stages the diseases of metropolitanism in Nashville will have been lost. Nashville can go the way of all metropolitan areas in a matter of a few years. While the more serious complications of metropolitan organization are still in Nashville's future, an opportunity still remains for a combination of vision and action.

LOS ANGELES, PROTOTYPE OF SUPERCITY

RICHARD AUSTIN SMITH

Richard Austin Smith is an associate editor of *Fortune* magazine. He is the author of *The Space Industry* (1962).

Ever since the first figures of the 1960 Census began to appear, the great cities of the East have been turning, with some of Balboa's "wild surmise," to discern what a whole new ocean of people has been doing to Los Angeles. To be sure, a simple superfluity of people was not enough in itself to make Los Angeles a cynosure of eastern interest — New York has been drowning in humanity for years, and Chicago is still America's second-biggest city, albeit by so narrow a margin that a busload of newcomers may next month put L.A. in that slot. The attraction Los Angeles holds for eastern metropoles is rather that of a rapidly unfolding pattern for megalopolis. L.A.'s population has shot up by 2,375,000 within a ten-year period, an influx of humanity almost massive enough to people present-day Boston. Borne upward by the greatest westward migration in U.S. history, the growth of Los Angeles has eclipsed that of every other metropole in the nation — double metropolitan Chicago's, more than New York's and San Francisco's put together. This one American city has accounted for 10 percent of the population increase in the sum total of our metropolitan areas, and now, with 6,740,000 people, its sheer size has given it the grandeur of a city-state; indeed it is bigger than all save seven of the states of the Union.

Under such circumstances, Los Angeles provides a scaled-down, speeded-up version of the process of urbanization that is even now engulfing the fewer and fewer islands of darkness in the vast sea of light that stretches from Philadelphia to Boston. L.A. in the grip of smog is no longer a special situation, but one impending for every city of size. L.A. struggling to handle more than three million automobiles — 80 percent of those employed in the area drive to work — is now regarded as providing a preview of traffic jams that, in a few years, might stretch a hundred miles along the Atlantic seaboard. L.A.'s long — and successful — battle to provide adequate water is no longer viewed as something apart from common experience, the consequence of 50 percent of a state's population being concentrated in a region that contains only 2 percent of its water resources; the dry hand of shortage has steadily tightened on eastern throats as population rises and the water table falls.

What gives Los Angeles added interest is the tremendous amount of

From "Los Angeles, Prototype of Supercity" by Richard Austin Smith, pp. 99-101, 200, 202, 207-208, 210. Reprinted from the March 1968 issue of *Fortune* magazine by special permission; ©1965 Time Inc.

territory it covers and the unexampled heterogeneity of its components. Here is no simple city set in a symmetrical matrix of suburbs, but a metropolitan area, covering far and away the largest acreage of any of the 216 listed in the U.S. Census. It begins at the northeastern border of Los Angeles County and ends some seventy miles to the south, thrust part way through neighboring Orange County. Roughly in the center of the Los Angeles metropolitan area—4,842 square miles of sun-drenched mountains, plains, valleys, and beaches—is the city of Los Angeles itself.

The city proper, 458 square miles in its own right, is an amalgam of sixty-four place-name communities—most of them absorbed between 1910 and 1927 as the city pushed ever outward, trading its precious water for territorial rights. Surrounding the city limits are seventy-five satellite cities ranging in size from Long Beach (population: 369,000) to the City of Industry (746). Because the oldest and sturdiest of these— Pasadena, Santa Monica, Burbank, Culver City, Beverly Hills, etc.— survived only be resisting Los Angeles" encroachment (and annexing a little territory of their own), they form something of an encircling ring of militantly independent communities. To these have been added a whole new crop of small cities, strung along the new freeways like trees along a river, their way to incorporation made easy by a state constitution that permits incorporation of any unincorporated area on petition of 500 citizens.

Untypical as this evolution has been by eastern standards, it has lately come to have a certain fascination. A new shape for urban ag-glomerations is in the making and Los Angeles may ultimately establish the pattern for it. Here is an obvious proving ground for metropolitan, even regional, government. It is perhaps no more than justice that Los Angeles, so long derided as "twenty-four suburbs in search of a city," may now be emerging as a forerunner of the urban world of tomorrow. Yet what can be learned from L.A. today, as it struggles with the prob-lems of size and change, regression and trail blazing, may well determine whether some sociologist of the Nineties will be deprecating the metro-poles of the *East* as "a half-dozen cities in search of a supercity."

The Struggle for the Center

Somewhat ironically, just at the time Los Angeles is attracting attention as a nascent supercity of the future, a group of influential citizens is trying to make it over in conformance with the "classic city" patterns of the past. The idea, promulgated in a series of "Centropolis" studies, was that every great city of the nation had a downtown core or center and L.A. would have to have one too. According to the reports, the central area, which had once held "a virtual monopoly on all major activities in Los Angeles," would have to be rejuvenated because "the future growth and prosperity of Los Angeles and the surrounding metropolitan region depend very largely upon the economic health and physical attraction of the central area." A sizable amount of new construction had already gone up since the first Centropolis study was published in 1960 — Welton Becket's lovely new Music Center, the bulk of a civic center, second in size only to that of the nation's capital, new additions to a group of banking headquarters, the Wilshire Metropolitan Medical Center, to mention a few. This past December the Los Angeles Central City Committee released its master plan: "a bold program," according to the Los Angeles *Times,* "to make its Central City one of the world's great centers for commerce, finance, and culture." The over-all space target for the downtown core: 18,137,000 net square feet of new construction.

The size of this target, building 1.7 times as much square footage in the next fifteen years as was built in the 1954-63 decade, suggests a major marshaling of civic effort. And certainly some downtown business-men believe the magnitude of the problem merits such effort. Retail sales, once 75 percent of those in the metropolitan area, have declined to 18.2 percent in thirty years' time, as new shopping centers prolif-erated outside the central-city area; the majority of new buildings have been erected elsewhere. As banker Robert Gordon, president of the Downtown Businessmen's Association, a prime backer of Centropolis, recently put it: "The only way we can preserve the property values is to keep the central city. We have seen building rentals go down from $6 a square foot to $2.75 a square foot. I could take you around downtown and show you buildings that are only 10 to 15 percent occupied. There is too much money invested in downtown to let it rot." Rot, of course, is a word calculated to give the average American the shivers, but the real question appears to be, what price so grand a re-establishment of downtown hegemony? Should all this effort be channeled into trying to re-establish a "central core"?

The average Angeleno would probably answer in the negative. Downtown stands as a firmly established center of such old-line business activities as banking, insurance, finance, oil, and publishing, and is where 160,000 people have jobs. It contains such essentials as the courts, the main offices of city and county government, the Stock Ex-change. But nobody "loves" downtown, and to the average citizen it is just 4,000 acres of parking lots, an abundance of bad restaurants, a paucity of good hotels. Downtown is something he and 380,000 other freeway drivers — 68 percent of those coming into the area — are pleased to hurtle by every day without stopping. The Angeleno's loyalty is to his suburb, where he can obtain most of the amenities of life, and anyway it would take him twice as long to drive downtown in search of entertain-ment as to cover the same distance on the city's periphery. Many thoughtful observers like Ruben Mettler, president of TRW Space

Technology Laboratories, believe it's too late for the establishment of a core city: geography would lick a central system.

James Gillies, professor of urban land economics at U.C.L.A.'s graduate school of business administration, reports similar skepticism. "I live in Encino, out in the San Fernando Valley but still within the city limits," he remarked recently. "Ninety percent of the people there enjoy all the advantages of life in a big city but identify with suburban Encino. They have no interest in the redevelopment of downtown. They see no need for any great rejuvenation. The slums are not a problem. Nor are they convinced of the central-city concept. The big developments in L.A. have been outside central-city planning." Fritz Burns, one of L.A.'s biggest builders, regards the natural trend as "away from the downtown core. It is in the interest of the downtown area to preserve itself, and that is justifiable, but I see no great reason to spend the taxpayers' money building up the central core. To try to revitalize the downtown area when the natural expression of public taste and preference is for other areas becomes a losing battle. Writing-down land values for some prospective buildings may reduce the trend away from the downtown core, but no such inducement can reverse it."

The truth of the matter would seem to be that if the promoters of the central core were to ask the general citizenry what kind of city they wanted it would probably look very much like the city they've got. Metropolitan Los Angeles is made up of a number of cores whose very existence indicates that the bulk of its citizens neither need nor want to be tied to downtown for employment, culture, social activities, and the good life. Wilshire Boulevard is one such core, a "linear" downtown, whose seventeen miles now include the new Los Angeles County Museum of Art, most of L.A.'s smart shops, plus impressive concentrations of highrise apartments and skyscraper offices, the newest of which represent defections from the central city. The University of California at Los Angeles, ably directed by Chancellor Franklin Murphy, provides the cultural center of another core; U.C.L.A. runs full blast with 24,000 regular students, 19,000 more taking extension courses, and no school night goes by that it doesn't offer a choice of one or more concerts, lectures, plays, musicales. The million people in the San Fernando Valley, where the population shot up 250 percent between 1950 and 1960, are now numerous enough to be considered a core; one of its shopping centers is a virtual downtown itself with four department-store branches, and its airfield ranks fourth after Chicago's O'Hare, L.A.'s International, and Long Beach. Alcoa's Century City, a complex of office buildings and shopping centers just west of Beverly Hills, will no doubt become a core upon completion, for this "city within a city" was designed to have a self-contained residential population of 12,000 plus a working population of 20,000. And the Los Angeles International Airport, twelve miles southwest of City Hall as the crow flies, must also be counted an incipient core, one already on the rise with tall new office buildings and hotels; more will come when completion of the San Diego freeway brings new areas within reach of this "air harbor."

On a smaller scale there is the contra-center pull of the innumerable urban concentrations either within the city limits or spilling over into the surrounding county. These are served by decentralized civic government (thirteen separate centers), decentralized banking (over 500 offices or branches), decentralized retailing (nearly 140 branch stores, part of forty-one regional shopping centers with anywhere from fifty to a hundred stores), decentralized journalism (212 newspapers operate in L.A. County). But self-oriented as the citizens of these communities are, when they do leave their own areas for downtown they are far more likely to be attracted by the older incorporated cities on L.A.'s border than by a rejuvenated central core. Beverly Hills offers the best hotels, intellectual excitement, the art galleries along La Cienega Boulevard, "restaurant row," and some of the loveliest houses on the West Coast. Santa Monica has its own symphony, the broad beaches of the Pacific, a good newspaper, a complex of aerospace and "think" factories with one of the nation's greatest concentrations of people holding scientific degrees. Pasadena has Caltech, the Rose Bowl, a symphony, and the world-renowned Huntington Library and Art Gallery.

The key problem of the city is not the downtown area, but learning how to live with movement. Here is a metropolis whose real shape has been dictated by the automobile and the limitless appetite of its citizens for outdoor living. Everyone has moved about as if personally pursued by haunting memories of winter immobility and the dreary row houses of the sunless East. As Reuben Lovret, of the city planning staff, shrewdly observed: "The prophets of the future show that if you have complete dependence on the automobile it can lead to nothing but change. As long as you are oriented toward the automobile, any location is subject to reorganization or redevelopment according to how the driver can exert pressure—for shopping centers or apartment houses. As long as unbridled fluidity exists, there can be no permanent pattern." Under such conditions of perpetual motion, what is needed is not the mystical pull of brick and mortar newly erected in a central core but government with speed to match that of the automobile and the scope to embrace the whole changing region: Los Angeles County, the city, and the seventy-five satellite municipalities. Cybernetics, the science of communication and control, could supply the speed and *metropolitan* government the framework.

Bridging the "Gulf of Ignorance"

Fortunately for Los Angeles, it is the first city to harness cybernetics to the expanding problems of municipal government. When the present mayor, Samuel W. Yorty, took office, it was apparent that something imaginative had to be done to keep the city from foundering under the sheer weight of people. Conventional planning simply could not cope with the demands for municipal services, much less plan for the future. The speed with which things were occurring in L.A. had already rendered worthless a plan of urban renewal: by the time its intricate maps and overlays had been prepared, the city's rapid evolution made them obsolete. Yorty decided to try to bridge the gulf of ignorance (borrowing Toynbee's phrase) through cybernetics coupled with the use of high-speed computers and other automated data-processing equipment. The basic approach was that cities such as L A. were living organisms or systems in which adjustments to social and economic conditions were rapid and incessant. Therefore they demanded quick and constant evaluation if planning were to be effective. Data would have to be compiled at a single source (so all units of information would be the same and compatible); and data would have to be delivered quickly enough to be current.

The Data Service Bureau, which the mayor set up in 1963 under the watchful eye of his executive assistant, Robert L. Goe, now has two I.B.M. 1401 computers at work, will shortly replace them with an even bigger unit, an I.B.M. 360. The bureau already has managed to make important savings through data-processing consolidation, ultimately expects to save a total of $2 million. More important, it intends to keep abreast of a volume of city information that one consultant characterized as nine times more complex than a Mars shot. Where it used to take 20 percent of all the managerial time in city government six months to produce a municipal budget, it can now be done in six weeks. Where cartography was once a roadblock in the path of planning, electronic mapping is years ahead of the game; the computers can, for example, deliver data on the industrial development of the San Fernando Valley for the next five years and do it in the next five minutes. Decision making on urban development and civic planning can now be balanced by information as fresh as today's newspaper, while the integration or interaction of the myriads of master plans covering a metropolitan area may be analyzed quickly and economically. Virtually any geographical area is susceptible to similar analysis.

The whole pace and efficiency of city government are being stepped up as the program makes it possible to accomplish more with the same number or fewer people. Previously two weeks of time and considerable commitment of manpower—fire inspectors, safety inspectors, health inspectors, ad infinitum—were required to determine whether an architect's drawings and specifications for a building were acceptable to the city; soon the code compliance of a complex structure will be checked out in only twenty minutes. The setting up of a machine language for the overburdened police communication system can .be expected to give law enforcement the speed and mobility essential to the effective coverage of a 458-square-mile area with a force of only 5,200 men. When the system is completed, data on traffic jams, wanted criminals, burglaries, stolen cars, will become available without delay.

Design for Weakness

The wonders of civic cybernetics, though, stop cold at the "city limits" of government structure; Los Angeles' own structure is too anachronistic for a central city, much less for coping with the problems of an incipient megalopolis. The trouble, specifically, is an archaic city charter. Created at a time when reform groups across the nation were intent upon stamping out boss rule, the Los Angeles charter is dedicated to the idea that the weaker the government the less harm it can do. Thus power is split between the mayor and a city council in such a way that neither can assume effective leadership. The fifteen councilmen are required to meet every morning (which gets them involved in administrative detail along with noisy debates on modern art, cat licenses, and dog inoculations) and are paid so little ($12,000 a year) as to make membership attractive to few first-rate people.

The mayor, for his part, is responsible for running the city. The charter, however, interposes an appointive but highly independent group of commissioners between the mayor and the general managers, the pros who really administer the city departments. The commissioners, who meet one day a week, must concur in the mayor's decisions before the general managers can move. U.C.L.A.'s Professor John Bollens has concluded, after an exhaustive study of the city charter: "It defies all modern rules of sound organization and management. The quality of the city employees is the only thing that makes it go." Superior Court Judge Fletcher Bowron, who spent fifteen years as mayor and six years ruminating about it from the long perspectives of the bench, considers the charter "the worst that any city possesses. It is a monstrosity and unless we get major changes in it, or a new charter, we are headed for municipal stagnation."

A Giant for a Gigantic Job

In contrast to the city's constricted governmental mechanism is the exemplary framework of government in Los Angeles County. Many people in southern California have come to look on the county as a model of the metropolitan government of the future. Here is power and efficiency and latitude of a degree seldom seen in our constitutional democracy. Los Angeles County is the largest county government in the nation, a colossus straddling 4,000 square miles of territory. Its five supervisors represent more people—nearly 1,300,000 apiece—than

their counterparts anywhere else in the U.S. and are almost too free of
the checks and balances so carefully built into our system of government.
They are executive and legislature all rolled into one and even function
as a quasi-judiciary in the matter of zoning. Last year they spent nearly
a billion dollars on such county-wide services as welfare, hospitals, jails,
and the world's largest sheriff's office.

Up until 1954, the county's government had concentrated most of
its services in the *un*incorporated areas of the county, leaving to the
fiercely independent incorporated cities the job of running things as
they saw fit. The success of this policy can be read in the fact that since
1939 no community in the unincorporated area had petitioned to become a city. But by 1954 the pressures were too strong: it appeared that
a whole flood of incorporations was building up. This confronted the
County Board of Supervisors with a difficult choice. It could continue to
fight a sort of delaying action against the inevitable day when all its
territory on the Los Angeles coastal plain would be preempted by
incorporations, or it could get into the city-making business itself. The
board decided the better part of wisdom was to join a trend it couldn't
beat and, for the first time, initiated a specific program of helping
communities become cities. The first beneficiaries were the 51,000
citizens of a postwar subdivision called Lakewood Park, adjacent to the
old-line city of Long Beach. Under what is now known as the Lakewood
Plan, the county offered Lakewood a whole package of municipal services so that the community could become an independent city rather
than be absorbed by Long Beach. Subsequently, a county-city co-
ordinator was set up in the County Administrator's Office. There embryo communities were offered everything from technical advice to
feasibility studies on proposed incorporations.

Then in 1955 the Board of Supervisors took another significant
step: it voted to assign cities part of the county's revenues from an
impending state sales tax, in effect providing them the means for
purchase of the necessary package of municipal services from the
county. The city-making business boomed. There were four incorporations under the Lakewood Plan in 1956, when the sales tax became law,
ten more in 1957. All together, thirty new "Lakewood cities" came into
being over the ten-year period 1954-64, all with municipal services
furnished by the county under contract.

Today it is the county's justifiable boast that the contract program
is still working in twenty-nine of the original thirty cities and these range
in population from 746 to 94,000. More than 1,500 city-county agreements for specific services to these and older municipalities are now in
effect, and matters have progressed to a point where the county publishes a regular catalogue offering cities anything from pest-control
helpers (at $4.54 per hour) to principal regional planners ($17.02).

Whether this county-fed form of urbanization is to be applauded or condemned depends on one's viewpoint. The 746 inhabitants of the city of Industry are doubtless content with their eighteen-mile-long jigsawed city, because the sales-tax support of municipal services keeps business from paying a property levy. Yet it is plainly just a tax shelter, a paper city—one visitor found its public library to contain only sixteen books—the ultimate example of home rule allowed to run wild. Fragmentation certainly never built any society worthy of the name and in the long view the people of the area would have been far better served by Industry's consolidation with adjoining La Puente (pop., 29,500). By the same token, there's much to question about fostering the formation of a city that has more cows than people, as does Dairy Village (pop., 3,603), or one with no public street, Rolling Hills (1,931).

But in the context of an expanding metropolis, the point to be remembered is that the county's contract-city program has brought about *functional consolidation of municipal governments to a degree thought impossible a decade ago.* An atmosphere of trust and cooperation now exists between the county and many municipalities, the result of day-to-day contact over problems of mutual interest. In sum, many people admire the efficiency and flexibility of the county's organization, the caliber of its nonpartisan supervisors, and applaud its reliance on civil-service professionals rather than the party hacks to fill most county posts elsewhere. In addition, they are confident that professionalism, and the advanced administrative techniques the county prides itself upon, could ultimately show the way to functional consolidation of the area's multifarious municipalities.

The Odds Against Unity

Functional consolidation, unfortunately, is a whole world removed from *political* consolidation. As noted, self-determinism has long been an article of faith among the incorporated cities of the area while metropolitan government is often viewed by local Birchers as a vast Communist take-over or at the very least as "Big Brother" government. As far back as 1959 the League of California Cities proclaimed its own belief that, "The best interests of the people . . . require the maintenance of strong healthy cities which have the right of home rule and which provide local governmental services and perform local governmental and policy-making functions. Local municipal affairs involving policy making, enforcement of laws and regulatory measures, and governmental activities are not proper subjects for inclusion in regional or metropolitan districts and should be retained by the cities. Any political consolidation of existing local governmental units (cities and/or counties) to form a regional government for any California metropolitan area is basically unsound."

In the considered opinion of Winston W. Crouch and Beatrice

Dinerman, expressed in their admirable study of government for a metropolitan area, *Southern California Metropolis* (1963), there is "little likelihood that a sufficiently large number of municipalities would agree to dissolve . . . in order to form a consolidated unit which would be truly area-wide in scope. . . . Political odds are very much in favor of maintaining the status quo." Nevertheless, they saw one possibility for change: widespread discontent with things as they are.

In the two years since their observation, the consequences of political fragmentation have become more onerous. Urban sprawl, costly in resources and ugly in appearance, meets the eyes almost anywhere one might look; prime agricultural land continues to give way to leapfrogging tract developments, characteristically forcing commitment of far more acreage to *urbanization* than the developments actually occupy—for the cities are powerless to control urban sprawl outside their borders and the county isn't strong enough to do so alone. Regional parks and recreational facilities remain unbuilt—though expert opinion holds southern California should increase them by 200 to 300 percent just to keep abreast of the current population. Secondary roads become increasingly clogged, a steadily tightening noose around everyone's area of operations, for unified traffic control is impossible with a different set of regulations every few miles; without coordination, big Los Angeles is individually as helpless as the tiny city of Vernon where 212 residents try to cope with a working population of 70,000. Millions of dollars continue to come out of the taxpayers' pockets for "crash" programs of reconstruction or simply to straighten the crooked street that must become a main artery—for in the absence of an area-wide governmental structure, the nature of municipalities is to act as if the world ended at their own city limits.

The multiplicity of cities would naturally be expected to produce such irritants, but Los Angeles is also crammed with special tax districts, usually single-purpose organizations perforce designed to provide local service at no risk to local sovereignties. There are now 246 of these in the county—cemetery districts, debris districts, hospital districts, garbage districts, library districts, ad infinitum; many overlap and most operate substantially without democratic control either by local government or by the individual resident—who, typically, finds he must support anywhere from six to ten of them.

The Silent Offensive

Working against the foreseeable day when local discontent shall reach such a pitch that political consolidation must ensue, the state, the county, and the central city itself have been pursuing a policy of saying little to offend home-rule sensibilities but pushing steadily toward greater functional consolidation. Los Angeles' City Planning Department has quietly undertaken a staff-level formulation of a plan of transportation, land use, zoning for the whole metropolitan area. The county itself has already taken over the city's public-health program, will shortly be operating all Los Angeles jails; the entire area's public-health programs and jails will then be run on a county-wide basis.*At the state level, Governor Brown's Commission on Metropolitan Area Problems had recommended the establishment of a multipurpose special district (a combination of two or more single-purpose districts) as the most politically practicable means of bringing some simplification to the metropolitan area, only to be thwarted by the militants of home rule and the combustible League of California Cities. But now the C.M.A.'s successor group, the Coordinating Council on Urban Policy, has come up with a broader means to the same end. Its first report issued this January strongly urged that powers of the Local Agency Formation Commission be expanded. These commissions, set up in each county by act of the 1963 legislature, had already been given the negative power to block municipal incorporations or new special districts; the coordinating council now recommended they be allowed to initiate proposals for the annexation, consolidation, and dissolution of special districts. The significant operational words are "initiation, consolidation, and dissolution."

Additionally, the state government has been trying to bring an integrated approach to area-wide problems by letting $100,000 study contracts to aerospace companies. Aerojet-General Corp. is taking a hard look at waste management in all its aspects—smokestacks, sewage, garbage, debris, smog, industrial effluents—for both California as a whole and a tactfully unidentified region, obviously Los Angeles. TRW Space Technology Laboratories was asked to propose a regional transportation study, embracing Los Angeles, San Bernardino, much of Orange County and based on every mode of transport—rapid transit, helicopters, highways, fixed-wing aircraft. Significantly it has done so with a special eye to the governmental handicaps. Said S.T.L.'s President Ruben Mettler recently: "There is to my mind one essential step that must be taken along with the technical analysis of this kind of integrated transportation system. That is the establishment of an organizational structure which has the same scope as the problem: an authority encompassing all the municipalities to be served by the system."

It should be evident at this juncture in the affairs of Los Angeles that the city was born to be big, but whether it becomes a viable supercity is for the future to decide. There is an uneasy feeling that the inordinate attention being given the reconstruction of downtown by civic leaders is draining off energies badly needed on the metropolitan front. The balance to be struck is certainly one that bedevils every major city

---

* The last hold-out, Long Beach, has now applied for inclusion in the county's public-health plan.

in quest of greatness, since it involves a measuring of the old against the new, but in Los Angeles the promise that looms on the horizon will demand an uncommon commitment of talent, good will, and hard work if it is ever to materialize. The city's leadership will have to put its prime efforts into rectifying the tangled mass of jurisdictions and cross purposes that divide the metropolitan area, sap its strength, and threaten the mobility on which every one of its seventy-six cities depends. The vital need, as expressed earlier, is for a framework of government big enough to embrace the whole region and for a cybernetic system of communication and control which possesses speed to match that of the automobile.

Whatever glass-and-steel monuments may be built downtown, the essence of Los Angeles, its true identifying characteristic, is mobility. Freedom of movement has long given life a special flavor there, liberated the individual to enjoy the sun and space that his environment so abundantly offered, put the manifold advantages of a great metropolitan area within his grasp. Perfection of this essential mobility will surely give Los Angeles an identity among the cities of the world such as no mere assemblage of buildings could ever match.

METROPOLITAN GOVERNMENT, 1975: AN EXTRAPOLATION OF TRENDS

The New Metropolis: Green Belts, Grass Roots or Gargantua?

ROBERT C. WOOD

Robert C. Wood is professor of political science, Massachusetts Institute of Technology. He is the author of *1400 Governments: The Political Economy of the New York Metropolitan Region* (1961) and *Suburbia: Its People and Their Politics* (1958).

Whatever the strengths and weaknesses in the study of urban government today, one fact seems clear: a process of transformation is underway. How fundamental a restructuring of research and teaching is involved is not yet certain, for the tide of debate still runs strong. At the very least however, the new model will be longer, wider and indelibly stamped with the forward look.

The boundaries of urban study are no longer limited to the formal structure and administrative processes of local government; they now

From "Metropolitan Government, 1975: An Extrapolation of Trends," Robert C. Wood, *The American Political Science Review*, LII (March 1958), 108-122. Reprinted by permission of the author and American Political Science Association. [Footnotes omitted.]

embrace the variety of public activities within metropolitan regions, whether local, state, or federal in origin. The ranks of political scientists are augmented by sociologists, economists, demographers, and planners demonstrating renewed interest in the field. And almost every analysis is dynamic in scope and method, designed to anticipate the policy problems yet to come.

This last characteristic deserves emphasis. Few areas in political science seem to have accepted more completely Harold Lasswell's injunction in the Presidential Address of 1956 to scan "the horizon of the unfolding future." Acutely aware of the abundant signs of technology at work, armed with indices of population shifts, economic growth, and new living patterns, the modern student of metropolitan affairs works in a changing world. In the atmosphere of apparent crisis which surrounds his subject, he accepts almost enthusiastically the responsibilities of forecasts and predictions—with all the problems of significance and inference these terms imply.

In the spirit of the times, this paper reports the results of a limited venture in such a projection. It is not an extrapolation in the exact sense of the word, for no explicit relationships among variables are established and no series of values are assigned each factor. Certainly, all the relevant factors have not been identified, nor have all the new forces emerging in the area been "discovered." Yet without claiming mathematical purity or substantive completeness, the analysis does try to summarize some of the important new data now available to identify some major trends, and to evaluate their significance on established doctrine respecting metropolitan government.

On balance, the effort to look ahead seems useful. For one thing, some inadequacies in existing doctrine come to light. For another, some of the shortcomings and uncertainties involved in the best of forecasts are revealed. Finally, and perhaps most important, it appears that while the ecology of the new metropolis will undoubtedly be different, the value issues which the new setting provokes will not. When the returns are in, political science remains free to repair to its traditional role of normative commentary and our obligation to render judgment is not diminished but intensified.

I

Growth and change in almost every aspect of American life form the backdrop of the studies of metropolitan regions and provide a concomitance of forces from which an analyst must choose. Innovations in transportation and communication, changes in housing construction and residential finance, mutations in the pattern of industrial development, almost instinctive aspirations for space and separate family accommodations, all play their part. So do the rising birth rate, the tradition of restlessness, nourished and intensified by the depression and the wars, the surging "upward mobility" within the middle class, prosperity and the family ethic.

From this concomitance, most of us who discuss the "metropolitan dilemma" and who call for radical reorganization of metropolitan government have traditionally selected three forces as being of major importance. The first is the pattern of population growth and distribution within the typical SMA, in particular the disproportionate increase in suburban residential population traceable for at least thirty years. The second is the slow diffusion of industry and large commercial activities throughout the area which has been taking place as new enterprises build their factories and shopping centers in fringe areas and old ones desert the central city to join them. The third is also diffusive in character, although less tangible: the gradual spread of the cultural ethos of the metropolis to enfold formerly independent communities and to blanket the hinterlands with a common set of mores and values. To most of us, each of these trends, taken alone, appears to have negative consequences for the fragmented pattern of government in metropolitan areas, and taken together, they seem to point positively in the direction of a common conclusion.

The now familiar negative aspects of suburban population growth are primarily three. The first concerns the costs of metropolitan governments. The journey to work, which the separation of residence and place of sustenance imposes, appears both to burden unfairly the central city and to impose crushing demands on the suburbs. The core is required to handle the cost of servicing a daytime population thirty to fifty percent in excess of its permanent number; the suburbs have unnecessarily large capital budgets since, in the welter of jurisdictions, economies of scale and size cannot be realized. Duplication and overlapping of facilities between suburbs and the core city and among suburbs result.

The population shift and the journey-to-work pattern which ensues appear to have a second negative effect. They seem to lead to a deterioration in the political process. The sturdy burgher class deserts the city, but the rigor of the commuting schedule makes its effective participation in suburban affairs unlikely. Big city politics is seen as becoming increasingly a struggle between the very rich and the very poor; suburban governments are held to be controlled by the old residents, merchants, and real-estate dealers, with only an occasional high-minded foray by the League of Women Voters. Most metropolitan inhabitants have their feet in at least two political jurisdictions; they are half-citizens, disfranchised either in law or in fact.

Third, what politics remains is likely to be bifurcated. As the suburban exodus goes on, we are told that the fringe and the central city are drifting farther and farther apart, the former increasingly Republican, the latter Democratic, so that the metropolitan areas are likely to be split into two warring camps. Prospects for mutual cooperation and understanding diminish, the metropolitan situation becomes cast in a rigid mold, and the opportunity for responsible consideration of regional problems diminishes.

These implications of suburban growth *per se* seem dismal enough, but the second force of industrial diffusion adds a further difficulty. It appears to compound the metropolitan fiscal problem by making impossible an orderly matching of resources to requirements, by taking away revenues from the jurisdictions which need them most. Again, the plight of the central city is highlighted. Its tax base, already weakened by a large proportion of tax-exempt property devoted to educational and cultural purposes, is weakened further by the departure of business. Slums and blighted areas take the place of busy commercial districts, renewal efforts become more difficult, and welfare and public safety costs increase. Meanwhile in the outer ring some suburbs receive windfalls from new industry, but adjoining ones are saddled with the expenses of the workers living in cracker-box houses and putting four children per family through school. Because population and economic location patterns do not coincide, the traditional inequities and inadequacies of the American local tax structure are further intensified.

As the metropolis extends its cultural influence, a third set of "negative" consequences ensues. Discrete local communities disappear; friendships become scattered randomly throughout the area; associations made in the course of work are different from those developed in residential neighborhoods. Only the ties of kinship and the stultifying communications of mass-media remain to bind men together. This development is thought to have two untoward effects: first, as men wander aimlessly in the lonely crowd, the capacity of existing units of government to function vigorously and effectively is impaired for they no longer engender civic consciousness and a sense of belonging. Second, without regional institutions, no loyalty to a high order is possible. All that remains is a weak notion of metropolitan patriotism, a New Yorker's superficial pride in being part of the Big Show. So regional problems find no vehicle for their solution and the capacity to look ahead, to plan rationally, to awake a regional consciousness is lost.

In a positive sense and in a broad way observers believe these trends are interrelated and that they lead to a common conclusion so far as political analysis is concerned. The separation of home and place of work, the rise of "nuclear centers of dominance" in the metropolitan economic system, the spread of metropolitan culture, taken together seem to signify that a metropolitan community has come — or is coming — into being. We have been imprecise about what the word "community" means. Rarely are political scientists as rigorous in their definitions as, for example, one of the panel members from a companion discipline has been. But generally, we have assumed that if an aggregate of people in a given area achieve economic autarchy, if social intercourse extends over the area, and if common mores and customs exist, the basic foundations for a genuine community are present. The three factors we have studied seem to indicate that fairly self-sufficient metropolitan economic systems have developed, that social interaction now takes place across the entire area, and that a growing consensus about values is at hand. The prerequisites for the metropolitan community appear imbedded then in the trends we emphasize today.

Given this positive interpretation, the common conclusion is that for a single community, there should be a rationally constructed set of political institutions. The metropolitan dilemma is defined as the existence of many governments within a common economic and social framework. The metropolitan solution has been seen in variations on the theme "one community — one government" by any one of the half dozen ingenious political inventions. Running through all these recommendations is the premise that if somehow present units of government are brought together, if they can share resources and administrative responsibilities, the negative consequences of the forces now at work will be avoided and their impact guided into useful channels. If such reorganization is not forthcoming, we have generally believed these areas face governmental crises of substantial proportions. To drift with the tide is to court political, financial, and administrative disaster for urban government in the United States.

II

The facts on which the case for metropolitan government depends are quite real, and we have not misread the figures. Yet nothing demonstrates the complexity of analysis so well as the results of our reliance on three trends, and three trends alone. Despite our predictions, disaster has not struck: urban government has continued to function, not well perhaps, but at least well enough to forestall catastrophe. Traffic continues to circulate; streets and sewers are built; water is provided; schools keep their doors open; and law and order generally prevail. Nor does this tolerable state of affairs result from an eager citizenry's acceptance of our counsel: we know only too well that our proposals for genuine reform have been largely ignored.

It may be, of course, that the breaking point has simply not been reached. There is certainly little sign that the tide of suburban growth is ebbing, or that industrial diffusion is slowing down, or that the representatives of the new American character are remorseful now that their values have been so cruelly exposed. If we are to look forward to 1975, we have good reason for believing that these trends will continue until the "linear city" is in being on both our coasts and probably in regions in between. Yet conditions were already serious enough in the nineteen-twenties to prompt investigation and to set loose prophecies of doom. Developments have continued unabated, and it is a fair question, given the technological changes of recent years and the stubborn public reluctance to listen to our counsel, to ask if we have discovered the whole story.

If we dip back into the arrays of factors and forces at work in metropolitan regions, other trends appear, and the more they are studied, the more important they appear. In effect, when other trends, formerly left unexplored, are reviewed, they seem to operate as countervailing forces that modify the trends on which we have concentrated our attention. At times they abate the consequences our basic factors imply; at times, they change the relationships we have assumed existed. And, at least in one important respect, they present a completely different picture of the SMA than we have been accustomed to portraying.

For example, while it is true that the disproportionate growth in suburban population has accelerated since World War II, that growth has been accompanied by an extraordinary period of prosperity. As the dominant feature of our economy for the past 15 years, inflation has swollen the cost of government, but it also swelled, although belatedly, the revenue. Urban governments have managed spectacular increases in their tax returns in the past few years, and we are told by no less authority than the President's Commission on Intergovernmental Relations that the potential of the property tax is by no means realized. Moreover, the rising level of income has an economic consequence quite apart from any particular tax structure: once basic necessities of life are satisfied, higher tax burdens, however imposed, are more tolerable, and borrowings become easier, so long as the market is not surfeited. Thus communities may be forced to a general reassessment of property values, or they may skate on fiscal thin ice, but they need not undertake a general structural reorganization. Metropolitan governments may be forced to pay the excessive costs which the fragmented pattern requires, but they have been able to do so without encountering municipal bankruptcy.

Nor should other forces which bolster the capacity of metropolitan governments to sustain themselves be overlooked. While no major structural reform has been accomplished, state and federal grants-in-aid have helped support critical services and new municipal tax sources have been discovered and utilized. The plight of the central city has been to some extent relieved by grants and shared taxes, and by state assumption of important responsibilities. The commuter has either directly by earnings taxes or indirectly through his payments to state and federal governments contributed some of his share to the core municipality. The special district has been used more and more frequently to sidestep statutory debt limits, to tap new revenue sources, and to scale jurisdictional barriers in important functional fields. And some suburbs have been content to forego services, to get along with amateur governments, and to ignore the welfare state in order to remain autonomous.

In less easily explicable ways, the deterioration of the urban political process seems to have been checked. Healthy signs of reinvigorated, capable political leadership have appeared in many of our large cities. Newcomers in suburbia have won important political battles, over schools and public improvements. Even the prophecy that the suburbs are irrevocably Republican and the central city irrevocably Democratic seems suspect in the light of the most recent election returns. The party battleground is more complex than previously supposed.

While the apparently obvious consequences of disproportionate suburban growth have been modified, other developments have affected the revenue side of the picture. Metropolitan areas as a whole have continued to hold their own in relative economic importance, and industry has continued to move out to the fringe. Yet, by concentrating on the pattern of industrial diffusion alone, we have overlooked even more important economic changes which sharply modify the "mismatched supply and demand" thesis.

The first of these is the shift in consumer demands. As output and income per worker have grown, and per capita consumption has risen, a relative decline has occurred in the consumption of agricultural products and a relative increase in the demand for "services." Employment has expanded dramatically in the fields of trade, amusement, research, education, medical care—the white collar category in general. Since these are the fields where real output per man has not increased very rapidly, the proportion of the labor force thus absorbed expands more rapidly than the absolute decrease in other categories would imply.

Second, the structure of manufacturing activities has changed. Not only have industry classifications included a larger number of truly white collar workers—management, advertising, special repair and maintenance staffs—but manufacturing processes and products have become increasingly specialized. An increasing number of specialists offer intermediate processes and products to a number of different industries, and their facilities provide the small manufacturer with "external economies" which allow him to compete effectively with larger firms. There are an increasing number of "unstandardized" final products, too, as firms depart from offering a few stable lines and present their customers with an array of choices.

Together with the decline in the pull of raw material sources as a locational factor, the relative increase in transportation costs, and the growing size of metropolitan markets, these changes in demand and in the structure of manufacturing help explain the continued growth of urban areas as entities. More important for our purposes, they move in the direction of counter-balancing the consequences of the industrial diffusion trend within metropolitan regions.

The rise in the importance of "services" in the urban economy means a broadening of the non-residential tax base exclusive of industrial plants. Offices, salesrooms, medical buildings, trade establishments of all sorts and sizes, while not as advantageous to municipalities in their cost-revenue ratios as manufacturing plants, still return more in taxes than they demand in public services. As the white collar occupations grow in importance, the facilities in which they work become part of the resource base, and as they are scattered through the region in general they provide additional sources for revenue quite apart from those supplied by factories. If only industrial location trends are studied, this growing number of service establishments is overlooked and important increments to the resource base omitted.

The changes within the structure of manufacturing also make an exclusive reliance on the industrial location trends undependable, particularly since, quite frequently, only larger firms are singled out for attention. The increasing specialization which characterizes more and more modern manufacturing means that the processes in any given industry from receipt of raw material to delivery of finished goods may be dispersed throughout a region. Large plants and service facilities may drift toward the suburbs in search of cheaper space, but this does not necessarily mean that former locations in the central city or inner ring remain deserted.

On the contrary, many small firms frequently find a location within the central city attractive, for here are available all the specialists in the intermediate stages of production whose services can be contracted for to permit competition with the larger plants. Other "external economies" arise: fractional use of transportation facilities at less-than-carload or truckload lots, urban public services — police and fire protection, water and sewage facilities — which might not exist in the suburbs, rented space, a larger labor market, and so on. The appearance of unstandardized end products also enhances the central city's position, for purchases usually depend on visual inspections, and when styles and grades of material are important, inventories have to be kept within strict limits. These conditions make the core attractive as a "seed-bed" for industrial development, and take up the slack as larger firms depart.

Moreover, for all firms, large and small, the central city offers certain unstandardized inputs which are best provided in a central location. Advertising agencies, law firms, banks, home offices, some types of salesrooms, are activities which require proximity with their competitors, both because of the irregular schedule in which they may be used, and because "knowledge of the industry," gossip of the trade, face-to-face confrontation are prerequisites for doing business.

Here again the central city offers advantages which few suburbs can yet supply.

When the changes in the manufacturing structure are considered, neither the central city nor the suburbs seem in such desperate straits as are often described. As industrial diffusion goes on, and available land is taken up, more suburbs will receive "windfalls." More will actively search them out as well, for changes in plant architecture and the elimination of unfavorable site conditions, smoke, smells, water pollution, mean that many suburbs formerly hostile to development, will become enamoured of "light industry." Those who do not want, or will not find, industry will have their resources bolstered by service establishments following the market or by special facilities within an industry which can be separated from the parent plant.

Meanwhile, the central city is likely to find alternative economic activities, plants of small firms, business offices of large ones, and the cluster of professional and semi-professional services on which both depend. Moreover, the overriding necessity of these economic activities to maintain their central location makes their response to tax changes highly inelastic. Existing levies can be increased, or even new taxes on earnings and income imposed, and these special groups will still "stay put." Together with continued prosperity and a rise in real income, this inelasticity helps explain the recent successes in discovering new revenue sources. It further reduces the "certain" consequences of financial crises, which population and industrial trends have been thought to portend, to the status of mere possibilities, less likely than alternative courses of development.

Not only are our demographic and economic series suspect, but the less tangible hypothesis of "metropolitan dominance" comes in for critical scrutiny also. Without questioning the accuracy of the measures of newspaper circulation, postal delivery areas, telephone exchanges and journey-to-work patterns which imply the existence of a metropolitan "community," contradictory trends can be established. It is possible to submit that each region is an economic entity, that it has a circulatory and communication system of its own, and still argue that a scatteration of society has accompanied the scatteration of government; that metropolitan growth promotes a "huge mosaic of massed segregation of size, class, and ethnic groups" a "crazy quilt of discontinuities."

Admittedly, as indicated earlier, when we speculate about community, we are talking about a nebulous term. The models used for the study of community are many; the essential elements of community life are still uncertain and their relative importance unweighed. Yet it is significant that when authorities speak of the break-up of local communities in the metropolitan area, and the onrush of metropolitan dominance, their departure point is almost always the primary community, preliterate society, savage village or feudal holding where economic autarchy, social isolation and consensus of values were most complete. Such a community, if it ever existed at all, never existed in the United States. Our archetype has been the New England town or the hamlet of the Old Northwest, both quite different in their organization of space and their feeling for community affairs, but both relatively sophisticated types, having substantial economic and social intercourse with the outside world, numbering speculators and entrepreneurs among their inhabitants, and displaying mature political systems. While their differences were many, the common elements of these communities were the qualities of propinquity, homogeneity, interdependence, and equality, which produced our ideal local government — grass-roots democracy.

If these qualities are taken as the essentials of smalltown life, then modern suburbs may be on the way to finding a substitute for economic self-sufficiency and social isolation to promote a sense of community consciousness. They may be using their political boundaries to differentiate the character of their residents from their neighbors and using governmental powers — zoning, residential covenants, taxation, selective industrial developments — to promote conscious segregation. From the variety of classes, occupations, income levels, races and creeds which the region contains, a municipality may isolate the particular variant it prefers and concentrate on one type of the metropolitan man. In a sense it may even produce a "purer" type of community than the American archetype, because it has a wider range of choice and it need not reproduce all the parts of a self-contained economic system. It can simply extract the particular function it chooses to support, and achieve a social homogeneity never before possible.

Moreover, growth itself may aid and abet the process of strengthening community bonds in subareas of metropolitan regions. To the extent that a feeling of fellowship waxes strong in the early stages of community growth, that "political democracy evolves most quickly while the process of organization and the solving of basic problems are still critical," many suburbs may resemble earlier American towns in their political and social processes. At any rate, provocative comparisons have been made between group and individual characteristics in modern housing developments — the acknowledgment of equality and the recognition of interdependence in Levittown and Park Forest — and frontier towns of old.

A thesis that small communities are reappearing in the metropolitan areas, that the high-water mark of the process of communal disintegration has passed, is conjectural. But so is the rationale for the new metropolitan man, unattached and unrooted, and some interesting statistics support the first hypothesis. For one thing, the existence of fragmented governments does break up the area into manageable proportions — more suburbanites live in towns between 10,000 and

25,000 than in towns of any other size. For another, modern suburbs have captured that portion of the middle class most oriented, in terms of education, occupation, income and family status, toward being responsible members of their locality. Third, subareas in metropolitan regions are displaying a tremendous variety in their economic functions, social rank and ethnic and occupational order. Most important of all, this variety does not seem to be random in nature, but the result of conscious coalescing according to a pattern of spatial homogeneity. In brief, each suburb may be gathering its chosen few to its bosom, and not just in the broad terms which Burgess and Hoyt have outlined. More specifically, a clustering according to occupations seems to be taking place, in which different occupations, representing different status points in the social spectrum, put space between each other; and the wider the social differences, the further apart the members of disparate occupations live within the metropolitan area. Tracing this development in the Chicago metropolitan area, Otis and Beverly Duncan found a consistent pattern of residential segregation among occupations and a preference for neighbors with closely related occupations.

If this process of natural neighborhoods goes on in an area in which each neighborhood is equipped with a local government, then instinctive feelings of community are enhanced by the fact of legal and political power. A cultural *sui generis* results, and the existence of separate political institutions, separate powers to be exercised, individual elections to be held, reinforces the bonds which make the neighborhood. Within the region as a whole, we may be witnessing a popular attempt to dissect the metropolitan giant into small pieces, and to cap each with legal authority and some degree of civic consciousness.

To the extent that this is true, the notion of one metropolitan community may be misleading, and the characterization of modern culture as new may be overdrawn. Economically the region may be one, but it may be powerless to bid for the loyalties of its residents against the claims of the smaller neighborhoods. Its inhabitants may be conformists, gregarious, adjusted, seeking approval from their peer groups, participating eagerly in every form of social endeavor; but these qualities may not signify a new dominant culture. Instead, they may mark a return to the smalltown life De Tocqueville found, an expression of protest against the stratified, pecuniary structure of the Victorian city, a desire to recreate again the " . . . opportunity for companionship and friendship, for easy access to local services, and for certain forms of security . . . , " a new vision of open-country culture to stand against the metropolis.

There are not enough reliable data over a long enough period of time to weigh the relative pulls of metropolitan dominance and grassroots renaissance. But there are enough data to allow us to be sceptical of the one community hypothesis, particularly when the history of public resistance to metropolitan reform is on our side. At least it seems clear that local loyalties are by no means abandoned, and that, if by some political sleight-of-hand, a metropolitan government is created, it may not find the instinctive springs of support and popular understanding which is supposed to be anxiously waiting for the creation of regional institutions.

III

So far this analysis has undertaken only to expand the frame of reference in which metropolitan politics and government is usually considered, to bring other factors and forces under review, and to qualify conclusions derived from a limited review of empirical facts. The results of the inquiry certainly do not unveil the metropolitan future, nor do they indicate what steps should be taken. Our findings to date have been tentative and negative. Seriously adverse financial or political effects may not be arising from suburban growth. There may be no shortage of resources for the central city or the inner ring. There may not be one community to bring into maturity. In short, there may not be the metropolitan crisis which so many of us have expected for so long, either now or in the future.

This does not mean that there are no metropolitan problems, nor that there is no case for reform. Problems there are aplenty: ugly implications of the growing segregation of classes, races, and occupations in suburban ghettoes; marginal costs and wastes and inefficiencies in government finance and organization to be eliminated, the overriding issue as to whether we will realize the potential, in politics, in land use, in social intercourse, in the amenities of existence which metropolitan regions promise. We may not face catastrophe, but this is no reason for countenancing one-hour commuting schedules, for permitting blight, for condoning the repellent sprawl of cheap commercial developments, inadequate parks, congested schools, mediocre administration, traffic jams, smog, pollution, and the hundred and one irritations which surround us. Even if we can exist in the present metropolis, the fact of survival does not excuse a failure to plan the future with more care, to avoid the mistakes we have made in the past and to bestow a more worthwhile legacy.

Yet while these are real problems and genuine issues, they are not categorical necessities. They are fundamentally questions of value and of judgment, of what we should and should not do, and of how much. In short they are issues for political science to tackle in its traditional way, and no trend is clear enough to give us the easy answer "we have to do it one way." Alternatives are before us; choice remains, and the burden of responsibility is off the shoulders of the economist and the sociologist and back again on ours.

Within this normative framework, the alternatives are several and, in this analysis, only a brief summary of their implications can be undertaken. But those which seem most important are three—greenbelts, grassroots or gargantua—and they are genuine alternatives. Quite frequently, we have tended to think of metropolitan planning, federation and consolidation as related steps to the single goal of achieving political institutions suitable to the metropolitan community. In practice, we have frequently chosen between them on grounds of political expediency. Yet, these reforms do not move in the same direction; they lead us down quite different paths and, in a certain sense, a choice among them can be "extrapolated" too. In a reasoned way we can explore the implications which a certain set of values have for the future, judged by the bench-mark of constitutional democracy. When this is done, though the task of metropolitan reform is complicated, its objectives are clarified. The discussion proceeds on the basis of a comparison of the values involved, in place of an excitable response to "inexorable" trends.

So far as the greenbelts alternative is concerned, the vision of order, balance, and beauty has timeless appeal for political philosophy as it has for the profession of planning. There are overtones of Plato and Aristotle, "an organic sense of structural differences," a corporate whole, in the concept, and there is the tough-minded insistence of Patrick Geddes, Ebenezer Howard, and Lewis Mumford that the vision is practical. When technology promises so much in terms of the capacity to shape nature to man's purposes, when the age of abundance is actuality, it seems reprehensible to permit the shapeless metropolitan sprawl. With such little effort, balanced communities could come into being, rational transportation systems provided, land set aside for recreational and cultural purposes, and the way cleared for Jefferson's common man to find "life" values in place of monetary values. The promise of individual dignity is combined with the aesthetics of a pastoral scene from which insects are banished and in which running water is supplied, and the metropolitan region becomes a true commingling of the best of rural and urban virtues.

There is of course a serpent in the garden of greenbelts as there was a crucial flaw in the Greek polis. Who defines the shape and substance of beauty, who determines the balance of each community, who arbitrates good taste, who decides the values of life? The advocates of greenbelts have always answered with injured innocence "the people," but they have been peculiarly reluctant to specify the means by which the people decide. They have, in modern times, reluctantly admitted that planning is properly a staff function; but when the chips are down, they have been scornful of the politician who curries votes, and indignant at his intrusion. The planners who have gained the most notoriety are those who have been the most ready to ignore the role of the elected official, to be contemptuous of the slow process of popular deliberations, and to hold themselves aloof from the electoral process. In short, while one implication of the greenbelt philosophy is harmony, another is in twentieth century socialism, American municipal style. Until the defenders of this alternative are much more specific as to the ways and means they can suggest to reconcile their values with the public's in a liberal tradition, we are rightly suspicious of their plans.

In contrast, the grassroots alternative clearly avoids the danger of professional controls imposed from above, and of an excessive commitment to communal order and balance. If we retain our belief in the efficacy of small communities and small governments which spring spontaneously into being, there is actually very little action called for at all. Given the accuracy of the economic and social statistics reviewed earlier, the likelihood of suburban governments disappearing or of crises forcing an expansion of public authority does not appear great. We can drift with the tide, fairly confident that the course of events will produce the best possible arrangement for the metropolitan complex.

This wedding of an ancient image in American political folklore to favorable modern trends makes the second approach both attractive and plausible. First the existence of all shapes and sizes of communities within the region offers an individual a freedom of choice as to where and how he wishes to live. Second, the continued segregation of occupations, classes, and races fits in well with modern doctrine on how to "manage" social conflict. Let each man find his own, abstain from social contact with antagonistic elements, abjure political disagreement and debate by joining a constituency which shares his values, and his tensions, anxieties, and uncertainties are relieved. The virtues of small-town life come to the fore, and the elemental qualities of neighborliness, friendship, and civic spirit are revived.

Yet even though the grassroots thesis has ample precedent in our history, underneath it lurk some assumptions which seem unpalatable. The individual who chooses his community in the metropolitan freemarket in the same way in which he buys his car is essentially a laissez-faire man. He pursues his own self-interest to the maximum, and depends on a natural order of events to provide for the common good. Local governments become truly a bundle of services, to be purchased by those who can afford them without regard to more general social consequences. Those with resources insulate themselves from those without them, and issues of equity and humanitarianism become muted. The garden city planners may place too much reliance on the social nature of man, but grassroots advocates reach toward the opposite extreme of unfettered individualism.

Further, given the general American consensus on values, our basic commitment to democracy and capitalism, the management of social conflict is not likely to be our most pressing public problem. The pressures for conformity, the profoundly anti-individualistic element which punishes the deviate so swiftly in our society, the absence of variety, are more serious issues. Encouraging a scatteration of communities and governments in the metropolitan area does not solve this problem; it intensifies it. The individual may be free to choose his community, but once this selection is made, it is difficult for him to change his values if he wishes to stay in his own home town. The small community is friendly and comfortable and it promises fraternity, but it is also intolerant, inquisitive, barren of privacy. It is at least an open question whether this creation of political boundaries around disparate groups and classes is an appropriate development in a democracy, or whether it truly frees the individual in the manner its advocates intend. Perhaps variety, disagreement, discussion, and debate are to be encouraged rather than avoided.

To the extent this proposition is true, there is something to be said for the third alternative — of gargantua — the creation of a single metropolitan government or at least the establishment of a regional superstructure which points in that direction. If genuine metropolitan political institutions and processes are provided, the excessive marginal costs which overlapping and duplication bring about are reduced, a genuine arena exists for debate about meaningful issues which affect the area as a whole, and there is an opportunity to realize the metropolitan potential which is at our disposal.

In this scheme, decisions about the regional destiny are not the exclusive province of professional value-makers; they lie with the constituency as a whole. Freedom of choice remains for the individual, for the entire variety of spectacles and experiences which a metropolis offers is open to him. But, in a political sense, this freedom is accompanied by responsibility. A man cannot escape his neighbor by retreating to an exclusive suburb; he has to face him, to persuade or be persuaded. Political parties cannot rest secure in the knowledge that they have preponderant majorities in particular jurisdictions; they compete in a region with so many diverse temperaments and outlooks, as almost to guarantee a close two-party fight. Harmony does not appear automatically, it is painfully put together by compromise, by adjustments, by trial and error.

A plea for gargantua is not an attack against neighborhoods, against the importance of "moral integration" or against the need for fellowship and companionship. It is simply a plea against confusing these socially desirable qualities with the prerequisites of good government, against equipping neighborhoods with political prerogatives. We do not have, in the philosophical sense, a conservative tradition in the United States which emphasizes communal purpose and morality or gradations in social status. We have instead a liberal tradition, however confused in its definition of individualism and beset with contradictions; and the essence of that tradition is a distinction between society and government, a preference for legal contractual relationships in public affairs in place of personal ones. Solutions which either in the name of the public good or paradoxically in the name of rampant individualism emphasize communal bonds excessively, seek harmony instinctive or contrived, and discourage variety, are alien to the highest purpose of that tradition. Men have always found privacy, civility, and urbanity, the marks of civilization, in great cities even though they have often paid the price of anonymity and loneliness. They are most likely to find the same qualities there today.

In the end, the case for metropolitan reform, the drive for larger governments and for one community is as strong as ever. It is not a case built on necessity, on the threat of impending disaster, or on the consequences of modern technology. It is a case dependent on value judgments and philosophical disputation. But it is a strong case and perhaps a more appealing and persuasive one once its norms have been frankly admitted, and pretensions of scientific objectivity left behind. Metropolitan reform may not have been right so far as its analysis of empirical data is concerned, but it has always been righteous in the best sense of the word, and it remains righteous today.

THE CASE FOR FEDERAL ACTION

ROBERT H. CONNERY AND RICHARD H. LEACH

Robert H. Connery is professor of government, Columbia University. His works include *The Navy and Industrial Mobilization in World War II* (1951). Richard H. Leach is an associate professor at Duke University. He is author of *Interstate Relations in Australia* (1965) and co-author of *The Administration of Interstate Compacts* (1959).

Nature of the Metropolitan Problem

Before the federal government's role can be delineated, there must be some clear thinking about the implications of metropolitan life in the United States today and the nature of the problem this new way of life has created. More and more of the nation's population is living in urban areas. This fact has been repeated until it has become almost trite. The metropolitan problem in one sense is a compound of urban problems. But it is more than that. Luther Gulick has recently described it as the discontent of millions of human beings, dissatisfied with life in the great cities.

Reprinted by permission of the publishers from Robert H. Connery and Richard H. Leach, *The Federal Government and Metropolitan Areas*, pp. 194-221. Cambridge, Mass.: Harvard University Press, Copyright, 1960, by the Governmental Affairs Institute. [Footnotes omitted.]

> *People are not satisfied with their homes and housing, with their trip to and from work, and with the aggravations, costs and delays of traffic and parking. They are distraught by the lack of schools and recreational facilities for their children and themselves, and they are concerned by social pressures, neighborhood condition, youthful delinquency and crime. People find shopping difficult and more regimented, and the ever more needed services hard to get and expensive. They struggle with water shortages, with bad drainage and sewer conditions, with dirt and noise which they don't like. They find the city centers "old style," inconvenient, dismal and repulsive, and the old buses, street-cars, trains and other methods of mass movement uncomfortable and slow. . . . And when people move to the suburbs and take work in a new suburban factory, store or other enterprise, they find that many of the evils they sought to escape move in right after them, with mounting taxes to plague them there too.*

To be sure, it is easy to picture current conditions against what people would want if economic resources were not scarce. But economic resources are scarce — as they have always been — and people who depend on material things for the satisfactions of life will always be unhappy. Nevertheless, this widespread social dissatisfaction is one aspect of the metropolitan problem.

In part, the metropolitan problem is a psychological problem. The ties that bind the metropolitan community are not those that bound the typical rural community of the last century. Though there may be and often is a certain degree of neighborhood consciousness, and even of loyalty to an individual city in the metropolitan complex, there is no loyalty to the metropolitan area as a whole. In a real sense, when one speaks about metropolitan areas, the line of Gertrude Stein, "There is no there there," applies. Ever since the days of ancient Greece, man's first loyalties have been to his city, and this tradition still prevails in our own culture. Thus the achievement of a solution to the problems of metropolitan areas is handicapped by the fact that the metropolitan area is not even a symbol which attracts men. There still is no awareness of the larger community in the minds of residents of metropolitan areas.

The metropolitan problem is also one of urban economics. The past decade has witnessed unprecedented demands for housing, schools, highways, streets, hospitals, parks, modern commercial and industrial facilities, and all the other amenities that go with community life in the second half of the twentieth century. These demands will continue and in all probability will even become greater. The tremendous increases in productivity in the American economy and the steady uptrend of the American standard of living will undoubtedly result in a steadily increasing need for community services. These new pressures come at a time when governments in metropolitan centers have still not solved the problems created by today's population. Millions of American city dwellers live in substandard housing. Schools are overcrowded. Traffic congestion is rampant. There is a large backlog of need for modern water and sewage treatment facilities. The strain on municipal finances is currently aggravated by tight money and skyrocketing interest rates. In the face of all this, there is hardly a city in the nation that has the economic resources to solve its present problems, let alone those just over the horizon.

But more than anything else, the metropolitan problem is a political problem, and its solution must be through political means. The system of local government in use in the United States today dates from the eighteenth century, from a time when the problems of government were chiefly those of a rural population. The times have changed, but the system still prevails, aided and abetted in its survival by powerful vested interests, determined to prevent accommodation to the present. As the years have gone by, the states have sought to meet problems arising in urban areas without reorganizing local governments. Cities, counties, and towns have been joined by myriad single-purpose special governmental districts, which are allowed not only to overlap one another in a crazy-quilt pattern, but to cross and recross city, county, and town lines with reckless abandon.

Between 1952 and 1957, 519 new special district governments were created in metropolitan areas alone. As of January 1958, there were more than 15,000 local governmental units of one sort or another in the then 174 metropolitan areas in the United States, an average of 86 per area. Nine metropolitan areas had 250 or more local governments each, including the New York-Northeastern New Jersey area with more than 1,400 local units and the Chicago area with more than 900. Everywhere, metropolitan areas are characterized by divided governments and diffused political power.

Moreover, the character of the thing called a "metropolitan area" has changed since it was first defined by the Bureau of the Census in 1910. Then it was regarded as a city having a population of at least 200,000 plus such densely populated places as lay within 10 miles of the boundaries of the central city. In 1910, no two metropolitan areas in the United States touched. Usually they were separated by miles of agricultural country or even wasteland. But today one metropolitan area grows into another until they form great metropolitan regions. By now, there are twenty-two such clusters in the United States. Where once each metropolitan area was a separate economic unit, today whole regions, composed of groups of metropolitan areas, are growing up. As a result, the time-honored formula that each metropolitan area is a separate unit and thus that its political needs can be met by annexing the suburbs no longer makes sense in many parts of the country. Certainly, annexation is no solution for a metropolitan cluster that runs from Springfield,

Massachusetts, to Washington, D.C., and on to Norfolk, Virginia, a distance of 600 miles, with a width ranging from 10 to 60 miles. In fact, what form of governmental structure at the local level could possibly meet the governmental needs of so vast a social and economic aggregation? To assert that the problems of these areas can best be solved by local governments is ridiculous.

The metropolitan problem is made particularly difficult, in short, because a metropolitan area is not a legal entity as such, and thus has no recognized status in the governmental apparatus. Cities, towns, and counties do have separate legal status, but they deal only with affairs within their physical boundaries. Although there may be hundreds of municipal corporations within a single metropolitan area, the whole area does not exist as a government unit. Though the metropolis is the dominant pattern of American life, it is a pattern without legal recognition.

Inability of States to Meet the Problem

Every state, of course, has the power to bring at least some order out of this jurisdictional chaos and thus to facilitate an attack on problems in its own metropolitan areas. Nor is there any way by which states can escape their responsibility for their failure to act. By and large, state legislators and state executive officers are more oriented toward the rural voter and thus more representative of rural interests and concerned about rural problems than they are of urban voters and about urban interests. Thus they either fail to see the need for action in the first place, or tend to give urban problems short shrift when they are finally brought to their attention. In part, the states have been slow to act on the metropolitan problem for the same reason pressure groups and Congress have not acted: because the problem is not a monolithic one. Probably, very often, state legislatures have been faced with a wide divergence of metropolitan opinions about what should be done. Until representatives in the legislatures from these areas themselves can come to terms on the approaches to be taken, it is futile to expect the rest of the state legislature to act for them. In part, the states have ignored their metropolitan problems because they have felt unable to accomplish a solution within the limitations of their financial resources. To be sure, in the immediate postwar years the states had a financial surplus, but increased activity in many areas since then has in many cases exhausted their resources. Moreover, the tax advantage has lain increasingly with the federal government. To obtain new sources of revenue, it has pushed into the fields heretofore occupied by the states and their subdivisions. This has meant for the states a contracting area of potential taxation within which to meet the demands of an expanding number of services. In 1940, state and local governments received 60.6 per cent of the tax dollar collected in the United States, and the federal government 39.4 per cent. In 1956, just sixteen years later, the federal government received 72.3 per cent of the tax dollar and the state and local governments only 27.7 per cent. This is a startling reversal, and it raises considerable doubt whether the states, even if they have the will to tackle metropolitan problems, can find a way to solve them alone.

Interstate Metropolitan Areas

The most important reason why the states cannot act, however, is that many metropolitan areas are not within the jurisdiction of any single state. According to the 1950 Census, 23 standard metropolitan areas extended across state boundary lines, and another 28 bordered very closely on a state line. Inevitably many of these will expand across state lines. Figure 2 shows five typical interstate metropolitan areas. Even in 1950, the population of the 23 areas which then crossed state lines amounted to almost 33 million, and of that number, more than one-fifth lived in a different state from the one in which the core city of the area was situated. The six largest accounted for over one-sixth of the total population of the United States, and the areas bordering on a state line accounted for almost another 10 million people. Thus a total of some 43 million people lived in such areas, or more than one out of every four people in the entire nation. The proportion is even higher today. Speculating upon the implications of these facts, Daniel R. Grant concluded that "with the bulk of our population increase presently taking place in the suburban fringes of metropolitan areas, there may well be more people living in interstate metropolitan areas than in intra-state cities of all sizes within the next generation or so." Thus the interstate area is rapidly becoming the pattern for urban living.

Yet innumerable difficulties confront state action in providing adequate arrangements for interstate areas, particularly if they would involve the creation of an interstate agency with general governmental powers. Some of the difficulties are constitutional—many state constitutions would have to be amended to permit such action; others are legal—an extensive revision of state statutes would be necessary to make it possible; and some are fiscal. It is all very well to set up a specialized interstate agency like the Port of New York Authority, which can live well on toll charges, but to create a general governmental agency on the interstate level and to grant it general taxing powers involves grave difficulties.

Perhaps even more important than these obstacles is the strength of popular emotional attachment to the present organization of government. People have always identified themselves with their city and their state. These are the traditional symbols to which their loyalties are given. A new interstate governing body for a whole metropolitan area would evoke no emotional response.

In addition, the American political party system is built on state lines. Rarely does a party organization cross the state line except for loose alliances made during national elections. An interstate agency would have no real political base and no political constituency. Consequently, the idea has little appeal to practical politicians. Nor does it attract political theorists, many of whom have doubts about interstate governing bodies, which are not subject to direct popular control. The only devices that have been developed for popular control, theorists point out, lie within state lines, and the question of how to make interstate agencies responsive to public opinion remains unanswered.

Finally, not only vested political but vested economic interests are tied to the present system. Differences in state regulations, tax systems, and license provisions in interstate areas all operate to the benefit of some business groups and to the disadvantage of others. Those who benefit would oppose change. Added to these vested interest groups are the thousands of officeholders in the many jurisdictions in interstate metropolitan areas. They would see a threat to their position in the creation of an interstate governmental agency.

In the light of this situation, state action to solve the problems of interstate areas is so beset with difficulties that many students of the problem agree with Professor Grant that "federal intervention is inevitable in one of two forms . . . [either] federal assumption of primary responsibility for those interstate metropolitan functions for which no adequate local authority exists . . . [or] federal stimulation, perhaps even coercion, of states and local governments toward creating new interstate instruments of integrated local government for the whole area." Either way, it appears that some sort of federal action with regard to interstate metropolitan areas is required if their problems are to be solved. . . .

Need for Federal Action

If the primary responsibility for solving the metropolitan area problem rests with the states and their local subdivisions, it is nevertheless true that by now the solution of the problem, not only for interstate and international metropolitan areas but for those within single states as well, has become too important to be put entirely on the shoulders of only one of the partners in the federal system. This new pattern of settlement is a national phenomenon and as such necessarily involves the other partner, the federal government, in its accommodation. Not that the entire problem of adjustment should simply be transferred to

Washington; it cannot and should not be. But neither can the federal government be indifferent to the fate of nearly two-thirds of the nation's population, which will shortly be living in those areas. After all, as Mayor Richard J. Daley of Chicago pointed out recently, metropolitan area problems concern the federal government "because they concern people. The Federal Government is concerned with people," and the bulk of those people "are in cities all over America." The effective government of so much of the country's population and the solution of the problems which face them are necessarily matters of prime importance to Washington. Indifference to the problem as a whole, or the extension of mere sympathy and encouragement to the states in their efforts to solve it, or even a continuation of the existing hit-and-miss program will no longer do. It has been obvious for some time not only that the "people and the governments of the metropolitan areas cannot solve their problems with the governmental and private devices now available," but also that the states, acting by themselves, can supply only part of the deficiency. The rest must be made up in Washington, if it is to be made up at all.

The lack of state action and the force of mere numbers are not the only reasons for federal action in the solution of the metropolitan area problem. The role metropolitan areas play in the national economy is enough in itself to make their fullest possible development a vital concern of the federal government. Indeed, "the problems of our metropolitan communities are so directly tied to growth in population, to growth in industry and commerce, to income, employment and unemployment, and to the movement of persons and goods . . . that the problems of any one metropolitan community cannot possibly be handled in isolation and apart from the whole national system of cities and regions. Both transportation and communication networks are centralized in the nation's metropolitan areas. In them is centered our industrial prowess. In them live the bulk of all our skilled artisans, as well as of our executive personnel. It does not exaggerate too much to say that on their welfare depends not only the welfare of the entire nation, but its security in the world of today.

Economic and Social Importance

Unfortunately, exact statistics are not available to demonstrate precisely the full economic stake which the nation has in its metropolitan areas. It is indicative of the general lack of recognition given to the problems of metropolitan areas that as yet no adequate statistical basis has been developed for urban research. However, enough of the relative position of the standard metropolitan areas in the national economy can be gleaned from the *County and City Data Book* of the Bureau of the Census to demonstrate that those areas account for over 75 per cent of the national total in manufactures, in wholesale and retail sales, and in receipts in the service trades, as well as for the bulk of all non-farm real estate in the country. In addition, a "crude effort" made in 1953 to derive a percentage of the national income originating in these areas set it "in a range of 65 to 70%." A government which is pledged by law to assume responsibility for full employment and national prosperity necessarily has a major interest in the areas which produce such a great majority of the nation's wealth.

Moreover, it is chiefly in the nation's metropolitan areas that the cultural, educational, and scientific centers of American life are found. The rest of the nation has long looked to the cities for cultural leadership through newspapers and radio, theaters and libraries, universities and museums. Hospitals and research groups are predominantly located in cities. In an era of increasing recognition of the importance of science and education to successful long-term competition for world leadership, the federal government's interest in maintaining the health of such centers is obvious. Although no tradition of direct governmental responsibility for the arts and sciences has developed in the United States, the dependence on them of both the nation's security and its future growth implies active governmental concern about their continued strength. To the degree that their strength is derived from their location in metropolitan areas, the federal government cannot avoid assuming some degree of responsibility for the development of those areas.

More than anything else, however, federal action with regard to government in metropolitan areas is demanded by the kind of problems those areas face today. Far from being matters of local or even state-wide concern, the most vital metropolitan area problems are at the same time problems of utmost concern to our national defense, to the conservation of natural resources, and to the maintenance of national health and welfare. They are problems of national dimensions, affecting the lives of all Americans, no matter where they live. So closely knit is our economic and industrial system today that what strikes at the metropolitan nerve centers of the nation is felt throughout the country. As shown above, it was demand for aid in solving these problems on the part of individual cities that first brought the federal government into the picture. The fact that many of them have become aggravated with the passage of time makes an integrated federal program imperative. Even if the theory of federalism would seem to allot the responsibility for some of the problems to the states, because of their very nature the federal government cannot avoid responsibility for aiding in their solution.

Defense Considerations

In case of the involvement of the United States in another major conflict, metropolitan mass transit, without substantial assistance, could not absorb the added burden that would be placed upon it by wartime industrial demands, handicapped as it would be by gasoline rationing and restriction of automobile production. Probably no problem is more readily apparent in most metropolitan areas than the inability of older transit systems to handle present-day traffic, to say nothing of future transportation requirements. Central cities in many metropolitan areas are ghost towns from 5 P.M. to 7 A.M. Workers flock to the suburbs after work—"the dormitory suburbs," they have been called—only to flock back again the next morning. Mass transit facilities must be able to accommodate the flood twice a day, yet are expected to remain idle and unused the rest of the time.

In recent years the trend toward private automobiles has further weakened the economic position of mass transit facilities, both by offering strenuous competition to them on the one hand and by clogging streets with surface traffic on the other, thereby making efficient service impossible. Clogged streets result in dropping downtown property values, and decreasing property values are quickly followed by economic readjustments which profoundly affect employment, sales, and production in downtown areas, which again react negatively upon mass transit facilities. A vicious circle of major proportions is thus well established in most metropolitan areas, yet no local body is competent to tackle the problem and to assure that the area as a whole will continue to be provided with a decent, effective, and economic mass transportation system. Today, metropolitan mass transit facilities have reached so low an ebb that it is doubtful in many cases whether they could be counted on in any future defense preparations this country might be forced to make. Yet, as President Eisenhower himself has said, "America is in an era when defensive and productive strength require the absolute best that we can have."

The mass transit problem is only one part of the nation's transportation problem, and it cannot be solved by itself. As Senator Keating has recently pointed out, the federal government, in its regulation of railroads, cannot overlook its responsibility to the commuter. Though some parts of the problem are susceptible to state and local action, in many metropolitan communities no solution can be found without the active participation of the federal government. Annoying as this whole situation is to everyday peacetime living, it is a matter of vital concern in considering the nation's defense.

The highway problem is equally serious, and here again, defense considerations alone make federal responsibility a necessity. The House

Committee on Public Roads, commenting in 1956 on the expanded National System of Interstate Highways, noted that it "contains only 1.2 per cent of total United States road mileage, [but] when completed . . . it may be expected to carry twenty per cent of the nation's total traffic load." The defense importance of that system is obvious. But defense is not the only consideration. As President Eisenhower told the Governors' Conference in 1954, in a message to the meeting held at Bolton's Landing, New York, the country urgently needs better and safer highways both to keep pace with its over-all economic development and to reduce the appalling toll of death and injury from traffic accidents. In 1952 President Eisenhower recognized the need for "a grand plan for a properly articulated highway system that solves the problems of speedy, safe, transcontinental travel . . . intercity transportation . . . access highways . . . and farm to farm movement . . . metropolitan area congestion . . . bottlenecks and parking." Since then the new highway program has been launched, but solution of the highway problems both of central cities and of their metropolitan fringes is requisite to the development of an adequate national highway program.

In many areas today, the demand for outdoor recreation resources and facilities far outstrips supply. Yet metropolitan communities, where the bulk of the American people live, are not generally able to develop adequate plans to meet their recreational needs. Because so many metropolitan areas are already interstate and international, and others are becoming so, to meet the demand for recreational facilities in time and on a large enough scale requires federal action. Moreover, because of the federal government's extensive commitments in highway construction in urban areas and in a variety of urban renewal and redevelopment projects, it must be a part of the team when plans for future land use to provide for recreational facilities are being formulated. In addition, as the Arden House Conference on Metropolitan Problems noted, the current concern with juvenile delinquency gives "added urgency" to the whole recreation problem. As one way to combat juvenile delinquency, which again has become a problem of national dimensions, the Conference suggested federal co-operation in meeting the recreational needs of school-age boys who otherwise would be confined to city streets all summer. Indeed, the creation of the National Outdoor Recreation Resources Review Commission by the Eighty-fifth Congress indicates a recognition of the need for federal action in this field.

Public Health Requirements

As noted above, almost every metropolitan area suffers to some degree from the lack of a sufficient supply of water. The rivers which supply many of the nation's most important metropolitan areas are interstate or international. For example, the Columbia and the Connecticut river basins are sources of water not for a single state but for entire regions, including a number of states. The Delaware, the Ohio, the St. Lawrence, and, of course, the Mississippi are further illustrations of the point. Every survey made in recent years of national water resources agrees that their most efficient development lies in comprehensive planning of an entire river system for many purposes. Such planning is very complex; it must include more than the local governments concerned, more than the states involved. For "it is the people that a Nation's water resources policy must be designed to serve." "A well-rounded national water resources policy . . . must be a broad reflection of the lives of the people on their farms, in their villages and cities, in their regions, and in the Nation as a whole." Such a policy can be evolved only by the initiative and under the leadership of the federal government.

Water pollution is closely related to the problem of water supply. "Pollution can be just as effective in reducing a water resource for use as drought. Pollution control, therefore, is now recognized as a key to the national problem of water conservation." The expansion of population and industry in the nation's metropolitan areas has been one of the prime causes for the tremendous increase in the amount of sewage and industrial waste dumped into the nation's waters in the past thirty years. Sewers and sewage disposal plants were largely designed for and confined to the central cities when they were originally constructed. As population expanded into the suburban fringes of those cities after 1920, vast problems of waste collection and sewage disposal arose as the result of the lower suburban density of population and of the unequal distribution of taxable property among the suburbs, as well as of the inadequate co-ordination which results from the maze of overlapping governmental jurisdictions characteristic of metropolitan areas. Even today, sewage and waste disposal plants are provided independently by municipalities and industries on a small-scale and uneconomic basis. As a result, the raw sewage equivalent dumped into American streams and rivers has increased by almost 50 per cent since 1920, and industrial wastes have increased by over 100 per cent in the same period. On the basis of such evidence, the Kestnbaum Commission concluded that stream pollution is "one of the Nation's most serious public health problems."

The House Committee on Public Works figured in 1955 that municipal pollution abatement needs for the next ten years, if met, would cost $5.33 billion, and that another $5.5 billion would be required for the construction of adequate new sewer systems in the same period. The fact that many of the rivers and streams involved are navigable streams already under federal jurisdiction, and the number of instances in which the waste from cities and industries in one state pollutes the waters of another state, led the Kestnbaum Commission to recommend "increased participation of the National Government in coping with this hazard to domestic and industrial water users." On the ground of the national health and welfare alone, the federal government's responsibility for action with regard to this problem in metropolitan areas is manifest.

Slum clearance and urban renewal, as has already been pointed out, is another metropolitan area problem of obvious importance to the federal government if national health is to be maintained and if cities are to remain the vital industrial workshops of the nation. At the core of every metropolitan area in the nation today are one or more old central cities, the hearts of which have been blighted more or less seriously by unsightly and unhealthy slums. It has been the desire of most city dwellers to have the modern equivalent of forty acres and a mule—a house of their own in the suburbs and a car to carry them back and forth to work—that has produced the metropolitan explosion. As thousands of people in downtown residential areas have realized their dreams and left the core cities to live in the suburbs, many old downtown residential areas have deteriorated to the point where they have become cancers gnawing at the vitals of the whole area's prosperity. Virtually every American community has felt the scourge of the slums. "Slums have spread so far, their costs have become so great, that they have become a problem of national dimensions and concern."

By now, urban blight and slums constitute one of the greatest peacetime economic problems that confront America. For cities must be renewed; they deteriorate more rapidly than they can be constructed, added to, or repaired. Yet the "real and total costs of urban renewal are almost beyond cities' and citizens' comprehension." They will total almost "two trillion dollars by 1970," concludes one expert in the field. Even though the "responsibilities and requirements involved are predominantly those of private enterprise . . . necessary Federal participation expenditures alone will rival those for national security." Slums have become more than an economic problem. They constitute a serious social problem as well, involving important considerations of human welfare. The Congress of the United States itself recognized these considerations in its "Declaration of National Housing Policy," prefacing the Housing Act of 1949, which states that "the general welfare and security of the Nation and the health and living standards of its people require . . . the elimination of substandard and other inadequate housing through the clearance of slums and blighted areas, and the realization as soon as possible of the goal of a decent home and a suitable living environment for every American family, thus contributing to the development and redevelopment of communities and to the advancement of the growth, wealth, and security of the Nation." That good housing and a sound living environment for American families are most important aspects of human welfare, and as such are areas of activity which cannot be ignored by the federal government, is no longer debatable. Many of the problems which the federal government is now attacking in the field of public health are but parts of the larger problem of slums. To solve them requires solution of the basic problem as well.

Although air pollution—"Garbage in the Sky"—is a relatively new metropolitan problem, it has already assumed alarming proportions. In his special message to Congress on national health problems, January 31, 1955, President Eisenhower noted that "as a result of industrial growth and urban development, the atmosphere over some population centers may be approaching the limit of its ability to absorb air pollutants with safety to health." Indeed, air pollution is now seen as a possible source of lung cancer, asthma, and other diseases. But, as the President observed, air pollution is primarily a problem of metropolitan areas. The effects of polluted air are not confined to the air over the metropolitan area from which it originates, nor indeed to the boundaries of any area or state. Polluted air moves wherever the winds carry it, with the result that air pollution is fast becoming a menace to the nation's health, and to the safety and comfort of people in many areas and in widely separated parts of the country. Nor are its effects interstate alone; they are even international. The problem is made all the more serious because of experiments with atomic explosions. In this connection, Dr. Alan T. Waterman, Director of the National Science Foundation, noted that "the problems of radio-active air pollution resulting from operations directly controlled by the Federal Government lie peculiarly within the province of the Federal Government. . . . therefore . . . the Federal Government should undertake responsibility for the control and prevention of such hazards." Both because of the growing danger of air pollution to national health in general and because of the federal government's part in creating the menace in the first place, the necessity of federal action to aid in solving the air pollution problem is beyond question.

Civil Defense

The 1950 Census showed that 40 per cent of the population of the United States and over half of all persons employed in manufacturing live in just forty metropolitan areas, and since then, the proportion has increased. It is obvious that in this thermonuclear age a single explosion can effectively destroy an entire metropolitan center, and prospective weapons promise the possibility of even more widespread destruction. Present legislation in the United States still leaves responsibility for solving the problem of civil defense divided between the states and the federal government. But there is increasing evidence that the possibilities of national catastrophe are so great that a larger and more active federal role is mandatory. A recent study by the House Military Operations Subcommittee predicts that a thermonuclear attack on the 150 largest cities in the United States could wipe out 70 per cent of the nation's industry and kill about 90 per cent of the population. In the face of such a threat, the Subcommittee concluded that "to save over 90 per cent of the population and restore the pre-attack American standard of living in less than ten years should be sufficient incentive to give civil defense its rightful place in the defense system." Only by the federal government's assumption of primary responsibility in this field can that place be assured.

Co-operative Federalism

The list of metropolitan area problems could be expanded much further, and in each case need for the assumption of federal responsibility could be demonstrated. The need is not for the federal government to take over the entire metropolitan area problem, lock, stock, and barrel. Democracy must of necessity resist the temptation to concentrate all powers of the state in one organ. The need is rather for the federal government to recognize and accept its share of responsibility on the one hand, and on the other hand to devise a coherent and comprehensive policy, within the framework of the federal system, to guide it in its actions. To date, Washington has done neither, nor does it appear that action in either direction will soon be forthcoming. Indeed, no consensus has yet been reached about what the federal government's role should be. Thus it has not been possible to devise any kind of policy. As Robert Daland noted recently, "It is almost a shock to realize that while we can turn to revealing analyses of [federal] agricultural policy, labor policy, tax policy or resources policy, we have no exposition of urbanism policy." Such a policy must be developed, however, if the federal government is to assist effectively in the solution of the metropolitan problem.